다빈출
코드

2025
학평대비

어법·어휘

전국의 많은 선생님께서
다빈출코드의 완성도를 함께 높여 주셨습니다.

Success is the sum of small efforts, repeated.

성공은 반복된 작은 노력들의 합이다.

\- Robert Collier

대학수학능력시험 영어 영역
절대평가의 의미와 학습 전략

01 수능 영어 절대평가의 목적

A. 지나친 경쟁을 지양하고 학습 부담을 경감시킴

B. 의사소통 중심의 수업 활성화 등 학생들의 실제 영어 능력을 향상시키는 방향으로 학교 영어교육이 정상화되는 계기를 마련

02 상대평가 vs. 절대평가

구분	상대평가	절대평가
점수 산정 방식	다른 학생들의 점수에 따라 등급이 달라짐	다른 학생들의 순위에 관계없이 본인의 점수에 따라 등급이 결정됨
시험 문항 출제	변별력을 위해 일정 수의 문항은 고난도로 출제하는 것이 불가피	학생 변별보다는 성취 수준을 달성했는지를 중점적으로 고려하여 출제
점수 제공 방식	백분위, 표준점수, 등급(9등급)	등급(9등급)

▶ 백분위와 표준점수를 활용하여 수험생들의 상대적 실력을 평가하는 상대평가 제도와 달리, 절대평가 제도에서는 학생 변별보다는 학력 성취 수준의 달성 여부가 문항 출제의 기준이 되며, 이는 곧 노력 여하에 따라 누구든 높은 등급을 받을 수 있음을 의미한다.

03 수능 영어 영역 대학별 반영 방식

모집시기	반영방법	대학 수
수시	최저학력기준	151개교
정시	최저학력기준	0개교
	비율반영	186개교
	가점부여	10개교
	감점부여	3개교

04 주요 대학 영역별 반영비율

대학명		2025학년도 수능 영역별 반영비율(%)				영어 영역 가점/감점 여부
		국어	수학	영어	탐구	
고려대	인문	36	36		29	등급당 3, 6, 9 …씩 감점 반영
	자연	31	38		31(과탐)	
서강대	인문	37	43		20	1등급에 100점 가점 부여 (9등급 92점)
	자연	37	43		20	

대학						
서울대		33	40		27	등급당 0.5, 2, 4 …씩 감점 반영
성균관대	인문	35	25	10	30	
		30	40	10	20	
	자연	20	40	10	30	
		30	40	10	20	
연세대	인문	37.5	25	12.5	25	1등급에 100점 부여 (등급별 감점 커짐)
	자연	22	33	11	33	
이화여대	인문	30	30	20	20	1등급에 100점 부여 (9등급 68점)
	자연	25	30	20	25	
한양대	인문	35	30	10	25	1등급에 100점 부여 (등급별 감점 커짐)
	자연	25	40	10	25	

*위 수치는 대략적인 수치이므로 전형별, 모집단위별 세부적인 내용은 각 대학 입시 요강 참고

▶ 2025학년도 정시모집에서는 비율로 반영하는 많은 학교가 영어 영역 반영비율을 이전 수준으로 유지한다. 서강대, 중앙대 등은 가점을 부여하는 방식으로 영어를 반영하며, 고려대, 서울대 등은 감점을 하는 방식으로 영어 영역 점수를 활용한다.

05 요약

A. 1등급 학생 수 증가

절대평가의 등급 산정 기준이 표준점수가 아닌 원점수이므로 상위권의 척도라 할 수 있는 1등급의 학생 수가 증가할 가능성이 있다.

B. 낮은 영어 비중의 유지

주요 대학들의 2025학년도 정시모집 전형을 보면 영어 영역 반영비율이 2024학년도와 유사한 수준이다. 이들 대학 대부분이 영어 영역 반영비율을 국어, 수학 등에 비해 낮게 유지하고 있어 영어의 입시 영향력이 약한 편이다.

★ 학습 전략 ★

A. 상위권

상위권 학생들의 경우 영어 1등급을 받는 것이 중요한데, 1·2점차로 당락이 좌우되므로 실수로 문제를 틀려 등급이 내려가지 않도록 주의해야 한다. 지금까지 공부해온 방식에서 크게 벗어나지 않되 EBS 교재 이외의 지문이나 변형 방식 등에 주목하고, 실수를 줄일 수 있도록 잘 틀리는 유형은 오답노트를 작성하는 것도 좋다.

B. 중위권 ~ 하위권

중위권 학생들의 경우 1~2등급으로 성적을 끌어 올려 상위권 대학 진입을 노려볼 수 있기 때문에 영어의 중요성이 더욱 클 수 있다. 중위권 학생들은 어휘와 구문을 탄탄하게 학습하고 어려운 유형(빈칸 추론 등)보다는 쉬운 유형을 모두 맞히는 전략을 세우는 것이 효율적이다. 또한 실제 시험과 같이 70분 안에 문제를 풀어보는 연습이 필요하다. 하위권 학생들의 경우 기초적인 문법과 어휘 학습을 통해 기본을 다지고 한 문장 한 문장 지문을 꼼꼼히 해석하는 연습을 할 필요가 있다.

구성과 특징

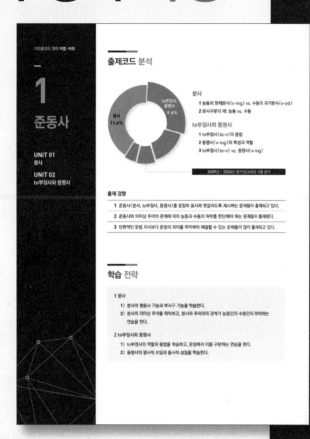

출제코드 분석과 학습 전략

출제코드 분석

출제코드 분석에서는 지난 14년간 출제된 모든 학력평가(교육청), 모의평가 · 수능(평가원) 문제를 모아 빅데이터를 만들고, 시험에 자주 나온 문법과 어휘를 추출하여 분석한 내용을 도표로 나타냈습니다. 시험에 자주 나오는 유형과 최신 시험의 출제 경향을 파악할 수 있습니다.

학습 전략

시험에 대비하기 위해 출제코드별로 똑똑하고 효율적으로 공부하는 방법을 제시했습니다.

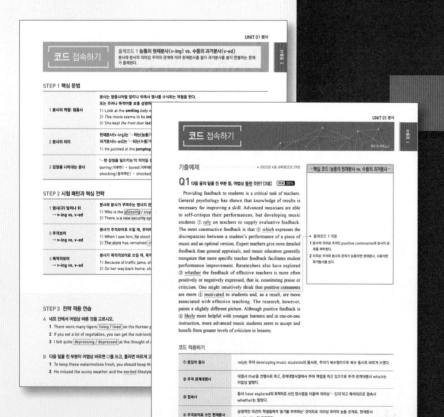

코드 접속하기

출제코드

3단계 전략적 접근으로 문제 해결 방법을 완벽하게 익힐 수 있습니다.
STEP 1: 문제 해결을 위해 꼭 알아야 할 핵심 내용 학습
STEP 2: 시험에 나오는 문제·패턴과 해결 전략 학습
STEP 3: STEP 1, 2를 적용하여 시험과 유사한 문제 연습

기출예제

출제코드가 적용된 기출문제와 코드 적용 해설을 제시했습니다. 출제코드에서 학습한 핵심 내용과 문제 해결 전략을 적용해서 문제를 풀어볼 수 있습니다.

코드 공략하기

출제코드가 적용되어 있는 학력평가(교육청), 모의평가 · 수능(평가원) 기출문제 중 우수한 문제를 선별하여 제시했습니다. 코드 접속하기에서 학습하고 연습한 핵심 내용과 전략을 적용하여 문제를 풀어보고, 실전 감각과 문제 해결 능력을 향상시킬 수 있습니다.

빠른 정답 찾기

문제집에 수록된 코드 공략하기 문제의 정답을 한 페이지에 모아 두었습니다. 문제를 풀어본 직후 정답을 빠르게 확인할 수 있습니다.

친절한 정답 해설

출제코드

다빈출코드 영어 어법 · 어휘 해설집은 수록된 모든 문제에 대해 자세하고 친절한 해설을 제공합니다. 문장별로 자세한 구문분석과 직독직해, 친절한 오답 풀이를 제공하고, 문제를 해결할 핵심 힌트를 하이라이트로 표시하여 문제 해결 능력을 한층 높일 수 있도록 했습니다.

코드+α

중요 문법과 구문 정보, 오답 피하기 Tips를 제공합니다. 문제에 나오지 않은 부분까지 꼼꼼히 학습하며 실력을 향상시킬 수 있습니다.

목차

1 준동사   p.8

UNIT 01   분사   p.9

UNIT 02   to부정사와 동명사   p.18

2 문장의 동사   p.26

UNIT 01   동사의 수 일치   p.27

UNIT 02   능동태와 수동태   p.39

UNIT 03   시제, 조동사, 대동사   p.45

3 관계사, 전치사, 접속사   p.50

UNIT 01   관계사 1   p.51

UNIT 02   관계사 2   p.63

UNIT 03   전치사와 접속사   p.70

4 문장 구조   p.76

UNIT 01   문장의 구조   p.77

UNIT 02   문장의 형식   p.87

UNIT 03   기타 주요 구문   p.95

5 대명사, 형용사, 부사   p.100

UNIT 01   대명사   p.101

UNIT 02   형용사, 부사   p.108

6 어휘   p.114

UNIT 01   어휘 의미   p.115

UNIT 02   어휘 형태   p.131

★ 모의고사   p.137

모의고사 1회   p.138

모의고사 2회   p.141

학습계획 하루 1시간, 23일 완성 프로젝트

	출제코드별 핵심 개념 학습	대표 기출예제 연습	코드 공략하기로 실전 감각 향상
	시험에 나오는 패턴과 핵심 개념 및 전략을 꼼꼼하게 학습하기	학습한 핵심 개념과 전략을 대표 기출문제에 적용하는 연습하기	다양한 기출문제를 풀어보며 문제 해결력을 높이고, 실전 감각을 상승시키기

PLANS				DAYS		CHECK
1 준동사	UNIT 01 분사	코드 공략하기 01	pp.9-14	월	일	☐
		코드 공략하기 02	pp.15-17	월	일	☐
	UNIT 02 to부정사와 동명사	코드 공략하기	pp.18-25	월	일	☐
2 문장의 동사	UNIT 01 동사의 수 일치	코드 공략하기 01	pp.27-34	월	일	☐
		코드 공략하기 02	pp.35-38	월	일	☐
	UNIT 02 능동태와 수동태	코드 공략하기	pp.39-44	월	일	☐
	UNIT 03 시제, 조동사, 대동사	코드 공략하기	pp.45-49	월	일	☐
3 관계사, 전치사, 접속사	UNIT 01 관계사 1	코드 공략하기 01	pp.51-59	월	일	☐
		코드 공략하기 02	pp.60-62	월	일	☐
	UNIT 02 관계사 2	코드 공략하기	pp.63-69	월	일	☐
	UNIT 03 전치사와 접속사	코드 공략하기	pp.70-75	월	일	☐
4 문장 구조	UNIT 01 문장의 구조	코드 공략하기 01	pp.77-83	월	일	☐
		코드 공략하기 02	pp.84-86	월	일	☐
	UNIT 02 문장의 형식	코드 공략하기	pp.87-94	월	일	☐
	UNIT 03 기타 주요 구문	코드 공략하기	pp.95-99	월	일	☐
5 대명사, 형용사, 부사	UNIT 01 대명사	코드 공략하기	pp.101-107	월	일	☐
	UNIT 02 형용사, 부사	코드 공략하기	pp.108-113	월	일	☐
6 어휘	UNIT 01 어휘 의미	코드 공략하기 01	pp.115-122	월	일	☐
		코드 공략하기 02	pp.123-126	월	일	☐
		코드 공략하기 03	pp.127-130	월	일	☐
	UNIT 02 어휘 형태	코드 공략하기	pp.131-136	월	일	☐
모의고사 1회			pp.138-140	월	일	☐
모의고사 2회			pp.141-143	월	일	☐

1
준동사

UNIT 01
분사

UNIT 02
to부정사와 동명사

출제코드 분석

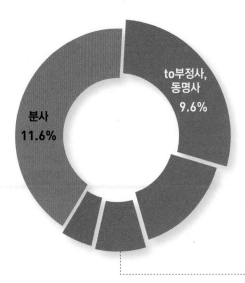

분사
1 능동의 현재분사(v-ing) vs. 수동의 과거분사(v-ed)
2 분사구문의 태: 능동 vs. 수동

to부정사와 동명사
1 to부정사(to-v)의 용법
2 동명사(v-ing)의 특성과 역할
3 to부정사(to-v) vs. 동명사(v-ing)

to부정사, 동명사 **9.6%**
분사 **11.6%**

2009년 – 2024년 평가원/교육청 기출 분석

출제 경향

1 준동사(분사, to부정사, 동명사)를 문장의 동사와 헷갈리도록 제시하는 문제들이 출제되고 있다.

2 준동사와 의미상 주어의 관계에 따라 능동과 수동의 여부를 판단해야 하는 문제들이 출제된다.

3 단편적인 문법 지식보다 문장의 의미를 파악해야 해결할 수 있는 문제들이 많이 출제되고 있다.

학습 전략

1 분사
1) 분사의 형용사 기능과 부사구 기능을 학습한다.
2) 분사의 의미상 주어를 파악하고, 분사와 주어와의 관계가 능동인지 수동인지 파악하는
연습을 한다.

2 to부정사와 동명사
1) to부정사의 역할과 용법을 학습하고, 문장에서 이를 구분하는 연습을 한다.
2) 동명사의 명사적 쓰임과 동사적 성질을 학습한다.

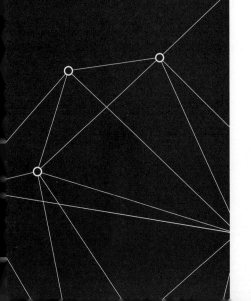

코드 접속하기

출제코드 1 능동의 현재분사(v-ing) vs. 수동의 과거분사(v-ed)
분사와 분사의 의미상 주어의 관계에 따라 현재분사를 쓸지 과거분사를 쓸지 판별하는 문제
가 출제된다.

STEP 1 핵심 문법

1 분사의 역할: 형용사	분사는 형용사처럼 앞이나 뒤에서 명사를 수식하는 역할을 한다. 또는 주어나 목적어를 보충 설명하는 보어 역할을 한다. 1) Look at the **smiling** *baby* who is lying on the bed. (명사 수식) 2) *This movie* seems to be **interesting**. (주격보어) 3) She kept *the front door* **locked** tightly. (목적격보어)
2 분사의 의미	현재분사(v-ing)는 '…하는(능동)'이나 '…하고 있는(진행)'의 의미를 나타낸다. 과거분사(v-ed)는 '…되는(수동)'이나 '…한(완료)'의 의미를 나타낸다. 1) He pointed at the **jumping** *dog*. 2) What is *the language* **spoken** in Quebec?
3 감정을 나타내는 분사	'…한 감정을 일으키는'의 의미일 경우 현재분사를, '…한 감정을 느끼는'의 의미일 경우 과거분사를 쓴다. boring(지루한) – bored(지루해하는) amazing(놀라운) – amazed(놀란) shocking(충격적인) – shocked(충격받은) disappointing(실망스러운) – disappointed(실망한)

STEP 2 시험 패턴과 핵심 전략

1 명사(구) 앞이나 뒤 → v-ing vs. v-ed	분사와 분사가 꾸며주는 명사의 관계가 능동이면 현재분사를, 수동이면 과거분사를 쓴다. 1) Who is the ⬭sleeping / slept boy in the corner of the classroom? 2) There is a new security system designing /⬭designed to protect privacy.
2 주격보어 → v-ing vs. v-ed	분사가 주격보어로 쓰일 때, 주어와 분사의 관계가 능동이면 현재분사를, 수동이면 과거분사를 쓴다. 1) When I saw him, he stood held an umbrella. (→ holding) 2) The store has remained closing /⬭closed for the last three months.
3 목적격보어 → v-ing vs. v-ed	분사가 목적격보어로 쓰일 때, 목적어와 분사의 관계가 능동이면 현재분사를, 수동이면 과거분사를 쓴다. 1) Because of traffic jams, she kept him ⬭waiting / waited for two hours. 2) On her way back home, she had her old bicycle fixing. (→ fixed)

정답 및 해설 p.2

STEP 3 전략 적용 연습

A 네모 안에서 어법상 바른 것을 고르시오.

1 There were many tigers living / lived on the Korean peninsula during the Joseon Dynasty.

2 If you eat a lot of vegetables, you can get the nutrients needing / needed to stay healthy. 기출 응용

3 I felt quite depressing / depressed at the thought of an "F" on my report card. 기출 응용

B 다음 밑줄 친 부분이 어법상 바르면 ○를 쓰고, 틀리면 바르게 고치시오.

1 To keep these watermelons fresh, you should keep them refrigerated.

2 He missed the sunny weather and the excited lifestyle of New York. 기출 응용

코드 접속하기

출제코드 2 분사구문의 태: 능동 vs. 수동
의미상 주어와 분사의 관계를 파악해 분사구문을 능동형으로 쓸지 수동형으로 쓸지 판별하는 문제가 출제된다.

STEP 1 핵심 문법

1 분사구문의 형태	분사구문은 「접속사 + 주어 + 동사 …」로 이루어진 부사절을 분사구로 간결하게 나타낸 것이다. 부사절의 주어는 주절의 주어와 다르면 생략하지 않으며, 의미를 분명히 하기 위해 접속사를 남기기도 한다. 1) **Walking** down the street, I met my homeroom teacher. (← When I walked down the street, ….) 2) ***It being*** hot outside, *we* decided not to go out. (← As it was hot outside, ….) 3) ***While* listening** to the speech, she took notes. (← While she listened to the speech, ….)
2 수동형 분사구문	부사절의 동사가 수동태인 경우, 분사구문은 being v-ed나 having been v-ed로 시작된다. 보통 being이나 having been은 생략되고 과거분사만 남게 되는데, 이 경우 수동형 분사구문이 된다. 1) (**Being**) **Surrounded** by fierce dogs, she shouted for help. (← As she *was surrounded* ….) 2) (**Having been**) **Raised** in France, he can speak French fluently. (← Because he *was raised* ….)
3 「with + (대)명사 + 분사」	'…가/을 ~한[된] 채로'의 의미로, 동시상황을 나타내는 일종의 분사구문이다. (대)명사와 분사가 능동 관계일 때 현재분사를 쓰고, 수동 관계일 때 과거분사를 쓴다. 1) Amy takes a walk every morning **with *her dog following*** her. 2) Jamie tries to study hard **with *his smartphone turned*** off.

STEP 2 시험 패턴과 핵심 전략

1 분사구문 → 능동형(v-ing) vs. 수동형(v-ed)	분사구문의 생략된 주어를 파악하고, 주어와 분사의 관계가 능동이면 현재분사를, 수동이면 과거분사를 쓴다. 1) Written / Writing in Old English, these poems are difficult to understand. 2) Moved to a big city, I missed my peaceful life in the country. (→ Moving[Having moved])
2 with + (대)명사 뒤 → v-ing vs. v-ed	(대)명사가 분사의 의미상 주어로, 분사가 '…하는'의 의미이면 현재분사를, '…되는'이면 과거분사를 쓴다. 1) Jenny stepped out on to the stage with every audience member staring / stared at her. 2) He always watches television on the sofa with his legs crossing. (→ crossed)

정답 및 해설 p.2

STEP 3 전략 적용 연습

A 네모 안에서 어법상 바른 것을 고르시오.

1 Asked / Asking what he wants to be in the future, he always says, "I want to be a great professor."

2 The boss raised the salary of her employees, thinking / thought that it would motivate them to work harder.

3 Many teenagers are addicted to smartphones with most used / using them to play games. 기출 응용

B 다음 밑줄 친 부분이 어법상 바르면 ○를 쓰고, 틀리면 바르게 고치시오.

1 After returning home from school, I have to go to an academy to learn how to write essays.

2 Comparing with other vegetables, beans contain high-quality proteins and nutrients. 기출 응용

3 With only 30 seconds leaving, the Korean soccer team finally scored a goal and won the game.

코드 접속하기

정답 및 해설 p.2

기출예제 ● 2023년 4월 교육청(고3) 29번

Q1 다음 글의 밑줄 친 부분 중, 어법상 틀린 것은? [3점] 정답률 28%

Providing feedback to students is a critical task of teachers. General psychology has shown that knowledge of results is necessary for improving a skill. Advanced musicians are able to self-critique their performances, but developing music students ① rely on teachers to supply evaluative feedback. The most constructive feedback is that ② which expresses the discrepancies between a student's performance of a piece of music and an optimal version. Expert teachers give more detailed feedback than general appraisals, and music educators generally recognize that more specific teacher feedback facilitates student performance improvement. Researchers also have explored ③ whether the feedback of effective teachers is more often positively or negatively expressed, that is, constituting praise or criticism. One might intuitively think that positive comments are more ④ motivated to students and, as a result, are more associated with effective teaching. The research, however, paints a slightly different picture. Although positive feedback is ⑤ likely more helpful with younger learners and in one-on-one instruction, more advanced music students seem to accept and benefit from greater levels of criticism in lessons.

핵심 코드: 능동의 현재분사 vs. 수동의 과거분사

● 출제코드 1 적용

1 분사의 의미상 주어인 positive comments와 분사의 관계를 파악한다.

2 의미상 주어와 분사의 관계가 능동이면 현재분사, 수동이면 과거분사를 쓴다.

코드 적용하기

① 문장의 동사	rely는 주어 developing music students의 동사로, 주어가 복수형이므로 복수 동사로 바르게 쓰였다.
② 주격 관계대명사	대명사 that을 선행사로 하고, 관계대명사절에서 주어 역할을 하고 있으므로 주격 관계대명사 which는 어법상 알맞다.
③ 접속사	동사 have explored의 목적어로 쓰인 명사절을 이끌며 의미상 '…인지'라고 해석되므로 접속사 whether는 알맞다.
④ 주격보어로 쓰인 현재분사	긍정적인 의견이 학생들에게 '동기를 부여하는' 것이므로 의미상 주어와 능동 관계로, 현재분사 motivating이 적절하다.
⑤ 부사	여기서 likely는 '아마도'라는 의미의 부사로 쓰여 뒤에 형용사 more helpful을 수식하고 있으므로 어법상 알맞다.

01 ◯△✕ ● 2024년 3월 교육청(고2) 29번

다음 글의 밑줄 친 부분 중, 어법상 틀린 것은? 정답률 **50%**

For years, many psychologists have held strongly to the belief ① that the key to addressing negative health habits is to change behavior. This, more than values and attitudes, ② is the part of personality that is easiest to change. Ingestive habits such as smoking, drinking and various eating behaviors are the most common health concerns targeted for behavioral changes. Process-addiction behaviors(workaholism, shopaholism, and the like) fall into this category as well. Mental imagery combined with power of suggestion was taken up as the premise of behavioral medicine to help people change negative health behaviors into positive ③ ones. Although this technique alone will not produce changes, when ④ using alongside other behavior modification tactics and coping strategies, behavioral changes have proved effective for some people. ⑤ What mental imagery does is reinforce a new desired behavior. Repeated use of images reinforces the desired behavior more strongly over time.

*ingestive: (음식) 섭취의 **premise: 전제

02 ◯△✕ ● 2014년 6월 교육청(고2) 21번

다음 글의 밑줄 친 부분 중, 어법상 틀린 것은? [3점] 정답률 **61%**

Jack Welch is considered to be one of the USA's top business leaders. In a gesture ① that was at once symbolic and real, Welch directed the ceremonial burning of the old-fashioned GE Blue Books. The Blue Books were a series of management training manuals that told how GE managers were to get tasks ② done in the organization. Despite the fact that these books for training ③ had not been used for some 15 years, they still had great influence over the actions of GE managers. ④ Cited the need for managers to write their own answers to day-to-day management challenges,

Welch swept away the old order by removing the Blue Books from the organization's culture. Now, GE managers are taught to find their own solutions rather than ⑤ look them up in a dusty old book.

03 ◯△✕ ● 2011년 11월 교육청(고2) 20번

다음 글의 밑줄 친 부분 중, 어법상 틀린 것은? [3점] 정답률 **55%**

While we don't all have the same amount of money, we do have access to the same twenty four hours in every day. Though some people have ① much less free time than others, nearly everyone has some opportunity to give. The gift of time can sometimes be more ② satisfied and more valuable than money. You can see this by watching those who have volunteered at homeless shelters or ③ brought meals on wheels to seniors. If you are willing to volunteer, there are many organizations and projects ④ that will be glad to welcome you. ⑤ Whatever you do, it will almost certainly be educational, enjoyable, and rewarding.

04 ◯△✕ ● 2021년 7월 교육청(고3) 29번

다음 글의 밑줄 친 부분 중, 어법상 틀린 것은? [3점] 정답률 **53%**

The idea that people ① selectively expose themselves to news content has been around for a long time, but it is even more important today with the fragmentation of audiences and the proliferation of choices. Selective exposure is a psychological concept that says people seek out information that conforms to their existing belief systems and ② avoid information that challenges those beliefs. In the past when there were few sources of news, people could either expose themselves to mainstream news — where they would likely see beliefs ③ expressed counter to their own — or they could avoid news altogether. Now with so many types of news constantly available to a full

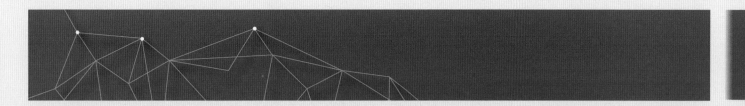

range of niche audiences, people can easily find a source of news ④ that consistently confirms their own personal set of beliefs. This leads to the possibility of creating many different small groups of people with each strongly ⑤ believes they are correct and everyone else is wrong about how the world works.

*fragmentation: 분열 **proliferation: 급증 ***niche: 틈새

05 ○△✕ •2010년 6월 교육청(고1) 21번

(A), (B), (C)의 각 네모 안에서 어법에 맞는 표현으로 가장 적절한 것은? 정답률 50%

The Republic of South Africa is a country located at the southern tip of Africa, with a 2,798 km coastline on the Atlantic and Indian Oceans. To the north (A) lay / lie Namibia, Botswana and Zimbabwe; to the east are Mozambique and Swaziland. This country is known for its diversity in languages. Eleven languages are (B) official / officially recognized. English is the most commonly spoken language in official and commercial public life; however, it is only the fifth most-spoken language at home. Although 79.5% of the South African population is black, the people are from various ethnic groups (C) speaking / spoken different Bantu languages.

	(A)	(B)	(C)
①	lay	official	spoken
②	lay	officially	speaking
③	lie	officially	spoken
④	lie	officially	speaking
⑤	lie	official	spoken

06 ○△✕ •2012년 7월 교육청(고3) 20번

다음 글의 밑줄 친 부분 중, 어법상 틀린 것은? 정답률 57%

Schoolteacher Carol Tateishi writes that in her Asian upbringing, she was taught ① that silence is a sign of self-reliance and strength. She interviewed five Asian American secondary school students from various ethnic backgrounds. Even though their families spanned 100 years of immigration, some recurrent themes ② emerged, such as "you're not supposed to say too much" and "talk could cause disrespect and harsh feelings." The girls who entered U.S. schools as English language learners ③ feared speaking up because they were self-conscious about their language skills. Another girl mentioned that girls "were not supposed to speak unless ④ speaking to." Restraint in speech was valued by these students and their families, whereas speaking in class ⑤ is taken as intellectual engagement and meaning-making in U.S. classrooms.

07 ○△✕ •2022년 7월 교육청(고3) 29번

다음 글의 밑줄 친 부분 중, 어법상 틀린 것은? 정답률 72%

The spider chart, also called a radar chart, is a form of line graph. It helps the researcher to represent their data in a chart ① that shows the relative size of a response on one scale for interrelated variables. Like the bar chart, the data needs to have one scale which is common to all variables. The spider chart is drawn with the variables spanning the chart, ② creating a spider web. An example of this is seen in a research study looking at self-reported confidence in year 7 students across a range of subjects ③ have taught in their first term in secondary school. The researcher takes the responses from a sample group and ④ calculates the mean to plot on the spider chart. The spider chart allows the researcher to easily compare and contrast the confidence level in different subjects for the sample group. The chart, like the pie chart, can then be broken down for different groups of students within the study ⑤ to elicit further analysis of findings.

08 고득점 ○△× ● 2012년 5월 평가원(고2) 27번

다음 글의 밑줄 친 부분 중, 어법상 틀린 것은? [3점] 정답률 37%

"Aerobic" means "with oxygen." It's not surprising that the demands you make on your body when you ask it to sustain an aerobic activity train your lungs to deliver oxygen and your heart ① to pump out greater amounts of blood to carry that oxygen to your working muscles. Your body also responds to this challenge by producing and storing something ② referred to as aerobic enzymes. These enzymes help you burn more fat, which is another reason why aerobic exercise has ③ such a pronounced effect on your body fat. This effect, which is often overlooked, is a primary reason why people ④ do aerobic exercises establish a new metabolism and a leaner body. Yet another benefit of aerobic training is ⑤ that it enables your muscles to better use oxygen to perform work over extended periods of time.

09 ○△× ● 2011년 9월 평가원(고3) 21번

다음 글의 밑줄 친 부분 중, 어법상 틀린 것은? 정답률 51%

Fieldwork is the hallmark of cultural anthropology. It is the way we explore and learn about the vast ① detailed intricacy of human culture and individual behavior. And it is, importantly, the way ② in which most cultural anthropologists earn and maintain their professional standing. Some of the early personal accounts of anthropologists in the field make fieldwork ③ sound exciting, adventuresome, certainly exotic, sometimes easy. Malinowski, the classic anthropological fieldworker, describes the early stages of fieldwork as 'a strange, sometimes unpleasant, sometimes intensely interesting adventure which soon ④ adopts quite a natural course.' He goes on to describe his daily routine of strolling through the village ⑤ observed the intimate details of family life, and as he tells it, such observations seem possible and accessible.

10 ○△× ● 2012년 3월 교육청(고3) 21번

(A), (B), (C)의 각 네모 안에서 어법에 맞는 표현으로 가장 적절한 것은? [3점] 정답률 69%

The observation that old windows are often thicker at the bottom than at the top (A) is / are often offered as supporting evidence for the view that glass flows over a time scale of centuries. However, this assumption is incorrect; once solidified, glass does not flow anymore. The reason for the observation is (B) that / what in the past, making uniformly flat glass was almost impossible. The technique used to make panes of glass was to spin molten glass so as to create a round, mostly flat plate. This plate was then cut to fit a window. However, the edges of the disk became thicker as the glass spun. When (C) installing / installed in a window frame, the glass would be placed thicker side down for the sake of stability.

*molten: 녹은, 용해된

	(A)		(B)		(C)
①	is	……	that	……	installing
②	is	……	what	……	installed
③	is	……	that	……	installed
④	are	……	what	……	installing
⑤	are	……	what	……	installed

코드 공략하기 02

01
● 2013년 6월 교육청(고2) 27번

다음 글의 밑줄 친 부분 중, 어법상 틀린 것은? [3점] 정답률 67%

When talking in general about Roman women, things break down by time periods and by classes. Whether a woman was a slave or ① came from a wealthier class made a great deal of difference. It also made a difference ② which period you're talking about. Rome's conquests meant ③ that men were often away for long periods of time and might not come back at all. Women were ④ left in charge of making sure that things got done. After the conquests, the enormous wealth ⑤ bringing back to Italy allowed middle- and upper-class women to run things with more independence and power.

02
● 2008년 4월 교육청(고3) 22번

다음 글의 밑줄 친 부분 중, 어법상 틀린 것은? 정답률 64%

Is quicksand for real? Yes, but it's not as deadly as it is in the movies. Quicksand forms when sand gets mixed with too much water and ① becomes loosened and soupy. It may look like normal sand, but if you were to step on it, the pressure from your foot would cause the sand ② to act more like a liquid, and you'd sink right in. Pressure from underground sources of water would separate and suspend the granular particles, ③ reduced the friction between them. In quicksand, the more you struggle, the ④ deeper you'll sink. But if you remain still, you'll start to float. So if you ever do fall into quicksand, remember to stay calm, and don't move until you've stopped ⑤ sinking.

03
● 2012년 3월 교육청(고2) 26번

다음 글의 밑줄 친 부분 중, 어법상 틀린 것은? 정답률 59%

In some cases two species are so dependent upon each other ① that if one becomes extinct, the other will as well. This nearly happened with trees that ② relied on the now-extinct Dodo birds. They once roamed Mauritius, a tropical island ③ situating in the Indian Ocean. However, Dodo birds became extinct during the late 19th century. They were overhunted by humans and other animals. After they ④ disappeared, the Calvaria Tree soon stopped sprouting seeds. Scientists finally concluded that, for the seeds of the Calvaria Tree ⑤ to sprout, they needed to first be digested by the Dodo bird.

04
● 2009년 6월 교육청(고2) 22번

다음 글의 밑줄 친 부분 중, 어법상 틀린 것은? 정답률 49%

Can you imagine ① what life was like 200 years ago? There was no electricity, and oil lamps ② were used at night. In addition, there were no cars or telephones, so travel was mostly on foot and communication was very difficult. These days, our lives are ③ completely different. We have jet planes, cell phones, the Internet, and many more aspects of life that our ancestors couldn't even dream of. However, have all these improvements had good results? Pollution and fossil fuels have given us global warming, ④ resulted in extreme weathers. Modern medicine lets us live longer, but governments are finding it hard ⑤ to look after the increasing number of old people.

05 고득점 ○△✕ •─────── • 2015년 3월 교육청(고2) 28번

다음 글의 밑줄 친 부분 중, 어법상 틀린 것은? [3점] 정답률 **22%**

Some researchers assumed early human beings ate mainly the muscle flesh of animals, as we ① do today. By "meat," they meant the muscle of the animal. Yet focusing on the muscle appears to be a ② relatively recent phenomenon. In every history on the subject, the evidence suggests that early human populations ③ preferred the fat and organ meat of the animal over its muscle meat. Vihjalmur Stefansson, an arctic explorer, found that the Inuit were careful to save fatty meat and organs for human consumption ④ while giving muscle meat to the dogs. In this way, humans ate as other large, meat-eating mammals eat. Lions and tigers, for instance, first eat the blood, hearts, livers, and brains of the animals they kill, often ⑤ leave the muscle meat for eagles. These organs tend to be much higher in fat.

06 ○△✕ •─────── • 2018년 6월 교육청(고2) 28번

(A), (B), (C)의 각 네모 안에서 어법에 맞는 표현으로 가장 적절한 것은? [3점] 정답률 **56%**

Getting in the habit of asking questions (A) transform / transforms you into an active listener. This practice forces you to have a different inner life experience, since you will, in fact, be listening more effectively. You know that sometimes when you are supposed to be listening to someone, your mind starts to wander. All teachers know that this happens frequently with students in classes. It's what goes on inside your head that makes all the difference in how well you will convert (B) what / that you hear into something you learn. Listening is not enough. If you

are constantly engaged in asking yourself questions about things you are hearing, you will find that even boring lecturers become a bit more (C) interesting / interested, because much of the interest will be coming from what you are generating rather than what the lecturer is offering. When someone else speaks, you need to be thought provoking!

*thought provoking: 생각을 불러일으키는

	(A)		(B)		(C)
①	transform	⋯⋯	what	⋯⋯	interesting
②	transform	⋯⋯	that	⋯⋯	interested
③	transforms	⋯⋯	what	⋯⋯	interesting
④	transforms	⋯⋯	that	⋯⋯	interesting
⑤	transforms	⋯⋯	what	⋯⋯	interested

07 고득점 ○△✕ •─────── • 2011년 9월 교육청(고2) 20번

다음 글의 밑줄 친 부분 중, 어법상 틀린 것은? [3점] 정답률 **25%**

A robot made in Japan can perform a journalist's tasks on its own by exploring its environment, determining ① what is relevant, and taking pictures with its built-in camera. It can even interview nearby people and perform Internet searches ② to improve its understanding. However, having a robot report news is not a new idea. Another robot called Stats Monkey can automatically use statistics to report sports news that ③ reads like it was written by a journalist. Furthermore, Australian scientist Ross Dawson points to News At Seven, a system ④ is developed by Northwestern University that automatically creates a virtual news show. ⑤ Using the resources available on the web, the system retrieves relevant images and blogs with comments on the topics to develop the text of the news stories.

08 고득점 ○△✕ ──── 2012년 10월 교육청(고3) 20번

다음 글의 밑줄 친 부분 중, 어법상 틀린 것은? 정답률 **27%**

Dropping your cell phone in water means you have to replace it, but sometimes if you're fast enough, you might be able to save the phone! If you want to suck the liquid out of the inner parts of the phone, try ① using a vacuum cleaner. Remove all residual moisture by drawing it away, with a vacuum cleaner ② holding over the affected areas for up to twenty minutes. This way you can completely dry out your phone and get it ③ working in thirty minutes. However, unless the exposure to water was extremely short, it's not recommended to attempt to turn your phone on ④ this soon. Be careful not to hold the vacuum too close to the phone, as a vacuum can create static electricity. It is even worse for the phone. The best way, of course, is ⑤ to bring your phone to the customer service center as soon as possible.

09 ○△✕ ──── 2017년 9월 교육청(고2) 29번

(A), (B), (C)의 각 네모 안에서 어법에 맞는 표현으로 가장 적절한 것은? 정답률 **64%**

English speakers have one of the simplest systems for describing familial relationships. Many African language speakers would consider it absurd to use a single word like "cousin" to describe both male and female relatives, or not to distinguish whether the person (A) described / describing is related by blood to the speaker's father or to his mother. To be unable to distinguish a brother-in-law as the brother of one's wife or the husband of one's sister would seem confusing within the structure of personal relationships existing in many cultures. Similarly, how is it possible to make sense of a situation (B) which / in which a single word "uncle" applies to the brother of one's father and to the brother of one's mother?

The Hawaiian language uses the same term to refer to one's father and to the father's brother. People of Northern Burma, who think in the Jinghpaw language, (C) has / have eighteen basic terms for describing their kin. Not one of them can be directly translated into English.

	(A)		(B)		(C)
①	described	······	which	······	have
②	described	······	in which	······	has
③	described	······	in which	······	have
④	describing	······	which	······	has
⑤	describing	······	in which	······	has

10 ○△✕ ──── 2008년 7월 교육청(고3) 21번

(A), (B), (C)의 각 네모 안에서 어법에 맞는 표현으로 가장 적절한 것은?

There are several events that take place while jury selection is proceeding. First, everyone who has been summoned to appear at jury duty must (A) arrive / have arrived by nine o'clock in the morning and assemble in the jury room. A few minutes later, the court clerk usually shows a movie (B) outlined / outlining what is going to happen throughout the day as the jury is chosen for a particular trial. At around ten o'clock, twenty people are chosen from the jurors in attendance and are taken to a courtroom where a judge describes (C) how / what the process is going to work. About thirty minutes later, ten people are called to sit in the jury box to be questioned by the lawyers in the case.

	(A)		(B)		(C)
①	arrive	······	outlined	······	what
②	arrive	······	outlining	······	how
③	arrive	······	outlining	······	what
④	have arrived	······	outlining	······	how
⑤	have arrived	······	outlined	······	what

코드 접속하기

출제코드 1 to부정사(to-v)의 용법
to부정사의 용법을 이해하고 문장에서 to부정사의 위치와 역할이 바른지 확인하는 문제가 출제된다.

STEP 1 핵심 문법

1 명사적 용법	명사적 용법의 to부정사는 문장에서 주어, 목적어, 보어로 쓰인다. ※ to부정사만 목적어로 취하는 동사: want, need, wish, hope, decide, expect, plan, agree, refuse 등 1) **To spend** too much time in the sun is harmful to your skin. (주어) 　(= **It** is harmful to your skin **to spend** too much time in the sun. It은 가주어, to spend가 진주어) 2) He decided **to get** a computer programming certificate. (목적어) 3) My plan is **to leave** early the next day. (보어)
2 형용사적 용법	형용사적 용법의 to부정사는 명사나 대명사를 뒤에서 수식한다. 또한 appear(…인 것 같다), seem(…처럼 보이다), come(…하게 되다), grow(…하게 되다)와 같은 불완전 자동사 뒤에 쓰여 보어 역할을 한다. 1) There was *no one* **to help** me out. (명사 수식) 2) She *seems* **to become** nervous when she is on the stage. (주격보어)
3 부사적 용법	부사적 용법의 to부정사는 부사처럼 동사, 형용사, 부사, 문장 전체 등을 수식한다. 1) People *waited* for an hour **to see the movie star**. (동사 수식) 2) The boy was too *young* **to ride the roller coaster**. (형용사 수식)

STEP 2 시험 패턴과 핵심 전략

1 동사(refuse, decide 등) 뒤 → to부정사	to부정사만을 목적어로 취하는 동사(refuse, decide 등)의 목적어 자리인 경우, to부정사가 와야 한다. The public official was so angry that he refused ~~talking~~ / to talk to reporters.
2 (대)명사 뒤 → to부정사	앞의 (대)명사를 수식하는 역할을 할 경우, to부정사가 와야 한다. There are still some reports ~~finish~~ / to finish tonight.
3 「주어 + 동사」 뒤 → 부사적 용법의 to부정사	앞에 주어와 서술어 역할을 하는 동사가 있을 경우, 뒤에 부사 역할을 하는 to부정사가 와야 한다. We visited lots of shops ~~find~~ / to find the cheapest radio.

정답 및 해설 p.16

STEP 3 전략 적용 연습

A 네모 안에서 어법상 바른 것을 고르시오.

1 The only way avoids / to avoid mistakes is to practice over and over again. 기출 응용

2 Customers were satisfied with the design, so we decided focusing / to focus on the quality.

3 There are lots of free antivirus programs, so you don't need to call an expert remove / to remove a computer virus. 기출 응용

B 다음 밑줄 친 부분이 어법상 바르면 ○를 쓰고, 틀리면 바르게 고치시오.

1 Whenever I visit my uncle, he always has lots of comic books to read. 기출 응용

2 To meet the deadline, I decided to do everything I could finish writing the term paper.

코드 접속하기

출제코드 2 동명사(v-ing)의 특성과 역할
동명사의 동사적, 명사적 성질과 동명사의 역할을 이해하는지 확인하는 문제가 출제된다.

STEP 1 핵심 문법

1 동명사의 명사적 특성	동명사는 명사처럼 문장에서 주어, 목적어, 보어 역할을 한다. 특히, 특정 동사와 전치사 뒤에서 목적어 역할을 한다. ※ 동명사만 목적어로 취하는 동사: enjoy, avoid, finish, give up, forgive, mind, imagine, consider, suggest 등 1) Poisonous frogs use their toxins to *avoid* **becoming** a meal. (동사의 목적어) 2) He finally succeeded *in* **finding** a reasonable solution to the problem. (전치사의 목적어)
2 동명사의 동사적 특성	동명사는 동사처럼 목적어를 가질 수 있으며, 수동태로 쓰일 수도 있다. 1) **Improving** *living conditions* is vital to both our society and economy. 2) He was afraid of **being scolded** in front of his classmates. (동명사의 수동태: being v-ed)
3 동명사를 포함한 관용표현	• spend + 시간[돈] + v-ing: …하는 데 시간[돈]을 쓰다 • keep[stop/prevent] + 목적어 + from v-ing: …가 ~하는 것을 막다 • cannot help v-ing: …하지 않을 수 없다 • be busy v-ing: …하느라 바쁘다 • keep v-ing: 계속해서 …하다 • (up)on v-ing: …하자마자

STEP 2 시험 패턴과 핵심 전략

1 주어, 보어 자리 → 동명사(또는 to부정사)	주어와 보어 자리인 경우, 명사 역할을 하는 동명사(또는 to부정사)가 와야 한다. 1) Invest / Investing in learning opportunities is the greatest gift you can give yourself. 2) The only part he enjoyed was made models of buildings. (→ making)
2 동사(enjoy, avoid 등) 뒤 → 동명사	동명사만을 목적어로 취하는 동사(enjoy, avoid 등)의 목적어 자리인 경우, 동명사가 와야 한다. They enjoy to travel / traveling from place to place on holidays.
3 전치사 뒤 → 동명사	전치사의 목적어 자리인 경우, 동명사가 와야 한다. He came up with the idea of post / posting notes with a simple message everywhere.

정답 및 해설 p.16

STEP 3 전략 적용 연습

A 네모 안에서 어법상 바른 것을 고르시오.

1 Cut / Cutting down the number of tourists would provide enough benefit to be worth the cost. 기출 응용

2 Avoid to touch / touching wounded wild animals even if you think it is safe to do so. 기출 응용

3 His stories were always aimed at encourage / encouraging children to use their creativity. 기출 응용

B 다음 밑줄 친 부분이 어법상 바르면 ○를 쓰고, 틀리면 바르게 고치시오.

1 Julie and her husband are considering adopting a second child.

2 Traditionally, intellectual property hasn't played much of a role in promote basic science. 기출 응용

3 Keep the lens covered when you aren't using your camera is highly recommended. 기출 응용

코드 접속하기

출제코드 3 to부정사(to-v) vs. 동명사(v-ing)
to부정사와 동명사의 의미를 구분하고, 문장에서 의미에 맞게 사용되었는지를 확인하는 문제가 출제된다.

STEP 1 핵심 문법

1 to부정사와 동명사 둘 다 목적어로 취하는 동사	like, love, hate, begin, start 등의 동사는 to부정사와 동명사를 모두 목적어로 취할 수 있다. All the children on the stage **began singing[to sing]** together.

2 to부정사와 동명사 둘 다 목적어로 취하지만 의미가 달라지는 동사

동사 remember/forget, regret, try는 뒤에 오는 목적어에 따라 의미가 달라진다.

동사	동사 + to-v (미래의 일)	동사 + v-ing (과거의 일)
remember/forget	…할 것을 기억하다/잊다	…한 것을 기억하다/잊다
regret	…하게 되어 유감이다	…한 것을 후회하다
try	…하려고 노력하다	(시험 삼아) …해보다

※ 동사 stop 뒤에는 to부정사(…하기 위해)와 동명사(…하는 것을)가 모두 올 수 있으나 의미 차이에 주의해야 한다.

1) She **remembered to pick** him up after work at six o'clock.
2) He **tried sending** her a message, but she didn't answer it.

3 be used to-v와 be used to v-ing	be used to-v는 '…하는 데 사용되다'라는 의미로, 목적을 나타내는 부사적 용법의 to부정사가 쓰였다. be used to v-ing는 '…하는 데 익숙하다'라는 의미로, 전치사 to와 동명사가 쓰였다. 1) Birds' feathers may **be used to attract** mates. 2) He **is used to making** presentations at public meetings.

STEP 2 시험 패턴과 핵심 전략

1 동사(remember, stop 등) 뒤 → to부정사 vs. 동명사	문맥상 미래의 일인 경우 to부정사를, 과거의 일인 경우 동명사를 목적어로 써야 한다. 1) If you fall into the swamp, don't move until you've stopped to sink /(sinking). 2) He remembered to say the same thing the other day. (→ saying)
2 be used 뒤 → to부정사 vs. 동명사	문맥상 '…하는 데 사용되다'의 의미일 경우 to부정사를, '…하는 데 익숙하다'의 의미일 경우 동명사를 써야 한다. 1) They were not used to eat /(eating) with chopsticks. 2) Ultrasound is often used to checking the baby of a pregnant woman. (→ check)

정답 및 해설 p.17

STEP 3 전략 적용 연습

A 네모 안에서 어법상 바른 것을 고르시오.

1 When you brush your teeth, don't forget to brush / brushing your tongue, too. 기출 응용

2 He regretted to say / saying such harsh things to his girlfriend when he saw her.

3 This program can be used to help / helping students who are not familiar with university life. 기출 응용

B 다음 밑줄 친 부분이 어법상 바르면 ○를 쓰고, 틀리면 바르게 고치시오.

1 The machine made a lot of noise, and finally it stopped to operate entirely. 기출 응용

2 If you want to suck the liquid out of your phone, try using a vacuum cleaner. 기출 응용

3 Most drivers are not used to drive in bad weather conditions.

코드 접속하기

기출예제 ● 2023년 9월 교육청(고2) 29번

Q1 다음 글의 밑줄 친 부분 중, 어법상 틀린 것은? 정답률 **45%**

There is little doubt that we are driven by the sell-by date. Once an item is past that date it goes into the waste stream, further ① increasing its carbon footprint. Remember those items have already travelled hundreds of miles ② reach the shelves and once they go into waste they start a new carbon mile journey. But we all make our own judgement about sell-by dates; those brought up during the Second World War ③ are often scornful of the terrible waste they believe such caution encourages. The manufacturer of the food has a view when making or growing something ④ that by the time the product reaches the shelves it has already been travelling for so many days and possibly many miles. The manufacturer then decides that a product can reasonably be consumed within say 90 days and 90 days minus so many days for travelling gives the sell-by date. But ⑤ whether it becomes toxic is something each individual can decide. It would seem to make sense not to buy large packs of perishable goods but non-perishable items may become cost-effective.

*sell-by date: 판매 유효 기한   **scornful: 경멸하는

• 핵심 코드 : to부정사의 용법 •

● **출제코드 1 적용**

1 앞에 동사 have travelled가 있으므로 동사 형태 reach 는 부적합하다.

2 앞에 동사 have travelled를 수식하는 부사적 용법의 to 부정사로 고쳐야 한다.

코드 적용하기

① 분사구문	increasing은 결과를 나타내는 분사구문의 분사이다. 앞 절 전체가 분사의 의미상 주어이며 주어와 분사의 의미상 관계가 능동이므로 현재분사가 바르게 쓰였다.
② 부사적 용법의 to부정사	앞에 동사 have travelled가 있으므로 동사 reach는 올 수 없다. 문맥상 '…하기 위해서'라는 목적의 의미를 나타내는 부사적 용법의 to부정사인 to reach가 되어야 한다.
③ 동사의 수 일치	주어는 뒤에 과거분사구의 수식을 받고 있는 those로 복수형이므로 복수 동사 are는 적절하다.
④ 접속사 that	앞의 명사 a view와 동격을 이루는 명사절을 이끄는 접속사로, 뒤에 완전한 절이 이어지고 있으므로 어법상 바르다.
⑤ 접속사	문장의 주어 역할을 하는 명사절을 이끌고 있으며, '~인지'로 해석되므로 접속사 whether는 어법상 바르다.

01 ○△✕ ● 2012년 3월 교육청(고1) 27번

다음 글의 밑줄 친 부분 중, 어법상 틀린 것은? [3점] 정답률 60%

Skateboarding is one of the best ways to replace snowboarding when there is no snow. They are almost the same in that the actions include riding and performing tricks ① using a board. However, the difference is that in skateboarding, the asphalt tends to hurt ② much more than snow when you fall on the ground. Be sure to wear protective equipment such as a helmet, wrist guards, and elbow pads even if your friends point and ③ laugh. Skate parks provide the safe environment without cars ④ keep your board skills improved. Also, a long downward road without cross streets could be the perfect area ⑤ where you practice basic skills.

02 ○△✕ ● 2007년 11월 교육청(고2) 21번

(A), (B), (C)의 각 네모 안에서 어법에 맞는 표현을 골라 짝지은 것으로 가장 적절한 것은?

Legend has it that, during the Chinese Tang dynasty, a poor public official was so honest that he refused (A) taking / to take bribes. He could not buy meat to feed his family. So, he invented tofu. To this day, some Chinese call honest government officials "tofu officials." (B) Knowing / Known as "the cow of China," tofu's protein is similar in quality to that of meat. But tofu is really more like cheese in the way it is made. Soy milk is thickened with a mineral salt, forming curds—that's (C) why / what tofu's other popular name is "bean curd."

	(A)	(B)	(C)
①	taking	Knowing	why
②	taking	Known	what
③	to take	Known	why
④	to take	Knowing	what
⑤	to take	Known	what

03 ○△✕ ● 2011년 6월 교육청(고2) 20번

다음 글의 밑줄 친 부분 중, 어법상 틀린 것은? [3점] 정답률 60%

Since his early childhood, Alvin was a keen model-maker. He made model cars, model railroad layouts, and model street scenes. When ① asked what he wanted to be, he would say, "I want to be a model-maker or run a store that sells model kits." Eventually, though, Alvin chose a "real" career: architecture. He was not very good at his work, nor ② did he seem to improve. The only part of his work he enjoyed was ③ made models of buildings to illustrate proposals. When a recession hit, Alvin was the first to be fired. Fortunately, one of his former employers did offer Alvin a contract ④ to take on his firm's model-making projects on a freelance basis. Now, Alvin makes models for the leading architectural firms in town. He does ⑤ what he loves, and he earns a good living.

04
◯△✕ ● 2011년 3월 교육청(고2) 21번

(A), (B), (C)의 각 네모 안에서 어법에 맞는 표현으로 가장 적절한 것은? 정답률 **60%**

There are lots of myths about taking care of bad breath. Here are two things you may have heard about bad breath that (A) | is / are | not true. One of them is that mouthwash will make bad breath go away. Mouthwash only gets rid of it temporarily. If you do use mouthwash, look for an antiseptic and plaque-reducing one. Secondly, as long as you brush your teeth, you are said not to have bad breath. The truth is (B) | that / what | most people only brush their teeth for 30 to 45 seconds, which just doesn't solve the problem. To sufficiently clean your teeth, you should brush for at least 2 minutes at least twice a day. Remember (C) | brushing / to brush | your tongue, too.

*antiseptic: 살균성분이 있는

	(A)		(B)		(C)
①	is	......	that	......	brushing
②	is	......	what	......	to brush
③	are	......	what	......	brushing
④	are	......	that	......	brushing
⑤	are	......	that	......	to brush

05 고득점
◯△✕ ● 2022년 9월 평가원(고3) 29번

다음 글의 밑줄 친 부분 중, 어법상 틀린 것은? 정답률 **43%**

Recognizing ethical issues is the most important step in understanding business ethics. An ethical issue is an identifiable problem, situation, or opportunity that requires a person to choose from among several actions that may ① be evaluated as right or wrong, ethical or unethical. ② Learn how to choose from alternatives and make a decision requires not only good personal values, but also knowledge competence in the business area of concern. Employees also need to know when to rely on their organizations' policies and codes of ethics or ③ have discussions with co-workers or managers on appropriate conduct. Ethical decision making is not always easy because there are always gray areas ④ that create dilemmas, no matter how decisions are made. For instance, should an employee report on a co-worker engaging in time theft? Should a salesperson leave out facts about a product's poor safety record in his presentation to a customer? Such questions require the decision maker to evaluate the ethics of his or her choice and decide ⑤ whether to ask for guidance.

06
◯△✕ ● 2007년 3월 교육청(고3) 22번

다음 글의 밑줄 친 부분 중, 어법상 틀린 것은? 정답률 **49%**

If you ever feel ill when ① traveling in remote foreign parts, just drop some gunpowder into a glass of warm, soapy water, and swallow it. That was the advice of Francis Galton in a book ② called *The Art of Travel*. Bee stings? Well, the tar scraped out of a tobacco pipe and ③ applied on the skin relieves the pain. Galton's book proved a bestseller. It covered every situation, from constructing boats, huts, and tents in a hurry ④ to catch fish without a line. It told readers how to find firewood in a rainstorm (under the roots of a tree) and where ⑤ to put your clothes when it's raining so that they don't get wet (just take them off and sit on them).

07 ○△✕ ······················· ● 2012년 4월 교육청(고3) 20번

(A) ~ (C)에서 어법에 맞는 표현을 바르게 짝지은 것은?

정답률 **56%**

Double Dutch is a style of jumping rope in which there are two participants turning two ropes while either one or two participants jump through the ropes. Double Dutch is a dynamic form of jumping rope that kids really love. In addition to its (A) | is / being | a beneficial cardiovascular exercise, Double Dutch also improves coordination and quickness. Furthermore, because it requires three to four participants working closely together, it is also great for (B) | development / developing | cooperative skills among children. At the most advanced levels, Double Dutch is also being done as an extreme competition sport (C) | where / which | groups of kids are doing high-energy dancing routines that are truly amazing.

*cardiovascular: 심장 혈관의

	(A)		(B)		(C)
①	is	······	development	······	where
②	is	······	developing	······	which
③	being	······	development	······	which
④	being	······	developing	······	which
⑤	being	······	developing	······	where

08 고득점 ○△✕ ···················· ● 2012년 9월 평가원(고3) 20번

(A), (B), (C)의 각 네모 안에서 어법에 맞는 표현으로 가장 적절한 것은?

정답률 **41%**

Remember what it was like to report on a daily deadline for the first time? Or to interview a city official for the first time? Or to begin to maneuver a desktop publishing program? We know that the journalism program at our college was a source of (A) | many / much | of these firsts for you. We're still providing these important first experiences to budding young writers and editors. And we're hoping you'll be willing to help these students make it through the program. As you know, the costs of providing first-rate education just keep going up. We've done everything we can (B) | contain / to contain | costs without compromising quality. One of those things is to set up a scholarship fund for students with special financial needs. We hope you would consider contributing generously to our fund. You'll get a great feeling (C) | known / knowing | you're helping support the formation of future leaders in the profession.

	(A)		(B)		(C)
①	many	······	contain	······	known
②	many	······	contain	······	knowing
③	many	······	to contain	······	knowing
④	much	······	contain	······	knowing
⑤	much	······	to contain	······	known

09 고득점 ○△× •—————• 2009년 7월 교육청(고3) 21번

(A), (B), (C)의 각 네모 안에서 어법에 맞는 표현으로 가장 적절한 것은? 정답률 **40%**

In China it has never been rare for emperors to paint, but Huizong took it so seriously that the entire Northern Song Dynasty is thought (A) to fall / to have fallen because of it. He was from a long line of artistic emperors, who added to the Imperial collections and held discussions about painting, calligraphy, and art collecting. Collecting was easy for Huizong—if he wanted a painting, the owner would have to hand it over. When he inherited the throne, at age nineteen, (B) it / which was expected that he would continue his ancestors' royal patronage. This he did, but spent so much of the next twenty-five years (C) involving / involved in art that he ignored his official duties.

	(A)		(B)		(C)
①	to fall	⋯⋯	it	⋯⋯	involved
②	to fall	⋯⋯	which	⋯⋯	involving
③	to have fallen	⋯⋯	it	⋯⋯	involving
④	to have fallen	⋯⋯	it	⋯⋯	involved
⑤	to have fallen	⋯⋯	which	⋯⋯	involved

10 고득점 ○△× •—————• 2008년 3월 교육청(고3) 23번

(A), (B), (C)의 각 네모 안에서 어법에 맞는 표현으로 가장 적절한 것은? 정답률 **31%**

Emma was very fond of singing. She had a very good voice, except that some of her high notes tended to sound like a gate which someone had forgotten (A) oiling / to oil . Emma was very conscious of this weakness and took every opportunity she could find to practice these high notes. As she lived in a small house, (B) where / which she could not practice without disturbing the rest of the family, she usually practiced her high notes outside. One afternoon, a car passed her while she was singing some of her highest and most difficult notes. She saw an anxious expression suddenly (C) come / to come over the driver's face. He put his brakes on violently, jumped out, and began to examine all his tires carefully.

	(A)		(B)		(C)
①	oiling	⋯⋯	where	⋯⋯	come
②	oiling	⋯⋯	which	⋯⋯	to come
③	oiling	⋯⋯	where	⋯⋯	to come
④	to oil	⋯⋯	which	⋯⋯	come
⑤	to oil	⋯⋯	where	⋯⋯	come

2
문장의 동사

UNIT 01
동사의 수 일치

UNIT 02
능동태 수동태

UNIT 03
시제, 조동사, 대동사

출제코드 분석

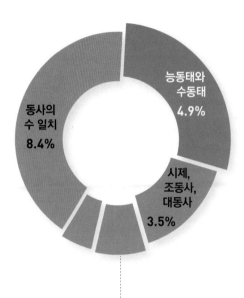

능동태와 수동태
4.9%

동사의 수 일치
8.4%

시제, 조동사, 대동사
3.5%

동사의 수 일치
1 주어가 수식어구로 길어진 경우
2 주어가 구나 절인 경우
3 주어와 동사가 도치된 경우

능동태와 수동태
1 능동태 vs. 수동태
2 4형식의 수동태

시제, 조동사, 대동사
1 완료시제
2 대동사 do

2009년 – 2024년 평가원/교육청 기출 분석

출제 경향

1 문장의 주어와 동사를 파악하고, 주어에 따라 동사의 형태가 바른지 판단하는 문제가 출제되고 있다.

2 문맥, 사건의 전후 관계를 파악하여 동사의 시제가 알맞게 쓰였는지 판단하는 문제가 출제되고 있다.

학습 전략

1 동사의 수 일치

1) 문장을 분석하여 주어와 수식어구를 구분하는 연습을 한다.
2) 문장의 주어가 될 수 있는 다양한 명사구와 명사절을 학습한다.
3) 주어와 동사의 순서가 바뀌는 도치구문을 학습하고 주어의 수를 파악하는 연습을 한다.

2 능동태와 수동태

1) 문장을 해석하여 주어와 동사의 의미 관계를 파악하는 연습을 한다.
2) 수동태 문장의 다양한 형태와 각 수동태의 주요 차이점을 학습한다.

3 시제, 조동사, 대동사

1) 단순시제와 완료시제의 차이점을 학습하고, 각 시제의 쓰임을 학습한다.
2) 일반동사를 대신하는 대동사의 쓰임을 학습한다.

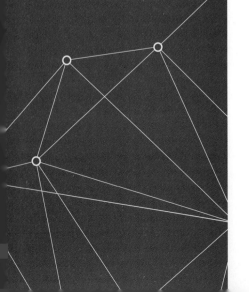

코드 접속하기

출제코드 1 주어가 수식어구로 길어진 경우
수식어구가 붙어 주어가 길어진 경우, 핵심 주어를 찾고 동사가 주어의 수와 일치하는지 확인하는 문제가 출제된다.

STEP 1 핵심 문법

1 주어를 길게 하는 수식어구[절]	주어에 붙는 수식어구로는 전치사구, to부정사구, 과거[현재]분사구, 관계사절 등이 있다. 보통 동사는 수식어구 뒤에 위치하며, 주어에 수를 일치시켜야 한다. 1) The Chinese people [**from** the upper class] *spend* a lot of money on luxuries. (전치사구) 　　　주어 ↑　　　　　　　　　　　동사 2) Volunteers [**to help** build the orphanage] *are* planning to have a meeting. (to부정사구) 3) The chocolate cupcakes [**covered** with whipped cream] *are* already sold out. (과거분사구) 4) The student [**who** is carrying heavy notebooks and textbooks] *is* my classmate. (관계대명사절)
2 「부분 표현 + of + 명사」	주어가 「부분 표현(all(전부)/most(대부분)/half(절반)/the rest(나머지)/the majority(대다수) 등) + of + 명사」인 경우, 동사를 of 뒤에 오는 명사의 수에 일치시킨다. ※ 「one of + 복수 명사」는 '…중 하나'라는 의미로, 항상 단수 동사가 뒤따른다. 1) **All of the soldiers** *are* ready to sacrifice their lives for their country. 2) **The rest of the villagers** *were* seriously injured in the earthquake. 3) **One of the reasons** *is* related to the lack of oxygen.

STEP 2 시험 패턴과 핵심 전략

1 주어 + 수식어구[절] 뒤 → 단수 동사 vs. 복수 동사	수식어구[절] 앞의 명사(주어)가 단수이면 단수 동사를, 복수이면 복수 동사를 쓴다. 1) The pictures hanging on the wall (were)/ was painted by members of a high school art club. 2) People who want to access this website has to have their own ID and password. (→ have to)
2 「부분 표현 + of + 명사」 뒤 → 단수 동사 vs. 복수 동사	「부분 표현 + of」 뒤에 오는 명사가 단수이면 단수 동사를, 복수이면 복수 동사를 쓴다. More than 64 percent of the students (are)/ is against wearing school uniforms.
3 「one of + 복수 명사」가 주어 → 단수 동사	「one of + 복수 명사」가 주어일 경우, 뒤에 단수 동사가 와야 한다. One of the most controversial issues in society (is)/ are the death penalty.

정답 및 해설 p.24

STEP 3 전략 적용 연습

A 네모 안에서 어법상 바른 것을 고르시오.

1 The most common reason to exchange gifts with each other is / are to express friendship.

2 Those who never achieve their dreams is / are the ones who don't try to overcome their difficulties.

3 One of the surest ways to get attention from people is / are to wear unique clothes.

B 다음 밑줄 친 부분이 어법상 바르면 ○를 쓰고, 틀리면 바르게 고치시오.

1 Most of the polar bears in the Arctic faces the danger of extinction.

2 These, in addition to other measures, has helped lower the possibility of future outbreaks. 기출 응용

3 Ignorance of other opinions that are different from our own views keep us from forming good relationships.

코드 접속하기

출제코드 2 주어가 구나 절인 경우
명사구와 명사절 형태의 주어를 파악하고, 뒤에 단수 동사가 쓰였는지 확인하는 문제가 출제된다.

STEP 1 핵심 문법

1 주어로 쓰이는 명사구	to부정사구, 동명사구와 같은 명사구는 문장의 주어로 쓰일 수 있으며, 단수 취급한다. 1) [**Finishing** the work in a day] *is* impossible. (동명사구) 　　　주어　　　　　　　　　　동사 2) [**To come** into contact with new people] *was* an exciting experience for me. (to부정사구)
2 주어로 쓰이는 명사절	관계대명사 what절, 의문사절, 접속사 whether절과 같은 명사절은 문장의 주어로 쓰일 수 있으며, 단수 취급한다. 1) [**What** she suggested in the class meeting] *is* a good idea. (관계대명사 what절) 　　　　　　　주어　　　　　　　　　동사 2) [**How** their children will do in school] *is* what parents worry about. (의문사절) 3) [**Whether** I will go out with him or not] *depends* on his appearance. (whether절)

STEP 2 시험 패턴과 핵심 전략

1 to부정사구, 동명사구 주어 뒤 → 단수 동사	to부정사구와 동명사구가 주어인 경우, 뒤에 단수 동사가 와야 한다. 1) Thinking about the terrible car accident make /⟨makes⟩ me feel guilty. 2) To know a lot of exceptions to grammar rules are useful when writing an essay. (→ is)
2 관계대명사 what/ 의문사/whether절 주어 뒤 → 단수 동사	관계대명사 what, 의문사, 접속사 whether로 시작하는 절이 주어인 경우, 뒤에 단수 동사가 와야 한다. 1) What you have to do ⟨is⟩/ are to think positively about your future. 2) Who stole the purse from my bag have remained a mystery. (→ has) 3) Whether they won the next game or not were not important to them. (→ was)

정답 및 해설 p.24

STEP 3 전략 적용 연습

A 네모 안에서 어법상 바른 것을 고르시오.

1 Who you heard the rumors about her from is / are an important matter.

2 Calculating the number of people in large countries have / has been a difficult job. 기출 응용

3 What makes him different from other journalists seem / seems to be his passion for his job.

B 다음 밑줄 친 부분이 어법상 바르면 ○를 쓰고, 틀리면 바르게 고치시오.

1 To exclude socially isolated people from voting destroys our democracy. 기출 응용

2 Why the Chinese think the color red brings them a lot of money are not exactly known.

3 Whether the government will change their annual plans is emerging as a major issue.

코드 접속하기

출제코드 3 주어와 동사가 도치된 경우
도치구문에서 주어를 파악하고, 동사가 주어의 수와 일치하는지 확인하는 문제가 출제된다.

STEP 1 핵심 문법

1 도치구문	강조하려는 어구가 문장 앞에 올 경우, 주어와 동사의 순서가 바뀌는 도치가 일어나기도 한다. 이때, 동사는 앞에 나온 어구가 아닌 뒤에 오는 주어에 수를 일치시켜야 한다. 1) *Around the corner* **is a coffee shop** called Caffeine. 　　　부사구　　　동사　　주어 2) *Never* **have I** ever **seen** such a handsome guy before. 　부정어　조동사 주어　　동사
2 be동사가 쓰인 경우	「be동사 + 주어」 형태로 도치되며, be동사는 뒤에 오는 주어의 수에 일치시킨다. 1) *Only then* **was she** aware of what was happening. 2) *Under a tree* **were a wooden table and a stool** that had been painted red.
3 일반동사가 쓰인 경우	부정어가 앞에 올 경우, 「조동사(do/does/have/has 등) + 주어 + 동사」 형태로 도치되며, 조동사를 주어의 수에 일치시킨다. 부사구가 앞에 올 경우, 「동사 + 주어」 형태로 도치된다. 1) *Not a single word* **do they say** when they are very nervous. 2) *Little* **have we dreamed** that our son would become a doctor. 3) *Next to the trees* **stands an old building** that was damaged in a fire.

STEP 2 시험 패턴과 핵심 전략

1 부사구, 부정어구 뒤 → **단수 동사 vs. 복수 동사**	부사구나 부정어구가 문장 앞에 올 경우, 동사 뒤에 오는 주어가 단수이면 단수 동사를, 복수이면 복수 동사를 쓴다. 1) In the back seat of the car next to mine was /(were) two little kids. 2) Never has his parents heard why he dropped out of school. (→ have)

정답 및 해설 p.24

STEP 3 전략 적용 연습

A 네모 안에서 어법상 바른 것을 고르시오.

1 Not only does / do she have good communication skills, but she also has good leadership skills.

2 Only after listening to the lecture for half an hour were / was they informed of the next step to be taken.

3 Our school has a big stage in the auditorium, on which is / are placed a podium for speakers.

B 다음 밑줄 친 부분이 어법상 바르면 ○를 쓰고, 틀리면 바르게 고치시오.

1 Nowhere in the world was they able to find the "elixir of eternal life."

2 From its 200-year-old trunk spreads branches in all directions.

3 Never are a machine more sensitive than a human in dealing with emotional issues.

코드 접속하기

정답 및 해설 p.25

기출예제 ●─────────── 2023년 3월 교육청(고1) 29번

Q1 다음 글의 밑줄 친 부분 중, 어법상 틀린 것은? [3점] 정답률 57%

The most noticeable human characteristic projected onto animals is ① that they can talk in human language. Physically, animal cartoon characters and toys ② made after animals are also most often deformed in such a way as to resemble humans. This is achieved by ③ showing them with humanlike facial features and deformed front legs to resemble human hands. In more recent animated movies the trend has been to show the animals in a more "natural" way. However, they still use their front legs ④ like human hands (for example, lions can pick up and lift small objects with one paw), and they still talk with an appropriate facial expression. A general strategy that is used to make the animal characters more emotionally appealing, both to children and adults, ⑤ are to give them enlarged and deformed childlike features.

*deform: 변형하다   **paw: (동물의) 발

● **핵심 코드 : 수식어구로 길어진 주어의 동사의 수 일치** ●

● **출제코드 1 적용**

1 수식어구를 제외한 핵심 주어가 무엇인지 파악한다.

2 that is used ... and adults는 주어 A general strategy를 수식하는 관계대명사절이다.

코드 적용하기

① 접속사	문장의 보어 역할을 하는 명사절을 이끌고 있으므로 접속사 that은 적절하다.
② 명사를 수식하는 과거분사	made는 앞의 명사 toys를 수식하는 과거분사로, 장난감은 '만들어지는' 것이므로 수동의 의미를 나타내는 과거분사가 알맞게 쓰였다.
③ 「전치사 + 동명사」	전치사 by의 목적어 역할을 하면서 뒤에 목적어 them을 취할 수 있는 동명사 showing이 오는 것이 알맞다.
④ 전치사	뒤에 전치사의 목적어 역할을 하는 명사구(human hands)가 있으므로 전치사 like는 어법상 바르다.
⑤ 동사의 수 일치	이 문장의 주어는 주격 관계대명사절의 수식을 받는 A general strategy이다. 주어가 단수이므로 복수 동사 are를 단수 동사 is로 고쳐야 한다.

코드 공략하기 01

01 ○△✕ ● 2018년 3월 교육청(고2) 28번

다음 글의 밑줄 친 부분 중, 어법상 틀린 것은? [3점] 정답률 **63%**

Although sports nutrition is a fairly new academic discipline, there have always been recommendations ① made to athletes about foods that could enhance athletic performance. One ancient Greek athlete is reported to ② have eaten dried figs to enhance training. There are reports that marathon runners in the 1908 Olympics drank cognac to improve performance. The teenage running phenomenon, Mary Decker, surprised the sports world in the 1970s when she reported ③ that she ate a plate of spaghetti noodles the night before a race. Such practices may be suggested to athletes ④ because of their real or perceived benefits by individuals who excelled in their sports. Obviously, some of these practices, such as drinking alcohol during a marathon, are no longer recommended, but others, such as a high-carbohydrate meal the night before a competition, ⑤ has stood the test of time.

*discipline: (학문의) 분야 **phenomenon: 천재

02 ○△✕ ● 2014년 3월 교육청(고1) 24번

(A), (B), (C)의 각 네모 안에서 어법에 맞는 표현으로 가장 적절한 것은? [3점] 정답률 **66%**

Three extremely important inventions came out of Mesopotamia: the wheel, the plow, and the sailboat. The wheel and the plow were possible (A) because / because of the availability of animal labor. Wheeled carts pulled by horses could transport more goods to market more quickly. Animals that pulled plows to turn the earth over for planting (B) was / were far more efficient than humans. The sail made it possible to trade with countries that could be reached only by sea. All three inventions made the cities of Mesopotamia powerful trading centers with as (C) much / many as 30,000 people each.

*plow: 쟁기

	(A)	(B)	(C)
①	because	…… was	…… much
②	because	…… were	…… many
③	because of	…… were	…… many
④	because of	…… were	…… much
⑤	because of	…… was	…… much

03 고득점 ○△✕ ● 2016년 9월 교육청(고1) 28번

다음 글의 밑줄 친 부분 중, 어법상 틀린 것은? [3점] 정답률 **40%**

What could be wrong with the compliment "I'm so proud of you"? Plenty. Just as it is misguided ① to offer your child false praise, it is also a mistake to reward all of his accomplishments. Although rewards sound so ② positive, they can often lead to negative consequences. It is because they can take away from the love of learning. If you consistently reward a child for her accomplishments, she starts to focus more on getting the reward than on ③ what she did to earn it. The focus of her excitement shifts from enjoying learning itself to ④ pleasing you. If you applaud every time your child identifies a letter, she may become a praise lover who eventually ⑤ become less interested in learning the alphabet for its own sake than for hearing you applaud.

04 [O△X] • 2019년 9월 교육청(고1) 29번

다음 글의 밑줄 친 부분 중, 어법상 틀린 것은? [3점] 정답률 52%

There are many methods for finding answers to the mysteries of the universe, and science is only one of these. However, science is unique. Instead of making guesses, scientists follow a system ① designed to prove if their ideas are true or false. They constantly reexamine and test their theories and conclusions. Old ideas are replaced when scientists find new information ② that they cannot explain. Once somebody makes a discovery, others review it carefully before ③ using the information in their own research. This way of building new knowledge on older discoveries ④ ensure that scientists correct their mistakes. Armed with scientific knowledge, people build tools and machines that transform the way we live, making our lives ⑤ much easier and better.

05 [O△X] • 2021년 9월 교육청(고2) 29번

다음 글의 밑줄 친 부분 중, 어법상 틀린 것은? [3점] 정답률 70%

Organisms living in the deep sea have adapted to the high pressure by storing water in their bodies, some ① consisting almost entirely of water. Most deep-sea organisms lack gas bladders. They are cold-blooded organisms that adjust their body temperature to their environment, allowing them ② to survive in the cold water while maintaining a low metabolism. Many species lower their metabolism so much that they are able to survive without food for long periods of time, as finding the sparse food ③ that is available expends a lot of energy. Many predatory fish of the deep sea are equipped with enormous mouths and sharp teeth, enabling them to hold on to prey and overpower ④ it. Some predators hunting in the residual light zone of the ocean ⑤ has excellent visual capabilities, while others are able to create their own light to attract prey or a mating partner.

*bladder: (물고기의) 부레

06 [O△X] • 2012년 4월 교육청(고3) 21번

다음 글의 밑줄 친 부분 중, 어법상 틀린 것은? 정답률 77%

Driving is, for most of us, what psychologists call an overlearned activity. It is something we are so well ① practiced at that we are able to do it without much conscious thought. That makes our life easier, and it is ② how we become good at things. Think of an expert tennis player. A serve is a complex maneuver with many different components, but ③ the better we become at it, the less we think of each individual step. One of the interesting things about learning and attention ④ are that once something becomes automated, it gets executed in a rapid string of events. If you try to pay attention, you ⑤ screw it up. This is why the best hitters in baseball do not necessarily make the best hitting coaches.

07 ○△× ● 2014년 6월 평가원(고3) 27번

다음 글의 밑줄 친 부분 중, 어법상 틀린 것은? [3점] 정답률 78%

In the twentieth century, advances in technology, from refrigeration to sophisticated ovens to air transportation ① that carries fresh ingredients around the world, contributed immeasurably to baking and pastry making. At the beginning of the twenty-first century, the popularity of fine breads and pastries ② are growing even faster than new chefs can be trained. Interestingly enough, many of the technological advances in bread making have sparked a reaction among bakers and consumers ③ alike. They are looking to reclaim some of the flavors of old-fashioned breads that ④ were lost as baking became more industrialized and baked goods became more refined, standardized, and—some would say—flavorless. Bakers are researching methods for ⑤ producing the handmade sourdough breads of the past, and they are experimenting with specialty flours in their search for flavor.

08 ○△× ● 2022년 3월 교육청(고2) 29번

다음 글의 밑줄 친 부분 중, 어법상 틀린 것은? [3점] 정답률 49%

Despite abundant warnings that we shouldn't measure ourselves against others, most of us still do. We're not only meaning-seeking creatures but social ① ones as well, constantly making interpersonal comparisons to evaluate ourselves, improve our standing, and enhance our self-esteem. But the problem with social comparison is that it often backfires. When comparing ourselves to someone who's doing better than we are, we often feel ② inadequate for not doing as well. This sometimes leads to what psychologists call *malignant envy*, the desire for someone ③ to meet with misfortune ("I wish she didn't have what she has"). Also, comparing ourselves with someone who's doing worse than we are ④ risk scorn, the feeling that others are something undeserving of our beneficence ("She's beneath my notice"). Then again, comparing ourselves to others can also lead to *benign envy*, the longing to reproduce someone else's accomplishments without wishing them ill ("I wish I had what she has"), ⑤ which has been shown in some circumstances to inspire and motivate us to increase our efforts in spite of a recent failure.

*backfire: 역효과를 내다 **scorn: 경멸

09 ○△× ● 2012년 9월 평가원(고3) 21번

다음 글의 밑줄 친 부분 중, 어법상 <u>틀린</u> 것은? [정답률 76%]

Today, the world of innovation is far different from what it was a century ago. The days of the solitary inventor working on his own are gone. To oversimplify, basic ideas bubble out of universities and laboratories ① <u>in which</u> a group of researchers work together: both major breakthroughs, like understanding the genetic structure of life, and smaller ② <u>ones</u>, such as advances in mathematics or basic chemistry. Traditionally, intellectual property has played little role in ③ <u>promoting</u> basic science. Academia believes in "open architecture," meaning ④ <u>that</u> the knowledge that research produces should be made public to encourage innovation. The great scientists are driven by an inner quest to understand the nature of the universe; the extrinsic reward that matters most to them ⑤ <u>are</u> the recognition of their peers.

10 ○△× ● 2021년 6월 교육청(고1) 29번

다음 글의 밑줄 친 부분 중, 어법상 <u>틀린</u> 것은? [3점] [정답률 66%]

There have been occasions ① <u>in which</u> you have observed a smile and you could sense it was not genuine. The most obvious way of identifying a genuine smile from an insincere ② <u>one</u> is that a fake smile primarily only affects the lower half of the face, mainly with the mouth alone. The eyes don't really get involved. Take the opportunity to look in the mirror and manufacture a smile ③ <u>using</u> the lower half your face only. When you do this, judge ④ <u>how</u> happy your face really looks — is it genuine? A genuine smile will impact on the muscles and wrinkles around the eyes and less noticeably, the skin between the eyebrow and upper eyelid ⑤ <u>are</u> lowered slightly with true enjoyment. The genuine smile can impact on the entire face.

01

● 2019년 6월 교육청(고1) 29번

다음 글의 밑줄 친 부분 중, 어법상 틀린 것은? 정답률 47%

Bad lighting can increase stress on your eyes, as can light that is too bright, or light that shines ① directly into your eyes. Fluorescent lighting can also be ② tiring. What you may not appreciate is that the quality of light may also be important. Most people are happiest in bright sunshine — this may cause a release of chemicals in the body ③ that bring a feeling of emotional wellbeing. Artificial light, which typically contains only a few wavelengths of light, ④ do not seem to have the same effect on mood that sunlight has. Try experimenting with working by a window or ⑤ using full spectrum bulbs in your desk lamp. You will probably find that this improves the quality of your working environment.

*fluorescent lighting: 형광등

02

● 2014년 11월 교육청(고1) 27번

(A), (B), (C)의 각 네모 안에서 어법에 맞는 표현으로 가장 적절한 것은? [3점] 정답률 74%

The biggest complaint of kids who don't read is that they can't find anything to read that (A) interest / interests them. This is where we parents need to do a better job of helping our kids identify the genres that excite (B) it / them. The children's librarian at your local public library, your school librarian, or the manager of the kids' section at a good bookstore can help you choose new material that isn't familiar to you. Also, think back on the books you liked

(C) when / what you were a child. My husband and I both enjoyed books by Beverly Cleary and it turns out our kids love them, too.

	(A)		(B)		(C)
①	interest	······	them	······	what
②	interest	······	it	······	when
③	interests	······	them	······	when
④	interests	······	it	······	when
⑤	interests	······	them	······	what

03

● 2022년 9월 교육청(고1) 29번

다음 글의 밑줄 친 부분 중, 어법상 틀린 것은? [3점] 정답률 71%

The human brain, it turns out, has shrunk in mass by about 10 percent since it ① peaked in size 15,000-30,000 years ago. One possible reason is that many thousands of years ago humans lived in a world of dangerous predators ② where they had to have their wits about them at all times to avoid being killed. Today, we have effectively domesticated ourselves and many of the tasks of survival — from avoiding immediate death to building shelters to obtaining food — ③ has been outsourced to the wider society. We are smaller than our ancestors too, and it is a characteristic of domestic animals ④ that they are generally smaller than their wild cousins. None of this may mean we are dumber — brain size is not necessarily an indicator of human intelligence — but it may mean that our brains today are wired up differently, and perhaps more efficiently, than ⑤ those of our ancestors.

04 ○△× ● 2017년 6월 교육청(고1) 28번

다음 글의 밑줄 친 부분 중, 어법상 틀린 것은? [3점] 정답률 60%

Are you honest with yourself about your strengths and weaknesses? Get to really know ① yourself and learn what your weaknesses are. Accepting your role in your problems ② mean that you understand the solution lies within you. If you have a weakness in a certain area, get educated and do ③ what you have to do to improve things for yourself. If your social image is terrible, look within yourself and take the necessary steps to improve ④ it, TODAY. You have the ability to choose how to respond to life. Decide today to end all the excuses, and stop ⑤ lying to yourself about what is going on. The beginning of growth comes when you begin to personally accept responsibility for your choices.

05 ○△× ● 2014년 3월 교육청(고2) 23번

다음 글의 밑줄 친 부분 중, 어법상 틀린 것은? 정답률 57%

Whenever I look into my daughter Emily's face, I think about the power of fatherhood. Her face reminds me ① that I have given her more than just my name. Like me, she has freckles stretching across the bridge of her nose almost like a Band-Aid. The skin around her eyes ② form small and thin lines, and the lines match mine. "When Emily smiles," my mother tells me, "she looks just like you." Other things in her are reflections of me. I see myself most ③ clearly in her eyes, the windows to her soul. Like me, Emily has a drive ④ to succeed and will try anything. "Who needs to wait for instructions?" she used to tell ⑤ herself as she attempted to do the high bar in gymnastics class; more than once, she failed. Also, more than once, she succeeded.

*high bar: (체조의) 철봉

06 고득점 ○△× ● 2011년 11월 교육청(고2) 21번

(A)~(C)에서 어법에 맞는 표현을 바르게 짝지은 것은? 정답률 44%

When I got back to my hotel room after taking a lot of pictures, I was eager to (A) upload / uploading the photos to my blog. I plugged my digital camera into my computer, and when the process was complete, no photos were there! Worse, the photos on my memory card were gone. When I told my friend what had happened, he sent me a certain program designed to recover photos that (B) was / were deleted from flash memory cards by mistake. I tried the program. It filled a folder with most of the photos I had lost. I hope you will never have an occasion to use this kind of program. But you need one to have lost files (C) to recover / recovered in case things go wrong.

	(A)		(B)		(C)
①	upload	……	were	……	recovered
②	upload	……	was	……	recovered
③	upload	……	were	……	to recover
④	uploading	……	was	……	recovered
⑤	uploading	……	were	……	to recover

07 ○△✕ ● 2013년 10월 교육청(고3) 27번

다음 글의 밑줄 친 부분 중, 어법상 틀린 것은? [3점] 정답률 75%

With all the passion for being slim, it is no wonder ① that many people view any amount of visible fat on the body as something to get rid of. However, the human body has evolved over time in environments of food scarcity; hence, the ability to store fat ② efficiently is a valuable physiological function that served our ancestors well for thousands of years. Only in the last few decades, in the primarily industrially developed economies, ③ have food become so plentiful and easy to obtain as to cause fat-related health problems. People no longer have to spend most of their time and energy ④ gathering berries and seeds and hoping that a hunting party will return with meat. All we have to do nowadays is drive to the supermarket or the fast-food restaurant, ⑤ where for very low cost we can obtain nearly all of our daily calories.

08 ○△✕ ● 2020년 3월 교육청(고2) 29번

다음 글의 밑줄 친 부분 중, 어법상 틀린 것은? 정답률 66%

Commercial airplanes generally travel airways similar to roads, although they are not physical structures. Airways have fixed widths and defined altitudes, ① which separate traffic moving in opposite directions. Vertical separation of aircraft allows some flights ② to pass over airports while other processes occur below. Air travel usually covers long distances, with short periods of intense pilot activity at takeoff and landing and long periods of lower pilot activity while in the air, the portion of the flight ③ known as the "long haul." During the long-haul portion of a flight, pilots spend more time assessing aircraft status than ④ searching out nearby planes. This is because collisions between aircraft usually occur in the surrounding area of airports, while crashes due to aircraft malfunction ⑤ tends to occur during long-haul flight.

*altitude: 고도 **long haul: 장거리 비행

09 고득점 ○△× ········· • 2013년 9월 평가원(고3) B형 27번

(A), (B), (C)의 각 네모 안에서 어법에 맞는 표현으로 가장 적절한 것은? [3점] 정답률 43%

It had long been something of a mystery where, and on what, the northern fur seals of the eastern Pacific feed during the winter, (A) when / which they spend off the coast of North America from California to Alaska. There is no evidence that they are feeding to any great extent on sardines, mackerel, or other commercially important fishes. Presumably four million seals could not compete with commercial fishermen for the same species without the fact (B) being / is known. But there is some evidence on the diet of the fur seals, and it is highly significant. Their stomachs have yielded the bones of a species of fish that has never been seen alive. Indeed, not even its remains (C) has / have been found anywhere except in the stomachs of seals. Ichthyologists say that this 'seal fish' belongs to a group that typically inhabits very deep water, off the edge of the continental shelf.

*ichthyologist: 어류학자

	(A)	(B)	(C)
①	when	⋯⋯ is	⋯⋯ have
②	when	⋯⋯ being	⋯⋯ have
③	which	⋯⋯ being	⋯⋯ have
④	which	⋯⋯ being	⋯⋯ has
⑤	which	⋯⋯ is	⋯⋯ has

10 고득점 ○△× ········· • 2017학년도 수능 28번

다음 글의 밑줄 친 부분 중, 어법상 틀린 것은? [3점] 정답률 38%

When people face real adversity — disease, unemployment, or the disabilities of age — affection from a pet takes on new meaning. A pet's continuing affection becomes crucially important for ① those enduring hardship because it reassures them that their core essence has not been damaged. Thus pets are important in the treatment of ② depressed or chronically ill patients. In addition, pets are ③ used to great advantage with the institutionalized aged. In such institutions it is difficult for the staff to retain optimism when all the patients are declining in health. Children who visit cannot help but remember ④ what their parents or grandparents once were and be depressed by their incapacities. Animals, however, have no expectations about mental capacity. They do not worship youth. They have no memories about what the aged once ⑤ was and greet them as if they were children. An old man holding a puppy can relive a childhood moment with complete accuracy. His joy and the animal's response are the same.

코드 접속하기

출제코드 1 능동태 vs. 수동태
주어와 동사의 관계를 파악하여 능동태와 수동태가 바르게 쓰였는지 확인하는 문제가 출제된다.

STEP 1 핵심 문법

1 수동태의 형태와 의미	주어가 동작의 주체이면 능동태를, 동작의 대상이면 수동태를 쓴다. 수동태는 「be동사 + v-ed」의 형태로 쓰며, '…되다, …당하다'라는 의미를 갖는다. 1) Our plan **was canceled** due to the sudden rain. 2) Many people **were injured** in the car accident.
2 수동태를 쓸 수 없는 동사	능동태 문장의 목적어가 수동태의 주어가 되므로, 목적어를 갖지 않는 자동사는 수동태로 쓸 수 없다. 타동사는 대부분 수동태로 쓸 수 있지만, 소유나 상태를 나타내는 일부 타동사는 수동태로 쓸 수 없다. ※ **수동태로 잘못 쓰기 쉬운 자동사:** appear(나타나다), disappear(사라지다), emerge(나오다), happen(발생하다), remain(남아있다), exist(존재하다) 등 ※ **수동태로 쓸 수 없는 타동사:** have(가지다), resemble(…와 닮다), suit(…와 어울리다), lack(…이 부족하다), fit(…에 맞다) 등

STEP 2 시험 패턴과 핵심 전략

1 동사가 '…되다'로 해석되는 경우 → 수동태	문장의 주어와 동사가 '…되다, …당하다'라는 의미일 경우, 수동태를 쓴다. 1) The famous picture stole / was stolen during the Korean War. 2) The youngest player chose as the MVP of the soccer game. (→ was chosen)
2 동사 뒤에 목적어가 오는 경우 → 능동태	동사 뒤에 '…을[를]'로 해석되는 목적어가 오는 경우, 능동태를 쓴다. ※ 수동태는 능동태 문장의 목적어가 주어로 나간 형태이므로, 동사 뒤에 목적어가 올 수 없다. William Shakespeare was written many great plays. (→ wrote)

정답 및 해설 p.39

STEP 3 전략 적용 연습

A 네모 안에서 어법상 바른 것을 고르시오.

1 Surprisingly, the question has remained / been remained unsettled for many years.

2 Information and knowledge should be sharing / shared rather than protected and controlled. 기출 응용

3 In the United States, parents recommend / are recommended to let their children sleep alone.

B 다음 밑줄 친 부분이 어법상 바르면 ○를 쓰고, 틀리면 바르게 고치시오.

1 At that time, the robots designed to be flexible in the tail and rigid in the midsection. 기출 응용

2 The listener is comparing to a teddy bear because toy bears would serve the same purpose. 기출 응용

3 An Internet company was introduced a new blogging service that allows users to easily start blogging. 기출 응용

코드 접속하기

출제코드 2 4형식의 수동태
간접목적어를 주어로 하는 4형식 문장의 수동태가 바르게 쓰였는지 확인하는 문제가 출제된다.

STEP 1 핵심 문법

1 4형식 문장 형태	4형식 문장은 「주어 + 동사 + 간접목적어(…에게) + 직접목적어(…을)」 형태로 쓴다. 4형식 문장은 간접목적어와 직접목적어를 각각 주어로 하는 수동태를 만들 수 있다.
2 간접목적어를 주어로 하는 수동태	「주어(← 간접목적어) + be동사 + v-ed + 직접목적어 (+ by + 행위자)」의 어순이 된다. *Amy* **was given** *a box of chocolates* **by** her boyfriend. 간접목적어　　　　　직접목적어 (← Her boyfriend gave Amy a box of chocolates.)
3 직접목적어를 주어로 하는 수동태	「주어(← 직접목적어) + be동사 + v-ed + to + 간접목적어 (+ by + 행위자)」의 어순이 된다. *cf.* make, buy, get, cook, find 등의 동사는 「주어(← 직접목적어) + be동사 + v-ed + for + 간접목적어 + (by + 행위자)」 형태의 수동태만 쓰며 간접목적어를 주어로 하는 수동태는 쓰지 않는다. 1) His new bike **was shown to** me **by** him. (← He showed me his new bike.) 　　　　　　직접목적어　　　　　간접목적어 2) This cheesecake **was made for** her **by** Sijin. (← Sijin made her this cheesecake.) 　　　　　직접목적어　　　　　간접목적어

STEP 2 시험 패턴과 핵심 전략

1 4형식 동사와 목적어의 해석이 '…을 ~받다/되다'로 해석되는 경우 → 수동태	4형식 문장의 간접목적어를 주어로 하는 수동태 문장이 주로 출제된다. 목적어 앞의 동사가 '…받다/되다'로 해석되면 동사는 수동태가 되어야 한다. 1) Those in charge of guarding the gate were giving / ⟨given⟩ a pistol and a rifle. 2) The participants told / ⟨were told⟩ what to do in case of emergency.

정답 및 해설 p.39

STEP 3 전략 적용 연습

A 네모 안에서 어법상 바른 것을 고르시오.

1 About 76 percent of the part-timers were not paying / paid extra for overtime work.

2 Debby sent / was sent a brand-new computer by her aunt as a birthday gift.

3 Chinese teaches / is taught to Julia by her grandfather who lived in China for five years.

B 다음 밑줄 친 부분이 어법상 바르면 ○를 쓰고, 틀리면 바르게 고치시오.

1 Several English comic books were bought for me by my friend Ashton.

2 The winners of the contest will give opportunities to study abroad.

3 I offered a job which requires good English conversation skills by my professor yesterday.

코드 접속하기

정답 및 해설 p.39

기출예제 ●────── **2023년 6월 교육청(고2) 29번**

Q1 다음 글의 밑줄 친 부분 중, 어법상 틀린 것은? [3점]　정답률 **38%**

　　Research psychologists often work with *self-report* data, made up of participants' verbal accounts of their behavior. This is the case ① <u>whenever</u> questionnaires, interviews, or personality inventories are used to measure variables. Self-report methods can be quite useful. They take advantage of the fact that people have a unique opportunity to observe ② <u>themselves</u> full-time. However, self-reports can be plagued by several kinds of distortion.　One of the most problematic of these distortions is the social desirability bias, which is a tendency to give ③ <u>socially</u> approved answers to questions about oneself. Subjects who are influenced by this bias work overtime trying to create a favorable impression, especially when subjects ④ <u>ask</u> about sensitive issues. For example, many survey respondents will report that they voted in an election or ⑤ <u>gave</u> to a charity when in fact it is possible to determine that they did not.

● 핵심 코드 : 능동태 vs. 수동태 ●

● **출제코드 1 적용**

1 주어가 동사의 주체인지 대상인지 파악한다.

2 주어가 동사의 대상이라면 동사는 수동태가 되어야 하며 '…되다, …당하다'의 의미가 된다.

코드 적용하기

① **복합관계부사**	복합관계부사 whenever가 부사절을 이끌고 있으므로 어법상 알맞다.
② **재귀대명사**	observe의 목적어가 주어(people)와 같은 대상을 가리키므로 재귀대명사 themselves가 오는 것이 적절하다.
③ **부사**	뒤의 형용사 approved를 수식하는 부사로 socially는 어법상 알맞다.
④ **능동태 vs. 수동태**	문맥상 주어인 피실험자들이 민감한 질문을 '하는' 주체가 아닌 '받는' 대상이므로, 동사는 수동태인 are asked가 되어야 한다. 주어가 복수이므로 복수형 be동사 are가 쓰였다.
⑤ **병렬구조**	등위접속사 or가 동사를 병렬 연결하고 있으므로, voted과 대등한 동사 gave는 어법상 적절하다.

코드 공략하기

● 2011년 9월 교육청(고1) 20번

01 ○△✕

다음 글의 밑줄 친 부분 중, 어법상 틀린 것은? 정답률 49%

The city of Pompeii is a ① partially buried Roman town-city near modern Naples. Pompeii was destroyed and buried ② during a long eruption of the volcano Mount Vesuvius in 79 AD. The eruption buried Pompeii under 4 to 6 meters of ash and stone, and it ③ lost for over 1,500 years before its accidental rediscovery in 1599. Since then, its rediscovery ④ has provided a detailed insight into the life at the height of the Roman Empire. Today, this UNESCO World Heritage Site is one of Italy's most popular tourist attractions, with about 2,500,000 people ⑤ visiting every year.

02 고득점 ○△✕

● 2019학년도 수능 29번

다음 글의 밑줄 친 부분 중, 어법상 틀린 것은? [3점] 정답률 32%

"Monumental" is a word that comes very close to ① expressing the basic characteristic of Egyptian art. Never before and never since has the quality of monumentality been achieved as fully as it ② did in Egypt. The reason for this is not the external size and massiveness of their works, although the Egyptians admittedly achieved some amazing things in this respect. Many modern structures exceed ③ those of Egypt in terms of purely physical size. But massiveness has nothing to do with monumentality. An Egyptian sculpture no bigger than a person's hand is more monumental than that gigantic pile of stones ④ that constitutes the war memorial in Leipzig, for instance. Monumentality is not a matter of external weight, but of "inner weight." This inner weight is the quality which Egyptian art possesses to such a degree that everything in it seems to be made of primeval stone, like a mountain range, even if it is only a few

inches across or ⑤ carved in wood.

*gigantic: 거대한 **primeval: 원시 시대의

03 ○△✕

● 2010년 3월 교육청(고2) 22번

다음 글의 밑줄 친 부분 중, 어법상 틀린 것은? 정답률 45%

Coffee is an important part of the Italian cuisine. Many of the different kinds of coffee drinks that we have around the world ① have originated from Italy. We commonly see people ② having coffee with milk. But it was the Italians ③ that first started the trend with the cappuccino which has coffee, milk, and an addition of milk foam on top. In the West and generally around the world, you can go for a cup of coffee ④ whenever you want. This attitude, however, will not ⑤ accept in Italy, where coffee is only a breakfast drink.

04 고득점 ○△✕

● 2014년 6월 교육청(고1) 24번

다음 글의 밑줄 친 부분 중, 어법상 틀린 것은? [3점] 정답률 35%

Ying Liu wanted to stop his six-year-old son, Jing, from watching so much TV. He also wanted to encourage Jing to play the piano and ① to do more math. The first thing Ying did was prepare. He made a list of his son's interests. It ② was included, in addition to watching TV, playing with Legos and going to the zoo. He then suggested to his son ③ that he could trade TV time, piano time, and study time for Legos and visits to the zoo. They established a point system, ④ where he got points whenever he watched less TV. Dad and son monitored the process together. As Jing got points, he felt valued and good about ⑤ himself and spent quality time with Dad.

05 ○△✕ ● 2015년 6월 교육청(고2) 28번

다음 글의 밑줄 친 부분 중, 어법상 틀린 것은? 정답률 47%

The process of job advancement in the field of sports ① is often said to be shaped like a pyramid. That is, at the wide base are many jobs with high school athletic teams, while at the narrow tip are the few, highly desired jobs with professional organizations. Thus there are many sports jobs altogether, but the competition becomes ② increasingly tough as one works their way up. The salaries of various positions reflect this pyramid model. For example, high school football coaches are typically teachers who ③ paid a little extra for their afterclass work. But coaches of the same sport at big universities can earn more than $1 million a year, causing the salaries of college presidents ④ to look small in comparison. One degree higher up is the National Football League, ⑤ where head coaches can earn many times more than their best-paid campus counterparts.

06 ○△✕ ● 2011년 4월 교육청(고3) 21번

(A)~(C)에서 어법에 맞는 표현을 바르게 짝지은 것은? 정답률 62%

People avoid feedback because they hate being criticized. Psychologists have a lot of theories about why people are so (A) sensitive / sensitively to hearing about their own imperfections. One is that they associate feedback with the critical comments received in their younger years from parents and teachers. (B) What / Whatever the cause of our discomfort is, most of us have to train ourselves to seek feedback and listen carefully when we hear it. Without that training, the very threat of critical feedback often leads us to (C) practice / be practiced destructive, maladaptive behaviors that negatively affect not only our work but the overall health of our organizations.

	(A)	(B)	(C)
①	sensitive	Whatever	practice
②	sensitive	Whatever	be practiced
③	sensitive	What	practice
④	sensitively	Whatever	practice
⑤	sensitively	What	be practiced

07 ○△✕ ● 2015년 10월 교육청(고3) 20번

다음 글의 밑줄 친 부분 중, 어법상 틀린 것은? [3점] 정답률 71%

In professional sports these days, it is not unusual ① to hear players and coaches talking about process. They talk about focusing on the process and following the process. Rarely ② do they talk about scoring a goal, a touchdown, a home run, a point, or achieving a good shot. It's all about process. So, what do they mean by this? What they mean by focusing on the process is that they focus on the actions they need to ③ be taken in order to achieve their desired result. They don't focus on the result itself. The reasoning here is ④ that if you follow the steps required, then the result will look after itself. This is one of the big differences between professional and amateur sportspeople. Amateurs often focus on the result and forget about ⑤ doing all the things that would almost automatically lead to the result.

08 고득점 ○△× • 2024년 6월 평가원(고3) 29번

다음 글의 밑줄 친 부분 중, 어법상 틀린 것은? 정답률 **23%**

What makes practicing retrieval so much better than review? One answer comes from the psychologist R. A. Bjork's concept of desirable difficulty. More difficult retrieval ① leads to better learning, provided the act of retrieval is itself successful. Free recall tests, in which students need to recall as much as they can remember without prompting, tend to result in better retention than cued recall tests, in which students ② give hints about what they need to remember. Cued recall tests, in turn, are better than recognition tests, such as multiple-choice answers, ③ where the correct answer needs to be recognized but not generated. Giving someone a test immediately after they learn something improves retention less than giving them a slight delay, long enough so that answers aren't in mind when they need ④ them. Difficulty, far from being a barrier to ⑤ making retrieval work, may be part of the reason it does so.

*retrieval: 불러오기 **retention: 보유력

09 고득점 ○△× • 2020년 9월 교육청(고1) 29번

다음 글의 밑줄 친 부분 중, 어법상 틀린 것은? [3점] 정답률 **44%**

Although it is obvious that part of our assessment of food is its visual appearance, it is perhaps surprising ① how visual input can override taste and smell. People find it very ② difficult to correctly identify fruit-flavoured drinks if the colour is wrong, for instance an orange drink that is coloured green. Perhaps even more striking ③ is the experience of wine tasters. One study of Bordeaux University students of wine and wine making revealed that they chose tasting notes appropriate for red wines, such as 'prune and chocolate', when they ④ gave white wine coloured with a red dye. Experienced New Zealand wine experts were similarly tricked into thinking ⑤ that the white wine Chardonnay was in fact a red wine, when it had been coloured with a red dye.

*override: ~에 우선하다 **prune: 자두

10 고득점 ○△× • 2010년 6월 교육청(고2) 22번

다음 글의 밑줄 친 부분 중, 어법상 틀린 것은? 정답률 **15%**

Imagine a school of fish weaving through a network of pipelines at the bottom of a bay. Only instead of ① live fish searching for food, these are robots patrolling for pipe damage and pollutant leaks. Robo-fish can fit in places divers and submarines can't. The newest ② are five to eighteen inches long, have about ten parts, and cost just hundreds of dollars. These robots made of a synthetic compound ③ designed to be flexible in the tail and rigid in the midsection. The motion of the material mimics the swimming motion of a real fish. Although the latest robotic fish are pretty close to ④ making a splash, they are not yet swimming in lakes and oceans. It'll be a few more years ⑤ before you can tell the story of the robo-fish that got away.

코드 접속하기

출제코드 1 완료시제
현재완료와 과거완료의 차이를 이해하고 조동사와 함께 쓰인 완료시제의 의미를 구분할 수 있는지 확인하는 문제가 출제된다.

STEP 1 핵심 문법

1 현재완료(have v-ed) vs. 과거완료(had v-ed)	완료시제는 기준 시점 이전의 일이 기준 시점까지 영향을 미치는 경우에 사용한다. 현재완료는 과거부터 현재까지, 과거완료는 과거 이전(대과거)부터 과거까지의 일을 나타낸다. 1) *Since he was fifteen*, he **has collected** Lego toys. (과거(15살)-현재까지) 2) Austin **had played** badminton *before he had a dinner with Lisa*. (대과거-과거(저녁 식사 전)) ※ 명백한 과거를 나타내는 부사구나 부사절이 쓰인 경우, 현재완료 시제를 쓰지 않는다. 3) He has visited(→ visited) numerous countries including Korea *last month*.
2 「조동사 + have v-ed」	「조동사 + 동사원형」은 현재나 미래 일에 대한 가능성, 추측 등을 나타낸다. 반면, 「조동사 + have v-ed」는 과거 일에 대한 추측이나 후회를 나타낸다. • may[might] have v-ed: ···했을지도 모른다(추측)　• must have v-ed: ···했음이 틀림없다(강한 추측) • cannot have v-ed: ···했을 리가 없다(강한 부정적 추측)　• could have v-ed: ···했을 수도 있다(불확실한 추측) • should have v-ed: ···했어야 했다(후회)　• shouldn't have v-ed: ···하지 말았어야 했다(후회) 1) She **should have visited** the Museum of Modern Art when she was in New York. 2) If you've ever climbed that mountain, you **may have seen** the great view from the top.

STEP 2 시험 패턴과 핵심 전략

1 과거 이전(대과거)의 일 → 과거완료	주절의 시제(과거)보다 더 앞선 일인 경우, 과거완료를 쓴다. Dad bought a toy car for me, which was what I has wanted / had wanted .
2 과거부터 현재까지의 일 → 현재완료	과거의 일이 현재까지 영향을 주는 경우, 현재완료를 쓴다. Since he was a little boy, he is / has been interested in soccer.
3 과거의 일 → 「조동사 + have v-ed」	과거 일에 대한 추측이나 후회를 나타내는 경우, 「조동사 + have v-ed」를 쓴다. He didn't answer my call. He might be / have been asleep.

정답 및 해설 p.47

STEP 3 전략 적용 연습

A 네모 안에서 어법상 바른 것을 고르시오.

1 Even though Julia have tried / had tried her best on her final exam, she got a poor grade.

2 Since 2002, they suggested / have suggested new ways to study the culture of the Middle Ages. 기출 응용

3 We should meet / have met the professor before he moved to another college.

B 다음 밑줄 친 부분이 어법상 바르면 ○를 쓰고, 틀리면 바르게 고치시오.

1 For last five years, she <u>practiced</u> dancing really hard to achieve her dream.

2 Paul lost the cellphone that his parents <u>have bought</u> for him the day before.

3 George had never seen Helena before, so he can't <u>have recognized</u> her.

코드 접속하기

출제코드 2 대동사 do
대동사 do의 쓰임을 이해하는지 확인하는 문제가 출제된다.

STEP 1 핵심 문법

1 대동사 do	대동사 do는 앞에 나온 일반동사(구)의 반복을 피하기 위해 사용되는 동사이다. 1) She *has* more shoes than I **do**. (= have) 2) I *like* dogs and so **does** my child. (= likes)
2 대동사의 시제와 수	대동사 do도 동사처럼 시제와 주어의 수에 따라 did, does로 변형하여 써야 한다. 1) He *earns* more money than he **did** *last year*. (과거시제) 2) Ben *works out* as hard as *an athlete* **does**. (3인칭 단수 주어, 현재시제)

STEP 2 시험 패턴과 핵심 전략

1 일반동사(구) 뒤 → 대동사 do[does/did]	주절의 동사가 일반동사(구)인 경우, 이를 대신하는 동사로 do[does/did]를 쓴다. 1) The kids didn't make noise as often as their parents were /did. 2) She talks a lot about her favorite singers as teenagers usually are. (→ do) 3) In August, it rains more in Seoul than it do in Daegu. (→ does)

정답 및 해설 p.47

STEP 3 전략 적용 연습

A 네모 안에서 어법상 바른 것을 고르시오.

1 As the machine has been repaired, it works as well as a new machine is / does now.

2 These days, people probably spend more time on the Internet than they do / are in their cars. 기출 응용

B 다음 밑줄 친 부분이 어법상 바르면 ○를 쓰고, 틀리면 바르게 고치시오.

1 I looked up the night sky, as do the people in the field.

2 People who are selfish do not make wise decisions as well as selfless people are. 기출 응용

3 It is assumed that early human beings ate mainly the muscle flesh of animals as we do today. 기출 응용

코드 접속하기

정답 및 해설 p.47

기출예제 ●━━━━━━━━━━━━━ ● 2017년 6월 교육청(고2) 28번

Q1 다음 글의 밑줄 친 부분 중, 어법상 틀린 것은? [3점] 　정답률 40%

Cutting costs can improve profitability but only up to a point. If the manufacturer cuts costs so deeply ① that doing so harms the product's quality, then the increased profitability will be short-lived. A better approach is to improve productivity. If businesses can get more production from the same number of employees, they're ② basically tapping into free money. They get more product to sell, and the price of each product falls. As long as the machinery or employee training ③ needed for productivity improvements costs less than the value of the productivity gains, it's an easy investment for any business to make. Productivity improvements are as important to the economy as they ④ do to the individual business that's making them. Productivity improvements generally raise the standard of living for everyone and ⑤ are a good indication of a healthy economy.

● 핵심 코드 : 대동사 do ●

● 출제코드 2 적용

1 do가 일반동사로 쓰였는지, 대동사로 쓰였는지 확인한다.

2 대동사 do가 앞에 어떤 동사를 대신하여 쓰였는지 확인한다.

코드 적용하기

① 「so + 부사 + that ...」	'너무 ~해서 …하다'의 의미인 「so + 부사 + that ...」 구문으로, 접속사 that이 오는 것이 알맞다.
② 부사	부사 basically가 동사(are tapping)를 수식하고 있으므로 어법상 바르다.
③ 명사를 수식하는 과거분사	앞의 명사구 the machinery or employee training을 수식하는 분사로, 수식받는 명사(구)와 분사가 의미상 수동 관계이므로 과거분사 needed가 오는 것이 어법상 바르다.
④ 대동사 do	대동사 do는 앞에 나온 일반동사(구)를 대신하는데, 밑줄 친 부분은 앞 절에 쓰인 are important가 반복되어 쓰이는 자리이므로, do를 are로 고쳐야 한다.
⑤ 병렬구조	등위접속사 and가 동사 raise와 are를 병렬 연결하고 있는 구조로 주어(Productivity improvements)가 복수 명사이므로 복수 동사 are는 어법상 바르다.

01 ○△✕ ● 2009년 3월 교육청(고1) 21번

(A), (B), (C)의 각 네모 안에서 어법에 맞는 표현으로 가장 적절한 것은? 정답률 54%

A driver saw two men carrying heavy bags on a lonely country road. This reminded him of the news (A) [what / that] he had heard on the radio: two thieves stopped a train and stole mailbags full of money. He at once called the police. The police soon arrived on the scene and arrested them. They questioned (B) [both / each] men but neither of them could speak English. They just kept shouting loudly at the police. Later, the police realized that they (C) [have made / had made] a terrible mistake. The men were French onion-sellers and their bags were full of onions!

	(A)		(B)		(C)
①	what	⋯⋯	each	⋯⋯	have made
②	what	⋯⋯	both	⋯⋯	had made
③	that	⋯⋯	each	⋯⋯	have made
④	that	⋯⋯	both	⋯⋯	have made
⑤	that	⋯⋯	both	⋯⋯	had made

02 고득점 ○△✕ ● 2013년 9월 교육청(고1) 27번

다음 글의 밑줄 친 부분 중, 어법상 틀린 것은? [3점] 정답률 44%

Grateful people are inclined to make healthy decisions. Life and sports present many situations ① where critical and difficult decisions have to be made. Selfish adults or kids do not make sound decisions as well as ② are grateful people. This includes the decision to be self-motivated. Frustrated parents ask: "How do I motivate my child to do sports or continue in sports? Sometimes my child gets ③ discouraged and does not want to put the required effort into his or her sports? What can I, as a parent, do or say to help?" It is difficult and almost impossible ④ to motivate kids or adults who are centered on their own narrow selfish desires. However, kids and adults who live as grateful people are able to motivate ⑤ themselves. They also welcome suggestions from others, even parents.

03 고득점 ○△✕ ● 2011년 3월 교육청(고3) 20번

다음 글의 밑줄 친 부분 중, 어법상 틀린 것은? 정답률 44%

Archaeologist Mark Aldenderfer set out last year to explore remote cliffside caves in Nepal's Mustang district, aiming to find human remains near an ancient settlement ① high in the Himalayas. Almost at once, he came face-to-face with ② what he was seeking: Sticking out from the rock, a skull was looking at him right ③ as he was looking at it. The skull, dating back perhaps 2,500 years, was among many human bones ④ piled inside several burial caves. Aldenderfer and his team hope that DNA analysis will pinpoint the origins of this isolated region's inhabitants, who may ⑤ migrate from the Tibetan Plateau or southern points.

04

다음 글의 밑줄 친 부분 중, 어법상 틀린 것은? [3점] 정답률 **40%**

Before the washing machine was invented, people used washboards to scrub, or they carried their laundry to riverbanks and streams, ① where they beat and rubbed it against rocks. Such backbreaking labor is still commonplace in parts of the world, but for most homeowners the work is now done by a machine that ② automatically regulates water temperature, measures out the detergent, washes, rinses, and spin-dries. With ③ its electrical and mechanical system, the washing machine is one of the most technologically advanced examples of a large household appliance. It not only cleans clothes, but it ④ is so with far less water, detergent, and energy than washing by hand requires. ⑤ Compared with the old washers that squeezed out excess water by feeding clothes through rollers, modern washers are indeed an electrical-mechanical phenomenon.

05

(A), (B), (C)의 각 네모 안에서 어법에 맞는 표현을 골라 짝지은 것으로 가장 적절한 것은? 정답률 **53%**

One day last summer when I was in the bathroom, the lock on the door jammed. I couldn't get it unlocked (A) how / however hard I tried. I thought about my predicament. I didn't think the neighbors could hear me if I shouted. Then I remembered the small window on the back wall. The basin (B) near / nearly the window provided an easy step up. After climbing out the window, I hung from the window sill for a few seconds and then easily dropped to the ground. Later my mother came home and asked me what I (C) have / had been doing. Laughing, I responded, "Oh, just hanging around." *predicament: 곤경

	(A)	(B)	(C)
①	how	near	have
②	how	nearly	had
③	however	nearly	have
④	however	near	have
⑤	however	near	had

06

(A), (B), (C)의 각 네모 안에서 어법에 맞는 표현으로 가장 적절한 것은? 정답률 **48%**

Most amateur speakers do not understand that when they are on stage they are actors and actresses. Most do have some idea that they should speak with more power on stage than they (A) are / do on a one-to-one basis, but they do not realize that their verbal eloquence must be matched with a nonverbal eloquence. If you move your hand two inches to emphasize a point when (B) speaking / to speak to one person, you may have to move it as much as two feet in front of a large audience. The general rule is, the bigger the audience, the bigger the motion. This is so difficult for people, especially businesspeople whose general style is that of understatement, (C) which / that they should take an acting course before they take a speech course.

	(A)	(B)	(C)
①	are	speaking	which
②	are	to speak	which
③	do	to speak	that
④	do	to speak	which
⑤	do	speaking	that

3
관계사, 전치사, 접속사

UNIT 01
관계사 1

UNIT 02
관계사 2

UNIT 03
전치사와 접속사

출제코드 분석

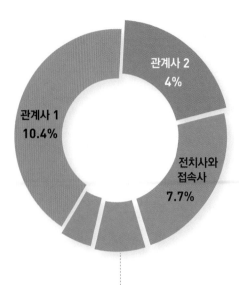

관계사 1

1 관계대명사의 쓰임
2 접속사와 관계대명사
3 주의해야 할 관계대명사

관계사 2

1 관계부사의 쓰임
2 복합관계대명사 vs. 복합관계부사

전치사와 접속사

1 전치사 vs. 접속사
2 종속접속사

2009년 – 2024년 평가원/교육청 기출 분석

출제 경향

1 문장의 구조와 성분을 파악하여, 절과 절을 연결하는 위치에 들어갈 알맞은 말을 찾는 문제가 출제되고 있다.

2 뒤에 연결되는 어구의 역할과 의미에 따라 접속사와 전치사를 구별하여 쓸 수 있는지 확인하는 문제가 출제되고 있다.

학습 전략

1 관계사

1) 여러 절이 연결된 문장의 경우, 절 단위로 문장성분을 분석하는 연습을 한다.
2) 대명사, 접속사, 관계대명사, 관계부사의 차이와 각각의 기능에 대해 학습한다.
3) 주의해야 할 관계사의 용법에 대해 학습한다.

2 전치사와 접속사

1) 구와 절의 차이와 전치사와 접속사의 기본적인 쓰임에 대해 학습한다.
2) 문장 안에서 접속사가 이끄는 절의 역할과 의미를 구별하는 연습을 한다.

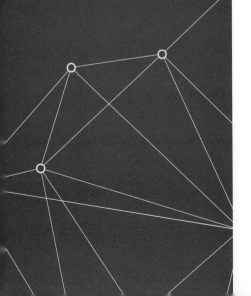

코드 접속하기

출제코드 1 관계대명사의 쓰임
대명사와 관계대명사의 차이를 구분하고, 관계대명사의 쓰임을 이해하는지 확인하는 문제가 출제된다.

STEP 1 핵심 문법

1 대명사 vs. 관계대명사	관계대명사는 절과 절을 연결하는 접속사 역할과 선행사를 대신하는 대명사 역할을 한다. 대명사는 명사를 대신하는 역할을 할 뿐, 절과 절을 연결하는 접속사 역할은 할 수 없다. There are two books on the desk. I have already read **them**(= two books). → There are two books on the desk **which** I have already read.

2 관계대명사의 격

관계대명사의 격은 관계대명사절 안에서의 역할에 따라 달라진다.

선행사	주격	소유격	목적격(생략 가능)
사람	who, that	whose	who(m), that
사물, 동물	which, that	whose, of which	which, that

1) *The boy* [**who**[**that**] is playing the guitar] is my brother. (주격)
2) She is *a famous writer* [**whose** works are read by people all around the world]. (소유격)
3) *The man* [(**whom**[**that**]) I met] doesn't let his child watch TV during the exam period. (목적격)

STEP 2 시험 패턴과 핵심 전략

1 절과 절을 연결하는 위치 → 대명사 vs. 관계대명사	대명사는 절과 절을 연결하는 기능이 없으므로, 「접속사 + 대명사」 역할을 하는 관계대명사를 쓴다. 1) They are scheduled to take a bus it / ⓦhich leaves at 10:30. 2) I have a sister her left eye is bigger than her right eye. (→ whose)

2 관계대명사의 격 → 주격 vs. 소유격 vs. 목적격

관계대명사는 뒤에 오는 절의 형태와 절 안에서의 역할에 따라 주격, 소유격, 목적격으로 써야 한다.

동사 앞에서 주어 역할 → 주격	뒤에 오는 명사를 수식 → 소유격	주어 + 동사 앞에서 동사의 목적어 역할 → 목적격

1) I saw the rich man ⓦho / whom lives on the top floor of the building.
2) Jenny is dating a man whom / ⓦhose father was a baseball player.
3) He couldn't find the wallet whose his wife left on the desk. (→ which[that])

정답 및 해설 p.52

STEP 3 전략 적용 연습

A 네모 안에서 어법상 바른 것을 고르시오.

1 This is the library it / that has now become the biggest in the city with over one million books.

2 Almost every evening she plays a game with her son who / which she calls the "memory game."

3 J. K. Rowling, who / whose novels have gained great popularity around the world, was born in 1965.

B 다음 밑줄 친 부분이 어법상 바르면 ○를 쓰고, 틀리면 바르게 고치시오.

1 He is a person whom I am sure does his best to overcome tough situations.

2 Some musicians their names you've heard earn more than $30,000 for a single performance. 기출 응용

코드 접속하기

출제코드 2 접속사와 관계대명사
접속사와 관계대명사의 차이를 구분하고, 관계대명사 what의 쓰임을 이해하는지 확인하는
문제가 출제된다.

STEP 1 핵심 문법

1 접속사 vs. 관계대명사	접속사는 절과 절을 연결하며 뒤에 문장성분이 완전한 절(주어 + 동사 …)이 이어진다. 관계대명사는 관계대명사절에서 빠진 성분을 대신하므로 뒤에 불완전한 절이 이어진다. 1) The rumor [**that** the two companies will merge] turned out to be true. 　　　　　　접속사　　　　　　완전한 절 2) I don't like people [**who** don't listen to other people]. 　　　주격 관계대명사　　　주어가 빠진 불완전한 절
2 관계대명사 what	what은 선행사를 포함하고 있는 관계대명사로, 앞에 선행사가 오지 않는다. what은 '…하는 것'이라는 의미로 명사절을 이끌며, 관계대명사절 안에서 주어나 목적어 역할을 한다. 1) [**What** makes him different from others] is his friendly manner. 　　관계대명사(주어)　　주어가 빠진 불완전한 절 2) This is [**what** I have learned from my English course this semester]. 　　관계대명사(목적어)　　목적어가 빠진 불완전한 절

STEP 2 시험 패턴과 핵심 전략

1 접속사(that) vs. 　관계대명사(what): 　1) 완전한 절 앞 → that 　2) 불완전한 절 앞 → what	뒤에 완전한 절이 이어지면 접속사 that을, 주어나 목적어가 빠진 불완전한 절이 오면 관계대명사 what을 쓴다. 1) The study shows (that)/ what frowning uses more muscles than smiling does. 2) That I really want to do is to go home early and get some rest. (→ what) 3) The truth is <u>what</u> most people only brush their teeth for less than a minute. (→ that)
2 관계대명사(which[that]) 　vs. 관계대명사(what): 　1) 선행사 뒤 → which[that] 　2) 선행사 없음 → what	앞에 선행사가 있으면 관계대명사 which나 that을, 선행사가 없으면 관계대명사 what을 쓴다. 1) My daughter never told me which /(what) she did this morning. 2) He bought his house with the money (that)/ what he earned through stock investment.

정답 및 해설 p.52

STEP 3 전략 적용 연습

A 네모 안에서 어법상 바른 것을 고르시오.

1 This class was so difficult for the students that / what many of them failed.

2 Leonardo had an unusual ability to see which / what ordinary people couldn't see. 기출 응용

3 Try to do something that / what you've been planning for a long time but haven't started.

B 다음 밑줄 친 부분이 어법상 바르면 ○를 쓰고, 틀리면 바르게 고치시오.

1 <u>Which</u> happened to me yesterday was so amazing that I can't describe it.

2 She thought she would be able to find another job <u>what</u> was a better match. 기출 응용

코드 접속하기

출제코드 3 주의해야 할 관계대명사
관계대명사의 기본 쓰임 외에 주의해야 할 관계대명사 용법들을 이해하는지 확인하는 문제가 출제된다.

STEP 1 핵심 문법

1 관계대명사의 계속적 용법	관계대명사 앞에 콤마(,)를 써서 나타내며, 선행사에 대한 부가적인 설명을 덧붙일 때 사용한다. 계속적 용법의 관계대명사는 생략할 수 없고, 관계대명사 which는 앞에 나온 절을 선행사로 하기도 한다. ※ 관계대명사 that과 what은 계속적 용법으로 쓸 수 없다. 1) I met *the new employee*, **who** had been hired to replace Tom. 2) *They want to go swimming over the safety line*, **which** is not a good idea. 3) He looks much better without *his beard*, **which** made him look older. (*He looks much better without his beard*, **that** *made him look older.* (×))
2 「전치사 + 관계대명사」	관계대명사절에서 관계대명사가 전치사의 목적어인 경우, 전치사는 관계대명사 앞에 위치한다. 이때 관계대명사는 생략할 수 없고, 관계대명사 that은 전치사 뒤에 쓸 수 없다. 전치사가 관계대명사와 떨어져 쓰일 경우, 관계대명사는 생략할 수 있고, that도 사용할 수 있다. *cf.*「부분을 나타내는 말(some/many/one/most 등)+ of」는 반드시 관계대명사 앞에 온다. 1) I can't find *the café* **of which** you took a nice picture. 　　　　　　　　= (**which**) you took a nice picture **of** 　　　　　　　　= (**that**) you took a nice picture **of** 2) He has *many foreign friends*, **one of whom** is a Chinese girl.

STEP 2 시험 패턴과 핵심 전략

1 콤마(,) 뒤 관계대명사	앞에 콤마(,)가 있는 경우, 관계대명사 that이나 what은 쓸 수 없다. 1) The baby was covered in a blanket, which / that kept out the cold. 2) He said he repaired his laptop, what turned out to be a lie. (→ which)
2 관계대명사 vs. 「전치사 + 관계대명사」	선행사가 관계대명사절에서 전치사의 목적어인 경우, 「전치사 + 관계대명사」를 쓴다. They went back to the restaurant which / in which they had dinner.

정답 및 해설 p.53

STEP 3 전략 적용 연습

A 네모 안에서 어법상 바른 것을 고르시오.

1 This workshop will be a time which / during which you can find yourselves.

2 He still thinks of his first love, that / whom he misses from time to time.

B 다음 밑줄 친 부분이 어법상 바르면 ○를 쓰고, 틀리면 바르게 고치시오.

1 Find something special about each day that you can be grateful. 기출 응용

2 Hippocrates prescribed willow bark, what contains a natural form of medicine. 기출 응용

3 His new album contains 10 songs, some of that have gained great popularity.

코드 접속하기

정답 및 해설 p.53

기출예제 ●2021학년도 수능 29번

Q1 다음 글의 밑줄 친 부분 중, 어법상 틀린 것은? [3점] 정답률 **60%**

Regulations covering scientific experiments on human subjects are strict. Subjects must give their informed, written consent, and experimenters must submit their proposed experiments to thorough examination by overseeing bodies. Scientists who experiment on themselves can, functionally if not legally, avoid the restrictions ① associated with experimenting on other people. They can also sidestep most of the ethical issues involved: nobody, presumably, is more aware of an experiment's potential hazards than the scientist who devised ② it. Nonetheless, experimenting on oneself remains ③ deeply problematic. One obvious drawback is the danger involved; knowing that it exists ④ does nothing to reduce it. A less obvious drawback is the limited range of data that the experiment can generate. Human anatomy and physiology vary, in small but significant ways, according to gender, age, lifestyle, and other factors. Experimental results derived from a single subject are, therefore, of limited value; there is no way to know ⑤ what the subject's responses are typical or atypical of the response of humans as a group.

*consent: 동의 **anatomy: (해부학적) 구조 ***physiology: 생리적 현상

● 핵심 코드 : 접속사 vs. 관계대명사 ●

● **출제코드 2 적용**

1 뒤에 이어지는 절이 완전한 절인지 불완전한 절인지 파악한다.

2 뒤에 완전한 절이 이어지면 접속사를, 불완전한 절이 이어지면 관계대명사를 쓴다.

코드 적용하기

① 명사를 수식하는 과거분사	앞의 명사구 the restrictions를 수식하는 분사로, 다른 사람을 실험하는 것과 '관련된' 규제라는 수동의 의미이므로 과거분사 associated가 오는 것은 어법상 알맞다.
② 대명사	문맥상 앞에 언급된 an experiment를 지칭하는 대명사로, 지칭하는 명사가 단수이므로 단수 대명사 it이 오는 것은 어법상 알맞다.
③ 부사	형용사 problematic을 수식하고 있으므로 부사 deeply의 쓰임은 어법상 바르다.
④ 동사의 수 일치	문장의 주어가 동명사구(knowing ... exists)이므로 단수 동사 does가 오는 것은 어법상 알맞다.
⑤ 접속사 vs. 관계대명사	뒤에 동사 know의 목적어로 쓰인 완전한 절이 이어지며, '…인지'라는 의미로 해석되므로 접속사 whether가 오는 것이 알맞다. 관계대명사 what은 불완전한 절을 이끌며 '…한 것'이라는 의미이다.

코드 접속하기

기출예제 ●————————————● 2023년 3월 교육청(고3) 29번

Q2 다음 글의 밑줄 친 부분 중, 어법상 틀린 것은? [3점] [정답률 31%]

From the 8th to the 12th century CE, while Europe suffered the perhaps overdramatically named Dark Ages, science on planet Earth could be found almost ① exclusively in the Islamic world. This science was not exactly like our science today, but it was surely antecedent to ② it and was nonetheless an activity aimed at knowing about the world. Muslim rulers granted scientific institutions tremendous resources, such as libraries, observatories, and hospitals. Great schools in all the cities ③ covering the Arabic Near East and Northern Africa (and even into Spain) trained generations of scholars. Almost every word in the modern scientific lexicon that begins with the prefix "al" ④ owes its origins to Islamic science — algorithm, alchemy, alcohol, alkali, algebra. And then, just over 400 years after it started, it ground to an apparent halt, and it would be a few hundred years, give or take, before ⑤ that we would today unmistakably recognize as science appeared in Europe — with Galileo, Kepler, and, a bit later, Newton.

*antecedent: 선행하는   * lexicon: 어휘 (목록)   ***give or take: 대략

● 핵심 코드 : 관계대명사 what ●

● 출제코드 2 적용

1 ⑤ 뒤에 동사 recognize의 목적어가 빠진 불완전한 절이 이어지고 있으므로 관계대명사가 와야 한다.

2 앞에 선행사 없이 주어 역할을 하는 명사절을 이끌 수 있는 관계대명사는 what이다.

코드 적용하기

① 부사	부사 exclusively는 동사 can be found를 수식하고 있으므로 어법상 알맞다.
② 대명사	it은 앞에 나온 our science를 지칭하는 대명사로, 지칭하는 명사가 단수이므로 단수 대명사 it은 어법상 알맞다.
③ 명사를 수식하는 현재분사	covering은 앞의 명사구 the cities를 수식하는 현재분사로, 분사와의 관계가 능동이므로 현재분사가 알맞다.
④ 동사의 수 일치	문장의 주어는 Almost every word이며 「every + 단수 명사」는 단수 취급하므로, 단수 동사 owes는 어법상 알맞다.
⑤ 관계대명사 what	뒤에 목적어가 빠진 불완전한 절이 이어지고 있으며 동사 appeared의 주어 역할을 하는 명사절을 이끌고 있으므로, 관계대명사 what이 와야 한다.

01 ☐○△✕ ● 2010년 6월 교육청(고1) 22번

다음 글의 밑줄 친 부분 중, 어법상 틀린 것은? [3점] 정답률 **63%**

　　Raised in a poor family, Confucius truly understood the suffering of the people. In his view, the lords of his country, only interested in their own personal gain, ① were responsible for it. Therefore, he gathered a group of intelligent followers ② what he trained in several subjects including ethics. He believed that government leaders must be humane, honest and ③ fair, not experts in administration. He taught his students that it is the role of rulers ④ to secure the happiness of their people. He had considerable success in placing his pupils in positions of power in government. When the men who ⑤ had been trained by him were sent into service, even immoral rulers valued their honesty.

02 ☐○△✕ ● 2015년 3월 교육청(고1) 28번

다음 글의 밑줄 친 부분 중, 어법상 틀린 것은? [3점] 정답률 **53%**

　　One cool thing about my Uncle Arthur was ① what he could always pick the best places to camp. One time, we went to Garrison Rock. Uncle Arthur said that the Indians stayed there. On trips like this, he would always have a good story ② to tell. His stories were always aimed at ③ helping us children use our brains to get out of trouble. For example, one story was about a guy being ④ chased by a big dog. They ran into a field. We kids were thinking that the dog would catch him. But the guy saw a bathtub in the field. He ran to the bathtub and ⑤ pulled it over himself. The dog just barked and barked until it went away. Then the guy came out of the bathtub, and went home.

03 고득점 ☐○△✕ ● 2013년 3월 교육청(고2) 27번

다음 글의 밑줄 친 부분 중, 어법상 틀린 것은? [3점] 정답률 **34%**

　　How you address your professors depends on many factors such as age, college culture, and their own preference. Some teachers will ask you ① to call them by their first names, especially if they're relatively young. They enjoy the informal atmosphere ② generated by having everyone in the class on the same level. Some colleges, in fact, pride themselves on having all their faculty and students on a first-name basis. But beware: one of the surest ways to upset professors ③ is to call them by their first names against their wishes. Most professors see themselves in a position of professional authority over their students ④ whom they earned by many years of study. They no more want to be called John or Maria than ⑤ does your average physician.

04 〇△✕ ────────── ● 2024년 6월 교육청(고1) 29번

다음 글의 밑줄 친 부분 중, 어법상 틀린 것은? 정답률 73%

The hunter-gatherer lifestyle, which can ① be described as "natural" to human beings, appears to have had much to recommend it. Examination of human remains from early hunter-gatherer societies ② has suggested that our ancestors enjoyed abundant food, obtainable without excessive effort, and suffered very few diseases. If this is true, it is not clear why so many humans settled in permanent villages and developed agriculture, growing crops and domesticating animals: cultivating fields was hard work, and it was in farming villages ③ what epidemic diseases first took root. Whatever its immediate effect on the lives of humans, the development of settlements and agriculture ④ undoubtedly led to a high increase in population density. This period, known as the New Stone Age, was a major turning point in human development, ⑤ opening the way to the growth of the first towns and cities, and eventually leading to settled "civilizations."

*remains: 유적, 유해 **epidemic: 전염병의

05 〇△✕ ────────── ● 2013년 11월 교육청(고2) 27번

다음 글의 밑줄 친 부분 중, 어법상 틀린 것은? [3점] 정답률 60%

An ambiguous term is one which has more than a single meaning and ① whose context does not clearly indicate which meaning is intended. For instance, a sign posted at a fork in a trail which ② reads "Bear To The Right" can be understood in two ways. The more probable meaning is that it is instructing hikers to take the right trail, not the left. But let us ③ say that the ranger who painted the sign meant to say just the opposite. He was trying to warn hikers against taking the right trail because there is a bear in the area through which it passes. The ranger's language was therefore careless, and open to misinterpretation ④ what could have serious consequences. The only way to avoid ambiguity is to spell things out as ⑤ explicitly as possible: "Keep left. Do not use trail to the right. Bears in the area."

06 〇△✕ ────────── ● 2022학년도 수능 29번

다음 글의 밑줄 친 부분 중, 어법상 틀린 것은? [3점] 정답률 54%

Like whole individuals, cells have a life span. During their life cycle (cell cycle), cell size, shape, and metabolic activities can change dramatically. A cell is "born" as a twin when its mother cell divides, ① producing two daughter cells. Each daughter cell is smaller than the mother cell, and except for unusual cases, each grows until it becomes as large as the mother cell ② was. During this time, the cell absorbs water, sugars, amino acids, and other nutrients and assembles them into new, living protoplasm. After the cell has grown to the proper size, its metabolism shifts as it either prepares to divide or matures and ③ differentiates into a specialized cell. Both growth and development require a complex and dynamic set of interactions involving all cell parts. ④ What cell metabolism and structure should be complex would not be surprising, but actually, they are rather simple and logical. Even the most complex cell has only a small number of parts, each ⑤ responsible for a distinct, well-defined aspect of cell life.

*metabolic: 물질대사의 **protoplasm: 원형질

07 ◯△✕ ● 2015년 3월 교육청(고3) 28번

다음 글의 밑줄 친 부분 중, 어법상 틀린 것은? [3점] 정답률 66%

Coming home from work the other day, I saw a woman trying to turn onto the main street and ① having very little luck because of the constant stream of traffic. I slowed and allowed her to turn in front of me. I was feeling pretty good until, a couple of blocks later, she stopped to let a few more cars into the line, causing us both to miss the next light. I found myself completely ② irritated with her. How dare she slow me down after I had so graciously let her into the traffic! As I was sitting there stewing, I realized ③ how ridiculous I was being. Suddenly, a phrase I once read ④ came floating into my mind: 'You must do him or her a kindness for inner reasons, not because someone is keeping score or because you will be punished if you don't.' I realized ⑤ what I had wanted a reward: If I do this nice thing for you, you (or someone else) will do an equally nice thing for me.

*stew: 안달하다

08 고득점 ◯△✕ ● 2020년 6월 교육청(고2) 29번

다음 글의 밑줄 친 부분 중, 어법상 틀린 것은? 정답률 40%

Every farmer knows that the hard part is getting the field ① prepared. Inserting seeds and watching ② them grow is easy. In the case of science and industry, the community prepares the field, yet society tends to give all the credit to the individual who happens to plant a successful seed. Planting a seed does not necessarily require overwhelming intelligence; creating an environment that allows seeds to prosper ③ does. We need to give more credit to the community in science, politics, business, and daily life. Martin Luther King Jr. was a great man. Perhaps his greatest strength was his ability ④ to inspire people to work together to achieve, against all odds, revolutionary changes in society's perception of race and in the fairness of the law. But to really understand ⑤ that he accomplished requires looking beyond the man. Instead of treating him as the manifestation of everything great, we should appreciate his role in allowing America to show that it can be great.

*manifestation: 표명

09 고득점 ○△✕ ● 2022년 6월 평가원(고3) 29번

다음 글의 밑줄 친 부분 중, 어법상 틀린 것은? [3점] 정답률 44%

Ecosystems differ in composition and extent. They can be defined as ranging from the communities and interactions of organisms in your mouth or ① those in the canopy of a rain forest to all those in Earth's oceans. The processes ② governing them differ in complexity and speed. There are systems that turn over in minutes, and there are others ③ which rhythmic time extends to hundreds of years. Some ecosystems are extensive ('biomes', such as the African savanna); some cover regions (river basins); many involve clusters of villages (micro-watersheds); others are confined to the level of a single village (the village pond). In each example there is an element of indivisibility. Divide an ecosystem into parts by creating barriers, and the sum of the productivity of the parts will typically be found to be lower than the productivity of the whole, other things ④ being equal. The mobility of biological populations is a reason. Safe passages, for example, enable migratory species ⑤ to survive.

*canopy: 덮개 **basin: 유역

10 고득점 ○△✕ ● 2014년 4월 교육청(고3) 24번

다음 글의 밑줄 친 부분 중, 어법상 틀린 것은? [3점] 정답률 33%

In some communities, music and performance have successfully transformed whole neighborhoods as ① profoundly as The Guggenheim Museum did in Bilbao. In Salvador, Brazil, musician Carlinhos Brown established several music and culture centers in formerly dangerous neighborhoods. In Candeal, ② where Brown was born, local kids were encouraged to join drum groups, sing, and stage performances. The kids, energized by these activities, ③ began to turn away from dealing drugs. Being a young criminal was no longer their only life option. Being musicians and playing together in a group looked like more fun and was more ④ satisfying. Little by little, the crime rate dropped in those neighborhoods; the hope returned. In another slum area, possibly inspired by Brown's example, a culture center began to encourage the local kids to stage musical events, some of ⑤ them dramatized the tragedy that they were still recovering from.

01 ○△✕ ● 2014년 3월 교육청(고1) 23번

다음 글의 밑줄 친 부분 중, 어법상 틀린 것은? 정답률 **65%**

It's important to remember that good decisions can still lead to bad outcomes. Here is an example. Soon after I got out of school, I ① was offered a job. I wasn't sure that was a great fit for me. After carefully considering the opportunity, I decided to ② turn it down. I thought that I would be able to find another job ③ what was a better match. Unfortunately, the economy soon grew worse quickly and I spent months ④ looking for another job. I kicked myself for ⑤ not taking that position, which started to look more and more appealing. I had made a good decision, based upon all the information I had at the time, but in the short run it didn't lead to a great outcome.

02 ○△✕ ● 2024년 9월 평가원(고3) 29번

다음 글의 밑줄 친 부분 중, 어법상 틀린 것은? 정답률 **75%**

Victorian England is characterised by the full development of the Industrial Revolution. England became the first industrial nation in the world and, by 1850, the first nation to have more people ① employed in industry than in agriculture. Expanding trade coincided with the growth of the Empire and brought great wealth to Britain, but this wealth was not ② evenly distributed. Many enterprising individuals (the 'self-made men') rose from humble origins to positions of wealth and influence, but large sections of the working class ③ were forced into the overcrowded slums of large cities where they worked long hours for low wages in unhealthy conditions. The manufacturing towns of the north of England provided some of the worst examples and ④ inspired such socially conscious novels as Kingsley's *Alton Locke*, Gaskell's *Mary Barton*, and Dickens's *Hard Times*. In the south there was London, already the largest city in the world, showing all the crime, evil, and misery ⑤ whose result from overpopulation and unplanned growth.

03 고득점 ○△✕ ● 2019년 3월 교육청(고2) 28번

다음 글의 밑줄 친 부분 중, 어법상 틀린 것은? 정답률 **27%**

If there's one thing koalas are good at, it's sleeping. For a long time many scientists suspected that koalas were so lethargic ① because the compounds in eucalyptus leaves kept the cute little animals in a drugged-out state. But more recent research has shown that the leaves are simply so low in nutrients ② that koalas have almost no energy. Therefore they tend to move as little as possible — and when they ③ do move, they often look as though they're in slow motion. They rest sixteen to eighteen hours a day and spend most of that unconscious. In fact, koalas spend little time thinking; their brains actually appear to ④ have shrunk over the last few centuries. The koala is the only known animal ⑤ its brain only fills half of its skull.

*lethargic: 무기력한 **drugged-out: 몽롱한, 취한

04 ○△✕ ● 2024학년도 수능 29번

다음 글의 밑줄 친 부분 중, 어법상 틀린 것은? 정답률 **58%**

A number of studies provide substantial evidence of an innate human disposition to respond differentially to social stimuli. From birth, infants will orient preferentially towards the human face and voice, ① seeming to know that such stimuli are particularly meaningful for them. Moreover, they register this connection actively, imitating a variety of facial gestures that are presented to them—tongue protrusions, lip tightenings, mouth openings. They will even try to match gestures ② which they have some difficulty, experimenting with their own faces until they succeed. When they ③ do succeed, they show pleasure by a brightening of their eyes; when

they fail, they show distress. In other words, they not only have an innate capacity for matching their own kinaesthetically experienced bodily movements with ④ those of others that are visually perceived; they have an innate drive to do so. That is, they seem to have an innate drive to imitate others whom they judge ⑤ to be 'like me'.

*innate: 타고난 **disposition: 성향 ***kinaesthetically: 운동감각적으로

05 ○△✕ ┈┈┈┈ ● 2009년 9월 교육청(고1) 21번

(A), (B), (C)의 각 네모 안에서 어법에 맞는 표현으로 가장 적절한 것은? [3점]   정답률 66%

We use many natural materials such as cotton, wool, and metal. They come from plants or animals, or they are (A) dug / digging from the ground. Plastics can be used in place of natural materials, and they are used to make clothes, parts for cars, and many other products. Plastics are synthetic materials, which means (B) that / what they are made from chemicals in factories. The chemicals come mainly from oil, but also from natural gas and coal. An important quality of plastics (C) is / are that they are easy to shape. They can be used to make objects of all kinds.

*synthetic: 합성의

	(A)	(B)	(C)
①	dug	that	is
②	dug	what	is
③	dug	that	are
④	digging	what	are
⑤	digging	that	are

06 ○△✕ ┈┈┈┈ ● 2021년 9월 교육청(고1) 29번

다음 글의 밑줄 친 부분 중, 어법상 틀린 것은? [3점]   정답률 50%

An economic theory of Say's Law holds that everything that's made will get sold. The money from anything that's produced is used to ① buy something else. There can never be a situation ② which a firm finds that it can't sell its goods and so has to dismiss workers and close its factories. Therefore, recessions and unemployment are impossible. Picture the level of spending like the level of water in a bath. Say's Law applies ③ because people use all their earnings to buy things. But what happens if people don't spend all their money, saving some of ④ it instead? Savings are a 'leakage' of spending from the economy. You're probably imagining the water level now falling, so there's less spending in the economy. That would mean firms producing less and ⑤ dismissing some of their workers.

*recession: 경기 후퇴

07 ○△✕ ┈┈┈┈ ● 2020년 3월 교육청(고3) 29번

다음 글의 밑줄 친 부분 중, 어법상 틀린 것은?   정답률 51%

When children are young, much of the work is demonstrating to them that they ① do have control. One wise friend of ours who was a parent educator for twenty years ② advises giving calendars to preschool-age children and writing down all the important events in their life, in part because it helps children understand the passage of time better, and how their days will unfold. We can't overstate the importance of the calendar tool in helping kids feel in control of their day. Have them ③ cross off days of the week as you come to them. Spend time going over the schedule for the day, giving them choice in that schedule wherever ④ possible. This communication expresses respect—they see that they are not just a tagalong to your day and your plans, and they understand what is going to happen, when, and why. As they get older, children will then start to write in important things for themselves, ⑤ it further helps them develop their sense of control.

08 [O△X] ● 2010년 10월 교육청(고3) 20번

다음 글의 밑줄 친 부분 중, 어법상 틀린 것은? 정답률 **61%**

Wherever the ad is placed, many members of the target market may miss it, so by increasing the frequency of an ad, advertisers increase the likelihood ① which members of the target market will be exposed to it. If advertising is on television, the more ② frequently a commercial is run, the more people it will reach. If advertising is on a bulletin board, the location will affect ③ how many people see the ad. If it is placed in a high-traffic zone, more people will see it, and if it is placed in a low-traffic zone, ④ fewer people will see it. However, ⑤ increasing the frequency of advertising costs more money, and advertising is most expensive where it is most effective. Therefore, careful planning is necessary when allocating funds for advertising.

09 고득점 [O△X] ● 2012년 11월 교육청(고2) 27번

다음 글의 밑줄 친 부분 중, 어법상 틀린 것은? [3점] 정답률 **35%**

The psychologist Gary Klein tells the story of a team of firefighters that entered a house ① where the kitchen was on fire. Soon after they started hosing down the kitchen, the commander heard ② himself shout, "Let's get out of here!" without realizing why. The floor collapsed almost immediately after the firefighters escaped. Only after the fact ③ did the commander realize that the fire had been unusually quiet and that his ears had been unusually hot. Together, these impressions prompted ④ that he called a "sixth sense of danger." He had no idea what was wrong, but he knew something was wrong. It turned out that the heart of the fire ⑤ had not been in the kitchen but in the basement below.

10 고득점 [O△X] ● 2019년 9월 교육청(고2) 29번

다음 글의 밑줄 친 부분 중, 어법상 틀린 것은? [3점] 정답률 **34%**

Not only are humans ① unique in the sense that they began to use an ever-widening tool set, we are also the only species on this planet that has constructed forms of complexity that use external energy sources. This was a fundamental new development, ② which there were no precedents in big history. This capacity may first have emerged between 1.5 and 0.5 million years ago, when humans began to control fire. From at least 50,000 years ago, some of the energy stored in air and water flows ③ was used for navigation and, much later, also for powering the first machines. Around 10,000 years ago, humans learned to cultivate plants and ④ tame animals and thus control these important matter and energy flows. Very soon, they also learned to use animal muscle power. About 250 years ago, fossil fuels began to be used on a large scale for powering machines of many different kinds, thereby ⑤ creating the virtually unlimited amounts of artificial complexity that we are familiar with today.

코드 접속하기

출제코드 1 관계부사의 쓰임
부사와 관계부사의 차이, 관계부사와 관계대명사의 차이를 구분할 수 있는지 확인하는 문제가 출제된다.

STEP 1 핵심 문법

1 부사 vs. 관계부사	관계부사는 절과 절을 연결하는 접속사 역할을 하고, 선행사를 수식하는 관계사절에서 부사 역할을 한다. 부사는 시간, 장소, 이유, 방법 등을 나타낼 뿐, 절과 절을 연결하는 접속사 역할은 할 수 없다. **New York** is located in the eastern United States. He lives **in that city**. → New York, **where** he lives, is located in the eastern United States.
2 관계부사의 종류와 쓰임	• when(시간) • where(장소) • why(이유) • how(방법) ※ 관계부사 how는 선행사 the way와 함께 쓰지 않으며, 관계부사는 「전치사 + 관계대명사」로 바꿔쓸 수 있다. 1) I told her *the reason* **why**(= **for which**) I couldn't attend the meeting. 2) Can you show me **how[the way]** you fixed the machine?
3 관계부사 vs. 관계대명사	관계사절에서 관계부사는 부사 역할을 하고, 관계대명사는 대명사 역할을 한다. 따라서 관계부사는 뒤에 완전한 절이, 관계대명사는 뒤에 불완전한 절이 이어진다. 1) *My grandparents' cabin*, [**where** I spend a summer vacation], is one of my favorite places. 　　　선행사　　　　　관계부사　　　　완전한 절 2) This is *the necklace* [**which** my mom gave me before she died]. 　　　선행사　　관계대명사　　직접목적어가 빠진 불완전한 절

STEP 2 시험 패턴과 핵심 전략

1 절과 절을 연결하는 위치 **→ 부사 vs. 관계부사**	부사는 절과 절을 이어주지 못하므로, 「접속사 + 부사」 역할을 하는 관계부사를 쓴다. 1) There is a park in the city, there /(where) you can take a walk with your dog. 2) She woke up at dawn then everyone in the room was still asleep. (→ when)
2 관계부사 vs. 관계대명사	뒤에 문장성분이 완전한 절이 오면 관계부사나 「전치사 + 관계대명사」를, 불완전한 절이 오면 관계대명사를 쓴다. 1) I forget the date which /(when) I had to turn in the term paper. 2) Is it true that the store (which)/ in which sells the instruments is closed?

정답 및 해설 p.69

STEP 3 전략 적용 연습

A 네모 안에서 어법상 바른 것을 고르시오.

1 In 2012, which / when she opened her second coffee shop, sales were higher than ever.

2 A long, downward road could be an area there / where you practice basic skateboarding skills. 기출 응용

B 다음 밑줄 친 부분이 어법상 바르면 ○를 쓰고, 틀리면 바르게 고치시오.

1 I will tell you the way how we became the best team.

2 She used to think about San Francisco, where she had spent three years working.

3 This is a building which people can do photo shoots or make movies.

코드 접속하기

출제코드 2 복합관계대명사 vs. 복합관계부사
복합관계대명사와 복합관계부사의 쓰임을 구분할 수 있는지 확인하는 문제가 출제된다.

STEP 1 핵심 문법

1 복합관계대명사 (관계대명사 + -ever)	복합관계대명사는 명사절(…든지)이나 부사절(…라도)을 이끌며, 관계대명사와 마찬가지로 뒤에 불완전한 절이 이어진다. *cf.* whichever와 whatever는 뒤에 오는 명사를 수식하는 복합관계형용사로도 쓰일 수 있다. 1) You can take [**whoever** you'd like] to the party. (명사절) 2) [**Whatever** happens], don't get discouraged. (부사절) 3) [**Whichever** bus you take], you will get to the station. (복합관계형용사가 이끄는 부사절)
2 복합관계부사 (관계부사 + -ever)	복합관계부사는 부사절을 이끌며, 뒤에 완전한 절이 이어진다. *cf.* however는 「however + 형용사/부사 + 주어 + 동사(아무리 …할지라도)」 형태로 자주 쓰인다. 1) She used to cheer me up [**whenever** I felt depressed]. (부사절) 2) [**However** hard he tried], he couldn't access the Internet. (부사절)

STEP 2 시험 패턴과 핵심 전략

1 복합관계대명사 vs. **복합관계부사**	뒤에 불완전한 절이 이어지면 복합관계대명사를, 완전한 절이 이어지면 복합관계부사를 쓴다. 뒤에 명사가 올 경우 whatever나 whichever를, 형용사나 부사가 올 경우 however를 쓴다. 1) Students must follow some guidelines whatever /(whenever) they work in the lab. 2) However /(Whatever) writers express in their work reflects their way of thinking. 3) (Whichever)/ Wherever team she wants to be on isn't important to me. 4) Whoever /(However) smart he is, he is only a ten-year-old child.
2 부사절을 이끄는 위치 → 의문사 vs. 복합관계사	부사절을 이끄는 경우 복합관계사를 써야 한다. 의문사는 명사절(의문사 + 주어 + 동사)을 이끌므로 쓸 수 없다. 1) What /(Whatever) others say, you should believe in yourself. 2) Everyone knows who he is where /(wherever) he goes.

정답 및 해설 p.69

STEP 3 전략 적용 연습

A 네모 안에서 어법상 바른 것을 고르시오.

1 I couldn't get the door unlocked how / however hard I tried. 기출 응용

2 Whatever / However you learn at the workshop, it will be educational, enjoyable, and rewarding. 기출 응용

3 There is a good Italian restaurant around the corner. Whichever / However dish you choose, you'll be happy.

B 다음 밑줄 친 부분이 어법상 바르면 ○를 쓰고, 틀리면 바르게 고치시오.

1 She is a social person and always makes new friends <u>wherever</u> she goes.

2 They are ready to offer <u>however</u> help we need to carry out our plans.

3 <u>Whichever</u> badly you want to go to the concert, there are no tickets left right now.

코드 접속하기

Q1 다음 글의 밑줄 친 부분 중, 어법상 틀린 것은? [3점] 정답률 43%

Competitive activities can be more than just performance showcases ① which the best is recognized and the rest are overlooked. The provision of timely, constructive feedback to participants on performance ② is an asset that some competitions and contests offer. In a sense, all competitions give feedback. For many, this is restricted to information about whether the participant is an award- or prizewinner. The provision of that type of feedback can be interpreted as shifting the emphasis to demonstrating superior performance but not ③ necessarily excellence. The best competitions promote excellence, not just winning or "beating" others. The emphasis on superiority is what we typically see as ④ fostering a detrimental effect of competition. Performance feedback requires that the program go beyond the "win, place, or show" level of feedback. Information about performance can be very helpful, not only to the participant who does not win or place but also to those who ⑤ do.

*foster: 조장하다 **detrimental: 유해한

핵심 코드 : 관계부사 vs. 관계대명사

● 출제코드 1 적용

1 뒤에 오는 절의 문장성분이 완전한지 불완전한지 파악해야 한다.

2 뒤에 완전한 절이 이어지면 관계부사를, 불완전한 절이 이어지면 관계대명사를 써야 한다.

코드 적용하기

① 관계대명사 vs. 관계부사	performance showcases가 선행사이고, 뒤에 수동태의 구조를 가진 완전한 절이 이어지므로, 관계대명사 which를 관계부사 where로 고쳐야 한다.
② 동사의 수 일치	문장의 주어(The provision)가 전치사구(of timely, constructive feedback)의 수식을 받는 단수 명사이므로, 단수 동사 is가 오는 것이 알맞다.
③ 부분부정 「not necessarily ...」	「not necessarily ...」는 '반드시 ...인 것은 아니다'라는 의미로 부분부정을 나타내며, necessarily와 excellence 사이에 반복되는 동명사 demonstrating이 생략된 것으로 볼 수 있으므로, 동명사 demonstrating을 수식하는 부사 necessarily는 어법상 바르다.
④ 「전치사 + 동명사」, 동명사의 동사적 성질	전치사 as의 목적어 역할을 하면서 명사구 a detrimental effect of competition을 목적어로 취할 수 있는 동명사 fostering이 오는 것이 알맞다.
⑤ 대동사 do	의미상 win or place를 대신하는 대동사로, 선행사가 복수 명사 those이므로 복수 동사 do가 오는 것이 어법상 바르다.

01 ○△✕ ● 2024년 9월 교육청(고1) 29번

다음 글의 밑줄 친 부분 중, 어법상 틀린 것은? 정답률 **48%**

From an organizational viewpoint, one of the most fascinating examples of how any organization may contain many different types of culture ① is to recognize the functional operations of different departments within the organization. The varying departments and divisions within an organization will inevitably view any given situation from their own biased and prejudiced perspective. A department and its members will acquire "tunnel vision" which disallows them to see things as others see ② them. The very structure of organizations can create conflict. The choice of ③ whether the structure is "mechanistic" or "organic" can have a profound influence on conflict management. A mechanistic structure has a vertical hierarchy with many rules, many procedures, and many levels of management ④ involved in decision making. Organic structures are more horizontal in nature, ⑤ which decision making is less centralized and spread across the plane of the organization.

*hierarchy: 위계

02 ○△✕ ● 2011년 9월 교육청(고1) 21번

(A), (B), (C)의 각 네모 안에서 어법에 맞는 표현으로 가장 적절한 것은? 정답률 **56%**

In living birds, feathers have many functions other than flight. They help to keep a bird (A) warm / warmly by trapping heat produced by the body close to the surface of the skin. Feathers may also be used to (B) attract / attracting mates. The tail of Caudipteryx carried a large fan of long feathers, a structure that would have made a very impressive display. The rest of the body seems to have been covered in much shorter feathers, (C) which / that would have kept out the cold. A few large feathers were present on the arms, and these might have been involved in display.

*Caudipteryx: 깃털공룡

	(A)		(B)		(C)
①	warm	⋯⋯	attract	⋯⋯	which
②	warm	⋯⋯	attracting	⋯⋯	which
③	warm	⋯⋯	attracting	⋯⋯	that
④	warmly	⋯⋯	attract	⋯⋯	that
⑤	warmly	⋯⋯	attracting	⋯⋯	which

03 ○△✕ ● 2012학년도 수능 20번

(A), (B), (C)의 각 네모 안에서 어법에 맞는 표현으로 가장 적절한 것은? 정답률 **67%**

On January 10, 1992, a ship (A) traveled / traveling through rough seas lost 12 cargo containers, one of which held 28,800 floating bath toys. Brightly colored ducks, frogs, and turtles were set adrift in the middle of the Pacific Ocean. After seven months, the first toys made landfall on beaches near Sitka, Alaska, 3,540 kilometers from (B) what / where they were lost. Other toys floated north and west along the Alaskan coast and across the Bering Sea. Some toy animals stayed at sea (C) even / very longer. They floated completely along the North Pacific currents, ending up back in Sitka.

	(A)		(B)		(C)
①	traveled	⋯⋯	what	⋯⋯	even
②	traveled	⋯⋯	what	⋯⋯	very
③	traveling	⋯⋯	what	⋯⋯	even
④	traveling	⋯⋯	where	⋯⋯	even
⑤	traveling	⋯⋯	where	⋯⋯	very

04 고득점 ○△× ● 2021년 3월 교육청(고2) 29번

다음 글의 밑줄 친 부분 중, 어법상 틀린 것은? 정답률 34%

While reflecting on the needs of organizations, leaders, and families today, we realize that one of the unique characteristics ① is inclusivity. Why? Because inclusivity supports ② what everyone ultimately wants from their relationships: collaboration. Yet the majority of leaders, organizations, and families are still using the language of the old paradigm in which one person — typically the oldest, most educated, and/or wealthiest — makes all the decisions, and their decisions rule with little discussion or inclusion of others, ③ resulting in exclusivity. Today, this person could be a director, CEO, or other senior leader of an organization. There is no need for others to present their ideas because they are considered ④ inadequate. Yet research shows that exclusivity in problem solving, even with a genius, is not as effective as inclusivity, ⑤ which everyone's ideas are heard and a solution is developed through collaboration.

05 고득점 ○△× ● 2014년 11월 교육청(고2) 27번

다음 글의 밑줄 친 부분 중, 어법상 틀린 것은? [3점] 정답률 40%

Debating is as old as language itself and has taken many forms throughout human history. In ancient Rome, debate in the Senate ① was critical to the conduct of civil society and the justice system. In Greece, advocates for policy changes would ② routinely make their cases before citizen juries composed of hundreds of Athenians. In India, debate was used to ③ settle religious controversies and was a very popular form of entertainment. Indian kings sponsored great debating contests, ④ offering prizes for the winners. China has its own ancient and distinguished tradition of debate. Beginning in the 2nd Century A.D., Taoist and Confucian scholars engaged in a practice known as 'pure talk' ⑤ which they debated spiritual and philosophical issues before audiences in contests that might last for a day and a night.

06 ○△× ● 2013년 6월 평가원(고3) 27번

다음 글의 밑줄 친 부분 중, 어법상 틀린 것은? [3점] 정답률 55%

Given that music appears to enhance physical and mental skills, are there circumstances where music is ① damaging to performance? One domain ② which this is of considerable significance is music's potentially damaging effects on the ability to drive safely. Evidence suggests an association between loud, fast music and reckless driving, but how might music's ability to influence driving in this way ③ be explained? One possibility is that drivers adjust to temporal regularities in music, and ④ that their speed is influenced accordingly. In other words, just as faster music causes people to eat faster, ⑤ so it causes people to drive at faster speeds, as they engage mentally and physically with ongoing repeated structures in the music.

07 ◯△✕ ● 2008년 6월 평가원(고3) 21번

(A), (B), (C)의 각 네모 안에서 어법에 맞는 표현으로 가장 적절한 것은? 정답률 **74%**

The most useful thing I brought out of my childhood was confidence in reading. Not long ago, I went on a weekend self-exploratory workshop, in the hope of getting a clue about how to live. One of the exercises we were given (A) | was / were | to make a list of the ten most important events of our lives. Number one was: "I was born," and you could put (B) | however / whatever | you liked after that. Without even thinking about it, my hand wrote at number two: "I learned to read." "I was born and learned to read" wouldn't be a sequence that occurs to many people, I imagine. But I knew what I meant to say. Being born was something (C) | done / doing | to me, but my own life began when I first made out the meaning of a sentence.

	(A)		(B)		(C)
①	was	……	however	……	done
②	was	……	whatever	……	done
③	was	……	whatever	……	doing
④	were	……	however	……	doing
⑤	were	……	however	……	done

08 고득점 ◯△✕ ● 2010년 6월 교육청(고2) 21번

(A), (B), (C)의 각 네모 안에서 어법에 맞는 표현으로 가장 적절한 것은? 정답률 **33%**

We spend an excessive amount of time browsing the Web every day. As a company's executive put it, "Many users probably spend more time on the Internet than they (A) | do / are | in their cars." Yet many of us barely notice what browser we're using. We tend to hold on to whatever comes loaded on our computer, as long as it allows us to check our email and do a little shopping. We live and work within a browser, and it doesn't matter (B) | whichever / however | browser it may be. As long as it gets the job done, it will be right. But for the companies (C) | concerning / concerned |, things are different. They are trying every effort to come up with the best browser with security and stability.

	(A)		(B)		(C)
①	do	……	however	……	concerning
②	do	……	whichever	……	concerned
③	do	……	whichever	……	concerning
④	are	……	however	……	concerned
⑤	are	……	however	……	concerning

09 고득점 O△X • 2012년 10월 교육청(고3) 21번

(A), (B), (C)의 각 네모 안에서 어법에 맞는 표현으로 가장 적절한 것은? [3점]　정답률 42%

Albert Einstein talked about what influenced his life as a scientist. He remembered seeing a pocket compass when he was five years old and (A) marveling / marveled that the needle always pointed north. In that moment, Einstein recalled, he "felt something deeply hidden behind things." Around the age of six, Einstein began studying the violin. When after several years he recognized the mathematical structure of music, the violin became a lifelong friend of his. When Einstein was ten, his family enrolled him in the Luitpold Gymnasium, (B) there / where he developed a suspicion of authority. The trait served Einstein well later in life as a scientist. His habit of skepticism made (C) him / it easy to question many long-standing scientific assumptions.

	(A)	(B)	(C)
①	marveling	there	him
②	marveled	there	him
③	marveling	where	him
④	marveled	where	it
⑤	marveling	where	it

10 고득점 O△X • 2013학년도 수능 20번

(A), (B), (C)의 각 네모 안에서 어법에 맞는 표현으로 가장 적절한 것은?　정답률 37%

In many countries, amongst younger people, the habit of reading newspapers has been on the decline and some of the dollars previously (A) spent / were spent on newspaper advertising have migrated to the Internet. Of course some of this decline in newspaper reading has been due to the fact that we are doing more of our newspaper reading online. We can read the news of the day, or the latest on business, entertainment or (B) however / whatever news on the websites of the *New York Times*, the *Guardian* or almost any other major newspaper in the world. Increasingly, we can access these stories wirelessly by mobile devices as well as our computers. Advertising dollars have simply been (C) followed / following the migration trail across to these new technologies.

	(A)	(B)	(C)
①	spent	however	followed
②	spent	whatever	following
③	were spent	however	following
④	were spent	whatever	followed
⑤	were spent	whatever	following

코드 접속하기

출제코드 1 전치사 vs. 접속사
문장 구조를 파악하여 전치사와 접속사의 자리를 구분하는 문제가 출제된다.

STEP 1 핵심 문법

1 전치사와 접속사의 구분	전치사 뒤에는 주로 명사 상당어구(명사(구), 대명사, 동명사(구), 명사절)가 목적어로 온다. 접속사 뒤에는 문장성분이 완전한 절이 온다. 1) I am planning to travel all around the country **during** *summer vacation*. (전치사) 2) **Though** *the service at the restaurant was poor*, the food was very delicious. (접속사)

2 뜻이 비슷한 전치사와 접속사

뜻	전치사	접속사
⋯ 때문에	because of	because
⋯ 동안에	during	while
⋯에도 불구하고	despite, in spite of	although, (even) though

3 전치사와 철자가 비슷한 형용사/부사	• like 전 ⋯ 같은 – alike 형 비슷한 부 똑같이 – likely 형 ⋯할 것 같은 • near 전 ⋯ 가까이 – nearly 부 거의 1) The final rehearsal last night was **like** *an actual concert*. (전치사) 2) She and her sister are **alike** in many ways. (형용사) 3) Kaka's house is **near** *my office*. It takes only two minutes on foot. (전치사)

STEP 2 시험 패턴과 핵심 전략

1 명사(구)나 완전한 절 앞 **→ 전치사 vs. 접속사**	뒤따르는 어구가 명사(구)일 경우 전치사를, 완전한 절일 경우 접속사를 쓴다. 1) Coffee is popular (because)/ because of it helps people feel awake and alert. 2) My grandfather took a bullet in his arm (during)/ while the Vietnam War. 3) Tom forgot to take his medication <u>although</u> warnings from his doctor. (→ despite/in spite of)

정답 및 해설 p.76

STEP 3 전략 적용 연습

A 네모 안에서 어법상 바른 것을 고르시오.

1 Teddy, like / alike many children in kindergarten, is sensitive about his toys.

2 Some children can't learn to be independent because / because of their parents, who do everything for them.

3 Though / In spite of the government has tried to discourage smoking, the number of smokers is on the rise.

B 다음 밑줄 친 부분이 어법상 바르면 ○를 쓰고, 틀리면 바르게 고치시오.

1 The basin <u>nearly</u> the window facing the garden provided an easy step up. 기출 응용

2 You have to keep in mind that drinking is strictly prohibited <u>while</u> you are using this medicine.

3 I fear that I won't finish my work by tomorrow <u>because of</u> I cannot concentrate on it.

코드 접속하기

출제코드 2 종속접속사
앞과 뒤에 오는 절의 의미를 살펴 알맞은 접속사를 고르는 문제가 출제된다.

STEP 1 핵심 문법

<table>
<tr><td rowspan="2">1 명사절을 이끄는
종속접속사</td><td colspan="2" align="center">that(…라는 것)</td><td colspan="2" align="center">whether[if] (…인지 (아닌지))</td></tr>
<tr><td colspan="2">주어(보통 진주어), 보어, 목적어, 동격의
명사절을 이끈다.</td><td colspan="2">주어, 보어, 목적어 역할을 하는 명사절을 이끌며, 동사 wonder, ask,
inquire 등과 자주 쓰인다.
※ 접속사 if는 문장 첫머리에 나오는 명사절, 그리고 보어절을 이끌 수 없다.</td></tr>
<tr><td></td><td colspan="4">1) The good news is [that I can withdraw the money from the bank]. (보어)
2) She asked [whether[if] he would have time to drink coffee after the meeting]. (목적어)</td></tr>
<tr><td rowspan="4">2 부사절을 이끄는
종속접속사</td><td>의미</td><td>접속사</td><td>의미</td><td>접속사</td></tr>
<tr><td>시간</td><td>when, as(…할 때), till(…까지)</td><td>이유</td><td>because(… 때문에), as(…이므로)</td></tr>
<tr><td>조건</td><td>if(…라면), unless(…가 아니라면),
as long as(…하는 한)</td><td rowspan="2">양보</td><td rowspan="2">(al)though(비록 …이지만),
whether … or ~(…이든 ~이든)</td></tr>
<tr><td>결과</td><td colspan="3">「so + 형용사/부사 + that ...」, 「such a(n) + 형용사 + 명사 + that ...」(너무 ~해서 …하다)</td></tr>
<tr><td></td><td colspan="4">1) Whether it is sunny or not, I will go out with my children.
2) I am so sick that I am not able to go to the party tonight.</td></tr>
</table>

STEP 2 시험 패턴과 핵심 전략

<table>
<tr><td>1 명사절을 이끄는 접속사
→ that vs. whether[if]</td><td>주어나 목적어 자리에 쓰인 명사절을 이끄는 접속사가 '…인지 (아닌지)'라고 해석되면 whether[if]를 쓴다.
I was wondering that /whether anyone knows the title of this movie.</td></tr>
<tr><td>2 so[such] ... that</td><td>가운데 형용사나 부사가 오면 so ... that을, 「a(n) + 형용사 + 명사」가 오면 such ... that을 쓴다.
1) This new program was so/ such efficient that we finished our work earlier than usual.
2) It was so a sad story that I couldn't help crying. (→ such)</td></tr>
<tr><td>3 or (not) 앞 접속사 →
whether</td><td>부사절 안에 or (not)이 쓰였고, '…이든 ~이든(아니든)'의 의미로 해석될 경우, 접속사 whether를 쓴다.
What you win or not, I am sure that you will enjoy running in the marathon. (→ Whether)</td></tr>
</table>

정답 및 해설 p.76

STEP 3 전략 적용 연습

A 네모 안에서 어법상 바른 것을 고르시오.

1 So / Such stupid was he that he rushed into the decision without thinking of what could happen.

2 He went to the front desk and asked that / if he could leave his wallet in the hotel safe. 기출 응용

3 It raises the question of which / whether we should listen to a minority opinion or ignore it.

B 다음 밑줄 친 부분이 어법상 바르면 ○를 쓰고, 틀리면 바르게 고치시오.

1 That his decision is right or wrong depends on your point of view.

2 It was such a cold day that no one went outside to walk along the river.

코드 접속하기

정답 및 해설 p.76

기출예제 ●━━━━━━━━ 2018학년도 수능28번

Q1 다음 글의 밑줄 친 부분 중, 어법상 틀린 것은? [3점] [정답률 **51%**]

Psychologists who study giving behavior ① <u>have</u> noticed that some people give substantial amounts to one or two charities, while others give small amounts to many charities. Those who donate to one or two charities seek evidence about what the charity is doing and ② <u>what</u> it is really having a positive impact. If the evidence indicates that the charity is really helping others, they make a substantial donation. Those who give small amounts to many charities are not so interested in whether what they are ③ <u>doing</u> helps others — psychologists call them warm glow givers. Knowing that they are giving makes ④ <u>them</u> feel good, regardless of the impact of their donation. In many cases the donation is so small — $10 or less — that if they stopped ⑤ <u>to think</u>, they would realize that the cost of processing the donation is likely to exceed any benefit it brings to the charity.

● 핵심 코드 : 접속사 whether ●

● **출제코드 2 적용**

1 뒤에 완전한 절이 이어지면 접속사가 와야 한다.

2 '…인지'의 의미를 나타내며, 전치사 about의 목적어 역할을 하는 명사절을 이끌 수 있는 접속사는 whether이다.

코드 적용하기

① 동사의 수 일치	주어는 뒤에 관계대명사절의 수식을 받는 Psychologists로 복수 명사이므로 수 일치하여 복수 동사 have가 왔다.
② 명사절을 이끄는 접속사	뒤에 완전한 절이 이어지고 있고 전치사 about의 목적어 역할을 하는 명사절을 이끌고 있으므로 접속사가 와야 한다. 문맥상 '…인지'의 의미가 들어가야 하므로 접속사 whether로 고쳐야 한다.
③ 현재진행 시제에 쓰이는 현재분사	현재진행 시제는 「be v-ing」로 나타내므로 be동사 뒤의 현재분사 doing은 어법상 알맞다.
④ 대명사	앞에 they를 받는 대명사로 동사 makes의 목적어이므로 목적격 them이 알맞다. 주어 Knowing that they are giving과 목적어가 가리키는 대상이 다르므로 재귀대명사가 쓰이지 않았다.
⑤ stop to-v	동사 stop은 뒤에 to부정사(…하기 위해)와 동명사(…하는 것을)가 모두 올 수 있는데, 문맥상 '생각하기 위해 멈추다, 곰곰이 생각하다'라는 의미가 자연스러우므로 to부정사 형태가 알맞다.

코드 공략하기

01 ☐△✕ ● 2008년 3월 교육청(고1) 22번

다음 글의 밑줄 친 부분 중, 어법상 틀린 것은? 정답률 **60%**

At what age should a child learn ① to use a computer? The answer seems to depend on whom you ask. Some early childhood educators believe ② that in modern society computer skills are a basic necessity for every child. But other educators say that children do not use their imagination enough ③ because of the computer screen shows them everything. Physically, children who type for a long time or use a computer mouse ④ too much can develop problems to their bodies. Perhaps the best way for young children to use computers is to use ⑤ them only for a short time each day.

02 ☐△✕ ● 2013년 6월 교육청(고1) 27번

(A), (B), (C)의 각 네모 안에서 어법에 맞는 표현으로 가장 적절한 것은? [3점] 정답률 **51%**

When I was a young girl, my room was always a mess. My mother was always trying to get me to straighten it up, telling me, "Go clean your room!" I resisted her at every opportunity. I hated to (A) tell / be told what to do. I was determined to have my room the way I wanted it. (B) Because / Whether I actually liked living in a messy room or not was another subject altogether. I never stopped to think about the benefits of having a clean room. To me, it was more important to get my own way. And my mother, (C) alike / like most other parents, did not get me to realize the benefits for myself. Instead, she decided on lecturing.

	(A)		(B)		(C)
①	tell	......	Because	......	alike
②	tell	......	Whether	......	like
③	be told	......	Because	......	alike
④	be told	......	Because	......	like
⑤	be told	......	Whether	......	like

03 ☐△✕ ● 2020년 3월 교육청(고1) 29번

다음 글의 밑줄 친 부분 중, 어법상 틀린 것은? [3점] 정답률 **63%**

"You are what you eat." That phrase is often used to ① show the relationship between the foods you eat and your physical health. But do you really know what you are eating when you buy processed foods, canned foods, and packaged goods? Many of the manufactured products made today contain so many chemicals and artificial ingredients ② which it is sometimes difficult to know exactly what is inside them. Fortunately, now there are food labels. Food labels are a good way ③ to find the information about the foods you eat. Labels on food are ④ like the table of contents found in books. The main purpose of food labels ⑤ is to inform you what is inside the food you are purchasing.

*manufactured: (공장에서) 제조된 **table of contents: (책 등의) 목차

04 고득점 ○△✕ ──────● 2010년 3월 교육청(고1) 22번

다음 글의 밑줄 친 부분 중, 어법상 틀린 것은? 정답률 **34%**

After moving to a new city, I ① joined the company baseball team. Being the oldest player, I had to play the outfield. During one game, I made a ② few mistakes. Then I kept ③ hearing someone shouting, "Way to go, Mr. Green" and "You can do it, Mr. Green." I was amazed someone would know my name in this strange city. After the game, I met my wife and son and asked ④ that they knew who was shouting encouragement in the stand. My son spoke up and said, "Dad, it was me." I asked why he was calling me Mr. Green and he replied, "I didn't want anyone ⑤ to know that I'm your son."

05 ○△✕ ──────● 2009년 10월 교육청(고3) 21번

(A), (B), (C)의 각 네모 안에서 어법에 맞는 표현으로 가장 적절한 것은? 정답률 **67%**

Unquestionably, the arts play a significant role in any society. They can be used to commemorate events or individuals. Or they often teach moral lessons or values (A) considered / considering important in a society and are also used to send political messages or draw attention to social issues. Yet the question is posed (B) which / whether the arts should reflect society's standards or question them. Art and artists are also severely criticized for being elitist, for not making art that would appeal to ordinary people. It is (C) because / because of their communicative properties that intense debates continue over the true role of the arts in today's world.

	(A)		(B)		(C)
①	considered	…	whether	…	because
②	considered	…	which	…	because
③	considered	…	whether	…	because of
④	considering	…	which	…	because of
⑤	considering	…	whether	…	because

06 ○△✕ ──────● 2010년 7월 교육청(고3) 22번

다음 글의 밑줄 친 부분 중, 어법상 틀린 것은? [3점] 정답률 **51%**

Do you think the new or used vehicle you are purchasing is safe? Since the introduction of automotive crash-testing, the number of people killed and injured by motor vehicles ① has decreased in many countries. Obviously, it would be ideal ② to have no car crashes. However, car crashes are a reality and you want the best possible chance of survival. How are cars becoming safer? One of the reasons cars have been getting safer ③ is that we can conduct a well-established crash test with test dummies. The dummy's job is to simulate a human being ④ while a crash, collecting data that would not be possible to collect from a human occupant. So far, they have provided invaluable data on how human bodies react in crashes and have contributed greatly to ⑤ improved vehicle design.

07 ○△✕ • 2010년 9월 평가원(고3) 21번

(A), (B), (C)의 각 네모 안에서 어법에 맞는 표현으로 가장 적절한 것은? 정답률 **69%**

Mr. Potter was sailing for Europe on one of the greatest transatlantic ocean liners. When he went on board, he found (A) another / other passenger was to share the cabin with him. After going to see the accommodations, he came up to the purser's desk and inquired (B) if / that he could leave his valuables in the ship's safe. Mr. Potter explained that ordinarily he never availed himself of that privilege, but he had been to his cabin and had met the man who was to occupy the other bed. Judging from his appearance, he was afraid that he might not be a very trustworthy person. The purser accepted the responsibility for the valuables and (C) remarking / remarked , "It's all right. I'll be very glad to take care of them for you. The other man has been up here and left his valuables for the same reason!"   *purser: 선박의 사무장

	(A)	(B)	(C)
①	another	⋯⋯ that	⋯⋯ remarking
②	another	⋯⋯ if	⋯⋯ remarked
③	another	⋯⋯ if	⋯⋯ remarking
④	other	⋯⋯ if	⋯⋯ remarked
⑤	other	⋯⋯ that	⋯⋯ remarked

08 고득점 ○△✕ • 2012년 3월 교육청(고2) 25번

(A), (B), (C)의 각 네모 안에서 어법에 맞는 표현으로 가장 적절한 것은? [3점] 정답률 **31%**

(A) Although / Despite various state-law bans and nationwide campaigns to prevent texting from behind the wheel, the number of people texting while driving is actually on the rise, a new study suggests. According to the Traffic Safety Administration (TSA), the percentage of drivers who send texts and use mobile devices while on the road (B) have / has jumped from 0.6% in 2009 to 0.9% in 2010. The news comes as automakers and lawmakers try to bring more awareness to the dangers of distracted driving. In fact, the Safety Board is working to make cellphone use from talking hands-free to texting (C) illegal / illegally in all states. The TSA said that drivers using mobile devices in any situation are four times more likely to have an accident and injure themselves or others.

	(A)	(B)	(C)
①	Although	⋯⋯ have	⋯⋯ illegally
②	Although	⋯⋯ has	⋯⋯ illegal
③	Despite	⋯⋯ have	⋯⋯ illegal
④	Despite	⋯⋯ has	⋯⋯ illegally
⑤	Despite	⋯⋯ has	⋯⋯ illegal

4

문장 구조

UNIT 01
문장의 구조

UNIT 02
문장의 형식

UNIT 03
기타 주요 구문

출제코드 분석

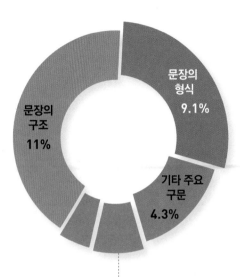

문장의 구조

1 문장의 동사

2 병렬구조

문장의 형식

1 5형식 문장구조와 목적격보어

2 2형식 문장구조와 주격보어

기타 주요 구문

1 간접의문문, 도치구문, 강조구문

2 가주어 진주어, 가목적어 진목적어 구문

문장의 형식 9.1%

문장의 구조 11%

기타 주요 구문 4.3%

2009년 – 2024년 평가원/교육청 기출 분석

출제 경향

1 문장을 분석하여 문장성분과 문장의 연결 구조를 파악해야 해결할 수 있는 문제가 출제되고 있다.

2 동사에 따라 달라지는 문장 구조를 파악하고, 보어가 알맞은 형태로 쓰였는지 확인하는 문제가 출제되고 있다.

3 특수 구문의 어순이나 절의 일부를 변형하여 어법에 맞는지 판단하는 문제가 출제되고 있다.

학습 전략

1 문장의 구조

1) 주어, 동사 등 문장의 필수성분을 파악하며 문장을 읽는 연습을 한다.

2) 병렬구조를 이루게 하는 접속사의 종류를 학습하고, 접속사가 연결하는 단위를 구분하며 문장을 읽는 연습을 한다.

2 문장의 형식

1) 보어가 필요한 문장 형식을 학습하고, 보어를 취하는 다양한 종류의 동사를 학습한다.

2) 목적어와 목적격보어, 주어와 주격보어 사이의 능동, 수동 관계를 파악하는 연습을 한다.

3 기타 주요 구문

1) 특수구문의 어순과 의미, 동사의 형태를 학습한다.

2) 가주어 진주어, 가목적어 진목적어 구문에서 진주어와 진목적어 자리에 쓰일 수 있는 형태를 학습한다.

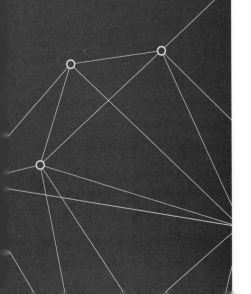

코드 접속하기

출제코드 1 문장의 동사

문장의 구조를 분석하여 문장의 필수 성분인 동사를 파악하는 문제가 출제된다.

STEP 1 핵심 문법

1 문장성분	영어 문장은 주어, 동사, 목적어, 보어와 같은 주요 문장성분과 이를 수식하는 수식어로 구성된다.

1) Fortunately, she became a doctor.
   수식어   주어   동사   보어
2) The policeman arrested the thief who stole the students' bags.
   주어   동사   목적어   수식어

2 문장의 형식

영어 문장은 동사에 따라 5가지 형태로 쓰인다. 동사는 문장의 필수 성분으로, 모든 문장 또는 절은 적어도 하나의 동사가 있어야 한다. 동사는 단독으로 쓰거나 조동사와 함께 쓰인다.

1형식	주어 + **동사**	1) My pencil / **disappeared**.
2형식	주어 + **동사** + 주격보어	2) They / **may seem** / very upset.
3형식	주어 + **동사** + 목적어	3) He / **enjoys** / playing the guitar.
4형식	주어 + **동사** + 간접목적어 + 직접목적어	4) I / **have sent** / Mr. Carl / some postcards.
5형식	주어 + **동사** + 목적어 + 목적격보어	5) My parents / **wanted** / me / to come earlier.

STEP 2 시험 패턴과 핵심 전략

1 문장의 동사 자리 → 동사 vs. 준동사	준동사는 문장에서 동사 역할을 할 수 없으므로 문장의 동사 자리에는 주어의 수, 문장의 시제에 맞는 동사가 와야 한다.

1) The best dish to turn / **turned** out to be the Fried Rice.
2) She said that the problem surrounding social issues **is** / to be their cultural sensitivity.
3) The oxygen which keeps us alive and active sending / **sends** out by-products when it combusts.

정답 및 해설 p.82

STEP 3 전략 적용 연습

A 네모 안에서 어법상 바른 것을 고르시오.

1 His determination to be a champion allowing / allows him to win. 기출 응용
2 People who frequently read a newspaper to improve / improve their ability to read. 기출 응용
3 Actually, almost everything you posted being / is available for everyone on the Internet to see. 기출 응용

B 다음 밑줄 친 부분이 어법상 바르면 ○를 쓰고, 틀리면 바르게 고치시오.

1 The volcano erupting so powerfully that people were surprised. 기출 응용
2 Suddenly, a phrase I once read in the newspaper came floating into my mind. 기출 응용
3 Mothers tending to respond immediately in any situation when their child begins to cry.

코드 접속하기

출제코드 2 병렬구조
접속사에 의한 문장의 병렬구조를 파악하고, 연결된 요소들이 문법적으로 대등한지 확인하는 문제가 출제된다.

STEP 1 핵심 문법

1 병렬구조	등위접속사, 상관접속사 등에 의해 문장의 일부 요소가 연결된 구조를 말한다. 단어와 단어, 구와 구, 절과 절 등 연결되는 요소는 문법적으로 대등해야 한다. 1) I wonder whether listening to music *helps* us focus on working **or** *interrupts* it. (동사와 동사) 2) Hailey likes **both** *reading books* **and** *writing stories*. (동명사구와 동명사구)
2 주요 등위접속사	등위접속사 형태와 기능이 같은 말들을 연결하는 접속사로 and, but, or, so(그래서), for(때문에) 등이 있다. 1) Sujin *gave* me a cupcake **and** *went* back home. 2) *He had a car accident*, **but** *he was pretty calm*.
3 주요 상관접속사	상관접속사는 떨어져 있는 어구들이 짝을 이루는 접속사로, 첨가나 선택의 의미를 나타낸다. • not only A but also B: A 뿐만 아니라 B도(= B as well as A) • both A and B: A와 B 둘 다 　　　　• not A but B: A가 아니라 B • either A or B: A 또는 B 둘 중 하나 　• neither A nor B: A도 B도 아닌 1) *Harry Potter* was a huge success **not only** *as a novel* **but also** *as a movie*. 2) The question is **not** *when to sleep* **but** *where to sleep*.

STEP 2 시험 패턴과 핵심 전략

1 동사 연결	접속사가 문장의 동사를 연결하는 경우, 접속사 뒤에는 앞의 동사와 수, 시제가 일치하는 동사가 와야 한다. 1) He ran to a big basket and (pulled)/ pulling it over himself. 2) This sanitizer not only removes germs but also to smell /(smells) good.
2 준동사 연결	목적어로 쓰인 to부정사나 동명사가 연결될 경우, 접속사 뒤의 형태가 앞의 형태와 일치해야 한다. We should think about renovating the restaurant and to develop /(developing) a new menu.
3 보어 연결	보어로 쓰인 형용사나 분사가 연결될 경우, 접속사 뒤의 단어의 품사나 형태가 앞에 오는 것과 같아야 한다. I found him exhausted and weaken /(weak) after working all night.

정답 및 해설 p.82

STEP 3 전략 적용 연습

A 네모 안에서 어법상 바른 것을 고르시오.

1 Stop thinking about things you don't have and try / trying to find a solution yourself. 기출 응용

2 Artificial intelligence has become capable of playing instruments and to make / making songs. 기출 응용

3 The campsite is surrounded by thick forests, and the fresh air keeps us energetic and healthy / healthily .

B 다음 밑줄 친 부분이 어법상 바르면 ○를 쓰고, 틀리면 바르게 고치시오.

1 Sleeping well and <u>eat</u> meals on a regular basis will make you feel better.

2 Climate change not only wiped out some oceanic fish but also <u>to change</u> the marine ecosystem.

3 Before joining the band and <u>played</u> in a concert, Dan wanted to change his old guitar.

코드 접속하기

기출예제 ● 2023년 6월 교육청(고1) 29번

Q1 다음 글의 밑줄 친 부분 중, 어법상 틀린 것은? [3점]　정답률 51%

Although praise is one of the most powerful tools available for improving young children's behavior, it is equally powerful for improving your child's self-esteem. Preschoolers believe what their parents tell ① them in a very profound way. They do not yet have the cognitive sophistication to reason ② analytically and reject false information. If a preschool boy consistently hears from his mother ③ that he is smart and a good helper, he is likely to incorporate that information into his self-image. Thinking of himself as a boy who is smart and knows how to do things ④ being likely to make him endure longer in problem-solving efforts and increase his confidence in trying new and difficult tasks. Similarly, thinking of himself as the kind of boy who is a good helper will make him more likely to volunteer ⑤ to help with tasks at home and at preschool.

*profound: 뜻 깊은　**sophistication: 정교화(함)

핵심 코드 : 문장의 동사

● 출제코드 1 적용

1 문장의 주어가 어디까지인지 파악하고, 그에 상응하는 동사가 있는지 확인한다.

2 Thinking of ... do things가 주어이므로, 준동사 being을 문장의 동사 역할을 할 수 있는 형태로 고쳐야 한다.

코드 적용하기

① 대명사	them은 앞의 Preschoolers를 지칭하는 대명사이다. 지칭하는 명사가 3인칭 복수이므로 복수 대명사 them은 어법상 알맞다.
② 부사	부사 analytically는 동사의 성질을 지닌 준동사인 to부정사 to reason을 수식하고 있으므로 어법상 알맞다.
③ 접속사	동사 hears의 목적어 역할을 하는 명사절을 이끌고 있으므로 접속사 that은 어법상 알맞다.
④ 문장의 동사	문장의 주어는 동명사구 Thinking of ... do things이다. 이 주어에 상응하는 동사가 와야 하며 동명사구는 단수 취급하므로 is로 고쳐야 한다.
⑤ 명사적 용법의 to부정사	동사 volunteer는 to부정사를 목적어로 취하므로 to help는 어법상 알맞다.

코드 접속하기

정답 및 해설 p.84

기출예제 ●──── 2021년 6월 평가원(고3) 29번

Q2 다음 글의 밑줄 친 부분 중, 어법상 **틀린** 것은? 정답률 **59%**

Most historians of science point to the need for a reliable calendar to regulate agricultural activity as the motivation for learning about what we now call astronomy, the study of stars and planets. Early astronomy provided information about when to plant crops and gave humans ① their first formal method of recording the passage of time. Stonehenge, the 4,000-year-old ring of stones in southern Britain, ② is perhaps the best-known monument to the discovery of regularity and predictability in the world we inhabit. The great markers of Stonehenge point to the spots on the horizon ③ where the sun rises at the solstices and equinoxes — the dates we still use to mark the beginnings of the seasons. The stones may even have ④ been used to predict eclipses. The existence of Stonehenge, built by people without writing, bears silent testimony both to the regularity of nature and to the ability of the human mind to see behind immediate appearances and ⑤ discovers deeper meanings in events.

*monument: 기념비 **eclipse: (해·달의) 식(蝕) ***testimony: 증언

● 핵심 코드 : 병렬구조 ●

● 출제코드 2 적용

1 바로 앞에 등위접속사 and가 쓰인 것에 주목한다.

2 접속사 and에 의해 to부정사인 to see와 병렬 연결된 구조이므로 이와 문법적으로 대등한 요소가 연결되어야 한다.

코드 적용하기

① 대명사	복수 명사인 humans의 소유격 대명사이므로, their는 어법상 알맞다.
② 동사의 수 일치	Stonehenge, the 4,000-year-old ring of stones in southern Britain에서 the 4,000-year-old 이하는 주어 Stonehenge를 부연 설명하는 동격어구이므로, 단수 동사 is는 어법상 알맞다.
③ 관계부사	the spots가 장소 역할을 하는 선행사이고, 뒤에 완전한 절이 왔으므로, 관계부사 where는 어법상 바르다.
④ 능동태 vs. 수동태	The stones는 use의 행위를 당하는 대상이므로 수동태를 써야 한다. 따라서, 현재완료 수동태 형태인 have been v-ed의 been used는 어법상 알맞다.
⑤ 병렬구조	등위접속사 and가 형용사적 용법의 to부정사인 to see와 (to) discover를 병렬 연결하고 있는 구조이므로, discovers를 discover로 고쳐야 한다.

01

다음 글의 밑줄 친 부분 중, 어법상 틀린 것은? [3점] 정답률 63%

Foraging is a means of searching for wild food resources. This is a method ① that has been used for a long time and is possibly the longest method of food searching, tracing back to thousands of years ago. In the past, people commonly foraged for food in forests, riversides, caves, and virtually any place where food could possibly ② be found. Most of the foods foraged before ③ were root crops, weeds, shrubs, and many more. Now, foraging has become a rising trend. People in today's fast-paced society ④ engaging in this either for necessity or for entertainment. Whatever purpose it may be, people are now slowly but surely getting acquainted with foraging. More and more people find it quite a fulfilling task and very ⑤ beneficial.

*forage: 식량을 찾아다니다

02

고득점 ○△✕ ● 2012년 6월 교육청(고1) 24번

다음 글의 밑줄 친 부분 중, 어법상 틀린 것은? [3점] 정답률 44%

Greg felt like a failure if he didn't receive every single point on every single assignment. A grade of 95 left him ① asking, "How did I fail to achieve 100?" Greg realized that his drive for perfectionism was putting him into a state of constant stress. He decided ② to work on stress management. He came up with the creative idea of ③ posting notes everywhere with the simple message, "92 is still an A." Gradually, these simple reminder notes allowed Greg to have a different point of view and ④ realized that he didn't have to be perfect at everything. He still could earn an "A" in class, but with ⑤ much less pressure.

03

다음 글의 밑줄 친 부분 중, 어법상 틀린 것은? 정답률 75%

While manned space missions are more costly than unmanned ① ones, they are more successful. Robots and astronauts use ② much of the same equipment in space. But a human is much more capable of operating those instruments correctly and ③ to place them in appropriate and useful positions. Rarely ④ is a computer more sensitive and accurate than a human in managing the same geographical or environmental factors. Robots are also not equipped with capabilities like humans to solve problems ⑤ as they arise, and they often collect data that are unhelpful or irrelevant.

04

○△✕ ● 2017년 3월 교육청(고2) 28번

다음 글의 밑줄 친 부분 중, 어법상 틀린 것은? [3점] 정답률 59%

The competition to sell manuscripts to publishers ① is fierce. I would estimate that less than one percent of the material ② sent to publishers is ever published. Since so much material is being written, publishers can be very selective. The material they choose to publish must not only have commercial value, but ③ being very competently written and free of editing and factual errors. Any manuscript that contains errors stands ④ little chance at being accepted for publication. Most publishers will not want to waste time with writers ⑤ whose material contains too many mistakes.

05

다음 글의 밑줄 친 부분 중, 어법상 틀린 것은? [정답률] 47%

Though he probably was not the first to do it, Dutch eyeglass maker Hans Lippershey gets credit for putting two lenses on either end of a tube in 1608 and ① creating a "spyglass." Even then, it was not Lippershey but his children who discovered ② that the double lenses made a nearby weathervane look bigger. These early instruments were not ③ much more than toys because their lenses were not very strong. The first person to turn a spyglass toward the sky was an Italian mathematician and professor named Galileo Galilei. Galileo, who heard about the Dutch spyglass and began making his own, ④ realizing right away how useful the device could be to armies and sailors. As he made better and better spyglasses, which were later named telescopes, Galileo decided ⑤ to point one at the Moon.

*weathervane: 풍향계

06

고득점 ○△✕ •2017년 3월 교육청(고1) 28번

다음 글의 밑줄 친 부분 중, 어법상 틀린 것은? [3점] [정답률] 44%

Take time to read the comics. This is worthwhile not just because they will make you laugh but ① because they contain wisdom about the nature of life. *Charlie Brown* and *Blondie* are part of my morning routine and help me ② to start the day with a smile. When you read the comics section of the newspaper, ③ cutting out a cartoon that makes you laugh. Post it wherever you need it most, such as on your refrigerator or at work—so that every time you see it, you will smile and feel your spirit ④ lifted. Share your favorites with your friends and family so that everyone can get a good laugh, too. Take your comics with you when you go to visit sick friends ⑤ who can really use a good laugh.

07

다음 글의 밑줄 친 부분 중, 어법상 틀린 것은? [3점] [정답률] 51%

In perceiving changes, we tend to regard the most recent ① ones as the most revolutionary. This is often inconsistent with the facts. Recent progress in telecommunications technologies is not more revolutionary than ② what happened in the late nineteenth century in relative terms. Moreover, in terms of the consequent economic and social changes, the Internet revolution has not been as ③ important as the washing machine and other household appliances. These things, by vastly reducing the amount of work needed for household chores, ④ allowing women to enter the labor market and virtually got rid of professions like domestic service. We should not "put the telescope backward" when we look into the past and underestimate the old and overestimate the new. This leads us ⑤ to make all sorts of wrong decisions about national economic policy, corporate policies, and our own careers.

08 ○△✕ • 2015년 9월 교육청(고2) 28번

다음 글의 밑줄 친 부분 중, 어법상 틀린 것은? [3점] 정답률 **50%**

The ability to think about why things work and what may be causing problems when events do not go as ① expected seems like an obvious aspect of the way we think. It is interesting that this ability to think about why things happen is one of the key abilities that separates human abilities from ② those of just about every other animal on the planet. Asking *why* allows people to create explanations. Issac Newton didn't just see an apple ③ fall from a tree. He used that observation to help him figure out why it fell. Your car mechanic doesn't just observe ④ that your car is not working. He figures out why it is not working using knowledge about why it usually does work properly. And anyone who has spent time with a five-year-old ⑤ knowing that children this age can test the limits of your patience by trying to get explanations for why everything works as it does.

09 ○△✕ • 2020년 6월 평가원(고3) 29번

다음 글의 밑줄 친 부분 중, 어법상 틀린 것은? 정답률 **68%**

People from more individualistic cultural contexts tend to be motivated to maintain self-focused agency or control ① as these serve as the basis of one's self-worth. With this form of agency comes the belief that individual successes ② depending primarily on one's own abilities and actions, and thus, whether by influencing the environment or trying to accept one's circumstances, the use of control ultimately centers on the individual. The independent self may be more ③ driven to cope by appealing to a sense of agency or control. However, people from more interdependent cultural contexts tend to be less focused on issues of individual success and agency and more motivated towards group goals and harmony. Research has shown ④ that East Asians prefer to receive, but not seek, more social support rather than seek personal control in certain cases. Therefore, people ⑤ who hold a more interdependent self-construal may prefer to cope in a way that promotes harmony in relationships.

*self-construal: 자기 구성

10 ○△✕ • 2013년 7월 교육청(고3) 27번

다음 글의 밑줄 친 부분 중, 어법상 틀린 것은? 정답률 **74%**

William H. Whyte turned video cameras on a number of spaces in New York City, watching to see ① how people used the spaces. He made a number of fascinating findings, and he had the video evidence to back ② them up. Even in the crowded city, he found that many urban spaces were usually deserted; people flocked to a few busy plazas even when they were planning to sit alone. Why? The most common activity among people observed by Whyte ③ turning out to be watching other people. And it was also found that people liked to be watched! Whyte expected lovers to ④ be found in private, isolated spaces, but most often they sat or stood right in the center of things for everyone to see. Further, people having private conversations would stand in the middle of the sidewalk, forcing people ⑤ to step around them.

01 ○△× • 2019년 6월 교육청(고2) 29번

다음 글의 밑줄 친 부분 중, 어법상 틀린 것은? 정답률 60%

Trying to produce everything yourself would mean you are using your time and resources to produce many things ① for which you are a high-cost provider. This would translate into lower production and income. For example, even though most doctors might be good at record keeping and arranging appointments, ② it is generally in their interest to hire someone to perform these services. The time doctors use to keep records is time they could have spent seeing patients. Because the time ③ spent with their patients is worth a lot, the opportunity cost of record keeping for doctors will be high. Thus, doctors will almost always find it ④ advantageous to hire someone else to keep and manage their records. Moreover, when the doctor specializes in the provision of physician services and ⑤ hiring someone who has a comparative advantage in record keeping, costs will be lower and joint output larger than would otherwise be achievable.

02 ○△× • 2024년 9월 교육청(고2) 29번

다음 글의 밑줄 친 부분 중, 어법상 틀린 것은? 정답률 58%

One well-known shift took place when the accepted view—that the Earth was the center of the universe—changed to one where we understood that we are only inhabitants on one planet ① orbiting the Sun. With each person who grasped the solar system view, ② it became easier for the next person to do so. So it is with the notion that the world revolves around the human economy. This is slowly being replaced by the view that the economy is a part of the larger system of material flows that connect all living things. When this perspective shifts into place, it will be obvious that our economic wellbeing requires that we account for, and ③ respond to, factors of ecological health. Unfortunately we do not have a century or two

④ make the change. By clarifying the nature of the old and new perspectives, and by identifying actions ⑤ on which we might cooperate to move the process along, we can help accelerate the shift.

03 고득점 ○△× • 2018년 6월 평가원(고3) 28번

다음 글의 밑줄 친 부분 중, 어법상 틀린 것은? 정답률 41%

Humans are so averse to feeling that they're being cheated ① that they often respond in ways that seemingly make little sense. Behavioral economists — the economists who actually study ② what people do as opposed to the kind who simply assume the human mind works like a calculator — have shown again and again that people reject unfair offers even if ③ it costs them money to do so. The typical experiment uses a task called the ultimatum game. It's pretty straightforward. One person in a pair is given some money — say $10. She then has the opportunity to offer some amount of it to her partner. The partner only has two options. He can take what's offered or ④ refused to take anything. There's no room for negotiation; that's why it's called the ultimatum game. What typically happens? Many people offer an equal split to the partner, ⑤ leaving both individuals happy and willing to trust each other in the future.

*averse to: ~을 싫어하는 **ultimatum: 최후통첩

04 ○△× • 2012년 9월 교육청(고1) 34번

다음 글의 밑줄 친 부분 중, 어법상 틀린 것은? [3점] 정답률 48%

Native people create legends to explain unusual events in their environment. A legend from the Hawaiian island of Kauai explains ① how the naupaka flower got its unusual shape. The flower looks like half a small daisy. The legend says that the marriage of two young lovers on the island ② was opposed by both sets of parents. The parents found the couple together on a beach one day, and ③ to

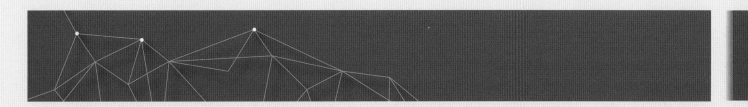

prevent them from being together, one of the families moved to the mountains, separating the young couple forever. As a result, the naupaka flower was separated into two halves; one half moved to the mountains, and the other half ④ staying near the beach. This story is a good example of a legend ⑤ which native people invented to make sense of the world around them.

05 ◯△✕ ────────•2020년 6월 교육청(고1) 29번

다음 글의 밑줄 친 부분 중, 어법상 틀린 것은? [3점] 정답률 54%

Positively or negatively, our parents and families are powerful influences on us. But even ① stronger, especially when we're young, are our friends. We often choose friends as a way of ② expanding our sense of identity beyond our families. As a result, the pressure to conform to the standards and expectations of friends and other social groups ③ is likely to be intense. Judith Rich Harris, who is a developmental psychologist, ④ arguing that three main forces shape our development: personal temperament, our parents, and our peers. The influence of peers, she argues, is much stronger than that of parents. "The world ⑤ that children share with their peers," she says, "is what shapes their behavior and modifies the characteristics they were born with, and hence determines the sort of people they will be when they grow up."

*temperament: 기질

06 ◯△✕ ────────•2014년 9월 교육청(고2) 27번

다음 글의 밑줄 친 부분 중, 어법상 틀린 것은? [3점] 정답률 62%

Language is one of the primary features that distinguishes humans from other animals. Many animals, including dolphins, whales, and birds, ① do indeed communicate with one another through patterned systems of sounds, scents, and other chemicals, or movements. Furthermore, some

nonhuman primates ② have been taught to use sign language to communicate with humans. However, the complexity of human language, its ability to convey nuanced emotions and ideas, and its importance for our existence as social animals ③ setting it apart from the communication systems used by other animals. In many ways, language is the essence of culture. It provides the single most common variable ④ by which different cultural groups are identified. Language not only facilitates the cultural diffusion of innovations, it also helps to shape the way we think about, perceive, and ⑤ name our environment.

07 ◯△✕ ────────•2010년 3월 교육청(고2) 21번

(A), (B), (C)의 각 네모 안에서 어법에 맞는 표현으로 가장 적절한 것은? [3점] 정답률 57%

"Oh, my! What can a "gym" teacher do without a gym?" Stop thinking about what you don't have and (A) find / finding a solution yourself! You weren't trained to be a "gym" teacher; you were trained to teach physical education. "Gym" teacher is an old-fashioned term that some people still (B) use / use it to describe a physical educator, and some people still use the word "gym" to describe physical education. If you were trained to be a physical education teacher, not having a gym (C) is / being not a huge problem. For example, you could teach your students the striking skills in tennis in the school parking lot and the dribbling skills in basketball in the old church.

	(A)		(B)		(C)
①	find	······	use	······	is
②	find	······	use it	······	being
③	find	······	use	······	being
④	finding	······	use it	······	being
⑤	finding	······	use	······	is

08 ○△✕ ● 2024년 3월 교육청(고1) 29번

다음 글의 밑줄 친 부분 중, 어법상 틀린 것은? 정답률 **73%**

It would be hard to overstate how important meaningful work is to human beings—work ① that provides a sense of fulfillment and empowerment. Those who have found deeper meaning in their careers find their days much more energizing and satisfying, and ② to count their employment as one of their greatest sources of joy and pride. Sonya Lyubomirsky, professor of psychology at the University of California, has conducted numerous workplace studies ③ showing that when people are more fulfilled on the job, they not only produce higher quality work and a greater output, but also generally earn higher incomes. Those most satisfied with their work ④ are also much more likely to be happier with their lives overall. For her book *Happiness at Work*, researcher Jessica Pryce-Jones conducted a study of 3,000 workers in seventy-nine countries, ⑤ finding that those who took greater satisfaction from their work were 150 percent more likely to have a happier life overall.

*numerous: 수많은

09 ○△✕ ● 2024년 6월 교육청(고2) 29번

다음 글의 밑줄 친 부분 중, 어법상 틀린 것은? 정답률 **59%**

The built-in capacity for smiling is proven by the remarkable observation ① that babies who are congenitally both deaf and blind, who have never seen a human face, also start to smile at around 2 months. However, smiling in blind babies eventually ② disappears if nothing is done to reinforce it. Without the right feedback, smiling dies out. But here's a fascinating fact: blind babies will continue to smile if they are cuddled, bounced, nudged, and tickled by an adult—anything to let ③ them know that they are not alone and that someone cares about them. This social feedback encourages the baby to continue smiling. In this way, early experience operates with our biology ④ to establish social behaviors. In fact, you don't need the cases of blind babies to make the point. Babies with sight smile more at you when you look at them or, better still, ⑤ smiling back at them.

*congenitally: 선천적으로 **cuddle: 껴안다
***nudge: 팔꿈치로 쿡쿡 찌르다

10 ○△✕ ● 2020년 9월 교육청(고2) 29번

다음 글의 밑줄 친 부분 중, 어법상 틀린 것은? [3점] 정답률 **56%**

All social interactions require some common ground upon which the involved parties can coordinate their behavior. In the interdependent groups ① in which humans and other primates live, individuals must have even greater common ground to establish and maintain social relationships. This common ground is morality. This is why morality often is defined as a shared set of standards for ② judging right and wrong in the conduct of social relationships. No matter how it is conceptualized — whether as trustworthiness, cooperation, justice, or caring — morality ③ to be always about the treatment of people in social relationships. This is likely why there is surprising agreement across a wide range of perspectives ④ that a shared sense of morality is necessary to social relations. Evolutionary biologists, sociologists, and philosophers all seem to agree with social psychologists that the interdependent relationships within groups that humans depend on ⑤ are not possible without a shared morality.

코드 접속하기

출제코드 1 5형식 문장 구조와 목적격보어

5형식 문장 구조에서 동사에 따라 목적격보어의 형태가 바르게 쓰였는지 확인하는 문제가 출제된다.

STEP 1 핵심 문법

1 5형식 구조: 「주어 + 동사 + 목적어 + 목적격보어」	5형식 문장에서 목적어와 목적어를 보충 설명하는 목적격보어는 의미상 주어, 서술어 관계가 성립한다. We / elected / him / president of the class. (him(목적어) = president of the class(목적격보어))	

2 목적격보어	목적격보어	목적격보어를 취하는 동사
	1) 형용사	make, get, turn, keep, leave, find, consider 등 His bright smile **makes** people **happy**.
	2) to부정사	want, ask, expect, cause, allow, enable, tell, order, encourage, advise 등 Her father **expected** her **to come** home before dinner.
	3) 동사원형	지각동사(feel, hear, see 등), 사역동사(make, have, let 등) The boss **had** his secretary **make** a reservation for lunch today.
	4) 현재분사	지각동사, have, get, keep, leave 등의 동사로, 목적어와 목적격보어가 능동 관계인 경우 She **noticed** someone **walking** toward her quietly. (동작이 진행 중임을 나타냄)
	5) 과거분사	지각동사, 사역동사, keep, leave, want 등의 동사로, 목적어와 목적격보어가 수동 관계인 경우 Amy **heard** her name **called** loudly through the speaker.

STEP 2 시험 패턴과 핵심 전략

1 동사(want, cause 등)의 목적격보어 → to부정사	want, ask, expect, cause, allow 등의 동사는 목적격보어로 to부정사를 써야 한다. The tragic car accident caused him lose his sight. (→ to lose)
2 목적격보어 자리 → 형용사 vs. 부사	5형식 문장의 목적격보어 자리에는 부사가 아닌 형용사를 써야 한다. Sijin considered himself (lucky)/ luckily to escape alive.
3 목적격보어 자리 → 동사원형 vs. 현재분사 vs. 과거분사	지각동사, 사역동사 등의 목적격보어는 목적어와 목적격보어가 능동 관계이면 동사원형이나 현재분사를, 수동 관계이면 과거분사를 쓴다. 1) I saw my sister (feed)/ to feed her cat. 2) Josh got his wisdom tooth pulling out two weeks ago. (→ pulled)

정답 및 해설 p.98

STEP 3 전략 적용 연습

A 네모 안에서 어법상 바른 것을 고르시오.

1 He needs to have the lost files recover / recovered by a computer expert.

2 Before long, he found it difficult / difficultly to see the fine details in small pictures.

3 If he had allowed himself become / to become frustrated by his failures, he would have never achieved his goal.

B 다음 밑줄 친 부분이 어법상 바르면 ○를 쓰고, 틀리면 바르게 고치시오.

1 I heard Tom, who is always late for school, punish for his wrong behavior.

2 Imagine, on your birthday, your parents give you a heart-warming, moving letter which makes you cry. 기출 응용

코드 접속하기

출제코드 2 2형식 문장 구조와 주격보어
2형식 동사의 주격보어 자리에 알맞은 품사의 단어가 들어갔는지 확인하는 문제가 출제된다.

STEP 1 핵심 문법

1 2형식 구조: 「주어 + 동사 + 주격보어」	2형식은 주어와 동사, 주어를 보충 설명하는 주격보어로 이루어진 문장이다. 주격보어로는 명사나 형용사를 쓴다. 1) She / is / a famous song writer. 　　　　　　　주격보어(명사) 2) I / kept / silent during the class meeting. 　　　　주격보어(형용사)
2 2형식에 쓰이는 동사	• 상태, 상태 변화를 나타내는 동사: be, keep, remain, become, grow 등 • 감각을 나타내는 동사: look, smell, taste, sound, feel 등 • 기타 동사: seem, appear 등 1) He **became** *angry* and wouldn't answer my calls. 2) If the grape jam **tastes** *too sweet*, try butter or margarine instead. 3) Jenny **seemed** *exhausted* when I met her in front of the library.

STEP 2 시험 패턴과 핵심 전략

1 주격보어 자리 → **형용사 vs. 부사**	2형식 동사 뒤의 주격보어 자리에는 부사가 아닌 형용사를 써야 한다. 1) The apple pie on the table looks very delicious / deliciously. 2) Perfume smells differently on different people's skin. (→ different) 3) The fat rabbit appears slow / slowly, but it can actually move very quickly.

정답 및 해설 p.98

STEP 3 전략 적용 연습

A 네모 안에서 어법상 바른 것을 고르시오.

1 Psychologists studied why people become so sensitive / sensitively about hearing their own flaws. 기출 응용

2 He was so anxious / anxiously to become a professor that his mother sent him back to school. 기출 응용

3 This sounds obvious / obviously, but only treating the symptoms ignores the problem. 기출 응용

B 다음 밑줄 친 부분이 어법상 바르면 ○를 쓰고, 틀리면 바르게 고치시오.

1 He thought it would be interesting to see the shark's life through the small video camera. 기출 응용

2 I'm sorry to wake you up, but I had to call because I'm going to be a little lately getting home tonight. 기출 응용

3 Many women worry about this scary world today and wonder how they can feel securely when going out alone. 기출 응용

코드 접속하기

정답 및 해설 p.99

기출예제 ●──────── **2022년 9월 교육청(고2) 29번**

Q1 다음 글의 밑줄 친 부분 중, 어법상 틀린 것은? [3점] 〔정답률 **50%**〕

By noticing the relation between their own actions and resultant external changes, infants develop self-efficacy, a sense ① that they are agents of the perceived changes. Although infants can notice the effect of their behavior on the physical environment, it is in early social interactions that infants most ② readily perceive the consequence of their actions. People have perceptual characteristics that virtually ③ assure that infants will orient toward them. They have visually contrasting and moving faces. They produce sound, provide touch, and have interesting smells. In addition, people engage with infants by exaggerating their facial expressions and inflecting their voices in ways that infants find ④ fascinated. But most importantly, these antics are responsive to infants' vocalizations, facial expressions, and gestures; people vary the pace and level of their behavior in response to infant actions. Consequentially, early social interactions provide a context ⑤ where infants can easily notice the effect of their behavior.

*inflect: (음성을) 조절하다 **antics: 익살스러운 행동

┌─────────────────────────────────────┐
│ **• 핵심 코드: 목적격보어 자리 현재분사 vs. 과거분사 •** │
│   │
│ **• 출제코드 1 적용**   │
│ **1** 밑줄 친 부분은 동사 find의 목적격보어 자리이다. │
│ **2** 목적어(ways)와 목적격보어의 의미상 관계가 능동이면 현 │
│   재분사를, 수동이면 과거분사를 쓴다.   │
└─────────────────────────────────────┘

코드 적용하기

① 접속사 that	앞의 명사구 a sense와 동격을 이루는 명사절을 이끄는 접속사로, 뒤에 완전한 절이 이어지고 있으므로 어법상 바르다.
② 부사	동사 perceive를 수식하고 있으므로 부사 readily가 오는 것이 알맞다.
③ 동사의 수 일치	assure은 perceptual characteristics를 선행사로 하는 주격 관계대명사절의 동사로, 선행사가 복수 명사이므로 복수 동사가 오는 것이 알맞다.
④ 목적격보어	동사 find의 목적격보어 자리이고, 목적어는 선행사인 ways이므로 목적어와 목적격보어가 의미상 능동 관계에 있다. 따라서 과거분사 fascinated를 현재분사 fascinating으로 고쳐야 한다.
⑤ 관계부사	where는 a context를 선행사로 하는 관계부사로, 뒤에 완전한 절이 이어지고 있으므로 어법상 바르다.

코드 접속하기

정답 및 해설 p.99

기출예제 ● 2011년 10월 교육청(고3) 21번

Q2 다음 글의 밑줄 친 부분 중, 어법상 틀린 것은? 정답률 **60%**

Democracies require more equality if they are ① to grow stronger. The problem is that globalization pushes in the opposite direction; by placing a premium on high skills that make workers more ② competitively, it increases income inequality between the highly skilled minority and the rest. In this situation, it is not sufficient ③ to reduce economic insecurity by expanding the social safety net. Instead, a country must begin to make the transition from a welfare state to a workfare state, with an emphasis on creating a more highly skilled labor force and ④ improving access to the labor market for women and low-income youth. To expand job creation, new social policies must also provide better incentives for entrepreneurship and innovation. Only then can social policies ⑤ be considered key factors of production, beyond their role as instruments of social protection.

*entrepreneurship: 창업 의욕

● 핵심 코드 : 목적격보어 ●

● **출제코드 1 적용**

1 make가 동사, workers가 목적어 역할을 하고 있고, ② 가 목적격보어 자리인 것을 파악한다.

2 목적격보어 자리에는 부사가 쓰일 수 없다.

코드 적용하기

① be to-v 용법	'…하려고 하다'의 의미로 의도를 나타내는 be to-v가 쓰였으므로 어법상 바르다.
② 목적격보어	동사 make의 목적격보어 자리이므로 부사 competitively를 형용사 competitive로 고쳐야 한다. 부사는 보어 자리에 쓰일 수 없다.
③ 가주어 진주어 구문	앞의 it이 가주어, to reduce 이하가 진주어로 쓰인 to부정사구로 어법상 바르다.
④ 병렬구조	등위접속사 and가 전치사 on의 목적어 역할을 하는 동명사를 병렬 연결하고 있는 구조로, 동명사 creating과 대등한 동명사 improving이 왔으므로 어법상 바르다.
⑤ 수동태	부사구 Only then이 강조를 위해 문장 앞으로 나가면서 「조동사 + 주어 + 동사」 형태로 도치가 일어난 문장이다. 사회 정책들이 '간주되는'이라는 수동의 의미이므로 수동태 be considered가 오는 것이 알맞다.

코드 공략하기

01

● 2009년 6월 교육청(고1) 21번

(A), (B), (C)의 각 네모 안에서 어법에 맞는 표현으로 가장 적절한 것은? 정답률 50%

Many parents worry about the state of the world today and wonder how they can feel (A) safe / safely when raising kids in this scary world. Yet, I found that there's still hope. When I was a brand-new mom, I was in an elevator with two teenage boys. When the door opened, one boy was about to get off first. The other boy put his arm in front of his friend, (B) motioned / motioning for me to go ahead. I was moved by his simple gesture of thoughtfulness and good manners. I thanked him, and also asked him to thank his mother for doing a wonderful job: raising such a polite young man. I promised myself at that moment (C) when / that I would raise my children to be like him.

	(A)	(B)	(C)
①	safe	motioning	that
②	safe	motioned	when
③	safe	motioning	when
④	safely	motioned	when
⑤	safely	motioning	that

02

● 2007년 4월 교육청(고3) 23번

다음 글의 밑줄 친 부분 중, 어법상 틀린 것은? 정답률 65%

The latest studies indicate that ① what people really want is a mate that has qualities like their parents. Women are ② after a man who is like their father and men want to be able to see their own mother in the woman of their dreams. Cognitive psychologist David Perrett studies what makes faces ③ attractively. He has developed a computerized morphing system that can endlessly adjust faces to suit his needs. Perrett suggests that we ④ find our own faces charming because they remind us ⑤ of the faces we looked at constantly in our early childhood years—Mom and Dad.

03 고득점

● 2010년 3월 교육청(고3) 23번

다음 글의 밑줄 친 부분 중, 어법상 틀린 것은? [3점] 정답률 39%

It was Mary's thirteenth birthday. It was also her first birthday at her uncle's house. Everyone brought out gifts for Mary: stockings from Elena, a purse from Steve, and a pair of very old silver earrings from Chris, who said she ① had had them since she was a little girl. Uncle Jack gave a lengthy speech about ② how Mary was like a daughter to him and to Aunt Barbara. And then, he handed her an envelope in ③ which was tucked a fifty-dollar bill. Mary was to buy ④ herself some new clothes with Aunt Barbara's help and advice. A miracle! So many presents and so much money all at once made her eyes ⑤ shone. She wanted to kiss everybody.

04 ○△✕ • 2011년 11월 교육청(고1) 21번

(A) ~ (C)에서 어법에 맞는 표현을 바르게 짝지은 것은? [3점]

정답률 **51%**

The Inchcape Rock is a great rock in the North Sea. Most of the time it is covered with water. That causes many boats and ships (A) | crash / to crash | onto the rock. The rock is so close to the top of the water that all the vessels that try to sail over it (B) | hit / hits | it. More than a hundred years ago, a kind-hearted man lived nearby. He thought that it was tragic for so many sailors to die on that hidden rock. So he fastened a floating mark to the rock with a strong chain, on top of (C) | it / which | a bell was attached. When ships came near, the waves made the mark float back and forth and the bell ring clearly. Now, sailors were no longer afraid to cross the sea there.

	(A)		(B)		(C)
①	crash	......	hit	......	which
②	crash	......	hits	......	it
③	to crash	......	hit	......	it
④	to crash	......	hits	......	it
⑤	to crash	......	hit	......	which

05 ○△✕ • 2012년 3월 교육청(고3) 20번

다음 글의 밑줄 친 부분 중, 어법상 틀린 것은? 정답률 **60%**

We do not hear with our eyes, but sometimes it almost seems as if we do. An environment-agency official tells a surprising incident about some people ① who lived in an apartment building close to a busy state highway. The families were made ② miserably by the noise, and they complained to the city government. City officials went to the state capital again and again to ask that something ③ be done about quieting the highway noise. They were put off repeatedly. At last the city officials had an idea. They planted a single row of trees in front of the apartment house. The trees made hardly any difference in the amount of noise, but they ④ did block the view of the highway. After that, there were very ⑤ few complaints from the people in the building.

06 ○△✕ • 2009년 10월 교육청(고3) 20번

다음 글의 밑줄 친 부분 중, 어법상 틀린 것은? 정답률 **64%**

Farmers plow more and more fields ① to produce more food for the increasing population. This increases pressure on our soil resources. Farmers plow soil to improve ② it for crops. They turn and loosen the soil, ③ leaving it in the best condition for farming. However, this process removes the important plant cover that holds soil particles in place, making soil ④ defenselessly to wind and water erosion. Sometimes, the wind blows soil from a plowed field. Soil erosion in many places occurs at a ⑤ much faster rate than the natural processes of weathering can replace it.

07 ○△✕ ●2009학년도 수능 21번

(A), (B), (C)의 각 네모 안에서 어법에 맞는 표현으로 가장 적절한 것은? 정답률 69%

Many social scientists have believed for some time (A) that / what birth order directly affects both personality and achievement in adult life. In fact, people have been using birth order to account for personality factors such as an aggressive behavior or a passive temperament. One might say, "Oh, I'm the eldest of three sisters, so I can't help that I'm so overbearing," or "I'm not very successful in business, because I'm the youngest child and thus less (B) aggressively / aggressive than my older brothers and sisters." Recent studies, however, have proved this belief to be false. In other words, birth order may define your role within a family, but as you mature into adulthood, (C) accepted / accepting other social roles, birth order becomes insignificant.

	(A)	(B)	(C)
①	that	aggressively	accepting
②	that	aggressive	accepting
③	that	aggressive	accepted
④	what	aggressive	accepted
⑤	what	aggressively	accepted

08 고득점 ○△✕ ●2008년 11월 교육청(고1) 21번

(A), (B), (C)의 각 네모 안에서 어법에 맞는 표현으로 가장 적절한 것은? 정답률 37%

A dilemma tale is an African story form that ends with a question. The question asks the listeners (A) choosing / to choose among several alternatives. By encouraging active discussion, a dilemma tale invites its audience to think about right and wrong behavior within society. Dilemma tales are (B) like / alike folk tales in that they are usually short, simple, and driven entirely by plot. As you read a dilemma tale, you need to keep in mind that most African cultures were traditionally oral ones: Their stories and tales are meant to (C) tell / be told aloud.

	(A)	(B)	(C)
①	choosing	like	be told
②	choosing	alike	tell
③	to choose	alike	tell
④	to choose	alike	be told
⑤	to choose	like	be told

09 ○△✕ ————————• 2012년 7월 교육청(고3) 21번

(A), (B), (C)의 각 네모 안에서 어법에 맞는 표현으로 가장 적절한 것은? 정답률 **70%**

Empathy is made possible by a special group of nerve cells called mirror neurons. These special cells enable us to "mirror" emotions. Mirror neurons were first discovered by Italian scientists who, while looking at the activity of individual nerve cells inside the brains of monkeys, (A) noticed / noticing that neurons in the same area of the brain were activated whether the animals were performing a particular movement or simply observing another monkey perform the same action. It appeared as though the cells in the observer's brain "mirrored" the activity in the performer's brain. A similar phenomenon takes place when we watch someone (B) experiencing / experienced an emotion and feel the same emotion in response. The same neural systems get activated in a part of the insula, (C) it / which is part of the mirror neuron system, and in the emotional brain areas associated with the observed emotion.

	(A)		(B)		(C)
①	noticed	⋯⋯	experiencing	⋯⋯	it
②	noticed	⋯⋯	experiencing	⋯⋯	which
③	noticed	⋯⋯	experienced	⋯⋯	which
④	noticing	⋯⋯	experiencing	⋯⋯	it
⑤	noticing	⋯⋯	experienced	⋯⋯	it

10 ○△✕ ————————• 2011년 9월 평가원(고3) 20번

(A), (B), (C)의 각 네모 안에서 어법에 맞는 표현으로 가장 적절한 것은? 정답률 **48%**

You have to pay close attention to someone's normal pattern in order to notice a deviation from it when he or she lies. Sometimes the variation is as (A) subtle / subtly as a pause. Other times it is obvious and abrupt. I recently saw a news interview with an acquaintance (B) who / whom I was certain was going to lie about a few particularly sensitive issues, and lie she did. During most of her interview she was calm and direct, but when she started lying, her manner changed dramatically: she threw her head back, laughed in 'disbelief,' and shook her head back and forth. It is true that the questions (C) dealt / dealing with very personal issues, but I have found that in general, no matter how touchy the question, if a person is telling the truth his or her manner will not change significantly or abruptly.

	(A)		(B)		(C)
①	subtle	⋯⋯	who	⋯⋯	dealt
②	subtle	⋯⋯	who	⋯⋯	dealing
③	subtle	⋯⋯	whom	⋯⋯	dealt
④	subtly	⋯⋯	who	⋯⋯	dealt
⑤	subtly	⋯⋯	whom	⋯⋯	dealing

코드 접속하기

출제코드 1 간접의문문, 도치구문, 강조구문
특수 구문을 파악하고 일반 문장과 다른 어순 및 특징을 이해하는지 묻는 문제가 출제된다.

STEP 1 핵심 문법

1 간접의문문 : 「의문사 + 주어 + 동사」	간접의문문은 다른 문장에 연결된 의문사절(명사절)로, 의문사가 이끄는 절은 평서문의 어순과 같다. 1) He finally realized [**why** his parents built their house]. (의문사 + 주어 + 동사) 2) She was curious about [**who** broke the window in her room]. (의문사(주어)+ 동사)
2 도치구문: 강조하려는 말이 문장 앞에 나오면서 주어와 동사의 어순이 바뀌는 것	• 부정어(never/no/rarely/hardly 등) 도치:「부정어 + 조동사(do/have 등) + 주어 + 동사」,「부정어 + be동사 + 주어」 • so/neither[nor] 도치:「so/neither[nor] + 조동사/be동사 + 주어」 ※ 조동사, be동사는 문장 전체의 시제와 주어의 수에 일치시킨다. 1) _Never_ **did I expect** John to come tonight. (부정어에 의한 도치) 2) I don't want to leave here, _neither_ **does he**. (neither에 의한 도치)
3 「It is ... that」 강조구문	'~한 것은 바로 …이다'의 의미로, 강조하려는 말(주어, 목적어, 부사(구))을 It is와 that 사이에 둔다. 1) **It was** _Nick_ **that**[who] I met at the theater. (강조 대상이 사람인 경우, that 대신 who 가능) 2) **It is** _the book_ **that**[which] I have been looking for. (강조 대상이 사물인 경우, that 대신 which 가능)

STEP 2 시험 패턴과 핵심 전략

1 간접의문문의 의문사 → 의문대명사 vs. 의문부사	뒤에 불완전한 절이 오면 의문대명사(which, what 등)를, 완전한 절이 오면 의문부사(when, how 등)를 쓴다. 1) Everyone looked at what /ⓗow she tried to hold her chopsticks. 2) We have wondered why /ⓦhat the moon is made of.
2 도치구문의 어순과 동사의 형태	부정어 뒤에서 도치가 일어난 경우, 부정어 뒤에 조동사(do/have 등)나 be동사가 온다. so/neither[nor] 도치의 경우, 앞에 쓰인 동사가 일반동사이면 do동사를, be동사이면 be동사를 쓴다. 1) Rarely they talk about politics, as they have contrasting opinions. (→ do they) 2) She felt safe when the plane landed, and so was her husband. (→ did)
3 강조구문의 형태 →「It is ... that」	'~한 것은 바로 …이다'라는 의미의 강조구문일 경우, 「It is ... that」의 형태로 써야 한다. It was the Italians while /ⓣhat first started making cappuccinos.

정답 및 해설 p.106

STEP 3 전략 적용 연습

A 네모 안에서 어법상 바른 것을 고르시오.

1 He was not very good at his studies, nor do / did he seem to improve. 기출 응용

2 It is the use of camera lenses what / that determines the "look" of any picture. 기출 응용

3 As lions chase a zebra, they cannot tell what / when it will run left or right. 기출 응용

B 다음 밑줄 친 부분이 어법상 바르면 ○를 쓰고, 틀리면 바르게 고치시오.

1 To make her dream come true, she always thinks about <u>how</u> celebrities succeeded.

2 It was a Hollywood star <u>when</u> I saw in the theater right after watching a movie.

코드 접속하기

출제코드 2 가주어 진주어, 가목적어 진목적어 구문
진주어의 형태가 바른지, 가목적어와 진목적어 구문이 바른 형태로 쓰였는지 확인하는 문제가 출제된다.

STEP 1 핵심 문법

1 가주어 진주어 구문	to부정사(구), that절 등이 주어인 경우, 가주어 it으로 대체하고 진주어(to부정사(구), that절)는 뒤로 보낸다. 이때 that은 접속사로 뒤에 완전한 절이 온다. 1) **It** is hard **to learn** how to read and write Chinese characters. 　가주어　　　　　　　진주어 2) **It** is unbelievable **that** he traveled around Egypt alone. 　가주어　　　　　　　진주어
2 가목적어 진목적어 구문	5형식 문장에서 to부정사(구)가 목적어인 경우, 가목적어 it으로 대체하고 진목적어(to부정사)는 뒤로 보낸다. think, make, find 등의 동사는 「동사 + it(가목적어) + 형용사/명사 + to-v(진목적어)」 구문으로 자주 쓰인다. They *found* **it** difficult **to translate** the language to English. 　　　　가목적어　　　　　　　진목적어

STEP 2 시험 패턴과 핵심 전략

1 진주어의 형태 　→ to부정사, that절 등	가주어 진주어 구문에서 진주어로 주로 to부정사나 that절을 쓴다. 1) It is common <u>see</u> heroes rise from the dead in movies. (→ to see) 2) It is well-known <u>what</u> people get the information they need on the web. (→ that)
2 가목적어 진목적어 구문의 　형태 → 「동사 + it + 　형용사/명사 + to-v」	가목적어 진목적어 구문에서 가목적어로는 it을, 진목적어로는 to부정사를 쓴다. 1) I found it more fun ⎡practice /⟨to practice⟩⎤ when I set a goal. 2) His curiosity made <u>him</u> easy for him to question lots of scientific assumptions. (→ it)

정답 및 해설 p.106

STEP 3 전략 적용 연습

A 네모 안에서 어법상 바른 것을 고르시오.

1 It is almost impossible ⎡persuade / to persuade⎤ them to participate in the campaign.

2 Zebra stripes actually make it easier for zebras ⎡recognize / to recognize⎤ one another. 기출 응용

3 It was really fortunate ⎡that / what⎤ there were no casualties from the train's derailment.

B 다음 밑줄 친 부분이 어법상 바르면 ○를 쓰고, 틀리면 바르게 고치시오.

1 It would be ideal <u>to have</u> clear roads while you drive on the freeway. 기출 응용

2 After some research, the scientists found <u>them</u> hard to make a conclusion.

코드 접속하기

정답 및 해설 p.106

기출예제 ●————— ● 2010년 9월 평가원(고3) 20번

Q1 다음 글의 밑줄 친 부분 중, 어법상 틀린 것은? [정답률 61%]

The phrase, 'jack-of-all-trades' is a ① shortened version of 'jack of all trades and master of none.' It refers to those who ② claim to be proficient at countless tasks, but cannot perform a single one of them well. The phrase was first used in England at the start of the Industrial Revolution. A large number of efficiency experts set up shop in London, ③ advertising themselves as knowledgeable about every type of new manufacturing process, trade, and business. For a substantial fee, they would impart their knowledge to their clients. But it soon became ④ evident that their knowledge was limited and of no practical value. Doubtful industrialists started calling these self-appointed experts 'jacks of all trades and masters of none.' These experts are still with us, and as a result so ⑤ does the phrase.

● 핵심 코드 : 도치구문 ●

● 출제코드 1 적용

1 「so + 동사 + 주어」 도치구문이 쓰였고, 앞 절의 동사가 be 동사임에 주목한다.

2 「so + 동사 + 주어」 도치구문의 동사는 주절의 동사가 일반 동사이면 조동사 do를, be동사이면 be동사를 써야 한다.

코드 적용하기

① 명사를 수식하는 과거분사	밑줄 친 부분은 뒤의 명사 version을 수식하는 분사로, '줄여진'이라는 수동의 의미이므로 과거분사 shortened가 오는 것이 알맞다.
② 동사의 수 일치	claim은 those를 선행사로 하는 주격 관계대명사절의 동사로, 선행사가 복수 대명사이므로 복수 동사가 오는 것이 알맞다.
③ 분사구문	advertising 이하는 연속동작을 나타내는 분사구문으로, 생략된 주어는 주절의 주어(A large ... experts)와 같다. 주어와 분사가 의미상 능동 관계이므로 현재분사 advertising이 오는 것이 알맞다.
④ 주격보어	became은 2형식 동사로 뒤에 보어를 취하므로 형용사 evident가 오는 것이 알맞다.
⑤ 「so + 동사 + 주어」 도치구문	「so + 동사 + 주어」 도치구문으로, 앞 절에 be동사 are가 쓰였으므로 도치구문의 동사도 be동사를 써야 한다. 주어(the phrase)가 단수이므로 does를 단수형 be동사 is로 고쳐야 한다.

01

● 2013년 11월 교육청(고1) 27번

(A), (B), (C)의 각 네모 안에서 어법에 맞는 표현으로 가장 적절한 것은? [3점] 정답률 64%

One way to make a pursuer work harder is to zigzag. A rabbit running from a coyote, for example, does not run endlessly in a straight line. Instead, it moves quickly back and forth, (A) forcing / forced the coyote to change direction and make sharp turns, too. Zigzagging is easier for a rabbit, which is small, than for the larger coyote. The coyote also cannot tell (B) what / when the rabbit will run this way or that, so it cannot plan its next move. In this way, the rabbit makes the chase more (C) difficult / difficultly and tiring for the coyote. Though a coyote may still succeed in catching its prey, there is a chance that it may tire out, give up, and go look for an easier meal.

	(A)	(B)	(C)
①	forcing	what	difficult
②	forcing	when	difficultly
③	forcing	when	difficult
④	forced	when	difficultly
⑤	forced	what	difficult

02

● 2009년 11월 교육청(고2) 21번

(A), (B), (C)에서 어법에 맞는 표현을 바르게 짝지은 것은? 정답률 52%

The university catalog can be used to (A) help / helping the freshman who is confused by university life. It is revised every year in order that it will be up-to-date. First of all, there is in this catalog a list of all the courses which are offered by the university. These courses are arranged (B) alphabetical / alphabetically by each department in order that the student may choose which courses he wants to take. It is also from this list of courses of each department (C) while / that a degree plan for the student can be devised, which will be within the limits of the regulations of the university.

	(A)	(B)	(C)
①	help	alphabetically	while
②	help	alphabetical	that
③	helping	alphabetically	that
④	help	alphabetically	that
⑤	helping	alphabetical	while

03

● 2015년 9월 평가원(고3) 28번

다음 글의 밑줄 친 부분 중, 어법상 틀린 것은? [3점] 정답률 83%

The Internet and communication technologies play an ever-increasing role in the social lives of young people in developed societies. Adolescents have been quick to immerse themselves in technology with most ① using the Internet to communicate. Young people treat the mobile phone as an essential necessity of life and often prefer to use text messages to communicate with their friends. Young people also ② increasingly access social networking websites. As technology and the Internet are a familiar resource for young people, it is logical ③ what they would seek assistance from this source. This has been shown by the increase in websites that provide therapeutic information for young people. A number of 'youth friendly' mental health websites ④ have been developed. The information ⑤ presented often takes the form of Frequently Asked Questions, fact sheets and suggested links. It would seem, therefore, logical to provide online counselling for young people.

04 고득점 ○△×
• 2011년 3월 교육청(고1) 20번

(A), (B), (C)의 각 네모 안에서 어법에 맞는 표현으로 가장 적절한 것은? 정답률 41%

For thousands of years, people have looked up at the night sky and looked at the moon. They wondered (A) if / what the moon was made of. They wanted to know how big it was and how far away it was. One of the most interesting questions was "Where did the moon come from?" No one knew for sure. Scientists developed (B) many / much different theories, or guesses, but they could not prove that their ideas were correct. Then, between 1969 and 1972, the United States sent astronauts to the moon for their studying the moon and (C) returned / returning to Earth with rock samples.

	(A)	(B)	(C)
①	if	many	returning
②	if	much	returned
③	what	many	returned
④	what	much	returned
⑤	what	many	returning

05 ○△×
• 2007년 6월 평가원(고3) 22번

다음 글의 밑줄 친 부분 중, 어법상 틀린 것은? 정답률 63%

College life is busy. There are too many demands on your schedule. Activities, friends, and pastimes may cause some difficulties in your ① performing the real job at hand. When you are feeling ② overwhelmed by presentations, paper deadlines, or tests, you will probably spend all your time studying ③ to deal with these pressures. However, this lack of time for relaxation makes it more difficult ④ get the most out of your studies. Promise ⑤ yourself that no matter how much work you have, you will always relax during one full evening. You will work better if you take time off for relaxation.

06 고득점 ○△×
• 2009년 3월 교육청(고3) 22번

다음 글의 밑줄 친 부분 중, 어법상 틀린 것은? 정답률 38%

In business settings, it's really easy to forget ① to take the time to say Thank-You, and yet, it's an essential part of interaction with others. It's important to people that they feel valid, important, and ② respected. Just as saying sorry matters, so does ③ remember to thank those who help you move forward. And I think it's much nicer to send along a physical card than an email. A personal note written by your own hand matters ④ far more than a few lines of typing into a window that's so easily available at your fingertips. One more thing: if you're going to go this route, put in the extra few minutes to purchase a nice card and ⑤ use a pen that gives you a decent flow.

5
대명사, 형용사, 부사

UNIT 01
대명사

UNIT 02
형용사, 부사

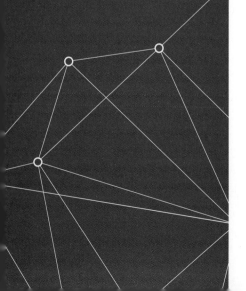

출제코드 분석

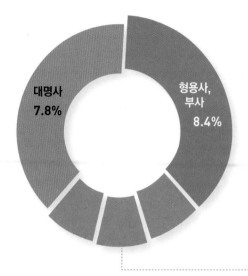

대명사
7.8%

형용사,
부사
8.4%

대명사

1 대명사의 수와 격
2 부정대명사
3 재귀대명사

형용사, 부사

1 형용사 vs. 부사
2 비교구문과 비교급을 강조하는 부사
3 수량형용사

2009년 – 2024년 평가원/교육청 기출 분석

출제 경향

1 문장의 세부 내용은 물론, 글의 문맥을 파악하여 대명사가 지칭하는 대상을 찾아야 풀 수 있는 문제들이 출제되고 있다.

2 함께 쓰인 명사, 동사의 수를 힌트로 하여 알맞은 대명사 또는 형용사가 쓰였는지 파악하는 문제가 출제되고 있다.

3 수식 대상에 따라 형용사와 부사를 구분하여 쓸 수 있는지 확인하는 문제가 출제되고 있다.

학습 전략

1 대명사

1) 대명사가 지칭하는 대상을 파악하며 문장을 읽는 연습을 한다.
2) 부정대명사별로 의미와 뒤에 올 수 있는 명사와 동사의 수를 구별하여 학습한다.
3) 재귀대명사의 기본 용법을 학습하고, 대명사가 지칭하는 대상을 파악하는 연습을 한다.

2 형용사, 부사

1) 형용사, 부사의 기본 용법과 형용사와 부사가 각각 수식할 수 있는 어구가 무엇인지 학습한다.
2) 비교급 앞에 쓰일 수 있는 부사와 쓰일 수 없는 부사를 구분하여 학습한다.
3) 수량형용사별로 의미와 뒤에 올 수 있는 명사와 동사의 수를 구별하여 학습한다.

코드 접속하기

출제코드 1 대명사의 수와 격
대명사의 수와 격이 대명사가 지칭하는 대상과 일치하는지 확인하는 문제가 출제된다.

STEP 1 핵심 문법

1 대명사의 단수와 복수	대명사는 사람이나 사물을 대신하여 나타내는 말이다. 지칭하는 대상이 단수이면 단수 대명사를, 복수이면 복수 대명사를 써야 한다.

단수 대명사	복수 대명사
I, you, he, she, it, this, that 등	we, you, they, these, those 등

※ 앞에 나온 구나 절을 대신할 경우, 대명사 it을 쓴다.

1) Hailey received *a bracelet*, but she didn't like **it**. (명사)
2) I tried on *many caps* in the shop, but none of **them** fit. (명사구)
3) *I exercise regularly*, and **it** keeps me healthy. (절)

2 대명사의 격	대명사의 격은 문장에서의 역할과 지칭 대상의 수에 맞게 써야 한다. 또한 소유대명사(…의 것)는 다른 대명사와 형태가 비슷하지만 의미와 쓰임이 다른 것에 주의한다.

1) *Her novel* was so popular that **it** made her a bestselling author.
2) *The smartphone* which I bought this morning is different from **his**.
   (his = his smartphone)

STEP 2 시험 패턴과 핵심 전략

1 단수 대명사 vs. 복수 대명사	대명사가 지칭하는 대상을 파악하고, 그 대상이 단수이면 단수 대명사를, 복수이면 복수 대명사를 쓴다. 1) She was so impressed by the movie that she has seen (it)/ them ten times. 2) The birth rate of European countries began to increase due to its various policies. (→ their)
2 목적어 자리 → 소유대명사 vs. 소유격 대명사	'…의 것'을 의미하고, 「소유격 + 명사」로 바꿨을 때 의미가 자연스러운 경우 소유대명사를 쓴다. Andrew thought his work should have won the award, but the judges preferred her /(hers).

정답 및 해설 p.111

STEP 3 전략 적용 연습

A 네모 안에서 어법상 바른 것을 고르시오.

1 What is justice? Different philosophers define it / them quite differently. 기출 응용

2 Entering the garden, I noticed that the grass was greener than that / those on the other side of the fence. 기출 응용

3 My friend looked at the pile of paper and said, "I'll help you with your work first. I can finish me / mine later."

B 다음 밑줄 친 부분이 어법상 바르면 ○를 쓰고, 틀리면 바르게 고치시오.

1 Do you have a friend whose name is the same as you?

2 I quickly wrote a note about my concerns and put them on the table. 기출 응용

3 The seats on the third floor of the theater are cheaper than those on the first floor.

코드 접속하기

출제코드 2 부정대명사
뒤따르는 명사나 동사의 수에 따라 알맞은 부정대명사가 사용되었는지 확인하는 문제가 출제된다.

STEP 1 핵심 문법

1 부정대명사

정해지지 않은 사람, 사물 및 수량을 나타낸다. 대명사이지만 명사를 수식하는 부정형용사로 쓰이기도 한다. 자주 쓰이는 부정대명사로 one, some, any, other, another, both, either, each 등이 있다.

1) She likes green apples more than red **ones**.
2) **Some** people like dog meat, while **others** really hate it.
3) **Both** of them are in the same school, but **each** has a different major.
4) I don't like the color of this shirt. Do you have this in **another** color?

2 부정대명사의 쓰임

부정대명사/부정형용사는 뒤에 오는 명사나 동사의 수에 영향을 준다.

• other(형용사) + 복수 명사 (+ 복수 동사)	• another(형용사) + 단수 명사 (+ 단수 동사)
• both(형용사) + 복수 명사 (+ 복수 동사)	• both of + 복수 명사 (+ 복수 동사)
• either(형용사) + 단수 명사 (+ 단수 동사)	• either of + 복수 명사 (+ 단수 동사)
• each(형용사) + 단수 명사 (+ 단수 동사)	• each of + 복수 명사 (+ 단수 동사)

1) **Another reason** I was annoyed *is* that the meeting was canceled without any notice.
2) **Either of the hotels** you suggested *looks* fine.
3) **Each box** *contains* several items that are chosen at random.

STEP 2 시험 패턴과 핵심 전략

1 복수 명사나 복수 동사 앞 → both, other(형용사)

복수 동사 앞이나 복수 명사 바로 앞에는 복수 취급하는 both, other(형용사) 등이 와야 한다.

1) Either /(Both) of them were fired after the strike.
2) Charley wants to know (other)/ another ways to show his appreciation.

2 단수 명사나 단수 동사 앞 → another, either, each

단수 동사 앞이나 단수 명사 바로 앞에는 단수 취급하는 another, either, each 등이 와야 한다.

1) There are orange trees on (either)/ both side of the road.
2) My family is moving to other city next month. (→ another)

정답 및 해설 p.111

STEP 3 전략 적용 연습

A 네모 안에서 어법상 바른 것을 고르시오.

1 Some write furiously in their notes, while other / another students give up writing in dismay. 기출 응용

2 The lens and the cornea are vulnerable parts; both / each are damaged if exposed to too much sunlight. 기출 응용

3 Each / Both of the boys were asked to attend the award ceremony on behalf of their team.

B 다음 밑줄 친 부분이 어법상 바르면 ○를 쓰고, 틀리면 바르게 고치시오.

1 Cake and ice cream are good desserts, so both one is fine with me.

2 If you are not satisfied with the restaurant, I will recommend other one to you.

3 Two thieves were finally caught and the policeman questioned each men. 기출 응용

코드 접속하기

출제코드 3 재귀대명사
문장의 목적어가 가리키는 대상을 파악하여 목적어 자리에 재귀대명사를 써야 하는지를 묻는 문제가 출제된다.

STEP 1 핵심 문법

1 재귀대명사의 용법	재귀대명사는 '… 자신'이라는 뜻으로, 인칭대명사(소유격, 목적격)에 -self/-selves를 붙여 만든다. 재귀대명사는 동작의 대상인 목적어가 주어와 같은 경우 사용한다. *cf.* 재귀대명사는 (대)명사를 강조하기 위해 사용하기도 하며, 이때 재귀대명사는 생략할 수 있다. 1) *Julia* bought **herself** a bunch of flowers. 2) I cried with pain when *I* cut **myself** with the knife by mistake. 3) Jamie tried to complete the work (**himself**). (강조 용법, 주어 강조)

STEP 2 시험 패턴과 핵심 전략

1 동사의 목적어 자리 → 재귀대명사 vs. 인칭대명사	동사의 주어와 목적어가 동일한 대상을 가리키는 경우 목적어로 재귀대명사를, 다른 대상을 가리키는 경우 목적어로 인칭대명사를 쓴다. 1) Angela always worries about small things and compares her / herself to others often. 2) When he opened the door, his little daughter came running toward himself. (→ him) 3) After winning the contest, he called him the best photographer. (→ himself)

정답 및 해설 p.111

STEP 3 전략 적용 연습

A 네모 안에서 어법상 바른 것을 고르시오.

1 To save him / himself from any embarrassment, the villagers at the banquet pretended nothing happened. **기출 응용**

2 Designers should be able to express them / themselves in their work.

3 When you fail, don't blame you / yourself for what you have done in the past.

B 다음 밑줄 친 부분이 어법상 바르면 ○를 쓰고, 틀리면 바르게 고치시오.

1 Some Korean parents force their children to study hard to prepare themselves to become "alpha kids."

2 David looked at himself in the mirror and realized he didn't resemble his mother at all.

3 Laura had always wanted to play the violin, so one day she decided to teach her.

코드 접속하기

정답 및 해설 p.112

기출예제 ● 2023학년도 수능 29번

Q1 다음 글의 밑줄 친 부분 중, 어법상 틀린 것은? 정답률 28%

Trends constantly suggest new opportunities for individuals to restage themselves, representing occasions for change. To understand how trends can ultimately give individuals power and freedom, one must first discuss fashion's importance as a basis for change. The most common explanation offered by my informants as to why fashion is so appealing is ① <u>that</u> it constitutes a kind of theatrical costumery. Clothes are part of how people present ② <u>them</u> to the world, and fashion locates them in the present, relative to what is happening in society and to fashion's own history. As a form of expression, fashion contains a host of ambiguities, enabling individuals to recreate the meanings ③ <u>associated</u> with specific pieces of clothing. Fashion is among the simplest and cheapest methods of self-expression: clothes can be ④ <u>inexpensively</u> purchased while making it easy to convey notions of wealth, intellectual stature, relaxation or environmental consciousness, even if none of these is true. Fashion can also strengthen agency in various ways, ⑤ <u>opening</u> up space for action.

*stature: 능력

● 핵심 코드 : 재귀대명사 ●

● 출제코드 3 적용
1 문장의 주어와 목적어가 동일한 대상인지 확인한다.
2 주어와 목적어가 동일한 대상을 가리키는 경우, 목적어는 재귀대명사를 써야 한다.

코드 적용하기

① 접속사	동사 is의 보어 역할을 하는 명사절을 이끌며, 뒤에 완전한 절이 이어지므로, 접속사 that은 어법상 알맞다.
② 재귀대명사	관계부사절 내의 주어 people과 목적어가 가리키는 대상이 같으므로, 목적어로는 재귀대명사 themselves가 와야 한다. people이 복수 명사이므로 대명사도 복수형이 와야 한다.
③ 명사를 수식하는 과거분사	과거분사 associated는 앞의 명사구 the meanings를 수식하고 있다. 의미는 '연관되어진' 것이므로 수식을 받는 명사와 분사의 의미상 관계가 수동이므로 과거분사 associated는 어법상 알맞다.
④ 부사	부사 inexpensively는 동사 can be purchased를 수식하고 있으므로 어법상 알맞다.
⑤ 분사구문	opening 이하는 결과를 나타내는 분사구문으로, 분사의 의미상 주어는 주절의 주어 Fashion과 동일하다. 의미상 주어와 분사의 관계가 능동이므로 현재분사 opening은 적절하다.

코드 공략하기

01 고득점 ○△✕ ····· ● 2018년 6월 교육청(고1) 28번

다음 글의 밑줄 친 부분 중, 어법상 틀린 것은? [3점] 정답률 35%

Plastic is extremely slow to degrade and tends to float, ① <u>which</u> allows it to travel in ocean currents for thousands of miles. Most plastics break down into smaller and smaller pieces when exposed to ultraviolet (UV) light, ② <u>forming</u> microplastics. These microplastics are very difficult to measure once they are small enough to pass through the nets typically used to collect ③ <u>themselves</u>. Their impacts on the marine environment and food webs are still poorly understood. These tiny particles are known to be eaten by various animals and to get into the food chain. Because most of the plastic particles in the ocean ④ <u>are</u> so small, there is no practical way to clean up the ocean. One would have to filter enormous amounts of water to collect a ⑤ <u>relatively</u> small amount of plastic.

*degrade: 분해되다

02 ○△✕ ····· ● 2008년 9월 교육청(고2) 21번

(A), (B), (C)의 각 네모 안에서 어법에 맞는 표현으로 가장 적절한 것은? 정답률 63%

Taking photos on sunny, hot days (A) | is / are | just as dangerous for you as it is for your camera. While you can deal with a simple sunburn, your camera can face permanent damages from too much sun exposure. (B) | Keep / Keeping | the lens covered when you aren't using it is recommended. Photos of sunrises and sunsets are always fun to take and are fun to view later, but pointing your lens directly at the sun may hurt the camera. The lens is related to the human eye; (C) | both / each | are damaged by directly peering at the light.

	(A)	(B)	(C)
①	is	Keep	each
②	is	Keeping	both
③	is	Keeping	each
④	are	Keeping	both
⑤	are	Keep	each

03 ○△✕ ····· ● 2008년 4월 교육청(고3) 21번

(A), (B), (C)의 각 네모 안에서 어법에 맞는 표현으로 가장 적절한 것은? 정답률 80%

Note taking is one of the activities by which students attempt to stay attentive, but it is also an aid to memory. "Working memory," or "short-term memory" is a term (A) | used / using | to describe the fact that one can hold only a given amount of material in mind at one time. When a lecturer presents a succession of new concepts, students' faces begin to show signs of anguish and frustration; some write furiously in their notebooks, while (B) | other / others | give up writing in complete discouragement. Note taking thus is dependent on one's ability to maintain attention, understand what is being said, and hold it in working memory long enough to (C) | write down it / write it down |.

	(A)	(B)	(C)
①	used	other	write down it
②	used	others	write it down
③	used	others	write down it
④	using	others	write it down
⑤	using	other	write down it

04 고득점 ○△✕ • 2009년 11월 교육청(고2) 20번

다음 글의 밑줄 친 부분 중, 어법상 틀린 것은? 정답률 26%

E-commerce is to the information revolution ① what the railroad was to the industrial revolution. While the railroad mastered distance, e-commerce eliminates it. The Internet provides enterprises with the ability to link one activity to another and to make real-time data widely ② available. It strengthens the move ③ to break up the big corporation of today. But, the greatest strength of e-commerce is that it provides the consumer with a whole range of products, ④ whoever makes them. E-commerce separates, for the first time, selling and producing. Selling is tied no longer to production but to distribution. There is absolutely no reason why any e-commerce enterprise should limit ⑤ themselves to marketing and selling one maker's products.

05 ○△✕ • 2009년 3월 교육청(고2) 21번

(A), (B), (C)의 각 네모 안에서 어법에 맞는 표현으로 가장 적절한 것은? 정답률 56%

Aging is a result of the gradual failure of the body's cells and organs to replace and repair (A) them / themselves . This is because there is a limit to the number of times that each cell can divide. As the body's cells begin to near this limit, the rate at which they divide slows down. Sometimes the new cells that are produced have defects or do not carry out their usual task (B) effective / effectively . Organs can then begin to fail, tissues change in structure, and the chemical reactions that power the body (C) become / becoming less efficient. Sometimes the blood supply to the brain is not effective. The brain cells become short of oxygen and nutrients, leading to forgetfulness.

	(A)	(B)	(C)
①	them	effective	become
②	themselves	effectively	become
③	them	effectively	become
④	themselves	effectively	becoming
⑤	themselves	effective	becoming

06 ○△✕ • 2010년 9월 교육청(고2) 21번

(A), (B), (C)의 각 네모 안에서 어법에 맞는 표현으로 가장 적절한 것은? 정답률 59%

In today's highly professionalized world, the term *amateur* invites rejection from business executives and economists. Yet throughout history, unpaid amateurs, (A) worked / working for themselves, their families or their communities, have made remarkable achievements in a wide variety of fields, including science and technology. Because science had not yet become a paying profession, early scientists were almost all amateurs. Many gained a living as paid professionals in one field but made (B) his / their greatest contributions to history as amateurs. Benjamin Franklin, as a politician, studied ocean currents on the side and demonstrated that lightning was a form of electricity. Pierre de Fermat, (C) who / whose 'last theorem' puzzled mathematicians for centuries, was a lawyer.

	(A)	(B)	(C)
①	worked	his	who
②	worked	their	who
③	working	their	who
④	working	his	whose
⑤	working	their	whose

07 ○△✕ • 2015년 11월 교육청(고2) 28번

(A), (B), (C)의 각 네모 안에서 어법에 맞는 표현으로 가장 적절한 것은? [3점] 정답률 46%

If we create a routine, we don't have to expend precious energy every day prioritizing everything. We must simply expend a small amount of initial energy to create the routine, and then all that is left to do is follow it. There is a huge body of scientific research to explain the mechanism (A) [which / by which] routine enables difficult things to become easy. One simplified explanation is that as we repeatedly do a certain task the neurons, or nerve cells, (B) [make / making] new connections through communication gateways called 'synapses.' With repetition, the connections strengthen and it becomes easier for the brain to activate them. For example, when you learn a new word it takes several repetitions at various intervals for the word to be mastered. To recall the word later you will need to activate the same synapses until eventually you know the word without consciously thinking about (C) [it / them].

	(A)		(B)		(C)
①	which	······	make	······	them
②	which	······	making	······	them
③	by which	······	make	······	them
④	by which	······	making	······	it
⑤	by which	······	make	······	it

08 고득점 ○△✕ • 2008년 6월 교육청(고2) 21번

(A), (B), (C)의 각 네모 안에서 어법에 맞는 표현으로 가장 적절한 것은? 정답률 41%

The summer Olympic Games contain many events with misleading names. For instance, the triple jump is a track and field event. The name implies (A) [what / that] the event includes three jumps, but it is made up of a hop, a skip, and a jump. The athletes who compete in this event look as if they are dancing as they bounce down the runway. (B) [Another / The other] event is the hammer throw. This event's name is misleading because the hammer does not look like a carpenter's tool at all. The hammer in the Olympic event is a metal ball that hangs from a wire handle. The athlete holds the handle with both of his or her hands, spins around to build power, and then (C) [releasing / releases] the hammer into the air.

	(A)		(B)		(C)
①	what	······	Another	······	releasing
②	what	······	The other	······	releasing
③	what	······	Another	······	releases
④	that	······	The other	······	releases
⑤	that	······	Another	······	releases

코드 접속하기 | 출제코드 1 형용사 vs. 부사
문장에서 형용사와 부사가 각각 알맞은 어구를 수식하고 있는지 확인하는 문제가 출제된다.

STEP 1 핵심 문법

1 형용사의 용법	형용사는 앞이나 뒤에서 명사를 수식한다. (한정적 용법) 또한 형용사는 주어나 목적어를 보충 설명하는 주격보어 혹은 목적격보어로 쓰인다. (서술적 용법) *cf.* a-로 시작하는 형용사(alive, alike, awake, asleep, afraid 등)는 서술적 용법으로만 쓰인다. 1) I eat **fresh** *fruit salad* for breakfast every day. (명사 수식) 2) *Teenage girls* are **sensitive** about their weight. (주격보어) 3) Because of his attitude, we considered *him* **fit** for the task. (목적격보어) 4) They made every effort to keep *the dolphin* **alive**. (서술적 용법으로만 쓰이는 형용사)
2 부사의 용법	부사는 동사, 형용사, 부사, 또는 구나 절을 수식한다. 1) He *reacts* **aggressively** in certain situations. (동사 수식) 2) She wanted to solve the problem in a **completely** *different* way. (형용사 수식) 3) Tom always solves complex math problems **amazingly** *quickly*. (부사 수식) 4) The focus of this policy is **mainly** *on anti-terrorism*. (구 수식) 5) **Fortunately**, *the police found the missing child in the cave*. (절 수식)

STEP 2 시험 패턴과 핵심 전략

1 형용사 vs. 부사	명사나 대명사를 수식하거나 보어 자리인 경우, 형용사를 써야 한다. 동사, 형용사, 부사, 구나 절을 수식할 경우, 부사를 써야 한다. 1) During ⟨regular⟩/ regularly meetings, club members share their opinions. 2) The ability to store fat efficient /⟨efficiently⟩ is a valuable physiological function.

정답 및 해설 p.117

STEP 3 전략 적용 연습

A 네모 안에서 어법상 바른 것을 고르시오.

1 The visit of a man in a Santa Claus suit made the children | happy / happily | last year.

2 The names of students are arranged | alphabetical / alphabetically | by each department. 기출 응용

3 Although carbon dioxide is criticized as a major pollutant, it is the | natural / naturally | occurring lifeblood of plants. 기출 응용

B 다음 밑줄 친 부분이 어법상 바르면 ○를 쓰고, 틀리면 바르게 고치시오.

1 Going fishing at every chance was quite <u>costly</u> for him.

2 These days, people are <u>increasing</u> accessing social networking websites. 기출 응용

3 This magazine is <u>high</u> recommended because it deals with the latest fashion trends around the world.

코드 접속하기

출제코드 2 비교구문과 비교급을 강조하는 부사
비교구문의 형태와 비교급을 강조하는 부사가 바르게 쓰였는지 확인하는 문제가 출제된다.

STEP 1 핵심 문법

1 비교구문의 형태	1) This book is **more interesting than** the previous one. (비교급) 2) Drinking enough water every day is **as important as** exercising every day. (원급 비교) 3) The shoes you picked out are **the most expensive** ones in our store. (최상급)
2 비교급과 최상급을 강조하는 부사	비교급을 강조할 때, 비교급 앞에 much, still, even, far, a lot 등의 부사를 쓴다. 최상급을 강조할 때, 「the + 최상급」 앞에 much, by far 등의 부사를 쓴다. ※ very는 비교급을 수식할 수 없으며, 최상급을 수식할 경우 「the very + 최상급」의 어순으로 쓴다. 1) The soil erosion in this region occurs at a **much faster** rate than normal. 2) This is **by far the best[the very best]** dictionary I have ever used.
3 비교구문을 이용한 표현	1) Please call me back **as soon as you can[as soon as possible]**. (가능한 한 …한[하게]) 2) The ice in the North Pole is melting **faster and faster**. (점점 더 …한[하게]) 3) **The more** you practice, **the better** you can perform. (…하면 할수록, 더 ~한[하게])

STEP 2 시험 패턴과 핵심 전략

1 비교급 앞 부사	비교급 앞에 올 수 있는 부사로는 much, still, even, far, a lot 등이 있고, very는 쓸 수 없다. 1) The government decided to introduce the rule (much)/ very more widely. 2) They developed toys which can stay in the water very /(even) longer than previous ones.
2 원급 비교구문 → 「as + 형용사 vs. 부사 + as」	원급 비교구문의 as와 as 사이에는 형용사와 부사가 모두 올 수 있다. as와 as 사이에 오는 말이 (대)명사를 수식하거나 보어로 쓰이면 형용사를, 동사나 부사 등을 수식하면 부사를 쓴다. 1) This creature's venom is as (poisonous)/ poisonously as a scorpion's. 2) Cold race car tires can't function as effective /(effectively) as when they are warm.

정답 및 해설 p.117

STEP 3 전략 적용 연습

A 네모 안에서 어법상 바른 것을 고르시오.

1 Some people have memories that can grow very / still sharper even as they age. 기출 응용

2 The only way to avoid ambiguity is to spell things out as explicit / explicitly as possible. 기출 응용

B 다음 밑줄 친 부분이 어법상 바르면 ○를 쓰고, 틀리면 바르게 고치시오.

1 Ironically, the more you struggle, the deep you'll sink in quicksand. 기출 응용

2 With this software, I can edit pictures as easy as an expert.

3 Minji thought her life would be much better if she could move to another city. 기출 응용

코드 접속하기

출제코드 3 수량형용사
뒤에 오는 명사에 따라 적절한 수량형용사가 쓰였는지 확인하는 문제가 출제된다.

STEP 1 핵심 문법

	many(셀 수 있는 명사의 '수')	much(셀 수 없는 명사의 '양')
1 many vs. much	many (of) + 복수 명사 (+ 복수 동사)	much (of) + 셀 수 없는 명사 (+ 단수 동사)

cf. many는 대명사로도 쓰이고, much는 대명사 또는 부사로도 쓰인다.
1) The scientists developed **many** *theories*, but they couldn't introduce all of them.
2) **Much of** *the equipment* for shooting the film *was* old and deficient.

	(a) few(셀 수 있는 명사의 '수')	(a) little(셀 수 없는 명사의 '양')
2 (a) few vs. (a) little	(a) few + 복수 명사 (+ 복수 동사)	(a) little + 셀 수 없는 명사 (+ 단수 동사)

※ a few와 a little은 '조금 있는'이라는 긍정의 의미를, few와 little은 '거의 없는'이라는 부정의 의미를 나타낸다. 또한 (a) little은 부사로도 쓰일 수 있다.
1) After carpeting the room, they received very **few** *complaints* about the noise.
2) **A little** *apple juice was* in the can, and it attracted some bees.
3) She seemed **a little** *afraid* of opening the door. (부사)

STEP 2 시험 패턴과 핵심 전략

1 복수 명사나 복수형 동사 앞 → many / (a) few	뒤에 복수 명사가 오거나 복수형 동사가 쓰인 경우, many나 (a) few를 써야 한다. 1) The professor gave us ⟨many⟩/ much books to read for our final exams. 2) There are ⟨few⟩/ little words to describe how I felt when I walked on stage.
2 셀 수 없는 명사나 단수형 동사 앞 → much / (a) little	뒤에 셀 수 없는 명사가 오거나 단수형 동사가 나온다면, much나 (a) little을 쓴다. 1) The airline received many /⟨much⟩ criticism after losing the passengers' luggage. 2) Even a few /⟨a little⟩ caffeine makes it difficult for me to sleep at night.

정답 및 해설 p.117

STEP 3 전략 적용 연습

A 네모 안에서 어법상 바른 것을 고르시오.

1 He didn't make | many / much | effort to qualify for the Olympics.

2 After the initial period, | few / little | ants continued to attack their enemies. 기출 응용

B 다음 밑줄 친 부분이 어법상 바르면 ○를 쓰고, 틀리면 바르게 고치시오.

1 Luckily, <u>many</u> patients were cured with the new drug.

2 Because of global warming, there are <u>little</u> areas for polar bears to inhabit.

3 The boss doesn't want people who don't have <u>many</u> experience in dealing with financial problems.

코드 접속하기

기출예제 ● 2021년 4월 교육청(고3) 29번

Q1 다음 글의 밑줄 친 부분 중, 어법상 틀린 것은? [3점] 정답률 **53%**

The world's first complex writing form, Sumerian cuneiform, followed an evolutionary path, moving around 3500 BCE from pictographic to ideographic representations, from the depiction of objects to ① that of abstract notions. Sumerian cuneiform was a linear writing system, its symbols usually ② set in columns, read from top to bottom and from left to right. This regimentation was a form of abstraction: the world is not a linear place, and objects do not organize ③ themselves horizontally or vertically in real life. Early rock paintings, thought to have been created for ritual purposes, were possibly shaped and organized ④ to follow the walls of the cave, or the desires of the painters, who may have organized them symbolically, or artistically, or even randomly. Yet after cuneiform, virtually every form of script that has emerged has been set out in rows with a clear beginning and endpoint. So ⑤ uniformly is this expectation, indeed, that the odd exception is noteworthy, and generally established for a specific purpose.

*cuneiform: 쐐기 문자 **regimentatio: 조직화

• 핵심 코드 : 형용사 vs. 부사 •

● 출제코드 1 적용

1 「so + 형용사/부사 + that ....」 구문에서 강조를 위해 so 이하가 문두로 나가 주어(this expectation)와 동사(is)의 도치가 일어난 것에 주목한다.

2 밑줄 친 부분은 동사 is의 보어 자리이므로 부사가 아닌 형용사가 와야 한다.

코드 적용하기

① 대명사	that은 앞에 언급된 the depiction을 지칭하는 대명사로, 지칭하는 명사가 단수이므로 단수 대명사 that이 오는 것은 어법상 알맞다.
② 분사구문	its symbols 이하는 주어가 남아있는 분사구문으로, 주어와 분사가 수동 관계에 있으므로 과거분사 set이 오는 것이 어법상 바르다. 이어지는 read 이하도 its symbols를 주어로 하는 분사구문이다.
③ 재귀대명사	동사의 목적어가 주어와 동일한 대상을 지칭하므로, 목적어로 쓰인 재귀대명사 themselves는 어법상 바르다.
④ 부사적 용법의 to부정사	to follow는 were possibly shaped and organized를 수식하는 부사적 용법의 to부정사로 어법상 바르다.
⑤ 형용사 vs. 부사	「so + 형용사/부사 + that ....」 구문에서 강조를 위해 so 이하가 문장 앞으로 나가 주어와 동사의 도치가 일어난 문장이다. be동사 is가 있으므로 부사 uniformly를 형용사 uniform으로 바꿔야 한다.

01

(A), (B), (C)의 각 네모 안에서 어법에 맞는 표현으로 가장 적절한 것은? [정답률 58%]

Every place on the earth is different. Just like people, no two places can be (A) exact / exactly alike. However, some places are similar in certain ways. There are patterns in the way people live and use the land. The design of buildings shows one pattern. Many large cities have very tall buildings (B) called / calling skyscrapers. There is not enough land, so people make more room by building up into the sky. Other patterns can be found in the foods we eat, the way we dress, or the way we grow crops. Learning about these patterns (C) help / helps us to understand the world a little better.

	(A)	(B)	(C)
①	exact	called	help
②	exact	calling	helps
③	exactly	called	helps
④	exactly	calling	help
⑤	exactly	called	help

02

다음 글의 밑줄 친 부분 중, 어법상 틀린 것은? [3점] [정답률 59%]

When I was growing up, one of the places I enjoyed most was the cherry tree in the back yard. Every summer ① when the cherries began to ripen, I would spend hours high in the tree ② picking and eating the sweet, sun-warmed cherries. My mother always worried about my falling out of the tree, but I never ③ did. But I had some competition for the cherries. Flocks of birds enjoyed them ④ as many as I did and would gather together in the tree, eating the fruit quickly and eagerly whenever I wasn't there. I used to wonder why the grown-ups never ate ⑤ any of the cherries.

03

(A), (B), (C)의 각 네모 안에서 어법에 맞는 표현으로 가장 적절한 것은? [정답률 86%]

When we enter a room, we immediately recognize the floor, chairs, furniture, tables, and so forth. But when a robot scans a room, it sees nothing but a vast collection of straight and curved lines, (A) which / what it converts to pixels. It takes an enormous amount of computing time to make sense out of this jumble of lines. A computer sees only a collection of circles, ovals, spirals, straight lines, curly lines, corners, and so on. (B) Spending / Spent an enormous amount of computing time, a robot might finally recognize the object as a table. But if you rotate the image, the computer has to start all over again. In other words, robots can see, and in fact they can see (C) much / very better than humans, but they don't understand what they are seeing.

*jumble: 혼잡, 뒤범벅

	(A)	(B)	(C)
①	what	Spent	very
②	what	Spending	much
③	which	Spending	much
④	which	Spent	very
⑤	which	Spending	very

04 ○△✕ • 2008년 9월 평가원(고3) 20번

(A), (B), (C)의 각 네모 안에서 어법에 맞는 표현으로 가장 적절한 것은? 정답률 71%

If you need to buy food, there is probably a shop or a department store close to your home that sells just (A) which / what you want. But shopping has not always been so easy. Shops started only with the introduction of money. In earlier times, people traded crops or objects they had made in exchange for the goods they needed. The first shops sold just (B) a few / a little products such as meat and bread. In 1850, the first department store, a shop which sells many different items under one roof, opened in Paris. Self-service stores developed in the United States in the 1930s. They replaced the old methods of serving customers individually by (C) selling / being sold prepackaged goods straight from the shelves.

	(A)	(B)	(C)
①	which	a little	being sold
②	what	a few	being sold
③	what	a few	selling
④	what	a little	selling
⑤	which	a little	selling

05 고득점 ○△✕ • 2007년 6월 교육청(고1) 23번

(A), (B), (C)의 각 네모 안에서 어법에 맞는 표현을 골라 짝지은 것으로 가장 적절한 것은? 정답률 43%

The more you read, the more you will build up your vocabulary and develop your reading skills. Wherever possible, (A) choose / choosing books or articles which encourage you to read on. Make sure they are at your level, or only a little above your level, neither too difficult nor too easy. Rather than working with word lists, it is (B) usually / usual best to see new words in context. Then you will understand how they are used. As you read a new word in context, there is a very good chance that you will be able to guess (C) its / their meaning.

	(A)	(B)	(C)
①	choose	usually	its
②	choose	usual	its
③	choosing	usually	their
④	choosing	usual	its
⑤	choosing	usual	their

06 ○△✕ • 2008년 3월 교육청(고2) 21번

(A), (B), (C)의 각 네모 안에서 어법에 맞는 표현으로 가장 적절한 것은? 정답률 59%

Dad came to football games whenever I played. He stood on the sidelines and watched the game attentively. I never told him how to get to a game; he just showed up. (A) Then / When I left the field at the end of a period, he would call me over with his hands. Not quite sure of what he was talking about, he always said the same thing. "You're playing good, Ron. Bend your knees (B) a few / a little more." I would respond to his comments by bending my knees more and (C) to run / running faster when I got back in the game.

	(A)	(B)	(C)
①	Then	a few	to run
②	Then	a little	running
③	When	a few	to run
④	When	a little	running
⑤	When	a few	running

6
어휘

UNIT 01
어휘 의미

UNIT 02
어휘 형태

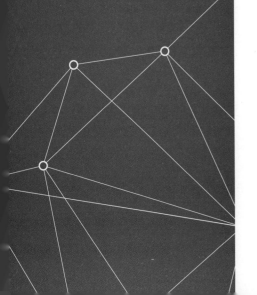

출제코드 분석

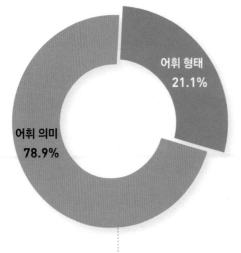

어휘 형태
21.1%

어휘 의미
78.9%

어휘 의미

1 반의어

2 문맥상 적절한 단어

어휘 형태

1 유사한 형태

2 파생어

2009년 – 2024년 평가원/교육청 기출 분석

출제 경향

1 단어의 의미는 물론 글의 전반적인 흐름이나 맥락을 이해해야 풀 수 있는 문제들이 출제되고 있다.

2 반의어들을 제시하거나 글의 전체 내용과 반대되는 단어를 제시하는 문제가 전체 어휘 문제의 절반 이상을 차지하고 있다.

3 의미상 관련이 없는 단어들을 제시하거나, 철자가 헷갈리는 단어들을 제시하는 문제도 다수 출제되고 있다.

학습 전략

1 어휘 의미와 형태

1) 반의어, 유의어, 철자가 비슷한 단어들을 정리하여 암기해둔다.

2) 평소 글을 읽을 때, 글 전체적인 내용과 흐름, 주제 등을 파악하며 읽는 연습을 한다.

3) 문제가 출제된 문장만을 읽을 것이 아니라, 앞이나 뒤에 오는 문장도 유심히 읽으며 문맥을 파악하는 연습을 한다.

코드 접속하기

출제코드 1 반의어
제시된 반의어들 중 문맥에 맞는 단어를 고르거나, 단어가 문맥상 반의어로 제시되는 문제가 출제된다.

STEP 1 핵심 기출 반의어

increase 증가하다	↔ decrease 감소하다	abandon 버리다	↔ maintain 유지하다
conceal 감추다, 숨기다	↔ reveal 드러내다	vulnerable 취약한	↔ immune 면역성이 있는
poverty 가난, 빈곤	↔ wealth 부	insufficient 불충분한	↔ adequate 충분한
fluid 액체	↔ solid 고체	encourage 격려하다	↔ discourage 좌절시키다
allow 허용하다	↔ forbid 금지하다	frequently 자주	↔ rarely 거의 …않는
broaden 넓히다	↔ narrow 좁히다	uncomplicated 복잡하지 않은	↔ intricate 복잡한
inferior 열등한	↔ superior 우월한	positive 긍정적인	↔ negative 부정적인
sustainable 지속 가능한	↔ unsustainable 지속 불가능한	damage 손상시키다	↔ recover 회복하다
overestimate 과대평가하다	↔ underestimate 과소평가하다	optimistic 낙관적인	↔ skeptical 회의적인
deflate 오므라들다	↔ inflate 부풀다	support 지지하다	↔ challenge 이의를 제기하다
disgrace 불명예	↔ honor 영예	exhale 숨을 내쉬다	↔ inhale 숨을 들이마시다
confident 자신감 있는	↔ insecure 자신이 없는	horizontal 수평의	↔ vertical 수직의
abundant 풍부한	↔ scarce 부족한	fluctuate 변동을 거듭하다	↔ stabilize 안정되다
maximum 최대	↔ minimum 최소	permanent 영구적인	↔ temporary 일시적인
acknowledge 인정하다	↔ disregard 무시하다	surrender 항복하다	↔ resist 저항하다
variable 변동이 심한	↔ constant 변함없는	enhance 향상시키다	↔ hinder 방해하다, 저지하다
accelerate 가속화하다	↔ slow 느리게 하다	solitary 혼자 하는	↔ social 사교적인
impoverished 빈곤한	↔ affluent 부유한	complexity 복잡성	↔ simplicity 단순함
abolishment 폐지	↔ establishment 설립, 수립	normal 표준의	↔ abnormal 비정상적인
tight 단단한, 꽉 조인	↔ loose 느슨한	prosper 번창하다	↔ wither 시들다
contract 수축시키다	↔ expand 확장시키다	accept 받아들이다	↔ deny 거부하다
hostile 적대적인	↔ favorable 호의적인	compete 경쟁하다	↔ cooperate 협력하다

정답 및 해설 p.122

STEP 2 전략 적용 연습

A 각 네모 안에서 문맥에 맞는 낱말로 가장 적절한 것을 고르시오.

1 Airlines must respond to problems swiftly. Their reputation can be [damaged / recovered] if they do not.

2 In winter, your blood vessels are more liable to [contract / expand], which makes your blood pressure rise. 기출 응용

3 Teenagers are particularly [vulnerable / immune] to drug use. Their brains are still maturing, and therefore drugs can have severe, long-term effects.

4 "When consumers get detailed information about ingredients in products, they are more [confident / insecure] about their decisions." said Harry M. Kaiser. 기출 응용

5 Reaching the summit of Mount Everest was considered an amazing achievement in the past. It was a national [disgrace / honor] to have a climber who succeeded in reaching the top. 기출 응용

6 A person who always cares about other people being above him has low self-confidence. Believing them to be [inferior / superior], he thinks he can never achieve their level of competence. 기출 응용

코드 접속하기

출제코드 2 문맥상 적절한 단어
의미상 연관성이 없는 두 단어 중 문맥에 맞는 적절한 단어를 고르는 문제가 출제된다.

STEP 1 핵심 풀이 전략

전체적인 글의 흐름을 파악하고, 앞뒤 문장을 통해 문맥을 파악하여 의미가 적절한 단어를 선택한다.
선택한 단어를 넣고 다시 읽어보고, 문맥이 자연스러운지 확인한다.

1 글의 주제 → 문맥 파악

> 2011년 4월 교육청(고3) 31번
>
> Some families work better together if there is a set of house rules. These prohibit / prescribe the expectations and guidelines which allow the family to live together as a group. Well-defined house rules can become quite important during the adolescent years. (중략)

• 주제: 가정 규칙의 필요성
• 문맥 파악: 앞뒤 문장들이 가정 규칙의 효과와 중요성에 대해 언급하고 있다.
→ 따라서 가정 규칙이 기대 행동과 가족 구성원으로서의 지침을 '규정한다'라는 의미의 prescribe가 들어가는 것이 문맥상 적절하다.

정답 및 해설 p.122

STEP 2 전략 적용 연습

A 각 네모 안에서 문맥에 맞는 낱말로 가장 적절한 것을 고르시오.

1 Have you ever thought about the functions of the skin? Most of us know that skin protects / selects us from heat, cold, and dirt. 기출 응용

2 Nobody likes to make others upset. Many people hesitate to say "no," but we should not continue / delay in delivering bad news.

3 Most women work long hours at home. However, a woman's contribution at home is often ignored / included when considering the prosperity of her family.

4 Most people think if they go on a long journey, they should take a tons of gear. But the absence / experience of professional backpackers teaches us the exact opposite.

5 The article was written to raise the public's admiration / awareness about smartphone addiction and to help prevent mental and physical health problems.

6 Research shows that pesticide use has tripled, while crop losses from pest damage have doubled. This shows that natural controls should be avoided / chosen over pesticide use. 기출 응용

7 One person can't do everything alone. Instead, we function as a society, with each person performing one highly specialized / urgent job such as baking bread or designing buildings. 기출 응용

코드 접속하기

정답 및 해설 p.122

기출예제 ● 2019학년도 수능 30번

Q1 다음 글의 밑줄 친 부분 중, 문맥상 낱말의 쓰임이 적절하지 <u>않은</u> 것은?

정답률 **55%**

Europe's first *Homo sapiens* lived primarily on large game, particularly reindeer. Even under ideal circumstances, hunting these fast animals with spear or bow and arrow is an ① <u>uncertain</u> task. The reindeer, however, had a ② <u>weakness</u> that mankind would mercilessly exploit: it swam poorly. While afloat, it is uniquely ③ <u>vulnerable</u>, moving slowly with its antlers held high as it struggles to keep its nose above water. At some point, a Stone Age genius realized the enormous hunting ④ <u>advantage</u> he would gain by being able to glide over the water's surface, and built the first boat. Once the ⑤ <u>laboriously</u> overtaken and killed prey had been hauled aboard, getting its body back to the tribal camp would have been far easier by boat than on land. It would not have taken long for mankind to apply this advantage to other goods.

*exploit: 이용하다 **haul: 끌어당기다

· 핵심 코드 : 반의어 ·

● 출제코드 1 적용
1 앞부분에서 언급된 순록 사냥 얘기에서 순록이 어렵게 잡히는지 확인한다.
2 물에 떠 있는 동안 순록은 공격받기 쉬운 상태가 되어 쉽게 따라 잡힌다고 했으므로 '쉽게' 따라 잡힌 먹이라는 내용이 이어지는 것이 자연스럽다.

코드 적용하기

① uncertain	앞에서 순록은 빠른 동물이라고 언급했으며, 이런 빠른 동물을 사냥하는 것은 '불확실한' 일일 것이므로 uncertain은 문맥상 자연스럽다.
② weakness	뒤에서 인류가 인정사정없이 이용할 수 있는 것이라고 했으므로, '약점'을 뜻하는 weakness는 문맥상 자연스럽다.
③ vulnerable	수영을 못하는 순록은 물에 떠 있는 동안 천천히 움직이며 쉽게 사냥의 표적이 되므로, '공격받기 쉬운'이라는 의미인 vulnerable은 문맥상 자연스럽다.
④ advantage	석기 시대의 한 천재가 최초의 배를 만듦으로써, 먹이의 이동을 수월하게 만들었다는 내용이 이어지고 있으므로 '이점'을 뜻하는 advantage는 문맥상 자연스럽다.
⑤ laboriously	앞에서 순록이 물에 떠 있는 동안에는 공격받기 쉬운 상태가 되고 '쉽게' 따라 잡힌다고 했으므로 laboriously(힘들게)를 easily(쉽게)와 같은 낱말로 고쳐야 한다.

코드 접속하기

정답 및 해설 p.123

기출예제 ●━━━━━━━━━━━ 2020년 6월 교육청(고1) 30번

Q2 (A), (B), (C)의 각 네모 안에서 문맥에 맞는 낱말로 가장 적절한 것은?

정답률 **70%**

The brain makes up just two percent of our body weight but uses 20 percent of our energy. In newborns, it's no less than 65 percent. That's partly why babies sleep all the time — their growing brains (A) [warn / exhaust] them — and have a lot of body fat, to use as an energy reserve when needed. Our muscles use even more of our energy, about a quarter of the total, but we have a lot of muscle. Actually, per unit of matter, the brain uses by far (B) [more / less] energy than our other organs. That means that the brain is the most expensive of our organs. But it is also marvelously (C) [creative / efficient] . Our brains require only about four hundred calories of energy a day — about the same as we get from a blueberry muffin. Try running your laptop for twenty-four hours on a muffin and see how far you get.

	(A)		(B)		(C)
①	warn	……	less	……	efficient
②	warn	……	more	……	efficient
③	exhaust	……	more	……	efficient
④	exhaust	……	more	……	creative
⑤	exhaust	……	less	……	creative

• 핵심 코드 : 문맥상 적절한 단어, 반의어 •

● **출제코드 2 적용**
앞에서 아기의 뇌는 전체 에너지의 65%를 쓴다고 했으므로 성장하는 뇌가 그들을 '기진맥진하게 만든다'라는 의미가 들어가는 것이 자연스럽다.

● **출제코드 1 적용**
뒤에서 뇌가 가장 에너지 소모가 많다고 했으므로 뇌는 다른 기관보다 훨씬 '더 많은' 에너지를 사용한다는 의미가 들어가는 것이 자연스럽다.

● **출제코드 2 적용**
뒤에서 뇌는 하루동안 약 400칼로리의 에너지만 필요로 한다고 했으므로 뇌가 '효율적인'이라는 의미가 들어가는 것이 자연스럽다.

코드 적용하기

(A) 문맥상 적절한 단어	아기의 뇌는 전체 에너지의 65퍼센트를 사용하기 때문에 성장하는 뇌가 그들을 '기진맥진하게 만든다'라는 의미가 문맥상 자연스럽다. 따라서 exhaust가 들어가야 한다. warn은 '경고하다'라는 의미이다.
(B) 반의어	뒤에 우리의 기관 중에 뇌가 가장 에너지 소모가 많다고 했으므로, 뇌는 다른 기관보다 훨씬 '더 많은' 에너지를 사용한다는 의미가 문맥상 자연스럽다. 따라서 more가 들어가야 한다. less는 '더 적은'이라는 의미이다.
(C) 문맥상 적절한 단어	뇌는 하루 동안 블루베리 머핀에서 얻을 수 있는 약 400칼로리의 에너지만을 필요로 한다고 했으므로, 뇌가 '효율적인'이라는 의미가 문맥상 자연스럽다. 따라서 efficient가 들어가야 한다. creative는 '창의적인'이라는 의미이다.

01 ○△× • 2015년 6월 교육청(고1) 30번

(A), (B), (C)의 각 네모 안에서 문맥에 맞는 낱말로 가장 적절한 것은? 정답률 51%

In Ontario, there is an old-growth forest near Temagami. Some people want to cut down the trees for lumber. Others want to keep it as it is: they believe it is (A) common / unique and must be protected for coming generations. Many people are somewhere in the middle, wanting some use and some protection. Most people are in favor of using our resources wisely. They prefer practices that make our resources (B) sustainable / unsustainable. That is, we should use our resources wisely now and we will still have more for the future. We are all responsible for looking after the environment. We can learn from First Nations' people who have long known the importance of (C) changing / preserving the environment for future generations. What you inherited and live with will become the inheritance of future generations.

*First Nations' people: 캐나다 원주민

	(A)	(B)	(C)
①	common	unsustainable	preserving
②	common	sustainable	changing
③	unique	unsustainable	preserving
④	unique	unsustainable	changing
⑤	unique	sustainable	preserving

02 ○△× • 2017년 3월 교육청(고2) 29번

(A), (B), (C)의 각 네모 안에서 문맥에 맞는 낱말로 가장 적절한 것은? 정답률 60%

Sometimes our judgments of ourselves are unreasonably negative. This is especially true for people with low self-esteem. Several studies have shown that such people tend to (A) ignore / magnify the importance of their failures. They often underestimate their abilities. And when they get negative feedback, such as a bad evaluation at work or a disrespectful remark from someone they know, they are likely to believe that it (B) accurately / inaccurately reflects their self-worth. People with low self-esteem also have a higher-than-average risk of being depressed. This (C) hurts / improves not only an individual's mental and emotional wellbeing but also his or her physical health and the quality of his or her social relationships.

	(A)	(B)	(C)
①	ignore	accurately	improves
②	ignore	inaccurately	hurts
③	magnify	accurately	improves
④	magnify	inaccurately	improves
⑤	magnify	accurately	hurts

03 ○△× • 2014년 11월 교육청(고1) 28번

다음 글의 밑줄 친 부분 중, 문맥상 낱말의 쓰임이 적절하지 않은 것은? [3점] 정답률 80%

When people share the same daily, weekly, monthly, and seasonal rhythms, connections among them form faster and stay stronger. The people trust each other more deeply, and ① coordination becomes easier. After all, they are ② frequently doing the same things and working on the same problems together. In fact, several organizations use regular stand-up meetings to maintain strong bonds and reinforce a ③ shared mindset. A CEO of a food company talks about his short daily meeting with his team. He explains, "The rhythm that frequency generates allows relationships to ④ weaken, personal habits to be understood, and stressors to be identified. All of this ⑤ helps the members of the team understand not only their roles but also how they can get the best out of one another."

04 고득점 ○△× ● 2014년 6월 교육청(고2) 28번

다음 글의 밑줄 친 부분 중, 문맥상 낱말의 쓰임이 적절하지 <u>않은</u> 것은? 정답률 43%

Suspense takes up a great share of our interest in life. A play or a novel is often robbed of much of its interest if you know the plot ① beforehand. We like to keep guessing as to the outcome. The circus acrobat employs this principle when he achieves a feat after purposely ② failing to perform it several times. Even the deliberate manner in which he arranges the opening scene ③ increases our expectation. In the last act of a play, a little circus dog balances a ball on its nose. One night when the dog ④ hesitated and worked with a long time before he would perform his feat, he got a lot more applause than when he did his trick at once. We not only like to wait, feeling ⑤ relieved, but we appreciate what we wait for.

05 ○△× ● 2020년 3월 교육청(고3) 30번

다음 글의 밑줄 친 부분 중, 문맥상 낱말의 쓰임이 적절하지 <u>않은</u> 것은? [3점] 정답률 55%

Random errors may be detected by ① repeating the measurements. Furthermore, by taking more and more readings, we obtain from the arithmetic mean a value which approaches more and more closely to the true value. Neither of these points is true for a systematic error. Repeated measurements with the same apparatus neither ② reveal nor do they eliminate a systematic error. For this reason systematic errors are potentially more ③ dangerous than random errors. If large random errors are present in an experiment, they will manifest themselves in a large value of the final quoted error. Thus everyone is ④ unaware of the imprecision of the result, and no harm is done — except possibly to the ego of the experimenter when no one takes notice of his or her results. However, the concealed presence of a systematic error may lead to an apparently ⑤ reliable result, given with a small estimated error, which is in fact seriously wrong.

*arithmetic mean: 산술 평균 **apparatus: 도구

06 고득점 ○△× ● 2021년 3월 교육청(고3) 30번

다음 글의 밑줄 친 부분 중, 문맥상 낱말의 쓰임이 적절하지 <u>않은</u> 것은? [3점] 정답률 29%

Those who limit themselves to Western scientific research have virtually ① ignored anything that cannot be perceived by the five senses and repeatedly measured or quantified. Research is dismissed as superstitious and invalid if it cannot be scientifically explained by cause and effect. Many continue to ② object with an almost religious passion to this cultural paradigm about the power of science — more specifically, the power that science gives them. By dismissing non-Western scientific paradigms as inferior at best and inaccurate at worst, the most rigid members of the conventional medical research community try to ③ counter the threat that alternative therapies and research pose to their work, their well-being, and their worldviews. And yet, biomedical research cannot explain many of the phenomena that ④ concern alternative practitioners regarding caring-healing processes. When therapies such as acupuncture or homeopathy are observed to result in a physiological or clinical response that cannot be explained by the biomedical model, many have tried to ⑤ deny the results rather than modify the scientific model.

*acupuncture: 침술 **homeopathy: 동종 요법

07 ○△✕ ● 2022년 6월 교육청(고2) 30번

다음 글의 밑줄 친 부분 중, 문맥상 낱말의 쓰임이 적절하지 않은 것은? 정답률 45%

The most advanced military jets are fly-by-wire: They are so unstable that they require an automated system that can sense and act more quickly than a human operator to maintain control. Our dependence on smart technology has led to a ① paradox. As technology improves, it becomes more reliable and more efficient, and human operators depend on it even more. Eventually they lose focus, become ② distracted, and check out, leaving the system to run on its own. In the most extreme case, piloting a massive airliner could become a ③ passive occupation, like watching TV. This is fine until something unexpected happens. The unexpected reveals the value of humans; what we bring to the table is the ④ flexibility to handle new situations. Machines aren't collaborating in pursuit of a joint goal; they are merely serving as tools. So when the human operator gives up oversight, the system is ⑤ less likely to have a serious accident.

*fly-by-wire: 전자식 비행 조종 장치

08 ○△✕ ● 2016년 9월 교육청(고2) 29번

(A), (B), (C)의 각 네모 안에서 문맥에 맞는 낱말로 가장 적절한 것은? [3점] 정답률 59%

Sadness in our culture is often considered an unnecessary and undesirable emotion. Numerous self-help books promote the benefits of positive thinking and positive behaviors, assigning negative affect in general, and sadness in particular, to the category of "problem emotions" that need to be (A) promoted / eliminated . Much of the psychology profession is employed in managing and relieving sadness. Yet some degree of sadness and depression has been far more (B) accepted / discouraged in previous historical ages than is the case today. From the classic philosophers through Shakespeare to the works of Chekhov, Ibsen, and the great novels of the 19th century, exploring the emotions of sadness, longing, and depression has long been considered (C) destructive / instructive . It is only recently that a thriving industry promoting positivity has managed to remove this earlier and more balanced view of human affectivity.

	(A)	(B)	(C)
①	promoted	accepted	destructive
②	promoted	discouraged	destructive
③	eliminated	accepted	destructive
④	eliminated	discouraged	instructive
⑤	eliminated	accepted	instructive

09 ○△✕ ● 2009년 6월 평가원(고3) 28번

(A), (B), (C)의 각 네모 안에서 문맥에 맞는 낱말로 가장 적절한 것은? 정답률 **50%**

A blind spot is not the same as a simple lack of knowledge. A blind spot emerges from a (A) resistance / connection to learning in a particular area. At the root of many of our blind spots are a number of emotions or attitudes — fear being the most obvious, but also pride, self-satisfaction, and anxiety. A manager, for example, might have unsurpassed knowledge in the financial field, but her understanding of people management might be (B) flooded / limited. Her people find her cold and aloof and want her to become more consultative and involved with the team. She, however, is not willing to accept feedback about her management style and refuses to even consider the (C) prospect / retrospect of changing her management style.

*aloof: 냉담한

	(A)	(B)	(C)
①	resistance	⋯⋯ limited	⋯⋯ prospect
②	resistance	⋯⋯ flooded	⋯⋯ retrospect
③	resistance	⋯⋯ limited	⋯⋯ retrospect
④	connection	⋯⋯ flooded	⋯⋯ prospect
⑤	connection	⋯⋯ limited	⋯⋯ retrospect

10 고득점 ○△✕ ● 2017학년도 수능 29번

(A), (B), (C)의 각 네모 안에서 문맥에 맞는 낱말로 가장 적절한 것은? [3점] 정답률 **40%**

When teachers work in isolation, they tend to see the world through one set of eyes — their own. The fact that there might be someone somewhere in the same building or district who may be more successful at teaching this or that subject or lesson is (A) based / lost on teachers who close the door and work their way through the school calendar virtually alone. In the absence of a process that (B) allows / forbids them to benchmark those who do things better or at least differently, teachers are left with that one perspective — their own. I taught various subjects under the social studies umbrella and had very little idea of how my peers who taught the same subject did what they did. The idea of meeting regularly to compare notes, plan common assessments, and share what we did well (C) mostly / never occurred to us. Rather, we spent much time in the social studies office complaining about a lack of time and playing the blame game.

	(A)	(B)	(C)
①	based	⋯⋯ allows	⋯⋯ never
②	based	⋯⋯ forbids	⋯⋯ mostly
③	lost	⋯⋯ allows	⋯⋯ mostly
④	lost	⋯⋯ allows	⋯⋯ never
⑤	lost	⋯⋯ forbids	⋯⋯ never

01 ○△✕ ● 2014년 3월 교육청(고1) 25번

다음 글의 밑줄 친 부분 중, 문맥상 낱말의 쓰임이 적절하지 않은 것은? 정답률 80%

It's a small world, and business brings people from all cultures together. You may attend a meeting with a ① foreign visitor, or you may be sent off to a country with a language you don't understand. A language ② gap is a great opportunity for good manners to shine. The best course of action is a little ③ preparation. You can obtain a phrase book and learn a few ④ basic expressions — "Good morning," "Please," "Thank you," "I'm pleased to meet you," and "Goodbye." Making an effort to communicate in another person's language shows your ⑤ disrespect for that person. *phrase book: (여행객을 위한) 상용 회화집

02 ○△✕ ● 2020년 3월 교육청(고2) 30번

다음 글의 밑줄 친 부분 중, 문맥상 낱말의 쓰임이 적절하지 않은 것은? [3점] 정답률 64%

I was sitting outside a restaurant in Spain one summer evening, waiting for dinner. The aroma of the kitchens excited my taste buds. My future meal was coming to me in the form of molecules drifting through the air, too small for my eyes to see but ① detected by my nose. The ancient Greeks first came upon the idea of atoms this way; the smell of baking bread suggested to them that small particles of bread ② existed beyond vision. The cycle of weather ③ disproved this idea: a puddle of water on the ground gradually dries out, disappears, and then falls later as rain. They reasoned that there must be particles of water that turn into steam, form clouds, and fall to earth, so that the water is ④ conserved even though the little particles are too small to see. My paella in Spain had inspired me, four thousand years too ⑤ late, to take the credit for atomic theory.

*taste bud: 미뢰(혀의 미각 기관) **molecule: 분자
***paella: 파에야(스페인 요리의 하나)

03 고득점 ○△✕ ● 2022년 6월 평가원(고3) 30번

다음 글의 밑줄 친 부분 중, 문맥상 낱말의 쓰임이 적절하지 않은 것은? 정답률 41%

In recent years urban transport professionals globally have largely acquiesced to the view that automobile demand in cities needs to be managed rather than accommodated. Rising incomes inevitably lead to increases in motorization. Even without the imperative of climate change, the physical constraints of densely inhabited cities and the corresponding demands of accessibility, mobility, safety, air pollution, and urban livability all ① limit the option of expanding road networks purely to accommodate this rising demand. As a result, as cities develop and their residents become more prosperous, ② persuading people to choose not to use cars becomes an increasingly key focus of city managers and planners. Improving the quality of ③ alternative options, such as walking, cycling, and public transport, is a central element of this strategy. However, the most direct approach to ④ accommodating automobile demand is making motorized travel more expensive or restricting it with administrative rules. The contribution of motorized travel to climate change ⑤ reinforces this imperative.

*acquiesce: 따르다 **imperative: 불가피한 것 ***constraint: 압박

04 ○△✕ • 2020년 3월 교육청(고1) 30번

다음 글의 밑줄 친 부분 중, 문맥상 낱말의 쓰임이 적절하지 않은 것은? [3점] 정답률 70%

We often ignore small changes because they don't seem to ① matter very much in the moment. If you save a little money now, you're still not a millionaire. If you study Spanish for an hour tonight, you still haven't learned the language. We make a few changes, but the results never seem to come ② quickly and so we slide back into our previous routines. The slow pace of transformation also makes it ③ easy to break a bad habit. If you eat an unhealthy meal today, the scale doesn't move much. A single decision is easy to ignore. But when we ④ repeat small errors, day after day, by following poor decisions again and again, our small choices add up to bad results. Many missteps eventually lead to a ⑤ problem.

05 고특점 ○△✕ • 2020년 9월 교육청(고2) 30번

다음 글의 밑줄 친 부분 중, 문맥상 낱말의 쓰임이 적절하지 않은 것은? 정답률 41%

Spine-tingling ghost stories are fun to tell if they are really scary, and even more so if you claim that they are true. People get a ① thrill from passing on those stories. The same applies to miracle stories. If a rumor of a miracle gets written down in a book, the rumor becomes hard to ② believe, especially if the book is ancient. If a rumor is ③ old enough, it starts to be called a "tradition" instead, and then people believe it all the more. This is rather odd because you might think they would realize that older rumors have had more time to get ④ distorted than younger rumors

that are close in time to the alleged events themselves. Elvis Presley and Michael Jackson lived too ⑤ recently for traditions to have grown up, so not many people believe stories like "Elvis seen on Mars."

06 ○△✕ • 2017년 3월 교육청(고3) 29번

(A), (B), (C)의 각 네모 안에서 문맥에 맞는 낱말로 가장 적절한 것은? [3점] 정답률 55%

Until the twentieth century, when composers began experimenting freely with form and design, classical music continued to follow basic rules relating to structure, not to mention harmony. There still was room for (A) conformity / individuality — the great composers didn't follow the rules, but made the rules follow them — yet there was always a fundamental proportion and logic behind the design. Even after many of the rules were (B) maintained / overturned by radical concepts in more recent times, composers, more often than not, still organized their thoughts in ways that produced an overall, unifying structure. That's one reason the atonal, incredibly complex works by Arnold Schönberg or Karlheinz Stockhausen, to name two twentieth-century Modernists, are nonetheless (C) approachable / inaccessible . The sounds might be very strange, but the results are still decidedly classical in terms of organization.

*atonal: 무조의, 장조나 단조 등의 조를 따르지 않는

	(A)	(B)	(C)
①	conformity	maintained	approachable
②	individuality	overturned	approachable
③	individuality	maintained	approachable
④	individuality	maintained	inaccessible
⑤	conformity	overturned	inaccessible

07 ○△✕ •——————— • 2015년 10월 교육청(고3) 35번

(A), (B), (C)의 각 네모 안에서 문맥에 맞는 낱말로 가장 적절한 것은? [3점] 정답률 88%

Until the mid-20th century, only a few immigrants paid a visit to their homeland once or twice before they died, but most never returned to the land of their birth. This pattern has completely changed with the advent of globalization, coupled with the digital revolution that has (A) enhanced / hindered communication. As a result, immigration is a very different experience from what it was in the past. The ability of immigrant families to (B) object / reconnect to their old culture via phone, television, and the Internet has changed their approach to integration into mainstream American society. This has also greatly influenced immigrant practices of socialization with children. Contacts with the country of origin are now more frequent, and result in more immigrant families being influenced to (C) abandon / maintain cultural patterns from the homeland, and to attempt to influence their children to keep them.

	(A)	(B)	(C)
①	enhanced	object	abandon
②	hindered	object	abandon
③	enhanced	reconnect	maintain
④	hindered	reconnect	maintain
⑤	enhanced	reconnect	abandon

08 고득점 ○△✕ •——————— • 2022년 4월 교육청(고3) 30번

다음 글의 밑줄 친 부분 중, 문맥상 낱말의 쓰임이 적절하지 <u>않은</u> 것은? 정답률 36%

One of the most productive strategies to build customer relationships is to increase the firm's share of customer rather than its market share. This strategy involves abandoning the old notions of ① <u>acquiring</u> new customers and increasing transactions to focus instead on more fully serving the needs of existing customers. Financial services are a great example of this. Most consumers purchase financial services from ② <u>different</u> firms. They bank at one institution, purchase insurance from another, and handle their investments elsewhere. To ③ <u>solidify</u> this purchasing pattern, many companies now offer all of these services under one roof. For example, Regions Financial Corporation offers retail and commercial banking, trust, mortgage, and insurance products to customers in a network of more than 1,500 offices. The company tries to more fully serve the financial needs of its ④ <u>current</u> customers, thereby acquiring a larger share of each customer's financial business. By creating these types of relationships, customers have ⑤ <u>little</u> incentive to seek out competitive firms to fulfill their financial services needs.

09 ○△✕ ● 2018년 6월 교육청(고1) 29번

(A), (B), (C)의 각 네모 안에서 문맥에 맞는 낱말로 가장 적절한 것은? [3점] 정답률 **55%**

People have higher expectations as their lives get better. However, the higher the expectations, the more difficult it is to be satisfied. We can increase the satisfaction we feel in our lives by (A) controlling / raising our expectations. Adequate expectations leave room for many experiences to be pleasant surprises. The challenge is to find a way to have proper expectations. One way to do this is by keeping wonderful experiences (B) frequent / rare. No matter what you can afford, save great wine for special occasions. Make an elegantly styled silk blouse a special treat. This may seem like an act of denying your desires, but I don't think it is. On the contrary, it's a way to make sure that you can continue to experience (C) familiarity / pleasure. What's the point of great wines and great blouses if they don't make you feel great?

	(A)	(B)	(C)
①	controlling	frequent	pleasure
②	controlling	rare	familiarity
③	controlling	rare	pleasure
④	raising	frequent	familiarity
⑤	raising	rare	pleasure

10 고득점 ○△✕ ● 2018년 9월 교육청(고2) 29번

(A), (B), (C)의 각 네모 안에서 문맥에 맞는 낱말로 가장 적절한 것은? 정답률 **37%**

A phenomenon in social psychology, the Pratfall Effect states that an individual's perceived attractiveness increases or decreases after he or she makes a mistake — depending on the individual's (A) perceived / hidden competence. As celebrities are generally considered to be competent individuals, and often even presented as flawless or perfect in certain aspects, committing blunders will make one's humanness endearing to others. Basically, those who never make mistakes are perceived as being less attractive and "likable" than those who make occasional mistakes. Perfection, or the attribution of that quality to individuals, (B) creates / narrows a perceived distance that the general public cannot relate to — making those who never make mistakes perceived as being less attractive or likable. However, this can also have the opposite effect — if a perceived average or less than average competent person makes a mistake, he or she will be (C) more / less attractive and likable to others.

*blunder: 부주의하거나 어리석은 실수

	(A)	(B)	(C)
①	perceived	creates	less
②	perceived	narrows	more
③	perceived	creates	more
④	hidden	creates	less
⑤	hidden	narrows	less

코드 공략하기 03

01 ○△✕ •2015년 3월 교육청(고2) 30번

(A), (B), (C)의 각 네모 안에서 문맥에 맞는 낱말로 가장 적절한 것은? [3점] 정답률 49%

Most of us play it safe by putting our needs aside when faced with the possibility of feeling guilty or disappointing others. At work you may (A) allow / forbid a complaining coworker to keep stealing your energy to avoid conflict — ending up hating your job. At home you may say yes to family members who give you a hard time to avoid their emotional rejection, only to feel (B) frustrated / satisfied by the lack of quality time that you have for yourself. We work hard to manage the perceptions of others, (C) ignoring / fulfilling our own needs, and in the end we give up the very thing that will enable us to live meaningful lives.

	(A)		(B)		(C)
①	allow	······	frustrated	······	ignoring
②	allow	······	frustrated	······	fulfilling
③	allow	······	satisfied	······	fulfilling
④	forbid	······	frustrated	······	ignoring
⑤	forbid	······	satisfied	······	fulfilling

02 ○△✕ •2020년 6월 평가원(고3) 30번

다음 글의 밑줄 친 부분 중, 문맥상 낱말의 쓰임이 적절하지 않은 것은? 정답률 69%

Chunking is vital for cognition of music. If we had to encode it in our brains note by note, we'd ① struggle to make sense of anything more complex than the simplest children's songs. Of course, most accomplished musicians can play compositions containing many thousands of notes entirely from ② memory, without a note out of place. But this seemingly awesome accomplishment of recall is made ③ improbable by remembering the musical *process*, not the individual notes as such. If you ask a pianist to start a Mozart sonata from bar forty-one, she'll probably have to ④ mentally replay the music from the start until reaching that bar — the score is not simply laid out in her mind, to be read from any random point. It's rather like describing how you drive to work: you don't simply recite the names of roads as an abstract list, but have to construct your route by mentally retracing it. When musicians make a mistake during rehearsal, they wind back to the ⑤ start of a musical phrase ('let's take it from the second verse') before restarting.

*chunking: 덩어리로 나누기 **bar: (악보의) 마디

03 고득점 ○△✕ •2019년 9월 교육청(고1) 30번

다음 글의 밑줄 친 부분 중, 문맥상 낱말의 쓰임이 적절하지 않은 것은? 정답률 34%

Technological development often forces change, and change is uncomfortable. This is one of the main reasons why technology is often resisted and why some perceive it as a ① threat. It is important to understand our natural ② hate of being uncomfortable when we consider the impact of technology on our lives. As a matter of fact, most of us prefer the path of ③ least resistance. This tendency means that the true potential of new technologies may remain ④ unrealized because, for many, starting something new is just too much of a struggle. Even our ideas about how new technology can enhance our lives may be ⑤ encouraged by this natural desire for comfort.

04 고득점 ○△× • 2024년 3월 교육청(고2) 30번

다음 글의 밑줄 친 부분 중, 문맥상 낱말의 쓰임이 적절하지 않은 것은? 정답률 30%

Emotion socialization—learning from other people about emotions and how to deal with them—starts early in life and plays a foundational role for emotion regulation development. Although extrafamilial influences, such as peers or media, gain in importance during adolescence, parents remain the ① primary socialization agents. For example, their own responses to emotional situations serve as a role model for emotion regulation, increasing the likelihood that their children will show ② similar reactions in comparable situations. Parental practices at times when their children are faced with emotional challenges also impact emotion regulation development. Whereas direct soothing and directive guidance of what to do are beneficial for younger children, they may ③ cultivate adolescents' autonomy striving. In consequence, adolescents might pull away from, rather than turn toward, their parents in times of emotional crisis, unless parental practices are ④ adjusted. More suitable in adolescence is ⑤ indirect support of autonomous emotion regulation, such as through interest in, as well as awareness and nonjudgmental acceptance of, adolescents' emotional experiences, and being available when the adolescent wants to talk.

05 ○△× • 2020년 6월 교육청(고2) 30번

다음 글의 밑줄 친 부분 중, 문맥상 낱말의 쓰임이 적절하지 않은 것은? [3점] 정답률 50%

Sudden success or winnings can be very dangerous. Neurologically, chemicals are released in the brain that give a powerful burst of excitement and energy, leading to the desire to ① repeat this experience. It can be the start of any kind of addiction or manic behavior. Also, when gains come quickly we tend to ② lose sight of the basic wisdom that true success, to really last, must come through hard work. We do not take into account the role that luck plays in such ③ hard-earned gains. We try again and again to recapture that high from winning so much money or attention. We acquire feelings of superiority. We become especially ④ resistant to anyone who tries to warn us—they don't understand, we tell ourselves. Because this cannot be sustained, we experience an inevitable ⑤ fall, which is all the more painful, leading to the depression part of the cycle. Although gamblers are the most prone to this, it equally applies to businesspeople during bubbles and to people who gain sudden attention from the public.

06 고득점 ○△× • 2021년 9월 교육청(고2) 30번

다음 글의 밑줄 친 부분 중, 문맥상 낱말의 쓰임이 적절하지 않은 것은? [3점] 정답률 43%

Human innovation in agriculture has unlocked modifications in apples, tulips, and potatoes that never would have been realized through a plant's natural reproductive cycles. This cultivation process has created some of the recognizable vegetables and fruits consumers look for in their grocery stores. However, relying on only a few varieties of cultivated crops can leave humankind ① vulnerable to starvation and agricultural loss if a harvest is destroyed. For example, a million people died over the course of three years during the Irish potato famine because the Irish relied ② primarily on potatoes and milk to create a nutritionally balanced meal. In order to continue its symbiotic relationship with cultivated plants, humanity must allow for biodiversity and recognize the potential ③ benefits that monocultures of plants

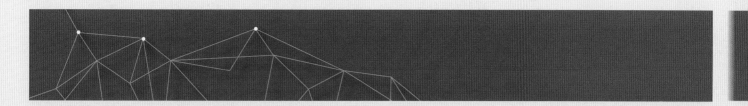

can introduce. Planting seeds of all kinds, even if they don't seem immediately useful or profitable, can ④ <u>ensure</u> the longevity of those plants for generations to come. A ⑤ <u>balance</u> must be struck between nature's capacity for wildness and humanity's desire for control.

*symbiotic: 공생의

07 ◯△✕ ● 2015년 11월 교육청(고2) 29번

(A), (B), (C)의 각 네모 안에서 문맥에 맞는 낱말로 가장 적절한 것은? [3점] 정답률 58%

Traditionally, most ecologists assumed that community stability — the ability of a community to withstand environmental disturbances — is a consequence of community (A) complexity / simplicity . That is, a community with considerable species richness may function better and be more stable than a community with less species richness. According to this view, the greater the species richness, the less critically important any single species should be. With many possible interactions within the community, it is (B) likely / unlikely that any single disturbance could affect enough components of the system to make a significant difference in its functioning. Evidence for this hypothesis includes the fact that destructive outbreaks of pests are more (C) common / uncommon in cultivated fields, which are low-diversity communities, than in natural communities with greater species richness.

*community: 군집, 군락

	(A)		(B)		(C)
①	complexity	……	likely	……	common
②	complexity	……	unlikely	……	common
③	complexity	……	unlikely	……	uncommon
④	simplicity	……	likely	……	common
⑤	simplicity	……	unlikely	……	uncommon

08 ◯△✕ ● 2020년 9월 교육청(고1) 30번

(A), (B), (C)의 각 네모 안에서 문맥에 맞는 낱말로 가장 적절한 것은? [3점] 정답률 60%

Social connections are so essential for our survival and well-being that we not only cooperate with others to build relationships, we also compete with others for friends. And often we do both at the same time. Take gossip. Through gossip, we bond with our friends, sharing interesting details. But at the same time, we are (A) creating / forgiving potential enemies in the targets of our gossip. Or consider rival holiday parties where people compete to see who will attend *their* party. We can even see this (B) harmony / tension in social media as people compete for the most friends and followers. At the same time, competitive exclusion can also (C) generate / prevent cooperation. High school social clubs and country clubs use this formula to great effect: It is through selective inclusion *and exclusion* that they produce loyalty and lasting social bonds.

	(A)		(B)		(C)
①	creating	……	harmony	……	prevent
②	creating	……	tension	……	generate
③	creating	……	tension	……	prevent
④	forgiving	……	tension	……	prevent
⑤	forgiving	……	harmony	……	generate

09 고득점 ○△×

• 2019년 6월 평가원(고3) 30번

다음 글의 밑줄 친 부분 중, 문맥상 낱말의 쓰임이 적절하지 <u>않은</u> 것은? 정답률 36%

Sometimes the awareness that one is distrusted can provide the necessary incentive for self-reflection. An employee who ① realizes she isn't being trusted by her co-workers with shared responsibilities at work might, upon reflection, identify areas where she has consistently let others down or failed to follow through on previous commitments. Others' distrust of her might then ② forbid her to perform her share of the duties in a way that makes her more worthy of their trust. But distrust of one who is ③ sincere in her efforts to be a trustworthy and dependable person can be disorienting and might cause her to doubt her own perceptions and to distrust herself. Consider, for instance, a teenager whose parents are ④ suspicious and distrustful when she goes out at night; even if she has been forthright about her plans and is not ⑤ breaking any agreed-upon rules, her identity as a respectable moral subject is undermined by a pervasive parental attitude that expects deceit and betrayal.

*forthright: 솔직한, 거리낌 없는 **pervasive: 널리 스며 있는

10 ○△×

• 2020년 9월 평가원(고3) 30번

다음 글의 밑줄 친 부분 중, 문맥상 낱말의 쓰임이 적절하지 <u>않은</u> 것은? 정답률 55%

If I say to you, 'Don't think of a white bear', you will find it difficult not to think of a white bear. In this way, 'thought suppression can actually increase the thoughts one wishes to suppress instead of calming them'. One common example of this is that people on a diet who try not to think about food often begin to think much ① more about food. This process is therefore also known as the *rebound effect*. The ② ironic effect seems to be caused by the interplay of two related cognitive processes. This dual-process system involves, first, an intentional operating process, which consciously attempts to locate thoughts ③ unrelated to the suppressed ones. Second, and simultaneously, an unconscious monitoring process tests whether the operating system is functioning effectively. If the monitoring system encounters thoughts inconsistent with the intended ones, it prompts the intentional operating process to ensure that these are replaced by ④ inappropriate thoughts. However, it is argued, the intentional operating system can fail due to increased cognitive load caused by fatigue, stress and emotional factors, and so the monitoring process filters the inappropriate thoughts into consciousness, making them highly ⑤ accessible.

코드 접속하기

출제코드 1 유사한 형태
형태는 유사하지만 서로 다른 의미를 가진 두 어휘 중 문맥에 맞는 것을 고르는 문제가 출제된다.

STEP 1 핵심 기출 어휘

접두사는 단어 앞에 붙어 단어의 의미를 바꾸고, 접미사는 단어 뒤에 붙어 품사를 바꾼다.

1 접두사나 접미사가 같은 단어

접두사가 같은 단어		접미사가 같은 단어	
abuse (남용)	– **ab**sence (결석)	atten**tion** (주목)	– inten**tion** (의도)
examine (조사하다)	– **ex**pect (기대하다)	original**ity** (독창성)	– util**ity** (유용성)
prevent (예방하다)	– **pre**serve (보존하다)	just**ify** (정당화하다)	– ident**ify** (확인하다)
combine (결합하다)	– **com**pare (비교하다)	accumu**late** (모으다)	– stimu**late** (자극하다)
encourage (격려하다)	– **en**counter (마주치다)	instinct**ive** (본능적인)	– inact**ive** (활동하지 않는)
prohibit (금지하다)	– **pro**vide (제공하다)	hesit**ancy** (주저함)	– consist**ency** (일관성)

철자가 유사하더라도 두 단어의 의미가 다르므로, 문맥에 어울리는 어휘를 선택해야 한다.

2 철자는 유사하지만 의미가 다른 단어

correct (수정하다)	– collect (수집하다)	initial (처음의)	– intimate (친밀한)
experience (경험)	– experiment (실험)	deliberate (의도적인)	– delicate (연약한)
sauce (소스)	– source (원천)	restrict (제한하다)	– restore (회복시키다)
suffer (고통 받다)	– differ (다르다)	stimulate (자극하다)	– simulate (…인 척하다)
optional (선택적인)	– optical (시각적인)	cruel (잔인한)	– crucial (중대한)
general (일반적인)	– generous (후한)	version (-판)	– vision (시력)
complaint (불평)	– compliment (칭찬)	pray (기도하다)	– prey (먹이)
blow (바람이 불다)	– glow (빛나다)	daybreak (새벽)	– outbreak (발생)
thorough (철저한)	– through (…을 통해)	thrive (번창하다)	– thrill (열광시키다)
assist (돕다)	– resist (저항하다)	attack (공격하다)	– attract (끌어들이다)
lack (부족하다)	– leak (새다)	poverty (가난)	– property (재산)

정답 및 해설 p.135

STEP 2 전략 적용 연습

A 네모 안에서 문맥에 맞는 낱말로 가장 적절한 것을 고르시오.

1 Finally, she identified her mistake and corrected / collected it.

2 The banana tree's trunk contains a large amount of water and is extremely deliberate / delicate . 기출 응용

3 Squirrels bury nuts during summer and fall to prohibit / provide food for themselves through the cold winter. 기출 응용

4 Some companies sponsor professional sports teams, which attracts attention / intention from the public.

5 According to the Olympic rules, people can transfer / transform a ticket to somebody else, but not for financial gain. 기출 응용

6 She felt the movie was boring because it was lacking / leaking an interesting storyline and realistic characters.

7 When we had almost finished building a domino house, Josh made such a cruel / crucial mistake that it collapsed.

코드 접속하기

출제코드 2 파생어
같은 어원을 가지지만 형태가 다른 파생어들을 짝으로 제시하여 문맥에 맞는 어휘를 고르는 문제들이 출제된다.

`기출 응용`

STEP 1 핵심 기출 어휘

접두사나 접미사가 붙으면 다른 뜻을 가지는 새로운 단어가 만들어지는데, 이를 파생어라 한다.
어원은 같더라도 접사에 따라 완전히 다른 뜻을 나타내기도 한다.

1 어원이 같은 파생어

· **sens**(느끼다)

sensation(느낌, 감각)	sensational(선풍적인)
sensible(분별 있는)	sensibility(감성)
sensitive(예민한)	sensitivity(예민함)
sensor(감지기)	sensory(감각의)
sensual(관능적인)	

· **tain**(가지다, 잡다)

contain(포함하다)	retain(유지하다)
maintain(유지하다)	obtain(얻다, 구하다)
sustain(지속시키다)	attain(이루다, 획득하다)
entertain(즐겁게 하다)	

· **popul**(사람들)

popular(인기 있는)	popularity(인기)
popularize(대중화하다)	popularly(일반적으로)
population(인구)	populous(인구가 많은)

· **scrib**(쓰다)

describe(묘사하다)	subscribe(구독하다)
prescribe(처방하다)	transcribe(기록하다)
inscribe(이름을 새기다)	

· **form**(형태, 구성)

perform(행하다)	inform(알리다)
reform(개선하다)	transform(변형시키다)

· **serv**(지키다)

observe(목격하다)	reserve(예약하다)
preserve(지키다)	

· **tend**(뻗다)

attend(출석하다)	extend(늘리다)
intend(의도하다)	pretend(…인 체하다)

· **quir**(묻다, 구하다)

require(요구하다)	acquire(습득하다)
inquire(묻다)	enquire(문의하다)

· **tribut**(할당하다)

contribute(기부하다)	distribute(분배하다)
attribute(…의 탓으로 돌리다)	

· **rupt**(깨다)

bankrupt(파산시키다)	corrupt(부패시키다)
erupt(분출하다)	interrupt(방해하다, 중단시키다)

정답 및 해설 p.135

STEP 2 전략 적용 연습

A 네모 안에서 문맥에 맞는 낱말로 가장 적절한 것을 고르시오.

1 Some medicines are prescribed / subscribed to slow the aging process of skin.

2 Many students intend / attend community colleges for vocational education.

3 The concert last night was interrupted / erupted by audio equipment failure.

4 Energy drinks sustain / contain high levels of caffeine and sugar which are harmful to your health.

5 The movie star is famous for contributing / attributing a lot of money to charity.

6 Researchers use satellite data to observe / preserve the environmental conditions that lead to disasters. `기출 응용`

7 Urban cycling has gained great popularity / population in the city thanks to the new bike share program.

8 You'll be able to inform / perform everyday activities without straining tight muscles if you maintain flexibility. `기출 응용`

코드 접속하기

정답 및 해설 p.136

기출예제 ● 2009학년도 수능 28번

Q1 (A), (B), (C)의 각 네모 안에서 문맥에 맞는 낱말로 가장 적절한 것은?

정답률 **53%**

The first experiments in television broadcasting began in France in the 1930s, but the French were slow to employ the new technology. There were several reasons for this (A) hesitancy / consistency . Radio absorbed the majority of state resources, and the French government was reluctant to shoulder the financial burden of developing national networks for television broadcasting. Television programming costs were too high, and program output correspondingly low. Poor (B) distribution / description combined with minimal offerings provided little incentive to purchase the new product. Further, television sets were priced beyond the means of a general public whose modest living standards, especially in the 1930s and 1940s, did not allow the acquisition of luxury goods. Ideological influences also factored in; elites in particular were (C) optimistic / skeptical of television, perceiving it as a messenger of mass culture and Americanization.

	· 핵심 코드 : 유사한 형태 ·	
	● 출제코드 1 적용	
	앞에서 프랑스인들은 새로운 기술 사용이 느렸다고 언급했다.	
	● 출제코드 1 적용	
	앞에서 프로그램 개발 비용은 높고, 산출 프로그램 수가 적었다고 언급했다.	

	(A)		(B)		(C)
①	hesitancy	……	distribution	……	optimistic
②	hesitancy	……	distribution	……	skeptical
③	hesitancy	……	description	……	optimistic
④	consistency	……	description	……	optimistic
⑤	consistency	……	distribution	……	skeptical

코드 적용하기

(A) 유사한 형태	앞에 프랑스인들은 새 기술을 쓰는 것이 느렸다고 언급했고, 이런 '주저함'에 몇 가지 이유가 있었다는 내용이 이어지는 것이 문맥상 자연스러우므로 hesitancy가 오는 것이 알맞다. consistency는 '일관성'이라는 의미이다.
(B) 유사한 형태	앞에 텔레비전 프로그램 개발 비용이 많이 들어 산출량이 적었다고 언급했고, 빈약한 '배급'으로 제품 구입을 유인하지 못했다는 내용이 이어지는 것이 문맥상 자연스러우므로 distribution이 오는 것이 알맞다. description은 '묘사'라는 의미이다.
(C) 반의어	프랑스 엘리트들이 텔레비전을 미국화와 대중문화의 전령으로 여겼다는 내용이 뒤에 이어지는 것으로 보아, 앞에 이들이 텔레비전에 대해 '회의적'이었을 것이라는 내용이 오는 것이 문맥상 자연스러우므로 skeptical이 오는 것이 적절하다. optimistic은 '낙관적인'이라는 의미의 반의어이다.

01 ○△✕ • 2008년 6월 교육청(고1) 28번

(A), (B), (C)의 각 네모 안에서 문맥에 맞는 낱말로 가장 적절한 것은? 정답률 73%

According to UNICEF(United Nations International Children's Fund), one of the keys to reducing (A) poverty / property in developing nations is improving educational opportunities for children, especially girls. It is often difficult for girls to (B) receive / deceive an education in poor countries. Girls often do not attend school or have to drop out because they must work or take care of their families. A great deal of research shows an important connection between increasing educational opportunities and improving the economic conditions of poor countries. Education can help girls grow into women with good jobs. This (C) strengthens / weakens the economy in the long term.

	(A)		(B)		(C)
①	poverty	⋯⋯	receive	⋯⋯	strengthens
②	poverty	⋯⋯	receive	⋯⋯	weakens
③	poverty	⋯⋯	deceive	⋯⋯	strengthens
④	property	⋯⋯	deceive	⋯⋯	weakens
⑤	property	⋯⋯	deceive	⋯⋯	strengthens

02 ○△✕ • 2011년 3월 교육청(고2) 31번

(A), (B), (C)의 각 네모 안에서 문맥에 맞는 낱말로 가장 적절한 것은? 정답률 54%

Can vitamin pills be dangerous to your health? Yes, if you take too many. With certain vitamins, the body uses as much as it needs and passes the rest out. Other vitamins, especially Vitamins A and D, (A) accumulate / stimulate in the body and can cause damage if taken in extremely high amounts over a period of time. Extremely high amounts of Vitamin A, for example, can eventually lead to liver damage and blurred (B) version / vision . On the other hand, it is safe to take a multiple-vitamin pill regularly, and some vitamins are even (C) prescribed / subscribed for medical purposes. For instance, niacin is used in very large dosages, under strict medical supervision, to lower cholesterol levels.

	(A)		(B)		(C)
①	accumulate	⋯⋯	vision	⋯⋯	prescribed
②	accumulate	⋯⋯	vision	⋯⋯	subscribed
③	accumulate	⋯⋯	version	⋯⋯	subscribed
④	stimulate	⋯⋯	vision	⋯⋯	prescribed
⑤	stimulate	⋯⋯	version	⋯⋯	prescribed

03 ○△✕ • 2010년 3월 교육청(고2) 31번

(A), (B), (C) 각 네모 안에서 문맥에 맞는 낱말로 가장 적절한 것은? 정답률 67%

It's well known that washing your hands with good old-fashioned soap and water is a great way to help prevent disease. What do you do when that's just not an option? There are plenty of wipes, creams, and sprays on store shelves that promise to (A) remove / reproduce germs without the addition of running water. While they're not a substitute for regular hand washing, they can be a (B) valuable / valueless second line of defense. Most of these products are alcohol-based. Alcohol is generally safe and effective, according to Sonya Lunder, a senior analyst at Environmental Working Group, a non-profit (C) organism / organization that has done extensive research on personal care products.

	(A)		(B)		(C)
①	remove	······	valuable	······	organism
②	remove	······	valuable	······	organization
③	remove	······	valueless	······	organism
④	reproduce	······	valueless	······	organism
⑤	reproduce	······	valuable	······	organization

04 ○△× • 2009년 3월 교육청(고2) 29번

(A), (B), (C)의 각 네모 안에서 문맥에 맞는 낱말로 가장 적절한 것은? 정답률 54%

When he was staying at an air base in Africa, author Saint-Exupéry (A) collected / corrected a thousand francs from his friends to help a Moroccan servant return to his home town. One of the pilots who flew the servant to his home town said, "As soon as he arrived, he went to the very best restaurant, handed out (B) general / generous tips, paid for food and drinks all round, and bought dolls for the children in his village. This man didn't have the slightest notion of economy."

"Quite the opposite," answered Saint-Exupéry, "He knew that the best (C) instrument / investment in the world is in people. Spending in that way, he managed to win all over again the respect of his countrymen, and they will offer him a job."

*franc: 프랑(프랑스의 옛 화폐 단위)

	(A)		(B)		(C)
①	collected	······	general	······	instrument
②	collected	······	generous	······	instrument
③	collected	······	generous	······	investment
④	corrected	······	generous	······	instrument
⑤	corrected	······	general	······	investment

05 ○△× • 2008년 11월 교육청(고2) 30번

(A), (B), (C)의 각 네모 안에서 문맥에 맞는 낱말로 가장 적절한 것은? 정답률 48%

It is often incorrectly quoted that mosquitoes kill more people than any other animal does. Actually, it is not mosquitoes that kill people but the parasite they carry that causes malaria. Approximately 300 million people worldwide are affected by malaria and about 1.5 million die from it every year. The greatest known (A) daybreak / outbreak of malaria happened in the 1920s in Russia when 13 million people were affected and 600,000 died. It also proved that mosquitoes (B) thrive / thrill in cold temperature. Mosquitoes are abundant in Antarctica. There are about 380 species of mosquitoes in the world, but only 60 (C) transmit / transcribe the parasite.

*parasite: 기생충

	(A)		(B)		(C)
①	daybreak	······	thrive	······	transcribe
②	outbreak	······	thrive	······	transmit
③	daybreak	······	thrive	······	transmit
④	outbreak	······	thrill	······	transcribe
⑤	daybreak	······	thrill	······	transmit

06 고득점 ○△× • 2008년 3월 교육청(고2) 28번

(A), (B), (C)의 각 네모 안에서 문맥에 맞는 낱말로 가장 적절한 것은? 정답률 35%

College sports are a big industry. Teams with nationwide (A) popularity / population can be worth millions of dollars. So, colleges invest in their players and, in return, the schools earn money and (B) attention / intention. The athletes often get a free education and gain experience that might lead to a chance to play professionally. But critics question the morality of a situation where college athletes may seem (C) valued / neglected more as athletes than as college students. They say that some players who finish college never really learn anything except their sport.

	(A)		(B)		(C)
①	popularity	······	attention	······	valued
②	population	······	attention	······	neglected
③	popularity	······	attention	······	neglected
④	population	······	intention	······	neglected
⑤	popularity	······	intention	······	valued

07 고득점 ○△✕ ● 2009년 6월 교육청(고2) 28번

(A), (B), (C)의 각 네모 안에서 문맥에 맞는 낱말로 가장 적절한 것은? 정답률 42%

Certain fears are normal during childhood. That is because fear can be a natural reaction to feeling unsure and much of what children experience is (A) familiar / unfamiliar . Young children often have fears of the dark, being alone, strangers, monsters, or other scary imaginary creatures. School-aged children might be afraid when it is stormy or at a first sleep-over. As they grow and learn, with the support of adults, most children are able to slowly conquer these fears and outgrow them. Some children are more (B) sensitive / sensible to fears and may have a tough time overcoming them. When fears last beyond the (C) expended / expected age, it might be a sign that someone is overly fearful, worried, or anxious. People whose fears are too intense or last too long might need help and support to overcome them.

	(A)		(B)		(C)
①	familiar	······	sensitive	······	expended
②	familiar	······	sensible	······	expended
③	unfamiliar	······	sensitive	······	expended
④	unfamiliar	······	sensible	······	expected
⑤	unfamiliar	······	sensitive	······	expected

08 ○△✕ ● 2012년 10월 교육청(고3) 34번

(A), (B), (C)의 각 네모 안에서 문맥에 맞는 낱말로 가장 적절한 것은? [3점] 정답률 65%

"The economist in me says the best gift is cash," writes Alex Tabarrok, an economist and blogger. "The rest of me (A) assists / resists ." He offers a good counterexample to the practical notion that the ideal gift is an item we would have bought for ourselves: Suppose someone gives you $100, and you buy a set of tires for your car. This is what maximizes your (B) originality / utility . Still, you might not be very happy if your lover gave you car tires for your birthday. In most cases, Tabarrok points out, we wish the gift giver would buy us something less (C) luxurious / ordinary . From our intimates at least, we'd rather receive a gift that speaks to "the wild self, the passionate self, the romantic self."

	(A)		(B)		(C)
①	assists	······	originality	······	luxurious
②	assists	······	utility	······	ordinary
③	resists	······	utility	······	ordinary
④	resists	······	originality	······	luxurious
⑤	resists	······	utility	······	luxurious

다빈출
코드

X

어법어휘

모의고사
1회
2회

01 고득점 · 2011년 3월 교육청(고1) 21번

다음 글의 밑줄 친 부분 중, 어법상 틀린 것은? 정답률 **39%**

I was working at a nursing home. It was late in the evening ① when I finished, so I ran down the street to the bus stop. I enjoyed the ride home and watched my fellow passengers ② got off at their stops. After a while, I was the only one ③ left on the bus. As the bus approached my stop, the driver called out to me, "Where do you live?" I explained to him ④ that I lived just up the next street. He then offered to drop me off outside my house. I was very grateful for his offer. I thanked the bus driver and walked to my door, ⑤ knowing that I would never forget his kindness.

02 · 2018년 9월 평가원(고3) 30번

(A), (B), (C)의 각 네모 안에서 문맥에 맞는 낱말로 가장 적절한 것은? 정답률 **51%**

For every toxic substance, process, or product in use today, there is a safer alternative — either already in existence, or waiting to be discovered through the application of human intellect, ingenuity, and effort. In almost every case, the safer alternative is (A) available / unavailable at a comparable cost. Industry may reject these facts and complain about the high cost of acting, but history sets the record straight. The chemical industry denied that there were practical alternatives to ozone-depleting chemicals, (B) predicting / preventing not only economic disaster but numerous deaths because food and vaccines would spoil without refrigeration. They were wrong. The motor vehicle industry initially denied that cars caused air pollution, then claimed that no technology existed to reduce pollution from vehicles, and later argued that installing devices to reduce air pollution would make cars extremely expensive. They were wrong every time. The pesticide industry argues that synthetic pesticides are absolutely (C) necessary / unnecessary to grow food. Thousands of organic farmers are proving them wrong.

*deplete: 고갈시키다 **synthetic pesticide: 합성 살충제

	(A)	(B)	(C)
①	available	predicting	necessary
②	available	preventing	necessary
③	available	predicting	unnecessary
④	unavailable	preventing	unnecessary
⑤	unavailable	predicting	necessary

03 · 2016년 3월 교육청(고1) 28번

다음 글의 밑줄 친 부분 중, 어법상 틀린 것은? [3점] 정답률 **62%**

Your parents may be afraid that you will not spend your allowance wisely. You may make some foolish spending choices, but if you ① do, the decision to do so is your own and hopefully you will learn from your mistakes. Much of learning ② occurs through trial and error. Explain to your parents that money is something you will have to deal with for the rest of your life. It is better ③ what you make your mistakes early on rather than later in life. Explain that you will have a family someday and you need to know how ④ to manage your money. Not everything ⑤ is taught at school!

04 · 2014년 3월 교육청(고2) 24번

(A), (B), (C)의 각 네모 안에서 문맥에 맞는 낱말로 가장 적절한 것은? 정답률 **82%**

It was once considered an amazing achievement to reach the summit of Mount Everest. It was even a national (A) disgrace / honor to have a climber waving a national flag there. But now that almost 4,000 people have reached its summit, the achievement means less than it did a half century ago. In 1963, six people reached the top, but in the spring of 2012, the summit was crowded with more than 500 people. Then what makes it (B) difficult / possible for so many people to reach the summit? One important factor is improved weather forecasting. In the past, (C) lack / presence of information led expeditions to attempt the summit whenever their team members were ready. Today, with hyper-accurate satellite forecasts, all teams know exactly when the weather will be perfect for climbing, and they often go for the top on the same days.

	(A)		(B)		(C)
①	disgrace	······	difficult	······	presence
②	disgrace	······	possible	······	lack
③	honor	······	difficult	······	lack
④	honor	······	possible	······	presence
⑤	honor	······	possible	······	lack

05

● 2021학년도 수능 30번

다음 글의 밑줄 친 부분 중, 문맥상 낱말의 쓰임이 적절하지 <u>않은</u> 것은? 정답률 72%

How the bandwagon effect occurs is demonstrated by the history of measurements of the speed of light. Because this speed is the basis of the theory of relativity, it's one of the most frequently and carefully measured ① <u>quantities</u> in science. As far as we know, the speed hasn't changed over time. However, from 1870 to 1900, all the experiments found speeds that were too high. Then, from 1900 to 1950, the ② <u>opposite</u> happened — all the experiments found speeds that were too low! This kind of error, where results are always on one side of the real value, is called "bias." It probably happened because over time, experimenters subconsciously adjusted their results to ③ <u>match</u> what they expected to find. If a result fit what they expected, they kept it. If a result didn't fit, they threw it out. They weren't being intentionally dishonest, just ④ <u>influenced</u> by the conventional wisdom. The pattern only changed when someone ⑤ <u>lacked</u> the courage to report what was actually measured instead of what was expected.

*bandwagon effect: 편승 효과

06 고득점

● 2019년 3월 교육청(고1) 28번

(A), (B), (C)의 각 네모 안에서 어법에 맞는 표현으로 가장 적절한 것은? 정답률 41%

Clothing doesn't have to be expensive to provide comfort during exercise. Select clothing appropriate for the temperature and environmental conditions (A) which / in which you will be doing exercise. Clothing that is appropriate for exercise and the season can improve your exercise experience. In warm environments, clothes that have a wicking capacity (B) is / are helpful in dissipating heat from the body. In contrast, it is best to face cold environments with layers so you can adjust your body temperature to avoid sweating and remain (C) comfortable / comfortably .

*wick: (모세관 작용으로) 수분을 흡수하거나 배출하다
**dissipate: (열을) 발산하다

	(A)		(B)		(C)
①	which	······	is	······	comfortable
②	which	······	are	······	comfortable
③	in which	······	are	······	comfortable
④	in which	······	is	······	comfortably
⑤	in which	······	are	······	comfortably

07

● 2011년 3월 교육청(고2) 20번

다음 글의 밑줄 친 부분 중, 어법상 틀린 것은? 정답률 47%

The U.S. space agency NASA is currently on the Hundred Years Starship, a project of exploring new habitable planets and ① <u>helping</u> people settle down there. If settlers succeed in making ② <u>another</u> planet their home, it will become one of the most revolutionary events in history. ③ <u>Assumed</u> to have a substantial amount of water, Mars is probably most habitable out of all the planets in our solar system. However, this project would take time since the cost will make a return flight to Earth almost ④ <u>impossible</u>. Although the living supplies for the settlers would ⑤ <u>send</u> from Earth, taking the risk of exchanging life for dreams is tough.

모의고사 1회 • 139

08

다음 글의 밑줄 친 부분 중, 문맥상 낱말의 쓰임이 적절하지 <ins>않은</ins> 것은? 정답률 **55%**

It has been suggested that "organic" methods, defined as those in which only natural products can be used as inputs, would be less damaging to the biosphere. Large-scale adoption of "organic" farming methods, however, would ① <ins>reduce</ins> yields and increase production costs for many major crops. Inorganic nitrogen supplies are ② <ins>essential</ins> for maintaining moderate to high levels of productivity for many of the non-leguminous crop species, because organic supplies of nitrogenous materials often are either limited or more expensive than inorganic nitrogen fertilizers. In addition, there are ③ <ins>benefits</ins> to the extensive use of either manure or legumes as "green manure" crops. In many cases, weed control can be very difficult or require much hand labor if chemicals cannot be used, and ④ <ins>fewer</ins> people are willing to do this work as societies become wealthier. Some methods used in "organic" farming, however, such as the sensible use of crop rotations and specific combinations of cropping and livestock enterprises, can make important ⑤ <ins>contributions</ins> to the sustainability of rural ecosystems.

*nitrogen fertilizer: 질소 비료 **manure: 거름
***legume: 콩과(科) 식물

09

(A), (B), (C)의 각 네모 안에서 어법에 맞는 표현으로 가장 적절한 것은? [3점] 정답률 **53%**

The first underwater photographs were taken by an Englishman named William Thompson. In 1856, he waterproofed a simple box camera, attached it to a pole, and (A) lowered / lowering it beneath the waves off the coast of southern England. During the 10-minute exposure, the camera slowly flooded with seawater, but the picture survived. Underwater photography was born. Near the surface, (B) where / which the water is clear and there is enough light, it is quite possible for an amateur photographer to take great shots with an inexpensive underwater camera. At greater depths — it is dark and cold there — photography is the principal way of exploring a mysterious deep-sea world, 95 percent of which has never (C) seen / been seen before.

*exposure: 노출

	(A)		(B)		(C)
①	lowered	⋯⋯	where	⋯⋯	seen
②	lowered	⋯⋯	where	⋯⋯	been seen
③	lowered	⋯⋯	which	⋯⋯	seen
④	lowering	⋯⋯	where	⋯⋯	seen
⑤	lowering	⋯⋯	which	⋯⋯	been seen

10

(A), (B), (C)의 각 네모 안에서 문맥에 맞는 낱말로 가장 적절한 것은? [3점] 정답률 **56%**

How soon is too soon to start kids on a computer? If your baby is less than a year old, the answer is (A) clear / unclear . That is because a baby's vision has not developed enough to focus on the screen, and they can't even sit up on their own. But after their first birthday, people have different answers to the question. Some people (B) agree / disagree with the idea of exposing three-year-olds to computers. They insist that parents stimulate their children in the traditional ways through reading, sports, and play — instead of computers. Others argue that early exposure to computers is helpful in adapting to our digital world. They believe the earlier kids start to use computers, the more (C) familiarity / reluctance they will have when using other digital devices.

	(A)		(B)		(C)
①	clear	⋯⋯	agree	⋯⋯	familiarity
②	clear	⋯⋯	disagree	⋯⋯	reluctance
③	clear	⋯⋯	disagree	⋯⋯	familiarity
④	unclear	⋯⋯	agree	⋯⋯	reluctance
⑤	unclear	⋯⋯	disagree	⋯⋯	reluctance

01

● 2016년 6월 교육청(고1) 28번

(A), (B), (C)의 각 네모 안에서 어법에 맞는 표현으로 가장 적절한 것은? [3점] 정답률 64%

A lot of customers buy products only after they are made aware that the products are available in the market. Let's say a product, even if it has been out there for a while, is not (A) advertising / advertised . Then what might happen? Not knowing that the product exists, customers would probably not buy it even if the product may have worked for (B) it / them . Advertising also helps people find the best for themselves. When they are made aware of a whole range of goods, they are able to compare them and make purchases so that they get (C) that / what they desire with their hard-earned money. Thus, advertising has become a necessity in everybody's daily life.

	(A)		(B)		(C)
①	advertising	......	it	......	that
②	advertising	......	them	......	what
③	advertised	......	them	......	what
④	advertised	......	it	......	what
⑤	advertised	......	them	......	that

02

● 2023학년도 수능 30번

다음 글의 밑줄 친 부분 중, 문맥상 낱말의 쓰임이 적절하지 않은 것은? [3점] 정답률 45%

Everywhere we turn we hear about almighty "cyberspace"! The hype promises that we will leave our boring lives, put on goggles and body suits, and enter some metallic, three-dimensional, multimedia otherworld. When the Industrial Revolution arrived with its great innovation, the motor, we didn't leave our world to go to some ① remote motorspace! On the contrary, we brought the motors into our lives, as automobiles, refrigerators, drill presses, and pencil sharpeners. This ② absorption has been so complete that we refer to all these tools with names that declare their usage, not their "motorness." These innovations led to a major socioeconomic movement precisely because they entered and ③ affected profoundly our everyday lives. People have not changed fundamentally in thousands of years. Technology changes constantly. It's the one that must ④ adapt to us. That's exactly what will happen with information technology and its devices under human-centric computing. The longer we continue to believe that computers will take us to a magical new world, the longer we will ⑤ maintain their natural fusion with our lives, the hallmark of every major movement that aspires to be called a socioeconomic revolution.

* hype: 과대광고　** hallmark: 특징

03

● 2016년 6월 교육청(고2) 28번

다음 글의 밑줄 친 부분 중, 어법상 틀린 것은? 정답률 46%

Architecture is generally conceived, designed, and realized in response to an existing set of conditions. These conditions may be ① purely functional in nature, or they may also reflect in varying degrees the social, political, and economic climate. In any case, it is assumed that the existing set of conditions is ② much less satisfactory and that a new set of conditions would be desirable. The initial phase of any design process is the recognition of a problematic condition and the decision ③ to find a solution to it. Design is above all a purposeful endeavor. A designer must first document the existing conditions of a problem and ④ collecting relevant data to be analyzed. This is the critical phase of the design process since the nature of a solution is related to how a problem ⑤ is defined.

다음 글의 밑줄 친 부분 중, 문맥상 낱말의 쓰임이 적절하지 않은 것은? [3점] 정답률 36%

Detailed study over the past two or three decades is showing that the complex forms of natural systems are essential to their functioning. The attempt to ① straighten rivers and give them regular cross-sections is perhaps the most disastrous example of this form-and-function relationship. The natural river has a very ② irregular form: it curves a lot, spills across floodplains, and leaks into wetlands, giving it an ever-changing and incredibly complex shoreline. This allows the river to ③ prevent variations in water level and speed. Pushing the river into tidy geometry ④ destroys functional capacity and results in disasters like the Mississippi floods of 1927 and 1993 and, more recently, the unnatural disaster of Hurricane Katrina. A $50 billion plan to "let the river loose" in Louisiana recognizes that the ⑤ controlled Mississippi is washing away twenty-four square miles of that state annually. *geometry: 기하학 **capacity: 수용능력

다음 글의 밑줄 친 부분 중, 어법상 틀린 것은? [3점] 정답률 64%

Most of us make at least three important decisions in our lives: where to live, what to do, and whom to do it with. We choose our towns, our jobs, and our spouses and friends. Making these decisions ① is such a natural part of adulthood that it is easy to forget that we are among the first human beings to make them. For most of recorded history, people lived ② where they were born, did what their parents had done, and associated with those who were doing the same. Social and physical structures were the great dictators ③ that determined how and where people would spend their lives. This left most folks with little to decide for ④ themselves. But the industrial and technological revolutions changed all that, and the resulting explosion of personal liberty ⑤ creating an array of options, alternatives, and decisions that our ancestors never faced.

(A), (B), (C)의 각 네모 안에서 문맥에 맞는 낱말로 가장 적절한 것은? [3점] 정답률 57%

Dworkin suggests a classic argument for a certain kind of equality of opportunity. From Dworkin's view, justice requires that a person's fate be determined by things that are within that person's control, not by luck. If differences in wellbeing are determined by circumstances lying outside of an individual's control, they are (A) fair / unjust . According to this argument, inequality of wellbeing that is driven by differences in individual choices or tastes is (B) acceptable / intolerable . But we should seek to eliminate inequality of wellbeing that is driven by factors that are not an individual's responsibility and which prevent an individual from achieving what he or she values. We do so by (C) ensuring / neglecting equality of opportunity or equality of access to fundamental resources.

	(A)		(B)		(C)
①	fair	……	acceptable	……	neglecting
②	unjust	……	acceptable	……	ensuring
③	unjust	……	intolerable	……	ensuring
④	fair	……	intolerable	……	neglecting
⑤	unjust	……	acceptable	……	neglecting

다음 글의 밑줄 친 부분 중, 어법상 틀린 것은? 정답률 42%

Not all organisms are able to find sufficient food to survive, so starvation is a kind of disvalue often found in nature. It also is part of the process of selection ① by which biological evolution functions. Starvation helps filter out those less fit to survive, those less resourceful in finding food for ② themselves and their young. In some circumstances, it may pave the way for genetic variants ③ to take hold in the population of a species and eventually allow the emergence of a new species in place of the old one. Thus starvation is a disvalue that can help make ④ possible the good of greater diversity. Starvation can be of practical or instrumental value, even as it is an intrinsic disvalue. ⑤ What some organisms must starve in nature is deeply regrettable and sad. The statement remains implacably true, even though starvation also may sometimes subserve ends that are good.

*implacably: 확고히 **subserve: 공헌하다

08 고득점 ● 2018학년도 수능 29번

다음 글의 밑줄 친 부분 중, 문맥상 낱말의 쓰임이 적절하지 않은 것은? 정답률 44%

Some prominent journalists say that archaeologists should work with treasure hunters because treasure hunters have accumulated valuable historical artifacts that can reveal much about the past. But archaeologists are not asked to cooperate with tomb robbers, who also have valuable historical artifacts. The quest for profit and the search for knowledge cannot coexist in archaeology because of the ① time factor. Rather incredibly, one archaeologist employed by a treasure hunting firm said that as long as archaeologists are given six months to study shipwrecked artifacts before they are sold, no historical knowledge is ② found! On the contrary, archaeologists and assistants from the INA (Institute of Nautical Archaeology) needed more than a decade of year-round conservation before they could even ③ catalog all the finds from an eleventh-century AD wreck they had excavated. Then, to interpret those finds, they had to ④ learn Russian, Bulgarian, and Romanian, without which they would never have learned the true nature of the site. Could a "commercial archaeologist" have ⑤ waited more than a decade or so before selling the finds?

*prominent: 저명한 **excavate: 발굴하다

09 ● 2014학년도 수능 B형 27번

다음 글의 밑줄 친 부분 중, 어법상 틀린 것은? [3점] 정답률 67%

Oxygen is what it is all about. Ironically, the stuff that gives us life eventually kills it. The ultimate life force lies in tiny cellular factories of energy, called mitochondria, ① that burn nearly all the oxygen we breathe in. But breathing has a price. The combustion of oxygen that keeps us alive and active ② sending out by-products called oxygen free radicals. They have Dr. Jekyll and Mr. Hyde characteristics. On the one hand, they help guarantee our survival. For example, when the body mobilizes ③ to fight off infectious agents, it generates a burst of free radicals to destroy the invaders very efficiently. On the other hand, free radicals move ④ uncontrollably through the body, attacking cells, rusting their proteins, piercing their membranes and corrupting their genetic code until the cells become dysfunctional and sometimes give up and die. These fierce radicals, ⑤ built into life as both protectors and avengers, are potent agents of aging.

*oxygen free radical: 활성 산소 **membrane: (해부학) 얇은 막

10 ● 2019년 3월 교육청(고2) 29번

다음 글의 밑줄 친 부분 중, 문맥상 낱말의 쓰임이 적절하지 않은 것은? [3점] 정답률 50%

Painters have in principle an infinite range of colours at their disposal, especially in modern times with the chromatic ① explosion of synthetic chemistry. And yet painters don't use all the colours at once, and indeed many have used a remarkably ② restrictive selection. Mondrian limited himself mostly to the three primaries red, yellow and blue to fill his black-ruled grids, and Kasimir Malevich worked with similar self-imposed restrictions. For Yves Klein, one colour was ③ enough; Franz Kline's art was typically black on white. There was nothing ④ new in this: the Greeks and Romans tended to use just red, yellow, black and white. Why? It's impossible to generalize, but both in antiquity and modernity it seems likely that the ⑤ expanded palette aided clarity and comprehensibility, and helped to focus attention on the components that mattered: shape and form.

*chromatic: 유채색의 **grid: 격자무늬

MEMO

필요충분한 수학유형서로
등급 상승각을 잡다!

'22개정
교육과정

시리즈 구성

공통수학1

공통수학2

교재구성
미리
보기

1 Goodness 빼어난 문제
'22 개정 교육과정에 맞춰 빼어난 문제를 필요한 만큼
충분하게 담아 완전 학습을 할 수 있습니다.

2 Analysis 철저한 분석
수학 시험지를 철저하게 분석하여 적확한 유형으로 구성,
가로로 익히고, 세로로 반복하는 학습을 할 수 있습니다.

3 Kindness 친절한 해설
선생님의 강의 노트 같은 깔끔한 해설로 알찬 학습,
정확하고 꼼꼼한 해설로 꽉 찬 학습을 할 수 있습니다.

BOOK LIST

도/서/목/록

어휘·문법·구문

능률VOCA

대한민국 어휘서의 표준
어원편 Lite | 어원편 | 고교기본 | 고교필수 2000 |
수능완성 2200 | 숙어 | 고난도

GRAMMAR ZONE

대한민국 영문법 교재의 표준
입문 | 기초 | 기본 1 | 기본 2 | 종합 (각 Workbook 별매)

필히 통하는

시험에 필히 통하는 고등 영문법과 서술형
필히 통하는 고등 영문법 기본편 | 실력편
필히 통하는 고등 서술형 기본편 | 실전편

문제로 미스터하는 고등영문법

고등학생을 위한 문법 연습의 길잡이

천문장

구문이 독해로 연결되는 해석 공식
입문 | 기본 | 완성

능률 기본 영어

최신 수능과 내신을 위한 고등 영어 입문서

다빈출코드

학평기출문제집

2025
학평대비

영어영역

어법·어휘

해설편

NE능률

다빈출코드

학평기출문제집

2025
학평대비

영어영역

어법·어휘

해설편

NE능률

1 준동사

UNIT 1 분사

코드 접속하기
pp.9~11

출제코드 1   능동의 현재분사(v-ing) vs. 수동의 과거분사(v-ed)

A 1 living 2 needed 3 depressed
B 1 ○ 2 ➡ exciting

해석과 정답 풀이

STEP 1

1 1) 침대에 누워 웃고 있는 아기를 봐라.
    2) 이 영화는 재미있을 것 같다.
    3) 그녀는 앞문을 단단히 잠가두었다.
2 1) 그는 점프하는 개를 가리켰다.
    2) 퀘벡에서 사용되는 언어는 무엇인가?

STEP 2

1 1) 교실 구석에서 자고 있는 소년은 누구니?
    2) 사생활을 보호하기 위해 고안된 새로운 보안 시스템이 있다.
2 1) 내가 그를 보았을 때, 그는 우산을 들고 서 있었다.
    2) 그 가게는 지난 3개월 동안 폐쇄되어 있었다.
3 1) 교통체증 때문에, 그녀는 그를 2시간 동안 계속 기다리게 했다.
    2) 집으로 돌아오는 길에, 그녀는 그녀의 오래된 자전거를 고쳤다.

STEP 3

A 1 조선시대에 한반도에는 많은 호랑이가 살았다.
    ➡ 앞의 명사 many tigers를 수식하는 분사로, 분사가 명사와 능동 관계이므로 현재분사 living이 알맞다.
    2 많은 채소들을 먹는다면, 당신은 건강하기 위해 필요한 영양분을 섭취할 수 있다.
    ➡ 앞의 명사 nutrients를 수식하는 분사로, 분사가 명사와 수동 관계이므로 과거분사 needed가 알맞다.
    3 나는 나의 성적표의 "F"학점 생각에 매우 우울했다.
    ➡ 감정을 나타내는 분사로, 주어(I)가 '우울한 감정을 느끼는' 것이므로 과거분사 depressed가 알맞다.
B 1 이 수박들을 신선하게 유지하려면, 당신은 그것들을 냉장 보관해야 한다.
    ➡ 앞의 목적어(them)의 상태를 설명하는 목적격보어로, 목적어와 수동 관계이므로 과거분사 refrigerated가 알맞다.
    2 그는 뉴욕의 화창한 날씨와 신나는 삶을 그리워했다.
    ➡ 뒤에 오는 명사 lifestyle을 수식하는 분사로, 명사가 '신나는 감정을 일으키는' 것이므로 현재분사 exciting이 알맞다.

출제코드 2   분사구문의 태: 능동 vs. 수동

A 1 Asked 2 thinking 3 using
B 1 ○ 2 ➡ Compared 3 ➡ left

해석과 정답 풀이

STEP 1

1 1) 길을 걸어갈 때, 나는 나의 담임 선생님을 만났다.
    2) 밖이 더워서, 우리는 나가지 않기로 결정했다.
    3) 연설을 듣는 동안, 그녀는 메모를 했다.
2 1) 사나운 개들에 둘러싸여, 그녀는 도와달라고 소리를 질렀다.
    2) 프랑스에서 자랐기 때문에, 그는 프랑스어를 유창하게 말할 수 있다.
3 1) Amy는 그녀의 강아지가 그녀를 따라오게 하면서 매일 아침 산책을 한다.
    2) Jamie는 그의 스마트폰을 끈 채로 열심히 공부하려고 노력한다.

STEP 2

1 1) 고대 영어로 쓰여져서, 이 시들은 이해하기 어렵다.
    2) 대도시로 이사간 후, 나는 시골에서의 평화로운 삶을 그리워했다.
2 1) 그녀를 향한 모든 관중들의 응시를 받으며 Jenny는 무대 위로 걸어 나갔다.
    2) 그는 항상 소파에 앉아 다리를 꼰 채로 TV를 본다.

STEP 3

A 1 미래에 무엇이 되기를 원하는지 질문을 받으면, 그는 항상 "나는 훌륭한 교수가 되기를 원해요."라고 말한다.
    ➡ 분사구문에서 생략된 주어는 주절의 주어(he)와 같다. 주어와 분사가 의미상 수동의 관계에 있으므로 과거분사 asked가 오는 것이 알맞다.
    2 직원들이 더 열심히 일하도록 동기를 부여할 것이라고 생각하면서, 사장은 그녀의 직원들의 월급을 올렸다.
    ➡ 분사구문에서 생략된 주어는 주절의 주어(The boss)와 같다. 주어와 분사가 의미상 능동의 관계에 있으므로 현재분사 thinking이 오는 것이 알맞다.
    3 대부분이 게임을 하기 위해 스마트폰을 사용하면서 많은 십 대들은 스마트폰에 중독되어 있다.
    ➡ 「with + (대)명사 + 분사」 구문으로, 대명사(most)와 분사가 의미상 능동의 관계에 있으므로 현재분사 using이 오는 것이 알맞다.
B 1 학교에서 집으로 돌아온 후, 나는 글 쓰는 법을 배우기 위해 학원에 가야 한다.
    ➡ 접속사 After가 남아있는 분사구문의 생략된 주어는 I로, 주어와 분사가 의미상 능동 관계이므로 현재분사 returning은 어법상 바르다.
    2 다른 채소들과 비교해서, 콩은 양질의 단백질과 영양소를 포함한다.
    ➡ 분사구문에서 생략된 주어는 beans로, 주어와 분사가 의미상 수동 관계이므로 Comparing을 과거분사 Compared로 고쳐야 한다.
    3 오직 30초만 남겨두고, 한국 축구팀은 마침내 골을 넣고 게임에 승리했다.
    ➡ 「with + (대)명사 + 분사」 구문으로, 명사(30 seconds)와 분사가 의미상 수동 관계이므로 leaving을 과거분사 left로 고쳐야 한다.

기출예제 Q1   정답 ④   정답률 28%

정답 풀이

④ 주격보어로 쓰인 현재분사

One might intuitively think / [that positive comments are more
                                     접속사   주어   동사1
사람들은 직관적으로 생각할지도 모른다   긍정적인 의견이 학생들에게
motivated(→ motivating) to students / and, as a result, / are more
                                                  동사2
더욱 동기를 부여하고   결과적으로
associated with effective teaching].
   …와 관련된
효과적인 가르침과 더욱 연관되어 있다고

➡ 긍정적인 의견이 학생들에게 '동기를 부여하는' 것이므로 의미상 주어와 능동 관계이므로 현재분사 motivating이 적절하다.

친절한 오답 풀이

① 문장의 동사

Advanced musicians are able to self-critique their performances, /
                   be able to-v: …할 수 있다
숙련된 음악가들은 자신의 연주를 스스로 비판할 수 있지만
but developing music students rely on teachers / to supply
          주어   동사   형용사적 용법의
                                                 to부정사
성장하고 있는 음악을 배우는 학생들은 교사에 의존한다   평가적 피드백을
evaluative feedback.
제공하는

➡ rely는 주어 developing music students의 동사로, 주어가 복수형이므로 복수동사로 바르게 쓰였다.

② 주격 관계대명사

The most constructive feedback / is that [which expresses the
　　　　　　　　　　　　　　　　　　　　　　　└─┘주격 관계대명사
가장 건설적인 피드백은　　　　　　　　　　불일치를 표현하는 것이다
discrepancies / between a student's performance of a piece of
　　　　　　　between A and B: A와 B 사이
　　　　　　　음악 한 곡에 대한 학생의 연주와 최적의 버전 사이의
music and an optimal version].

➡ 대명사 that을 선행사로 하고, 관계대명사절에서 주어 역할을 하고 있으므로 주격 관계대명사 which는 어법상 알맞다.

③ 접속사

Researchers also have explored / [whether the feedback of
　　　　　　　　　　　　　　　　　명사절을 이끄는 접속사　주어
연구자들은 또한 탐구했다　　　　　　　　유능한 교사의 피드백이 …인지
effective teachers / is more often positively or negatively
　　　　　　　　　　동사
　　　　　　　　　더 자주 긍정적으로 혹은 부정적으로 표현되는지
expressed, / that is, constituting praise or criticism].
be v-ed: 수동태
　　　　　　즉 칭찬 혹은 비판을 이루는지

➡ 동사 have explored의 목적어로 쓰인 명사절을 이끌고 있고, 의미상 '…인지'라고 해석되므로 접속사 whether는 알맞다.

⑤ 부사

[Although positive feedback is likely more helpful with younger
접속사(…이지만)　　　　　　　　　　　└───┘
긍정적인 피드백이 어린 학습자와 일대일 교수에서는 아마도 더욱 도움이 되는 것 같지만
learners and in one-on-one instruction], more advanced music
　　　　　　　　　　　　　　　　　　　　　음악을 배우는 더 숙련된 학생들은
students / seem to accept and (to) benefit from / greater levels of
　　　　seem to-v: …인 것 같다
　　　　받아들이고 이익을 얻는 것처럼 보인다　　　　수업에서 더 높은 수준의
criticism in lessons.
비평을

➡ 여기서 likely는 '아마도'라는 의미의 부사로 쓰여 뒤에 형용사 more helpful을 수식하고 있으므로 어법상 알맞다.

지문 해석

학생들에게 피드백을 제공하는 것은 교사에게 중요한 과제이다. 일반 심리학은 결과에 대한 지식이 기량을 향상시키는 데 필요하다는 것을 보여 주었다. 숙련된 음악가들은 자신의 연주를 스스로 비판할 수 있지만 성장하고 있는 음악을 배우는 학생들은 평가적 피드백을 제공하는 교사에 의존한다. 가장 건설적인 피드백은 음악 한 곡에 대한 학생의 연주와 최적의 버전 사이의 불일치를 표현하는 것이다. 숙련된 교사는 일반적인 평가보다 더 상세한 피드백을 주고 음악 교육자는 더 구체적인 교사 피드백이 학생의 연주 향상을 촉진한다고 보통 인정한다. 연구자들은 또한 유능한 교사의 피드백이 더 자주 긍정적으로 혹은 부정적으로 표현되는지, 즉 칭찬 혹은 비판을 이루는지 탐구했다. 사람들은 긍정적인 의견이 학생들에게 더욱 동기를 부여하고 결과적으로 효과적인 가르침과 더욱 연관되어 있다고 직관적으로 생각할지도 모른다. 그러나 그 연구는 약간 다른 그림을 그린다. 긍정적인 피드백이 어린 학습자와 일대일 교수에서는 더욱 도움이 되는 것 같지만 음악을 배우는 더 숙련된 학생들은 수업에서 더 높은 수준의 비평을 받아들이고 이익을 얻는 것처럼 보인다.

어휘

critical 📋 대단히 중요한　advanced 📋 고급[상급]의　self-critique 📋 스스로를 비평하다　evaluative 📋 평가하는　discrepancy 📋 차이　optimal 📋 최선의, 최적의　appraisal 📋 평가, 판단　facilitate 📋 가능하게 하다　effective 📋 효과적인; 유능한　constitute 📋 구성하다, 이루다　intuitively 📋 직감적으로

01
정답 ④　　정답률 50%

정답 풀이

④ 분사구문

Although this technique alone will not produce changes, / [when
접속사(비록 …이긴 하지만)　　　　　　　　　　　　　　　접속사+
이 기술만으로는 변화를 만들어 내지는 않지만
(being) using(→ used) alongside other behavior modification
분사구문　　　　　　　　　　　　　　　　　…와 함께
다른 행동 수정 기법 및 대응 전략과 함께 사용되면
tactics and coping strategies], / behavioral changes have proved
　　　　　　　　　　　　　　　행동 변화가 일부 사람들에게의 효과를 입증했다
effective for some people.

➡ 밑줄 친 부분은 접속사를 생략하지 않은 분사구문의 분사로, 생략된 주어는 주절의 주어(behavioral changes)와 같다. 주어와 분사의 관계가 수동이므로, 현재분사 using이 아닌 과거분사 used가 되어야 한다.

친절한 오답 풀이

① 접속사 that

For years, / many psychologists have held strongly to the belief /
　　　　　　　　　　　　　hold to: …을 유지하다　　　└─ 동격
수년 동안　　　많은 심리학자들이 믿음을 굳게 유지했다
[that the key to addressing negative health habits / is to change
└─ 전치사 …로의 동명사(전치사의 목적어)　　　　　명사적 용법의 to부정사(보어)
부정적인 건강 습관을 해결하기 위한 열쇠는　　　　행동을 바꾸는 것이라는
behavior].

➡ 앞의 명사구 the belief와 동격을 이루는 명사절을 이끄는 접속사로, 뒤에 완전한 절이 이어지고 있으므로 어법상 바르다.

② 동사의 수 일치

This, / [more than values and attitudes], / is the part of
　　　　　　　　　　　　　　　　　　삽입구
이것이　가치관이나 태도보다　　　　　　성격의 한 부분이다
personality / [that is easiest to change].
　　　　　　└─ 주격 관계대명사 ↑　　└─ 부사적 용법의 to부정사(형용사 수식)
　　　　　　　　가장 바꾸기 쉬운

➡ This가 주어이므로 단수형 is는 어법상 바르다.

③ 부정대명사

Mental imagery [combined with power of suggestion] was
　　　　　　　└─ 과거분사구
암시의 힘과 결합된 마음 속 이미지는　　받아들여졌다
taken up / as the premise of behavioral medicine / to help people
　　　　　　　　　　　　　　　　　　　　　└─ 형용사적 용법의 to부정사
　　　　　행동 의학의 전제로　　　　　　사람들이
change negative health behaviors into positive ones.
change A into B: A를 B로 바꾸다
사람들이 부정적인 건강 행동을 긍정적인 것으로 바꾸는 데 도움을 주는

➡ 앞에 나온 복수 명사 health behaviors를 대신하므로, 복수형 부정대명사 ones는 어법상 알맞다.

⑤ 관계대명사 what

[What mental imagery does] / is reinforce a new desired behavior.
마음 속 이미지가 하는 일은　　　　새로운 바람직한 행동을 강화하는 것이다

➡ 앞에 선행사가 없고, 뒤에 목적어가 빠진 불완전한 절이 이어지므로, 선행사를 포함하는 관계대명사 What이 오는 것이 어법상 바르다.

수년 동안 많은 심리학자들이 부정적인 건강 습관을 해결하기 위한 열쇠는 행동을 바꾸는 것이라는 믿음을 굳게 유지했다. 가치관이나 태도보다, 이것이 가장 바꾸기 쉬운 성격의 한 부분이다. 흡연, 음주, 그리고 다양한 섭식 행동과 같은 섭취 습관은 행동 변화의 대상이 되는 가장 일반적인 건강 문제이다. 과정 중독 행동(일 중독, 쇼핑 중독 등) 또한 이 범주에 속한다. 암시의 힘과 결합된 마음 속 이미지는 사람들이 부정적인 건강 행동을 긍정적인 것으로 바꾸는 데 도움을 주는 행동 의학의 전제로 받아들여졌다. 이 기술만으로는 변화를 만들어 내지는 않지만, 다른 행동 수정 기법 및 대응 전략과 함께 사용되면, 행동 변화가 일부 사람들에게 효과를 입증했다. 마음 속 이미지가 하는 일은 새로운 바람직한 행동을 강화하는 것이다. 이미지의 반복적 사용은 시간이 지남에 따라 그 바람직한 행동을 더욱 강력하게 강화한다.

psychologist 명 심리학자 **target** 동 대상으로 하다 **addiction** 명 중독 **combined with** …와 결합된 **suggestion** 명 암시 **alongside** 전 …와 함께 **modification** 명 수정 **tactic** 명 기법 **reinforce** 동 강화하다

02 정답 ④ 정답률 61%

정답 풀이

④ 분사구문

[Cited(→ Citing) the need for managers to write their own
동시동작을 나타내는 분사구문(= As Welch cited …) 형용사적 용법의 to부정사
관리자들이 그들 자신의 해답을 써야 할 필요성을 언급하면서
answers / to day-to-day management challenges], / Welch swept
                                                         sweep away: 완전히 없애다
그날그날의 경영 문제들에 대한   Welch는 낡은 제도를
away the old order / by removing the Blue Books / from the
       by v-ing: …함으로써
없애버렸다   Blue Books를 제거함으로써   조직 문화에서
organization's culture.

➡ 밑줄 친 부분은 동시동작을 나타내는 분사구문의 분사로, 생략된 주어는 주절의 주어(Welch)와 같다. Welch가 필요성을 '언급하면서'라는 능동의 의미가 적절하므로 과거분사 Cited를 현재분사 Citing으로 고쳐야 한다.

친절한 오답 풀이

① 주격 관계대명사

In a gesture [that was at once symbolic and real], / Welch directed
                   주격 관계대명사
상징적이면서 동시에 실제적인 제스처로   Welch는 불태우기 의식을 지시했다
the ceremonial burning / of the old-fashioned GE Blue Books.
                           구식의 GE의 Blue Books의

➡ that은 주격 관계대명사로, 선행사 a gesture를 수식하는 관계대명사절에서 주어 역할을 하고 있으므로 어법상 바르다.

② 「get + 목적어 + 목적격보어(분사)」

The Blue Books were a series of management training manuals / {that
                        a series of: 일련의   주격 관계대명사
Blue Books는 여러 권의 경영 훈련 매뉴얼이었다
told [how GE managers were to get tasks done in the organization]}.
간접의문문(의문사 + 주어 + 동사) be to-v용법(의무, …해야 한다)
GE의 관리자들이 조직에서 과업을 어떻게 해내야 할지를 말해주는

➡ 동사 get은 '…하게 하다'라는 뜻으로, 뒤에 오는 목적어와 목적격보어의 관계가 수동이면 목적격보어로 과거분사를 쓴다. 문맥상 과업이 '수행되는'이라는 수동의 의미가 적절하므로 과거분사 done이 알맞다.

③ 과거완료 수동태

                        ┌── 동격 ──┐
Despite the fact [that these books for training had not been used /
전치사(…임에도 불구하고) 동격의 접속사   had been v-ed: 과거 완료 수동태
이 훈련용 책들이 사용되지 않았다는 사실에도 불구하고
for some 15 years], / they still had great influence over the
                                    have influence over: …에 대한 영향력이 있다
약 15년 동안   그것들은 여전히 GE 관리자들의 행동에 지대한 영향력을 발휘했다
actions of GE managers.

➡ 밑줄 친 부분은 주절의 시제(과거)보다 앞선 시점의 일을 나타내고 있고, 책이 '사용되지 않은'이라는 수동의 의미가 적절하므로, 과거완료 수동태를 쓰는 것이 알맞다.

⑤ 병렬구조

Now, GE managers are taught / to find their own solutions /
                               teach A to-v의 수동태
이제, GE의 관리자들은 배운다   그들 자신만의 해결책을 찾도록
rather than (to) look them up / in a dusty old book.
A rather than B: B보다는 A
그것들(해결책)을 찾기보다는   먼지투성이의 낡은 책에서

➡ rather than이 보어로 쓰인 to부정사 to find와 원형부정사 look을 병렬 연결하고 있는 구조로, look 앞에 to가 생략되어 있다.

 코드+α 구문 분석 Plus

1행
Jack Welch **is considered to be** one of the USA's top business leaders.
➡ be considered to-v: …로 여겨지다, 간주되다
➡ one of + 복수 명사: … 중 하나

지문 해석

Jack Welch는 미국 최고의 기업주 중 한 사람으로 여겨진다. 상징적이면서 동시에 실제적인 제스처로, Welch는 구식의 GE(General Electric)의 Blue Books의 불태우기 의식을 지시했다. Blue Books는 GE의 관리자들이 조직에서 과업을 어떻게 해내야 할지를 말해주는 여러 권의 경영 훈련 매뉴얼이었다. 이 훈련용 책들이 약 15년 동안 사용되지 않았다는 사실에도 불구하고, 그것들은 여전히 GE관리자들의 행동에 지대한 영향력을 발휘했다. 관리자들이 그날그날의 경영 문제들에 대한 그들 자신의 해답을 써야 할 필요성을 언급하면서, Welch는 조직 문화에서 Blue Books를 제거함으로써 낡은 제도를 없애버렸다. 이제, GE의 관리자들은 먼지투성이의 낡은 책에서 해결책을 찾기보다는 그들 자신만의 해결책을 찾도록 배운다.

consider 동 고려하다; *여기다 **symbolic** 형 상징적인 **direct** 동 지시하다 **ceremonial** 형 의식의 **old-fashioned** 형 구식의 **management** 명 경영 **organization** 명 조직, 단체 **influence** 명 영향; *영향력 **cite** 동 인용하다, 언급하다 **day-to-day** 형 그날그날의 **remove** 동 없애다, 제거하다 **solution** 명 해결책 **dusty** 형 먼지투성이인

03 정답 ② 정답률 55%

정답 풀이

② 감정을 나타내는 분사

The gift of time can sometimes be more satisfied(→ satisfying)
시간이라는 선물은 때때로 더 만족스럽고 더 가치 있을 수 있다
and more valuable / than money.
                     돈보다

➡ 감정을 나타내는 분사는 의미상 주어와의 관계가 능동(…한 감정을 일으키는)일 경우 현재분사를, 수동(…한 감정을 느끼는)일 경우 과거분사로 쓴다. 밑줄 친 부분은 감정을 나타내는 분사로, 의미상 주어(The gift of time)와 능동 관계(만족스러운)이므로 과거분사 satisfied를 현재분사 satisfying으로 고쳐야 한다.

① 비교급 강조 부사

[Though some people have much less free time than others], /
접속사(비록 …일지라도) ┗━━━┛↑ little의 비교급
비록 어떤 사람들은 남들보다 훨씬 더 적은 자유 시간을 갖지만,

nearly everyone has some opportunity to give.
everyone + 단수 동사 ┗━━━━┛ 형용사적 용법의 to부정사
거의 모든 사람들은 약간의 베풀 기회를 가지고 있다

➡ much는 '훨씬'이라는 의미로 뒤에 오는 비교급 less를 강조하는 부사로 어법상 바르다.

③ 병렬구조

You can see this / by watching those [who have volunteered at
by v-ing: …함으로써 ↑ 주격 관계대명사
당신은 이것을 알 수 있다 노숙자쉼터에서 자원봉사를 하는 사람들을 보면서

homeless shelters / or (have) brought meals on wheels to seniors].
등위접속사
또는 노인들에게 배달 식사를 가져다주는

➡ 등위접속사는 문법적으로 대등한 것들을 병렬 연결하는데, or는 등위접속사로 주격 관계대명사절의 동사 have volunteered와 brought를 연결하고 있다. 반복을 피하기 위해 brought 앞에 have가 생략된 것으로 어법상 바르다.

④ 주격 관계대명사

[If you are willing to volunteer], / there are many organizations
be willing to-v: 기꺼이 …하다
만약 당신이 기꺼이 자원봉사를 하고자 한다면, 많은 단체와 프로젝트가 있다

and projects / [that will be glad to welcome you].
↑ 주격 관계대명사
당신을 기쁘게 환영할

➡ that은 주격 관계대명사로, 선행사 many organizations and projects를 수식하는 관계대명사절에서 주어 역할을 하고 있으므로 어법상 바르다.

⑤ 복합관계대명사

[Whatever you do], / it will almost certainly be educational,
복합관계대명사(무엇을 …하더라도, = No matter what)
당신이 무엇을 하더라도 그것은 거의 확실히 교육적이고, 즐거우며, 보람이 있을 것이다

enjoyable, and rewarding.
and에 의해 연결된 병렬구조(A, B, and C)

➡ Whatever는 부사절을 이끄는 복합관계대명사로 어법상 바르다.

 코드+α 구문 발견 Plus

2행	…, we **do have** access to the same twenty four hours …. ➡ do + 동사원형: '정말 …하다'의 의미로, do는 동사의 의미를 강조하는 조동사 ➡ have access to: …에 접근할 수 있다

지문 해석

우리는 모두 같은 양의 돈을 가지고 있지는 않지만, 매일 똑같은 24시간을 이용할 수 있다. 비록 어떤 사람들은 남들보다 훨씬 더 적은 자유 시간을 갖지만, 거의 모든 사람들은 약간의 베풀 기회를 가지고 있다. 시간이라는 선물은 때때로 돈보다 더 만족스럽고 더 가치 있을 수 있다. 당신은 노숙자쉼터에서 자원봉사를 하거나 노인들에게 배달 식사를 가져다주는 사람들을 보면서 이것을 알 수 있다. 만약 당신이 기꺼이 자원봉사를 하고자 한다면, 당신을 기쁘게 환영할 많은 단체와 프로젝트가 있다. 당신이 무엇을 하더라도, 그것은 거의 확실히 교육적이고, 즐거우며, 보람이 있을 것이다.

 어휘

opportunity 명 기회 satisfied 형 만족하는 valuable 형 소중한, 귀중한 volunteer 동 자원 봉사로 하다 homeless 형 노숙자의 shelter 명 주거지; *(노숙자 등을 위한) 쉼터 senior 명 연장자; *노령자 certainly 부 틀림없이, 분명히 educational 형 교육적인 enjoyable 형 즐거운 rewarding 형 보람 있는

04 　　　정답 ⑤　　　정답률 53%

정답 풀이

⑤ 「with + (대)명사 + 분사」

This leads to the possibility / of creating many different small
이것은 가능성으로 이어진다 사람들의 많은 다양한 소집단을 만들 수 있는

groups of people / with each strongly believes(→ believing) /
with + (대)명사 + 분사: …가 ~하는 채로
각자 강하게 믿는

{(that) they are correct / and everyone else is wrong / about [how
명사절(목적어)을 이끄는 접속사 that 생략
자신들이 옳다는 것을 그리고 다른 모든 사람들이 틀리다고

the world works]}.
간접의문문(의문사 + 주어 + 동사)
세상이 어떻게 돌아가는지에 대해

➡ '…가 ~한[된] 채로'라는 의미의 「with + (대)명사 + 분사」 구문으로, (대)명사와 분사의 관계가 능동이면 현재분사를, 수동이면 과거분사를 쓴다. 문맥상 각자가 자신의 신념을 강하게 '믿는'이라는 능동의 의미이므로 현재분사 believing이 오는 것이 알맞다.

① 부사

The idea [that people selectively expose themselves to news
주어 동격의 접속사
사람들이 선택적으로 뉴스 콘텐츠에 자신을 노출시킨다는 생각이

content] / has been around for a long time, / but it is even more
동사 비교급 강조 부사
오랫동안 있어 왔다 하지만 오늘날 훨씬 더 중요하다

important today / with the fragmentation of audiences / and the
구독자의 분열과 함께

proliferation of choices.
그리고 선택의 급증으로

➡ 부사 selectively가 접속사절의 동사 expose를 수식하고 있으므로 어법상 바르다.

② 병렬구조

명사절(목적어)을 이끄는 접속사 that 생략
Selective exposure is a psychological concept / that says {(that)
선택적 노출은 심리학적 개념이다 ↑ 주격 관계대명사

people seek out information / [that conforms to their existing
↑ 주격 관계대명사
사람들이 정보를 찾으려 한다는 자신의 기존 신념 체계에 부합하는

belief systems] / and avoid information [that challenges those
↑ 주격 관계대명사
그리고 그러한 신념에 도전하는 정보를 피한다는

beliefs]}.

➡ 등위접속사 and가 명사절 안의 동사 seek와 avoid를 병렬 연결하고 있으므로 어법상 바르다.

③ 명사를 수식하는 과거분사

> In the past [when there were few sources of news], / people could
> 　　　　　　　└─ 관계부사
> 뉴스의 공급처가 얼마 없었던 과거에는
> either expose themselves to mainstream news — / {where they
> └─ either A or B: A 또는 B 둘 중 하나　　　　　　　　　└─ 관계부사
> 사람들은 주류 뉴스에 자신을 노출시키거나
> would likely see beliefs [expressed counter to their own]} — / or
> 　　　　　　　　　　　└─ 과거분사
> 사람들이 자신의 신념과 상반되게 표현된 신념을 보게 될 수도 있는
> they could avoid news altogether.
> 또는 그들은 뉴스를 전적으로 피할 수 있었다

➡ 앞에 나온 명사 beliefs를 수식하는 분사로, 상반되게 '표현된'이라는 수동의 의미이므로 과거분사 expressed가 오는 것이 알맞다.

④ 주격 관계대명사

> Now with so many types of news (being) constantly available /
> 　　　└─ with + (대)명사 + 분사: …가 ~하는 채로
> 지금은 아주 많은 종류의 뉴스들이 끊임없이 이용 가능해지면서
> to a full range of niche audiences, / people can easily find a
> 매우 다양한 틈새 구독자들에게　　　　　　사람들은 쉽게 뉴스의 공급처를 찾을 수 있다
> source of news / [that consistently confirms their own personal
> 　　　　　　　　└─ 주격 관계대명사
> 　　　　　　　　　자신의 개인적인 신념들을 지속적으로 확인해주는
> set of beliefs].

➡ that은 앞의 명사 a source of news를 선행사로 하는 주격 관계대명사로, 관계대명사절에서 동사의 주어 역할을 하므로 어법상 바르다.

지문 해석

사람들이 선택적으로 뉴스 콘텐츠에 자신을 노출시킨다는 생각이 오랫동안 있어 왔지만, 구독자의 분열과 선택의 급증으로 그것은 오늘날 훨씬 더 중요하다. 선택적 노출은 사람들이 자신의 기존 신념 체계에 부합하는 정보를 찾으려 하고 그러한 신념에 도전하는 정보를 피한다는 심리학적 개념이다. 뉴스의 공급처가 얼마 없었던 과거에는, 그들 자신의 신념과 상반되게 표현된 신념을 보게 될 수도 있는 주류 뉴스에 자신을 노출시키거나 뉴스를 전적으로 피할 수 있었다. 아주 많은 종류의 뉴스들이 매우 다양한 틈새 구독자들에게 끊임없이 이용 가능해지면서 사람들은 자신의 개인적 신념들을 지속적으로 확인해주는 뉴스의 공급처를 쉽게 찾을 수 있다. 이것은 각자가 세상이 어떻게 돌아가는지에 대해 자신들이 옳고 다른 모든 사람들이 틀리다고 강하게 믿는 사람들의 많은 다양한 소집단을 만들 수 있는 가능성으로 이어진다.

selectively 🔒 선택적으로　expose 🔒 노출시키다　psychological 🔒 심리적인; *심리학적인　conform to …에 일치[부합]하다　mainstream 🔒 주류를 이루는　counter to …과 반대로　constantly 🔒 끊임없이　consistently 🔒 일관되게, 지속적으로

05　　　　　정답 ④　　　정답률 50%

정답 풀이

(A) 문장의 동사

> To the north ~~lay~~ / lie Namibia, Botswana and Zimbabwe; /
> 전치사구(부사)　　동사　　　　　주어
> 북쪽으로 나미비아, 보츠와나, 짐바브웨가 있고
> to the east are Mozambique and Swaziland.
> 전치사구(부사)　동사　　　　　　주어
> 동쪽으로는 모잠비크와 스와질란드가 있다

➡ 전치사구(To the north)가 문장의 첫머리에 오면서 주어와 동사의 순서가 바뀌는 도치가 일어난 문장으로, 네모 부분이 동사, Namibia, Botswana and Zimbabwe가 주어이다. 의미상 '놓여있다'가 적절하므로 자동사 lie가 알맞다. lay는 '…을 놓다'라는 의미의 타동사로, 목적어가 필요하다.

(B) 부사

> Eleven languages are ~~official~~ / officially recognized.
> 　　　　주어　　　　　　　　　부사
> 11개의 언어가 공식적으로 인정된다

➡ 수동태의 과거분사 recognized를 수식하고 있으므로 부사 officially가 오는 것이 알맞다.

(C) 명사를 수식하는 현재분사

> [Although 79.5% of the South African population is black], /
> 접속사(비록 …이긴 하지만)
> 비록 남아프리카 인구의 79.5퍼센트가 흑인이지만
> the people are from various ethnic groups / speaking / ~~spoken~~
> 주어　　　동사　　　　　　　　　　　　　　　　　현재분사
> 그 사람들도 다양한 민족 집단 출신이다　　　　　각기 다른 반투어를 사용하는
> different Bantu languages.

➡ 네모 부분은 앞의 명사구(various ethnic groups)를 수식하는 분사로, 다른 반투어를 '사용하는'이라는 능동의 의미이므로 현재분사 speaking이 알맞다.

지문 해석

남아프리카 공화국은 아프리카 남쪽 끝에 위치해 있는 나라로, 2,798km의 해안선이 대서양과 인도양에 접해있다. 북쪽으로 나미비아, 보츠와나, 짐바브웨가 있고, 동쪽으로는 모잠비크와 스와질란드가 있다. 이 나라는 다양한 언어를 사용하는 것으로 알려져 있다. 11개의 언어가 공식적으로 인정된다. 영어는 공사와 상거래에서 가장 흔하게 쓰이는 언어이지만, 가정에서는 5번째로 많이 쓰이는 언어일 뿐이다. 비록 남아프리카 인구의 79.5퍼센트가 흑인이지만, 그 사람들도 각기 다른 반투어를 사용하는 다양한 민족 집단 출신이다.

republic 🔒 공화국　coastline 🔒 해안 지대, 해안선　Atlantic 🔒 대서양의　Indian 🔒 인도양의　be known for …로 알려져 있다　diversity 🔒 다양성　recognize 🔒 알아보다; *인정[공인]하다　commonly 🔒 흔히　commercial 🔒 상업적인　ethnic 🔒 인종의, 민족의

06　　　　　정답 ④　　　정답률 57%

정답 풀이

④ 수동형 분사구문

> Another girl mentioned / {that girls "were not supposed to speak /
> └─ another + 단수 명사　　　접속사　　　└─ be supposed to-v: …해야 한다
> 또 다른 여학생은 말했다　　　　　　여자아이들은 '말해서는 안 된다
> [unless speaking(→ spoken) to.”]}
> 접속사(…하지 않으면), 접속사가 남아있는 분사구문(= Unless girls were spoken to)
> (누가) 말을 걸어오지 않으면'

➡ unless 이하는 의미를 분명히 하기 위해 접속사를 남겨놓은 분사구문으로, 생략된 주어는 that절의 주어(girls)와 같다. 여자아이들이 '말하게 되는'이라는 수동의 의미가 적절하므로, 현재분사 speaking을 과거분사 spoken으로 고쳐야 한다.

│친절한 오답 풀이│

① 접속사 that

> Schoolteacher Carol Tateishi writes / {that in her Asian upbringing, /
> 　　　　　　　　　　　　　　　　　　　　　명사절(목적어)을 이끄는 접속사
> 교사인 Carol Tateishi는 쓴다　　　　자신이 받은 아시아식 교육에서,
> she was taught [that silence is a sign of self-reliance and strength]}.
> 　　　　　　　　　명사절(목적어)을 이끄는 접속사
> 그녀는 침묵은 자립과 힘의 표시라는 것을 배웠다

➡ 밑줄 친 that은 문장에서 목적어 역할을 하는 명사절을 이끄는 접속사로, 뒤에 완전한 절(silence … strength)이 이어지고 있으므로 어법상 바르다.

② 문장의 동사

> [Even though their families spanned 100 years of immigration], /
> 접속사(비록 …일지라도)
> 비록 그들의 가문들이 이주 100년에 걸쳐 이어졌지만,
> some recurrent themes emerged, / such as "you're not supposed to
> 주어　　　　　　　　동사　전치사(…와 같이)
> 몇몇 반복적인 주제가 등장했다　　　　　　'너는 말을 너무 많이 해서는 안 된다'와 같은
> say too much" and "talk could cause disrespect and harsh feelings."
> '말은 무례와 불쾌한 감정을 일으킬 수 있다'와 같은

➡ 접속사 Even though 이하는 양보를 나타내는 부사절이고 some recurrent themes 이하가 주절인 문장으로, emerged는 주절의 동사로 바르게 쓰였다.

③ 문장의 동사

> The girls / [who entered U.S. schools as English language
> 주어 ↑　　주격 관계대명사　　　　　 전치사(…로서)
> 여학생들은　영어 학습자로 미국의 학교에 들어온
> learners] / feared speaking up / [because they were self-conscious /
> 동사　목적어(동명사)　　부사절(이유)
> 소리 내어 말하기를 두려워했다　왜냐하면 그들은 의식하고 있었기 때문에
> about their language skills].
> 자신들의 언어 능력에 대해

➡ 주어는 The girls이고 who 이하는 The girls를 수식하는 주격 관계대명사절로, 뒤에 문장의 동사 feared가 이어지고 있으므로 어법상 바르다.

⑤ 동사의 수 일치

> Restraint in speech was valued / by these students and their
> 말하기에 있어서 절제는 가치 있게 여겨졌다　　이 학생과 그들의 가족에게
> families, / [whereas speaking in class is taken / as intellectual
> 접속사(반면에)　주어(동명사구)　동사　전치사(…로)
> 반면에 수업시간에 말하는 것은 여겨진다　　지적인
> engagement and meaning-making / in U.S. classrooms].
> 지적인 참여와 의미 형성으로　　　　미국의 교실에서

➡ 동명사(구)가 주어인 경우 단수 취급하는데, 접속사 whereas가 이끄는 절의 주어가 동명사구(speaking in class)이므로 뒤에 단수 동사인 is가 오는 것이 알맞다.

지문 해석

교사인 Carol Tateishi는 자신이 받은 아시아식 교육에서, 침묵은 자립과 힘의 표시라는 것을 배웠다고 쓴다. 그녀는 다양한 인종 배경 출신의 아시아계 미국인 중등학교 학생 5명을 인터뷰했다. 비록 그들의 가문들이 이주 100년에 걸쳐 이어졌지만, '너는 말을 너무 많이 해서는 안 된다'와 '말은 무례와 불쾌한 감정을 일으킬 수 있다'와 같은 몇몇 반복적인 주제가 등장했다. 영어 학습자로 미국의 학교에 들어온 여학생들은 자신들의 언어 능력에 대해 의식하고 있었기 때문에 소리 내어 말하기를 두려워했다. 또 다른 여학생은 여자아이들은 '(누가) 말을 걸어오지 않으면 말해서는 안 된다'고 말했다. 말하기에 있어서 절제는 이 학생들과 그들의 가족에게 가치 있게 여겨졌던 반면에, 수업시간에 말을 하는 것은 미국의 교실에서 지적인 참여와 의미 형성으로 여겨진다.

upbringing 명 양육, 훈육　self-reliance 명 자립　strength 명 힘　interview
동 인터뷰하다　ethnic 형 민족[종족]의　span 동 (얼마의 기간에) 걸쳐 이어지다
immigration 명 이주, 이민　recurrent 형 되풀이되는, 반복되는　emerge 동
나오다　disrespect 명 무례, 결례　self-conscious 형 남의 시선을 의식하는
restraint 명 규제; *절제　value 동 가치있게 여기다　intellectual 형 지적인
engagement 명 약속; *참여

정답 풀이

③ 명사를 수식하는 과거분사

> An example of this / is seen in a research study / [looking at self-
> 주어　　　　　동사　　　　　↑　현재분사
> 이것의 예는　　　　 연구에서 보여진다　　　스스로 보고된
> reported confidence] / in year 7 students / across a range of
> 자신감을 조사한　　　　7학년 학생들의　　　다양한 과목에 걸쳐
> subjects / [have taught(→ taught) in their first term / in secondary
> 　　　　　　　　過去分詞
> 첫 학기에 가르쳐진　　　　　　　중등학교에서
> school].

➡ 이 문장의 동사는 is seen이므로 동사 have taught는 올 수 없다. 따라서 have taught는 앞의 명사구 a range of subjects를 수식하는 분사가 되어야 하는데 다양한 과목들이 '가르쳐지는' 것이므로 수동의 의미를 지닌 과거분사 taught가 되어야 한다.

친절한 오답 풀이

① 주격 관계대명사

> It helps the researcher to represent their data in a chart / [that
> help A to-v: A가 …하도록 돕다　　　　　　　　　↑　　주격
> 그것은 연구자가 차트로 그들의 데이터를 설명하도록 도와준다　　　관계대명사
> shows the relative size of a response / on one scale / for
> 응답의 상대적 크기를 보여주는　　　　하나의 척도에서
> interrelated variables].
> 상호 연관된 변수에 대해

➡ a chart를 선행사로 하고 관계대명사절 안에서 동사 shows의 주어 역할을 할 수 있는 주격 관계대명사 that이 쓰였으므로 어법상 바르다.

② 분사구문

> The spider chart is drawn / with the variables spanning the chart, /
> 스파이더 차트는 그려진다　with + (대)명사 + v-ing: …가 ~한 채로
> 변수들이 차트에 걸치면서
> [creating a spider web].
> 연속동작을 나타내는 분사구문
> 그리고 거미줄을 만든다

➡ creating 이하는 연속동작을 나타내는 분사구문으로, 생략된 주어는 주절의 주어(The spider chart)와 같다. 주어와 분사가 의미상 능동 관계이므로 현재분사 creating이 오는 것이 알맞다.

④ 병렬구조

> The researcher takes the responses from a sample group / and
> 주어　　동사1
> 연구자는 표본 집단으로부터 응답값들을 가져온다　　　　　　　그리고
> calculates the mean / to plot on the spider chart.
> 동사2　　　　　형용사적 용법의 to부정사
> 평균치를 계산한다　　스파이더 차트에 나타낼

➡ 등위접속사 and가 동사를 병렬 연결하고 있으므로, 앞의 단수 동사 takes와 대등하도록 동사 calculates가 오는 것이 알맞다.

⑤ 부사적 용법의 to부정사

> The chart, like the pie chart, can then be broken down / for
> be v-ed: 수동태
> 이후, 파이 차트와 마찬가지로, 이 차트는 세분화될 수 있다
> different groups of students / within the study / to elicit further
> 전치사(… 안에)　　부사적 용법의 to부정사(목적)
> 다른 학생 집단으로　　　연구 내의　　　연구 결과의 추가
> analysis of findings.
> 분석을 도출하기 위해

➡ 앞의 동사 can be broken down을 수식하는 부사적 용법의 to부정사로 어법상 바르다.

방사형 차트라고도 불리는 스파이더 차트는 선 그래프의 한 형태이다. 그것은 연구자가 상호 연관된 변수에 대해 하나의 척도에서 응답의 상대적 크기를 보여주는 차트로 그들의 데이터를 설명하도록 도와준다. 막대 그래프와 마찬가지로 데이터는 모든 변수에 공통인 하나의 척도를 가져야 한다. 스파이더 차트는 변수들이 차트에 걸치면서 그려지며 거미줄을 만든다. 이것의 예는 중등학교에서 첫 학기에 가르쳐진 다양한 과목에 걸쳐 7학년 학생들의 스스로 보고된 자신감을 조사한 연구에서 보여진다. 연구자는 표본 집단으로부터 응답값들을 가져와 스파이더 차트에 나타낼 평균치를 계산한다. 스파이더 차트는 연구자가 표본 집단의 여러 다른 과목에서의 자신감 정도를 쉽게 비교하고 대조할 수 있도록 한다. 이후, 파이 차트와 마찬가지로, 이 차트는 연구 결과의 추가 분석을 도출하기 위해 연구 내의 다른 학생 집단으로 세분화될 수 있다.

represent 통 나타내다; 설명하다   relative 형 비교상의, 상대적인   scale 명 규모; *척도   interrelate 통 밀접한 연관을 갖다   variable 명 변수, 변인   span 통 (얼마의 기간에) 걸쳐 이어지다   self-reported 형 자가 보고된, 스스로 보고하는 형식의   calculate 통 계산하다   plot 통 (좌표를) 나타내다, (그래프를) 그리다   elicit 통 도출하다, 이끌어내다

08 　　　　　정답 ④　　　정답률 37%

정답 풀이

④ 명사를 수식하는 현재분사

> This effect, [which is often overlooked], / is a primary reason / {why
> 주어, 선행사　　계속적 용법의 주격 관계대명사　　동사　　　　　관계부사
> 종종 간과되는 이런 효과는　　　　　　　　주요한 이유이다
> people [do(→ doing) aerobic exercises] / establish a new
> 주어　　　현재분사　　　　　　동사
> 유산소 운동을 하는 사람들이
> metabolism and a leaner body}.
> 새로운 신진대사와 더 날씬한 몸을 확립하는

➡ why 이하의 관계부사절의 주어는 people이고 동사는 establish로, 밑줄 친 do는 동사 역할을 할 수 없다. 따라서 앞에 오는 명사(people)를 수식하는 현재분사 doing으로 고쳐야 한다.

친절한 오답 풀이

① 목적격보어로 쓰인 to부정사

> It's not surprising / {that the demands [(which/that) you make on
> 가주어　　　명사절(진주어)를 이끄는 접속사　　주어　　목적격 관계대명사 생략
> 놀라운 일이 아니다　　당신이 당신의 몸에 하는 요구들은
> your body / when you ask it to sustain an aerobic activity] / train
> 접속사　　ask A to-v: A에게 …하도록 요구하다　　동사
> 당신이 몸에 유산소 활동을 지속하라고 할 때　　당신의 폐가
> your lungs to deliver oxygen / and (train) your heart to pump out
> 목적어1　　목적격보어1　　접속사　　목적어2　　목적격보어2
> 산소를 나르도록 훈련하고　　당신의 심장이 더 많은 양의 혈액을 퍼내도록 훈련한다
> greater amounts of blood / to carry that oxygen to your working
> 부사적 용법의 to부정사(목적)
> 그 산소를 활동 중인 근육으로 나르기 위해서
> muscles}.

➡ It이 가주어, that 이하가 진주어인 문장으로, that절에서 밑줄 친 to pump는 동사 train의 두 번째 목적어(your heart)에 대한 목적격보어로 어법상 적절하다. 반복을 피하기 위해 접속사 and 뒤에 동사 train이 생략되어 있다.

② 대명사를 수식하는 과거분사

> Your body also responds to this challenge / by producing and
> 주어　　　동사　　　　　　by v-ing: …함으로써
> 당신의 몸은 또한 이런 도전에 반응한다　　어떤 것을 생산하고 저장함으로써
> storing something / [referred to as aerobic enzymes].
> 과거분사　전치사(…로)
> 유산소 효소라고 불리는

➡ 밑줄 친 referred는 앞의 대명사 something을 수식하는 과거분사로, 어떤 것이 유산소 효소라고 '불리는'이라는 수동의 의미가 적절하므로 과거분사로 쓰는 것이 알맞다.

③ 「such a(n) + 형용사 + 명사」

> These enzymes help you burn more fat, / which is
> help + 목적어 + 동사원형: …가 ~하도록 돕다　　앞 절 전체를 선행사로 하는
> 이런 효소는 당신이 더 많은 지방을 연소하도록 돕는데　　계속적 용법의 주격 관계대명사
> another reason / [why aerobic exercise has such a pronounced
> 　　　　　　　　　　관계부사
> 이는 또 다른 이유이다　　유산소 운동이 당신의 체지방에 매우 현저한 효과를 가지는
> effect on your body fat].

➡ such는 '매우 …한'의 의미로 「such a(n) + 형용사 + 명사」의 어순으로 써야 하는데, 뒤에 a pronounced effect가 쓰였으므로 어법상 바르다.

⑤ 접속사 that

> Yet another benefit of aerobic training / is [that it enables your
> 　　　　　　　　　　　　　　　　　명사절(보어)를 이끄는 접속사
> 유산소 훈련의 또 다른 이점은　　그것이 당신의 근육으로 하여금
> muscles to better use oxygen / to perform work / over extended
> enable A to-v: A가 …할 수 있게 하다　　부사적 용법의 to부정사(목적)
> 산소를 더 잘 사용할 수 있도록 해준다는 점이다　　일을 수행하기 위해서　　장기간의 시간에 걸쳐
> periods of time].

➡ 밑줄 친 that은 문장의 보어 역할을 하는 명사절을 이끄는 접속사로, 뒤에 완전한 절이 이어지고 있으므로 어법상 바르다.

지문 해석

'Aerobic'은 '산소를 가지고 있는'이라는 뜻이다. 당신이 당신의 몸에 유산소 활동을 지속하라고 할 때 당신이 몸에 하는 요구들은 당신의 폐가 산소를 나르도록 훈련하고, 활동 중인 근육으로 그 산소를 나르기 위해서 당신의 심장이 더 많은 양의 혈액을 퍼내도록 훈련한다는 것은 놀라운 일이 아니다. 당신의 몸은 또한 유산소 효소라고 불리는 것을 생산하고 저장함으로써 이런 도전에 반응한다. 이런 효소는 당신이 더 많은 지방을 연소하도록 돕는데, 이는 유산소 운동이 당신의 체지방에 매우 현저한 효과를 가지는 또 다른 이유이다. 종종 간과되는 이런 효과는 유산소 운동을 하는 사람들이 새로운 신진대사와 더 날씬한 몸을 확립하는 주요한 이유이다. 유산소 훈련의 또 다른 이점은 그것이 당신의 근육으로 하여금 장기간의 시간에 걸쳐 일을 수행하기 위해서 산소를 더 잘 사용할 수 있도록 해준다는 점이다.

aerobic 형 유산소의   demand 명 요구   sustain 통 지속하다   lung 명 폐   muscle 명 근육   respond 통 반응하다   challenge 명 도전   enzyme 명 효소   pronounced 형 현저한   overlook 통 간과하다   primary 형 주된, 주요한   establish 통 확립하다   metabolism 명 신진대사   lean 형 날씬한   benefit 명 혜택, 이득   extend 통 연장하다

09 　　　　　정답 ⑤　　　정답률 51%

정답 풀이

⑤ 분사구문

> He goes on to describe his daily routine of strolling through the
> go on to-v: 계속해서 …하다　　　동격　　of는 동격의 전치사
> 그는 마을을 걸어 다니는 그의 매일의 일과를 계속해서 기술한다
> village / [observed(→ observing) the intimate details of family
> 동시동작을 나타내는 분사구문(= as he observes …)
> 가정생활의 사소한 세부 사항들을 관찰하면서
> life], / and [as he tells it], such observations seem possible and
> 접속사(…듯이)　　　　　　　　seem + 형용사: …하게 보이다
> 그리고 그가 말하듯이, 그러한 관찰들은 가능하고 쉬운 것처럼 보인다
> accessible.

➡ 밑줄 친 부분은 동시동작을 나타내는 분사구문으로, 생략된 주어는 문장의 주어(He)와 같다. 의미상 그가 '관찰하면서'라는 능동의 의미가 적절하므로, 과거분사 observed를 현재분사 observing으로 고쳐야 한다.

┃친절한 오답 풀이┃

① 명사를 수식하는 과거분사

It is the way [we explore and learn / about the vast detailed intricacy /
선행사   관계부사절, 선행사가 쓰여 관계부사 how가 쓰이지 않음 과거분사
그것은 우리가 탐구하고 배우는 방법이다   방대하고 세세한 복잡함에 대해
of human culture and individual behavior].
인류 문화와 개인의 행동의

➡ 밑줄 친 detailed는 뒤에 오는 명사 intricacy를 수식하는 분사로, 명사와의 관계가
수동이므로 과거분사가 오는 것이 적절하다.

② 「전치사 + 관계대명사」

And it is, importantly, the way / in which most cultural
                              선행사   which는 목적격 관계대명사
그리고 중요하게도 그것은 방법이다   대부분의 문화 인류학자들이
anthropologists earn and maintain / their professional standing.
획득하고 유지하는   자신들의 전문적인 입장을

➡ which는 the way를 선행사로 하고 관계대명사절 안에서 전치사 in의 목적어로
쓰였으므로 「전치사 + 관계대명사」 형태인 in which는 어법상 바르다.

③ 「make(사역동사) + 목적어 + 동사원형」

Some of the early personal accounts of anthropologists in the
「some of + 명사」 주어는 of 뒤 명사에 동사 수 일치
현장에서 인류학자들의 초기의 개인적인 설명 중 일부는
field / make fieldwork sound exciting, adventuresome, certainly
       make(사역동사) + 목적어 + 동사원형: …가 ~하게 하다
       현지조사가 흥미롭고, 모험적이며, 분명히 색다르고, 때로는 쉬운 것처럼 들리게 한다
exotic, sometimes easy.

➡ 사역동사는 목적격보어로 동사원형을 쓰는데, 밑줄 친 부분은 사역동사 make의
목적격보어 자리이므로 동사원형 sound는 어법상 바르다.

④ 동사의 수 일치

Malinowski, the classic anthropological fieldworker, /
주어 └──동격──┘
전형적인 인류학 현지 탐험가인 Malinowski는
describes the early stages of fieldwork / as 'a strange, sometimes
동사, describe A as B: A를 B로 묘사하다
현지 조사의 초기 단계들을 묘사하고 있다
unpleasant, sometimes intensely interesting adventure / [which
낯설고, 때로는 불쾌하고, 때로는 강렬하게 흥미로운 모험으로   주격 관계대명사
soon adopts quite a natural course].'
곧 아주 자연스러운 방식을 취하는

➡ 주격 관계대명사절의 동사는 선행사에 수를 일치시켜야 하는데, 선행사(a strange …
adventure)가 3인칭 단수이므로 3인칭 단수형 adopts가 알맞다.

지문 해석

현지 조사는 문화 인류학의 특징이다. 그것은 인류 문화와 개인의 행동의 방대하고 세세한
복잡함에 대해 우리가 탐구하고 배우는 방법이다. 그리고 중요하게도 그것은 대부분의
문화 인류학자들이 자신들의 전문적인 입장을 획득하고 유지하는 방법이다. 현장에서
인류학자들의 초기의 개인적인 설명 중 일부는 현지조사가 흥미롭고, 모험적이며,
분명히 색다르고, 때로는 쉬운 것처럼 들리게 한다. 전형적인 인류학 현지 탐험가인
Malinowski는 현지 조사의 초기 단계들을 '곧 아주 자연스러운 방식을 취하는, 낯설고,
때로는 불쾌하고, 때로는 강렬하게 흥미로운 모험'으로 묘사하고 있다. 그는 가정생활의
사소한 세부 사항들을 관찰하면서 마을을 걸어 다니는 그의 매일의 일과를 계속해서
기술하는데, 그가 말하듯이, 그러한 관찰들은 가능하고 쉬운 것처럼 보인다.

---

fieldwork 몡 현지[실지] 조사 hallmark 몡 특징, 특질 anthropology 몡 인류학
(anthropologist 몡 인류학자 anthropological 혱 인류학의) vast 혱 어마어마한,
방대한 intricacy 몡 복잡함 standing 몡 입장 account 몡 기술, 설명
adventuresome 혱 모험적인 exotic 혱 이국적인 classic 혱 일류의; *전형적인
intensely 閈 강렬하게, 격하게 adopt 통 입양하다; *(방식 등을) 쓰다, 취하다
stroll 통 거닐다, 산책하다 intimate 혱 친밀한 accessible 혱 다가가기 쉬운

10   정답 ③   정답률 69%

정답 풀이

(A) 동사의 수 일치

The observation / [that old windows are often thicker at the
주어 └─동격─┘   that은 동격의 접속사
관찰 결과는   오래된 창은 아랫부분이 윗부분보다 종종 더 두껍다는
bottom than at the top] / is / are often offered as supporting
                          동사   전치사(…로써)
                          종종 견해를 뒷받침하는 증거로 제시된다
evidence for the view / [that glass flows over a time scale of
       └─동격─┘   that은 동격의 접속사
                         유리가 여러 세기에 걸쳐 흘러내린다는
centuries].

➡ 문장의 주어는 The observation이고, 뒤에 오는 that … the top은 주어를 보충하기
위한 동격의 명사절이다. 주어가 단수이므로 단수 동사 is가 오는 것이 알맞다.

(B) 접속사 that

The reason for the observation / is [that / what] in the past,
주어   동사 명사절(보어)을 이끄는 접속사
관찰 결과에 대한 이유는   …라는 것이다   과거에
making uniformly flat glass was almost impossible].
명사절의 주어(동명사구)   명사절의 동사
고르게 평평한 유리를 만드는 것이 거의 불가능했다

➡ 문장에서 보어 역할을 하는 명사절을 이끌고 있고, 뒤에 완전한 절이 이어지고 있으므로
접속사 that이 오는 것이 알맞다. what은 관계대명사로 뒤에 불완전한 절이 온다.

(C) 수동형 분사구문

[When (being) installing / installed in a window frame], / the glass
접속사가 남아있는 분사구문(= When the glass was installed …)   주어
창틀에 설치될 때,
would be placed thicker side down / for the sake of stability.
                                   … 때문에, …을 위해서
그 유리는 더 두꺼운 쪽을 아래로 하여 설치되었다   안정성을 위해서

➡ When … frame은 때를 나타내는 분사구문으로, 생략된 주어는 주절의 주어(the
glass)와 같다. 유리가 '설치되는'이라는 수동의 의미가 적절하므로 과거분사 installed
가 오는 것이 알맞다.

코드+α 구문 분석 Plus

5행	…; once (being) solidified, glass does not flow anymore. ➡ 접속사 once(일단 …하면)가 남아있고 being이 생략된 수동형 분사구문(= once the glass is solidified) ➡ not … anymore: 더 이상 … 않다
8행	The technique [used to make panes of glass] was to spin molten glass so as to create a round, mostly flat plate. ➡ used 이하는 The technique을 수식하는 과거분사구 ➡ so as to-v: …하기 위하여

지문 해석

오래된 창은 아랫부분이 윗부분보다 종종 더 두껍다는 관찰 결과는 유리가 여러 세기에
걸쳐서 흘러내린다는 견해를 뒷받침하는 증거로 종종 제시된다. 그러나 이런 가정은
정확하지 않다. 일단 굳어지면, 유리는 더 이상 흐르지 않는다. 관찰 결과에 대한 이유는

과거에 고르게 평평한 유리를 만드는 것이 거의 불가능했기 때문이다. 유리창을 만드는 데 사용된 기술은 둥글고 거의 평평한 판유리를 만들기 위해 녹은 유리를 회전시키는 것이었다. 그리고 이 판유리는 창문에 맞게 절단되었다. 그러나 그 원판의 가장자리는 유리가 회전할 때 점점 더 두꺼워졌다. 창틀에 설치될 때, 그 유리는 안정성을 위해서 더 두꺼운 쪽을 아래로 하여 설치되었다.

어휘

observation 명 관찰   offer 통 제공하다   supporting 형 뒷받침하는   evidence 명 증거   assumption 명 가정   incorrect 형 부정확한   solidify 통 굳히다   uniformly 부 한결같이, 균등하게   pane 명 (한 장의) 판유리   spin 통 회전시키다   molten 형 녹은   disk 명 동글납작한 판, 원반   install 통 설치하다   stability 명 안정, 안정성

코드 공략하기 02   pp.15~17

01 ⑤	02 ③	03 ③	04 ④	05 ⑤	06 ③	07 ④	08 ②
09 ③	10 ②						

01   정답 ⑤   정답률 67%

정답 풀이

⑤ 명사를 수식하는 과거분사

After the conquests, the enemous wealth / [bringing(→ brought)
주어   과거분사
정복 후, 엄청난 부는   이탈리아로 다시 들어온
back to Italy] / allowed middle- and upper-class women to run
동사, allow A to-v : A가 …하는 것을 허용하다
중상류층의 여성들이 일을 처리하는 것을 허용했다
things / with more independence and power.
        더 많은 독립성과 권한을 가지고

➡ 밑줄 친 부분은 앞에 오는 명사구(the enormous wealth)를 수식하는 분사로, 의미상 엄청난 부가 이탈리아로 '들여온' 것이므로 수동의 의미를 나타내는 과거분사 brought로 고쳐야 한다.

친절한 오답 풀이

① 병렬구조

[Whether a woman was a slave or came from a wealthier class] /
접속사(…이든 아니든), 명사절(주어)을 이끌고 있음
여성이 노예인지 더 부유한 계층 출신인지가
made a great deal of difference.
동사   대단히 큰   make a difference: 중요하다
대단히 중요했다

➡ 등위접속사 or가 명사절의 동사 was와 came을 병렬 연결하고 있으므로 어법상 바르다.

② 가주어 진주어 구문

It also made a difference / [which period you're talking about].
가주어   진주어(의문(형용)사 + 주어 + 동사)
또한 중요했다   어느 시기를 언급하고 있는지가

➡ 가주어 진주어 구문으로, 의문사 which가 이끄는 명사절이 문장의 진주어 역할을 하고 있으므로 어법상 바르다.

③ 접속사 that

Rome's conquests meant / [that men were often away for long
                        명사절(목적어)을 이끄는 접속사
로마의 정복은 의미했다   남자들이 자주 오랜 기간 동안 멀리 나가 있고
periods of time / and might not come back at all].
                                not ... at all: 결코 … 않다
                그리고 결코 돌아올 수도 모른다는 것을

➡ 밑줄 친 that은 동사 meant의 목적어 역할을 하는 명사절을 이끄는 접속사로, 뒤에 완전한 절이 이어지고 있으므로 어법상 바르다.

④ 수동태

Women were left / in charge of making sure / [that things got done].
      be v-ed: 수동태   …을 책임지는   접속사
여성들에게 맡겨졌다   확실히 되도록 책임지는 것이   일이 처리되도록

➡ 의미상 여자들에게 책임이 '맡겨진' 것이므로 수동태가 어법상 적절하다.

지문 해석

일반적으로 로마 여성들에 관해 이야기할 때, 모든 것은 기간과 계층에 의해 나누어진다. 여성이 노예인지 부유한 계층 출신인지가 대단히 중요했다. 어느 시기를 언급하고 있는지가 또한 중요했다. 로마의 정복은 남자들이 자주 오랜 기간 동안 멀리 나가 있고 다시 돌아올 수 없을지도 모른다는 것을 의미했다. 일들이 확실히 처리되도록 책임지는 것은 여성들에게 맡겨졌다. 정복 후, 이탈리아로 다시 들어온 엄청난 부는 중상류층의 여성들이 더 많은 독립성과 권한을 가지고 일을 처리하는 것을 허용했다.

어휘

in general 일반적으로   break down 고장나다; *나누다   class 명 수업; *계층   conquest 명 정복   leave 통 떠나다; *남기다   enormous 형 거대한   wealth 명 부, 재산   independence 명 독립

02   정답 ③   정답률 64%

정답 풀이

③ 분사구문

Pressure from underground sources of water / would separate and
주어   동사
지하수원에서 나오는 압력은   알갱이 입자를 분리하고
suspend the granular particles, / [reduced(→ reducing) the friction].
                                                  결과를 나타내는 분사구문
뜨게 만들어서   마찰력을 감소시킬 것이다

➡ 밑줄 친 부분은 결과를 나타내는 분사구문의 분사로, 생략된 주어는 주절의 주어(Pressure)와 같다. 주어와 분사가 의미상 능동 관계에 있으므로 과거분사 reduced를 현재분사 reducing으로 고쳐야 한다.

친절한 오답 풀이

① 병렬구조

Quicksand forms / [when sand gets mixed with too much water /
                          접속사
유사는 형성된다   모래가 너무 많은 물과 섞여
and becomes loosened and soupy].
느슨하고 걸쭉해질 때

➡ 등위접속사 and가 접속사 when이 이끄는 절의 동사 gets와 becomes를 병렬 연결하고 있으므로 어법상 바르다.

② 목적격보어로 쓰인 to부정사

..., if you were to step on it, / the pressure from your foot would
      가정법 과거(…라면 ~할 텐데)
      당신이 그것에 한 걸음 디디면,   발의 압력이 모래를 움직이게 한다
cause the sand to act / more like a liquid, / and you'd sink right in.
cause A to-v: A가 …하도록 하다   전치사(…처럼)   부사(바로)
                      좀 더 액체처럼   그리고 당신은 바로 가라앉을 것이다

➡ 동사 cause는 목적격보어로 to부정사를 취하므로 밑줄 친 to act는 어법상 바르다.

Grammar Tips

가정법 과거

「If + 주어 + were to + 동사원형, 주어 + 조동사의 과거형 + 동사원형」은 '…라면 ~할 텐데'라는 의미로, 미래에 일어날 가능성이 없는 일을 가정할 때 쓴다.

④ 「the + 비교급 …, the + 비교급 ~」

In quicksand, / the more you struggle, / the deeper you'll sink.
유사 속에서　　당신이 발버둥을 치면 칠수록　　당신은 더 깊게 가라앉을 것이다

➡ '…하면 할수록 더 ~하다'라는 의미의 「the + 비교급 …, the + 비교급 ~」 구문으로, 앞 절에 the more가 쓰였고 the 뒤에 비교급 deeper가 쓰였으므로 어법상 적절하다.

⑤ stop v-ing

So if you ever do fall into quicksand, / remember to stay calm,
　　동사를 강조하는 조동사　　remember to-v: (미래에) …할 것을 기억하다
그러므로 당신이 유사에 빠지기라도 한다면　　침착하게 있을 것을 기억하고
and don't move / until you've stopped sinking.
　　접속사(…할 때까지)
움직이지 마라　　당신이 가라앉는 것이 멈출 때까지

➡ 동사 stop 뒤에는 to부정사(…하기 위해)와 동명사(…하는 것)가 모두 올 수 있으나, 문맥상 '가라앉는 것을 멈출'이라는 의미이므로 동명사 sinking이 오는 것이 적절하다.

지문 해석

유사(流砂)는 정말로 있는가? 그렇다. 그러나 그것은 영화에서만큼 치명적이지는 않다. 유사는 모래가 너무 많은 물과 섞여 느슨하고 걸쭉해질 때 형성된다. 그것은 일반적인 모래처럼 보일지도 모르지만, 당신이 그것에 한 걸음 디디면, 발의 압력이 모래를 좀 더 액체처럼 움직이게 하고, 당신은 바로 가라앉을 것이다. 지하수원에서 나오는 압력은 알갱이 입자를 분리하고 뜨게 만들어서 마찰력을 감소시킬 것이다. 유사 속에서, 당신이 발버둥을 치면 칠수록, 더 깊게 가라앉을 것이다. 그러나 가만히 있으면, 당신은 떠오르기 시작할 것이다. 그러므로 당신이 유사에 빠지기라도 한다면, 침착하게 있을 것을 기억하고, 당신이 가라앉는 것이 멈출 때까지 움직이지 마라.

quicksand 명 유사(流砂)　deadly 형 치명적인　loosen 동 느슨하게 하다　soupy 형 걸쭉한　normal 형 평범한　liquid 명 액체　sink 동 가라앉다　pressure 명 압력　separate 동 분리하다　suspend 동 매달다; *떠 있게 하다　granular 형 알갱이 모양의　particle 명 입자　friction 명 마찰　struggle 동 투쟁하다; *발버둥을 치다　float 동 떠가다; *뜨다

03　정답 ③　정답률 59%

정답 풀이

③ 명사를 수식하는 과거분사

They once roamed Mauritius, a tropical island / [situating
　　　　　　　　　　　　　　　　　　동격
그들은 한 때 열대섬인 Mauritius를 배회했다
(→ situated) in the Indian Ocean].
　　과거분사
인도양에 위치되어 있는

➡ 밑줄 친 부분은 앞의 명사(a tropical island)를 수식하는 분사로, 의미상 섬이 인도양에 '위치된'이라는 수동의 의미가 적절하므로, 현재분사 situating을 과거분사 situated로 고쳐야 한다.

---

① 「so + 형용사 + that …」

In some cases / two species are so dependent upon each other /
　　　　　　　be dependent (up)on: …에 의존하다　so + 형용사 + that …: 너무 ~해서 …하다
몇몇의 경우에　　두 종이 너무 상호의존적이어서
{that [if one becomes extinct], / the other will (become extinct)
접속사　　부사절　　　　　　　　　　　동사구 생략
만약 한 종이 멸종하면　　다른 한 종도 또한 그럴 것이다
as well}.
또한(= too)

➡ 「so + 형용사 + that …」 구문으로, that은 결과를 나타내는 절을 이끄는 접속사이다. that 뒤에 주어가 the other이고 반복을 피하기 위해 동사구(become extinct)가 생략된 절이 이어지고 있으므로 어법상 바르다.

② 주격 관계대명사절의 동사

This nearly happened with trees / [that relied on the now-extinct
　　　　　　　　　　　　　　　　　　主격 관계대명사　rely on: …에 의존하다
이러한 현상은 나무에서 거의 발생했다　　현재 멸종해버린 도도새에 의존했던
Dodo birds].

➡ 밑줄 친 relied는 선행사 trees를 수식하는 주격 관계대명사절의 동사로 어법상 바르다.

④ 부사절의 동사

[After they disappeared], / the Calvaria Tree soon stopped sprouting
접속사　　　　　　　　　　　　　　　　stop v-ing: …하는 것을 멈추다
그들이 사라진 이후에　　Calvaria 나무는 머지않아 씨앗을 싹 틔우기를 멈추었다
seeds.

➡ 밑줄 친 disappeared는 접속사 After가 이끄는 부사절의 동사로 어법상 바르다.

⑤ 부사적 용법의 to부정사

Scientists finally concluded / [that, for the seeds of the Calvaria
　　　　　　　　　　　　　　명사절(목적어)을 이끄는 접속사　to부정사의 의미상의 주어
과학자들이 최종적으로 결론 내렸다　　Calvaria 나무의 씨앗이 싹트기 위해서는
Tree to sprout, / they needed to first be digested by the Dodo bird].
부사적 용법의 to부정사(목적)
　　　　　　　　　그것들이 우선 도도새에 의해 소화되어야 했다

➡ 밑줄 친 to sprout는 뒤에 오는 절 전체를 수식하는 부사적 용법의 to부정사로 어법상 바르다.

지문 해석

두 종이 너무 상호의존적인 몇몇 경우에, 한 종이 멸종하면 다른 한 종도 또한 그럴 것이다. 이러한 현상은 현재 멸종해버린 도도새에 의존했던 나무에서 거의 발생했다. 그들은 한 때 인도양에 위치되어 있는 열대섬인 Mauritius를 배회했다. 그러나 도도새는 19세기 후반에 멸종되었다. 그들은 인간과 다른 동물들에 의해 지나치게 사냥되었다. 그들이 사라진 이후에, Calvaria 나무는 머지않아 씨앗을 싹 틔우기를 멈추었다. Calvaria 나무의 씨앗이 싹트기 위해서는, 그 씨앗이 도도새에 의해 우선 소화되어야 했다고 과학자들이 최종적으로 결론을 내렸다.

dependent 형 의존하는　extinct 형 멸종된　roam 동 배회하다　tropical 형 열대의　situate 동 위치시키다　sprout 동 싹트다　seed 명 씨앗　conclude 동 결론을 내리다　digest 동 (음식을) 소화하다

정답 풀이

④ 분사구문

> Pollution and fossil fuels have given us global warming, /
> 주어   동사
> 오염과 화석 연료는 우리에게 지구 온난화를 가져왔다
> resulted(→ resulting) in extreme weathers.
> 결과를 나타내는 분사구문, result in: …한 결과를 낳다
> 극심한 기후를 초래했다

➡ 밑줄 친 부분은 결과를 나타내는 분사구문의 분사로, 생략된 주어는 주절의 주어(Pollution and fossil fuels)와 같다. 주어와 분사가 의미상 능동 관계에 있으므로 과거분사 resulted를 현재분사 resulting으로 고쳐야 한다.

▮친절한 오답 풀이▮

① 간접의문문

> Can you imagine / [what life was like 200 years ago]?
>   간접의문문(의문사 + 주어 + 동사)
> 당신은 상상할 수 있는가   200년 전에는 삶이 어떠했는지?

➡ what 이하는 동사 imagine의 목적어로 쓰인 간접의문문으로, 간접의문문 안에서 what은 전치사 like의 목적어로 쓰인 의문대명사로 어법상 바르다.

② 수동태

> There was no electricity, / and oil lamps were used at night.
>   주어
> 전기가 없었다   그리고 밤에는 기름 램프가 사용되었다

➡ 기름 램프가 '사용되었다'라는 수동의 의미이므로 수동태 were used는 어법상 바르다.

③ 부사

> These days, our lives are completely different.
> 오늘날, 우리의 삶은 완전히 다르다

➡ 부사 completely가 뒤에 오는 형용사 different를 수식하고 있으므로 어법상 바르다.

⑤ 가목적어 진목적어 구문

> Modern medicine lets us live longer, / but governments are
>   let(사역동사) + 목적어 + 동사원형: …가 ~하게 하다
> 현대 의학은 우리가 더 오래 살게 한다   그러나 정부는 어렵다고 생각하고 있다
> **finding it hard** / [**to look** after the increasing number of old people].
> 가목적어   진목적어, look after: …을 돌보다
>   늘어나는 노령인구의 수를 보살피는 것이

➡ finding 뒤에 쓰인 it은 가목적어이고 to look 이하가 진목적어인 to부정사구로 어법상 바르다.

Grammar Tips

자주 쓰이는 가목적어 진목적어 구문

「think[find] it + 형용사 + to-v」는 '…하는 것이 ~라고 생각하다[알게 되다]'라는 의미로, it은 뒤에 오는 진목적어인 to부정사(구)를 대신하는 가목적어이다.

지문 해석

200년 전에는 삶이 어떠했는지 당신은 상상할 수 있는가? 전기가 없었고, 밤에는 기름 램프가 사용되었다. 게다가, 자동차나 전화기도 없어서, 여행은 주로 걸어서 다녔고 통신도 매우 어려웠다. 오늘날, 우리의 삶은 완전히 다르다. 우리는 우리의 조상들이 꿈조차 꾸지 못했던 제트기, 휴대전화, 인터넷, 그리고 더 많은 생활 양상들을 갖게 되었다. 하지만, 이 모든 발전들이 좋은 결과를 가져왔을까? 오염과 화석 연료는 우리에게 지구 온난화를 가져왔고, 극심한 기후를 초래했다. 현대의학은 우리가 더 오래 살게 하지만, 정부는 늘어나는 노령인구의 수를 보살피는 것이 어렵다고 생각하고 있다.

imagine 통 상상하다   communication 명 의사소통; *통신, 소통   completely 부 완전히   jet plane 제트기   aspect 명 측면, 양상   ancestor 명 조상 improvement 명 개선, 호전   pollution 명 오염   fossil fuel 화석 연료 extreme 형 극심한

정답 풀이

⑤ 분사구문

> Lions and tigers, for instance, / first eat the blood, hearts, livers,
> 주어   동사
> 사자나 호랑이는, 예를 들어,   먼저 동물의 피, 심장, 간, 그리고 뇌를 먹는다
> and brains of the animals / [(which/that) they kill], /
>   목적격 관계대명사 생략
>   그들이 죽인
> [often leave(→ leaving) the muscle meat for eagles].
>   동시동작을 나타내는 분사구문(= as lions and tigers leave …)
> 종종 근육덩이 고기는 독수리를 위해 남기면서

➡ 문장의 동사는 eat이고 또 다른 동사를 연결해줄 접속사가 없으므로 밑줄 친 leave는 동사로 쓰일 수 없다. 따라서 leave 이하는 문장에서 부사구 역할을 하는 분사구문으로 고쳐야 하는데, 주어 Lions and tigers와 leave가 의미상 능동 관계에 있으므로 동사 leave는 현재분사 leaving으로 고쳐야 한다.

▮친절한 오답 풀이▮

① 대동사 do

> Some researchers assumed / [(that) early human beings ate mainly /
>   명사절(목적어)을 이끄는 접속사 that 생략
> 몇몇 연구가들은 추정했다   초창기 인류가 주로 먹었을 것이라고
> the muscle flesh of animals], / [as we do today].
>   접속사(…처럼)   = eat
> 동물의 근육덩이 살코기를   오늘날 우리가 그러는 것처럼

➡ 밑줄 친 do는 대동사로, 앞에 나온 동사 ate을 대신하고 있는데, 뒤에 현재를 나타내는 부사 today가 와서 현재시제로 쓰였으므로 어법상 바르다.

② 부사

> Yet focusing on the muscle / appears to be a relatively recent
>   동명사 주어   appear to-v: …인 것 같다   형용사
> 하지만 근육덩이에 주목하는 것은   비교적 최근 현상인 것 같다
> phenomenon.

➡ 부사 relatively가 뒤에 오는 형용사 recent를 수식하고 있으므로 어법상 적절하다.

③ 문장의 동사

> In every history on the subject, / the evidence **suggests** / [that early
>   = about   명사절(목적어)을 이끄는 접속사
> 그 주제에 관한 모든 역사에서   증거는 시사한다
> human populations **preferred** the fat and organ meat of the animal /
>   that절의 주어   that절의 동사
> 초창기 인류가 동물의 비계와 내장을 선호했다는 것을
> over its muscle meat].
> 그것의 근육덩이 고기보다는

➡ that은 문장 전체의 동사 suggests의 목적어 역할을 하는 명사절을 이끄는 접속사로, that 뒤에는 주어와 동사를 가지는 완전한 절이 와야 한다. 밑줄 친 preferred는 that절에서 동사 역할을 하고 있으므로 어법상 바르다.

오답 피하기 Tips

> **suggest 뒤에 오는 절의 동사는 무조건 동사원형?**
>
> 제안(suggest), 요구(demand), 주장(insist), 명령(order) 등을 나타내는 동사 뒤에 오는 that절에서, 동사는 「should + 동사원형」 형태로 쓰며, 종종 should는 생략된다. 그러나 that절이 현재나 과거의 '사실'을 나타내는 경우, 동사는 「should + 동사원형」으로 쓰지 않고 시제 일치의 원칙에 따른다.
>
> 예) Research **suggests** that there **are** health benefits to losing small amount of weight. (연구는 약간의 체중 감소에 건강상 이점이 있다는 점을 시사한다.)

④ 접속사

> Vihjalmur Stefansson, an arctic explorer, found / {that the Inuit
> ─── 동격 ───────── ── 명사절(목적어)을 이끄는 접속사
> 북극 탐험가인 Vihjalmur Stefansson은 발견했다   이누이트 족이
> were careful to save fatty meat and organs / for human
> 지방이 많은 고기와 내장을 주의 깊게 보관한다는 것을   인간의 섭취를 위해
> consumption / [while giving muscle meat to the dogs]}.
> 소비   접속사(…인 반면에) 접속사가 남아있는 분사구문(= while the Inuit gave …)
>   근육덩이 고기를 개에게 주는 반면에

➡ while 이하는 부사절 while the Inuit gave muscle meat to the dogs를 분사구문으로 바꾼 것이며, while은 분사구문의 의미를 분명하게 하기 위해 남겨둔 접속사로 어법상 바르다.

지문 해석

몇몇 연구가들은 초창기 인류가 오늘날 우리가 그러는 것처럼 주로 동물의 근육덩이 살코기를 먹었을 것이라고 추정했다. 그들에게 '고기'는 동물의 근육덩이를 의미했다. 하지만 근육덩이에 주목하는 것은 비교적 최근 현상인 것 같다. 그 주제에 관한 모든 역사에서, 증거는 초창기 인류가 동물의 근육덩이 고기보다는 비계와 내장을 선호했다는 것을 시사한다. 북극 탐험가인 Vihjalmur Stefansson은 이누이트족이 근육덩이 고기는 개에게 주는 반면에 지방이 많은 고기와 내장은 인간의 섭취를 위해 주의 깊게 보관한다는 것을 발견했다. 이런 식으로, 인간은 다른 큰 육식 포유동물이 먹는 것처럼 먹었다. 예를 들어, 사자나 호랑이는 먼저 그들이 죽인 동물의 피, 심장, 간, 그리고 뇌를 먹고, 근육덩이 고기는 독수리를 위해 종종 남긴다. 이런 내장은 지방이 훨씬 많은 경향이 있다.

 어휘

researcher 명 연구가   **assume** 통 추정하다   **flesh** 명 살코기   **recent** 형 최근의   **phenomenon** 명 현상   **population** 명 인구   **prefer** 통 선호하다   **organ** 명 (인체의) 장기, 기관   **arctic** 형 북극의   **explorer** 명 탐험가   **consumption** 명 소비   **mammal** 명 포유동물   **liver** 명 간

06   정답 ③   정답률 56%

정답 풀이

(A) 동사의 수 일치

> [Getting in the habit of asking questions] / ~~transform~~ / transforms
> ── 동명사구 주어 ──   transform A into B: A를 B로 바꾸다
> 질문하는 습관을 갖는 것은   당신을 바꾸다
> you / into an active listener.
>   적극적 청자로

➡ 문장의 주어가 동명사구(Getting … questions)이며 동명사구는 단수 취급하므로 단수 동사 transforms를 쓰는 것이 알맞다.

(B) 관계대명사 what

> It's [what goes on inside your head] / that makes all the difference /
> 「It is … that」 강조구문, 관계대명사(…하는 것)
> 바로 당신의 머릿속에서 일어나는 것이다   전적으로 차이를 만들어내는 것은
> in how well you will convert / [what / ~~that~~ you hear] / into
> 얼마나 잘 전환할 것인가에 있어서   관계대명사
>   당신이 듣는 것을
> something [(that) you learn].
>   ── 목적격 관계대명사 생략
> 당신이 배우는 것으로

➡ 동사 convert의 목적어 역할을 하면서 뒤에 목적어가 빠진 불완전한 절이 이어지므로 선행사를 포함하는 관계대명사 what이 오는 것이 어법상 바르다.

(C) 감정을 나타내는 분사

> {If you are constantly engaged / in asking yourself questions /
> 접속사(만약 …라면), be engaged in: …로 바쁘다
> 만약 당신이 끊임없이 몰두한다면   스스로 질문하는 것에
> about things [(that) you are hearing]}, / you will find / [that even
>   ── 목적격 관계대명사 생략   명사절(목적어)을 이끄는 접속사
> 당신이 듣고 있는 것에 대하여   당신은 생각할 것인데
> boring lecturers become a bit more [interesting / ~~interested~~], /
>   현재분사
> 따분한 강연자조차도 약간 더 흥미로워진다고
> because much of the interest will be coming / from [what you
> 왜냐하면 그 흥미 중 많은 부분이 올 것이기 때문이다   관계대명사(…하는 것)
>   당신이 만들어내고
> are generating] / rather than [what the lecturer is offering].
> 있는 것으로부터   접속사(…보다는) 관계대명사
>   강연자가 제공하고 있는 것보다는

➡ 감정을 나타내는 분사는 의미상 주어와의 관계가 능동(…한 감정을 일으키는)일 경우 현재분사를, 수동(…한 감정을 느끼는)일 경우 과거분사로 쓴다. 주어(boring lecturers)가 약간 더 '흥미를 일으키는' 것이므로 현재분사 interesting이 오는 것이 적절하다.

지문 해석

질문하는 습관을 갖는 것은 당신을 적극적 청자로 바꾼다. 이러한 습관은 당신이 다른 내적 삶의 경험을 갖도록 하는데, 왜냐하면 사실상 당신이 더욱 효과적으로 듣고 있을 것이기 때문이다. 당신은 때때로 어떤 이의 말을 들어야 할 때, 당신의 마음이 산만해지기 시작한다는 것을 안다. 모든 교사는 이러한 것이 수업 중에 학생들에게서 빈번하게 발생한다는 것을 알고 있다. 당신이 듣는 것을 배우는 것으로 얼마나 잘 전환할 것인가에 있어서 전적으로 차이를 만들어내는 것은 바로 당신의 머릿속에서 일어나는 것이다. 듣는 것은 충분하지 않다. 만약 당신이 듣고 있는 것에 대하여 스스로 질문하는 것에 끊임없이 몰두한다면, 당신은 따분한 강연자조차도 약간 더 흥미로워진다고 생각할 것인데, 왜냐하면 그 흥미 중 많은 부분이 강연자가 제공하고 있는 것보다는 당신이 만들어내고 있는 것으로부터 올 것이기 때문이다. 다른 누군가가 말할 때, 당신은 생각을 불러일으킬 필요가 있다!

 어휘

transform 통 바꾸다, 변형시키다   **practice** 명 실행; *습관   **wander** 통 돌아다니다; *산만해지다   **frequently** 부 자주, 빈번히   **go on** 일어나다   **convert** 통 전환하다   **constantly** 부 끊임없이   **lecturer** 명 강연자   **generate** 통 발생시키다, 만들어내다

정답 풀이

④ 명사를 수식하는 과거분사

Furthermore, / Australian scientist Ross Dawson points to News
                                                주어   동사
게다가,   호주의 과학자인 Ross Dawson은 News At Seven을 언급한다
At Seven, / a system is developed(→ developed) by Northwestern
              동격   과거분사
             Northwestern University에 의해 개발된 시스템인
University / [that automatically creates a virtual news show].
           a system을 선행사로 하는 주격 관계대명사
           자동으로 가상 뉴스를 만드는

➡ 밑줄 앞의 명사 a system은 전치사 to의 목적어인 News At Seven과 동격으로, 동사가 필요하지 않다. 따라서 is developed는 a system을 수식하는 분사로 고쳐야 하는데, 시스템이 '개발된'이라는 수동의 의미이므로 과거분사 developed로 고쳐야 한다.

친절한 오답 풀이

① 관계대명사 what

A robot [made in Japan] / can perform a journalist's tasks on its
             과거분사   on one's own: 스스로
일본에서 만들어진 한 로봇은   스스로 기자들의 과업을 수행할 수 있다
own / by exploring its environment, determining [what is
         by v-ing: …함으로써   관계대명사 what
         주변 환경을 탐지하고, 관련 있는 것을 판단하고
relevant], / and taking pictures with its built-in camera.
          and에 의해 연결된 병렬구조(A, B and C)
          그리고 내장된 카메라로 사진을 찍음으로써

➡ what은 선행사를 포함한 관계대명사로, 동명사 determining의 목적어 역할을 하는 명사절을 이끌고 있으므로 어법상 바르다.

② 부사적 용법의 to부정사

It can even interview nearby people and perform Internet
                                 and에 의해 연결된 병렬구조
그것은 심지어 근처 사람들을 인터뷰하고 인터넷 검색까지 수행할 수 있다
searches / to improve its understanding.
          부사적 용법의 to부정사(목적)
          이해력을 높이기 위해

➡ to improve는 동사구 perform Internet searches를 수식하는 부사 용법의 to부정사로 어법상 바르다.

③ 동사의 수 일치

Another robot [called Stats Monkey] can automatically use
                       과거분사
Stats Monkey라고 불리는 또 다른 로봇은 자동으로 통계 자료를 사용할 수 있다
statistics / to report sports news / [that reads like it was written
                          주격 관계대명사   접속사(…처럼)
          스포츠 뉴스를 보도하기 위해   기자에 의해 쓰여진 것처럼 읽히는
by a journalist].

➡ 주격 관계대명사절의 동사는 선행사에 수를 일치시켜야 한다. reads는 sports news를 선행사로 하는 주격 관계대명사절의 동사로, 선행사가 단수 명사이므로 단수형 동사 reads를 쓰는 것이 알맞다.

⑤ 분사구문

[Using the resources available on the web], / the system retrieves /
동시동작을 나타내는 분사구문(= As the system uses …)   주어   동사
웹 상에서 이용할 수 있는 자료를 활용하여   그 시스템은 검색한다
relevant images and blogs with comments on the topics / to develop
                                    부사적 용법의 to부정사(목적)
관련된 이미지와 주제에 관한 논평이 있는 블로그를
the text of the new stories.
새로운 이야기의 원고를 작성하기 위해

➡ Using 이하는 동시동작을 나타내는 분사구문으로, 생략된 주어(the system)와 분사가 의미상 능동 관계이므로 현재분사인 Using을 쓰는 것이 어법상 바르다.

 구문 분석 Plus

6행	However, ***having a robot report*** news *is* not a new idea.
	➡ have(사역동사) + 목적어 + 동사원형: …가 ~하게 하다
	➡ having은 동명사 주어로 단수 취급함

지문 해석

일본에서 만들어진 한 로봇은 스스로 주변 환경을 탐지하고, 관련 있는 것을 판단하고, 내장된 카메라로 사진을 찍음으로써 기자들의 과업을 수행할 수 있다. 그것은 심지어 근처 사람들을 인터뷰하고 이해력을 높이기 위해 인터넷 검색까지 수행할 수 있다. 그러나 로봇이 뉴스를 보도하게 하는 것은 새로운 생각이 아니다. Stats Monkey라고 불리는 또 다른 로봇은 기자에 의해 쓰여진 것처럼 읽히는 스포츠 뉴스를 보도하기 위해 자동으로 통계 자료를 사용할 수 있다. 게다가, 호주의 과학자인 Ross Dawson은 Northwestern University에 의해 개발된, 자동적으로 가상 뉴스를 만드는 시스템인 News At Seven을 언급한다. 그 시스템은 웹 상에서 이용할 수 있는 자료를 활용하여, 새로운 이야기의 원고를 작성하기 위해, 관련된 이미지와 주제에 관한 논평이 있는 블로그를 검색한다.

 어휘

perform 통 수행하다   **journalist** 명 기자   **determine** 통 결정하다   **relevant** 형 관련 있는   **built-in** 형 붙박이의   **automatically** 부 자동으로   **statistics** 명 《*pl.*》 통계 (자료)   **furthermore** 부 게다가   **virtual** 형 사실상의; *가상의   **available** 형 구할[이용할] 수 있는   **retrieve** 통 되찾아오다, 회수하다; *검색하다   **comment** 명 논평

정답 풀이

②「with + (대)명사 + 분사」

Remove all residual moisture / by drawing it away, /
                                     by v-ing: …함으로써
남아있는 모든 습기를 제거해라   그것을 빨아냄으로써
with a vacuum cleaner holding(→ held) / over the affected areas /
with + (대)명사 + v-ed: …가 ~된 채로   과거분사
진공청소기가 들린 채로   영향을 받은 부분 위로
for up to twenty minutes.
    전치사(…까지)
    20분 정도까지

➡ '…가 ~한[된] 채로'라는 의미의「with + (대)명사 + 분사」구문으로, (대)명사와 분사의 관계가 능동이면 현재분사를, 수동이면 과거분사를 써야 한다. 의미상 진공청소기가 '들린 채로'라는 수동의 의미가 적절하므로 현재분사 holding을 과거분사인 held로 고쳐야 한다.

친절한 오답 풀이

① try v-ing

If you want to suck the liquid / out of the inner parts of the phone, /
                                 …에서(= from)
당신이 물을 빨아내고자 한다면   전화기의 내부 부품에서
try using a vacuum cleaner.
try v-ing: (시험 삼아) …해보다
진공청소기를 사용해 보아라

➡ 문맥상 진공청소기를 '사용해 보라'라는 의미이므로 동사 try 뒤에 동명사 using이 오는 것이 어법상 바르다. try to-v는 '…하려고 노력하다'라는 의미이다.

③ 「get + 목적어 + 목적격보어(분사)」

> This way / you can completely dry out your phone / and
> ···을 말리다
> 이리하여　　　당신은 완전히 당신의 전화기를 말릴 수 있다
> get it working in thirty minutes.
> get + 목적어 + v-ing: ···가 ~하게 하다
> 그리고 그것을 삼십분 안에 작동시킬 수 있다

➡ 동사 get은 '···하게 하다'라는 뜻으로, 뒤에 오는 목적어와 목적격보어의 관계가 능동이면 목적격보어로 현재분사를 쓴다. get의 목적어 it은 앞에 your phone을 지칭하며, 전화기가 '작동하는'이라는 능동의 의미이므로 현재분사 working이 알맞다.

④ 부사

> However, / [unless the exposure to water was extremely short], / it's
> 접속사(···하지 않으면, = if ... not)　　　　　　　　　　　가주어
> 하지만　　　물에 노출된 것이 아주 짧은 것이 아니라면
> not recommended / [to attempt to turn your phone on / this soon].
> 진주어　　　　turn on: ···을 켜다　　부사
> 권장되지 않는다　　전화기를 켜려고 시도하는 것은　　이렇게 빨리

➡ 부사 this가 '이렇게'라는 의미로 부사 soon을 수식하고 있으므로 어법상 바르다.

⑤ 명사적 용법의 to부정사

> The best way, of course, / is [to bring your phone to the customer
> 주어　　　　　　동사　주격보어
> 최선의 방법은, 물론　　전화기를 고객 서비스센터로 가져가는 것이다
> service center / as soon as possible].
> 가능한 한 빨리

➡ to bring 이하는 주격보어의 역할을 하는 명사적 용법의 to부정사로 어법상 바르다.

 구문 분석 Plus

| 2행 | ..., but sometimes if you're **fast enough**, you might be able to save the phone!
➡ 부사 enough는 형용사나 부사를 뒤에서 수식 |
| 14행 | It is **even** worse for the phone.
➡ even: '훨씬'의 의미로 비교급을 강조하는 부사 |

지문 해석

휴대전화를 물에 빠뜨리는 것은 그것을 교체해야 한다는 것을 의미하지만, 때로는 당신이 신속하기만 하다면, 전화기를 살릴 수도 있을 것이다! 당신이 전화기 내부 부품에서 물을 빨아내고자 한다면, 진공청소기를 사용해 보아라. 영향을 받은 부분 위로 20분 정도까지 진공청소기를 든 채로 남아있는 모든 습기를 빨아냄으로써 제거해라. 이리하여 당신은 전화기를 완전히 말릴 수 있고 삼십 분 안에 작동시킬 수 있다. 하지만 물에 노출된 것이 아주 짧은 것이 아니라면, 이렇게 빨리 전화기를 켜려고 시도하는 것은 권장되지 않는다. 진공청소기는 정전기를 유발할 수 있으므로, 진공청소기를 전화기에 너무 가까이 들고 있지 않도록 주의하라. 그것은 전화기에 훨씬 더 좋지 않다. 최선의 방법은 물론 가능한 한 빨리 전화기를 고객 서비스센터로 가져가는 것이다.

어휘

replace 동 바꾸다, 교체하다　suck 동 빨아내다　vacuum cleaner 진공청소기
residual 형 남은, 잔여의　moisture 명 수분, 습기　exposure 명 노출
extremely 부 극도로, 극히　recommend 동 추천하다; *(행동 방침 등을)
권고[권장]하다　attempt 동 시도하다　static electricity 정전기

정답 풀이

(A) 명사를 수식하는 과거분사

> Many African language speakers would consider it absurd /
> 주어　　　　　　　　　　　　　　　　　　가목적어
> 많은 아프리카 언어 사용자들은 불합리하다고 여길 것이다
> {to use a single word [like "cousin"] / to describe both male
> 진목적어1　　　　전치사(···와 같은)　　　남성과 여성 친척 양쪽 모두를 묘사하는 데
> 'cousin'과 같은 한 단어를 사용하는 것을
> and female relatives, / or not to distinguish / [whether
> 접속사　　진목적어2　　　　　whether A or B: A이든 B이든
> 혹은 구별하지 않는 것을
> the person described / describing is related by blood /
> 묘사되는 사람이 혈연관계인지
> to the speaker's father or to his mother]}.
> 말하는 사람의 아버지 혹은 어머니와

➡ 네모는 앞의 명사 the person을 수식하는 분사로, '묘사되는'이라는 수동의 의미이므로 과거분사 described가 알맞다.

(B) 「전치사 + 관계대명사」

> Similarly, how is it possible {to make sense of a situation /
> 가주어　　　진주어　　선행사
> 마찬가지로, 상황을 이해하는 것이 어떻게 가능하겠는가
> [which / in which a single word "uncle" applies to the brother of
> 주어　　　동사
> 'uncle'이라는 한 단어가 아버지의 형제에게 적용되는
> one's father / and to the brother of one's mother]}?
> 그리고 어머니의 형제에게

➡ 네모 이하는 선행사 a situation을 수식하는 관계대명사절로, 네모 뒤에 완전한 절이 이어지므로 「전치사 + 관계대명사」의 형태인 in which가 와야 한다. 관계대명사 뒤에는 불완전한 절이 온다.

(C) 동사의 수 일치

> People of Northern Burma, / [who think in the Jinghpaw language], /
> 주어　　　　　계속적 용법의 주격 관계대명사
> Northern Burma의 사람들은　　　그들은 Jinghpaw 언어로 사고한다
> has / have eighteen basic terms / for describing their kin.
> 동사
> 18개의 기본 용어가 있다　　　　그들의 친족을 묘사하기 위한

➡ 네모는 문장의 동사 자리로, 문장의 주어에 수를 일치시켜야 한다. 문장의 주어(People)가 복수이므로 복수 동사 have가 알맞다.

 구문 분석 Plus

| 7행 | [**To be** unable to distinguish a brother-in-law as the brother of one's wife or the husband of one's sister] **would seem** confusing within the structure of personal relationships [*existing* in many cultures].
➡ To be ... one's sister가 주어, would seem이 동사
➡ existing 이하는 앞의 명사구(the structure of personal relationships)를 수식하는 현재분사구 |

지문 해석

영어 사용자들은 가족 관계를 묘사하기 위한 가장 단순한 체계들 중 하나를 갖고 있다. 많은 아프리카 언어 사용자들은 남성과 여성 친척 양쪽 모두를 묘사하는 데 'cousin'과 같은 한 단어를 사용하는 것, 또는 묘사되는 사람이 말하는 사람의 아버지와 혈연관계인지 아니면 어머니와 혈연관계인지를 구별하지 않는 것을 불합리하다고 여길 것이다. brother-in-law를 아내의 남자 형제인지 여자 형제의 남편인지를 구별할 수 없다는 것은 많은 문화에 존재하는 인간관계의 구조 내에서 혼란스럽게 보일 것이다. 마찬가지로, 'uncle'이라는 한 단어가 아버지의 형제와 어머니의 형제에게 적용되는 상황을 이해하는 것이 어떻게 가능하겠는가? 하와이 언어는 아버지와 아버지의 남자 형제를 지칭하는 데 동일한 용어를 사용한다. Jinghpaw 언어로 사고하는 Northern Burma의 사람들은 그들의 친족을 묘사하기 위한 18개의 기본 용어가 있다. 이 용어 중 어떤 것도 영어로 바로

번역될 수 없다.

describe 통 묘사하다 familial 형 가족의 relationship 명 관계 consider 통 사려하다; *…로 여기다 absurd 형 불합리한 relative 명 친척 distinguish 통 구별하다 confusing 형 혼란스러운 similarly 부 마찬가지로 apply 통 신청하다; *적용되다 term 명 용어, 말 kin 명 친족 translate 통 번역하다

10
정답 ②

정답 풀이

(A) 병렬구조

First, everyone / [who has been summoned to appear at jury duty] /
└─ 주격 관계대명사
우선 모든 사람들은   배심원의 임무로 출두하도록 소집된

must [arrive / ~~have arrived~~] by nine o'clock in the morning /
오전 9시까지 도착해야 한다

and assemble in the jury room.
그리고 배심원실에 모여야 한다

➡ 등위접속사 and가 문장의 동사를 병렬 연결하고 있는 구조로, and 뒤에 동사원형 assemble이 왔으므로 arrive가 오는 것이 적절하다. must have v-ed는 '…했음에 틀림없다'라는 과거 사실에 대한 강한 추측의 의미를 나타내므로 적절하지 않다.

(B) 명사를 수식하는 현재분사

..., the court clerk usually shows a movie / {~~outlined~~ / outlining}
                    주어   동사   ↑   현재분사
법원 서기는 보통 동영상 하나를 보여준다

[what is going to happen throughout the day] / [as the jury is
간접의문문(의문사(주어) + 동사)   전치사(…하는 내내)   접속사(…할 때)
하루 종일 어떤 일이 진행되는지를 대략 설명하는   배심원이 특정 재판에 선정될 때

chosen for a particular trial]}.

➡ 어떤 일이 진행될지 '대략 설명하는'이라는 능동의 의미가 적절하므로 현재분사 outlining이 오는 것이 알맞다.

(C) 간접의문문

..., twenty people are chosen from the jurors in attendance /
                                          참석한
20명의 사람들이 참석한 배심원단에서 선정된다

and are taken to a courtroom / [where a judge describes /
                                          관계부사
그리고 법정으로 이동한다   판사가 설명해주는

[how / ~~what~~] the process is going to work].
간접의문문(의문사 + 주어 + 동사)
어떻게 과정이 진행되는지를

➡ 네모 이하는 동사 describes의 목적어 역할을 하는 간접의문문으로, 의문사 뒤에 완전한 절이 이어지고 있으므로, 의문부사 how가 오는 것이 적절하다. 의문대명사 what 뒤에는 불완전한 절이 온다.

지문 해석

배심원 선정이 진행되는 동안에 일어나는 몇 가지 일들이 있다. 우선 배심원의 임무로 출두하도록 소집된 모든 사람들은 오전 9시까지 도착해야 하고, 배심원실에 모여야 한다. 몇 분 후에, 법원의 서기는 보통 배심원이 특정 재판에 선정될 때 하루 종일 어떤 일이 진행되는지를 대략 설명하는 동영상 하나를 보여준다. 10시쯤에, 20명의 사람들이 참석한 배심원단에서 선정되고 그들은 판사가 어떻게 과정이 진행되는지를 설명해주는 법정으로 이동한다. 약 30분 후에, 10명의 사람들이 배심원석에 앉아서 그 사건의 변호사들로부터 심문을 받도록 요구된다.

jury 명 배심원단 (juror 명 배심원) proceed 통 진행하다 summon 통 (의회 등을) 소집하다 duty 명 의무 assemble 통 모이다, 모으다 court clerk 법원 서기 outline 통 개요를 서술하다 particular 형 특정한 trial 명 재판 attendance 명 출석, 참석 courtroom 명 법정 jury box 배심원석

UNIT 2 to부정사와 동명사

코드 접속하기
pp.18~21

출제코드 1   to부정사(to-v)의 용법

A 1 to avoid 2 to focus 3 to remove
B 1 ○ 2 ➡ to finish

해석과 정답 풀이

STEP 1
1 1) 햇빛을 받으며 너무 많은 시간을 보내는 것은 당신의 피부에 해롭다.
   2) 그는 컴퓨터 프로그래밍 자격증을 따기로 결심했다.
   3) 나의 계획은 다음날 일찍 떠나는 것이다.
2 1) 나를 도와줄 사람이 아무도 없었다.
   2) 그녀는 무대에 오르면 긴장되는 것처럼 보인다.
3 1) 사람들은 그 영화배우를 보기 위해 한 시간 동안 기다렸다.
   2) 그 소년은 너무 어려서 롤러코스터를 탈 수 없었다.

STEP 2
1 그 공무원은 너무 화가 나서 기자들과 말하는 것을 거부했다.
2 아직 오늘 밤에 끝내야 할 보고서가 조금 있다.
3 우리는 가장 저렴한 라디오를 찾기 위해 많은 가게들을 방문했다.

STEP 3
A 1 실수를 피하는 유일한 방법은 반복해서 연습을 하는 것이다.
   ➡ 앞의 명사(The only way)를 수식하는 형용사적 용법의 to부정사 to avoid가 오는 것이 알맞다.
   2 고객들은 그 디자인에 만족해서 우리는 품질에 집중하기로 결정했다.
   ➡ 동사 decide는 to부정사만을 목적어로 취하는 동사이므로 목적어로 to focus가 오는 것이 알맞다.
   3 많은 무료 바이러스 퇴치용 프로그램들이 있으므로, 당신은 컴퓨터 바이러스를 제거하기 위해 전문가를 부를 필요가 없다.
   ➡ 동사 call을 수식하여 목적(…하기 위하여)의 의미를 나타내는 부사적 용법의 to부정사로 to remove가 오는 것이 알맞다.
B 1 내가 삼촌 집에 방문할 때마다, 그는 항상 읽을 많은 만화책들을 가지고 있다.
   ➡ 앞에 나오는 명사(comic books)를 수식하는 형용사적 용법의 to부정사이므로 어법상 적절하다.
   2 마감일을 맞추기 위해서, 나는 학기말 레포트 쓰는 것을 끝내기 위해 내가 할 수 있었던 모든 것을 하기로 결심했다.
   ➡ 앞에 주어와 서술어 역할을 하는 동사(I decided)가 있으므로 동사 finish를 목적을 나타내는 부사적 용법의 to부정사인 to finish로 고쳐야 한다.

출제코드 2   동명사(v-ing)의 특성과 역할

A 1 Cutting 2 touching 3 encouraging
B 1 ○ 2 ➡ promoting 3 ➡ Keeping[To keep]

해석과 정답 풀이

STEP 1
1 1) 독 개구리는 먹이가 되는 것을 피하기 위해 그들의 독을 사용한다.
   2) 그는 마침내 그 문제의 합리적인 해결책을 찾는 데 성공했다.
2 1) 생활 여건을 개선하는 것은 우리 사회와 경제 모두에 중요하다.
   2) 그는 반 친구들 앞에서 혼나는 것을 두려워했다.

STEP 2
1 1) 배움의 기회에 투자하는 것은 당신이 당신 자신에게 줄 수 있는 가장 훌륭한 선물이다.
   2) 그가 좋아했던 유일한 부분은 건물의 모형을 만드는 것이었다.
2 그들은 휴일에 이곳저곳을 여행 다니는 것을 좋아한다.
3 그는 간단한 메시지가 담긴 메모를 곳곳에 붙이는 생각을 떠올렸다.

STEP 3
A 1 관광객의 수를 줄이는 것은 그 비용만큼의 가치가 있는 충분한 혜택을 제공할 것이다.
➡ 명사처럼 문장에서 주어 역할을 하며, 뒤에 목적어(the number of tourists)를 가질 수 있는 동명사 Cutting이 오는 것이 알맞다.

2 심지어 당신이 그렇게 하는 것이 안전하다고 생각할지라도 다친 야생동물들을 만지는 것을 피해라.
➡ 동사 avoid는 동명사만을 목적어로 취하는 동사이므로, 목적어로 동명사 touching이 오는 것이 알맞다.

3 그의 이야기는 항상 아이들이 그들의 창의력을 사용하도록 장려하는 것을 목표로 삼았다.
➡ 앞의 전치사(at)의 목적어 역할을 하며, 뒤에 목적어(children)가 이어지고 있으므로 동명사 encouraging이 오는 것이 알맞다.

B 1 Julie와 그녀의 남편은 둘째 아이를 입양하는 것을 고려하고 있다.
➡ 동사 consider는 동명사만을 목적어로 취하는 동사이므로, 목적어로 동명사 adopting이 오는 것이 알맞다.

2 전통적으로, 지적 재산은 기초 과학을 육성하는 데 큰 역할을 하지 않았다.
➡ 앞의 전치사(in)의 목적어 역할을 하며, 뒤에 목적어(basic science)가 이어지고 있으므로 promote를 동명사 promoting으로 고쳐야 한다.

3 당신이 카메라를 사용하고 있지 않을 때 렌즈를 닫힌 상태로 유지하는 것이 매우 권장된다.
➡ 문장에서 주어 역할을 하며 뒤에 목적어(the lens)가 이어지므로, Keep을 동명사 Keeping이나 to부정사 To keep으로 고쳐야 한다.

출제코드 3 　to부정사(to-v) vs. 동명사(v-ing)

A 1 to brush **2** saying **3** help
B 1 ➡ operating **2** ○ **3** ➡ to driving

해석과 정답 풀이

STEP 1
1 무대 위의 모든 아이들이 함께 노래하기 시작했다.
2 1) 그녀는 퇴근 후 6시에 그를 데리러 갈 것을 기억했다.
　2) 그는 그녀에게 메시지를 보내봤지만, 그녀는 그것에 응답하지 않았다.
3 1) 새의 깃털은 짝을 유혹하는 데 쓰일 수 있다.
　2) 그는 공개 회의에서 발표를 하는 데 익숙하다.

STEP 2
1 1) 당신이 늪에 빠진다면, 가라앉는 것이 멈출 때까지 움직이지 마라.
　2) 그는 일전에 같은 말을 한 것이 기억났다.
2 1) 그들은 젓가락으로 먹는 것에 익숙하지 않았다.
　2) 초음파는 종종 임신부의 아기를 검진하는 데 사용된다.

STEP 3
A 1 당신이 양치질을 할 때, 또한 당신의 혀를 닦는 것도 잊지 마라.
➡ '혀를 닦을 것을 잊다'라는 의미이므로 to부정사인 to brush가 오는 것이 알맞다.
2 그가 그녀를 보았을 때 그는 그의 여자친구에게 그렇게 심한 말을 한 것을 후회했다.
➡ '말을 한 것을 후회하다'라는 의미이므로 동명사인 saying이 오는 것이 알맞다.
3 이 프로그램은 대학 생활에 친숙하지 않은 학생들을 돕는 데 사용될 수 있다.
➡ '돕는 데 사용되다'라는 의미이므로 to부정사인 to help가 오는 것이 알맞다.
B 1 그 기계는 많은 소음을 냈고, 마침내 작동하던 것을 완전히 멈추었다.
➡ 문맥상 '작동하던 것을 멈추다'라는 의미이므로 to operate를 동명사 operating으로 고쳐야 한다.
2 만약 당신이 당신의 휴대폰에서 액체를 빨아들이고 싶다면, 진공청소기를 사용해보아라.
➡ 동사 try는 to부정사와 동명사 둘 다 목적어로 취할 수 있지만, '(시험 삼아) …해보다'라는 의미이므로 동명사 using이 오는 것이 알맞다.
3 대부분의 운전자들은 악천후에 운전하는 것에 익숙하지 않다.
➡ be used 뒤에는 to부정사와 to v-ing 모두 올 수 있지만, 문맥상 '…하는 데 익숙하다'라는 의미이므로 to drive를 to driving으로 고쳐야 한다.

기출예제 Q1　　정답 ②　　정답률 45%

정답 풀이

② 부사적 용법의 to부정사

Remember (that) those items have already travelled hundreds of
명사절 접속사 that 생략　　주어　　동사
그러한 품목들이 이미 수백 마일을 이동했다는 것을 기억하라
miles / reach(→ to reach) the shelves / and [once they go into
　　부사적 용법의 to부정사(목적)　　접속사 = those items
　　선반에 도달하기 위해　　　그리고 일단 그것들이 버려지게 되면
waste] / they start a new carbon mile journey.
　　그것들은 새로운 탄소 마일 여정을 시작한다는 것을

➡ 앞에 동사 have travelled가 있으므로 동사 reach는 올 수 없다. 문맥상 '…하기 위해서'라는 목적의 의미를 나타내는 부사적 용법의 to부정사 형태인 to reach가 되어야 한다.

친절한 오답 풀이

① 분사구문

[Once an item is past that date] / it goes into the waste stream, /
접속사　　　　　　주어 동사
일단 어떤 품목이 그 기한을 지나면　　폐기물 흐름으로 들어가고
[further increasing its carbon footprint].
결과를 나타내는 분사구문
이는 그것의 탄소 발자국을 더욱더 증가시킨다

➡ increasing은 결과를 나타내는 분사구문의 분사이다. 앞 절 전체가 분사의 의미상 주어이며 주어와 분사의 의미상 관계가 능동이므로 현재분사가 바르게 쓰였다.

③ 동사의 수 일치

But we all make our own judgement about sell-by dates; / those
　　　　　판단을 내리다　　　　　　　　　　　　　　주어↑
그러나 우리 모두는 판매 유효 기한에 대해 자신만의 판단을 내린다
[brought up during the Second World War] / are often scornful
　　　과거분사구　　　　　　　　　　　　동사
제2차 세계대전 중에 자란 사람들은　　　끔찍한 낭비를 자주 경멸한다
of the terrible waste / they believe / [(which/that) such caution
　　　　　　　　　　삽입절　　　　　목적격 관계대명사 생략
　　　　　　　　그들이 생각하기에 그러한 경고가 조장하는
encourages].

➡ 주어는 뒤에 과거분사구의 수식을 받고 있는 those로 복수형이므로 복수 동사 are는 적절하다.

④ 접속사 that

　　　　　　　　　　　　　　　접속사를 생략하지 않은 분사구문
The manufacturer of the food has a view / [when making or
식품 제조업자는 관점을 가지고 있다 ┗━━ 동격 ━━┛　무엇인가를 만들거나
growing something] [that by the time the product reaches the
재배할 때　　　　동격의 접속사　　제품이 선반에 도달할 때에는
shelves / it has already been travelling for so many days and
　　　　have been v-ing: 현재완료 진행형
　　　　그것은 이미 매우 오랫동안 그리고 아마도 상당한 거리를 이동해 왔다는
possibly many miles].

➡ 앞의 명사구 a view와 동격을 이루는 명사절을 이끄는 접속사로, 뒤에 완전한 절이 이어지고 있으므로 어법상 바르다.

⑤ 접속사

But [whether it becomes toxic] / is something [(that/which) each
　　　　　주어　　　　　　동사 ┗━━━━┛　목적격 관계대명사
그러나 그것이 유독해지는지는　　　각 개인이 결정할 수 있는 것이다
individual can decide].

➡ 문장의 주어 역할을 하는 명사절을 이끌고 있으며, '~인지'로 해석되므로 접속사 whether는 어법상 바르다.

지문 해석

우리가 판매 유효 기한에 따라 움직인다는 것은 의심할 여지가 거의 없다. 일단 어떤 품목이 그 기한을 지나면 폐기물 흐름으로 들어가고, 이는 그것의 탄소 발자국을 더욱더 증가시킨다. 그러한 품목들이 선반에 도달하기 위해 이미 수백 마일을 이동했고 일단 그것들이 버려지게 되면 그것들은 새로운 탄소 마일 여정을 시작한다는 것을 기억하라. 그러나 우리 모두는 판매 유효 기한에 대해 자신만의 판단을 내린다. 가령, 제2차 세계대전 중에 자란 사람들은 그들이 생각하기에 그러한 경고가 조장하는 끔찍한 낭비를 자주 경멸한다. 식품 제조업자는 무엇인가를 만들거나 재배할 때 제품이 선반에 도달할 때에는 그것은 이미 매우 오랫동안 그리고 아마도 상당한 거리를 이동해 왔다는 관점을 가지고 있다. 그래서 제조업자는 제품이 이를테면 90일 이내에는 무리 없이 소비될 수 있고 90일에서 이동에 필요한 많은 날들을 뺀 것이 판매 유효 기한이 된다고 결정한다. 그러나 그것이 유독해지는지는 각 개인이 결정할 수 있는 것이다. 큰 묶음의 상하기 쉬운 제품을 사지 않는 것이 이치에 맞는 것으로 보이겠지만, 상하지 않는 품목들의 경우에는 비용 효율이 높아질 수도 있다.

어휘

carbon footprint 탄소 발자국(온실 효과를 유발하는 이산화탄소의 배출량)
manufacturer 몡 제조자   **reasonably** 뷔 합리적으로; *무리없이   **toxic** 혱
유독성의   **make sense** 타당하다   **perishable** 혱 잘 상하는   **cost-effective** 혱
비용 효율이 높은

코드 공략하기

pp.22~25

| 01 ④ | 02 ③ | 03 ③ | 04 ⑤ | 05 ② | 06 ④ | 07 ⑤ | 08 ③ |
| 09 ④ | 10 ⑤ |

---

01   정답 ④   정답률 60%

정답 풀이

④ 부사적 용법의 to부정사

Skate parks provide the safe environment without cars /
주어   동사   전치사(…없이)
스케이트 공원은 차가 없는 안전한 환경을 제공한다
keep(→ to keep) your board skills improved.
부사적 용법의 to부정사(결과), keep + 목적어 + v-ed: …을 ~되게 하다
(그 결과) 당신의 보드 기술이 지속적으로 향상되도록 해준다

➡ 문장의 주어와 동사(Skate parks provide)가 있으므로 밑줄 친 keep은 동사가 될 수 없다. 그러므로 keep 이하를 부사구 역할을 하는 부사적 용법의 to부정사로 고쳐야 한다.

▌친절한 오답 풀이▐

① 동명사구를 수식하는 현재분사

They are almost the same / in that the actions include riding and
…라는 점에서, that은 접속사
그것들은 거의 똑같다   동작이 타는 것과 기술을 구사하는 것을 포함한다는 점에서
performing tricks / [using a board].
현재분사
보드를 사용하여

➡ 밑줄 친 using은 앞에 나온 동명사구(riding ... tricks)를 수식하는 분사로, 수식을 받는 동명사구와 의미상 능동 관계이므로 현재분사 using을 쓰는 것이 어법상 바르다.

② 비교급을 강조하는 부사

However, the difference / is {that in skateboarding, the asphalt
명사절(보어)을 이끄는 접속사
그러나, 차이점은   스케이트보드에서 아스팔트가
tends to hurt much more than snow / [when you fall on the ground]}.
tend to-v: …하는 경향이 있다   접속사
눈보다 훨씬 더 다치게 하는 경향이 있다는 것이다   당신이 땅에 넘어질 때

➡ much는 '훨씬'의 의미로 뒤에 오는 비교급 more를 수식하여 비교의 의미를 강조하는 부사로 어법상 바르다.

---

③ 병렬구조

Be sure to wear protective equipment / such as a helmet, wrist
be sure to-v: (명령문으로 쓰여) 반드시 …해라   전치사(…와 같은)
반드시 보호장비를 착용해라   헬멧, 손목 보호대,
guards, and elbow pads / [even if your friends point and laugh].
접속사(비록 …일지라도)   동사1 접속사 동사2
그리고 팔꿈치 패드와 같은   비록 당신의 친구들이 손가락질하고 웃더라도

➡ even if 절 안에 등위접속사 and가 동사 point와 laugh를 병렬 연결하고 있으므로, 동사 point와 대등한 laugh는 어법상 바르다.

⑤ 관계부사

Also, a long downward road without cross streets / could be
또한, 교차로가 없는 긴 내리막길은
the perfect area / [where you practice basic skills].
관계부사
완벽한 장소가 될 수 있다   당신이 기본 기술을 연습하는

➡ 선행사(the perfect area)가 장소를 나타내고, 뒤에 완전한 절이 이어지고 있으므로 관계부사 where는 어법상 바르다.

지문 해석

스케이트보드 타기는 눈이 없을 때 스노보드 타기를 대체할 최선의 방법들 중 하나이다. 그것들은 동작이 보드를 사용하여 타는 것과 기술을 구사하는 것을 포함한다는 점에서 거의 똑같다. 그러나 차이점은 스케이트보드에서 당신이 땅에 넘어질 때 아스팔트가 눈보다 훨씬 더 다치게 하는 경향이 있다는 것이다. 비록 당신의 친구들이 손가락질하고 웃더라도, 헬멧, 손목 보호대, 그리고 팔꿈치 패드와 같은 보호장비를 반드시 착용해라. 스케이트 공원은 차가 없는 안전한 환경을 제공하여 당신의 보드 기술이 지속적으로 향상되도록 해준다. 또한, 교차로가 없는 긴 내리막길은 당신이 기본 기술을 연습하는 완벽한 장소가 될 수 있다.

어휘

replace 됭 대체하다   **include** 됭 포함하다   **difference** 몡 차이점   **protective**
혱 보호하는   **equipment** 몡 장비   **wrist guard** 손목 보호대   **elbow pad**
팔꿈치 보호대   **environment** 몡 환경   **improve** 됭 향상시키다   **downward** 혱
내리막의   **cross street** 교차로

---

02   정답 ③

정답 풀이

(A) 명사적 용법의 to부정사

Legend / has it {that, during the Chinese Tang dynasty, a poor public
have it (that ...): …라고 주장하다
전설은   중국 당 왕조에 한 가난한 관리가 너무 정직해서
official was so honest / [that he refused taking / to take bribes]}.
so + 형용사 + that ...: 너무 ~해서 …하다
뇌물 수수를 거부했다고 한다

➡ 동사 refuse는 to부정사를 목적어로 취하므로 to take가 오는 것이 알맞다.

(B) 수동형 분사구문

[(Being) Knowing / Known as "the cow of China,"] / tofu's
Being이 생략된 분사구문(= As tofu's protein is known as ...), be known as: …로 알려지다
'중국의 소'로 알려져 있는 것처럼   두부의
protein is similar / in quality to that of meat.
be similar to: …와 비슷하다   = protein
단백질은 비슷하다   질적인 면에서 고기의 그것과

➡ 네모 부분은 분사구문의 분사로, 생략된 주어는 주절의 주어(tofu's protein)와 같다. 주어와 분사가 의미상 수동 관계이므로, 과거분사 known이 오는 것이 알맞다.

(C) 관계부사

Soy milk is thickened with a mineral salt, / [forming curds] — /
동시동작을 나타내는 분사구문(= as soy milk forms ...)
두유는 무기염을 넣으면 걸쭉해진다   응고물을 만들면서
that's (the reason) why / ~~what~~ tofu's other popular name is "bean
선행사 생략
그것이 두부의 다른 유명한 이름이 'bean curd'인 이유이다
curd]."

➡ 뒤에 완전한 절이 이어지고 있으므로 관계부사 why가 오는 것이 알맞다. 관계대명사 what 뒤에는 불완전한 절이 이어진다.

지문 해석

전설에 따르면 중국 당 왕조에 한 가난한 관리가 너무 정직해서 뇌물 수수를 거부했다고 한다. 그는 가족을 먹일 고기를 살 수 없었다. 그래서 그는 두부를 발명했다. 오늘날까지 어떤 중국인들은 정직한 국가 관리들을 '두부 공무원'이라 부른다. '중국의 소'로 알려져 있는 것처럼, 두부의 단백질은 질적인 면에서 고기의 단백질과 비슷하다. 그러나 두부는 만들어지는 방식에 있어서 실제로는 치즈와 더 유사하다. 두유는 무기염을 넣으면 응고물을 만들면서 걸쭉해지는데, 그것이 두부의 다른 유명한 이름이 'bean curd'인 이유이다.

어휘

legend 명 전설   dynasty 명 왕조   public official 공무원   refuse 동 거절하다
bribe 명 뇌물   feed 동 먹이다, 먹여 살리다   protein 명 단백질   soy milk 두유
thicken 동 걸쭉해지다   mineral salt 무기염   curd 명 응유(우유가 산이나 효소에 의하여 응고된 것)   bean curd 두부

03   정답 ③   정답률 60%

정답 풀이

③ 준동사의 명사적 성질

The only part of his work [(that) he enjoyed] / was made
주어   목적격 관계대명사 생략 동사
그의 일 중 그가 좋아했던 유일한 부분은
(→ making) models of buildings / to illustrate proposals.
주격보어   형용사적 용법의 to부정사
건물 모형을 만드는 것이었다   계획안을 설명할

➡ 문장의 주어는 The only ... work이고 동사가 was로, 뒤에 주격보어가 필요한 문장이다. 따라서 밑줄 친 made를 명사처럼 보어 역할을 할 수 있는 동명사 making으로 고쳐야 한다.

친절한 오답 풀이

① 수동형 분사구문

{When (being) asked / [what he wanted to be]}, / he would say, /
분사구문(= When he was asked) 간접의문문(의문사+주어+동사) ···하곤 했다(과거의 습관)
질문을 받으면   무엇이 되고 싶은지   그는 말하곤 했다
"I want to be a model-maker or run a store / [that sells model kits]."
주격 관계대명사
저는 모형 제작자가 되거나 가게를 운영하고 싶어요   모형 조립 세트를 파는

➡ 밑줄 친 asked는 때를 나타내는 분사구문의 분사로, 의미를 명확하게 하기 위해 앞에 접속사를 남겨두었다. 생략된 주어는 주절의 주어(he)와 같은데, 그가 질문을 '받을' 때라는 수동의 의미이므로 과거분사 asked가 알맞다.

② 도치구문

He was not very good at his work, / nor did he seem to improve.
be good at: ···에 능숙하다, 잘하다   부정어 주어 동사
그는 일을 그리 잘 하지 못했으며   나아지는 것 같지도 않았다

➡ nor와 같은 부정어가 문장의 첫머리에 오면, 주어와 동사의 어순이 바뀌는 도치가 일어나는데, 동사가 일반동사일 경우 주어 앞에 do동사를 써서 시제를 나타낸다. 주절의 시제가 과거이므로 과거형 did를 쓰는 것이 어법상 바르다.

④ 형용사적 용법의 to부정사

..., one of his former employers / did offer Alvin
one of + 복수 명사: ··· 중의 하나   동사를 강조하는 조동사
그의 이전 고용주 중 한 명이   Alvin에게 계약을 제안했다
a contract / to take on his firm's model-making projects /
형용사적 용법의 to부정사, take on: ···을 맡다
자기 회사의 모형 제작 업무를 맡는
on a freelance basis.
프리랜서로

➡ 밑줄 친 to take는 앞에 나온 명사(a contract)를 수식하는 형용사적 용법의 to부정사로 어법상 바르다.

⑤ 관계대명사 what

He does [what he loves], / and he earns a good living.
관계대명사(···하는 것)   earn a living: 생활비를 벌다
그는 자신이 좋아하는 것을 하고   그는 충분한 생활비를 번다

➡ what은 선행사를 포함한 관계대명사로, 명사절을 이끌어 문장에서 주어, 목적어, 보어의 역할을 한다. 밑줄 친 관계대명사 what은 동사 does의 목적어 역할을 하는 명사절을 이끌고 있으므로 어법상 바르다.

 구문 분석 Plus

10행 When a recession hit, Alvin was the first **to be fired**.
➡ 앞에 나온 명사(the first)를 수식하는 형용사적 용법의 to부정사로, 명사와 수동 관계이므로 수동태(to be v-ed)로 쓰임

지문 해석

어린 시절부터 Alvin은 열렬한 모형 제작자였다. 그는 모형 자동차, 모형 철로 설비, 모형 거리 풍경 등을 만들었다. 무엇이 되고 싶은지 질문을 받으면, "저는 모형 제작자가 되거나 모형 조립 세트를 파는 가게를 운영하고 싶어요."라고 말하곤 했다. 그러나 결국 Alvin은 건축이라는 '현실적인' 직업을 선택했다. 그는 일을 그리 잘 하지 못했으며, 나아지는 것 같지도 않았다. 그의 일 중 그가 좋아했던 유일한 부분은 계획안을 설명할 건물 모형을 만드는 것이었다. 불경기가 닥치자, 그는 제일 먼저 해고되었다. 다행히도, 그의 이전 고용주 중 한 명이 Alvin에게 프리랜서로 자기 회사의 모형 제작 업무를 맡는 계약을 제안했다. 이제 Alvin은 그 지역의 일류 건축사들을 위해 모형을 만든다. 그는 자신이 좋아하는 일을 하면서 충분한 생활비를 번다.

어휘

keen 형 열정적인, 열렬한   layout 명 (건물 등의) 배치   run 동 달리다; *운영하다
kit 명 조립 용품 세트   eventually 부 마침내   career 명 직업   architecture 명
건축 (architectural 형 건축학[술]의)   improve 동 개선되다, 나아지다   illustrate
동 (도해 등으로) 설명하다   proposal 명 제안, 계획안   recession 명 불경기   fire
동 해고하다   contract 명 계약   firm 명 회사   leading 형 선두적인

04   정답 ⑤   정답률 60%

정답 풀이

(A) 동사의 수 일치

Here are two things / [(which/that) you may have heard about bad
선행사   목적격 관계대명사 생략 may have v-ed: ···했을지도 모른다
여기 두 가지가 있다   당신이 입 냄새에 대해 들어봤을지도 모르는
breath] / [that is / are not true].
two things를 선행사로 하는 주격 관계대명사
사실이 아닌

➡ 네모 앞의 that은 two things를 선행사로 하는 주격 관계대명사이고, 네모는 주격 관계대명사절의 동사이다. 주격 관계대명사절의 동사는 선행사에 수를 일치시켜야 하므로 복수형인 are가 알맞다.

(B) 접속사 that

The truth is [[that / ~~what~~] most people only brush their teeth /
　　　　　　　 　접속사
사실은 대부분의 사람들이 오직 이를 닦는다는 것인데
for 30 to 45 seconds], / which just doesn't solve the problem.
30~45초 정도만　　　　앞의 절을 선행사로 하는 계속적 용법의 주격 관계대명사
　　　　　　　　　　　　그것은 문제를 해결하지 않는다

➡ 주격보어 역할을 하는 명사절을 이끌고 있고, 뒤에 완전한 절이 이어지고 있으므로
접속사 that이 알맞다.

(C) remember to-v

Remember / [~~brushing~~ / to brush] your tongue, too.
기억해라　　　　당신의 혀를 닦는 것 또한

➡ 동사 remember는 to부정사(…할 것을)와 동명사(…한 것을)를 모두 목적어로 취할
수 있는데, 이 문장에서는 '닦을 것을' 기억하라는 의미이므로 to brush가 알맞다.

 구문 분석 Plus

7행
Secondly, **as long as** you brush your teeth, [you are said not
to have bad breath].
➡ as long as: …하기만 하면
➡ they **say that you** do not have bad breath (원문)
　→ **you are said** not to have bad breath (that절의 주어를
　　수동태의 주어로 한 문장)

지문 해석

입 냄새를 해결하는 것에 대해 많은 속설들이 있다. 당신이 입 냄새에 대해 들어봤을지도
모르는, 사실이 아닌 두 가지가 여기 있다. 그 중 하나는 구강청결제가 입 냄새를 사라지게
한다는 것이다. 구강청결제는 단지 일시적으로만 입 냄새를 없애준다. 당신이 구강
청결제를 그래도 사용한다면, 살균 성분이 있고 치석을 줄여주는 것을 찾아라. 둘째,
당신이 양치질을 하기만 하면 입 냄새가 나지 않는다고 하는 것이다. 사실은 대부분의
사람들이 오직 30~45초 정도만 이를 닦는데, 그것은 문제를 해결하지 않는다. 이를
충분히 청결하게 하기 위해서, 당신은 적어도 하루 두 번 최소한 2분간 양치질을 해야
한다. 혀를 닦는 것 또한 기억해라.

어휘

myth 명 신화; *근거 없는 속설　**take care of** …을 돌보다; *…을 처리하다
bad breath 입 냄새　**mouthwash** 명 구강청결제　**get rid of** …을 제거하다
temporarily 부 일시적으로　**plaque** 명 플라크, 치석　**sufficiently** 부 충분히
at least 적어도　**tongue** 명 혀

05　　정답 ②　　정답률 43%

정답 풀이

② 준동사의 명사적 성질

<u>Learn(→ Learning[To learn])</u> how to choose from alternatives
　　　주어　　　　　　　　　　　　how to-v: …하는 법
대안 중에서 선택하고 결정을 내리는 방법을 배우는 것은
and (to) make a decision / requires / not only good personal
접속사 and에 의해 to choose와　　동사　　not only A but also B: A뿐만 아니라 B도
병렬 연결됨　　　　　　　　　필요로 한다　　훌륭한 개인적 가치관뿐만 아니라
values, / but also knowledge competence / in the business area of
지식 역량도　　　　　　　　　　　　관계가 있는 비즈니스 분야의
concern.

➡ 밑줄 친 부분은 동사 requires의 주어 역할을 하는 부분이다. 따라서 명사처럼 주어
역할을 할 수 있는 동명사 Learning이나 to부정사 To learn으로 고쳐야 한다.

① 수동태

An ethical issue is an identifiable problem, situation, or
윤리적 문제는 식별 가능한 문제, 상황 또는 기회이다
opportunity /{that requires a person to choose from among
　　　　　　　　주격 관계대명사 require A to-v: A가 …하는 것을 요구하다
　　　　　　　　여러 가지 행동들 가운데에서 한 사람이 선택하기를 요구하는
several actions / [that may be evaluated as right or wrong, ethical
　　　　　　　　　주격 관계대명사 be v-ed: 수동태
　　　　　　　　　옳거나 그르다고, 윤리적 또는 비윤리적이라고 평가될 수 있는
or unethical]}.

➡ 밑줄 친 부분은 주격 관계대명사절의 동사 자리이며 선행사 several actions가 주어
역할을 하고 있다. several actions는 평가되는 대상이므로 수동태 be evaluated는
어법상 바르다.

③ 병렬구조

Employees also need to know / when to rely on their
　　　　　　need to-v: …해야 한다　when to-v: 언제 …할지
또한 직원들은 알아야 한다　　　　언제 자신이 속한
organizations' policies and codes of ethics / or (to) have
　　　　　　　　　　　　　　　　접속사 or에 의해 to rely on과 병렬 연결됨
조직의 정책과 윤리 강령에 의존할지　　　　혹은
discussions with co-workers or managers / on appropriate conduct.
　　　　　　　　　　　　　　　　　　전치사(…에 관해)
언제 동료 또는 관리자와 논의해야 할지를　　　적절한 행동에 대해

➡ when to rely on 구문에서 to rely on과 접속사 or로 병렬 연결된 구조이며 이때
to는 반복을 피하므로 주로 생략되므로 동사 have는 어법상 바르다.

④ 주격 관계대명사

Ethical decision making is not always easy / because there are
　　　　　　　　　　'언제나 …인 것은 아니다'라는 의미의 부분부정
윤리적 의사결정이 항상 쉬운 것은 아니다　　　　　　　왜냐하면
always gray areas [that create dilemmas], / no matter how
　　　　　　　　　　주격 관계대명사　　　　= however(어떤 식으로 …하든)
딜레마를 만드는 회색 영역이 늘 있기 때문이다　　결정이 어떻게 내려지든
decisions are made.

➡ that은 앞의 명사 gray areas를 수식하는 관계대명사절에서 주어 역할을 하는 주격
관계대명사로 어법상 바르다.

⑤ 접속사

Such questions require the decision maker to evaluate the ethics
　　　　　　　　　require A to-v: A가 …할 것을 요구하다
그러한 질문은 의사결정자가 자신이 선택한 윤리를 평가하기를 요구한다
　　　　　　　　　　　　　　　　whether to-v: …할 것인지
of his or her choice / and (to) decide whether to ask for guidance.
접속사 and에 의해 to evaluate와 병렬 연결됨
그리고 지침을 요청할 것인지 말지의 여부를 결정할 것을 요구한다

➡ 「whether to-v」는 '…할 것인지'의 의미로 decide의 목적어 역할을 하므로 어법상
적절하다.

지문 해석

윤리적 문제를 인식하는 것은 비즈니스 윤리를 이해하는 데 가장 중요한 단계이다. 윤리적
문제는 옳거나 그르다고, 윤리적 또는 비윤리적이라고 평가될 수 있는 여러 가지 행동들
가운데에서 한 사람이 선택하기를 요구하는 식별 가능한 문제, 상황 또는 기회이다.
대안 중에서 선택하고 결정을 내리는 방법을 배우는 것은 훌륭한 개인적 가치관 뿐만
아니라 관계가 있는 비즈니스 분야에 대한 지식 역량도 필요로 한다. 또한 직원들은 언제
자신이 속한 조직의 정책과 윤리 강령에 의존할지 혹은 언제 동료 또는 관리자와 적절한
행동에 대해 논의해야 할지를 알아야 한다. 윤리적 의사결정이 항상 쉬운 것은 아닌데,
왜냐하면 결정이 어떻게 내려지든 딜레마를 만드는 회색 영역이 늘 있기 때문이다. 예를
들어, 직원은 시간 훔치기를 하는 동료에 대해 보고해야 하는가? 판매원은 고객에게
프레젠테이션을 할 때 어떤 제품의 안전 상태가 좋지 않다는 기록에 대한 사실을 생략해야
하는가? 그러한 질문은 의사결정자가 자신이 선택한 윤리를 평가하여 지침을 요청할
것인지 말지의 여부를 결정할 것을 요구한다.

ethical 혱 윤리적인   identifiable 혱 식별 가능한   evaluate 통 평가하다
alternative 몡 대안   values 몡 (pl.) 가치관   competence 몡 능력, 역량
policy 몡 정책   dilemma 몡 딜레마, 진퇴양난   time theft 시간 훔치기(근무하지
않은 시간에 대하여 급여를 타는 행위)

06　　　　정답 ④　　　정답률 49%

정답 풀이

④ 「전치사 + 동명사」

It covered every situation, / from constructing boats, huts, and
그것은 모든 상황을 다루었다　　　　　　배, 오두막, 그리고 텐트를 빠르게 만들기부터
from A to B: A부터 B까지
tents in a hurry / to catch(→ to catching) fish without a line.
　　　　　　　　　　낚싯줄 없이 물고기 잡기까지

➡ 「from A to B」 구문에서 from과 to는 전치사로 각각 뒤에 목적어가 와야 한다. 전치사
to의 목적어 역할을 하면서 뒤에 목적어(fish)를 가져야 하므로, to catch를 「전치사 +
동명사」 형태인 to catching으로 고쳐야 한다.

친절한 오답 풀이

① 분사구문

If you ever feel ill / [when traveling in remote foreign parts], /
당신이 속이 안 좋다면　　　　접속사가 생략되지 않은 분사구문(= when you travel ...)
　　　　　　　　　　　　　외국의 외진 지역을 여행할 때
just drop some gunpowder into a glass of warm, soapy water,
약간의 화약을 따뜻한 비눗물 한 잔에 넣고 그것을 마셔라
and swallow it.

➡ 접속사가 남아있는 분사구문으로, 생략된 주어는 앞 절의 주어(you)와 같다. 주어와
분사가 의미상 능동 관계이므로 현재분사 traveling이 오는 것이 알맞다.

② 명사를 수식하는 과거분사

That was the advice of Francis Galton / in a book [called *The Art*
　　　　　　　　　　　　　　　　　　　　　　　　　　　과거분사
그것은 Francis Galton의 조언이었다　　　여행의 기술이라 불리는 책에서
of Travel].

➡ called 이하는 앞의 명사 a book을 수식하는 분사구로, 명사와 분사가 의미상 수동
관계이므로 과거분사 called가 오는 것이 알맞다.

③ 병렬구조

Well, the tar [scraped out of a tobacco pipe and applied on the
　　　　　　　　　과거분사　　　　　　　　　접속사　과거분사
담뱃대에서 긁어내어 피부에 바른 타르는
skin] / relieves the pain.
　　　　　　고통을 줄여준다

➡ 등위접속사 and가 명사 the tar를 수식하는 과거분사를 병렬 연결하고 있으므로, 앞의
과거분사 scraped와 대등한 과거분사 applied가 오는 것이 알맞다.

⑤ 「의문사 + to-v」

It told readers / [how to find firewood in a rainstorm (under the
동사　간접목적어　직접목적어1, how to-v: …하는 법
그것은 독자들에게 알려주었다　　폭우 속에서 땔나무를 찾는 법(나무 뿌리 아래서)을
roots of a tree)] / and {where to put your clothes [when it's raining] /
　　　　　　　　　　접속사　직접목적어2, where to-v: 어디서 …할지
그리고 비가 올 때 어디에 옷을 두어야 할지를
so that they don't get wet (just take them off and sit on them)}.
목적을 나타내는 접속사(…하도록)
그것들이 젖지 않도록 (그냥 옷을 벗어서 깔고 앉는다)

➡ 「의문사 + to-v」는 명사적 용법의 to부정사 구문으로 '(의문사) …할지'의 의미이다.
where to put 이하는 4형식 동사 told의 두 번째 직접목적어로 어법상 바르다.

지문 해석

당신이 외국의 외진 지역을 여행할 때 속이 안 좋다면, 약간의 화약을 따뜻한 비눗물 한
잔에 넣고 그것을 마셔라. 그것은 *여행의 기술*이라고 불리는 책에서 Francis Galton의
조언이었다. 벌에 쏘였다면? 담뱃대에서 긁어내어 피부에 바른 타르가 통증을 줄여준다.
Galton의 책은 베스트셀러가 되었다. 그것은 배, 오두막, 그리고 텐트를 빠르게
만들기부터 낚싯줄 없이 물고기 잡기까지 모든 상황을 다루었다. 그것은 독자들에게 폭우
속에서 땔나무를 찾는 법(나무 뿌리 아래서)과 비가 올 때 옷을 젖지 않게 어디에 두어야
할지(그냥 옷을 벗어서 깔고 앉는다)를 알려주었다.

remote 혱 외진, 외딴   foreign 혱 외국의   gunpowder 몡 화약   soapy water
비눗물   swallow 통 삼키다   art 몡 예술; *기술   sting 통 (곤충 등이) 쏘다, 찌르다
scrape 통 벗기다   tobacco pipe 담뱃대   apply 통 적용하다; *바르다   relieve 통
완화하다   construct 통 건설하다   firewood 몡 땔나무   rainstorm 몡 폭풍우

07　　　　정답 ⑤　　　정답률 56%

정답 풀이

(A) 「전치사 + 동명사」

In addition to its is / being a beneficial cardiovascular exercise, /
… 이외에도　　　동명사의 의미상의 주어
그것이 유익한 심혈관 운동인 것 이외에도
Double Dutch also improves coordination and quickness.
Double Dutch는 조정능력과 민첩성 또한 향상시킨다

➡ In addition to의 to는 전치사로, 뒤에는 전치사의 목적어의 역할을 하는 동명사
being이 와야 한다.

(B) 「전치사 + 동명사」, 동명사의 동사적 성질

..., / {because it requires three to four participants / [working
　　　　　　　　　　　　　　　　　　　　　　　　　　　현재분사
　　　그것은 서너 명의 참가자가 필요하기 때문에　　　함께 긴밀하게 움직이는
closely together]}, / it is also great for development / developing
　　　　　　　　　　　　　　　　　　　　　　전치사
　　　　　　　　　　　그것은 아이들 사이의 협력하는 기술을 개발하는 데도 좋다
cooperative skills among children.
동명사의 목적어

➡ 전치사 for의 목적어 역할을 하면서 명사 cooperative skills를 목적어로 취할 수
있는 동명사 developing이 오는 것이 알맞다.

(C) 관계부사

At the most advanced levels, / Double Dutch is also being done /
　　　　　　　　　　　　　　　　　　　be being v-ed: 진행형 수동태
최상급 수준에서　　　　　　　　　　Double Dutch는 또한 행해지고 있다
as **an extreme competition sport** / {where / which groups of kids
전치사(…로)　　　　　　　　　　　　　　　　관계부사
격렬한 스포츠 경기로　　　　　　　　　아이들 무리가
are doing high-energy dancing routines / [that are truly amazing]}.
많은 에너지를 요하는 춤 동작을 하는　　　　　　주격 관계대명사
　　　　　　　　　　　　　　　　　　정말로 놀라운

➡ 선행사 an extreme competition sport를 수식하고 있고, 뒤에 완전한 절이
이어지고 있으므로 관계부사 where가 오는 것이 알맞다. which는 관계대명사로 뒤에
불완전한 절이 와야 한다.

물리적인 장소가 아닌 situation(상황), case(경우), point(점) 등 추상적인 의미의 선행사에도 관계부사 where가 쓰일 수 있다.

예) That's **the point where** we disagreed.
(바로 그것이 우리가 동의하지 않았던 점이다.)

지문 해석

Double Dutch는 한 명이나 두 명의 참가자가 줄을 통과해 뛰어넘는 동안 참가자 두 명이 두 개의 줄을 돌리는 줄넘기의 한 방법이다. Double Dutch는 아이들이 매우 좋아하는 역동적인 형태의 줄넘기다. 그것이 유익한 심혈관 운동인 것 이외에도, Double Dutch는 조정능력과 민첩성 또한 향상시킨다. 더욱이 그것은 함께 긴밀하게 움직이는 서너 명의 참가자가 필요하기 때문에, 아이들 사이의 협력하는 기술을 개발하는 데도 좋다. 최상급 수준에서 Double Dutch는 또한 아이들 무리가 많은 에너지를 요하는 정말로 놀라운 춤 동작을 하는 격렬한 스포츠 경기로도 행해지고 있다.

 어휘

jumping rope 줄넘기 participant 몡 참가자 dynamic 혭 역동적인 beneficial 혭 유익한 coordination 몡 합동; *(신체 동작의) 조령력 quickness 몡 민첩성 furthermore 팀 더욱이 cooperative 혭 협력하는 advanced 혭 고급의, 상급의 extreme 혭 극도의, 극심한 competition 몡 경쟁; *대회, 시합

08 　　　　정답 ③ 　　정답률 41%

정답 풀이

(A) 「many of + 복수 명사」

We know / [that the journalism program at our college was a
　　　　　　　명사절(목적어)을 이끄는 접속사
우리는 알고 있습니다　우리 대학의 언론 프로그램이 원천이었다는 것을
source / of [many / ~~much~~ of these firsts for you].
　　　　　　　당신의 이런 첫 경험들 중 많은 것들의

➡ 「many of + 복수 명사」 또는 「much of + 셀 수 없는 명사」의 형태로 쓰는데, of 뒤에 복수 명사(these firsts)가 이어지고 있으므로 many가 오는 것이 알맞다.

(B) 부사적 용법의 to부정사

We've done everything / [(that) we can (do)] / [~~contain~~ / to contain]
주어　　동사　　　　　목적격 관계대명사 생략　부사적 용법의 to부정사(목적)
우리는 모든 일을 다했습니다　　우리가 할 수 있는　　　비용을 억제하기 위해
costs / without compromising quality.
　　　　without v-ing: …하지 않고
　　　　품질을 양보하지 않으면서

➡ 문장의 동사는 have done으로 또 다른 동사가 필요하지 않으므로, 네모에는 문장 전체를 수식하는 부사적 용법의 to부정사가 오는 것이 적절하다.

(C) 분사구문

You'll get a great feeling / [{~~known~~ / knowing} [(that) you're
주어　　동사　　　　　조건을 나타내는 분사구문(= if you know ...)　접속사 that 생략
당신은 기분이 정말 좋아질 것입니다　　　당신이 돕고 있다는 것을 안다면
helping / (to) support the formation of future leaders / in the
help 뒤에 오는 to부정사에서 to는 종종 생략됨
　　　미래의 지도자 양성을 지원하는 것을　　　　　　　　이 직종에서
profession]}.

➡ 네모 이하는 조건을 나타내는 분사구문으로, 생략된 주어는 주절의 주어(You)와 같다. 당신이 '안다면'이라는 능동의 의미가 적절하므로 현재분사인 knowing이 오는 것이 적절하다.

1행	Remember {**what** *it* was **like** [*to report* on a daily deadline for the first time]}? ➡ what ... like?: '…은 어떤가?'의 의미로, 동사 Remember의 목적어 역할을 하는 「의문사 + 주어 + 동사」 형태의 간접의문문 ➡ it은 가주어, to report 이하가 진주어
8행	And we're hoping you'll **be willing to** *help* these students (to) *make* it through the program. ➡ be willing to-v: 기꺼이 …하다 ➡ help + 목적어 + (to) 동사원형: '…가 ~하도록 돕다'의 의미로, help의 목적격보어 자리에 to부정사가 올 경우, to는 종종 생략됨 ➡ make it through: …을 통과하다

지문 해석

처음으로 일일 마감에 맞춰 보도했던 것이 어땠는지 기억하십니까? 혹은 처음으로 시 공무원을 인터뷰했던 것은요? 혹은 컴퓨터 출판 프로그램을 쓰기 시작했던 것은요? 우리 대학의 언론 프로그램이 당신의 이런 많은 첫 경험들 중 많은 것들의 원천이었다는 것을 우리는 알고 있습니다. 우리는 여전히 이런 중요한 첫 경험들을 젊은 신진 작가들과 편집자들에게 제공하고 있습니다. 그리고 우리는 당신이 이 학생들이 프로그램을 끝낼 수 있도록 기꺼이 도와주기를 바라고 있습니다. 아시다시피, 최고 수준의 교육을 제공하는 비용은 계속 오르고 있습니다. 우리는 품질을 양보하지 않으면서 비용을 억제하기 위해 우리가 할 수 있는 모든 일을 다했습니다. 그것들 중 하나가 특별 재정적 지원이 필요한 학생들을 위해 장학기금을 설립하는 일입니다. 우리는 당신이 기금에 후하게 기부하는 것을 고려해 주시기를 바랍니다. 당신이 이 직종에서 미래의 지도자 양성을 지원하는 것을 돕고 있다는 것을 안다면 당신은 기분이 정말 좋아질 것입니다.

 어휘

deadline 몡 기한, 마감 시간 maneuver 톰 움직이다, 조종하다 publishing 몡 출판 journalism 몡 언론 budding 혭 싹트기 시작하는; *신예의 editor 몡 편집자 first-rate 혭 일류의, 최고의 contain 톰 포함하다; *방지[억제]하다 compromise 톰 타협하다; *굽히다, 양보하다 quality 몡 품질 set up …을 설립하다 scholarship 몡 장학금 financial 혭 금융의, 재정의 contribute 톰 기부[기증]하다 generously 팀 후하게 formation 몡 형성 profession 몡 직업, 직종

09 　　　　정답 ④ 　　정답률 40%

정답 풀이

(A) 완료부정사

In China / it has never been rare for emperors to paint, / but
　　　　　가주어　　　　　　　　　　　　to부정사의 의미상 주어　진주어
중국에서　　황제가 그림을 그리는 것은 결코 드문 일이 아니었지만
Huizong took it so seriously / [that the entire Northern Song
　　　　　　　　　so ... that ~: 너무 …해서 ~하다
휘종은 그것을 너무 진지하게 받아들여서　　　북송 왕조 전체가 무너졌다고 여겨진다
Dynasty is thought [~~to fall~~ / to have fallen] / because of it].
　　　　　　　　　　　　　　　　　　　　그것 때문에

➡ that절에서 네모 앞 동사의 시제는 현재이고, 북송이 멸망한 시점은 그 이전의 일이므로, 완료부정사 to have fallen이 오는 것이 적절하다.

Grammar Tips

to부정사의 시제

1 단순부정사(to-v): 서술어 역할을 하는 동사와 같은 시점의 일을 나타낸다.

예) He *seems* **to be satisfied** with his job.
(그는 자신의 직업에 만족한 것처럼 보인다.)

2 완료부정사(to have v-ed): 서술어 역할을 하는 동사가 나타내는 시점보다 앞선 시점의 일을 나타낸다.

예) He *seems* **to have been satisfied** with his job.
(그는 자신의 직업에 만족했던 것처럼 보인다.)

(B) 가주어 진주어 구문

[When he inherited the throne, at age nineteen], / it / ~~which~~ was
접속사　　　　　　　　　　　　　　　　　　　　　　　　　가주어
그가 19세에 왕위를 물려받았을 때　　　　　　　　　　　　예상되었다

expected / [that he would continue his ancestors' royal patronage].
　　　　　　진주어, that은 접속사
　　　　　　그가 자기 선조들의 왕실 (예술) 애호를 계속 할 것이라고

➡ 뒤에 오는 that절이 진주어로, 네모에는 진주어를 대신할 가주어 it이 오는 것이 적절하다.

(C) 주격보어로 쓰인 과거분사

This he did, / but **spent** so much of the next twenty-five years /
주어 동사　　　　 동사　 so ... that ~: 너무 …해서 ~하다
그는 이렇게 했지만　　 그 후 25년의 너무 많은 시간을 보냈다

~~involving~~ / **involved** in art / [that he ignored his official duties].
　　　　　　　　　　　　　　　　接續詞
예술에 몰입되어　　　　　　　　그래서 그는 공적 의무를 소홀히 했다

➡ 네모는 주어(he)에 대해 보충 설명하는 주격보어로, 그가 예술에 '몰입되어'라는 수동의 의미가 적절하므로 과거분사 involved가 오는 것이 알맞다.

 오답 피하기 Tips

「spend + 시간」 뒤에는 무조건 v-ing가 온다?

「spend + 시간」 뒤에 반드시 v-ing가 오는 것은 아니다. 「spend + 시간 + v-ing」는 '…하는 데 시간을 보내다'라는 의미로 v-ing는 명사이지만, 위 문장에서처럼 「spend + 시간」 뒤에 분사가 주어의 상태를 보충 설명하는 주격보어로 오기도 한다.

지문 해석

중국에서 황제가 그림을 그리는 것은 결코 드문 일이 아니었지만, 휘종은 그것을 너무 진지하게 받아들여서 북송 왕조 전체가 그것 때문에 무너졌다고 여겨진다. 그는 예술적 감각이 있는 오랜 황제 가문 출신으로, 이 황제들은 황제의 소장품을 늘렸으며, 그림, 서예, 예술품 수집에 대해 논의를 했다. 휘종에게 수집은 쉬운 일이었다. 그가 그림을 원하면, 그림의 주인은 그것을 넘겨야 했다. 그가 19세에 왕위를 물려받았을 때, 그가 자기 선조들의 왕실 (예술) 애호를 계속 할 것이라고 예상되었다. 그는 이렇게 했지만, 그 후 25년의 너무 많은 시간을 예술에 몰입되어 보내서 그의 공적 의무를 소홀히 했다.

 어휘

emperor 뗑 황제　**line** 뗑 선; *가계, 계통　**artistic** 혱 예술적인　**add to** …을 늘리다　**imperial** 혱 제국의, 황제의　**collection** 뗑 수집품; *소장품　**discussion** 뗑 논의　**calligraphy** 뗑 서예　**hand over** …을 넘겨주다　**inherit** 통 상속받다, 물려받다　**throne** 뗑 왕좌; *왕위, 보위　**ancestor** 뗑 조상, 선조　**royal** 혱 왕족의　**patronage** 뗑 후원; *애호　**official** 혱 공식적인; *공무상의　**duty** 뗑 임무

10　　　정답 ⑤　　　정답률 31%

정답 풀이

(A) forget to-v

She had a very good voice, / except that some of her high notes
　　　　　　　　　　　　　…라는 것을 제외하면
그녀는 매우 좋은 목소리를 가지고 있었다　일부 고음들이 문 소리처럼 들리는 경향이 있다는 것을

tended to sound like a gate / [which someone had forgotten
sound like + 명사: …처럼 들리다 　　 목적격 관계대명사
제외하면　　　　　　　　　　　　누군가가 기름칠할 것을 잊은

~~oiling~~ / to oil].

➡ 동사 forget은 to부정사(…할 것을)와 동명사(…한 것을)를 모두 목적어로 취할 수 있는데, 이 문장에서는 '기름칠할 것을' 잊었다는 의미이므로 to부정사 to oil이 알맞다.

(B) 관계부사 vs. 관계대명사

As she lived in a small house, / [where / ~~which~~ she could not
접속사(…때문에)　　　　선행사　　　계속적 용법의 관계부사
그녀는 작은 집에서 살았기 때문에　　　그곳에서 그녀는 연습할 수 없었다

practice / without disturbing the rest of the family], / she usually
　　　　 without v-ing: …하지 않고
　　　　 나머지 가족들을 방해하지 않고　　　　　　그녀는 보통

practiced her high notes outside.
밖에서 고음을 연습했다

➡ 장소를 나타내는 a small house를 선행사로 하고, 뒤에 완전한 절이 이어지므로 관계부사 where가 오는 것이 알맞다.

(C) 「see(지각동사) + 목적어 + 동사원형」

She saw an anxious expression suddenly come / ~~to come~~ /
　　　　　　　목적어　　　　　　　　　　　목적격보어
그녀는 불안해하는 표정이 갑자기 떠오르는 것을 보았다

over the driver's face.
운전자의 얼굴에

➡ 지각동사 saw의 목적격보어의 자리이므로 동사원형 come이 오는 것이 알맞다.

지문 해석

Emma는 노래 부르는 것을 매우 좋아했다. 일부 고음들이 누군가가 기름칠할 것을 잊은 문 소리처럼 들리는 경향이 있다는 것을 제외하면, 그녀는 매우 좋은 목소리를 가지고 있었다. Emma는 이 약점을 무척 의식해서 기회가 날 때마다 이러한 고음을 연습했다. 그녀는 작은 집에 살았고, 그곳에서 나머지 가족을 방해하지 않고 연습할 수 없었기 때문에 보통 밖에서 고음을 연습했다. 어느 날 오후, 그녀가 가장 높고 어려운 음조를 노래하는 동안 자동차 한 대가 그녀를 지나쳤다. 그녀는 운전자의 얼굴에 불안해하는 표정이 갑자기 떠오르는 것을 보았다. 그는 브레이크를 세게 밟더니, 뛰어 나와, 모든 타이어를 주의 깊게 점검하기 시작했다.

 어휘

be fond of …을 좋아하다　**note** 뗑 음, 음조　**tend** 통 (…하는) 경향이 있다　**oil** 통 기름칠하다　**conscious** 혱 의식하는　**weakness** 뗑 약점　**opportunity** 뗑 기회　**disturb** 통 방해하다　**the rest of** 나머지의　**anxious** 혱 불안해하는　**violently** 붠 격렬하게, 맹렬히　**jump out** 뛰어나오다　**examine** 통 점검하다　**carefully** 붠 주의 깊게

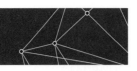

2 문장의 동사

UNIT 1 동사의 수 일치

코드 접속하기

pp.27~30

출제코드 1 　주어가 수식어구로 길어진 경우

A **1** is **2** are **3** is
B **1** ➡ face **2** ➡ have **3** ➡ keeps

해석과 정답 풀이

STEP 1
1 1) 상류층 출신의 중국 사람들은 사치품에 많은 돈을 쓴다.
　2) 고아원을 짓는 것을 도울 자원봉사자들이 회의를 할 계획이다.
　3) 생크림으로 덮여있는 초콜릿 컵케이크들은 이미 품절되었다.
　4) 무거운 공책과 교과서를 나르고 있는 학생은 나의 반 친구다.
2 1) 모든 군인들은 그들의 조국을 위해 목숨을 희생할 준비가 되어있다.
　2) 나머지 마을 사람들은 지진으로 심각하게 부상을 당했다.
　3) 이유들 중 하나는 산소 부족과 관련이 있다.

STEP 2
1 1) 벽에 걸린 그림들은 고등학교 미술 동아리 회원들에 의해 그려졌다.
　2) 이 웹사이트에 접속하기를 원하는 사람들은 각자의 ID와 비밀번호를 가지고 있어야 한다.
2 64퍼센트 이상의 학생들이 교복을 입는 것에 반대한다.
3 사회에서 가장 논란이 많은 문제들 중 하나는 사형 제도다.

STEP 3
A 1 서로 선물을 교환하는 가장 흔한 이유는 우정을 표현하는 것이다.
　➡ 주어는 to부정사구(to exchange ... other)의 수식을 받는 The most common reason으로, 주어가 단수 명사이므로 단수 동사 is가 오는 것이 알맞다.
　2 자신의 꿈을 이루지 못한 사람들은 그들의 고난을 극복하려고 노력하지 않은 사람들이다.
　➡ 주어는 관계사절(who ... dreams)의 수식을 받는 Those로, 주어가 복수 대명사이므로 복수 동사 are가 오는 것이 알맞다.
　3 사람들의 관심을 얻는 가장 확실한 방법 중 하나는 특이한 옷을 입는 것이다.
　➡ 「one of + 복수 명사」가 주어이므로 단수 동사 is가 오는 것이 알맞다.
B 1 북극 지방의 북극곰들의 대부분은 멸종 위기에 직면해 있다.
　➡ Most of 뒤에 복수 명사(the polar bears)가 왔으므로 단수 동사 faces를 복수 동사 face로 고쳐야 한다.
　2 다른 조치들 외에도, 이것들은 미래의 발생 확률을 낮추도록 도왔다.
　➡ 문장의 주어가 복수 대명사(These)이므로 단수 동사 has를 복수 동사 have로 고쳐야 한다.
　3 우리 자신의 견해와 다른 의견을 무시하는 것은 우리가 좋은 관계를 형성하지 못하게 한다.
　➡ 문장의 주어가 단수 명사(Ignorance)이므로 복수 동사 keep을 단수 동사 keeps로 고쳐야 한다.

출제코드 2 　주어가 구나 절인 경우

A **1** is **2** has **3** seems
B **1** ○ **2** ➡ is **3** ○

해석과 정답 풀이

STEP 1
1 1) 그 일을 하루에 마치는 것은 불가능하다.
　2) 새로운 사람들과 만나는 것은 나에게 신나는 경험이었다.
2 1) 그녀가 학급 회의에서 제안했던 것은 좋은 생각이다.

---

　2) 아이들이 학교에서 어떻게 지낼 것인지가 부모들이 걱정하는 것이다.
　3) 내가 그와 데이트를 할지 말지는 그의 외모에 달려있다.

STEP 2
1 1) 그 끔찍한 교통사고에 대해 생각하는 것은 내가 죄책감을 느끼게 한다.
　2) 문법 규칙의 많은 예외 사항을 아는 것은 글을 쓸 때 유용하다.
2 1) 당신이 해야 하는 것은 당신의 미래에 대해 긍정적으로 생각하는 것이다.
　2) 누가 내 가방에서 지갑을 훔쳤는지는 수수께끼로 남았다.
　3) 그들이 다음 게임을 이겼는지 아니었는지는 그들에게 중요하지 않았다.

STEP 3
A 1 당신이 누구에게 그녀에 관한 소문을 들었는지는 중요한 문제이다.
　➡ 의문사절(Who you ... from)이 주어이므로 뒤에 단수 동사 is가 오는 것이 알맞다.
　2 큰 나라의 인구 수를 계산하는 것은 어려운 일이었다.
　➡ 동명사구(Calculating ... countries)가 주어이므로 뒤에 단수 동사 has가 오는 것이 알맞다.
　3 그를 다른 기자들과 다르게 만드는 것은 직업에 대한 그의 열정으로 보인다.
　➡ 관계대명사 What절(What ... journalists)이 주어이므로 뒤에 단수 동사 seems가 오는 것이 알맞다.
B 1 사회적으로 고립된 사람들을 투표에서 배제하는 것은 우리의 민주주의를 망친다.
　➡ to부정사구(To exclude ... voting)가 주어이므로 뒤에 단수 동사 destroys가 오는 것이 알맞다.
　2 왜 중국인들이 빨간색이 그들에게 많은 돈을 가져다 준다고 생각하는지는 정확히 알려져 있지 않다.
　➡ 의문사절(Why ... money)이 주어이므로 복수 동사 are를 단수 동사 is로 고쳐야 한다.
　3 정부가 연간 계획을 변경할지가 중요한 문제로 떠오르고 있다.
　➡ 접속사 Whether절(Whether ... plans)이 주어이므로 뒤에 단수 동사 is가 오는 것이 알맞다.

출제코드 3 　주어와 동사가 도치된 경우

A **1** does **2** were **3** is
B **1** ➡ were **2** ➡ spread **3** ➡ is

해석과 정답 풀이

STEP 1
1 1) 모퉁이에 Caffeine이라 불리는 커피숍이 있다.
　2) 나는 이전에 그렇게 잘생긴 남자를 본 적이 없었다.
2 1) 그제서야 그녀는 무슨 일이 일어나고 있는지를 알았다.
　2) 나무 아래에 나무 탁자와 빨간색으로 칠해진 의자가 있었다.
3 1) 그들은 매우 긴장하면 한 마디도 말하지 않는다.
　2) 우리는 우리의 아들이 의사가 되리라고는 꿈도 꾸지 않았다.
　3) 나무 옆에는 화재로 훼손된 오래된 건물이 서 있다.

STEP 2
1 1) 내 차 옆에 있는 차의 뒷좌석에 두 명의 어린 아이들이 있었다.
　2) 그의 부모님은 왜 그가 학교를 그만두었는지 들어본 적이 없다.

STEP 3
A 1 그녀는 좋은 의사소통 능력뿐만 아니라 훌륭한 리더십 능력을 가지고 있다.
　➡ 부정어구(Not only)가 문장 앞으로 나오면서 주어와 동사가 도치된 구문으로, 주어가 단수 대명사(she)이므로 단수 동사 does가 오는 것이 적절하다.
　2 30분 동안 강연을 들은 후에야 그들은 취해져야 할 다음 조치에 대해 안내받았다.
　➡ Only를 포함한 부사구가 문장 앞으로 나오면서 주어와 동사가 도치된 구문으로, 주어가 복수 대명사(they)이므로 복수 동사 were가 오는 것이 적절하다.
　3 우리 학교 강당에는 큰 무대가 있는데, 그 위에는 연설자들을 위한 연단이 놓여있다.
　➡ 관계대명사 which의 선행사는 a big stage로, on which가 장소를 나타내는 부사구 역할을 하여 뒤에 주어와 동사가 도치된 구문이다. 주어가 단수 명사(a podium)이므로 단수 동사 is가 오는 것이 알맞다.
B 1 세상 어디에서도 그들은 "불로장생약"을 구할 수 없었다.
　➡ 부정어구(Nowhere)가 문장 앞으로 나와 주어와 동사가 도치된 구문으로, 주어가 복수 대명사(they)이므로 단수 동사 was를 복수 동사 were로 고쳐야 한다.
　2 200년된 나무 줄기로부터 가지들이 사방으로 뻗어 있다.
　➡ 부사구(From its 200-year-old trunk)가 문장 앞으로 나와 주어와 동사가

도치된 구문으로, 주어가 복수 명사(branches)이므로 단수 동사 spreads를 복수 동사 spread로 고쳐야 한다.

3 감정적인 문제들을 다루는 데에 있어서 기계는 인간보다 결코 더 세심할 수 없다.

➡ 부정어구(Never)가 문장 앞으로 나와 주어와 동사가 도치된 구문으로, 주어가 단수 명사(a machine)이므로 복수 동사 are를 단수 동사 is로 고쳐야 한다.

기출예제 Q1 　　정답 ⑤　　정답률 57%

정답 풀이

⑤ 동사의 수 일치

A general strategy / [that is used to make the animal characters
주어　　　　　　주격 관계대명사　make + 목적어 + 형용사: …을 ~하게 만들다
일반적인 전략은　　　　　　　동물 캐릭터를 더 감정적으로 매력적이게 만들기 위해 이용하는
more emotionally appealing, / both to children and adults], /
　　　　　　　　　　아이와 어른 모두에게
are(→ is) to give them enlarged and deformed childlike features.
동사　　　　동사　간접목적어　　　　　　직접목적어
그것들에 확대되고 변형된 어린이 같은 특징을 부여하는 것이다

➡ 이 문장의 주어는 주격 관계대명사절의 수식을 받는 A general strategy이다. 주어가 3인칭 단수이므로 복수 동사 are를 단수 동사 is로 고쳐야 한다.

친절한 오답 풀이

① 접속사

The most noticeable human characteristic [projected onto
주어　　　　　　　　　　　　　과거분사
동물에게 투영된 가장 눈에 띄는 인간의 특징은
animals] / is [that they can talk in human language].
　　　　동사 접속사
동물이 인간의 언어로 대화할 수 있다는 점이다

➡ 문장의 보어 역할을 하는 명사절을 이끌고 있으므로 접속사 that은 적절하다.

② 명사를 수식하는 과거분사

Physically, animal cartoon characters and toys [made after
　　　　　　　　　　　　　　　　　　　　　과거분사
신체적으로도, 동물 만화 캐릭터와 동물을 본떠 만든 장난감은
animals] / are also most often deformed / in such a way as to
　　　　be v-ed: 수동태　　　　　　= in such a way that they resemble
　　　　또한 변형되는 경우가 아주 많다　　인간을 닮게 하는 방식으로
resemble humans.

➡ made는 앞의 명사 toys를 수식하는 과거분사로, 장난감은 '만들어지는' 것이므로 수동의 의미를 나타내는 과거분사가 알맞게 쓰였다.

③ 「전치사 + 동명사」

This is achieved / by showing them with humanlike facial
be v-ed: 수동태　전치사　동명사의 목적어
이것은 달성된다　　인간과 같은 얼굴 특징과 변형된 앞다리를 가지고 있는 것으로
features and deformed front legs / to resemble human hands.
　　　　　　　　　　　　　　　형용사적 용법의 to부정사
그것들을 보여줌으로써　　　　　　사람의 손을 닮게

➡ 전치사 by의 목적어 역할을 하면서 뒤에 목적어 them을 취할 수 있는 동명사 showing이 오는 것이 알맞다.

④ 전치사

However, / they still use their front legs like human hands / (for
　　　　　　　　　　　　　　전치사　전치사의 목적어
그러나　　그것들은 여전히 사람의 손처럼 앞다리를 사용한다
example, lions can pick up and lift small objects with one paw), /
　　　　　　　　　　　　　　　　　　　　　　　전치사구(부사)
예를 들어, 사자가 한 발로 작은 물체를 집어 들어 올릴 수 있는 것처럼
and they still talk with an appropriate facial expression.
　　　　　　　　　　　　　전치사구(부사)
그리고 그것들은 여전히 적절한 표정을 지으며 이야기한다

➡ 뒤에 전치사의 목적어 역할을 하는 명사구(human hands)가 있으므로 전치사 like는 어법상 바르다.

지문 해석

동물에게 투영된 가장 눈에 띄는 인간의 특징은 동물이 인간의 언어로 대화할 수 있다는 점이다. 신체적으로도, 동물 만화 캐릭터와 동물을 본떠 만든 장난감은 또한 인간을 닮게 하는 방식으로 변형되는 경우가 아주 많다. 이것은 인간과 같은 얼굴 특징과 사람의 손을 닮게 변형된 앞다리를 가지고 있는 것으로 그것들을 보여줌으로써 달성된다. 더 최근의 만화 영화에서 추세는 동물을 더 '자연스러운' 방식으로 묘사하는 것이었다. 그러나 그것들은 (예를 들어 사자가 한 발로 작은 물체를 집어 들어 올릴 수 있는 것처럼) 여전히 사람의 손처럼 앞다리를 사용하고, 여전히 적절한 표정을 지으며 이야기한다. 동물 캐릭터를 아이와 어른 모두에게 더 감정적으로 매력적이게 만들기 위해 이용하는 일반적인 전략은 그것들에 확대되고 변형된 어린이 같은 특징을 부여하는 것이다.

어휘

noticeable 형 눈에 띄는　**characteristic** 명 특징, 특성　**project** 동 투영하다
physically 부 신체적으로　**resemble** 동 닮다　**achieve** 동 달성하다, 이루다
facial 형 얼굴의　**animated** 형 만화 영화의　**appropriate** 형 적절한, 적당한
appealing 형 매력적인　**enlarge** 동 확대하다　**childlike** 형 어린이 같은

코드 공략하기 01 　　　　pp.31~34

01 ⑤　**02** ③　**03** ⑤　**04** ④　**05** ⑤　**06** ④　**07** ②　**08** ④
09 ⑤　**10** ⑤

01 　　정답 ⑤　　정답률 63%

정답 풀이

⑤ 동사의 수 일치

Obviously, some of these practices, / [such as drinking alcohol /
　　　　　　주어　　　　　　전치사(…와 같은)　　　삽입구
분명 이러한 관행 중 일부는　　　　　술을 마시는 것과 같은
during a marathon], / are no longer recommended, / but others, /
　　　　　　　　　동사　더 이상 … 않다　　　　주어
마라톤 중에　　　더는 권장되지 않지만　　　　다른 관행은
[such as a high-carbohydrate meal / the night before a
　　　　　　삽입구
고(高)탄수화물 식사와 같은　　　　경기 전날 밤의
competition], / has(→ have) stood the test of time.
　　　　　　　동사
　　　　　세월의 검증을 견뎌냈다

➡ 문장의 주어는 삽입구(such as ... competition) 앞에 오는 복수 명사(others)이므로, 단수 동사 has를 복수 동사 have로 고쳐야 한다.

친절한 오답 풀이

① 명사를 수식하는 과거분사

[Although sports nutrition is a fairly new academic discipline], /
접속사(비록 …이긴 하지만)
비록 운동 영양학이 상당히 새로운 학문 분야이긴 하지만
there have always been recommendations / {made to athletes /
　　　　현재완료(계속)　　　　　　　　　　과거분사
권고는 늘 있어 왔다　　　　　　　　　운동선수들에게 제시된
about foods / [that could enhance athletic performance]}.
　　　　　　　주격 관계대명사
음식에 관해　　　운동 기량을 향상할 수 있는

➡ 앞에 나온 명사(recommendations)를 수식하는 분사로, 운동선수들에게 '제시된' 권고라는 수동의 의미이므로 과거분사 made가 오는 것이 알맞다.

② 완료부정사

One ancient Greek athlete is reported / to have eaten dried figs /
고대 그리스의 한 운동선수는 전해진다 　　　　말린 무화과를 먹었다고
완료부정사

to enhance training.
부사적 용법의 to부정사(목적)
컨디션을 향상하기 위해

➡ 고대 그리스의 한 운동선수에 관한 내용이 전해지는 시점은 현재이고, 그 선수가 말린 무화과를 먹은 시점은 그 이전의 일이므로, 완료부정사 to have eaten은 어법상 바르다.

③ 접속사 that

The teenage running phenomenon, / Mary Decker, / surprised
십 대 달리기 천재인 　　　　Mary Decker는
동격

the sports world / in the 1970s / {when she reported / [that she
스포츠계를 놀라게 했는데 　1970년대에 　그녀는 전했다 　접속사
관계부사

ate a plate of spaghetti noodles / the night before a race]}.
스파게티 한 접시를 먹었다고 　경주 전날 밤에

➡ that은 동사 reported의 목적어 역할을 하는 명사절을 이끄는 접속사로, 뒤에 완전한 절이 이어지므로 어법상 바르다.

④ 전치사

Such practices may be suggested / to athletes / because of their
그러한 관행은 권고될 수도 있다 　운동선수들에게 　그것의 실제적인

real / or perceived benefits / by individuals / [who excelled in
혹은 인식된 이득 때문에 　개인들에 의해 　자신의 운동 분야에서
주격 관계대명사

their sports].
탁월한 능력을 보인

➡ 뒤에 명사구(their real ... sports)가 이어지므로 전치사 because of가 오는 것이 알맞다.

지문 해석

비록 운동 영양학이 상당히 새로운 학문 분야이긴 하지만, 운동 기량을 향상할 수 있는 음식에 관해 운동선수들에게 제시된 권고는 늘 있어 왔다. 고대 그리스의 한 운동선수는 컨디션을 향상하기 위해 말린 무화과를 먹었다고 전해진다. 1908년 올림픽에서 마라톤 주자들은 기량을 향상하기 위하여 코냑을 마셨다는 보고가 있다. 십 대 달리기 천재인 Mary Decker는 1970년대에 스포츠계를 놀라게 했는데, 그녀는 경주 전날 밤에 스파게티 한 접시를 먹었다고 전했다. 그러한 관행은 그것의 실제적인 이득 혹은 자신의 운동 분야에서 탁월한 능력을 보인 개인들이 인식한 이득 때문에 운동선수들에게 권고될 수도 있다. 분명, 마라톤 중에 술을 마시는 것과 같은 이러한 관행 중 일부는 더는 권장되지 않지만, 경기 전날 밤의 고(高)탄수화물 식사와 같은 다른 관행은 세월의 검증을 견뎌냈다.

어휘

sports nutrition 운동 영양학　fairly 틧 상당히, 꽤　recommendation 閏 권고 (recommend 튕 권장하다)　enhance 튕 높이다, 향상하다　fig 閏 무화과　practice 閏 실행; *관행　perceive 튕 지각하다, 인지하다　excel 튕 뛰어나다, 탁월하다　carbohydrate 閏 탄수화물　competition 閏 경쟁; *경기, 시합

02　　　정답 ③　　　정답률 66%

정답 풀이

(A) 접속사 vs. 전치사

The wheel and the plow were possible / because / because of
　　　　주어　　　　동사　　　보어
바퀴와 쟁기는 가능했다

the availability of animal labor.
동물 노동력의 이용 가능성 때문에

➡ because와 because of는 모두 '… 때문에'라는 뜻이지만, because는 접속사로 뒤에 주어와 동사를 가지는 절이 와야 하고, because of는 전치사로 뒤에 명사(구)가 와야 한다. 뒤에 명사구(the availability ... labor)가 왔으므로 전치사 because of를 쓰는 것이 알맞다.

(B) 동사의 수 일치

Animals [that pulled plows to turn the earth over for planting] /
주어 ↑ 　　주격 관계대명사 　부사적 용법의 to부정사(목적), turn over: …을 뒤집다
파종을 위한 흙을 뒤집기 위해 쟁기를 끌었던 동물들은

was / were far more efficient than humans.
동사 　비교급 강조 부사(훨씬)
인간들보다 훨씬 더 효율적이었다

➡ 주어는 관계대명사절(that pulled ... planting)의 수식을 받고 있는 Animals로, 주어가 복수 명사이므로 복수 동사인 were가 오는 것이 알맞다.

(C) 수량형용사

All three inventions made the cities of Mesopotamia powerful
make + 목적어 + 명사: …을 ~로 만들다
모든 3개 발명품들은 메소포타미아의 도시들을 강력한 무역 중심지들로 만들었다

trading centers / with as much / many as 30,000 people each.
as many as: 무려 …나 되는 　　　　　부사
각각 3만 명이나 되는 많은 인구를 가진

➡ much는 셀 수 없는 명사와 함께 쓰이고, many는 셀 수 있는 명사의 복수형과 함께 쓰이는 수량형용사이다. 뒤에 나온 30,000 people은 셀 수 있는 명사의 복수형이므로 형용사 many가 오는 것이 알맞다.

 구문 분석 Plus

The sail **made** **it** **possible** {to trade with countries [that could be reached only by sea]}.

8행

➡ make + 목적어 + 형용사: …을 ~하게 만들다
➡ it은 가목적어, to trade 이하가 진목적어
➡ that 이하는 선행사 countries를 수식하는 주격 관계대명사절

지문 해석

바퀴, 쟁기, 그리고 범선이라는 세 가지 매우 중요한 발명품이 메소포타미아에서 나왔다. 바퀴와 쟁기는 동물 노동력의 이용 가능성 때문에 가능했다. 말이 끄는 바퀴가 달린 수레는 더 많은 상품을 더 빠르게 시장으로 운반할 수 있었다. 파종을 위한 흙을 뒤집기 위해 쟁기를 끌었던 동물들은 인간들보다 훨씬 더 효율적이었다. 돛은 바다를 통해서만 닿을 수 있는 나라들과 무역하는 것을 가능하게 했다. 세 가지 발명품은 모두 메소포타미아의 도시들을 각각 무려 3만 명이나 되는 인구를 가진 강력한 무역 중심지로 만들었다.

어휘

extremely 틧 극도로, 극히　invention 閏 발명품　wheel 閏 바퀴 (wheeled 閺 바퀴 달린)　sailboat 閏 범선, 요트　availability 閏 이용 가능성　labor 閏 노동; *노동력　transport 튕 수송하다　goods 閏 (pl.) 상품, 제품　earth 閏 지구; *흙　plant 튕 (나무·씨앗 등을) 심다　efficient 閺 효율적인　sail 閏 돛　trade 튕 거래 [무역]하다　reach 튕 도달하다

03　　　정답 ⑤　　　정답률 40%

정답 풀이

⑤ 동사의 수 일치

{If you applaud / [every time your child identifies a letter],} / she
　　　　　…할 때마다
당신이 박수를 친다면 　당신의 자녀가 글자를 알아볼 때마다 　그녀는

may become a praise lover / [who eventually become(→ becomes)
주격 관계대명사
칭찬 애호가가 될지도 모른다 　결국 흥미를 덜 갖게 되는

less interested / in learning the alphabet for its own sake /
for one's sake: …을 위해
그 자체를 위해 알파벳을 배우는 데에

than for hearing you applaud].
hear(지각동사) + 목적어 + 동사원형: …가 ~하는 것을 듣다
당신이 칭찬하는 것을 듣기 위함보다

➡ 밑줄 친 부분은 a praise lover를 선행사로 하는 주격 관계대명사절의 동사로,

선행사에 동사의 수를 일치시켜야 한다. 선행사가 단수 명사이므로 become을 단수 동사 becomes로 고쳐야 한다.

▌친절한 오답 풀이▐

① 가주어 진주어 구문

{Just as it is misguided / [to offer your child false praise]}, /
꼭 …처럼 가주어　　　　진주어
잘못된 판단인 것처럼　　　　당신의 자녀에게 거짓된 칭찬을 하는 것이

it is also a mistake / [to reward all of his accomplishments].
가주어　　　　진주어
또한 실수이다　　　　그의 모든 성취에 대해 보상하는 것은

➡ Just as절에서 to offer 이하는 가주어 it에 대한 진주어로 쓰인 to부정사구로 어법상 바르다.

② 주격보어

[Although rewards sound so positive], / they can often lead to
접속사(…이지만)　　　sound + 형용사: …하게 들리다　　　…로 이어지다
보상이 아주 긍정적으로 들리기는 하지만,　　　그것들은 종종 부정적인

negative consequences.
결과로 이어질 수 있다

➡ 감각동사 sound의 보어 자리이므로 형용사 positive가 오는 것이 알맞다. 보어의 자리에는 부사가 올 수 없다.

③ 관계대명사 what

…, she starts to focus more on getting the reward / than on [what
focus on: …에 집중하다　　　관계대명사
그녀는 보상을 받는 것에 좀 더 집중하기 시작한다　　　그녀가 한 것보다는

she did] / to earn it.
부사적 용법의 to부정사 = the reward
보상을 얻기 위해

➡ 전치사 on의 목적어 역할을 하면서 뒤에 오는 불완전한 절의 목적어 역할을 하고 있으므로 관계대명사 what은 어법상 바르다.

④ 「전치사 + 동명사」

The focus of her excitement / shifts from enjoying learning itself /
from A to B: A에서 B로
그녀의 즐거움의 초점이　　　배움 그 자체를 즐기는 것에서 옮겨간다

to pleasing you.
전치사
당신을 기쁘게 하는 것으로

➡ 「from A to B」 구문에서 from과 to는 전치사로 각각 뒤에 목적어가 와야 한다. to의 목적어 역할을 하면서 뒤에 목적어(you)를 가져야 하므로 「전치사 + 동명사」 형태인 to pleasing이 오는 것이 알맞다.

지문 해석

"나는 네가 참 자랑스러워."라는 칭찬에 있어 잘못된 점이 무엇일까? 많다. 당신의 자녀에게 거짓된 칭찬을 하는 것이 잘못된 판단인 것처럼, 자녀의 모든 성취에 대해 보상하는 것은 또한 실수이다. 보상이 아주 긍정적으로 들리기는 하지만, 그것은 종종 부정적인 결과로 이어질 수 있다. 이는 그것들이 배움의 즐거움을 앗아갈 수 있기 때문이다. 당신이 자녀의 성취에 대해 지속적으로 보상을 해준다면, 자녀는 보상을 얻기 위해 그녀가 한 것보다는 보상을 받는 것에 좀 더 집중하기 시작한다. 자녀의 즐거움의 초점이 배움 그 자체를 즐기는 것에서 당신을 기쁘게 하는 것으로 옮겨간다. 당신의 자녀가 글자를 알아볼 때마다 당신이 박수를 친다면, 그녀는 결국 당신이 칭찬하는 것을 듣기 위함보다 그 자체를 위해 알파벳을 배우는 데에 흥미를 덜 갖게 되는 칭찬 애호가가 될지도 모른다.

compliment 뗑 칭찬　plenty 뗑 풍부한 양　misguided 뗑 잘못 이해한[판단한]　reward 뗑 보상하다 뗑 보상　accomplishment 뗑 성취, 업적　positive 뗑 긍정적인　negative 뗑 부정적인　consequence 뗑 결과　consistently 뛷 지속적으로　shift 뗑 옮기다　applaud 뗑 박수를 치다　identify 뗑 확인하다; *분간[식별]하다

정답 풀이

④ 동사의 수 일치

This way of building new knowledge on older discoveries /
주어 └ 동격 ┘
더 이전의 발견들에 새로운 지식을 쌓아가는 이러한 방법은

ensure(→ ensures) / [that scientists correct their mistakes].
동사　　　명사절(목적어)을 이끄는 접속사
보장한다　　　과학자들이 그들의 실수를 바로잡는 것을

➡ 문장의 주어는 This way이고, 뒤에 오는 of … discoveries는 주어를 보충하기 위한 동격의 전치사구이다. 주어가 단수 명사이므로 복수 동사 ensure를 단수 동사 ensures로 고쳐야 한다.

▌친절한 오답 풀이▐

① 명사를 수식하는 과거분사

Instead of making guesses, / scientists follow a system / {designed
… 대신에　　　　과거분사
추측하는 대신에　　　과학자들은 체계를 따른다

to prove [if their ideas are true or false]}.
접속사(…인지)
그들의 생각이 사실인지 거짓인지 증명하도록 고안된

➡ 앞에 나온 명사(a system)를 수식하는 분사로, 시스템이 '고안되는'이라는 수동의 의미가 적절하므로 과거분사 designed가 오는 것이 알맞다.

② 목적격 관계대명사

Old ideas are replaced / when scientists find new information /
be v-ed: 수동태
기존의 생각들은 대체된다　　　과학자들이 새로운 정보를 찾을 때

[that they cannot explain].
목적격 관계대명사
그들이 설명할 수 없는

➡ that은 new information을 선행사로 하고 관계대명사절에서 동사 explain의 목적어 역할을 하는 목적격 관계대명사로, 어법상 바르다.

③ 「전치사 + 동명사」

[Once somebody makes a discovery], / others review it carefully /
접속사(일단 …하면)　　　= the discovery
누군가가 발견을 하면　　　다른 사람들은 그것을 주의 깊게 검토한다

before using the information in their own research.
전치사 동명사
그들 자신의 연구에서 그 정보를 사용하기 전에

➡ using은 전치사 before의 목적어로 쓰인 동명사이므로 어법상 바르다.

⑤ 비교급 강조 부사

[Armed with scientific knowledge], / people build tools and
동시동작을 나타내는 분사구문(= As people are armed …)
과학적 지식으로 무장해서　　　사람들은 도구와 기기를 만든다

machines / {that transform the way [we live]}, / making our lives
주격 관계대명사　　　관계부사절
우리가 사는 방식을 변화시키는

much easier and better.
그리고 그것은 우리의 삶을 훨씬 더 쉽고 나아지게 한다

➡ 부사 much는 '훨씬'의 의미로 뒤에 오는 비교급 easier와 better를 수식하고 있으므로 어법상 바르다.

지문 해석

우주의 불가사의한 것들에 관한 답을 찾는 많은 방법이 있고, 과학은 이러한 것들 중 단지 하나이다. 그러나 과학은 독특하다. 추측하는 대신에 과학자들은 그들의 생각이 사실인지 거짓인지 증명하도록 고안된 체계를 따른다. 그들은 그들의 이론과 결론을 끊임없이 재검토하고 시험한다. 기존의 생각들은 과학자들이 그들이 설명할 수 없는 새로운 정보를 찾을 때 대체된다. 누군가가 발견을 하면, 다른 사람들은 그들 자신의 연구에서 그 정보를

사용하기 전에 그것을 주의 깊게 검토한다. 더 이전의 발견들에 새로운 지식을 쌓아가는 이러한 방법은 과학자들이 그들의 실수를 바로잡는 것을 보장한다. 과학적 지식으로 무장해서, 사람들은 우리가 사는 방식을 변화시키는 도구와 기기를 만들고, 그것은 우리의 삶을 훨씬 더 쉽고 나아지게 한다.

어휘

method 명 방법   unique 형 독특한   make a guess 추측을 해보다   prove 동 입증하다   false 형 틀린   constantly 부 끊임없이   reexamine 동 재검토하다   replace 동 대체하다   make a discovery 발견하다   ensure 동 보장하다   transform 동 변형시키다

05   정답 ⑤   정답률 70%

정답 풀이

⑤ 동사의 수 일치

Some predators [hunting in the residual light zone of the ocean] /
주어 / 현재분사
해양의 잔광 구역에서 먹이를 잡는 일부 포식자들은
has(→ have) excellent visual capabilities, / [while others are
동사 / 접속사(…하는 반면에)
뛰어난 시력을 가지고 있다 / 반면 나머지 포식자들은
able to create their own light / to attract prey or a mating partner].
부사적 용법의 to부정사(목적)
자신의 빛을 만들어 낼 수 있다 / 먹이감이나 짝을 끌어들이기 위해

➡ 주어는 현재분사구(hunting in ... the ocean)의 수식을 받고 있는 Some predators로, 주어가 복수 명사이므로 단수 동사 has를 복수 동사 have로 고쳐야 한다.

친절한 오답 풀이

① 분사구문

Organisms [living in the deep sea] have adapted / to the high
현재분사
심해에 사는 유기체들은 적응해 왔나 / 고압에
pressure / by storing water in their bodies, / some consisting
by v-ing: …함으로써 / 분사구문(= and some consist ...)
몸에 물을 저장함으로써 / 일부는 거의 물만으로
almost entirely of water.
구성되어 있다

➡ 주어(some)가 생략되지 않은 분사구문으로, consist는 자동사이므로 현재분사 consisting이 오는 것이 알맞다.

② 목적격보어로 쓰인 to부정사

They are cold-blooded organisms / [that adjust their body
주격 관계대명사
그들은 냉혈 유기체이다 / 체온을 맞추는
동시동작을 나타내는 분사구문
temperature / to their environment], / {allowing them to survive
allow A to-v: A가 …하는 것을 허용하다
주변 환경에 / 그들이 차가운 물에 생존하게 하면서
in the cold water / [while maintaining a low metabolism]}.
접속사가 남아있는 분사구문(= while they maintain ...)
낮은 신진대사를 유지하고 있는 동안

➡ 동사 allow는 목적격보어로 to부정사를 취하므로 to survive는 어법상 알맞다.

③ 주격 관계대명사

Many species lower their metabolism so much / [that they are
so + 형용사 + that ...: 접속사
~할 만큼 …한
많은 종들은 그들의 신진대사를 매우 많이 낮춘다 / 그들이 생존할 수 있도록
able to survive / without food / for long periods of time], / {as
접속사(… 때문에)
음식 없이 / 오랜 기간 동안
finding the sparse food [that is available] / expends a lot of energy}.
동명사구 주어 / 주격 관계대명사 / 동사
먹을 수 있는 드문 음식을 찾는 것이 / 많은 에너지를 소비하기 때문에

➡ the sparse food를 선행사로 하고, 관계대명사절에서 주어 역할을 하고 있으므로 주격 관계대명사 that은 어법상 알맞다.

④ 대명사

Many predatory fish of the deep sea / are equipped with
be equipped with: …을 갖추고 있다
심해의 많은 포식성 물고기는 / 결과를 나타내는 분사구문
enormous mouths and sharp teeth, / [enabling them to hold on
enable A to-v: A가 …할 수 있게 하다
거대한 입과 날카로운 이빨을 가지고 있다 / 그것들이 먹이를 붙잡고 제압하게 한다
to prey and overpower it].
= prey

➡ it은 앞에 언급된 prey를 지칭하는 대명사로, 지칭하는 명사가 단수이므로 단수 대명사 it이 오는 것은 어법상 알맞다.

지문 해석

심해에 사는 유기체들은 몸에 물을 저장하여 고압에 적응해 왔고, 일부는 거의 물만으로 구성되어 있다. 대부분의 심해 유기체들은 부레가 없다. 그들은 냉혈 유기체로 주변 환경에 체온을 맞추어, 낮은 신진대사를 유지하고 있는 동안 차가운 물에 생존하게 한다. 많은 종들은 먹을 수 있는 드문 음식을 찾는 것이 많은 에너지를 소비하기 때문에 오랜 기간동안 음식 없이 생존이 가능하도록 그들의 신진대사를 매우 많이 낮춘다. 심해의 많은 포식성 물고기는 거대한 입과 날카로운 이빨을 가지고 있는데 그것들이 먹이를 붙잡고 제압하게 한다. 해양의 잔광 구역에서 먹이를 잡는 일부 포식자들은 뛰어난 시력을 가지고 있고, 반면 나머지 포식자들은 먹이감이나 짝을 끌어들이기 위해 자신의 빛을 만들어 낼 수 있다.

어휘

organism 명 유기체, 생물(체)   adapt 동 적응하다   pressure 명 압력   adjust 동 조절하다, 맞추다   survive 동 생존하다   metabolism 명 신진대사   sparse 형 드문   expend 동 (많은 돈·시간·에너지를) 쓰다, 들이다   predatory 형 포식성의 (predator 명 포식자)   enormous 형 거대한   hold on to …을 꼭 잡다   prey 명 먹이   overpower 동 제압하다   residual light zone 잔광 구역   capability 명 능력

06   정답 ④   정답률 77%

정답 풀이

④ 동사의 수 일치

One of the interesting things about learning and attention /
주어, one of + 복수 명사: … 중의 하나
학습과 주의에 대한 흥미로운 사실 중 하나는
are(→ is) {that [once something becomes automated], / it gets
동사 접속사 접속사(일단 …하면) / get v-ed: 수동태
일단 어떤 일이 자동화되면 / 그것은 실행된다는
executed / in a rapid string of events}.
것이다 / 빠른 일련의 행위로

➡ 문장의 주어가 「one of + 복수 명사」이므로 복수 동사 are를 단수 동사 is로 고쳐야 한다.

친절한 오답 풀이

① 수동태

It is something / {(that) we are so well practiced at / [that we are
목적격 관계대명사 생략 주어 / so ... that ~: 너무 …해서 ~하다
그것은 어떤 것이다 / 우리가 너무 잘 훈련돼있어서 / 우리는 그것을 할 수 있다
able to do it / without much conscious thought]}.
be able to-v: …할 수 있다
많은 의식적인 사고 없이도

➡ something을 선행사로 하는 관계대명사절 안의 주어는 we로, 우리가 잘 '훈련된' 이라는 수동의 의미가 적절하므로 수동태의 과거분사 practiced가 오는 것이 알맞다.

② 관계부사

> That makes our life easier, and it is how we become good at things.
> make + 목적어 + 형용사: …을 ~하게 만들다   관계부사
> 그것은 우리의 삶을 보다 용이하게 만들고, 그것은 우리가 일을 잘하게 되는 방법이다

➡ how는 선행사 the way를 대신해서 쓰인 관계부사로, 뒤에 완전한 절이 이어지고 있으므로 어법상 바르다.

③ 「the + 비교급 …, the + 비교급 ~」

> A serve is a complex maneuver with many different components, /
> 서브는 많은 다른 구성 요소가 결합된 복잡한 동작이다
> but the better we become at it, / the less we think of each
> the + 비교급 …, the + 비교급 ~: …하면 할수록 더 ~하다
> 그러나 우리가 그것을 잘하게 되면 될수록   우리는 각각의 개별적인 단계에 대해서는 덜
> individual step.
> 생각하게 된다

➡ 「the + 비교급 …, the + 비교급 ~」 구문으로, 「the + 비교급」 형태의 the better는 어법상 바르다.

⑤ 구동사와 목적어

> [If you try to pay attention], / you screw it up.
> 접속사(만약 …라면)   screw up: ~을 망치다
> 당신이 주의를 기울이려고 한다면,   당신은 그 일을 망쳐버리게 된다

➡ 「동사 + 부사」로 이루어진 구동사의 목적어가 대명사인 경우 목적어는 동사와 부사 사이에 위치해야 하므로, screw it up은 어법상 바르다.

 구문 분석 Plus

12행	This is (the reason) why the best hitters in baseball do *not necessarily* make the best hitting coaches. ➡ This is why …: '이것이 …한 이유다'라는 의미로, why는 앞에 생략된 선행사 the reason을 수식하는 관계부사 ➡ not necessarily …: '반드시 …인 것은 아니다'라는 의미의 부분부정

지문 해석

우리들 대부분에게 있어서, 운전은 심리학자들이 과잉 학습된 행동이라고 말하는 것이다. 그것은 우리가 너무나 잘 훈련돼있어서 많은 의식적인 사고 없이도 할 수 있는 어떤 것이다. 그것은 우리의 삶을 보다 용이하게 만들고, 그것은 우리가 일을 잘하게 되는 방법이다. 전문 테니스 선수를 생각해 보자. 서브는 많은 다른 구성 요소가 결합된 복잡한 동작이지만, 우리가 그것을 잘하게 되면 될수록, 우리는 각각의 개별적인 단계에 대해서는 덜 생각하게 된다. 학습과 주의에 대한 흥미로운 사실 중 하나는 일단 어떤 일이 자동화되면, 그것은 빠른 일련의 행위로 실행된다는 것이다. 주의를 기울이려고 한다면, 당신은 그 일을 망쳐버리게 된다. 이것이 야구에서 최고의 타자들이 반드시 최고의 타격 코치가 되지는 않는 이유이다.

 어휘

psychologist 명 심리학자   overlearned 형 과잉 학습된   conscious 형 의식적인
thought 명 (특정한) 생각   expert 형 전문적인   complex 형 복잡한   maneuver 명 동작, 움직임   component 명 구성요소   individual 형 개인의, 개별적인
attention 명 주의   automate 동 자동화하다   execute 동 실시하다, 실행하다
a string of 일련의, 연속된   hitter 명 타자   necessarily 부 반드시

07   정답 ②   정답률 78%

정답 풀이

② 동사의 수 일치

> …, the popularity of fine breads and pastries are(→ is) growing /
> 주어   동사
> 고급 빵과 페이스트리의 인기는 상승하고 있다
> even faster / than new chefs can be trained.
> 비교급 강조 부사(훨씬)
> 훨씬 더 빠르게   새로운 요리사들이 훈련될 수 있는 것보다

➡ 문장의 주어는 전치사구(of … pastries)의 수식을 받고 있는 the popularity로, 주어가 단수 명사이므로 복수 동사 are를 단수 동사 is로 고쳐야 한다.

친절한 오답 풀이

① 주격 관계대명사

> …, advances in technology, / from refrigeration to sophisticated
> 주어   from A to B to C: A에서부터 B, C까지
> 기술의 진보는   냉장부터 고성능 오븐, 항공 수송에 이르기까지
> ovens to air transportation / [that carries fresh ingredients
>   주격 관계대명사
>   신선한 재료를 전 세계에 실어 나르는
> around the world], / contributed immeasurably to baking and
>   동사
>   제빵과 페이스트리 제조에 헤아릴 수 없을 정도로 기여했다
> pastry making.

➡ that은 앞의 명사 air transportation을 선행사로 하는 주격 관계대명사로, 관계대명사절에서 동사의 주어 역할을 하고 있으므로 어법상 바르다.

③ 부사 alike

> Interestingly enough, / many of the technological advances in
> 아주 흥미롭게도,   주어, 「many of + 복수 명사」
>   제빵에서의 많은 기술적 발전은
> bread making / have sparked a reaction / among bakers and
>   동사
>   하나의 반응을 촉발했다   제빵사와 소비자에게 똑같이
> consumers alike.

➡ 「A and B alike」는 'A와 B 둘 다, 똑같이'라는 뜻으로, 밑줄 친 alike는 앞의 동사(have sparked)를 수식하는 부사로 쓰였다.

 Grammar Tips

like vs. alike

단어	품사	뜻	용법
like	전치사	… 같은	like + (동)명사 예) He eats **like** a pig. (그는 돼지처럼 먹는다.)
alike	형용사	비슷한	be동사/2형식 동사 + alike 예) These books *are* **alike**. (이 책들은 비슷하다.) 예) They *look* **alike**. (그들은 비슷해 보인다.)
	부사	똑같이	동사 수식 예) She *treats* her children **alike**. (그녀는 아이들을 똑같이 대한다.)

④ 수동태

> They are looking to reclaim / some of the flavors of old-fashioned
> look to-v: …하기를 바라다   선행사
> 그들은 되찾기를 원하고 있다   옛날 빵의 맛 몇 가지를
> breads / [that were lost] / [as baking became more industrialized …].
>   주격 관계대명사   접속사(…하면서)
>   사라진   제빵이 더 산업화되면서

➡ were lost는 주격 관계대명사절의 동사로, 선행사 some of the flavors가 were lost의 의미상 주어이다. 맛 몇 가지가 '사라지는'이라는 수동의 의미가 적절하므로 수동태를 쓰는 것이 알맞다.

⑤ 「전치사 + 동명사」

> Bakers are researching methods / for producing the handmade
>   전치사
> 제빵사들은 방법을 찾고 있다   시큼한 수제 반죽 빵을 생산하기 위한
> sourdough breads / of the past, ….
>   과거의

➡ 앞에 나온 전치사 for의 목적어 역할을 하고, 뒤에 목적어(the handmade sourdough breads)를 가지므로 동명사 producing이 오는 것이 적절하다.

20세기에, 냉장부터 고성능 오븐, 신선한 재료를 전 세계에 실어 나르는 항공 수송에 이르기까지 기술의 진보는 제빵과 페이스트리 제조에 헤아릴 수 없을 정도로 기여했다. 21세기 초에, 고급 빵과 페이스트리의 인기는 새로운 요리사들이 훈련될 수 있는 것보다 훨씬 더 빠르게 상승하고 있다. 아주 흥미롭게도 제빵에서의 많은 기술적 발전은 제빵사와 소비자에게 똑같이 하나의 반응을 촉발했다. 제빵이 더 산업화되고, 제빵 제품이 더 개선되고, 표준화되고, 어떤 사람들이 말하기를 풍미가 없어지면서 그들은 옛날 빵의 사라진 맛 몇 가지를 되찾기를 원하고 있다. 제빵사들은 과거의 시큼한 수제 반죽 빵을 생산하는 방법을 찾고 있으며, 그들은 풍미를 찾기 위해 특제 밀가루로 실험하고 있다.

어휘

advance 뗑 진보 refrigeration 뗑 냉장, 냉동 sophisticated 톙 고성능의 transportation 뗑 수송 ingredient 뗑 재료, 성분 contribute 톰 기여하다 immeasurably 튀 헤아릴 수 없을 정도로 popularity 뗑 인기 spark 톰 촉발하다, 유발하다 reclaim 톰 되찾다 flavor 뗑 풍미, 맛 (flavorless 톙 맛이 없는) old-fashioned 톙 옛날식의, 구식의 industrialize 톰 산업화하다 refine 톰 정제하다; *개선하다 standardize 톰 표준화하다 sourdough 뗑 시큼한 맛이 나는 반죽 experiment 톰 실험하다 specialty 뗑 전문; *특제품 flour 뗑 밀가루

08　　정답 ④　　정답률 49%

④ 동사의 수 일치

Also, {comparing ourselves with someone / [who's doing worse
　　　동명사구 주어　　　　　　　　　　주격 관계대명사
마찬가지로 자신을 누군가와 비교하는 것은　　　우리보다 더 못하고 있는
than we are]} / risk(→ risks) scorn, / the feeling [that others are
　　　　　　　　　　동사
경멸을 가질 위험이 있다　　　즉 다른 사람이 우리의 호의를
something undeserving of our beneficence / ("She's beneath my
받을 가치가 없는 것이라는 느낌　　　　　그녀는 내가 주목할 가치가 없어
notice")].

➡ 문장의 주어는 comparing ... we are로 동명사구이며 동명사구는 단수 취급하므로 동사 risk를 단수 동사 risks로 고쳐야 한다.

친절한 오답 풀이

① 부정대명사

We're not only meaning-seeking creatures but social ones as
　　not only A but (also) B: A뿐만 아니라 B도　　　= creatures
우리는 의미를 추구하는 존재일 뿐만 아니라 사회적인 존재라서
well, / [constantly making interpersonal comparisons / to evaluate
　　　　　결과를 나타내는 분사구문　　　부사적 용법의 to부정사(목적)
　　　끊임없이 사람들끼리 비교한다
ourselves, (to) improve our standing, and (to) enhance our
우리 자신을 평가하고 우리 지위를 개선하며 우리의 자존감을 높이기 위해
self-esteem].

➡ 앞에 나온 복수 명사 creatures를 대신하므로, 복수형 부정대명사 ones가 오는 것이 알맞다.

② 주격보어

{When comparing ourselves to someone [who's doing better
접속사가 생략되지 않은 분사구문(= When we compare ...)　　　주격 관계대명사
우리보다 더 잘하고 있는 사람과 우리 자신을 비교할 때
than we are]}, / we often feel inadequate / for not doing as well.
　　　　　　　　　　　　　　주격보어　　　전치사(…에 대해)
우리는 흔히 무능하다고 느낀다　　그만큼 잘하지 못하는 것에 대해서

➡ 2형식 동사 feel의 주격보어로 형용사 inadequate이 왔으므로 어법상 알맞다.

③ 형용사적 용법의 to부정사

This sometimes leads to {what psychologists call *malignant*
　　　　　…로 이어지다　　관계대명사
이것은 때로는 심리학자들이 '악성 질투'라고 부르는 것으로 이어진다
envy, / the desire for someone to meet with misfortune / ("I wish
　　동격　　　　　형용사적 용법의 to부정사　　　나는
즉 누군가가 불행을 만나기를 바라는 욕망
she didn't have [what she has])}.
　　　　　　관계대명사
그녀가 가진 것을 가지고 있지 않으면 좋을 텐데

➡ 앞의 명사 the desire를 수식하는 형용사적 용법의 to부정사로 어법상 적절하다.

⑤ 계속적 용법의 주격 관계대명사

..., the longing / to reproduce someone else's accomplishments /
　　　　열망　　형용사적 용법의 to부정사　　　선행사
　　　　　　　　다른 사람의 성취를 재생산하려는
without wishing them ill / ("I wish I had what she has"), / [which
without v-ing: …하지 않고　　　　계속적 용법의 주격 관계대명사
그들이 불행해지기를 바라지 않고　그녀가 가진 것을 나도 가지면 좋을 텐데
has been shown in some circumstances to inspire and motivate
그리고 그것은 몇몇 상황에서 우리에게 영감을 주고 동기를 부여하는 것으로 보여져 왔다
us / to increase our efforts / in spite of a recent failure].
부사적 용법의 to부정사(목적)　　　에도 불구하고
우리의 노력을 늘리도록　　　최근의 실패에도 불구하고

➡ the longing ... what she has를 선행사로 하고, 관계대명사절에서 동사(has been shown)의 주어 역할을 하고 있으므로 주격 관계대명사 which가 오는 것이 어법상 바르다.

타인과 견주어 우리 자신을 평가해서는 안 된다는 많은 경고에도 불구하고 우리 대부분은 여전히 그렇게 하고 있다. 우리는 의미를 추구하는 존재일 뿐만 아니라 사회적인 존재라서 우리 자신을 평가하고 우리 지위를 개선하며 우리의 자존감을 높이기 위해 끊임없이 사람들끼리 비교를 한다. 그러나 사회적 비교의 문제는 그것이 흔히 역효과를 낸다는 것이다. 우리보다 더 잘하고 있는 사람과 우리 자신을 비교할 때, 우리는 흔히 그만큼 잘하지 못하는 것에 대해서 무능하다고 느낀다. 이것은 때로는 심리학자들이 '악성 질투'라고 부르는 것, 즉 누군가가 불행을 만나기를 바라는 욕망("나는 그녀가 가진 것을 가지고 있지 않으면 좋을 텐데.")으로 이어진다. 마찬가지로 우리보다 더 못하고 있는 사람과 자신을 비교하는 것은 경멸, 즉 다른 사람이 우리의 호의를 받을 가치가 없는 것이라는 느낌("그녀는 내가 주목할 가치가 없어.")을 가질 위험이 있다. 그렇지 않고 우리 자신을 타인과 비교하는 것은 또한 '양성 질투' 즉, 그들이 불행해지기를 바라지 않고 다른 사람의 성취를 재생산하려는 열망("그녀가 가진 것을 나도 가지면 좋을 텐데.")으로 이어질 수 있으며 그것은 몇몇 상황에서 최근의 실패에도 불구하고 우리의 노력을 늘리도록 우리에게 영감을 주고 동기를 부여하는 것으로 보여져 왔다.

어휘

abundant 톙 풍부한 measure 톰 측정하다; *평가하다 meaning-seeking 톙 의미를 추구하는 interpersonal 톙 사람과 사람 사이의; 대인 관계의 evaluate 톰 평가하다 standing 뗑 지위, 평가 enhance 톰 높이다, 향상하다 inadequate 톙 부적절한; *무능한 malignant 톙 악성의 risk 톰 위태롭게 하다 beneficence 뗑 선행, 자선 reproduce 톰 재생하다, 재형성하다

09　　정답 ⑤　　정답률 76%

⑤ 동사의 수 일치

...; the extrinsic reward / [that matters most to them] / are(→ is)
　　　　주어　　　　　　주격 관계대명사　　　　　동사
　　　외적 보상은　　　　그들에게 가장 중요한
the recognition of their peers.
그들의 동료들의 인정이다

➡ 주어는 관계대명사절(that ... them)의 수식을 받는 the extrinsic reward로, 주어가 단수 명사이므로 복수 동사 are를 단수 동사인 is로 고쳐야 한다.

① 「전치사 + 관계대명사」

To oversimplify, / basic ideas bubble out of universities and
…에서(= from)
과하게 단순화시키자면,   기본적 아이디어들이 대학과 실험실에서 넘쳐 나온다
laboratories / [in which a group of researchers work together]: ....
= where(관계부사)
한 집단의 연구자들이 함께 일하는

➡ which는 universities and laboratories를 선행사로 하고, 관계대명사절에서 전치사 in의 목적어로 쓰였으므로, 「전치사 + 관계대명사」 형태인 in which는 어법상 바르다. 「전치사 + 관계대명사」 뒤에는 완전한 절이 온다.

② 부정대명사

...: both major breakthroughs, / [like understanding the genetic
both A and B: A와 B 둘 다   전치사(…와 같은)
중대한 발견과   생명체의 유전자 구조 이해와 같은
structure of life], / and smaller ones, / [such as advances in
전치사(…와 같은)
그리고 보다 작은 것들   수학이나 기초 화학에서의 진보와 같은
mathematics or basic chemistry].

➡ 상관접속사 「both A and B」에 의해 major breakthroughs와 smaller ones가 병렬 연결된 구조로, 복수 부정대명사 ones가 앞에 나온 복수 명사 breakthroughs를 대신하고 있으므로 어법상 바르다.

③ 「전치사 + 동명사」, 동명사의 동사적 성질

Traditionally, intellectual property has played little role /
play a role in: …에서 역할을 하다
전통적으로, 지적 재산은 별로 역할을 하지 못했다   little(형용사, 거의 없는[아닌])
in promoting basic science.
기초 과학의 증진에 있어서

➡ 앞에 나온 전치사 in의 목적어 역할을 하고, 뒤에 목적어(basic science)를 가지므로 동명사 promoting은 어법상 바르다.

④ 접속사 that

Academia believes in "open architecture," / meaning / {that
분사구문   접속사
학계는 '공개된 구조'를 믿는다   그리고 ("공개된 구조"는) 의미한다
the knowledge [that research produces] should be made public /
목적격 관계대명사   make public: 공표하다
연구가 산출한 지식이 공개되어야 한다는 것을
to encourage innovation}.
부사적 용법의 to부정사(목적)
기술 혁신을 장려하도록

➡ that은 분사 meaning의 목적어 역할을 하는 명사절을 이끄는 접속사로, 뒤에 완전한 절이 이어지고 있으므로 어법상 바르다.

구문 별너 Plus

| 1행 | Today, the world of innovation is **far** different from [*what* it was a century ago].
➡ far: '훨씬'이라는 의미의 부사
➡ what: 선행사를 포함한 관계대명사로, 전치사 from의 목적어 역할을 하는 명사절을 이끌고 있음 |

지문 해석

오늘날, 혁신의 세계는 한 세기 전의 것과 아주 다르다. 혼자서 작업하는 고독한 발명가의 시대는 지나갔다. 과하게 단순화시키자면, 기본적 아이디어들이 한 집단의 연구자들이 함께 일하는 대학과 실험실에서 넘쳐 나온다. 생명체의 유전자 구조 이해와 같은 중대한 발견과 수학이나 기초 화학에서의 진보와 같은 보다 작은 것들 모두가 그렇다. 전통적으로 지적 재산은 기초 과학의 증진에 있어서 별로 역할을 하지 못했다. 학계는 '공개된 구조'를 믿는데, 이는 연구가 산출한 지식이 기술 혁신을 장려하도록 공개되어야 한다는 것을 의미한다. 위대한 과학자들은 우주의 본질을 이해하려는 내적 탐구에 의해 동기를 부여받으며, 그들에게 가장 중요한 외적 보상은 그들의 동료들의 인정이다.

어휘

innovation 몡 혁신 solitary 혱 혼자 하는 oversimplify 통 지나치게 단순화하다 laboratory 몡 실험실 breakthrough 몡 돌파구; *획기적 발견 genetic 혱 유전의 chemistry 몡 화학 intellectual property 지적 재산 academia 몡 학계 architecture 몡 건축학; *구조 quest 몡 탐구 extrinsic 혱 외적인 matter 통 중요하다 recognition 몡 인식; *인정 peer 몡 동료

10   정답 ⑤   정답률 66%

정답 풀이

⑤ 동사의 수 일치

A genuine smile will impact / on the muscles and wrinkles /
진짜 미소는 영향을 줄 것이다   근육과 주름에
around the eyes / and less noticeably, / the skin [between the
주어
눈 주변의   그리고 티가 덜 나게   눈썹과 윗눈꺼풀 사이의 피부가
eyebrow and upper eyelid] / are(→ is) lowered slightly / with true
between A and B: A와 B 사이   동사
살짝 내려온다   진정한 즐거움으로
enjoyment.

➡ 문장의 주어는 전치사구(between the ... eyelid)의 수식을 받고 있는 the skin으로 주어가 단수 명사이므로, 복수 동사 are를 단수 동사 is로 고쳐야 한다.

① 「전치사 + 관계대명사」

There have been occasions / [in which you have observed a smile] /
which는 목적격 관계대명사
경우가 있었다   당신이 미소를 관찰한
and you could sense / [(that) it was not genuine].
명사절(목적어)을 이끄는 접속사 that 생략
그리고 당신은 느낄 수 있었다   그것이 진짜가 아니라고

➡ which는 occasions를 선행사로 하고, 관계대명사절에서 전치사 in의 목적어로 쓰였으므로, 「전치사 + 관계대명사」 형태인 in which는 어법상 바르다. 「전치사 + 관계대명사」 뒤에는 완전한 절이 온다.

② 부정대명사

The most obvious way / of identifying a genuine smile / from an
주어
가장 명확한 방법은   진짜 미소를 알아보는   진실하지 못한 미소로부터
insincere one / is [that a fake smile primarily only affects / the
동사 명사절(보어)을 이끄는 접속사
가짜 미소는 주로 ~에만 영향을 미친다는 것이다
lower half of the face, / mainly with the mouth alone].
얼굴의 절반 아래쪽 부분   주로 입에만

➡ 앞에 나온 명사 smile을 대신하므로, 단수형 부정대명사 one이 오는 것이 알맞다.

③ 분사구문

Take the opportunity / to look in the mirror / and manufacture a
형용사적 용법의 to부정사
기회를 잡아라   거울을 볼   그리고 미소를 지어봐라
smile / [using the lower half your face only].
동시동작을 나타내는 분사구문(= as you use)
당신의 얼굴 아랫부분만을 사용하여

➡ using 이하는 동시동작을 나타내는 분사구문으로, 생략된 주어는 주절인 명령문에서 생략된 주어(you)와 같다. 주어와 분사가 능동 관계이므로 현재분사 using이 오는 것이 알맞다.

④ 간접의문문

> When you do this, / judge [how happy your face really looks] — /
> 간접의문문(의문사 + 주어 + 동사)
> 당신이 이렇게 할 때　당신의 얼굴이 실제로 얼마나 행복해 보이는지를 판단해 봐라
> is it genuine?
> 그것은 진짜인가?

➡ how 이하는 동사 judge의 목적어 역할을 하는 간접의문문으로, 의문부사 how가 형용사 happy를 수식하고 있으므로 어법상 바르다.

지문 해석

당신이 미소를 관찰했는데 그것이 진짜가 아니라고 느낄 수 있는 경우가 있었다. 진짜 미소와 진실하지 못한 미소를 알아보는 가장 명확한 방법은 가짜 미소는 주로 입에만, 얼굴의 절반 아래쪽 부분에만, 주로 영향을 미친다는 것이다. 눈은 실제 관련이 없다. 거울을 볼 기회를 잡아서 당신의 얼굴 아랫부분만을 사용하여 미소를 지어봐라. 당신이 이렇게 할 때, 당신의 얼굴이 실제로 얼마나 행복해 보이는지를 판단해 봐라. 그것은 진짜인가? 진짜 미소는 눈가 근육과 주름에 영향을 주며, 티가 덜 나게 눈썹과 윗눈꺼풀 사이의 피부가 진정한 즐거움으로 살짝 내려오는 것이다. 진짜 미소는 얼굴 전체에 영향을 줄 수 있다.

어휘

occasion 명 때, 경우　sense 동 감지하다, 느끼다　genuine 형 진짜의　obvious 형 분명한, 명백한　identify 동 확인하다, 알아보다　insincere 형 진실되지 못한　primarily 부 주로　involved 형 관련이 있는　manufacture 동 짓다, 만들어내다　impact 동 영향을 주다　wrinkle 명 주름　noticeably 부 눈에 띄게　slightly 부 살짝, 약간

코드 공략하기 02　　pp.35~38

| 01 ④ | 02 ③ | 03 ③ | 04 ② | 05 ② | 06 ① | 07 ③ | 08 ⑤ |
| 09 ③ | 10 ⑤ |

01　　정답 ④　　정답률 47%

정답 풀이

④ 동사의 수 일치

> Artificial light, [which typically contains only a few wavelengths
> 주어　계속적 용법의 주격 관계대명사
> 전형적으로 단지 몇 개의 빛 파장만 있는 인공 조명이
> of light], / do(→ does) not seem to have the same
> 동사　seem to-v: …인 것 같다
> 분위기에 미치는 효과가 똑같지 않을 수 있다
> effect on mood / [that sunlight has].
> └───────┘ 목적격 관계대명사
> 햇빛이 미치는

➡ 문장의 주어는 Artificial light이고 뒤에 오는 which ... light는 선행사 Artificial light를 부연 설명하는 계속적 용법의 관계대명사절이다. 주어가 단수 명사이므로 복수 동사 do를 단수 동사 does로 고쳐야 한다.

친절한 오답 풀이

① 부사

> 동사
> Bad lighting can increase stress on your eyes, / {as can light [that
> 접속사 (…듯이)　주어1 주격
> 나쁜 조명은 여러분의 눈에 스트레스를 증가시킬 수 있다　너무 밝은 빛이나 관계대명사
> is too bright], or light [that shines directly into your eyes]}.
> 주어2　동사↑
> 눈에 직접적으로 비추는 빛이 (증가시킬) 수 있듯이

➡ 동사 shines를 수식하고 있으므로 부사 directly가 오는 것이 알맞다.

---

② 감정을 나타내는 분사

> Fluorescent lighting can also be tiring.
> 주어
> 형광등 또한 피로감을 줄 수 있다

➡ 주어인 Fluorescent lighting이 '피곤하게 하는' 것이므로 능동의 의미인 현재분사 tiring은 어법상 바르다.

③ 주격 관계대명사

> Most people are happiest in bright sunshine / — this may cause
> = bright sunshine
> 대부분의 사람들은 밝은 햇빛 속에서 가장 행복하다　이것은 아마
> a release of chemicals in the body / [that bring a feeling of
> └────┐ 주격 관계대명사
> 체내의 화학물질을 분비시킬지도 모른다　정서적인 행복감을 주는
> emotional well-being].

➡ that은 chemicals를 선행사로 하는 주격 관계대명사로, 관계대명사절에서 주어 역할을 하고 있으므로 어법상 바르다.

⑤ 병렬구조

> Try experimenting with working by a window / or using full
> try v-ing: (시험 삼아) …해보다　동명사　동명사
> 창가에서 작업하며 실험해 봐라　혹은
> spectrum bulbs in your desk lamp.
> 책상 전등에 있는 모든 파장이 있는 전구를 사용하여

➡ 접속사 or가 전치사 with의 목적어로 쓰인 동명사를 병렬 연결하고 있으므로, 앞의 동명사 working과 대등한 동명사 using은 어법상 바르다.

 구문 분석 Plus

> [**What** you may not appreciate] is [that the quality of light
> 4행　may also be important].
> ➡ What: '…하는 것'의 의미로 선행사를 포함한 관계대명사
> ➡ that: 문장의 보어 역할을 하는 명사절을 이끄는 접속사

지문 해석

너무 밝은 빛이나, 눈에 직접적으로 비추는 빛처럼, 나쁜 조명은 여러분의 눈에 스트레스를 증가시킬 수 있다. 형광등 또한 피로감을 줄 수 있다. 여러분이 모를 수도 있는 것은 빛의 질 또한 중요할 수 있다는 것이다. 대부분의 사람들은 밝은 햇빛 속에서 가장 행복하다 — 이것은 아마 정서적인 행복감을 주는 체내의 화학물질을 분비시킬지도 모른다. 전형적으로 단지 몇 개의 빛 파장만 있는 인공 조명이 분위기에 미치는 효과는 햇빛(이 미치는 효과)과 똑같지 않을 수 있다. 창가에서 작업하거나 책상 전등에 있는 모든 파장이 있는 전구를 사용하여 실험해 보아라. 이것이 여러분의 작업 환경의 질을 향상시킨다는 것을 아마도 알게 될 것이다.

어휘

lighting 명 조명　appreciate 동 진가를 알아보다; *인식하다　quality 명 질　release 명 방출, 유출　artificial 형 인공의　contain 동 …이 들어있다　wavelength 명 파장　mood 명 분위기　experiment 동 실험하다　bulb 명 전구

02　　정답 ③　　정답률 74%

정답 풀이

(A) 동사의 수 일치

> The biggest complaint of kids [who don't read] / is {that they
> └──┐ 주격 관계대명사　명사절(보어)을 이끄는 접속사
> 책을 읽지 않는 아이들의 가장 큰 불만은　그들이 읽을 것을 찾을 수
> └───┐ 주격 관계대명사
> can't find anything to read / [that interest / interests them]}.
> └───┘ 형용사적 용법의 to부정사
> 없다는 것이다　그들에게 흥미를 일으키는

➡ 네모는 anything을 선행사로 하는 주격 관계대명사절의 동사로, 선행사에 동사의

수를 일치시켜야 한다. 대명사 anything은 단수이므로 단수 동사 interests가 오는 것이 적절하다.

(B) 대명사

> This is (the place) {where we parents need to do a better job /
> 선행사 생략　　　　　관계부사
> 여기가 부모인 우리가 일을 더 잘할 필요가 있는 곳이다
> of helping our kids identify the genres / [that excite it / them]}.
> help + 목적어 + 동사원형: ~가 ~하도록 돕다　　　주격 관계대명사
> 우리 아이들이 그 장르를 찾도록 도와주는　　　그들을 신나게 하는

➡ 네모의 대명사가 지칭하는 대상이 앞에 나온 복수 명사 our kids이므로 복수 대명사 them이 오는 것이 적절하다.

 Grammar Tips

> **관계부사의 선행사 생략**
>
> the time(시간), the place(장소), the reason(이유) 등 일반적인 선행사의 경우, 생략되는 경우가 많다.
>
> 예) That is (the reason) **why** I didn't call you last night.
> 　(그것이 어젯밤 내가 네게 전화하지 않았던 이유이다.)
>
> 예) This is (the place) **where** the accident happened.
> 　(여기가 그 사고가 일어났던 곳이다.)

(C) 접속사 vs. 관계대명사

> Also, think back on the books / [that you liked] / when / what
> 　…을 회상하다　　　목적격 관계대명사　　접속사
> 또한, 그 책들을 회상해 봐　　　당신이 좋아했던
> you were a child.
> 당신이 아이였을 때

➡ 네모 뒤에 완전한 절이 이어지므로 접속사 when이 들어가는 것이 적절하다. 관계대명사 what 뒤에는 불완전한 절이 온다.

지문 해석

책을 읽지 않는 아이들의 가장 큰 불만은 그들에게 흥미를 일으키는 읽을 것을 찾을 수 없다는 것이다. 여기가 바로 부모인 우리가 아이들이 자신들을 신나게 하는 장르를 찾도록 도와주는 일을 더 잘할 필요가 있는 곳이다. 당신의 지역 공공 도서관의 어린이 서적 사서, 학교 사서, 혹은 좋은 서점의 아동 도서 부분의 관리자가 당신에게 익숙하지 않은 새로운 읽을거리를 선택하도록 도울 수 있다. 또한, 당신이 아이였을 때 좋아했던 책들을 회상해 봐라. 남편과 나 둘 다 Beverly Cleary가 쓴 책들을 좋아했고 우리 아이들도 역시 그 책들을 좋아하는 것이 드러난다.

complaint 몡 불평, 불만　**interest** 통 …의 관심[흥미]을 끌다　**identify** 통 (신원을) 확인하다; *찾다, 발견하다　**excite** 통 흥분시키다, 들뜨게 하다　**librarian** 몡 사서　**turn out** …임이 드러나다

03　정답 ③　정답률 71%

정답 풀이

③ 동사의 수 일치

> Today, we have effectively domesticated ourselves / and many
> 오늘날 우리는 우리 자신을 효율적으로 길들여 왔다　　그리고
> of the tasks of survival / — from avoiding immediate death
> 주어, many of + 복수 명사　　　from A to B: A부터 B까지
> 생존의 많은 과업이　　　즉각적인 죽음을 피하는 것부터
> to building shelters to obtaining food — / has(→ have) been
> 은신처를 짓는 일과 음식을 얻어 내는 일까지　　　동사
> outsourced to the wider society.
> 위탁되어 왔다　　　더 넓은 사회로

➡ 밑줄 친 부분은 문장의 동사 자리로 주어는 many of the tasks이다. 「many of + 복수 명사」는 복수 취급하므로 단수 동사 has를 복수 동사 have로 고쳐야 한다.

┃친절한 오답 풀이┃

① 과거 시제

> The human brain, it turns out, has shrunk in mass / by about
> 인간의 뇌는 부피가 줄어들었다는 것이　삽입절　현재완료(계속)　약 10퍼센트 만큼
> 밝혀졌다
> 10 percent / since it peaked in size 15,000-30,000 years ago.
> 접속사(…한 이래로)
> 15,000년에서 30,000년 전 크기가 정점에 도달한 이래

➡ 15,000-30,000 years ago라는 명백한 과거 시점을 나타내는 부사구가 있으므로 과거 시제 peaked는 어법상 바르다.

② 관계부사

> One possible reason / is that many thousands of years ago /
> 한 가지 가능한 이유는　접속사　수천 년 전에 …라는 것이다
> humans lived in a world of dangerous predators / [where they
> 　　　　　　　　　　　　　　　　　관계부사
> 인간은 위험한 포식자의 세계에서 살았다　항상 그들(위험한 포식자)에
> had to have their wits about them at all times / to avoid being
> 　　　= dangerous predators　부사적 용법의
> 　　　　　　　　　　　　　　　　　to부정사(목적)
> 대한 그들의 기지를 발휘했어야 하는　　죽임을 당하는 것을 피하기 위
> killed].
> being v-ed: 동명사의 수동태
> 해

➡ where는 앞의 명사 a world of dangerous predators를 선행사로 하는 관계부사로, 뒤에 완전한 절이 이어지고 있으므로 어법상 바르다.

 Grammar Tips

> **동명사의 수동태: being v-ed**
>
> 동명사의 의미상 주어와 동명사의 의미 관계가 수동일 때, 수동태 being v-ed를 쓴다.
>
> 예) People object to **being charged** for parking in the area.
> 　(사람들은 이 지역에서 주차 요금을 내게 되는 것을 반대한다.)
> → 동명사의 의미상 주어 people이 주차 요금을 '청구받는' 것이므로 수동태가 쓰임

④ 가주어 진주어 구문

> We are smaller than our ancestors too, / and it is a characteristic
> 　　　　　　　　　　　　　　　　가주어
> 우리는 우리 조상보다 더 작기도 하다　　그리고 가축의 한 특징이다
> of domestic animals / [that they are generally smaller than their
> 　　　　　진주어 = domestic animals
> 　　　　　가축이 그들의 야생 사촌보다 일반적으로 더 작다는 것은
> wild cousins].

➡ 가주어 진주어 구문으로, 접속사 that이 이끄는 명사절이 문장의 진주어 역할을 하고 있으므로 어법상 바르다.

⑤ 대명사

> ... but it may mean / that our brains today are wired up differently,
> 　　　　　명사절(목적어)을 이끄는 접속사
> 그러나 그것은 의미할지도 모른다 오늘날 우리의 뇌가 다르게
> and perhaps more efficiently, / than those of our ancestors.
> 　　　　　　비교급 + than …: …보다 더 ~한　= brains
> 그리고 아마도 더 효율적으로 타고났다는 것을　우리 조상들의 그것들보다

➡ 복수 대명사 those는 앞에 언급된 복수 명사 brains를 대신하므로 어법상 바르다.

Grammar Tips

that vs. those

앞에 언급한 명사의 반복을 피하기 위해 대명사 that이나 those를 쓴다. 이때, 대신하는 명사가 단수이면 that, 복수이면 those를 쓴다.

예) *The population* of China is much larger than **that** of Korea.
(중국의 인구는 한국의 그것(인구)보다 훨씬 더 많다.)
This year's *sales* were more than **those** of last year.
(올해 판매량은 작년의 그것들(판매량)보다 더 많았다.)

지문 해석

인간의 뇌는 15,000년에서 30,000년 전 크기가 정점에 도달한 이래 부피가 약 10퍼센트만큼 줄어들었다는 것이 밝혀졌다. 한 가지 가능한 이유는 수천 년 전에 인간은 죽임을 당하는 것을 피하기 위해 항상 그들(위험한 포식자)에 대한 그들의 기지를 발휘했어야 하는 위험한 포식자의 세계에서 살았다는 것이다. 오늘날, 우리는 우리 자신을 효율적으로 길들여 왔고 생존의 많은 과업이 — 즉각적인 죽음을 피하는 것부터 은신처를 짓는 일과 음식을 얻어 내는 일까지 — 더 넓은 사회로 위탁되어 왔다. 우리는 우리의 조상보다 더 작기도 한데, 가축이 그들의 야생 사촌보다 일반적으로 더 작다는 것은 가축의 한 특징이다. 이것의 어떤 것도 우리가 더 어리석다는 것을 의미하지는 않지만 — 뇌 크기가 반드시 인간의 지능의 지표는 아니다 — 그것은 오늘날 우리의 뇌가 다르게, 그리고 우리 조상들의 그것들보다 아마도 더 효율적으로 타고났다는 것을 의미할지도 모른다.

shrink 통 줄어들다, 작아지다 peak 통 절정에 달하다 predator 명 포식자
wit 명 기지, 재치 domesticate 통 (동물을) 길들이다 shelter 명 주거지; 은신처
outsource 통 외부에 위탁하다 characteristic 명 특징 indicator 명 지표

04   정답 ②   정답률 60%

정답 풀이

② 동사의 수 일치

[Accepting your role in your problems] / mean(→ means) /
　　　　　동명사구 주어　　　　　　　　　　　동사
당신의 문제에 있어 자신의 역할을 받아들이는 것은　　　의미한다
{that you understand / [(that) the solution **lies** within you]}.
명사절(목적어)을 이끄는 접속사　접속사 생략
당신이 이해함을　　　해결책이 당신 안에 있다는 것을

➡ 문장의 주어가 동명사구(Accepting ... problems)이며 동명사구는 단수 취급하므로 동사 mean은 단수 형태 means로 고쳐야 한다.

 Grammar Tips

주의해야 할 자동사와 타동사

동사	뜻	과거	과거분사	현재분사
lie(자동사)	눕다, …에 있다	lay	lain	lying
lie(자동사)	거짓말하다	lied	lied	lying
lay(타동사)	놓다, (알을) 낳다	laid	laid	laying

친절한 오답 풀이

① 재귀대명사

Get to really know yourself / and learn [what your weaknesses are].
명령문의 동사1　　　재귀대명사　　동사2　간접의문문(의문사+주어+동사)
자신을 확실히 알아라　　　　　그리고 당신의 약점이 무엇인지를 파악하라

➡ 명령문에 생략된 주어(you)와 목적어가 가리키는 대상이 같으므로, 목적어로 재귀대명사 yourself가 오는 것이 어법상 바르다.

---

③ 관계대명사 what

[If you have a weakness in a certain area], / get educated and
접속사(만약 …라면)
만약 당신이 특정 분야에 약점이 있다면　　　　　　　　　배워서
do [what you have to do] / to improve things / for yourself.
　　관계대명사　　　　　　부사적 용법의 to부정사(목적)
해야 할 것을 행하라　　　상황을 개선하기 위해　　스스로

➡ 앞에 선행사가 없고, 뒤에 목적어가 빠진 불완전한 절이 이어지므로 선행사를 포함하는 관계대명사 what이 오는 것이 어법상 바르다.

④ 대명사

[If your social image is terrible], / look within yourself and
　　　　　　　　　　　　　　　　　동사1　　　　접속사
만약 당신의 사회적 이미지가 형편없다면　자신을 들여다보고
take the necessary steps to improve it, TODAY.
동사2　　　　　　　　　　　　　형용사적 용법의 to부정사
그것을 개선하기 위한 필요한 조치들을 취하라, 오늘 당장

➡ it은 앞에 언급된 your social image를 지칭하는 대명사로, 지칭하는 명사가 단수이므로 단수 대명사 it이 오는 것이 어법상 바르다.

⑤ stop v-ing

Decide today to end all the excuses, / and stop lying to yourself /
　동사1　　　　　　　　　　　　　　　　동사2, stop v-ing: …하는 것을 멈추다
모든 변명을 끝내기로 오늘 결심해라　　　그리고 자신에게 거짓말하는 것을 멈춰라
about [what is going on].
　　관계대명사
일어나고 있는 일에 대해

➡ 동사 stop은 뒤에 to부정사(…하기 위해)와 동명사(…하는 것을)가 모두 올 수 있는데, 문맥상 거짓말하는 것을 멈춘다는 의미이므로 stop 뒤에 동명사 lying이 오는 것이 적절하다.

지문 해석

당신은 당신의 강점과 약점에 대하여 자신에게 솔직한가? 자신을 확실히 알고 당신의 약점이 무엇인지를 파악하라. 당신의 문제에 있어 자신의 역할을 받아들이는 것은 해결책도 당신 안에 있다는 것을 이해함을 의미한다. 만약 당신이 특정 분야에 약점이 있다면, 배워서 상황을 개선하기 위해 해야만 할 것을 스스로 행하라. 만약 당신의 사회적 이미지가 형편없다면, 오늘 당장 자신을 들여다보고 그것을 개선하기 위한 필요한 조치들을 취하라. 당신은 삶에 대응하는 방법을 선택할 능력이 있다. 오늘 모든 변명을 끝내기로 결심하고, 일어나고 있는 일에 대해 자신에게 거짓말하는 것을 멈춰라. 성장의 시작은 당신이 자신의 선택에 대한 책임을 직접 받아들이기 시작할 때 일어난다.

strength 명 강점, 장점 weakness 명 약점 solution 명 해결책 lie 통 (…에)
있다 improve 통 개선하다 social 형 사회적인 respond 통 대답하다; *대응하다
excuse 명 변명 personally 부 직접, 개인적으로 responsibility 명 책임

05   정답 ②   정답률 57%

정답 풀이

② 동사의 수 일치

The skin around her eyes form(→ forms) small and thin lines, /
　　주어　　　　　　　　　　동사
그녀의 눈 주변의 피부에는 작고 가는 주름들이 생기는데,
and the lines match mine.
그 주름들은 내 것과 일치한다

➡ 문장의 주어는 전치사구(around her eyes)의 수식을 받는 명사 The skin으로, 주어가 단수 명사이므로 복수 동사 form을 단수 동사 forms로 고쳐야 한다.

34 • 다빈출코드

① 접속사 that

Her face reminds me / [that I have given her more than just my name].
　　　4형식 동사　　간접목적어　　　　　　직접목적어
그녀의 얼굴은 내게 상기시킨다　　　내가 그녀에게 단지 이름 이상의 것을 주었다는 것을

➡ that은 동사 reminds의 직접목적어 역할을 하는 명사절을 이끌고 있는 접속사로, 뒤에 완전한 절이 이어지므로 어법상 바르다.

③ 부사

I see myself most clearly in her eyes, / the windows to her soul.
나는 그녀의 눈에서 나 자신을 가장 분명하게 본다　　그녀의 영혼의 창인

➡ 부사 clearly는 동사 see를 수식하므로 어법상 바르다.

④ 형용사적 용법의 to부정사

..., Emily has a drive to succeed / and will try anything.
Emily는 성공하려는 의욕을 가지고 있고　　어떤 것이든 시도하려고 한다

➡ to succeed는 형용사적 용법의 to부정사로, 앞의 명사 a drive를 수식하고 있으므로 어법상 바르다.

⑤ 재귀대명사

"Who needs to wait for instructions?"/ she used to tell herself /
　　　　　　　　　　　　　　　　　　　　　　　…하곤 했다(과거의 습관)
"누가 지시를 기다릴 필요가 있나요?"　　그녀는 자기 자신에게 말하곤 했다
[as she attempted to do the high bar / in gymnastics class];
접속사(…할 때) attempt to-v: …하려고 시도하다
그녀가 철봉을 하려고 시도했을 때　　　　　체조 시간에

➡ 주어(she)와 목적어가 가리키는 대상이 같으므로 재귀대명사 herself가 오는 것이 어법상 바르다.

지문 해석

내 딸 Emily의 얼굴을 볼 때마다, 나는 부성(父性)의 힘에 대해 생각한다. 그녀의 얼굴은 내가 그녀에게 단지 이름 이상의 것을 주었다는 것을 내게 상기시킨다. 나처럼, 그녀는 거의 반창고같이 그녀의 콧날을 가로질러 펼쳐있는 주근깨를 가지고 있다. 그녀의 눈 주변의 피부에는 작고 가는 주름들이 생기는데, 그 주름들은 내 것과 일치한다. 어머니는 내게 "Emily가 웃으면, 너랑 아주 똑같아."라고 말씀하신다. 그녀의 다른 것들도 내 모습들이다. 나는 그녀의 영혼의 창인 그녀의 눈에서 나 자신을 가장 분명하게 본다. 나처럼, Emily는 성공하려는 의욕을 가지고 있고 어떤 것이든 시도하려고 한다. 체조 시간에 철봉을 하려고 시도했을 때, 그녀는 "누가 지시를 기다릴 필요가 있나요?"라고 자기 자신에게 말하곤 했다. 그녀는 한 번 이상 실패했다. 또한 그녀는 한 번 이상 성공했다.

fatherhood 몡 아버지임, 부성　**remind** 동 상기시키다　**freckle** 몡 주근깨
stretch 동 늘이다; *펼쳐지다　**bridge** 몡 다리; *콧대, 콧날　**match** 동 일치하다
reflection 몡 상, 모습　**drive** 몡 드라이브; *욕구　**instruction** 몡 설명; *지시
gymnastics 몡 체조

06　　　　정답 ①　　　정답률 44%

정답 풀이

(A) be eager to-v

[When I got back to my hotel room / after taking a lot of pictures], /
접속사　　get back: 돌아오다　　　　　전치사(… 후에)
내가 호텔방으로 돌아왔을 때　　　　　　많은 사진을 찍은 후
I was eager to upload / ~~uploading~~ the photos to my blog.
be eager to-v: …하고 싶어 하다
나는 그 사진들을 내 블로그에 올리고 싶었다

➡ 「be eager to-v」구문으로 to 뒤에 동사원형인 upload가 오는 것이 적절하다.

(B) 동사의 수 일치

{When I told my friend / [what had happened],} / he sent me
접속사　　　　　　　　간접의문문(의문사(주어) + 동사)
내가 친구에게 이야기했을 때　　무슨 일이 일어났는지　　　　그는 나에게
a certain program / {designed to recover photos / that was / were
　　　　　　　　　　　과거분사 부사적 용법(목적)　　　　　주격 관계대명사
어떤 프로그램을 보내주었다　　사진들을 복구하도록 고안된
deleted from flash memory cards by mistake]}.
실수로, 잘못하여
플래시 메모리카드에서 실수로 지워진

➡ 네모는 photos를 선행사로 하는 주격 관계대명사절의 동사로, 선행사에 수를 일치시켜야 한다. 선행사가 복수 명사이므로 복수 동사 were가 오는 것이 적절하다.

(C) 「have(사역동사) + 목적어 + v-ed」

But you need one / to have lost files ~~to recover~~ / recovered /
　　　　　　　　　　형용사적 용법의 to부정사　have(사역동사) + 목적어 + v-ed:
그러나 당신은 하나가 필요하다　잃어버린 파일이 복구되게 할　　…가 ~되게 하다
in case things go wrong.
접속사(…할 경우에 대비하여)
일이 잘못될 경우를 대비하여

➡ 사역동사 have는 보통 「have + 목적어 + 동사원형(목적격보어)」 형태로 쓰지만, 목적어와 목적격보어가 수동 관계일 경우, 목적격보어로 과거분사를 쓴다. 잃어버린 파일이 '복구된다'는 수동의 의미가 적절하므로 과거분사 recovered가 오는 것이 알맞다.

지문 해석

내가 많은 사진을 찍은 후 호텔방으로 돌아왔을 때, 나는 그 사진들을 내 블로그에 올리고 싶었다. 나는 디지털 카메라를 컴퓨터에 연결했고, 과정이 끝났을 때, 거기에는 사진이 없었다! 더 심각한 것은, 내 메모리 카드에 있는 사진들도 사라져버렸다는 것이다. 내가 친구에게 무슨 일이 일어났는지 이야기했을 때, 그는 나에게 플래시 메모리카드에서 실수로 지워진 사진들을 복구하도록 고안된 어떤 프로그램을 보내주었다. 나는 그 프로그램을 실행해보았다. 그것은 내가 잃어버린 대부분의 사진들로 폴더를 채웠다. 나는 당신이 이런 종류의 프로그램을 사용할 일이 결코 없기를 바란다. 그러나 당신은 일이 잘못될 경우를 대비하여 잃어버린 파일이 복구되게 할 프로그램이 필요하다.

upload 동 업로드하다　**plug** 동 끼워 넣다　**process** 몡 과정　**complete** 형 완벽한; *완료된　**certain** 형 확실한; *어떤　**recover** 동 회복하다; *복구하다
delete 동 삭제하다　**occasion** 몡 (특정한) 때, 경우

07　　　　정답 ③　　　정답률 75%

정답 풀이

③ 동사의 수 일치

Only in the last few decades, / in the primarily industrially
부사구
겨우 지난 몇 십 년 동안,　　　주요 선진 공업국에서
developed economies, / have(→ has) food become so plentiful
　　　　　　　　　　　　조동사　주어　　so ... as to-v: 너무 …해서 ~하다
　　　　　　　　　　　　식량이 너무 풍부하고 구하기 쉬워져서
and easy to obtain / as to cause fat-related health problems.
부사적 용법의 to부정사
지방 관련 건강 문제를 일으키게 되었다

➡ Only가 이끄는 부사구가 문장 앞에 나와서, 조동사가 주어 앞으로 나온 도치 구문이다. 문장의 주어 food는 단수 명사이므로, 복수형 조동사 have를 단수형인 has로 고쳐야 한다.

① 접속사 that

..., it is no wonder / [that many people view any amount of
가주어　　　　　　　　　진주어, that은 접속사　　view A as B: A를 B라고 여기다
놀랄 일이 아니다　　　　　　많은 사람들이 눈에 보이는 어떤 양의 지방을 여기는 것은
visible fat / on the body / as something to get rid of].
　　　　　　　　　　　　　　　　　　　　형용사적 용법의 to부정사
몸에 있는　　　없애야 하는 것으로　　get rid of: …을 제거하다, 없애다

➡ that은 가주어 it에 대한 진주어절을 이끄는 접속사로, 뒤에 완전한 절이 이어지므로 어법상 적절하다. 「It is no wonder that ....은 '…하는 것은 놀랄 일이 아니다'라는 뜻의 구문이다.

② 부사

..., the ability to <u>store</u> fat <u>efficiently</u> / is a valuable physiological
부사
형용사적 용법의 to부정사
지방을 효율적으로 저장하는 능력은 　　　　　 소중한 생리적인 기능이다
function / [that served our ancestors well / for thousands of years].
주격 관계대명사
우리 조상에게 큰 도움을 주었던 　　　　　　　 수천 년 동안

➡ 부사 efficiently가 동사 store를 수식하고 있으므로 어법상 바르다.

④ 「spend + 시간 + v-ing」

People no longer have to <u>spend</u> most of their time and energy /
더 이상 …않다　　　 spend + 시간 + v-ing: …하는 데 시간을 쓰다
사람들은 더 이상 그들의 시간과 에너지 대부분을 쓸 필요가 없다
<u>gathering</u> berries and seeds and hoping / [that a hunting party will
명사절(목적어)을 이끄는 접속사
열매와 씨앗을 모으고 바라는 데에 　　　　　　 사냥 나간 무리가
return with meat].
고기를 가지고 돌아오기를

➡ 「spend + 시간 + v-ing」 구문으로 동명사 gathering은 어법상 바르다.

⑤ 관계부사

<u>All</u> [(that) we have to do nowadays] / is (to) drive to
목적격 관계대명사 생략　　　　　 보어로 쓰인 원형부정사
오늘날 우리가 해야 할 모든 것은　　　 슈퍼마켓이나 패스트푸드점으로
the supermarket or the fast-food restaurant, / [where for very low
선행사　　　　　　　　　 계속적 용법의 관계부사
운전해서 가는 것이다　　　　　　　　 거기서 아주 적은 비용으로
cost / we can obtain nearly all of our daily calories].
우리는 하루 열량의 거의 전부를 얻을 수 있다

➡ where는 the supermarket or the fast-food restaurant를 선행사로 하는 계속적 용법의 관계부사로, 뒤에 완전한 절이 이어지고 있으므로 어법상 바르다.

 Grammar Tips

> **주격보어로 쓰이는 원형부정사**
>
> 주어에 동사 do를 포함하고 be동사가 뒤따르는 경우, 주격보어로 쓰인 to부정사에서 to는 주로 생략한다.
>
> 예) All I want to do is (to) take a rest for a while.
> (내가 하고 싶은 모든 것은 잠시 쉬는 것이다.)

지문 해석

날씬해지고 싶은 모든 열정으로, 많은 사람들이 몸에 있는 눈에 보이는 어떤 양의 지방도 없어야 하는 것으로 여기는 것은 놀랄 일이 아니다. 그러나 인류의 몸은 식량이 부족한 환경에서 시간에 걸쳐 진화해 왔다. 따라서, 지방을 효율적으로 저장하는 능력은 수천 년 동안 우리 조상에게 큰 도움을 주었던 소중한 생리적인 기능이다. 겨우 지난 몇 십 년 동안, 주요 선진 공업국에서 식량이 너무 풍부하고 구하기 쉬워져서 지방 관련 건강 문제를 일으키게 되었다. 사람들은 더 이상 그들의 시간과 에너지 대부분을 열매와 씨앗을 모으고, 사냥 나간 무리가 고기를 가지고 돌아오기를 바라는 데에 쓸 필요가 없다. 오늘날 우리가 해야 할 모든 것은 슈퍼마켓이나 패스트푸드점으로 운전해서 가는 것인데, 거기서 우리는 아주 적은 비용으로 하루 열량의 거의 전부를 얻을 수 있다.

 어휘

passion 명 열정, 격정　visible 형 보이는　fat 명 지방　evolve 동 발달하다; *진화하다　scarcity 명 부족, 결핍　hence 부 그러므로, 따라서　efficiently 부 효율적으로　valuable 형 소중한　physiological 형 생리적인　function 명 기능　serve 동 제공하다; *도움이 되다　ancestor 명 조상　primarily 부 주로　industrially 부 산업에 관련하여　economy 명 경제; *국가　plentiful 형 풍부한　party 명 정당; *단체, 일행　obtain 동 획득하다

08　　　정답 ⑤　　　정답률 66%

정답 풀이

⑤ 동사의 수 일치

This is because collisions between aircraft usually occur / in the
부사구
이는 왜냐하면 항공기 간의 충돌은 대개 발생하지만
surrounding area of airports, / [while crashes due to aircraft
접속사　주어　 전치사(…로 인해)
공항 주변 지역에서　　　 반면에 항공기 오작동으로 인한 사고는
malfunction / tends(→ tend) to occur during long-haul flight].
동사　　　 전치사(… 동안)
　　　　 장거리 비행 동안에 발생하는 경향이 있기 때문이다

➡ 문장의 주어(crashes)가 복수이므로, 단수 동사 tends를 복수 동사 tend로 고쳐야 한다.

▌친절한 오답 풀이▐

① 계속적 용법의 주격 관계대명사

Airways have fixed widths and defined altitudes, / {which
선행사　　　　　 계속적 용법의 주격 관계대명사
항로에는 고정된 폭과 규정된 고도가 있고
separate traffic / [moving in opposite directions]}.
현재분사
그것들이 통행을 분리한다　 반대 방향으로 움직이는

➡ fixed widths and defined altitudes를 선행사로 하고, 관계대명사절에서 동사(separate)의 주어 역할을 하고 있으므로 주격 관계대명사 which가 오는 것이 어법상 바르다.

② 목적격보어로 쓰인 to부정사

Vertical separation of aircraft / allows some flights to pass over
allow A to-v: A가 …하는 것을 허용하다
항공기 간의 수직 분리는　　　　 일부 비행기가 공항 위를 통과할 수 있게 한다
airports / [while other processes occur below].
접속사(…하는 동안)
아래에서 다른 과정이 이루어지는 동안

➡ 동사 allow는 목적격보어로 to부정사를 취하므로 to pass는 어법상 바르다.

③ 명사를 수식하는 과거분사

Air travel usually covers long distances, / with short periods of
항공 여행은 보통 장거리에 걸치며
intense pilot activity / at takeoff and landing / and (with) long
반복으로 인한 생략
짧은 시간의 고강도 조종사 활동과　 이륙과 착륙 시
periods of lower pilot activity / while in the air, / the portion of
동격
긴 시간의 저강도 조종사 활동이 있다　 공중에 있는 동안
the flight [known as the "long haul."]
과거분사
'장거리 비행'이라고 알려진 비행 부분인

➡ known은 앞에 오는 명사구(the portion of the flight)를 수식하는 분사로, 장거리 비행이라고 '알려진'이라는 수동의 의미가 적절하므로 과거분사가 오는 것이 어법상 바르다.

④ 병렬구조

During the long-haul portion of a flight, / pilots spend more time /
전치사(… 동안)　　　　　　　　　spend + 시간 + v-ing: …하는 데 시간을 쓰다
장거리 비행 부분 동안　　　　　　　조종사들은 더 많은 시간을 보낸다
assessing aircraft status / than searching out nearby planes.
항공기 상태를 평가하는 데　　　근처의 비행기를 탐색하는 것보다

➡ 「spend + 시간 + v-ing」 구문이 than으로 병렬 연결되어 있는 구조로, 동명사 searching은 어법상 바르다.

지문 해석

민간 항공기는 물리적 구조물은 아니지만 일반적으로 도로와 유사한 항로로 운항한다. 항로에는 고정된 폭과 규정된 고도가 있고, 그것들이 반대 방향으로 움직이는 통행을 분리한다. 항공기 간의 수직 분리는 아래에서 다른 과정이 이루어지는 동안 일부 비행기가 공항 위를 통과할 수 있게 한다. 항공 여행은 보통 장거리에 걸치며, 이륙과 착륙 시 짧은 시간의 고강도 조종사 활동과, '장거리 비행'이라고 알려진 비행 부분인, 공중에 있는 동안 긴 시간의 저강도 조종사 활동이 있다. 장거리 비행 부분 동안 조종사들은 근처의 비행기를 탐색하는 것보다 항공기 상태를 평가하는 데 더 많은 시간을 보낸다. 이는 항공기 간의 충돌은 대개 공항 주변 지역에서 발생하는 반면 항공기 오작동으로 인한 사고는 장거리 비행 동안에 발생하는 경향이 있기 때문이다.

commercial ⓗ 민간의, 상업적인　airway ⓜ 항로　structure ⓜ 구조(물)
fixed ⓗ 고정된　width ⓜ 폭　define ⓥ 규정하다　separate ⓥ 분리하다
(separation ⓜ 분리)　opposite ⓗ 반대의　vertical ⓗ 상하의, 수직의　aircraft
ⓜ 항공기　intense ⓗ 고강도의, 강렬한　takeoff ⓜ 이륙　landing ⓜ 착륙
long-haul ⓗ 장거리의　assess ⓥ 평가하다　status ⓜ 지위; *상태　collision
ⓜ 충돌　crash ⓜ (자동차 충돌·항공기 추락) 사고　malfunction ⓜ 오작동, 고장

09　　정답 ③　　정답률 43%

정답 풀이

(A) 관계부사 vs. 관계대명사

It had long been something of a mystery / [where, and on what,
가주어　　　　　　　　　　　　　　　진주어(의문사절)
오랫동안 다소 불가사의한 것이었다　　어디에서 그리고 무엇을
the northern fur seals of the eastern Pacific feed /
동태평양 북부의 물개들이 먹고 사는지
during the winter], / [when / which] they spend /
전치사(… 동안) 선행사　　　계속적 용법의 목적격 관계대명사
겨울 동안　　　　　　　그들은 보낸다
off the coast of North America / from California to Alaska].
북아메리카 연안에서　　　　　　　캘리포니아에서 알래스카까지의

➡ the winter를 선행사로 하면서 동사 spend의 목적어 역할을 하는 목적격 관계대명사가 필요하므로 which가 오는 것이 적절하다. 네모 뒤에 목적어가 빠진 불완전한 절이 이어지고 있으므로 관계부사 when은 올 수 없다.

코드+α 오답 피하기 Tips

선행사가 때를 나타내면 뒤에는 무조건 관계부사 when이다?

선행사만 보고 성급하게 관계부사를 써야 한다고 생각하면 안 된다. 관계사절의 문장성분을 확인하고 완전한 절이 오면 관계부사, 불완전한 절이 오면 관계대명사를 써야 한다.

예) Who will compensate **the time** *which* we wasted to solve the wrong problems.
(잘못된 문제를 풀기 위해 우리가 낭비한 시간을 누가 보상해 줄 것인가?)

(B) 명사를 수식하는 현재분사

Presumably four million seals could not compete with
　　　　　　　　　　　　　　　　　compete with: …와 경쟁하다
아마도 4백만 마리의 물개들이 상업적 어부들과 경쟁할 수 없었을 것이다
commercial fishermen / for the same species / without
　　　　　　　　　　　　　　　　　　　　전치사(… 없이)
　　　　　　　　　　같은 종을 놓고　　　알려진 사실은 없지만
the fact [being / is] known].
　　　　　　　　현재분사

➡ without은 전치사이므로, 뒤에 목적어로 명사(구)가 와야 한다. 따라서 네모 이하는 동사가 아닌 앞의 명사 the fact를 수식하는 분사구가 되어야 하므로, 현재분사 being이 오는 것이 적절하다.

(C) 동사의 수 일치

Indeed, not even its remains [has / have] been found anywhere /
　　　　　　　　　　주어　　　　have been v-ed: 현재완료 수동태
사실, 심지어 그것의 잔존물조차 어느 곳에서도 발견된 적이 없었다
except in the stomachs of seals.
물개들의 위 속을 제외하고

➡ 문장의 주어는 복수 명사 its remains이므로 복수 동사 have가 오는 것이 알맞다.

지문 해석

동태평양 북부의 물개들이 겨울 동안 어디에서, 그리고 무엇을 먹고 사는지는 오랫동안 다소 불가사의한 것이었는데, 그들은 그 계절을 캘리포니아에서 알래스카까지의 북아메리카 연안에서 보낸다. 그들이 정어리, 고등어 또는 다른 상업적으로 중요한 물고기를 얼마만큼이나 많이 먹고 살고 있다는 증거는 없다. 아마도, 알려진 사실은 없지만 4백만 마리의 물개들이 같은 종을 놓고 상업적 어부들과 경쟁할 수 없었을 것이다. 그러나 물개들의 먹이에 관한 약간의 증거는 있고, 그것은 대단히 의미심장하다. 그들의 위에서 살아있는 채로는 발견된 적이 없는 한 종의 물고기 뼈들이 나왔다. 사실, 물개들의 위 속을 제외하고 심지어 그것의 잔존물조차 어느 곳에서도 발견된 적이 없었다. 어류학자들은 이 '물개 어류'가 대륙붕 가장자리에서 떨어진 아주 깊은 물에서 보통 서식하는 한 집단에 속한다고 말한다.

mystery ⓜ 신비, 불가사의　fur seal 물개　to an extent … 정도까지　sardine
ⓜ 정어리　mackerel ⓜ 고등어　commercially ⓦ 상업적으로 (commercial ⓗ
상업적인)　presumably ⓦ 아마도, 짐작건대　evidence ⓜ 증거　significant ⓗ
중요한; *의미심장한　yield ⓥ 내다, 산출하다　remains ⓜ 《pl.》 남은 것, 나머지
belong to …에 속하다　inhabit ⓥ 살다, 서식하다　continental shelf 대륙붕

10　　정답 ⑤　　정답률 38%

정답 풀이

⑤ 동사의 수 일치

They have no memories / about [what **the aged** once was
　　　　　　　　　　　간접의문문(의문사 + 주어 + 동사)
그들은 기억이 없다　　고령자들이 한때 무엇이었는지에 관한
(→ were)] / and greet them / as if they were children.
　　　　　　　　　　　　as if + 가정법 과거: 마치 …인[하는] 것처럼
　　　　　그리고 그들을 반긴다　마치 그들이 어린아이인 것처럼

➡ 의문사 what이 이끄는 의문사절의 주어는 the aged(= aged people)로, 절의 주어가 복수이므로 단수 동사 was를 복수 동사 were로 고쳐야 한다.

코드+α Grammar Tips

「the + 형용사/분사」
'…한 사람들'이라는 의미로, 사람을 나타내는 복수보통명사이다.

예) The article says that **the unemployed** want their jobs back.
(그 기사에는 실업자들이 다시 일자리를 원한다고 쓰여 있다.)

▌친절한 오답 풀이▐

① 대명사

> [When people face real adversity ...]. / A pet's continuing
> 접속사(…할 때)
> 사람들이 진짜 역경에 직면할 때　　　　　애완동물의 계속적인 애착은
> affection / becomes crucially important / for those [enduring
> 　　　　　결정적으로 중요해진다　　　　　어려움을 견디는 사람들에게
> 　　　　　　　　　　　　　　　　　　　　　　　　　　　　현재분사
> hardship] / because it reassures them / [that their core essence
> 　　　　　　　　　　　　　　　　　　　　　　명사절을 이끄는 접속사
> 　　왜냐하면 그것이 그들을 안심시키기 때문이다　그들의 핵심적인 본질이
> has not been damaged].
> 손상되지 않았다고

➡ 앞 문장에 나온 people을 지칭하는 대명사로, 지칭하는 대상이 복수이므로 복수형 대명사 those는 어법상 바르다.

② 명사를 수식하는 과거분사

> Thus pets are important / in the treatment /
> 따라서 애완동물은 중요하다　　　　　치료에서
> of depressed or chronically ill patients.
> 　과거분사
> 우울증을 앓거나 만성적인 병이 있는 환자들의

➡ 밑줄 친 depressed는 뒤에 오는 명사 patients를 수식하는 과거분사로, 환자들이 우울증을 '겪게 되는'이라는 수동의 의미가 적절하므로 과거분사로 쓰는 것이 알맞다.

③ 수동태

> In addition, pets are used / to great advantage /
> 　　　　　　　　　　　　　to advantage: 유리하게
> 게다가, 애완동물은 사용된다　　크게 유리하게
> with the institutionalized aged.
> 　　　= aged people[the elderly]
> 시설로 보내진 고령자들에게

➡ 주어는 pets이고, 애완동물이 '사용된다'라는 수동의 의미가 적절하므로 수동태 are used는 어법상 바르다.

④ 간접의문문

> 　　　　　주격 관계대명사
> Children [who visit] / cannot help but remember / [what their
> 　　　cannot (help) but + 동사원형: …하지 않을 수 없다　동사1
> 방문하는 아이들은　　　기억하지 않을 수 없다　　　그들의 부모님이나
> parents or grandparents once were] / and be depressed by their
> 간접의문문(의문사 + 주어 + 동사)　　　　접속사 동사2
> 조부모님이 한때 무엇이었는지를　　　　그리고 그들의 불능 상태로 인해 우울해진다
> incapacities.

➡ what 이하는 앞의 동사 remember의 목적어 역할을 하는 간접의문문으로, 간접의문문 안에서 what은 동사 were의 보어로 쓰인 의문대명사로 어법상 바르다.

지문 해석

사람들이 질병, 실업, 나이로 인한 장애와 같은 진짜 역경에 직면할 때, 애완동물의 애착은 새로운 의미를 가지게 된다. 애완동물의 계속적인 애착은 어려움을 견디고 있는 사람들에게 결정적으로 중요해지는데, 그것이 그들의 핵심적인 본질이 손상되지 않았다고 안심시키기 때문이다. 따라서 애완동물은 우울증을 앓거나 만성적인 병이 있는 환자들의 치료에서 중요하다. 게다가, 애완동물은 시설로 보내진 고령자들에게 크게 유리하게 사용된다. 이런 시설에서 모든 환자들이 건강상 쇠퇴하고 있는데 직원들이 낙관주의를 유지하기는 어렵다. 방문하는 아이들은 한때 그들의 부모님이나 조부모님이 무엇이었는지 기억하고 그들의 불능 상태로 인해 우울해지지 않을 수 없다. 그러나 동물들은 지능에 대한 기대가 없다. 그들은 젊음을 흠모하지 않는다. 그들은 고령자들이 한때 무엇이었는지에 관한 기억이 없으며 마치 그들이 어린 아이들인 것처럼 그들을 반긴다. 강아지를 안고 있는 노인은 유년시절의 순간을 완전히 정확하게 다시 체험한다. 그의 즐거움과 동물의 반응은 똑같다.

 어휘

adversity 몡 역경　unemployment 몡 실업　disability 몡 장애　affection 몡 애착, 애정　continuing 혱 연속적인, 계속적인　crucially 凰 결정적으로, 중대하게　endure 통 견디다, 참다　hardship 몡 어려움, 곤란　reassure 통 안심시키다　core 혱 핵심적인　essence 몡 본질, 정수　treatment 몡 치료　depressed 혱 우울한; 우울증을 앓는　chronically 凰 만성적으로　institutionalize 통 보호 시설로 보내다　institution 몡 기관; *보호 시설　retain 통 유지하다　optimism 몡 낙관론, 낙관주의　decline 통 감소하다; *쇠퇴하다　incapacity 몡 무능력; *불능 상태　expectation 몡 예상; *기대　mental capacity 지능　worship 통 흠모하다, 숭배하다　relive 통 다시 체험하다

UNIT 2 능동태와 수동태

코드 접속하기

pp.39~41

출제코드 1
능동태 vs. 수동태

A 1 remained 2 shared 3 are recommended
B 1 → were designed 2 → is compared 3 → introduced

해석과 정답 풀이

STEP 1
1 1) 우리의 계획은 갑작스러운 비 때문에 취소되었다.
　2) 많은 사람들이 자동차 사고로 부상을 당했다.

STEP 2
1 1) 유명한 그림이 한국 전쟁 동안 도난 당했다.
　2) 가장 어린 선수가 축구 경기의 MVP로 선정되었다.
2 윌리엄 셰익스피어는 많은 위대한 희곡을 썼다.

STEP 3
A 1 놀랍게도, 그 문제는 수년 동안 풀리지 않은 채로 남아있었다.
　➡ remain은 자동사이므로 수동태로 쓸 수 없으므로 remained가 오는 것이 알맞다.
　2 정보와 지식은 보호되고 통제되기보다는 공유되어야 한다.
　➡ 주어인 정보와 지식은 공유하는 주체가 아니라 '공유되는' 대상이므로 수동태가 오는 것이 알맞다.
　3 미국에서, 부모들은 그들의 아이들이 혼자 자게 하도록 권장 받는다.
　➡ 주어인 부모님들이 권장하는 주체가 아니라 '권장 받는' 대상이므로 수동태가 오는 것이 알맞다.
B 1 그 당시에 로봇들은 꼬리 부분은 유연하고 중간 부분은 뻣뻣하도록 디자인되었다.
　➡ 주어인 로봇들이 디자인했던 주체가 아니라 '디자인되었던' 대상이므로 능동태 designed을 수동태 were designed로 고쳐야 한다.
　2 듣는 사람은 곰 인형에 비유되는데 왜냐하면 장난감 곰이 같은 목적을 행할 것이기 때문이다.
　➡ 주어인 듣는 사람이 비유하는 주체가 아니라 '비유되는' 대상이므로 능동태 is comparing을 수동태 is compared로 고쳐야 한다.
　3 한 인터넷 회사는 사용자들이 쉽게 블로그를 시작하도록 하는 새로운 블로그 서비스를 도입했다.
　➡ 주어인 회사가 '도입하는' 주체이고, 동사 뒤에 목적어(a new blogging service)가 있으므로 수동태 was introduced를 능동태 introduced로 고쳐야 한다.

출제코드 2
4형식의 수동태

A 1 paid 2 was sent 3 is taught
B 1 ○ 2 → be given 3 → was offered

해석과 정답 풀이

STEP 1
2 Amy는 그녀의 남자친구에 의해 초콜릿 한 상자를 받았다.
　(그녀의 남자친구는 Amy에게 초콜릿 한 상자를 주었다.)
3 1) 그의 새 자전거는 그에 의해 나에게 보여졌다.
　　(그는 나에게 그의 새 자전거를 보여주었다.)
　2) 이 치즈케이크는 그녀를 위해 시진에 의해 만들어졌다.
　　(시진은 그녀에게 이 치즈케이크를 만들어주었다.)

STEP 2
1 1) 정문 수비를 책임지는 사람들은 권총과 소총을 받았다.
　2) 참가자들은 위기의 상황에서 무엇을 해야 하는지 들었다.

STEP 3
A 1 대략 76%의 파트 타임 직원들이 초과 근무에 대한 추가 수당을 지급받지 못했다.
　➡ 간접목적어(About 76 percent of the part-timers)가 주어이고, '지급받지'

못한다고 해석되므로 수동태가 오는 것이 알맞다.
2 Debby는 그녀의 이모에 의해 신형 컴퓨터를 생일 선물로 받았다.
➡ 간접목적어(Debby)가 주어이고, 선물을 '받은' 것이므로 수동태 was sent가 오는 것이 알맞다.
3 중국어는 중국에서 5년 동안 살았던 할아버지에 의해 Julia에게 가르쳐진다.
➡ 직접목적어(Chinese)가 주어이고, 중국어가 '가르쳐지는' 것이므로 수동태 is taught가 오는 것이 알맞다.
B 1 영어 만화책 몇 권이 나를 위해 친구 Ashton에 의해 구입되었다.
➡ 동사 buy의 직접목적어(Several English comic books)가 주어이고, 만화책이 '구입되는' 것이므로 수동태 were bought가 오는 것이 알맞다.
2 대회의 우승자들은 해외 유학을 할 수 있는 기회가 주어질 것이다.
➡ 동사 give의 간접목적어(The winners of the contest)가 주어이고, 기회가 '주어질' 것이므로 능동태 give를 수동태 be given으로 고쳐야 한다.
3 나는 어제 나의 교수님에 의해 능숙한 영어 회화 실력을 요구하는 일자리를 제안받았다.
➡ 동사 offer의 간접목적어(I)가 주어이고, 일자리를 '제안받은' 것이므로 능동태 offered를 수동태 was offered로 고쳐야 한다.

기출예제 Q1
정답 ④　　정답률 38%

정답 풀이

④ 능동태 vs. 수동태

Subjects [who are influenced by this bias] / work overtime [trying
　주어↑　　└─주격 관계대명사　　　　　　　　　　동사　　　동시동작을 나타내는
이러한 편향에 영향을 받은 피실험자들은　　　　　　호의적인 인상을 만들기 위해 분사구문
to create a favorable impression], / especially [when subjects
　　　　　　　　　　　　　　　　　　　　접속사
노력하면서 추가적으로 애쓴다　　　　　　특히 피실험자들이
ask(→ are asked) about sensitive issues].
민감한 문제에 대해 질문받을 때

➡ 문맥상 주어인 피실험자들이 민감한 질문을 '하는' 주체가 아닌 '받는' 대상이므로, 동사는 수동태인 are asked가 되어야 한다. 주어가 복수이므로 복수형 be동사 are가 쓰였다.

친절한 오답 풀이

① 복합관계부사

This is the case / [whenever questionnaires, interviews, or
　　　　　　　　　복합관계부사(…할 때마다)
이에 해당한다　　　　　설문지, 면접 또는
personality inventories are used / to measure variables].
　　　　　　　　　　　　　부사적 용법의 to부정사(목적)
성격 목록이 사용될 때마다　　　　변인을 측정하기 위해

➡ 복합관계부사 whenever가 부사절을 이끌고 있으므로 어법상 알맞다.

② 재귀대명사

They take advantage of the fact / [that people have a unique
　　　　　　　　　　　　　　　└─동격──┘접속사
그것은 사실을 이용한다　　　　　사람들이 자신을 풀타임으로 관찰할 수 있는 유일한
opportunity to observe themselves full-time].
　　　↑──┘형용사적 용법의 to부정사
기회를 가진다는

➡ observe의 목적어가 주어(people)와 같은 대상을 가리키므로 재귀대명사 themselves가 오는 것이 적절하다.

③ 부사

One of the most problematic of these distortions / is the social
　　　one of + 복수 명사: … 중 하나　　　　　　　단수 동사　선행사
이러한 왜곡 중 가장 문제가 되는 하나는　　　　　　사회적 바람직성
desirability bias, / [which is a tendency / to give socially approved
　　　　　　　주격 관계대명사(계속적 용법)　　　　　　　　↑──형용사
편향인데　　　　이것은 경향이다　　　사회적으로 승인된 답을
answers to questions about oneself].
자신에 관한 질문에 제공하는

정답 및 해설 • 39

➜ 뒤의 형용사 approved를 수식하는 부사로 socially는 어법상 알맞다.

⑤ 병렬구조

For example, many survey respondents will report / {that they
　　　　　　　　　　　　　　　　　　　　　　　　　　　　　접속사
예를 들어, 많은 설문 조사 응답자들은 보고할 것이다　　　　자신이 선거에서

voted in an election or gave to a charity / [when in fact it is
동사1　　　　　　　　　　　동사2　　　　　　　접속사　　　가주어
투표했다거나 자선 단체에 기부했다고　　　　　　사실은 하지 않았다고

possible to determine that they did not]}.
　　　　　　　　　　　　　　진주어
결정하는 것이 가능할 때

➜ 등위접속사 or가 동사를 병렬 연결하고 있으므로, voted과 대등한 동사 gave는 어법상 적절하다.

지문 해석

연구 심리학자들은 종종 '자기 보고' 데이터로 작업을 하는데, 이는 참가자들의 행동에 대한 구두 설명으로 구성되어 있다. 변인을 측정하기 위해 설문지, 면접 또는 성격 목록이 사용될 때마다 이에 해당한다. 자기 보고 방법은 꽤 유용할 수 있다. 그것들은 사람들이 자신을 풀타임으로 관찰할 수 있는 유일한 기회를 가진다는 사실을 이용한다. 그러나, 자기 보고는 몇 가지 종류의 왜곡으로 인해 오염될 수 있다. 이러한 왜곡 중 가장 문제가 되는 하나는 사회적 바람직성 편향인데, 이것은 사회적으로 승인된 답을 자신에 관한 질문에 제공하는 경향이다. 이러한 편향에 영향을 받은 피실험자들은 특히 민감한 문제에 대해 질문받을 때 호의적인 인상을 만들기 위해 추가적으로 노력한다. 예를 들어, 많은 설문 조사 응답자들은 사실은 하지 않았다고 결정하는 것이 가능할 때 선거에서 투표했다거나 자선 단체에 기부했다고 보고할 것이다.

self-report 몡 자기보고　verbal 뼹 언어의, 말로 된　questionnaire 몡 설문지
measure 동 측정하다　variable 몡 변수　full-time 뷔 풀타임으로　plague 동 괴롭히다; *역병에 걸리게 하다　distortion 몡 왜곡　problematic 뼹 문제가 있는
desirability 몡 바람직함　bias 몡 편견

코드 공략하기
pp.42~44

| 01 ③ | 02 ② | 03 ⑤ | 04 ② | 05 ③ | 06 ① | 07 ③ | 08 ② |
| 09 ④ | 10 ③ | | | | | | |

01
정답 ③　　정답률 49%

정답 풀이

③ 능동태 vs. 수동태

The eruption buried Pompeii / under 4 to 6 meters of ash and
　　　　　　　　　　　　　　전치사(… 아래에)
그 분출은 폼페이를 묻었다　　4~6미터의 화산재와 돌 아래에

stone, / and it lost(→ was lost) for over 1,500 years / before its
　　　　　= Pompeii　　　　　　　　　　　　　　　전치사(… 전에)
　　　　그리고 그것은 1,500년 넘도록 잊혀졌다

accidental rediscovery / in 1599.
우연한 재발견 전에　　　　1599년에

➜ 주어 it(= Pompeii)이 1,500년 동안 '잊혀지다'라는 수동의 의미가 적절하므로 동사를 수동태인 was lost로 고쳐야 한다. 동사 lose(과거형, 과거분사형 lost)는 '…을 잃다'라는 의미의 타동사로 뒤에 목적어가 와야 하지만 위 문장에는 목적어가 없으므로, 수동태를 쓰는 것이 알맞다.

친절한 오답 풀이

① 부사

The city of Pompeii is a partially buried Roman town-city /
　　　　　　　　　　　　　　　　↑ 과거분사
폼페이라는 도시는 부분적으로 파묻힌 로마의 도시이다
near modern Naples.
현대의 나폴리 근처에 있는

➜ 부사 partially가 뒤에 오는 과거분사 buried를 수식하고 있으므로 어법상 바르다.

② 전치사

Pompeii was destroyed and buried / during a long eruption of the
　　　　　　　　　　　　　　　　전치사(… 동안)
폼페이는 파괴되고 파묻혔다　　베수비오 화산의 오랜 폭발 기간 동안
volcano Mount Vesuvius / in 79 AD.
　　　　　　　　　　　서기 79년에

➜ during은 '… 동안'이라는 의미를 가진 전치사로, 뒤에 기간을 나타내는 명사구 a long eruption이 목적어로 왔으므로 어법상 바르다.

④ 현재완료 시제

Since then, its rediscovery has provided / a detailed insight
전치사(… 이후로)　　　　　　　현재완료(계속)　　과거분사
그때 이후로, 그것의 재발견은 제공해 왔다　　　생활상에 대한 자세한 이해를
into the life / at the height of the Roman Empire.
　　　　　　　로마 제국의 전성기의

➜ 현재완료와 자주 쓰이는 전치사 since가 쓰였고, 과거부터 계속되고 있는 일에 대해 이야기하고 있으므로 현재완료 시제인 has provided는 어법상 바르다.

⑤ 「with + (대)명사 + 분사」

Today, this UNESCO World Heritage Site / is one of Italy's most
　　　　　　　　　　　　　　　　　　　one of + 복수 명사: … 중의 하나
오늘날, 이 UNESCO 세계 문화 유적지는　　　이탈리아의 가장
popular tourist attractions, / with about 2,500,000 people visiting
　　　　　　　　　　　　　　with + (대)명사 + v-ing: …가 ~하는 채로
인기 있는 관광명소 중의 하나이다　　약 2백 5십만 명의 사람들이 매년 방문하는
every year.

➜ 「with + (대)명사 + 분사」는 '…가 ~한[된] 채로'라는 의미의 분사구문으로, (대)명사와 분사가 능동 관계일 경우 현재분사를, 수동 관계일 경우 과거분사를 써야 한다. 이 문장에서는 2백 5십만 명의 사람들이 '방문하는'이라는 능동의 의미가 적절하므로 현재분사 visiting은 어법상 바르다.

지문 해석

폼페이라는 도시는 현대의 나폴리 근처에 있는 부분적으로 파묻힌 로마 도시이다. 서기 79년에 베수비오 화산의 오랜 화산 폭발 기간 동안 폼페이는 파괴되고 파묻혔다. 그 분출은 폼페이를 4~6미터의 화산재와 돌 아래에 묻었고, 1599년에 우연히 재발견되기 전까지 1,500년 넘도록 잊혀졌다. 그때 이후로, 그것의 발견은 전성기 로마 제국의 생활상에 대한 자세한 이해를 제공해 왔다. 오늘날, 이 유네스코 세계 문화유산 유적지는 매년 약 2백 5십만 명의 사람들이 방문하는 이탈리아의 가장 인기 있는 관광명소 중의 하나이다.

partially 뷔 부분적으로　bury 동 묻다, 매장하다　destroy 동 파괴하다
eruption 몡 분출, 분화　ash 몡 재　accidental 뼹 우연한　rediscovery 몡 재발견　detailed 뼹 상세한　insight 몡 통찰력; *이해, 간파　height 몡 높이; *최고조, 절정　empire 몡 제국　heritage 몡 유산　tourist attraction 관광 명소

정답 풀이

② 능동태 vs. 수동태

> Never before and never since / has the quality of monumentality
> 　　　　부정어　　　　　　　　　　조동사　　　　　　　주어
> 그전에도 그 이후에도　　　　　　　　　기념성이라는 특성이 달성된 적이 없었다
> been achieved / as fully as it did(→ was) (achieved) in Egypt.
> 동사(현재완료 수동태)　　　　　　　　　　생략(수동태)
> 　　　　　이집트에서 그랬던 것처럼 완전히

➡ 부정어가 문장 앞으로 나와 조동사와 주어가 도치된 문장이다. 종속절의 주어 it은 앞서 언급된 the quality of monumentality를 가리키며 문맥상 그것이 '달성되었다'라는 의미가 되어야 하므로 수동태인 was achieved를 대신하도록 did를 was로 고쳐야 한다.

┃친절한 오답 풀이┃

① 「전치사 + 동명사」

> "Monumental" is a word / {that comes very close / to
> 　　　　　　　　　　　　　　　주격 관계대명사　　　전치사
> '기념비적'이라는 말은 단어이다　　　매우 근접한
> [expressing the basic characteristic of Egyptian art]}.
> 동명사(전치사의 목적어)
> 이집트 예술의 기본적 특징을 표현하는 것에

➡ 전치사 to의 목적어로, 동명사 expressing은 어법상 바르다.

③ 대명사

> Many modern structures exceed / those of Egypt / in terms of
> 　　　　　　　　　　　　　　　= structures
> 많은 현대의 구조물은 능가한다　　이집트의 구조물을　　… 면에서
> purely physical size.
> 순전히 물리적 크기 면에서

➡ 앞서 언급된 structures를 대신하여 쓰인 복수형 대명사로 those는 어법상 바르다.

④ 주격 관계대명사

> An Egyptian sculpture [(which/that is) no bigger than a
> 　　　　　　　　　　　　　　「주격 관계대명사 + be동사」 생략
> 사람 손 크기만한 이집트의 조각품이
> person's hand] / is more monumental than that gigantic pile of
> 　　　　　　　　　그 거대한 돌무더기보다 더 기념비적이다
> stones / [that constitutes the war memorial in Leipzig], /
> 　　　　　　주격 관계대명사
> 　　　　　Leipzig의 전쟁 기념비를 구성하는
> for instance.
> 예를 들어

➡ that은 앞의 명사 that gigantic pile of stones를 선행사로 하는 주격 관계대명사로, 관계대명사절에서 동사의 주어 역할을 하므로 어법상 바르다.

⑤ 병렬구조

> This inner weight is the quality {which Egyptian art possesses /
> 　　　　　　　　　　　　　　　　　목적격 관계대명사
> 이 내적 무게는 특성인데　　　　　　　이집트 예술이 지닌
> to such a degree that everything in it seems / to be made of
> such + 명사 + that …: …할 만큼의 ~　　= Egyptian art
> 그 안에 있는 모든 작품이 보일 정도이다　　　원시 시대의 돌로
> primeval stone, / like a mountain range, / [even if it is only a few
> 　　　　　　　　　　　　　　　　　　접속사(비록 …일지라도)
> 만들어진 것처럼　　　마치 산맥처럼　　　비록 폭이 몇 인치에 불과하거나
> inches across or (is) carved in wood]}.
> 　　　　　　접속사　　수동태
> 나무에 새겨져 있을지라도

➡ 등위접속사 or에 의해 병렬 연결된 구조로, 수동의 의미를 나타내는 carved는 어법상 바르다. 반복을 피하기 위해 carved 앞에 be동사 is가 생략되었다.

지문 해석

'기념비적'이라는 말은 이집트 예술의 기본적 특징을 표현하는 것에 매우 근접한 단어이다. 그전에도 그 이후에도 기념성이라는 특성이 이집트에서 그랬던 것처럼 완전히 달성된 적은 없었다. 비록 이집트인들이 이 점(외적 크기와 거대함)에 있어서 틀림없이 몇 가지 대단한 업적을 달성했지만 이에 대한 이유는 그들 작품의 외적 크기와 거대함이 아니다. 많은 현대의 구조물은 순전히 물리적 크기 면에서 이집트의 구조물을 능가한다. 그러나 거대함은 기념성과는 아무 관련이 없다. 예를 들어, 사람 손 크기만한 이집트의 조각품이 Leipzig의 전쟁 기념비를 구성하는 그 거대한 돌무더기보다 더 기념비적이다. 기념성은 외적 무게의 문제가 아니라 '내적 무게'의 문제이다. 이 내적 무게는 이집트 예술이 지닌 특성인데, 이집트 예술 안에 있는 모든 작품이 비록 폭이 몇 인치에 불과하거나 나무에 새겨져 있을지라도 마치 산맥처럼 원시 시대의 돌로 만들어진 것처럼 보일 정도이다.

monumental 형 기념비적인 (monumentality 명 기념성)　characteristic 명 특징　quality 명 질; *특성　achieve 동 달성하다　external 형 외적인　massiveness 명 거대함　admittedly 부 틀림없이, 확실히　respect 명 존경; *측면, 점　structure 명 구조; *구조물　exceed 동 능가하다　purely 부 순전히　physical 형 신체의; *물리적인　sculpture 명 조각품　constitute 동 구성하다　war memorial 전쟁 기념비　inner 형 내적인　possess 동 소유하다; *(특징을) 지니다　mountain range 산맥　carve 동 (나무·돌 등에) 새기다

정답 풀이

⑤ 능동태 vs. 수동태

> This attitude, however, will not accept(→ be accepted) in Italy, /
> 　　주어
> 하지만, 이런 태도는 이탈리아에서 받아들여지지 않을 것이다　　　선행사
> [where coffee is only a breakfast drink].
> 계속적 용법의 관계부사
> 그곳에서 커피는 오직 아침식사 음료일 뿐이다

➡ 주어는 This attitude이고, 태도가 '받아들여지지 않는'이라는 수동의 의미가 적절하므로, 능동태 accept를 수동태인 be accepted로 고쳐야 한다.

┃친절한 오답 풀이┃

① 동사의 수 일치

> Many of the different kinds / of coffee drinks / [that we have
> 　주어, many of + 복수 명사　　　　　　　　　목적격 관계대명사
> 다양한 종류의 많은 것들이　　　　　커피 음료의　　　우리가 세계 곳곳에서 마시는
> around the world] / have originated from Italy.
> 　　　　　　　　　　　동사
> 　　　　　　　　　이탈리아에서 기원했다

➡ 문장의 주어로 쓰인 「many of + 복수 명사」는 복수 취급하므로, 복수형 조동사 have가 오는 것이 적절하다.

② 「see(지각동사) + 목적어 + v-ing」

> We commonly see people having coffee with milk.
> 　　　　　　　지각동사　목적어　목적격보어로 쓰인 현재분사
> 우리는 흔히 사람들이 우유와 함께 커피를 마시는 것을 본다

➡ 지각동사 see의 목적격보어로, 목적어와 목적격보어가 능동 관계이므로 현재분사 having은 어법상 바르다.

③ 강조구문

> But it was the Italians / that first started the trend with
> 　　It is ... that 강조구문
> 하지만 바로 이탈리아 사람들이었다　처음 카푸치노의 유행을 시작한 것은
> cappuccino ....

➡ the Italians를 강조하는 「It is ... that」 강조구문이므로, that은 어법상 쓰임이 적절하다.

Grammar Tips

강조구문과 가주어 진주어 구문의 구별

「It is ... that ~」 형태가 강조구문인지, 가주어 진주어 구문인지 구별해야 할 때는 It is와 that을 생략해보면 된다. 생략한 나머지 부분이 완전한 문장이면, 강조구문이고, 불완전한 문장이면 가주어 진주어 구문이다.

예) **It is** at noon **that** he will leave. (강조구문)
　　(바로 정오에 그가 떠날 것이다.)
예) **It is** certain **that** he will leave. (가주어 진주어 구문)
　　(그가 떠날 것이 확실하다.)

④ 복합관계부사

In the West and generally around the world, / you can go for a cup
서구와 일반적으로 세계 곳곳에서,　　　　　　　　당신은 커피 한 잔을 마시러 갈 수 있다
　　　　　　　　　　　　　　　　　　　　　　　…하러 가다
of coffee / [whenever you want].
　　　　　　복합관계부사(…할 때는 언제든지)
　　　　　　당신이 원할 때는 언제든지

➡ 복합관계부사 whenever가 부사절을 이끌고 있으므로 어법상 바르다.

지문 해석

커피는 이탈리아 요리의 중요한 한 부분이다. 우리가 세계 곳곳에서 마시는 다양한 종류의 커피 음료의 많은 것들이 이탈리아에서 기원했다. 우리는 흔히 사람들이 우유와 함께 커피를 마시는 것을 본다. 그러나 커피, 우유, 그리고 맨 위에 우유 거품을 첨가한 카푸치노로 그 유행을 처음 시작한 것은 바로 이탈리아 사람들이었다. 서구와 일반적으로 세계 곳곳에서는, 당신이 원할 때는 언제든지 커피 한 잔을 마시러 갈 수 있다. 하지만 이런 태도는 이탈리아에서는 받아들여지지 않을 텐데, 그곳에서 커피는 오직 아침식사 음료일 뿐이다.

cuisine 명 요리법; *요리　originate 동 비롯되다, 유래하다　commonly 부 흔히, 보통　trend 명 동향, 추세　addition 명 첨가　foam 명 거품　attitude 명 태도

04　　　　　정답 ②　　　정답률 35%

정답 풀이

② 능동태 vs. 수동태

It was included(→ included), / in addition to watching TV, /
= a list of his son's interests　　　전치사(… 외에도)
그것은 포함했다　　　　　　　　　　　TV 시청 외에도
playing with Legos and going to the zoo.
　　　　　　　　목적어
레고 가지고 놀기와 동물원 가기를

➡ 리스트가 '포함하는'이라는 능동의 의미가 적절하고, 뒤에 목적어(playing ... zoo)가 이어지므로, 수동태 was included를 능동태 included로 고쳐야 한다.

┃친절한 오답 풀이┃

① 병렬구조

He also wanted to encourage Jing / to play the piano and to do
　　　　　　　encourage A to-v: A가 …하도록 격려하다
그는 또한 Jing을 격려하기를 원했다　　　피아노도 치고 수학도 더 많이 하도록
more math.

➡ 등위접속사 and가 동사 encourage의 목적격보어로 쓰인 to부정사 to play와 to do를 병렬 연결하고 있는 구조로, to do는 어법상 바르다.

---

③ 접속사 that

He then suggested to his son / [that he could trade TV time, piano
　　　　　　　　　　　　　명사절(목적어)을 이끄는 접속사　trade A for B: A를 B와 교환하다
그는 그러고 나서 그의 아들에게 제안했다　　그가 TV 시간, 피아노 시간,
time, and study time / for Legos and visits to the zoo].
공부 시간을 교환할 수 있다고　　　레고와 동물원 방문과

➡ 밑줄 친 that은 동사 suggested의 목적어 역할을 하는 명사절을 이끄는 접속사로, 뒤에 완전한 절이 이어지고 있으므로 어법상 바르다.

④ 관계부사

They established a point system, / {where he got points /
　　　　　　　　선행사　　　　　계속적 용법의 관계부사
그들은 포인트 시스템을 만들었다　　　그가 점수를 획득했다
[whenever he watched less TV]}.
복합관계부사(…할 때는 언제든지)
그가 TV를 덜 볼 때마다

➡ a point system이 장소 역할을 하는 선행사이고, 뒤에 완전한 절이 오고 있으므로, 관계부사 where는 어법상 바르다.

⑤ 재귀대명사

[As Jing got points], / he felt valued and good about himself / and
접속사(…하면서)　　　　feel + 형용사: …하게 느끼다, valued는 형용사처럼 쓰인 과거분사
Jing이 점수를 획득하면서,　　　그는 자기 자신에 대해 가치 있고 훌륭하다고 느꼈다
spent quality time with Dad.
그리고 아빠와 함께 귀중한 시간을 보냈다

➡ 주어와 목적어가 동일한 대상을 지칭하는 경우 목적어로 재귀대명사를 쓰는데, 전치사 about의 목적어가 주어(he)와 같은 대상이므로, 재귀대명사 himself를 쓰는 것이 알맞다.

 구문 분석 Plus

1행	Ying Liu wanted to **stop** his six-year-old son, Jing, **from watching** so much TV. ➡ stop A from v-ing: A가 …하는 것을 막다
4행	[The first thing (**that**) Ying did] was (**to**) prepare. ➡ 목적격 관계대명사 that이 생략돼 있음 ➡ prepare: be동사의 보어로 쓰인 원형부정사로, 주어에 동사 do가 쓰이고 뒤따르는 be동사의 보어로 to부정사가 쓰인 경우, to부정사에서 to를 생략하기도 함

지문 해석

Ying Liu는 그의 여섯 살짜리 아들 Jing이 TV를 너무 많이 보는 것을 멈추게 하고 싶었다. 그는 또한 Jing이 피아노도 치고 수학도 더 많이 하도록 격려하기를 원했다. Ying이 가장 먼저 했던 일은 준비하는 것이었다. 그는 아들의 관심사들의 목록을 만들었다. 그것은 TV 시청 외에도 레고 가지고 놀기와 동물원 가기를 포함했다. 그러고 나서 그는 아들에게 TV 시간, 피아노 시간, 공부 시간을 레고와 동물원 방문과 교환할 수 있다고 제안했다. 그들은 포인트 시스템을 만들었는데, 그 시스템에서 그는 TV를 덜 볼 때마다 점수를 획득했다. 아빠와 아들은 그 과정을 함께 관찰했다. Jing이 점수를 획득하면서, 그는 자기 자신에 대해 가치 있고 훌륭하다고 느꼈고 아빠와 함께 귀중한 시간을 보냈다.

interest 명 흥미　establish 동 설립[설정]하다　monitor 동 추적 관찰하다
process 명 과정　valued 형 존중되는, 소중한　quality 형 고급[양질]의

05   정답 ③   정답률 47%

정답 풀이

③ 능동태 vs. 수동태

> ..., high school football coaches are typically teachers / [who
> 고등학교 축구 코치들은 일반적으로 교사이다   주격 관계대명사
> paid(→ are paid) a little extra / for their afterclass work].
> 약간의 추가 급여를 지급받는   그들의 방과 후 일에 대해

➡ 밑줄 친 paid는 teachers를 선행사로 하는 주격 관계대명사절의 동사로, 선행사가 동사의 의미상 주어 역할을 한다. 교사들이 추가 급여를 '지급하는' 것이 아니라 '지급받는' 것이므로 능동태 paid를 수동태 are paid로 고쳐야 한다.

친절한 오답 풀이

① 동사의 수 일치

> The process of job advancement in the field of sports is often
> 주어   동사
> 스포츠 분야에서 직업 상승의 과정은 종종 말해진다
> said / to be shaped like a pyramid.
> 전치사(…와 같은)
> 피라미드와 같은 모양으로 만들어졌다고

➡ 주어는 전치사구(of … sports)의 수식을 받고 있는 The process로, 주어가 단수 명사이므로 단수 동사 is는 어법상 바르다.

② 부사

> ..., but the competition becomes increasingly tough / [as one
>   ↑ 형용사   접속사(…하면서)
> 그러나 경쟁은 점점 더 치열해진다
> works their way up].
> 사람들이 올라갈수록

➡ 부사 increasingly가 형용사 tough를 수식하고 있으므로 어법상 바르다.

④ 목적격보어로 쓰인 to부정사

> But coaches of the same sport at big universities / can earn
> 하지만 큰 대학의 같은 스포츠의 코치들은
> more than $1 million a year, / [causing the salaries of college
> … 이상   결과를 나타내는 분사구문, cause A to-v: A가 …하게 하다
> 일 년에 백만 달러 이상을 벌 수 있다   대학 총장의 봉급을 작아 보이게 하는
> presidents to look small / in comparison].
>   look + 형용사: …하게 보이다
>   비교적으로

➡ 동사 cause는 목적격보어로 to부정사를 취하므로 to look은 어법상 바르다.

⑤ 관계부사

> One degree higher up is the National Football League, / [where
>   선행사   계속적 용법의 관계부사
> 한 단계 더 높은 것이 전미 미식축구 연맹이다   그곳에서
> head coaches can earn / many times more than their best-paid
> 수석 코치들은 돈을 벌 수 있다   가장 잘 받는 대학 감독들보다 몇 배 더 많이
> campus counterparts].

➡ where는 the National Football League를 선행사로 하는 계속적 용법의 관계부사로, 뒤에 완전한 절이 이어지고 있으므로 어법상 바르다.

구문 분석 Plus

> ..., at the wide base are many jobs with high school athletic
> teams, *while* at the narrow tip are the few, highly desired
> jobs with professional organizations.

3행   ➡ 각각 장소를 나타내는 부사구(at the wide base / at the narrow tip)가 절 앞에 나오면서 주어(many jobs / the few, highly desired jobs)와 동사(are)가 도치됨
➡ while: '반면에'라는 의미의 접속사

지문 해석

스포츠 분야에서 직업 상승의 과정은 피라미드와 같은 모양으로 만들어졌다고 흔히 말해진다. 즉, 넓은 하단부에는 고등학교 운동팀과 함께 많은 직업이 있는 반면에, 좁은 꼭대기에는 프로 단체들과 함께 사람들이 몹시 원하는 극소수의 직업이 있다. 그래서 합치면 많은 스포츠 관련 일자리가 있지만, 사람들이 올라갈수록 경쟁이 점점 더 치열해진다. 다양한 직종의 봉급이 이러한 피라미드 모델을 반영하고 있다. 예를 들어, 일반적으로 고등학교 축구 코치들은 그들의 방과 후 일에 대해 약간의 추가 급여를 지급받는 교사들이다. 하지만 큰 대학과 같은 스포츠의 코치들은 일 년에 백만 달러 이상을 벌 수 있는데, 이는 비교적으로 대학 총장의 봉급을 작아 보이게 한다. 한 단계 더 높은 것이 전미 미식축구 연맹인데, 그곳에서 수석 코치들은 가장 잘 받는 대학 감독들보다 몇 배 더 많이 벌 수 있다.

어휘

advancement 몡 전진; *상승   **athletic** 혱 (몸이) 탄탄한; *운동 경기의   **tip** 몡 끝, 꼭대기   **highly** 뷘 매우   **desired** 혱 바랐던, 희망했던   **professional** 혱 직업의; *(스포츠에서) 프로의   **organization** 몡 조직, 단체   **altogether** 뷘 완전히, 전적으로; *모두 합치면   **competition** 몡 경쟁   **reflect** 통 반사하다; *반영하다   **in comparison** …와 비교하여   **counterpart** 몡 상대, 대응하는 것

06   정답 ①   정답률 62%

정답 풀이

(A) 형용사

> Psychologists have a lot of theories / about [why people are so
>   간접의문문(의문사 + 주어 + 동사)
> 심리학자들은 많은 이론을 가지고 있다   왜 사람들이 그렇게 민감한지에 대한
> sensitive / sensitively / to hearing about their own imperfections].
> 주격보어   전치사(…에 대해)
>   자기 자신의 결함에 대해 듣는 것에 대해

➡ 네모는 의문사절 안에서 주격보어 자리로, 형용사 sensitive가 적절하다. 부사는 보어로 쓰일 수 없다.

(B) 복합관계대명사

> [What / Whatever the cause of our discomfort is], / most of us
> 복합관계대명사(무엇이 …하더라도) 주어   동사   우리들 대부분은
> 우리의 불편함의 원인이 무엇이라도
> have to train ourselves / to seek feedback and listen carefully /
> 자신을 훈련시켜야 한다   피드백을 구하고 주의 깊게 듣도록
> [when we hear it].
> 접속사
> 우리가 그것을 들을 때

➡ 문장의 부사절을 이끌고, 절 안에서 주격보어 역할을 해야 하므로 복합관계대명사 Whatever가 오는 것이 적절하다.

(C) 능동태 vs. 수동태

> Without that training, / the very threat of critical feedback /
>   바로 그(명사 강조) 주어
> 그런 훈련 없이는   비판적인 피드백에 대한 바로 그 위험이
> often leads us to practice / be practiced destructive, maladaptive
>   lead A to-v: A가 …하도록 이끌다   to부정사의 목적어
> 종종 우리가 파괴적이고 부적응적 행동을 하게 한다
> behaviors / [that negatively affect / not only our work but the
>   주격 관계대명사   not only A but (also) B: A뿐만 아니라 B도
>   부정적으로 영향을 미치는   우리의 일뿐만 아니라 전반적인 건강에도
> overall health / of our organizations].
>   우리 조직의

➡ 「lead + 목적어 + to-v(목적격보어)」 구문으로, 목적어와 to부정사는 주어와 서술어 관계가 성립한다. 우리가 행동을 '행하는'이라는 능동의 의미가 적절하므로 능동태인 practice가 알맞다. 네모 뒤의 명사구(destructive … behaviors)가 to부정사의 목적어이므로 수동태는 쓰일 수 없다.

지문 해석

사람들은 비판받는 것을 싫어하기 때문에 피드백을 회피한다. 심리학자들은 왜 사람들이

자기 자신의 결함에 대해 듣는 것에 대해 그렇게 민감한지에 대한 많은 이론을 가지고 있다. 하나는 그들이 피드백을 어린 시절에 부모와 교사로부터 받았던 비판적인 말과 연관 짓는다는 것이다. 우리의 불편함의 원인이 무엇이라도, 우리들 대부분은 피드백을 구하고 그것을 들을 때 주의 깊게 듣도록 자신을 훈련시켜야 한다. 그러한 훈련 없는 비판적인 피드백에 대한 바로 그 위협이 종종 우리가 우리의 일부뿐 아니라 우리 조직의 전반적인 건강에도 부정적으로 영향을 미치는 파괴적이고 부적응적 행동을 하게 한다.

feedback 몡 피드백　criticize 통 비판하다 (critical 혱 비판적인)　psychologist 몡 심리학자　theory 몡 이론　sensitive 혱 예민한, 민감한　imperfection 몡 결함　associate 통 연상하다, 연관짓다　comment 몡 논평, 언급　cause 몡 원인　discomfort 몡 불편　threat 몡 위협　destructive 혱 파괴적인　maladaptive 혱 부적응의　affect 통 영향을 미치다　overall 혱 전반적인

07　정답 ③　정답률 71%

정답 풀이

③ 능동태 vs. 수동태

> [What they mean by focusing on the process] / is {that they focus
> 관계대명사　　　　by v-ing: …함으로써　　　명사절(보어)를 이끄는 접속사
> 그들이 과정에 집중함으로써 의도한 것은　　　그들이 행동에 집중한다는 것이다
> on the actions / [(which/that) they need to be taken(→ take), /
> 목적격 관계대명사 생략
> 그들이 취할 필요가 있는,
> in order to achieve their desired result]}.
> in order to-v: …하기 위하여
> 그들이 바라는 결과를 얻기 위해

➡ they need 앞에 목적격 관계대명사가 생략돼 있고, 선행사 the actions가 관계대명사절에서 목적어 역할을 하고 있으므로, 목적어를 가질 수 없는 수동태 be taken은 적절하지 않다. 따라서 수동태 be taken을 능동태 take로 고쳐야 한다.

┃친절한 오답 풀이┃

① 가주어 진주어 구문

> ..., it is not unusual / [to hear players and coaches talking about
> 가주어　　　　　진주어, hear(지각동사) + 목적어 + v-ing: …가 ~하는 것을 듣다
> 특이하지 않다　　　선수와 코치가 과정에 대해 이야기하는 것을 듣는 것은
> process].

➡ to hear 이하는 가주어 it에 대한 진주어로 쓰인 to부정사구이므로, to hear는 어법상 바르다.

② 도치 구문

> **Rarely** do they talk / about scoring a goal, a touchdown, a home
> 부정어(좀처럼 … 않다)
> 좀처럼 그들은 이야기하지 않는다　골 넣기, 터치다운, 홈런,
> run, a point, or achieving a good shot.
> 점수, 혹은 명중시키는 것에 대해서

➡ 부정어 Rarely가 문장 앞에 나와서 주어와 동사의 어순이 바뀌는 도치가 일어난 구문으로, 일반동사가 쓰인 문장은 「do[does/did] + 주어 + 동사원형」의 어순으로 도치되므로, do they는 어법상 바르다.

 Grammar Tips

> **부정의 의미를 나타내는 부사**
>
> rarely, seldom(좀처럼 … 않다), hardly, scarcely, barely(거의 … 않다), never(결코 … 않다)와 같은 부사는 부정의 의미를 포함하고 있어서 not 등의 부정어와 함께 쓰지 않는다.
>
> 예) He **seldom** calls me. (그는 나에게 거의 전화하지 않는다.)

---

④ 접속사 that

> The reasoning here / is {that [if you follow the steps required], /
> 　　　　　　　　　　　명사절(보어)를 이끄는 접속사　　　　　　　과거분사
> 여기에서의 추론은　　　　당신이 요구되는 단계들을 따른다면
> then the result will look after itself}.
> 　　　　　주어(the result)를 받는 재귀대명사
> 그러면 결과는 저절로 나올 것이라는 것이다

➡ that은 주격보어로 쓰이는 명사절을 이끄는 접속사로, that 뒤에 완전한 절이 이어지고 있으므로 어법상 바르다.

⑤ 「전치사 + 동명사」

> Amateurs often focus on the result / and forget about doing all
> 　　　　　　　　　　　　　　　　　　　전치사
> 아마추어들은 종종 결과에 집중하고　　　　모든 것들을 행하는 것에 대해 잊어버린다
> the things / [that would almost automatically lead to the result].
> 　　　　　주격 관계대명사　　　　　　　　　　…로 이어지다
> 　　　　　거의 자동으로 결과로 이어질

➡ doing은 전치사 about의 목적어로 쓰인 동명사로 어법상 바르다.

지문 해석

요즘에는 프로 스포츠에서, 선수와 코치가 과정에 대해 이야기하는 것을 듣는 것은 특이하지 않다. 그들은 과정에 집중하는 것과 과정을 따르는 것에 대하여 이야기한다. 그들은 골 넣기, 터치다운, 홈런, 점수, 혹은 명중시키는 것에 대해서는 좀처럼 이야기하지 않는다. 그것은 모두 과정에 관한 것이다. 그러면 그들은 이것으로 무엇을 말하려는 것인가? 그들이 과정에 집중함으로써 의도한 것은 그들이 바라는 결과를 얻기 위해 취할 필요가 있는 행동에 집중한다는 것이다. 그들은 결과 자체에 집중하지 않는다. 여기에서의 추론은 당신이 요구되는 단계들을 따른다면, 결과는 저절로 나올 것이라는 것이다. 이것이 프로 스포츠인과 아마추어 스포츠인 사이의 큰 차이 중 하나이다. 아마추어들은 종종 결과에 집중하고 거의 자동으로 결과로 이어질 모든 것들을 행하는 것에 대해서는 잊어버린다.

unusual 혱 특이한, 흔치 않은　achieve 통 달성하다, 성취하다　reasoning 몡 추론　require 통 필요[요구]하다　difference 몡 차이　amateur 혱 아마추어의 몡 아마추어　sportsperson 몡 운동선수　automatically 뷔 자동적으로

08　정답 ②　정답률 23%

정답 풀이

② 수동태

> Free recall tests, / [in which students need to recall as much as
> 주어　　　　　　　　전치사+관계대명사　　　as+원급+as: 가능한 한 …한[하게]
> 자유 회상 테스트는　　학생들이 별다른 힌트 없이 가능한 많은 것을 기억해야 하는
> they can remember without prompting], / tend to result in better
> 　　　　　　　　　　　　　　　　　　　동사
> 　　　　　　　　　　　　　　더 나은 기억 유지 결과를 낳는
> retention / than cued recall tests, / {in which students give(→ are
> 　　　　　　　　　　　　　　　　　　전치사+관계대명사
> 경향이 있다　단서 회상 테스트보다　　　학생들이 힌트를 받는
> given) hints / about [what they need to remember]}.
> 　　　　　　　관계대명사
> 　　　　　　그들이 기억해야 할 내용에 관한

➡ 주어인 students가 힌트를 주는 주체가 아니라 대상이므로 수동태 are given이 되어야 한다.

┃친절한 오답 풀이┃

① 동사의 수 일치

> More difficult retrieval leads to better learning, / provided the
> 　　　주어　　　　　　동사　　　　　　　　　　　접속사(만약) …라면
> 더 어려운 기억의 재생은 더 나은 학습으로 이어진다　　그 재생 행위 자체가
> act of retrieval is itself successful.
> 성공적이라면

➡ provided는 '(만약) …라면'이라는 의미의 접속사로 부사절을 이끌고, More difficult retrieval이 주절의 주어이다. 주절의 동사가 필요하며, 주어가 단수 명사이므로 leads는 어법상 바르다.

③ 관계부사

Cued recall tests, in turn, are better / than recognition tests, / such
        삽입구
결국 단서 회상 테스트는 더 효과적이다   인식 테스트보다
as multiple-choice answers, / [where the correct answer needs to
              관계부사
객관식 테스트와 같은   정답을 인식할 필요는 있지만 생성할 필요는 없는
be recognized but not generated].
      병렬구조

➡ 구체적인 상황을 나타내는 recognition test를 선행사로 하고, 뒤에 완전한 절이 이어지고 있으므로 관계부사 where은 어법상 바르다.

④ 대명사

{Giving someone a test immediately [after they learn
동명사구(주어)   접속사
무언가를 학습한 직후에 테스트를 하는 것은
something]} / improves retention less / than giving them a slight
           동사
    기억 유지에 덜 도움이 된다   약간의 시간 지연을 주는 것보다
delay, / {long enough so that answers aren't in mind / [when they
          부사구   하도록   접속사
      답을 떠올릴 수 없을 정도로 충분히 긴   답이 필요할 때
need them]}.

➡ 복수 명사 answers를 대신하므로 복수형 대명사 them은 어법상 바르다.

⑤ 「전치사 + 동명사」

Difficulty, / [far from being a barrier to making retrieval work], /
주어   삽입구
어려움은   기억의 재생이 효과를 발하게 하는 데 있어 장애물이 아니라
                  = retrieval
may be part of the reason [it does so].
동사   관계부사절
                  = works
그것(재생)이 그렇게 되는(효과가 있는) 이유의 일부일 수 있다

➡ to는 전치사로 쓰였으므로, 전치사의 목적어로 동명사 making은 어법상 바르다.

지문 해석

무엇이 복습보다 연습을 통한 기억의 재생을 훨씬 더 나은 것으로 만드는가? 하나의 답은 심리학자 R. A. Bjork의 바람직한 어려움이란 개념에서 나온다. 더 어려운 기억의 재생은, 그 재생 행위 자체가 성공적이라면, 더 나은 학습으로 이어진다. 학생들이 별다른 힌트 없이 가능한 많은 것을 기억해야 하는 자유 회상 테스트는, 학생들이 기억해야 할 내용에 관한 힌트를 받는 단서 회상 테스트보다 더 나은 기억 유지 결과를 낳는 경향이 있다. 결국 단서 회상 테스트는, 객관식 테스트와 같은 정답을 인식할 필요는 있지만 생성할 필요는 없는 인식 테스트보다 더 효과적이다. 무언가를 학습한 직후에 테스트를 하는 것은, 답이 필요할 때 그것을 떠올릴 수 없을 정도로 충분히 긴 약간의 시간 지연을 주는 것보다 기억 유지에 덜 도움이 된다. 어려움은 기억의 재생이 효과를 발하게 하는 데 있어 장애물이 아니라, 그것이 그렇게 되는(효과가 있는) 이유의 일부일 수 있다.

desirable 형 바람직한 **prompt** 동 (질문·힌트 등을 주어 말을 하도록) 유도하다
cued 형 단서가 제공되는 **recognition** 명 인식 **generate** 동 생성하다 **delay**
명 지연 **barrier** 명 장애물

정답 풀이

④ 능동태 vs. 수동태

One study of Bordeaux University students of wine and wine
포도주와 포도주 제조에 관해 공부하는 Bordeaux University 학생들을 대상으로 한 연구는
making / revealed {that they chose tasting notes / [(which were)
               접속사   「주격 관계대명사 + be동사」 생략
        그들이 시음표를 선택했다는 것을 보여주었다
appropriate for red wines]}, / such as 'prune and chocolate', /
                      전치사(…와 같은)
적포도주에 적합한   '자두와 초콜릿'과 같은
{when they gave(→ were given) white wine / [coloured with a
      접속사   과거분사
그들이 백포도주를 받았을 때   붉은색 색소로 물든
red dye]}.

➡ 동사 give의 간접목적어(they)가 주어이고, 문맥상 백포도주를 '받았다'라는 의미가 되어야 하므로 능동태 gave를 수동태 were given으로 고쳐야 한다.

친절한 오답 풀이

① 가주어 진주어 구문

Although it is obvious / [that part of our assessment of food /
         가주어   진주어
비록 분명하지만   음식에 대한 우리 평가의 일부가
is its visual appearance], / it is perhaps surprising / [how visual
                 가주어   진주어(의문사 + 주어 + 동사)
음식의 시각적 외관인 것은   아마도 놀라울 것이다   어떻게 시각적인 입력 정보가
input can override taste and smell].
맛과 냄새에 우선할 수 있는가는

➡ 가주어 진주어 구문으로, 의문사 how가 이끄는 명사절이 문장의 진주어 역할을 하고 있으므로 어법상 바르다.

② 「find + 목적어 + 형용사」

People find it very difficult / [to correctly identify fruit-flavoured
           가목적어 목적격보어   진목적어
사람들은 매우 어렵다는 것을 알게 된다   과일 맛이 나는 음료를 정확하게 식별하는 것이
drinks] / if the colour is wrong, / for instance an orange drink /
           색깔이 잘못되어 있다면   예를 들어 오렌지 음료와 같이
[that is coloured green].
    주격 관계대명사
초록색으로 물든

➡ 동사 find의 목적격보어 자리에는 명사와 형용사가 모두 올 수 있으므로 형용사 difficult는 어법상 바르다.

③ 도치구문의 동사

Perhaps even more striking is / the experience of wine tasters.
            주격보어   동사   주어
아마 훨씬 더 놀라울 것이다   포도주 맛을 감정하는 사람들의 경험은

➡ 주격보어가 문장 앞에 나오면서 주어와 동사가 도치된 구문으로, 주어가 전치사구(of wine tasters)의 수식을 받는 the experience이므로 단수 동사 is가 오는 것이 알맞다.

⑤ 접속사 that

Experienced New Zealand wine experts / were similarly tricked
                          be tricked into: ~하도록 속임을 당하다
숙련된 뉴질랜드 포도주 전문가들도   마찬가지로 속아서 생각하게 되었다
into thinking / [that the white wine Chardonnay was in fact a red
             명사절(목적어)을 이끄는 접속사
             백포도주 Chardonnay를 실제로 적포도주라고
wine], / [when it had been coloured with a red dye].
         접속사   had been v-ed: 과거완료 수동태
      그것이 붉은색 색소로 물들었을 때

➡ 동명사 thinking의 목적어 역할을 하는 명사절을 이끄는 접속사로, 뒤에 완전한 절(the

white ... a red wine)이 이어지고 있으므로 접속사 that은 어법상 바르다.

비록 음식에 대한 우리 평가의 일부가 음식의 시각적 외관인 것은 분명하지만, 어떻게 시각적인 입력 정보가 맛과 냄새에 우선할 수 있는가는 아마도 놀라울 것이다. 만약 예를 들어 초록색으로 물든 오렌지 음료와 같이 색깔이 잘못되어 있다면, 사람들은 과일 맛이 나는 음료를 정확하게 식별하는 것이 매우 어렵다는 것을 알게 된다. 포도주 맛을 감정하는 사람들의 경험은 아마 훨씬 더 놀라울 것이다. 포도주와 포도주 제조에 관해 공부하는 Bordeaux University 학생들을 대상으로 한 연구는 그들이 붉은색 색소로 물든 백포도주를 받았을 때, '자두와 초콜릿'과 같은 적포도주에 적합한 시음표를 선택했다는 것을 보여주었다. 숙련된 뉴질랜드 포도주 전문가들도 마찬가지로 백포도주 Chardonnay가 붉은색 색소로 물들었을 때, 속아서 그것을 실제로 적포도주라고 생각하게 되었다.

obvious 혱 분명한, 명백한   assessment 몡 평가   visual 혱 시각의   input 몡 입력; *입력 정보   identify 됭 확인하다; *식별하다   flavoured …맛이 나는   striking 혱 인상적인; *놀라운   wine taster 포도주 맛[품질] 감정가   tasting 몡 시음   note 몡 표, 기호   dye 몡 염료; *색깔

---

10   정답 ③   정답률 15%

③ 능동태 vs. 수동태

These robots / [made of a synthetic compound] / designed(→ are
주어   과거분사, made of: …로 만들어진   동사
이 로봇들은   인조 합성물로 만들어진   설계되어 있다
designed) / to be flexible in the tail and rigid in the midsection.
부사적 용법의 to부정사(목적)
꼬리 부분은 유연하고 중앙부는 딱딱하도록

➡ 주어는 과거분사구(made of ... compound)의 수식을 받는 These robots로, 로봇들이 '설계한' 것이 아니라 '설계된' 것이므로 능동태 designed를 수동태 are designed로 고쳐야 한다.

친절한 오답 풀이

① 형용사

Only instead of **live** fish / [searching for food], / these are
형용사   현재분사
단순히 살아있는 물고기 대신에   먹이를 찾아다니는   이들은 로봇들이다
robots / [patrolling for pipe damage and pollutant leaks].
현재분사
파이프 손상과 오염 물질의 유출을 찾아 순찰하는

➡ live는 형용사로 쓰여 뒤따르는 명사 fish를 수식하고 있으므로 어법상 바르다.

 오답 피하기 Tips

live의 품사와 쓰임

단어	품사	뜻	쓰임
live	형용사	살아 있는	뒤에 오는 명사 수식 예) **live** *birds* (살아있는 새들)
	자동사	살다	동사 단독으로 쓰거나 뒤에 전치사구가 붙음 예) He **lives** alone. (그는 혼자 산다.) 예) She **lives** in London. (그녀는 런던에 산다.)
	타동사	…한 생활을 하다	동족목적어와 함께 쓰임 예) I **lived** a happy *life*. (나는 행복한 생활을 했다.)

---

② 동사의 수 일치

The newest (robo-fish) are five to eighteen inches long, / have
주어   동사1   동사2
최신형(로봇 물고기들)은 길이가 5~18인치이고,
about ten parts, and cost just hundreds of dollars.
등위접속사 and에 의해 연결된 병렬구조(A, B, and C), 동사3
약 10개의 부분으로 되어 있고, 비용이 단지 수백 달러만 든다

➡ The newest (robo-fish)가 주어이고, 등위접속사 and가 동사 are, have, cost를 병렬 연결하고 있다. 명사 fish는 단수형과 복수형이 같은데, 뒤에 오는 두 번째, 세 번째 동사가 복수형인 것으로 보아 '로봇 물고기들'이라는 의미로 복수형으로 쓰인 것으로 볼 수 있으므로, 복수 동사 are가 오는 것이 알맞다.

④ 「전치사 + 동명사」

[Although the latest robotic fish are pretty close **to** making a
접속사(비록 …일지라도)   전치사
비록 최신의 로봇 물고기들이 첨벙거리는 것에 꽤 근접하기는 하지만
splash], / they are not yet swimming / in lakes and oceans.
그들은 아직 헤엄쳐 다니지 못한다   호수나 바다에서

➡ 앞의 전치사 to의 목적어 역할을 하는 동명사가 와야 하므로 making이 오는 것이 적절하다.

 Grammar Tips

자주 나오는 전치사 to 표현

He's **dedicated to** developing invention.
(그는 발명품을 개발하는 데 전념하고 있다.)
They **object to** paying unfair tax.
(그들은 부당한 세금을 지불하는 것에 반대한다.)
This is the **key to** brewing great coffee.
(이것이 좋은 커피를 만드는 핵심이다.)
Reusable bottles can **contribute to** reducing the amount of plastic waste. (재사용컵은 플라스틱 쓰레기 양을 줄이는 데 기여할 수 있다.)

⑤ 접속사

It'll be a few more years / {before you can tell the story of
접속사
몇 년은 더 있어야 할 것이다   당신이 로봇 물고기에 대해 이야기를 할 수 있기 전까지
the robo-fish / [that got away]}.
주격 관계대명사
도망가버린

➡ before는 접속사로 뒤에 완전한 절이 이어지고 있으므로 어법상 바르다.

 구문 분석 Plus

5행
Robo-fish can fit in places [(**which/that**) divers and submarines *can't* (*fit in*)].
➡ places 뒤에 목적격 관계대명사가 생략됨
➡ can't 뒤에 동사구 fit in이 생략됨

만의 바닥에 있는 파이프라인의 망을 통과하여 헤엄쳐 다니는 물고기 떼를 상상해 보라. 단순히 먹이를 찾아다니는 살아있는 물고기 대신, 이들은 파이프 손상과 오염 물질의 유출을 찾아 순찰하는 로봇들이다. 로봇 물고기들은 잠수부나 잠수함이 갈 수 없는 장소에 적합하다. 최신형은 길이가 5~18인치이며, 약 10개의 부분으로 되어 있고, 비용이 단지 수백 달러만 든다. 인조 합성물로 만들어진 이 로봇은 꼬리 부분은 유연하고 중앙부는 딱딱하도록 설계되어 있다. 그 물질의 동작은 실제 물고기의 헤엄치는 동작을 흉내 낸다. 비록 최신의 로봇 물고기들이 첨벙거리는 것에 꽤 근접하기는 하지만, 그들은 아직 호수나 바다에서 헤엄쳐 다니지 못한다. 당신이 도망가버린 로봇 물고기에 대해 이야기를 할 수 있기 전까지 몇 년은 더 있어야 할 것이다.

school 뗑 학교; *(물고기의) 떼　weave 똥 (옷감 등을) 짜다; *누비며 가다　bay 뗑
만(灣)　patrol 똥 순찰을 돌다　pollutant 뗑 오염 물질　leak 뗑 누출
submarine 뗑 잠수함　synthetic 뼹 인조의, 합성의　compound 뗑 혼합물
flexible 뼹 유연한　rigid 뼹 단단한　midsection 뗑 중간부　material 뗑 물질
mimic 똥 흉내 내다　splash 뗑 첨벙하는 소리

UNIT 3 시제, 조동사, 대동사

코드 접속하기   pp.45~47

출제코드 1   완료시제

A 1 had tried   2 have suggested   3 have met
B 1 ➡ has practiced   2 ➡ had bought   3 ○

해석과 정답 풀이

STEP 1
1 1) 그는 15살 때부터 레고 장난감을 수집해 왔다.
   2) Austin은 Lisa와 저녁을 먹기 전에 배드민턴을 쳤다.
   3) 지난달 그는 한국을 포함하여 많은 나라들을 방문했다.
2 1) 그녀가 New York에 있었을 때 현대 미술관에 갔어야 했다.
   2) 만약 당신이 그 산을 등반해본 적이 있다면, 정상에서 멋진 광경을 봤을지도 모른다.

STEP 2
1 아빠는 나에게 장난감 자동차를 사주었는데, 그것은 내가 원했던 것이었다.
2 그는 어릴 때부터 축구에 관심이 있었다.
3 그는 내 전화를 받지 않았다. 그는 아마 잠들었을지도 모른다.

STEP 3
A 1 Julia가 기말고사에서 최선을 다했음에도 불구하고, 그녀는 나쁜 성적을 받았다.
   ➡ Julia가 성적을 받은 것보다 시험에 최선을 다한 것이 더 앞선 과거의 일이므로
      과거완료 had tried가 오는 것이 알맞다.
   2 2002년 이래로, 그들은 중세 시대의 문화를 연구할 새로운 방법들을 제안해왔다.
   ➡ 2002년 이후 계속된 일을 나타내므로 현재완료 have suggested가 오는 것이
      알맞다.
   3 우리는 교수님이 다른 대학으로 옮기기 전에 그를 만났어야 했다.
   ➡ 과거 일에 대한 후회를 나타내고 있으므로, should 뒤에 have met이 오는 것이
      알맞다.
B 1 지난 5년 동안, 그녀는 그녀의 꿈을 이루기 위해 정말로 열심히 춤을 연습해왔다.
   ➡ 지난 5년 동안 계속된 일을 나타내므로 practiced를 현재완료 has practiced로
      고쳐야 한다.
   2 Paul은 그 전날 부모님이 그를 위해 사주셨던 휴대폰을 잃어버렸다.
   ➡ 휴대폰을 잃어버린 것보다 부모님이 휴대폰을 사주신 것이 더 이전의 일이므로
      현재완료 have bought를 과거완료 had bought로 고쳐야 한다.
   3 George는 Helena를 전에 본 적이 없었으므로, 그녀를 알아봤을 리가 없다.
   ➡ 과거 사실에 대한 강한 부정적 추측을 나타내므로, can't 뒤에 have recognized가
      오는 것이 알맞다.

출제코드 2   대동사 do

A 1 does   2 do
B 1 ➡ did   2 ➡ do, 또는 are 삭제   3 ○

해석과 정답 풀이

STEP 1
1 1) 그녀는 내가 가진 것보다 훨씬 더 많은 신발들을 가지고 있다.
   2) 나는 개를 좋아하고 나의 아이도 그렇다.
2 1) 그는 작년에 그랬던 것보다 돈을 더 많이 번다.
   2) Ben은 운동선수가 하는 것만큼 열심히 운동한다.

STEP 2
1 1) 아이들은 그들의 부모들이 그랬던 것만큼 자주 떠들지 않았다.
   2) 그녀는 십 대들이 보통 그러는 것처럼 그녀가 좋아하는 가수들에 대해 많이
      이야기한다.
   3) 8월에, 서울에는 대구에서 그러는 것보다 더 많은 비가 내린다.

STEP 3
A 1 그 기계가 수리되었기 때문에, 그것은 지금 새 기계만큼 잘 작동한다.
   ➡ 앞에 나온 동사 works를 대신하므로 대동사 does가 오는 것이 알맞다.

2 요즘, 사람들은 아마도 그들의 차 안에서 그러는 것보다 인터넷에서 더 많은 시간을 쓴다.
➡ 앞에 나온 동사 spend를 대신하므로 대동사 do가 오는 것이 알맞다.

B 1 사람들이 들판에서 그랬던 것처럼, 나는 밤하늘을 올려다 보았다.
➡ 앞에 나온 동사구 looked up .... sky를 대신하고, 문장 전체가 과거시제이므로 과거형 대동사 did로 고쳐야 한다.

2 이기적인 사람들은 이타적인 사람들이 그러는 것만큼 현명한 결정을 내리지 않는다.
➡ 앞에 나온 동사구 make wise decisions를 대신하고, 주어(selfless people)가 복수이므로 복수형 대동사 do로 고쳐야 한다. 혹은 as well as 뒤에 비교 대상인 selfless people만 남기고 are를 삭제한다.

3 초기 인류들은 오늘날의 우리가 그러는 것처럼 주로 동물의 근육덩이 살코기를 먹었을 것으로 추정된다.
➡ 앞에 나온 동사구 ate ... of animals를 대신하며, 현재를 나타내는 부사 today가 쓰였으므로 현재형 대동사 do가 오는 것이 알맞다.

기출예제 Q1   정답 ④   정답률 40%

정답 풀이

④ 대동사 do

> Productivity improvements are as important to the economy /
>   as ... as 비교구문
> 생산성 향상은 경제에도 중요하다
> as they do(→ are) to the individual business [that's making
>   주격 관계대명사
> 그것을 만들어 내는 개별 기업에 중요한 만큼
> them].
> = productivity improvements

➡ 대동사 do는 앞에 나온 일반동사(구)를 대신하는데, 밑줄 친 부분은 앞 절에 쓰인 are important가 반복되어 쓰이는 자리이므로, do를 are로 고쳐야 한다.

친절한 오답 풀이

① 「so + 부사 + that...」

> [If the manufacturer cuts costs so deeply that doing so harms
>   = cutting costs so deeply
> 만약 제조업자가 비용을 너무 많이 절감해서 그렇게 하는 것이
> the product's quality], / then the increased profitability will be
>   주어
> 제품의 질을 손상하게 된다면   그러면 그 증가된 수익성은 단기적일 것이다
> short-lived.

➡ '너무 ~해서 …하다'의 의미인 「so + 부사 + that …」 구문으로, 접속사 that이 오는 것이 알맞다.

② 부사

> {If businesses can get more production / [from the same number
> 만약 기업이 더 많은 생산을 얻을 수 있다면   똑같은 수의 직원들로부터
> of employees]}, / they're basically tapping into free money.
>   =businesses   tap into: …에 다가가다
>   그들은 기본적으로 돈을 거저 얻게 되는 것이다

➡ 부사 basically가 동사(are tapping)를 수식하고 있으므로 어법상 바르다.

③ 명사를 수식하는 과거분사

> {As long as the machinery or employee training [needed
>   …이기만 하면   주어   과거분사
> 생산성 향상에 필요한 기계 또는 직원 연수가 …하기만 하면
> for productivity improvements] / costs less than the value of
>   동사
> 생산성 향상으로 얻는 이윤의 가치보다 비용이 적게 들기만 하면
> the productivity gains}, / it's an easy investment for any business
>   to부정사의 의미상 주어
>   이것은 어떤 기업이든 할 수 있는 쉬운 투자이다
> to make.
> 형용사적 용법의 to부정사

➡ 앞의 명사구 the machinery or employee training을 수식하는 분사로, 수식받는 명사(구)와 분사가 의미상 수동 관계이므로 과거분사 needed가 오는 것이 어법상 바르다.

⑤ 병렬구조

> Productivity improvements generally raise the standard of living
>   주어   동사1
> 생산성 향상은 일반적으로 생활 수준을 모두를 위해 향상시킨다
> for everyone / and are a good indication of a healthy economy.
>   동사2
> 그리고 건강한 경제의 좋은 지표이다

➡ 등위접속사 and가 동사 raise와 are를 병렬 연결하고 있는 구조로 주어(Productivity improvements)가 복수 명사이므로 복수 동사 are는 어법상 바르다.

 구문 분석 Plus

4행   A better approach is **to improve** productivity.
➡ to improve: 문장의 보어 역할을 하는 명사적 용법의 to부정사

지문 해석

비용 절감은 수익성을 향상시킬 수 있지만, 단지 어느 정도까지다. 만약 제조업자가 비용을 너무 많이 절감해서 그렇게 하는 것이 제품의 질을 손상하게 된다면 그 증가된 수익성은 단기적일 것이다. 더 나은 접근법은 생산성을 향상시키는 것이다. 만약 기업이 똑같은 수의 직원들로부터 더 많은 생산을 얻을 수 있다면 그들은 기본적으로 돈을 거저 얻게 되는 것이다. 그들은 판매할 상품을 더 많이 얻고, 각 상품의 가격은 내려간다. 생산성 향상에 필요한 기계 또는 직원 연수가 생산성 향상으로 얻는 이윤의 가치보다 비용이 적게 들기만 하면, 이것은 어떤 기업이든 할 수 있는 쉬운 투자이다. 생산성 향상은 그것을 만들어 내는 개별 기업에 중요한 만큼 경제에도 중요하다. 생산성 향상은 일반적으로 모두를 위해 생활 수준을 향상시키며 건강한 경제의 좋은 지표이다.

어휘

profitability 몡 수익성   **up to a point** 어느 정도(는)   **manufacturer** 몡 제조자 **short-lived** 혱 오래가지 못하는   **productivity** 몡 생산성   **tap into** …에 다가가다; *…을 이용하다   **improvement** 몡 향상, 개선   **investment** 몡 투자   **standard of living** 생활 수준   **indication** 몡 지표

코드 공략하기   pp.48~49

01 ⑤   **02** ②   **03** ⑤   **04** ④   **05** ⑤   **06** ⑤

01   정답 ⑤   정답률 54%

정답 풀이

(A) 목적격 관계대명사

> This reminded him of the news / { what / that he had heard on
> remind A of B: A에게 B를 연상하게 하다   목적격 관계대명사   과거완료
> 이것은 그가 뉴스를 연상하게 했다   그가 라디오에서 들었던
> the radio: / two thieves stopped a train and stole mailbags [full of
>   full of: …로 가득 찬
> 두 명의 도둑이 열차를 세우고 돈으로 가득 찬 우편물 가방들을 훔쳤다
> money]}.

➡ 네모는 the news를 선행사로 하는 관계대명사로, 관계대명사절에서 동사의 목적어 역할을 하므로 목적격 관계대명사 that이 오는 것이 적절하다. 관계대명사 what은 선행사를 포함하고 있으므로 앞에 명사가 올 수 없다.

(B) 부정형용사

> They questioned both / each men / but neither of them could
>   neither of: …의 어느 쪽도 아니다
> 그들은 두 남자들을 모두 심문했다   하지만 그들 중 누구도 영어를 할 수 없었다
> speak English.

➡ both는 '둘 다'의 뜻으로 뒤에 복수 명사가 오고, each는 '각각의'라는 뜻으로 뒤에 단수

명사가 와야 한다. 네모 뒤에 오는 명사(men)가 복수형이므로 both가 오는 것이 알맞다.

(C) 과거완료 시제

Later, the police **realized** / [that they ~~have made~~ / **had made**]
　　　　　　　　 과거　　　　　 접속사　　過거완료(주절보다 한 시제 앞선 일을 나타냄)
나중에, 경찰은 깨달았다　　　　 그들이 심한 실수를 저질렀다는 것을
a terrible mistake].

➡ 경찰이 실수를 저지른 것은 그 사실을 깨달은 것(과거)보다 앞선 일이므로, 과거완료 시제인 had made가 와야 한다.

 구문 분석 Plus

> 1행
> A driver **saw** two men **carrying** heavy bags on a lonely country road.
> ➡ see(지각동사) + 목적어 + v-ing: '…가 ~하고 있는 것을 보다'의 의미로, 어떤 동작이 진행 중임을 나타냄

지문 해석

한 운전자가 한적한 시골 도로에서 남자 두 명이 무거운 가방들을 나르고 있는 것을 보았다. 이것은 그가 라디오에서 들었던, 두 명의 도둑이 열차를 세우고 돈으로 가득 찬 우편물 가방들을 훔쳤다는 뉴스를 연상하게 했다. 그는 즉시 경찰에 전화를 했다. 경찰이 곧 현장에 도착했고 그들을 체포했다. 그들은 두 남자들을 모두 심문했지만 그들 중 누구도 영어를 할 수 없었다. 그들은 그저 계속해서 경찰에게 소리만 질러댔다. 나중에, 경찰은 그들이 심한 실수를 저질렀다는 것을 깨달았다. 그 남자들은 프랑스인 양파 상인들이었고 그들의 가방은 양파로 가득 차 있었다!

 어휘

lonely 톙 외로운; *인적이 드문 **thief** 몡 도둑, 절도범 **mailbag** 몡 우편물 **scene** 몡 현장 **arrest** 통 체포하다 **question** 통 질문하다, 심문하다 **terrible** 톙 끔찍한; *심한

02　　　　　정답 ②　　　정답률 44%

정답 풀이

② 대동사 do

Selfish adults or kids **do** not make sound decisions / as well as
　　　　　　　　　　 make a decision: 결정을 내리다　　　 …만큼 잘
이기적인 어른이나 아이들은 건전한 결정을 잘 내리지 못한다
are(→ **do**) grateful people.
감사할 줄 아는 사람들이 그러는 만큼 잘

➡ 밑줄 친 동사는 주절의 동사구 make sound decisions를 대신하는 동사 자리이므로 대동사 do를 써야 한다.

친절한 오답 풀이

① 관계부사

Life and sports present **many situations** / [where critical and
　　　　　　　　　　　　　　　　　↑_____ 관계부사
인생과 스포츠는 많은 상황들을 제시한다
difficult decisions have to be made].
중요하고 어려운 결정이 내려져야 하는

➡ where는 앞의 명사 many situations를 선행사로 하는 관계부사로, 뒤에 완전한 절이 이어지므로 어법상 바르다.

 오답 피하기 Tips

> 관계부사 where의 선행사는 무조건 장소이다?
> 물리적 장소 외에도 point(점), case(경우), circumstance(사정), situation (상황) 등 추상적인 의미의 장소를 나타내는 선행사에도 관계부사 where가 사용될 수 있다.

---

③ 수동태

Sometimes my child **gets discouraged** / and does not want to put
　　　　　　　　　　 get v-ed: 수동태
때때로 내 아이가 낙심하고　　　　　　　　 요구되는 노력을 들이기를 원하지 않는다면
the required effort / into his or her sports?
　　과거분사 └_____┘
　　　　　　　　 그 스포츠에

➡ 주어(my child)가 '낙담하게 되는'이라는 수동의 의미가 적절하므로, 과거분사 discouraged가 알맞다.

④ 가주어 진주어 구문

It is difficult and almost impossible / {to motivate kids or adults /
가주어　　　　　　　　　　　　　　　 진주어　　　　 선행사
어렵고 거의 불가능하다　　　　　　　　 아이들이나 성인들에게 동기를 유발하는 것은
[who are centered on their own narrow selfish desires]}.
주격 관계대명사
자기들만의 편협하고 이기적인 욕구에 집중돼있는

➡ to motivate 이하는 앞의 가주어 It에 대한 진주어 역할을 하고 있는 to부정사로 어법상 바르다.

⑤ 재귀대명사

However, kids and adults [who live as grateful people] / are able
　　　　　　　 주어 ↑_____ 주격 관계대명사　 be able to-v: …할 수 있다(= can)
그러나, 감사할 줄 아는 사람들로 살아가는 아이들과 성인들은
to motivate **themselves**.
스스로에게 동기를 유발할 수 있다

➡ 주어와 동사의 목적어가 동일한 대상을 지칭하므로, 목적어로 쓰인 재귀대명사 themselves는 어법상 바르다.

지문 해석

감사할 줄 아는 사람들은 건전한 결정을 내리는 경향이 있다. 인생과 스포츠는 중요하고 어려운 결정이 내려져야 하는 많은 상황들을 제시한다. 이기적인 어른이나 아이들은 감사할 줄 아는 사람들이 그러는 만큼 건전한 결정을 잘 내리지 못한다. 이것은 스스로 동기를 부여하는 결정을 포함한다. 좌절한 부모는 묻는다. "어떻게 내가 나의 아이에게 스포츠를 하거나 스포츠를 계속하도록 동기를 부여할까? 때때로 내 아이가 낙심하여 그 스포츠에 요구되는 노력을 들이기를 원하지 않는다면? 부모로서 돕기 위해 내가 무엇을 하거나 말해야 하지?" 자기들만의 편협하고 이기적인 욕구에 집중돼있는 아이들이나 성인들에게 동기를 유발하는 것은 어렵고 거의 불가능하다. 그러나, 감사할 줄 아는 사람들로 살아가는 아이들과 성인들은 스스로에게 동기를 유발할 수 있다. 그들은 또한 다른 사람들 심지어는 부모로부터의 제안을 환영한다.

 어휘

grateful 톙 고마워하는, 감사하는 **be inclined to-v** …하는 경향이 있다 **present** 통 제시하다 **critical** 톙 비판적인; *중요한 **selfish** 톙 이기적인 **sound** 톙 건전한 **frustrate** 통 좌절감을 주다 **motivate** 통 동기를 부여하다 **discourage** 통 막다; *의욕을 꺾다, 좌절시키다 **narrow** 톙 좁은; *편협한 **desire** 몡 욕구, 갈망 **welcome** 통 환영하다

03　　　　　정답 ⑤　　　정답률 44%

정답 풀이

⑤「조동사 + have v-ed」

Aldenderfer and his team hope / that DNA analysis will
　　　　　　　　　　　　　　 명사절(목적어)을 이끄는 접속사
Aldenderfer와 그의 팀은 기대한다　 DNA 분석이 정확히 찾아줄 것으로
pinpoint / the origins of this isolated region's inhabitants, / who
　　　　　　　　　　　　　　　 선행사　　 계속적 용법의 주격 관계대명사
　　　　　　 이 고립된 지역 거주자들의 기원을
may migrate(→ **have migrated**) from the Tibetan Plateau or
may have v-ed: …했을지도 모른다
이들은 티베트 고원이나 남부 지역에서 이주해 왔을지도 모른다
southern points.

→ 문맥상 고립 지역 거주자들이 다른 지역에서 '이주해 왔을지도 모르는'이라는 과거 일에 대한 추측의 의미를 나타내야 하므로 may migrate는 may have migrated가 되어야 한다.

친절한 오답 풀이

① 「주격 관계대명사 + be동사」 생략

Archaeologist Mark Aldenderfer set out last year / to explore
고고학자 Mark Aldenderfer는 지난해에 떠났다   출발하다   부사적 용법의 to부정사(목적)
remote cliffside caves / in Nepal's Mustang district, / {aiming to
                                       동시동작을 나타내는 분사구문(= as he aimed ...)   인간의 유해
동굴을 탐사하려고   네팔의 Mustang 지역에 있는
find human remains / near an ancient settlement [(which was)
                                       「주격 관계대명사 +
발견을 목표로 하면서   히말라야 높이 있는 고대 정착지 근처에서   be동사」 생략
high in the Himalayas]}.

→ an ancient settlement를 선행사로 하는 주격 관계대명사와 be동사(which was)가 생략된 구문으로, high 이하 형용사구가 선행사를 수식하고 있으므로 어법상 바르다.

② 관계대명사 what

Almost at once, he came face-to-face / with [what he was seeking]:
                   come face-to-face with: …와 맞닥뜨리다   관계대명사
거의 즉시, 그는 맞닥뜨렸다   자신이 찾고 있던 것과

→ 전치사 with의 목적어 역할을 하면서 뒤에 오는 불완전한 절의 목적어 역할을 하고 있으므로 관계대명사 what은 어법상 바르다.

③ 접속사

[Sticking out from the rock], / a skull was looking at him right /
동시동작을 나타내는 분사구문(= As a skull was sticking ...)
바위에서 툭 튀어 나온 채   해골 하나가 그를 똑바로 바라보고 있었다
as he was looking at it.
접속사(= when)
그가 그것을 볼 때

→ as는 접속사로, 뒤에 완전한 절이 이어지므로 어법상 바르다.

④ 명사를 수식하는 과거분사

The skull, / [dating back perhaps 2,500 years], / was among many
주어   현재분사   동사
해골은   아마도 2,500년까지 거슬러 올라가는   많은 사람 뼈 사이에 있었다
human bones / [piled inside several burial caves].
                           과거분사
                   몇몇 매장 굴의 내부에 쌓여있는

→ 앞의 명사구 many human bones를 수식하는 분사로, 명사와 분사가 수동 관계에 있으므로 과거분사 piled가 오는 것이 어법상 바르다.

지문 해석

고고학자 Mark Aldenderfer는 지난해에 히말라야 높이 있는 고대 정착지 근처에 인간의 유해 발견을 목표로 하면서 네팔 Mustang 지역에 있는 외진 절벽의 동굴을 탐사하려고 떠났다. 거의 즉시, 그는 자신이 찾고 있는 것에 맞닥뜨렸다. 바위에서 툭 튀어 나온 채, 해골 하나가 그가 그것을 볼 때 그를 똑바로 바라보고 있었다. 아마도 2,500년까지 거슬러 올라가는 그 해골은 몇몇 매장 굴의 내부에 쌓여있는 많은 사람 뼈 사이에 있었다. Aldenderfer와 그의 팀은 DNA 분석이 이 고립된 지역 거주자들의 기원을 정확히 찾아줄 것으로 기대하고 있는데, 그들은 티베트 고원이나 남부 지역에서 이주해 왔을지도 모른다.

어휘

archaeologist 몡 고고학자   explore 동 탐험하다   remote 혱 외진, 외딴
cliffside 몡 절벽   cave 몡 동굴   district 몡 지구, 지역   remains 몡 유골, 유해
settlement 몡 정착지   stick out 툭 튀어나오다   skull 몡 두개골   date back
(역사가) …까지 거슬러 올라가다   pile 동 쌓다   burial 몡 매장   pinpoint 동 정확히
찾아내다   origin 몡 기원   isolate 동 격리하다, 고립시키다   inhabitant 몡 주민,
거주자   migrate 동 이주하다   plateau 몡 고원

정답 풀이

④ 대동사 do

It not only cleans clothes, but it is(→ does) so / with far less water,
     not only A but (also) B: A뿐만 아니라 B도   비교급 강조 부사
그것은 옷을 깨끗하게 할 뿐만 아니라, 그렇게 한다   훨씬 적은 양의 물과
detergent, and energy / [than washing by hand requires].
                          접속사   주어(동명사구)   동사
세제, 에너지를 가지고   손으로 빠는 것이 요구하는 것보다

→ 밑줄 친 동사는 앞 문장의 동사구(cleans clothes)를 대신하는 동사 자리이므로, is를 대동사 does로 고쳐야 한다.

친절한 오답 풀이

① 관계부사

[Before the washing machine was invented], / people used
접속사(… 전에)
세탁기가 발명되기 전   사람들은 빨래판을 사용했다
washboards / to scrub, / or they carried their laundry to riverbanks
             부사적 용법의 to부정사   선행사
            문질러 빨기 위해   또는 그들은 세탁물을 강가나 개울가로 가져갔다
and streams, / where they beat and rubbed it against rocks.
                   계속적 용법의 관계부사(= and there)
                   그곳에서 그들은 그것을 바위에 때리거나 문질렀다

→ 장소를 나타내는 명사 riverbanks and streams를 선행사로 하고 있고, 뒤에 완전한 절이 이어지므로 계속적 용법의 관계부사 where는 어법상 바르다.

② 부사

Such backbreaking labor is still commonplace / in parts of the
such (+ a(n)) + 형용사 + 명사: 그러한, 그와 같은 …
그런 대단히 힘든 노동은 아직도 흔하다   세계 각지에서
world, / but for most homeowners / the work is now done by
        하지만 대부분의 주택 소유자들에게   그 일은 이제 기계에 의해 행해진다
a machine / [that automatically regulates water temperature,
            주격 관계대명사   동사1
              자동으로 물의 온도를 조절하고, 세제를 덜어내고
measures out the detergent, washes, rinses, and spin-dries].
     동사2   동사3   동사4   접속사   동사5
빨고, 헹구고, 원심력으로 탈수하는

→ a machine을 선행사로 하는 주격 관계대명사절에서 부사 automatically가 동사들(regulates, measures, washes, spin-dries)을 수식하고 있으므로 어법상 바르다.

③ 대명사

[With its electrical and mechanical system], / the washing
전치사(… 때문에)
그것의 전기적이고 기계적인 체계 때문에   세탁기는
machine is one of the most technologically advanced examples /
             one of + 복수 명사: … 중의 하나
가장 기술적으로 진보한 예 중 하나이다
of a large household appliance.
대형 가전제품 중

→ 단수형 소유격 대명사인 its가 단수 명사인 the washing machine을 대신하고 있으므로 어법상 바르다.

⑤ 수동형 분사구문

(Being) Compared with the old washers / [that squeezed out excess
분사구문(= When modern washers are compared ...) 주격 관계대명사
구식 세탁기와 비교할 때   과한 물기를 짜냈던
water / by feeding clothes through rollers], / modern washers are
       by v-ing: …함으로써
           롤러에 빨래를 넣어서   현대식 세탁기는 정말로
indeed an electrical-mechanical phenomenon.
경이로운 전기적 · 기계적 물건이다

➡ 때를 나타내는 분사구문으로, 생략된 주어는 주절의 주어(modern washers)와 같다. 현대식 세탁기가 구식 세탁기와 '비교되는' 것으로 주어와 분사가 수동 관계이므로 과거분사 Compared가 오는 것이 알맞다.

세탁기가 발명되기 전, 사람들은 문질러 빨기 위해 빨래판을 이용하거나, 세탁물을 강가나 개울가로 가져가서, 그곳에서 세탁물을 바위에 때리거나 문질렀다. 그런 대단히 힘든 노동은 세계 각지에서 아직도 흔하지만, 대부분의 주택 소유자들에게 그 일은 이제 자동으로 물의 온도를 조절하고, 세제를 덜어내고, 빨고, 헹구고, 원심력으로 탈수하는 기계에 의해 행해진다. 세탁기는 전기적이고 기계적인 체계 때문에 대형 가전제품 중 가장 기술적으로 진보한 예 중 하나이다. 그것은 옷을 깨끗하게 할 뿐만 아니라, 손으로 빠는 것이 요구하는 것보다 훨씬 적은 양의 물과 세제, 에너지를 가지고 그렇게 한다. 롤러에 빨래를 넣어서 과한 물기를 짜냈던 구식 세탁기와 비교할 때, 현대식 세탁기는 정말로 경이로운 전기적·기계적 물건이다.

washing machine 세탁기   washboard 명 빨래판   scrub 동 문질러 씻다
laundry 명 세탁물   stream 명 개울, 시내   backbreaking 형 매우 힘든
commonplace 형 아주 흔한   homeowner 명 주택 보유자   regulate 동
규제하다; *조절하다   detergent 명 세제   measure out …을 덜어내다   rinse 동
헹구다   spin-dry 동 원심력으로 탈수하다   electronical 형 전기적   mechanical
형 기계로 작동되는   household appliance 가전제품   squeeze out 짜내다
excess 형 초과한   feed 동 먹이를 주다; *(기계에) 넣다   indeed 부 정말, 참으로
phenomenon 명 경이로운 사람[것]

05   정답 ⑤   정답률 53%

(A) 복합관계부사

I couldn't get it unlocked / [how / **however** hard I tried].
get + 목적어 + v-ed: ~가 ~되게 하다   however + 부사 + 주어 + 동사: 아무리 …할지라도
나는 그것을 열 수가 없었다   아무리 열심히 노력해도

➡ 문장에서 의문사절(의문사 + 주어 + 동사)은 명사 역할을, 복합관계부사절(복합관계부사 + 주어 + 동사)은 부사 역할을 한다. 앞에 문장성분이 완전한 절이 있으므로 네모 이하는 문장에서 부사절이 되어야 하므로 복합관계부사 however가 오는 것이 알맞다.

(B) 전치사

The basin [**near** / ~~nearly~~ the window] / provided an easy step up.
전치사구
창문 근처에 있는 세면대는   쉽게 올라갈 수 있는 발판을 제공했다

➡ 뒤에 목적어(the window)를 가지면서 앞의 명사(the basin)를 수식하므로, 전치사 near가 알맞다. nearly는 '거의'라는 뜻의 부사로, 뒤에 목적어를 취하거나 명사를 수식할 수 없다.

(C) 과거완료진행

Later my mother came home and asked me / [what I ~~have~~ / **had**
동사 asked의 직접목적어로 역할을 하는 의문사절(의문사 + 주어 + 동사)
나중에 어머니가 집에 와서 나에게 물어보셨다   내가 무엇을 하고 있었는지를
been doing].

➡ what 이하는 어머니가 물었던 것보다 더 앞선 과거에 진행되고 있던 일을 나타내고 있으므로, 과거완료진행(had been v-ing) 시제가 알맞다.

 구문 분석 Plus

11행 **Laughing**, I responded, "Oh, just hanging around."
➡ Laughing: 동시동작을 나타내는 분사구문(= As I laughed)

지난 여름의 어느 날 내가 화장실에 있었을 때, 문의 잠금 장치가 움직이지 않았다. 아무리 열심히 노력해도 나는 그것을 열 수가 없었다. 나는 내가 처한 곤경에 대해 생각했다.

소리를 지른다 해도 이웃 사람들이 내 소리를 들을 수 있을 것 같지 않았다. 그때 나는 뒤쪽 벽에 있는 작은 창문이 생각났다. 창문 근처에 있는 세면대는 쉽게 올라갈 수 있는 발판을 제공했다. 창문 밖으로 기어나간 후, 창턱에 몇 초간 매달려 있다가 쉽게 땅으로 뛰어 내렸다. 나중에 어머니가 돌아와서 나에게 무엇을 하고 있었는지 물어보셨다. 웃으면서 "아, 그냥 돌아다녔어요."라고 나는 대답했다.

lock 명 자물쇠; *잠금 장치 (unlock 동 (열쇠로) 열다)   jam 동 밀다; *움직이지 [작동하지] 못하게 되다   basin 명 대야, 세면대   sill 명 창턱   hang around 어슬렁거리다, 돌아다니다

06   정답 ⑤   정답률 48%

(A) 대동사 do

Most do have some idea / [that they should speak with more
동사를 강조하는 조동사   동격   접속사
대부분은 어떤 생각을 가지고 있다   그들이 무대에서 더 강력하게 말해야 한다는
power on stage / than they are / **do** on a one-to-one basis], ...
접속사(…보다)
그들이 일대일로 말할 때보다

➡ 접속사 than 앞 절의 동사 speak를 대신하는 대동사 do가 오는 것이 알맞다.

(B) 분사구문

{If you move your hand two inches to emphasize a point /
부사적 용법의 to부정사(목적)
당신이 한 부분을 강조하기 위해 손을 2인치 움직인다면
[when speaking / ~~to speak~~ to one person]}, / you may have to
접속사를 생략하지 않은 분사구문(= when you speak …)
한 사람에게 말할 때   당신은 그것을 움직여야 할지도 모른다
move it / as much as two feet / in front of a large audience.
…만큼
2피트만큼   많은 청중 앞에서

➡ when … person은 접속사가 남아있는 분사구문으로, 생략된 주어는 앞 절의 주어(you)와 같다. 당신이 한 사람에게 '말할' 때라는 능동의 의미가 적절하므로 현재분사 speaking이 알맞다.

(C)「so + 형용사 + that …」

This is so difficult / for people, [especially businesspeople / whose
so + 형용사 + that …: 너무 ~해서 …하다   삽입구   소유격 관계대명사
이것은 너무 어렵다   사람들, 특히 사업가들에게
general style is that of understatement], / {~~which~~ / **that** they should
접속사
일반적인 스타일이 말을 적게 하는 것인
take an acting course / [before they take a speech course]}.
take a course: 강습을 받다   접속사
그들은 연기 수업을 받아야 한다   연설 수업을 받기 전에

➡ 주절에 '너무 ~해서'라는 의미의「so + 형용사」가 쓰였으므로, '…하다'라는 결과를 나타내는 접속사 that이 오는 것이 알맞다.

 구문 분석 Plus

10행 The general rule is, **the bigger** (becomes) the audience, **the bigger** (becomes) the motion.
➡ the + 비교급 …, the + 비교급 ~: …하면 할수록 더 ~하다

대부분의 아마추어 연사들은 무대 위에 있을 때 자신들이 남자 배우 그리고 여자 배우라는 것을 이해하지 못한다. 대부분은 일대일로 말할 때보다 무대에서 더 강력하게 말해야 한다는 어떤 생각은 갖고 있지만, 언어적 유창함이 비언어적 유창함과 연결되어야 한다는 것은 깨닫지 못한다. 한 사람에게 말할 때 당신이 한 부분을 강조하기 위해 손을 2인치 움직인다면, 많은 청중 앞에서는 손을 2피트만큼 움직여야 할지도 모른다. 일반적인

규칙은 청중의 규모가 크면 클수록 동작이 더욱 더 커진다는 점이다. 이것은 사람들, 특히 일반적인 스타일이 말을 적게 하는 것인 사업가들에게 너무 어려워서, 그들은 연설 수업을 받기 전에 연기 수업을 받아야 한다.

어휘

one-to-one 형 1대 1의 verbal 형 언어의 (nonverbal 형 말로 할 수 없는, 비언어적인) eloquence 명 유창한 화술 emphasize 동 강조하다 audience 명 청중 general 형 일반적인 motion 명 동작 understatement 명 절제된 표현

UNIT 1 관계사 1

코드 접속하기   pp.51~55

출제코드 1   관계대명사의 쓰임

A **1** that   **2** which   **3** whose
B **1** ➡ who[that]   **2** ➡ whose

해석과 정답 풀이

STEP 1
1 책상 위에 2권의 책이 있다. 나는 그것들을 이미 읽었다.
　책상 위에 내가 이미 읽은 2권의 책이 있다.
2 1) 기타를 연주하고 있는 소년은 나의 남동생이다.
　2) 그녀는 그녀의 작품이 전 세계 사람들에 의해 읽히는 유명 작가이다.
　3) 내가 만난 남자는 그의 아이가 시험 기간에 TV를 못 보게 한다.

STEP 2
1 1) 그들은 10시 30분에 떠나는 버스를 타기로 예정되어 있다.
　2) 나는 왼쪽 눈이 오른쪽 눈보다 더 큰 여동생이 있다.
2 1) 나는 건물의 꼭대기 층에 사는 부유한 남자를 보았다.
　2) Jenny는 아버지가 야구선수였던 남자와 데이트하고 있다.
　3) 그는 그의 아내가 책상에 놓아둔 지갑을 찾을 수 없었다.

STEP 3
A 1 이곳은 이제 백 만권 이상의 책을 소장한, 도시에서 가장 큰 도서관이 되었다.
　➡ 접속사 역할과 뒤에 오는 절에서 주어 역할을 할 수 있는 주격 관계대명사 that이 오는 것이 알맞다.
　2 거의 매일 저녁에 그녀는 아들과 함께 그녀가 '기억력 게임'이라고 부르는 게임을 한다.
　➡ 접속사 역할과 관계대명사절에서 5형식 동사 call의 목적어 역할을 할 수 있는 목적격 관계대명사 which가 오는 것이 알맞다.
　3 그녀의 소설이 전 세계에서 큰 인기를 얻은 J. K. Rowling은 1965년에 태어났다.
　➡ 선행사 J. K. Rowling과 관계대명사 뒤의 명사 novels가 소유 관계에 있으므로 소유격 관계대명사 whose가 오는 것이 알맞다.
B 1 그는 힘든 상황을 극복하기 위해 최선을 다할 것이라고 내가 확신하는 사람이다.
　➡ 명사 a person을 선행사로 하고, 동사 does의 주어 역할을 하므로 whom을 주격 관계대명사 who나 that으로 고쳐야 한다. I am sure은 삽입절이다.
　2 당신이 이름을 들어본 몇몇 음악가들은 1회 공연에 30,000달러 이상을 번다.
　➡ 접속사 역할을 하고 있고, 선행사 Some musicians와 뒤에 오는 명사 names가 소유 관계에 있으므로 their를 소유격 관계대명사 whose로 고쳐야 한다.

출제코드 2   접속사와 관계대명사

A **1** that   **2** what   **3** that
B **1** ➡ What   **2** ➡ which[that]

해석과 정답 풀이

STEP 1
1 1) 두 회사가 합병될 것이라는 소문은 사실로 드러났다.
　2) 나는 다른 사람들의 말을 듣지 않는 사람들을 좋아하지 않는다.
2 1) 그를 다른 사람들과 다르게 하는 것은 그의 친절한 매너이다.
　2) 이것이 내가 이번 학기 영어 수업에서 배운 것이다.

STEP 2
1 1) 그 연구는 찡그리는 것이 웃는 것이 그러는 것보다 더 많은 근육을 사용한다는 것을 보여준다.

2) 내가 정말로 하고 싶은 것은 집에 일찍 가서 좀 쉬는 것이다.
3) 진실은 대부분의 사람들이 단지 1분 미만으로 양치질을 한다는 것이다.
2 1) 나의 딸은 그녀가 오늘 아침에 한 일을 결코 내게 말하지 않았다.
2) 그는 주식투자를 통해 번 돈으로 그의 집을 샀다.

STEP 3
A 1 이 수업은 학생들에게 너무 어려워서 많은 학생들이 낙제했다.
➡ 뒤에 완전한 절이 이어지고 있으므로 접속사 that이 오는 것이 알맞다. 「so + 형용사 + that ...」은 '너무 ~해서 …하다'라는 의미를 나타낸다.
2 Leonardo에게는 평범한 사람들이 보지 못하는 것을 볼 수 있는 특별한 능력이 있었다.
➡ 앞에 선행사가 없고 관계대명사절에 동사 couldn't see의 목적어 역할을 하고 있으므로 선행사를 포함한 관계대명사 what이 오는 것이 알맞다.
3 당신이 오랫동안 계획해왔으나 시작하지 못한 것을 시도해라.
➡ 앞에 오는 대명사 something을 선행사로 하고, 뒤에 오는 절에서 목적어 역할을 하므로 목적격 관계대명사 that이 오는 것이 알맞다.
B 1 어제 나에게 일어났던 것은 너무 놀라워서 나는 그것을 묘사할 수 없다.
➡ 앞에 선행사가 없고 뒤에 주어가 빠진 불완전한 절이 이어지고 있으므로 Which를 관계대명사 What으로 고쳐야 한다.
2 그녀는 더 잘 맞는 또 다른 직업을 찾을 수 있을 것이라 생각했다.
➡ 명사 another job을 선행사로 하고, 관계대명사절에서 동사 was의 주어 역할을 하고 있으므로 what을 주격 관계대명사 which나 that으로 고쳐야 한다. 관계대명사 what은 선행사를 포함하므로 앞에 선행사가 오지 않는다.

출제코드 3 · 주의해야 할 관계대명사
A 1 during which 2 whom
B 1 ➡ for which 2 ➡ which 3 ➡ which

해석과 정답 풀이

STEP 1
1 1) 나는 새로운 직원을 만났는데, 그 직원은 Tom을 대신하기 위해 고용되었다.
2) 그들은 안전선을 넘어 수영하러 가기를 원하는데, 그것은 좋은 생각이 아니다.
3) 그는 턱수염이 없는 것이 훨씬 더 나아 보이는데, 그것은 그를 나이 들어 보이게 했다.
2 1) 나는 당신이 멋진 사진을 찍었던 카페를 찾을 수가 없다.
2) 그는 많은 외국인 친구들이 있는데, 그들 중 하나는 중국 여자아이이다.

STEP 2
1 1) 그 아기는 담요로 싸여 있었는데, 그것은 추위를 막아주었다.
2) 그는 자신의 노트북 컴퓨터를 고쳤다고 말했지만, 그것은 거짓말로 드러났다.
2 그들은 저녁을 먹었던 식당으로 돌아갔다.

STEP 3
A 1 이 워크숍은 그 기간 동안 당신이 자신을 발견할 수 있는 시간이 될 것이다.
➡ 앞의 명사 a time이 선행사로, 관계대명사절 안에 '… 동안'이라는 의미의 전치사가 필요하므로 「전치사 + 관계대명사」인 during which가 오는 것이 알맞다.
2 그는 그의 첫사랑에 대해 여전히 생각하고, 그 사람을 때때로 그리워한다.
➡ 앞의 명사 his first love를 선행사로 하는 계속적 용법의 목적격 관계대명사이므로 whom이 오는 것이 알맞다. 관계대명사 that은 계속적 용법으로 쓸 수 없다.
B 1 매일 당신이 감사할 수 있는 어떤 특별한 것을 찾아라.
➡ 선행사 something은 관계대명사절의 동사 be grateful의 의미상 목적어이지만 '…에 대해'라는 의미의 전치사가 필요하므로, 관계대명사 that을 「전치사 + 관계대명사」인 for which로 고쳐야 한다.
2 히포크라테스는 버드나무 껍질을 처방했는데, 그것은 천연 형태의 약품을 함유하고 있다.
➡ 명사 willow bark를 선행사로 하는 계속적 용법의 주격 관계대명사이므로 what을 which로 고쳐야 한다.
3 그의 새 앨범은 10곡을 담고 있는데, 그 중 일부는 큰 인기를 얻었다.
➡ 명사 10 songs를 선행사로 하는 계속적 용법의 관계대명사로, 관계대명사절에서 전치사 of의 목적어 역할을 하고 있으므로 that을 목적격 관계대명사 which로 고쳐야 한다.

기출예제 Q1 · 정답 ⑤ · 정답률 60%

정답 풀이

⑤ 접속사 vs. 관계대명사
...; there is no way to know / [what(→ whether) the subject's
　　　　　　　　　　　　형용사적 용법의 to부정사　　　접속사
알 방법은 없다　　　　　　　피험자의 반응이 전형적인 것인지 이례적인 것인지
responses are typical or atypical / of the response of humans /
　　　　　　　　　　　　　　　인간 반응의
as a group].
전치사(…로서)
집단으로서

➡ 뒤에 동사 know의 목적어로 쓰인 완전한 절이 이어지며, '…인지'라는 의미로 해석되므로 접속사 whether가 오는 것이 알맞다. 관계대명사 what은 불완전한 절을 이끌며 '…한 것'이라는 의미이다.

친절한 오답 풀이

① 명사를 수식하는 과거분사
Scientists [who experiment on themselves] / can, functionally if
　　　　　↑___주격 관계대명사
자신을 실험하는 과학자들은　　　　　　　　　　법률적으로는 아니지만 기능적으로는
not legally, avoid / the restrictions [associated with experimenting
　　　　　　　　　　　　　↑___과거분사　　　　동명사(전치사의 목적어)
피할 수 있다　　　　다른 사람을 실험하는 것과 관련된 규제를
on other people].

➡ 앞의 명사구 the restrictions를 수식하는 분사로, 다른 사람을 실험하는 것과 '관련된' 규제라는 수동의 의미이므로 과거분사 associated가 오는 것은 어법상 알맞다.

② 대명사
They can also sidestep / most of the ethical issues involved: /
그들은 또한 피할 수 있다　　　　대부분의 관련된 윤리적인 문제도
nobody, presumably, is more aware of / an experiment's potential
　　　　　　　　　　be aware of: …를 알다
아무도 아마 더 잘 알고 있지 않을 것이다　　　실험의 잠재적인 위험을
hazards / than the scientist [who devised it].
　　　　　　　　　　　　　　　↑___주격 관계대명사
그것을 고안한 과학자보다

➡ 문맥상 앞에 언급된 an experiment를 지칭하는 대명사로, 지칭하는 명사가 단수이므로 단수 대명사 it이 오는 것은 어법상 알맞다.

③ 부사
Nonetheless, experimenting on oneself / remains deeply
부사(그럼에도 불구하고)　　　　　　　　　　　부사
그럼에도 불구하고, 자신을 실험하는 것은　　　여전히 심각한 문제로 남아있다
problematic.

➡ 형용사 problematic을 수식하고 있으므로 부사 deeply의 쓰임은 어법상 바르다.

④ 동사의 수 일치
One obvious drawback is the danger involved; / knowing [that
　　　　　　　　　　　　　　　　　　　　　동명사구 주어　접속사
한 가지 명백한 문제점은 수반되는 위험이다　　　　위험이 존재하는 것을 아는 것은
it exists] / does nothing to reduce it.
= the danger　동사　　　　　　　　= the danger
　　　그것을 줄이는 데 아무런 도움이 되지 않는다

➡ 문장의 주어가 동명사구(knowing ... exists)이므로 단수 동사 does가 오는 것은 어법상 알맞다.

지문 해석

인간 피험자에 관한 과학적 실험을 다루는 규정은 엄격하다. 피험자는 충분한 설명에 입각하며 서면으로 된 동의를 해야 하고, 실험자는 자신들의 계획된 실험을 제출해 감독 기관에 의한 철저한 정밀 조사를 받아야 한다. 자신을 실험하는 과학자들은 법률적으로는 아니지만 기능적으로는 다른 사람을 실험하는 것과 관련된 규제를 피할 수 있다. 그들은

또한 관련된 윤리적인 문제도 대부분 피할 수 있다. 실험을 고안한 과학자보다 그것의 잠재적인 위험을 더 잘 알고 있는 사람은 아마 없을 것이다. 그럼에도 불구하고, 자신을 실험하는 것은 여전히 심각한 문제로 남아있다. 한 가지 명백한 문제점은 (실험에) 수반되는 위험이다. 위험이 존재하는 것을 아는 것은 그것을 줄이는 데 아무런 도움이 되지 않는다. 덜 명백한 문제점은 실험이 만들어 낼 수 있는 데이터의 제한된 범위이다. 인체의 해부학적 구조와 생리적 현상은 성별, 나이, 생활 방식, 그리고 기타 요인에 따라 사소하지만 의미 있는 방식으로 다르다. 따라서, 단 한 명의 피험자로부터 얻어진 실험 결과는 가치가 제한적이며, 피험자의 반응이 집단으로서 인간 반응의 전형적인 것인지 이례적인 것인지 알 방법은 없다.

어휘

regulation 몡 규정, 규제 **subject** 몡 피험자, 대상 **informed** 혭 충분한 설명에 입각한 **submit** 됭 제출하다 **proposed** 혭 계획된, 제안된 **thorough** 혭 철저한 **oversee** 됭 감독하다 **body** 몡 단체[조직] **functionally** 뭐 기능적으로 **restriction** 몡 규제, 제한 **sidestep** 됭 피하다 **ethical** 혭 윤리적인 **involved** 혭 수반되는 **presumably** 뭐 아마, 짐작건대 **potential** 혭 잠재적인 **hazard** 몡 위험 **devise** 됭 고안하다, 생각해 내다 **drawback** 몡 문제점, 결점 **generate** 됭 만들어 내다, 발생시키다 **derive** 됭 얻다, 끌어내다 **typical** 혭 전형적인, 대표적인 (↔ **atypical** 혭 이례적인)

기출예제 Q2 정답 ⑤ 정답률 31%

정답 풀이

⑤ 관계대명사 what

And then, just over 400 years [after it started], / it ground to an
　　　　　　　　　　　　　 접속사　　　　　　　　　　　grind to a halt:
그리고 그것이 시작된 지 막 400년이 넘었던 그때　　　　　그것은 서서히 멈춘 것
apparent halt, / and it would be a few hundred years, give or
서서히 멈추다
같았고　　　　　　　대략 몇 백 년 후였을 것이다　　　　　 대략
take, / before [that(→ what) we would today unmistakably
　　　　　　　 관계대명사　　　　주어
우리가 오늘날 과학이라고 확실히 인식하게 될 것이
recognize as science] / appeared in Europe — with Galileo,
전치사(…로서)　　　　　 동사
　　　　　　　　　　 갈릴레오, 케플러, 그리고 조금 후에 뉴턴과 함께 유럽에서 출현했다
Kepler, and, a bit later, Newton.

➡ 뒤에 목적어가 빠진 불완전한 절이 이어지고 있으며 동사 appeared의 주어 역할을 하는 명사절을 이끌고 있으므로, 관계대명사 what이 와야 한다.

친절한 오답 풀이

① 부사

From the 8th to the 12th century CE, / [while Europe suffered
from A to B: A에서 B까지　　　　　　　　　　 접속사
서기 8세기부터 12세기까지　　　　　　　　　　 유럽이 아마도 지나치게
the perhaps overdramatically named Dark Ages], science on
　　　　　　　　　　　　　　　　　　　　　 주어 ┘└전치사구
극적인 이름이 붙여진 '암흑시대'를 겪는 동안
planet Earth / could be found almost exclusively in the Islamic
　　　　　　　 동사　　　　　　　　　 부사
지구상의 과학은　　 거의 오로지 이슬람 세계에서만 발견될 수 있었다
world.

➡ 부사 exclusively는 동사 can be found를 수식하고 있으므로 어법상 알맞다.

② 대명사

This science was not exactly like our science today, / but it was
　　　　　　　　　　 … 같은(전치사)　　　　　　　 = this science
이 과학이 오늘날 우리의 과학과 똑같지는 않았다　　　　　 하지만 그것은
surely antecedent to it / and was nonetheless an activity [aimed
　　　　　　　 = our science　　　　　　　　　　　　　 과거분사
확실히 그것에 선행했다　 그리고 그러기는 했지만 세계에 대해 아는 것을 목표로 한 활동이었다
at knowing about the world].
동명사(전치사의 목적어)

➡ it은 앞에 나온 our science를 지칭하는 대명사로, 지칭하는 명사가 단수이므로 단수 대명사 it은 어법상 알맞다.

③ 명사를 수식하는 현재분사

Great schools [in all the cities] / [covering the Arabic Near East
　주어 ┘　　　　　 전치사구　　　　　 현재분사
모든 도시의 훌륭한 학교는　　　　　 근동 아랍과
and Northern Africa (and even into Spain)] / trained generations
　　　　　　　　　　　　　　　　　　　　　　　 동사
북아프리카(와 심지어 스페인까지)에 걸친　　　 여러 세대의 학자들을 훈련시켰다
of scholars.

➡ covering은 앞의 명사구 the cities를 수식하는 현재분사로, 분사와의 관계가 능동이므로 현재분사가 알맞다.

④ 동사의 수 일치

Almost every word / {in the modern scientific lexicon [that
　주어 ┘　　　　　　 전치사구　　　　　　　　　 주격 관계대명사
거의 모든 단어는　　 접두사 'al'로 시작하는 현대 과학 어휘 목록의
begins with the prefix "al"]} / owes its origins to Islamic science
　　　　　　　　　　　　　　　 동사
　　　　　　　　　　　　　　 이슬람 과학에 그 기원을 두고 있다
— / algorithm, alchemy, alcohol, alkali, algebra.
즉 알고리즘, 연금술, 알코올, 알칼리, 대수학은

➡ 문장의 주어는 Almost every word이며 「every + 단수 명사」는 단수 취급하므로, 단수 동사 owes는 어법상 알맞다.

코드 +α 구문 분석 Plus

6행
Muslim rulers **granted scientific institutions tremendous resources**, *such as* libraries, observatories, and hospitals.
➡ 동사 grant는 4형식 동사로 scientific institutions는 간접목적어이며, tremendous resources는 직접목적어이다.
➡ such as는 전치사로 '… 같은'의 의미이며, 뒤에 명사(구)가 온다.

지문 해석

서기 8세기부터 12세기까지 유럽이 아마도 지나치게 극적인 이름이 붙여진 '암흑시대'를 겪고 있던 시기에, 지구상의 과학은 거의 오로지 이슬람 세계에서만 발견될 수 있었다. 이 과학이 오늘날 우리의 과학과 똑같지는 않았지만, 그것(이 과학)은 확실히 그것(우리의 과학)에 선행했고, 그러기는 했지만 세계에 대해 아는 것을 목표로 한 활동이었다. 무슬림 통치자들은 엄청난 물자를 도서관, 천문대, 병원과 같은 과학 기관에 주었다. 근동 아랍과 북아프리카(와 심지어 스페인까지)에 걸친 모든 도시의 훌륭한 학교는 여러 세대의 학자들을 훈련시켰다. 접두사 'al'로 시작하는 현대 과학 어휘 목록의 거의 모든 단어, 즉 알고리즘, 연금술, 알코올, 알칼리, 대수학은 이슬람 과학에 그 기원을 두고 있다. 그리고 그것이 시작된 지 막 400년이 넘었던 그때, 그것은 서서히 멈춘 것 같았고, 대략 몇 백 년 후에 우리가 오늘날 과학이라고 확실히 인식하게 될 것이 갈릴레오, 케플러, 그리고 조금 후에 뉴턴과 함께 유럽에서 출현했다.

어휘

exclusively 뭐 오로지, 배타적으로 **grant** 됭 주다, 수여하다 **institution** 몡 기관 **tremendous** 혭 엄청난 **observatory** 몡 천문대 **generation** 몡 세대 **prefix** 몡 접두사 **alchemy** 몡 연금술 **algebra** 몡 대수학 **grind to a halt** 서서히 멈추다 **apparent** 혭 …인 것 같은, …인 것으로 보이는 **unmistakably** 뭐 확실히

01 ②	02 ①	03 ④	04 ③	05 ④	06 ④	07 ⑤	08 ⑤
09 ③	10 ⑤						

01   정답 ②   정답률 63%

[정답 풀이]

② 목적격 관계대명사

> Therefore, he gathered a group of intelligent followers / [what
> 선행사
> 그래서, 그는 한 무리의 똑똑한 제자들을 모았다
> (→ who(m)/that) he trained in several subjects including ethics].
> 목적격 관계대명사   전치사(…을 포함하여)
> 그가 윤리학을 포함하여 여러 과목을 가르쳤던

➡ 사람(a group ... followers)을 선행사로 하고 있고, 뒤에 목적어가 빠진 불완전한 절이 이어지고 있으므로, what을 목적격 관계대명사 who(m)이나 that으로 고쳐야 한다. 관계대명사 what은 선행사를 포함하고 있으므로 앞에 선행사가 오지 않는다.

∥친절한 오답 풀이∥

① 동사의 수 일치

> In his view, / the lords of his country, / [only interested in their
> 주어 ↑   과거분사
> 그의 관점에서,   그의 나라의 지배자들이,   오로지 자기 자신의 이익에만 관심이 있는
> own personal gain], / were responsible for it.
> 동사   be responsible for: …에 책임이 있다
> 그것에 대한 책임이 있었다

➡ 문장의 주어는 전치사구(of his country)와 과거분사구(only interested ... gain)의 수식을 받는 the lords로, 주어가 복수 명사이므로 복수 동사 were가 오는 것이 알맞다.

③ 병렬구조

> He believed / [that government leaders must be humane, honest
> 명사절(목적어)을 이끄는 접속사   and에 의해 연결된 병렬구조(A, B, and C)
> 그는 믿었다   정부의 지도자들이 인간적이고, 정직하고 그리고 공정해야 한다고
> and fair, / not experts in administration].
> 행정 전문가들이 아닌

➡ that절 안에서 등위접속사 and에 의해 주격보어로 쓰인 형용사 humane, honest, fair가 병렬 연결된 구조로, fair는 어법상 바르다.

④ 가주어 진주어 구문

> He taught his students / {that it is the role of rulers / [to secure the
> 접속사 가주어   진주어
> 그는 그의 제자들에게 가르쳤다   지도자의 역할이라고
> happiness of their people]}.
> 그들의 백성들의 행복을 보장해 주는 것이

➡ that절에서 it이 가주어이고, to secure는 진주어로 쓰인 to부정사로 어법상 바르다.

⑤ 과거완료 수동태

> {When the men [who had been trained by him] were sent into
> 주격 관계대명사 had been v-ed: 과거완료 수동태   동사(과거)
> 그에게 교육을 받았던 사람들이 공직에 나갔을 때
> service,} / even immoral rulers valued their honesty.
> 심지어 부도덕한 지배자들조차도 그들의 정직함을 가치 있게 생각했다

➡ 공직에 나간 것(과거)보다 교육을 받은 것이 더 앞선 일이므로, 과거완료 시제가 알맞다. 또한 사람들이 '교육을 받은'이라는 수동의 의미가 적절하므로 과거완료 수동태인 had been trained가 오는 것이 알맞다.

코드+α 구문 분석 Plus

> 1행   [(Being) **Raised** in a poor family], Confucius truly understood the suffering of the people.
> ➡ Raised 이하는 이유를 나타내며, 앞에 Being이 생략되어 있는 수동형 분사구문(= Because Confucius was raised ...)

[지문 해석]

가난한 가정에서 자랐기 때문에, 공자는 백성들의 고통을 진심으로 이해했다. 그의 관점에서, 오로지 자기 자신의 이익에만 관심이 있는 그의 나라의 지배자들이 그것에 대한 책임이 있었다. 그래서, 그는 윤리학을 포함하여 여러 과목을 가르쳤던 한 무리의 똑똑한 제자들을 모았다. 그는 정부의 지도자들이 행정 전문가들이 되는 것이 아니라, 인간적이고, 정직하고 그리고 공정해야 한다고 믿었다. 그는 제자들에게 백성들의 행복을 보장해 주는 것이 지도자의 역할이라고 가르쳤다. 그는 자신의 제자들을 정부 권력의 지위에 위치시키는 데 상당한 성공을 거두었다. 공자에게 교육을 받았던 사람들이 공직에 나갔을 때, 심지어 부도덕한 지배자들조차도 그들의 정직함을 가치 있게 생각했다.

어휘

Confucius 몡 공자   **suffering** 몡 (육체적·정신적) 고통   **lord** 몡 지배자, 주인 **gain** 몡 증가; *(재정적) 이익   **intelligent** 혱 똑똑한   **ethics** 몡 윤리학   **humane** 혱 인간적인   **administration** 몡 관리, 행정   **secure** 동 보장하다   **considerable** 혱 상당한   **pupil** 몡 (어린) 학생; *제자   **immoral** 혱 부도덕한

02   정답 ①   정답률 53%

[정답 풀이]

① 접속사

> One cool thing about my Uncle Arthur / was [what(→ that) he
> 주어   동사   접속사
> Arthur 삼촌의 한 가지 멋진 점은   그가 항상 고를 수 있다는 것이었다
> could always pick / the best places to camp].
> ↑ 형용사적 용법의 to부정사
> 야영하기에 가장 좋은 장소를

➡ 뒤에 완전한 절이 이어지고 있으므로 what을 접속사 that으로 고쳐야 한다. 앞에 선행사 역할을 하는 명사는 없지만 뒤에 완전한 절이 이어지므로 관계대명사 what은 올 수 없다.

∥친절한 오답 풀이∥

② 형용사적 용법의 to부정사

> On trips like this, / he would always have a good story to tell.
> …하곤 했다(과거의 반복적인 행동)   ↑
> 이와 같은 여행에서   그에게는 항상 말해줄 멋진 이야기가 있곤 했다

➡ 앞의 명사(a good story)를 수식하는 형용사적 용법의 to부정사로 어법상 바르다.

③ 「전치사 + 동명사」

> His stories were always aimed at helping us children use our
> be aimed at: …을 목표로 삼다   help + 목적어 + 동사원형:…가 ~하도록 돕다
> 그의 이야기는 항상 아이인 우리가 우리의 머리를 쓰도록 돕는 데에 목표를 두었다
> brains / to get out of trouble.
> 부사적 용법(목적), get out of trouble: 곤경에서 벗어나다
> 곤경에서 벗어나기 위해

➡ 전치사 at의 목적어가 와야 하고, 뒤에 목적어(us children)을 취해야 하므로 명사적 성질과 동사적 성질을 가지는 동명사 helping이 오는 것이 알맞다.

④ 수동태

> ..., one story was about a guy / [being chased by a big dog].
> 현재분사
> 한 이야기는 한 남자에 관한 것이었다   큰 개에게 쫓기는

➡ being 이하는 명사 a guy를 수식하는 현재분사구로, 남자가 개에게 '쫓기는'이라는

수동의 의미이므로 being 뒤에 과거분사 chased가 오는 것이 알맞다.

⑤ 병렬구조

> He ran to the bathtub / and pulled it over himself.
> 그는 욕조로 달려갔다   그리고 자신 위로 그것을 뒤집어썼다

➡ 등위접속사 and가 과거형 동사 ran과 pulled를 병렬 연결하고 있는 구조로, 어법상 바르다.

지문 해석

Arthur 삼촌의 한 가지 멋진 점은 그가 항상 야영하기에 가장 좋은 장소를 고를 수 있다는 것이었다. 우리는 한 번 Garrison Rock에 갔다. Arthur 삼촌은 원주민들이 그곳에 머물렀다고 말했다. 이와 같은 여행에서, 그에게는 항상 말해줄 멋진 이야기가 있곤 했다. 그의 이야기는 항상 아이인 우리가 곤경에서 벗어나기 위해 우리의 머리를 쓰도록 돕는 데에 목표를 두었다. 예를 들어, 한 이야기는 큰 개에게 쫓기는 한 남자에 관한 것이었다. 그들은 들판으로 달렸다. 아이인 우리는 그 개가 그 남자를 잡을 것으로 생각하고 있었다. 그러나 그 남자는 들판에서 욕조를 보았다. 그는 욕조로 달려가 그것을 자신 위로 뒤집어썼다. 그 개는 떠날 때까지 계속 짖기만 했다. 그런 다음 그 남자는 욕조에서 나와, 집으로 갔다.

 어휘

pick 통 고르다, 선택하다 chase 통 쫓다, 추적하다 bathtub 명 욕조 pull 통 당기다 bark 통 짖다

03
정답 ④   정답률 34%

정답 풀이

④ 목적격 관계대명사

> Most professors see themselves in **a position of professional**
>   선행사
> 대부분의 교수들은 그들 자신을 전문가적 권위의 위치에 있다고 생각한다
> **authority** / over their students / [whom(→ which/that) they earned /
>   전치사구   목적격 관계대명사 주어 동사
> 학생들보다   그들이 얻은
> by many years of study].
> 여러 해 동안의 연구를 통해

➡ 선행사(a position ... authority)가 사물이므로, 목적격 관계대명사 whom을 which나 that으로 고쳐야 한다.

 오답 피하기 Tips

> **관계대명사 바로 앞에 오는 명사가 무조건 선행사다?**
> 선행사는 관계대명사절의 수식을 받는 명사로 주로 관계대명사절 앞에 쓰이지만, 명사 뒤에 전치사구나 분사구 등의 수식어구가 이어질 수도 있다. 따라서 관계대명사의 선행사는 문장 구조와 전체적인 의미를 따져보고 찾아야 한다.

┃친절한 오답 풀이┃

① 목적격보어로 쓰인 to부정사

> Some teachers will **ask you to call** them by their first names, /
>   ask A to-v : A가 …하도록 요청하다
> 몇몇 교수들은 당신에게 그들의 이름으로 부르라고 요청할 것이다
> especially if they're relatively young.
> 특히 그들이 비교적 젊다면

➡ 동사 ask는 5형식 문장에 쓰일 때 목적격보어로 to부정사를 취하므로 to call은 어법상 바르다.

② 명사를 수식하는 과거분사

> They enjoy the informal atmosphere / [generated by having
>   주어   동사   과거분사 by v-ing: …함으로써
> 그들은 스스럼 없는 분위기를 즐긴다   교실 안의 모든 사람들을 동등한 수준에
> everyone in the class on the same level].
> 둠으로써 만들어지는

➡ generated는 앞에 오는 명사구(the informal atmosphere)를 수식하는 분사로, 명사와의 관계가 수동이므로 과거분사가 어법상 바르다.

③ 동사의 수 일치

> But beware: / one of the surest ways to upset professors / is to call
>   주어, one of + 복수 명사: … 중의 하나 형용사적 용법의 to부정사   명사적 용법의
>   to부정사(보어)
> 그러나 유의해라   교수들을 속상하게 하는 가장 확실한 방법들 중 하나는
> them by their first names / against their wishes.
>   against one's wishes: …의 바람과 반대로
> 그들을 그들의 이름으로 부르는 것이다   그들의 바람과 반대로

➡ 주어가 「one of + 복수 명사」이므로 뒤에 단수 동사 is가 오는 것이 적절하다.

⑤ 대동사 do

> They no more want to be called John or Maria / than does your
>   A no more … than B ~: A가 …하지 않은 것은 B가 ~하지 않은 것과 같다
> 그들은 John이나 Maria로 불리기를 원하지 않는다   보통의 의사가 원하지
> average physician.
> 않는 것처럼

➡ does는 앞에 나오는 동사구 want to be called를 대신하는 대동사로, 주어(your average physician)가 단수 명사이므로 단수형 does가 오는 것이 어법상 바르다.

 구문 분석 Plus

> 1행
> [**How** you address your professors] depends on many factors
> *such as* age, college culture, and their own preference.
> ➡ How 이하는 주어 역할을 하는 「의문사 + 주어 + 동사」 어순의 간접
> 의문문
> ➡ such as: …와 같은

지문 해석

당신이 교수들을 어떻게 부르는지는 나이, 대학 문화, 그들 자신의 선호도와 같은 많은 요소에 달려있다. 몇몇 교수들은 특히 그들이 비교적 젊다면, 당신에게 그들의 이름으로 부르라고 요청할 것이다. 그들은 교실 안의 모든 사람들을 동등한 수준에 둠으로써 만들어지는 스스럼 없는 분위기를 즐긴다. 사실, 몇몇 대학은 모든 교수진과 학생들이 서로 이름을 부르는 사이라는 것에 대해 자랑스러워한다. 그러나 교수들을 속상하게 하는 가장 확실한 방법들 중 하나는 그들의 바람과는 반대로 이름으로 부르는 것이라는 점에 유의하라. 대부분의 교수들은 그들을 학생들보다는 여러 해 동안의 연구를 통해 얻은 전문가적 권위의 위치에 있다고 생각한다. 보통의 의사들이 이름으로 불리기를 원하지 않는 것처럼, 그들은 John이나 Maria로 불리기를 원하지 않는다.

 어휘

address 통 주소를 쓰다; *(호칭으로) 부르다 factor 명 요소, 요인 preference 명 선호(도) relatively 부 비교적 informal 형 격식에 얽매이지 않는, 편안한 atmosphere 명 대기; *분위기 generate 통 발생시키다, 만들어내다 pride oneself on …을 자랑하다 faculty 명 교수진 a first-name basis 서로 이름을 부르는 가까운 사이 beware 통 조심[주의]하다 upset 통 속상하게 하다 authority 명 권위 average 형 평균의; *보통의 physician 명 의사

정답 풀이

③ 강조구문

...: cultivating fields was hard work, / and it was in farming
　　　동명사구(주어)　　　　　　　　　　「it was ... that」 강조구문
밭을 경작하는 것은 힘든 일이었다　　　　그리고 농경 마을에서였다
villages / [what(→ that) epidemic diseases first took root].
　　　　　　　　　　전염병이 처음 뿌리를 내린 곳은

➡ in farming villages를 강조하는 「it is/was ... that」 강조구문이므로, what이 아닌 that이 되어야 한다.

친절한 오답 풀이

① 수동태

The hunter-gatherer lifestyle, / [which can be described as "natural"
　　　주어, 선행사　　　　　　　　계속적 용법의 주격 관계대명사
수렵 채집 생활 방식은　　　　　　인류에게 '자연스러운' 것으로 묘사될 수 있으며
to human beings], / appears to have had much to recommend it.
　　　동사　　　　　　　　　　　　형용사적 용법의 to부정사
　　　　　　그것을 추천할 만한 많은 것(장점)이 있는 것으로 보인다

➡ 주어 which는 앞의 The hunter-gatherer lifestyle을 가리키며, 이는 동작의 주체가 아니라 대상으로, '묘사되는'이라는 수동의 의미가 적절하므로 수동태가 와야 하며 앞에 조동사 can이 있으므로 be described가 어법상 바르다.

② 동사의 수 일치

Examination [of human remains from early hunter-gatherer
　주어　　　　　　전치사구
초기 수렵 채집 사회의 유적 조사는 알려준다
societies] has suggested / [that our ancestors enjoyed abundant
　　　　　　동사　　　　　　　명사절(목적어)을 이끄는 접속사
　　　　　　　　　　　　인류의 조상들이 과도한 노력 없이도 구할 수 있는
food, obtainable without excessive effort, / and suffered very few
　　　　　　　형용사구　　　　　　　　　　　　　　거의 없는
풍족한 식량을 누렸다는 것을　　　　　그리고 질병에 걸리는 일도 거의
diseases].
없었다는 것을

➡ 문장의 주어는 전치사구(of ... societies)의 수식을 받고 있는 Examination으로, 주어가 단수 명사이므로 단수 동사 has는 어법상 바르다.

④ 부사

[Whatever its immediate effect (was) on the lives of humans], /
복합관계대명사(…하는 것은 무엇이든)
인간의 삶에 미치는 즉각적인 영향이 무엇이든
the development of settlements and agriculture / undoubtedly led
　　　　　　　　주어　　　　　　　　　　　　의심의 여지없이　　동사
정착지와 농업의 발전은　　　　　　　　　　　의심의 여지없이
to a high increase in population density.
인구 밀도의 높은 증가로 이어졌다

➡ 부사 undoubtedly는 동사 led를 수식하고 있으므로 어법상 바르다.

⑤ 분사구문

This period, [known as the New Stone Age], / was a major
　　　　　　　과거분사구
신석기 시대로 알려진 이 시기는　　　　　　　　　인류 발전의 중요한
turning point in human development, / [opening the way to the
　　　　　　　　　　　　　　　　　　　동시동작을 나타내는 분사구문
전환점이었다　　　　　　　　　　　최초의 마을과 도시가 성장하는
growth of the first towns and cities], / and [eventually leading to
　　　　　　　　　　　　　　　　　　　결과를 나타내는 분사구문
길을 연　　　　　　　　　　그리고 결국 정착된 '문명'으로 이어졌다
settled "civilizations."]

➡ opening은 동시동작을 나타내는 분사구문의 분사로, 생략된 주어는 주절의 주어(This period)와 같다. 주어와 분사가 능동 관계에 있으므로 현재분사 opening은 어법상 바르다.

 구문 분석 Plus

7행
If this is true, **it** is not clear / {**why** so many humans settled in permanent villages and developed agriculture, [*growing* crops] and [*domesticating* animals]}: ...
➡ it은 가주어, why 이하가 진주어
➡ growing crops와 domesticating animals는 동시동작을 나타내는 분사구문

지문 해석

수렵 채집 생활 방식은 인류에게 '자연스러운' 것으로 묘사될 수 있으며, 그것을 추천할 만한 많은 것(장점)이 있는 것으로 보인다. 초기 수렵 채집 사회의 유적 조사는 인류의 조상들이 과도한 노력 없이도 구할 수 있는 풍족한 식량을 누렸고 질병에 걸리는 일도 거의 없었다는 것을 알려준다. 이것이 사실이라면, 왜 그렇게 많은 인류가 영구적으로 마을에 정착하여 농작물을 재배하고 동물을 기르면서 농업을 발달시켰는지는 분명하지 않다. 밭을 경작하는 것은 힘든 일이었고, 전염병이 처음 뿌리를 내린 곳은 농경 마을이었다. 인간의 삶에 미치는 즉각적인 영향이 무엇이든, 정착지와 농업의 발전은 의심의 여지없이 인구 밀도의 높은 증가로 이어졌다. 신석기 시대로 알려진 이 시기는 인류 발전의 중요한 전환점으로, 최초의 마을과 도시가 성장하는 길을 열었고, 결국 정착된 '문명'으로 이어졌다.

어휘

ancestor 몡 조상　abundant 몧 풍부한　obtainable 몧 구할 수 있는
excessive 몧 과도한　disease 몡 질병　settle in …에 정착하다　permanent 몧 영구적인　agriculture 몡 농업　crop 몡 농작물　domesticate 동 길들이다
cultivate 동 경작하다　take root 뿌리를 내리다　undoubtedly 뵘 의심의 여지없이
density 몡 밀도　civilization 몡 문명

정답 풀이

④ 주격 관계대명사

The ranger's language was therefore careless,
그 삼림 관리인의 말은 따라서 부주의했고
and open to misinterpretation / [what(→ which/that) could have
　　　　　　　　　　　　　　　　　　　　주격 관계대명사
오역의 소지도 있었다　　　　　　　　　　심각한 결과를 가져올 수도 있었던
serious consequences].

➡ 앞에 선행사(misinterpretation)가 있고, 뒤에 주어가 빠진 불완전한 절이 이어지고 있으므로, what을 주격 관계대명사 which나 that으로 고쳐야 한다. 관계대명사 what은 선행사를 포함하고 있으므로, 앞에 선행사가 오지 않는다.

친절한 오답 풀이

① 소유격 관계대명사

An ambiguous term is one / {which has more than a single
　　　　　　　　　　　　　　　　주격 관계대명사　… 이상의
모호한 용어는 …인 것이다　　　　　단 하나 이상의 의미를 가지고 있는
meaning} / and {whose context does not clearly indicate / [which
　　　　　　　　소유격 관계대명사　　　　　　　　　동사 indicate의 목적어로 쓰인 간접의문문
　　　　　　　　　그리고 그것의 문맥이 명확하게 보여주지 못하는
meaning is intended]}.
어떤 의미가 의도되었는지를

➡ whose는 대명사 one을 선행사로 하는 소유격 관계대명사로, '그것의 문맥'이라는 의미로 선행사와 뒤에 오는 명사 context가 소유 관계에 있으므로 어법상 바르다.

② 동사의 수 일치

..., a sign [posted at a fork in a trail] / [which reads "Bear To The
　　　　　　　　과거분사　　　　　　　　　　　주격 관계대명사
어느 산길의 갈림길에 세워진 표지는　　　　　　　　　"Bear To The Right"라고 쓰여 있는

Right"] / can be understood in two ways.
　　　　　　두 가지 방식으로 이해될 수 있다

➡ 주격 관계대명사절의 동사는 선행사에 수를 일치시켜야 한다. 선행사가 a sign으로
3인칭 단수 명사이므로 3인칭 단수 동사 reads가 오는 것이 알맞다.

③ 「let(사역동사) + 목적어 + 동사원형」

But let us say / {that the ranger [who painted the sign] / meant to
let + 목적어 + 동사원형 접속사　　　　　　　↑　주격 관계대명사
그러나 …라고 해보자　　그 표지판을 만든 삼림 관리인이

say just the opposite}.
정반대로 말하려 했다고

➡ 사역동사 let은 목적격보어로 동사원형을 취하므로 동사원형 say가 오는 것이 알맞다.

⑤ 부사

The only way to avoid ambiguity / is to spell things out as explicitly
　　　　　　　　　　형용사적 용법의 to부정사
모호함을 피하는 유일한 방법은　　　　　　　가능한 한 명쾌하게 설명하는 것이다

as possible: ....
as + 형용사/부사 + as possible: 가능한 한 …한/하게

➡ as와 as 사이의 부사 explicitly가 구동사 spell out을 수식하고 있으므로 어법상
바르다.

 코드+α 구문 분석 Plus

9행

He was trying to warn hikers against taking the right trail
{because there is a bear in the area [through which it
passes]}.
➡ which는 the area를 선행사로 하고, 관계대명사절에서 전치사
through의 목적어 역할을 하는 관계대명사

지문 해석

모호한 용어란 단 하나 이상의 의미를 가지고 있고 어떤 의미가 의도되었는지를 그것의
문맥이 명확하게 보여주지 못하는 것이다. 예를 들어, 어느 산길의 갈림길에 세워진
"Bear To The Right"라고 쓰여 있는 표지는 두 가지 방식으로 이해될 수 있다. 좀
더 그럴듯한 의미는 그것이 등산객들에게 왼쪽이 아니라 오른쪽 길로 가라고 알려주고
있다는 것이다. 그러나 그 표지판을 만든 삼림 관리인이 정반대로 말하려 했다고 해보자.
그 길이 통과하는 지역에 곰이 있기 때문에 그는 등산객들에게 오른쪽 길로 가지 말라고
경고하려고 했다. 따라서 그 삼림 관리인의 말은 부주의했고, 심각한 결과를 가져올
수도 있었던 오역의 소지가 있었다. 모호함을 피하는 유일한 방법은 가능한 한 명쾌하게
설명하는 것이다. "왼쪽으로 가시오. 오른쪽 길로 가지 마시오. 곰이 있는 지역임."

어휘

ambiguous 형 모호한 (ambiguity 명 모호함)　term 명 용어　context 명 문맥
indicate 동 나타내다, 보여주다　intend 동 의도하다　fork 명 포크; *분기점, 갈림길
read 동 읽다; *(…라고) 적혀[쓰여] 있다　probable 형 (어떤 일이) 있을[사실일] 것
같은　trail 명 자국; *산길　ranger 명 공원[삼림] 관리원　opposite 명 반대
careless 형 부주의한, 조심성 없는　misinterpretation 명 오해; *오역
consequence 명 (발생한 일의) 결과　explicitly 부 명쾌하게

정답 풀이

④ 접속사 that

[What(→ That) cell metabolism and structure should be complex] /
　　접속사　　　　　　　　　　주어
세포의 물질대사와 구조가 복잡할 것임은

would not be surprising, / but actually, / they are rather simple
　　동사
놀라운 것이 아닐 것이다　　　하지만 실제로　　그것들은 꽤 간단하고 논리적이다

and logical.

➡ 문장의 주어 역할을 하는 명사절을 이끌고 있고, 뒤에 완전한 절이 이어지므로 What을
접속사 That으로 고쳐야 한다.

친절한 오답 풀이

① 분사구문

A cell is "born" as a twin / [when its mother cell divides, /
　　　　　　　　　　　　　　　접속사
세포는 쌍둥이로 '탄생'한다　　　모세포가 분열할 때

producing two daughter cells].
동시동작을 나타내는 분사구문(= as it produces ...)
두 개의 딸세포를 생성하면서

➡ producing 이하는 동시동작을 나타내는 분사구문으로, 생략된 주어는 접속사절에
있는 주어(its mother cell)와 같다. 주어와 분사가 능동 관계에 있으므로 현재분사
producing이 오는 것이 어법상 바르다.

② 보어의 생략

Each daughter cell is smaller than the mother cell, / and except
　　　　　　　　　　　　　　　　　　　　　전치사(…을 제외하고는)
각각의 딸세포는 모세포보다 더 작다

for unusual cases, / each grows / [until it becomes as large as the
　　　　　　　　　　　　　　　　　　접속사
특이한 경우를 제외하고는　각각은 자란다　그것이 모세포가 컸던 만큼 커질 때까지

mother cell was (large)].

➡ the mother cell was large에서 large가 생략된 것으로 be동사 was는 어법상
바르다.

③ 병렬구조

[After the cell has grown to the proper size], / its metabolism
　　접속사
세포가 적절한 크기로 성장한 후　　　　　　　　　그것의 물질대사가 변화한다

shifts / [as it either prepares to divide / or matures and
　　　접속사　either A or B: A 또는 B 둘 중 하나
　　　　그것은 분열할 준비를 하면서　　　혹은 성숙하여

differentiates into a specialized cell].
특화된 세포로 분화하면서

➡ 등위접속사 or, and가 3인칭 단수형 동사 prepares, matures, differentiates를
병렬 연결하고 있는 구조로, 어법상 바르다.

⑤ 분사구문

Even the most complex cell / has only a small number of parts, /
가장 복잡한 세포조차도　　　　　　　그저 몇몇 부분만을 가지고 있다
[each (being) responsible for a distinct, well-defined aspect of
각각은 세포 생명의 뚜렷하고 명확한 측면을 맡고 있다
cell life].

➡ each responsible 이하는 주절의 주어와 분사구문의 주어가 달라 주어를 생략하지
않은 독립분사구문이며, responsible 앞에 being이 생략되어 있다. 분사구문에서
being이 생략되는 경우 형용사만 남는 경우도 있으므로 responsible은 어법상 바르다.

지문 해석

개체 전체와 마찬가지로, 세포도 수명을 가지고 있다. 그것의 생명 주기(세포 주기)
동안에, 세포의 크기, 모양, 물질대사 활동이 극적으로 변할 수 있다. 세포는 모세포가

분열할 때 두 개의 딸세포를 생성하면서 쌍둥이로 '탄생'한다. 각각의 딸세포는 모세포보다 더 작으며, 특이한 경우를 제외하고는 각각은 모세포가 컸던 만큼 커질 때까지 자란다. 이 기간 동안, 세포는 물, 당, 아미노산, 그리고 다른 영양소들을 흡수하고 그것들을 새로운 살아있는 원형질로 조합한다. 세포가 적절한 크기로 성장한 후, 그것은 분열할 준비를 하거나 혹은 성숙하여 특화된 세포로 분화하면서 그것의 물질대사가 변화한다. 성장과 발달 둘 다 모든 세포 부분을 포함하는 일련의 복잡하고 역동적인 상호 작용을 필요로 한다. 세포의 물질대사와 구조가 복잡할 것임은 놀라운 것이 아니겠지만, 실제로 그것들은 꽤 간단하고 논리적이다. 가장 복잡한 세포조차도 그저 몇몇 부분만을 가지고 있는데, 각각은 세포 생명의 뚜렷하고 명확한 측면을 맡고 있다.

life span 수명   dramatically 뷔 극적으로   absorb 툉 흡수하다   amino acid
아미노산   nutrient 몡 영양소, 영양분   assemble 툉 조합[구성]하다   mature
툉 (충분히) 발달[성숙]하다   differentiate 툉 구별하다; *(세포·조직이) 분화하다
complex 혱 복잡한   interaction 몡 상호 작용   structure 몡 구조   distinct 혱
뚜렷한   well-defined 명확한

07 　　정답 ⑤ 　　정답률 66%

정답 풀이

⑤ 접속사 that

> I realized / [what(→ that) I had wanted a reward]: ....
> 나는 깨달았다　　접속사　주어　　동사　　목적어
> 　　　　　　　　내가 보상을 원했다는 것을

➡ 동사 realized의 목적어 역할을 하는 명사절을 이끌고 있고, 뒤에 완전한 절이 이어지므로 what을 접속사 that으로 고쳐야 한다.

친절한 오답 풀이

① 병렬구조

> [Coming home from work the other day], / I saw a woman trying
> 때를 나타내는 분사구문(= When I came ...) see(지각동사) + 목적어 + v-ing: …가 ~하는 것을 보다
> 며칠 전 퇴근할 때　　　　　　　　　　　나는 어떤 여자가
> to turn onto the main street / and having very little luck / [because
> 큰 길로 들어오려고 애쓰는 것을 보았다　그리고 운이 별로 없는 것을　　전치사(… 때문에)
> of the constant stream of traffic].
> 끊임없는 차량 흐름 때문에

➡ 등위접속사 and가 지각동사 saw의 목적격보어로 쓰인 현재분사를 병렬 연결하고 있는 구조로, trying과 대등한 having은 어법상 바르다.

② 「find + 목적어 + v-ed」

> I found myself completely irritated / with her.
> 동사　목적어　　　　　　목적격보어　　　　목적어
> 나는 나 자신이 완전히 짜증난 것을 발견했다　　그녀에게

➡ 동사 found 뒤에 오는 myself가 목적어, irritated가 목적격보어로, 나 자신이 '짜증나게 된'이라는 수동의 의미이므로 과거분사 irritated가 오는 것이 알맞다.

③ 간접의문문의 의문사

> [As I was sitting there stewing], / I realized [how ridiculous I
> 접속사(…할 때)　　　　　주격보어　　　간접의문문(의문사 + 주어 + 동사)
> 내가 안달하면서 앉아 있을 때　　　　나는 내가 얼마나 어리석게 굴고 있는지 깨달았다
> was being].

➡ how 이하는 동사 realized의 목적어 역할을 하는 간접의문문으로, 형용사 ridiculous 앞에 의문부사 how가 오는 것이 적절하다.

④ 문장의 동사

> Suddenly, a phrase [(which/that) I once read] / came floating
> 　　　　　주어　↑　　　　　목적격 관계대명사 생략　　동사
> 갑자기, 내가 언젠가 읽었던 문구가　　　　　　　　　마음 속에 떠올랐다
> into my mind: ....

➡ came은 문장의 동사로, 글 전체가 과거의 일을 이야기하고 있으므로 과거시제로 바르게 쓰였다.

 구문 분석 Plus

> 5행
> I was feeling pretty good until, a couple of blocks later, she stopped to let a few more cars into the line, [*causing* us both *to miss* the next light].
> ➡ causing 이하는 결과를 나타내는 분사구문
> ➡ cause A to-v: A가 …하게 하다

지문 해석

며칠 전 퇴근할 때, 나는 어떤 여자가 큰 길로 들어오려고 애쓰는데 끊임없는 차량 흐름 때문에 운이 별로 없는 것을 보았다. 나는 속도를 줄이고 그녀가 내 앞에 들어오게 해주었다. 그때까지 나는 기분이 꽤 좋았는데, 두 블록을 간 후 그녀가 차 몇 대를 더 끼워주려고 차를 멈췄고, 우리 둘 다 다음 신호를 놓치게 되었다. 나는 나 자신이 그녀에게 완전히 짜증난 것을 발견했다. 내가 그렇게 친절하게 그녀가 차선으로 들어오게 해주었는데 어떻게 감히 그녀가 나를 느리게 가게 한단 말인가! 내가 안달하면서 앉아 있을 때, 나는 얼마나 어리석게 굴고 있는지 깨달았다. 갑자기, 내가 언젠가 읽었던 문구가 마음 속에 떠올랐다. '누군가 점수를 매기고 있기 때문이거나, 하지 않으면 벌을 받기 때문이 아니라, 내적인 이유로 사람들에게 친절을 베풀어야 한다.' 나는 내가 보상을 원했다는 것을 깨달았다. 내가 당신에게 이런 친절을 베푼다면, 당신(또는 어떤 다른 사람)이 나에게 동등하게 친절을 베풀 것이라는 생각이었다.

the other day 일전에, 며칠 전에   constant 혱 끊임없는   stream 몡 흐름
traffic 몡 차량, 교통(량)   irritated 혱 짜증난   slow down (속도를) 낮추다
graciously 뷔 친절하게   ridiculous 혱 어리석은   phrase 몡 구절   float 툉
떠오르다   keep score 점수를 기록하다   punish 툉 처벌하다   reward 몡 보상
equally 뷔 똑같이, 동등하게

08 　　정답 ⑤ 　　정답률 40%

정답 풀이

⑤ 관계대명사 what

> But to really understand / [that(→ what) he accomplished] /
> 명사적 용법의 to부정사(주어)　　　선행사를 포함하는 관계대명사
> 그러나 진정으로 이해하는 것은　　　그가 성취한 것을
> requires looking beyond the man.
> 동사　　　　전치사(…을 넘어서)
> 그 사람을 넘어서 보는 것을 필요로 한다

➡ 앞에 동사 understand의 목적어이자 선행사의 역할을 하는 명사가 없고, 뒤에 동사 accomplished의 목적어가 없는 불완전한 절이 이어지므로, 관계대명사 that을 선행사를 포함하는 관계대명사 what으로 고쳐야 한다.

친절한 오답 풀이

① 「get + 목적어 + 목적격보어(분사)」

> Every farmer knows / [that the hard part is getting the field
> every + 단수 명사 + 단수 동사　접속사　　　　　　　　　　목적어
> 모든 농부들은 안다　　　　어려운 부분은 밭이 준비되도록 하는 것임을
> prepared].
> 목적격보어

➡ 동사 get은 '…하게 하다'라는 뜻으로, 뒤에 오는 목적어와 목적격보어의 관계가 수동이면 목적격보어로 과거분사를 쓴다. 문맥상 밭이 '준비되는'이라는 수동의 의미가 적절하므로 과거분사 prepared가 알맞다.

② 대명사

> Inserting seeds and watching them grow is easy.
> 　　　　　　　watch(지각동사) + 목적어 + 동사원형: …가 ~하는 것을 보다
> 씨앗을 심고 그것들이 자라는 것을 보는 것은 쉽다

→ 앞에 오는 복수 명사 seeds를 지칭하므로 복수 대명사 them이 오는 것은 어법상 바르다.

③ 대동사 do

Planting a seed / does not necessarily require overwhelming
동명사구 주어　　　　　반드시 …인 것은 아니다(부분부정)
씨앗을 심는 것이　　　　반드시 엄청난 지성을 필요로 하는 것은 아니다
intelligence; / creating an environment / [that allows seeds to
　　　　　　　　동명사구 주어, 선행사　　　주격 관계대명사
　　　　　　　　환경을 만드는 것은　　　　씨앗이 번성하게 하는
prosper] / does.
　　　　= requires overwhelming intelligence
　　　　그러하다

→ does는 앞에 나오는 동사구 require overwhelming intelligence를 대신하는 대동사로, 동명사구(creating an environment)가 문장의 주어이므로 단수 동사 does가 오는 것이 어법상 바르다.

④ 형용사적 용법의 to부정사

Perhaps his greatest strength / was his ability to inspire people
　　　　　　　　　　　　　　　　　　　　　형용사적 용법의 to부정사
아마도 그의 가장 큰 강점은　　　　사람들이 함께 일하도록 고무시키는 그의 능력이었다
to work together / to achieve, ...
inspire A to-v: A가 …하도록 고무하다　부사적 용법의 to부정사(목적)
　　　　　　　　　　　　　성취하기 위해서

→ 앞의 명사(his ability)를 수식하는 형용사적 용법의 to부정사로 어법상 바르다.

지문 해석

모든 농부들은 밭이 준비되도록 하는 것이 어려운 부분임을 안다. 씨앗을 심고 그것들이 자라는 것을 보는 것은 쉽다. 과학과 산업의 경우, 공동체가 밭을 준비하지만, 사회는 우연히 성공적인 씨앗을 심은 개인에게 모든 공로를 돌리는 경향이 있다. 씨앗을 심는 것이 반드시 엄청난 지성을 필요로 하는 것은 아니다. 씨앗이 번성하게 하는 환경을 만드는 것은 그러하다. 우리는 과학, 정치, 사업 그리고 일상에서 공동체에 좀 더 많은 공로를 돌릴 필요가 있다. Martin Luther King Jr.는 위대한 사람이었다. 아마도 그의 가장 큰 강점은 모든 역경에 맞서, 사회의 인종에 대한 인식과 법의 공정성에 있어 혁명적인 변화들을 성취하기 위해서 사람들이 함께 일하도록 고무시키는 그의 능력이었다. 그러나 그가 성취한 것을 진정으로 이해하는 것은 그 사람을 넘어서 보는 것을 필요로 한다. 그를 모든 위대한 것들의 표명으로 여기는 대신에 우리는 미국이 위대해질 수 있음을 보여주게 하는 데 있어서 그의 역할을 인정해야 한다.

어휘

insert 통 끼우다, 넣다　in the case of …에 관하여 말하면　credit 명 공(적)
plant 통 (나무·씨앗 등을) 심다　overwhelming 형 압도적인, 굉장한　intelligence
명 지능; *지성　prosper 통 번영[번성]하다　odds 명 가능성; *역경　revolutionary
형 혁명적인　perception 명 인식　fairness 명 공정성　appreciate 통 인정하다

09　　정답 ③　　정답률 44%

정답 풀이

③ 소유격 관계대명사

There are systems [that turn over in minutes], / and there are
　　　　　　　　　　　주격　　바뀌다
　　　　　　　　　관계대명사
몇 분 안에 바뀌는 시스템이 있다　　　　　　　　　　그리고 다른 것들도 있다
others / [which(→ whose) rhythmic time extends to hundreds of
　　　　　　　　　　　　　소유격 관계대명사
　　　　그것의 규칙적으로 순환하는 시간이 수백 년까지 연장되는
years].

→ 선행사 others와 관계사절 안에서 뒤에 이어지는 명사 rhythmic time이 소유 관계에 있으므로, 소유격 관계대명사 whose로 고쳐야 한다.

┃ 친절한 오답 풀이 ┃

① 대명사

They can be defined / as ranging / from the communities and
= ecosystems　　　　　　　　range from A to B: A에서 B까지의 범위에 이르다
그것들은 정의될 수 있다　　　범위에 이르는 것으로　여러분의 입안에 있는 유기체들의 군집과
interactions of organisms in your mouth / or those in the canopy
　　　　　　　　　　　　　　　　　　　　　　　　　= the communities and
　　　　　　　　　　　　　　　　　　　　　　　　　interactions of organisms
상호작용에서부터　　　　　　　　혹은 열대 우림의 덮개 안에 있는
of a rain forest / to all those in Earth's oceans.
그것들　　　　지구의 바다에 있는 모든 그것들까지

→ 앞에 있는 the communities and interactions of organisms를 대신하는 대명사로 복수 대명사 those는 어법상 적절하다.

② 명사를 수식하는 현재분사

The processes [governing them] / differ in complexity and speed.
　　　　　　　　현재분사　　　　　　　…에 대해 다르다
그것들을 지배하는 과정들은　　　　　　복잡성과 속도의 면에서 차이가 있다

→ governing은 앞의 명사 The processes를 수식하는 분사로, 그것들을 '지배하는' 과정들이라는 능동의 의미이므로 현재분사 governing이 오는 것이 알맞다.

④ 분사구문

…, and the sum of the productivity of the parts / will typically
　　그 부분들의 생산성의 총합은　　　　　　　　　　일반적으로
be found to be lower / than the productivity of the whole, / [other
find A to-v의 수동태　　　　　　　　　　　　　　　　　분사의 의미상 주어
더 낮다는 것이 발견될 것이다　　조건을 나타내는 분사구문(= if other things are equal)
things being equal].
다른 것이 동일하다면

→ other things를 의미상의 주어로 하면서 조건을 나타내는 분사구문을 만드는 being은 어법상 적절하다.

 Grammar Tips

주어를 함께 쓰는 분사구문

분사구문과 주절의 주어가 다를 때 분사구문의 주어를 분사 앞에 쓴다.

예) **Weather permitting**, the soccer game will be held tomorrow.
(= If weather permits, ...)
(날씨가 허락하면, 내일 축구 경기가 열릴 것이다.)

⑤ 목적격보어로 쓰인 to부정사

Safe passages, / for example, / enable migratory species to survive.
　　　　　　　　　　　　　　enable A to-v: A가 …할 수 있게 하다
안전한 통행은　　　　예를 들어　　이동하는 생물 종들이 생존할 수 있게 한다

→ 동사 enable은 목적격보어로 to부정사를 취하므로 to survive는 어법상 적절하다.

지문 해석

생태계들은 구성과 범위에 있어 차이가 있다. 그것[생태계]들은 여러분의 입안에 있는 유기체들의 군집과 상호작용 혹은 열대 우림의 덮개 안에 있는 그것[유기체들의 군집과 상호작용]들에서부터 지구의 바다에 있는 모든 그것[유기체들의 군집과 상호작용]들까지의 범위에 이르는 것으로 정의될 수 있다. 그것들을 지배하는 과정들은 복잡성과 속도의 면에서 차이가 있다. 몇 분 안에 바뀌는 시스템도 있고, 규칙적으로 순환하는 시간이 수백 년까지 연장되는 시스템도 있다. 어떤 생태계는 광범위하고(아프리카 사바나 같은 '생물군계'), 어떤 생태계는 지역들에 걸쳐 있으며(강의 유역), 많은 생태계가 마을 군집을 포함하고(작은 분수령들), 다른 생태계들은 단 하나의 마을 차원으로 국한된다(마을 연못). 각각의 사례에는 불가분성이라는 요소가 있다. 어떤 생태계를 장벽을 만들어 부분들로 나누면, 그 부분들의 생산성의 총합은 일반적으로, 다른 것이 동일하다면, 전체의 생산성보다 더 낮다는 것이 발견될 것이다. 생물학적 개체군의 이동성이 한 가지 이유이다. 예를 들어, 안전한 통행은 이동하는 생물 종들을 생존하게 한다.

어휘

composition 몡 구성 extent 몡 범위 community 몡 군집 organism 몡
유기체 govern 동 지배하다, 관리하다 complexity 몡 복잡성 turn over 바뀌다
rhythmic 혱 규칙적으로 순환하는 extend 동 연장되다 extensive 혱 광범위한
biome 몡 (숲·사막 같은 특정 환경 내의) 생물계 cluster 몡 무리 watershed
몡 분수령 confine 동 제한하다 indivisibility 몡 불가분성 barrier 몡 장벽
productivity 몡 생산성 mobility 몡 이동성 population 몡 개체군 migratory
혱 이동[이주]하는

10　　　　　　　　　　정답 ⑤　　　정답률 33%

정답 풀이

⑤ 대명사 vs. 관계대명사

In another slum area, / [possibly inspired by Brown's example], /
　　　　　　　　　　　　　　　　　　　　　　　↑과거분사
또 다른 빈민가 지역에서　　　아마도 Brown의 본보기에 영감을 받은
a culture center began to encourage the local kids to stage musical
　　　　　　　　　　　　　　encourage A to-v: A가 …하도록 격려하다
문화센터는 지역 아이들이 음악 공연을 무대에 올리도록 격려하기 시작했다
events, / {some of them(→ which) dramatized the tragedy / [that
선행사　　　　　　　　　　　　　　　　　　　　목적격 관계대명사
　　　그 중 몇몇은 비극을 극화했다
they were still recovering from]}.
그들이 아직 회복 중인

➡ 절(a culture … events)과 절(some of … from)을 연결하는 접속사 역할과 앞 절의
musical events를 받는 대명사 역할을 해야 하므로, them을 관계대명사 which로
고쳐야 한다.

▮친절한 오답 풀이▮

① 부사

In some communities, / music and performance have successfully
일부 지역 사회에서　　　음악과 공연이 성공적으로 전체 지역을 바꿔 놓았다
transformed whole neighborhoods / as profoundly as
동사　　　　　　　　　　　　　　as + 형용사/부사 + as: …만큼 ~한/하게
　　　　　　　　　　　　　　　　구겐하임 박물관이 빌바오에서
The Guggenheim Museum did in Bilbao.
　　　　　　　　　　　　　대동사
그랬던 것만큼 완전히

➡ as와 as 사이에 온 부사 profoundly가 동사 have transformed를 수식하므로
어법상 바르다.

② 관계부사

In Candeal, [where Brown was born], / local kids were
선행사　　관계부사
Brown이 태어난 Candeal에서　　　　지역 아이들은 권장되었다
encouraged / to join drum groups, sing, and stage performances.
be encouraged to-v: …하도록 권장되다
　　　　　　　드럼 동호회에 가입하고, 노래하고, 공연을 무대에 올리도록

➡ where 이하는 관계부사절로, 장소(Candeal)를 선행사로 하고 있고 뒤에 완전한 절이
이어지므로 관계부사 where는 어법상 바르다.

③ 문장의 동사

The kids, [energized by these activities], / began to turn away
주어　　　　과거분사　　　　　　　　　동사　　　…을 외면하다
이런 활동에 활력을 얻은 아이들은　　　　　마약 거래를 외면하기 시작했다
from dealing drugs.

➡ began은 문장의 동사로 글 전체가 과거의 일을 이야기하고 있으므로, 과거시제로
바르게 썼다.

---

④ 감정을 나타내는 분사

Being musicians and playing together in a group / looked like
　　　　　　　　　　　　주어
음악가가 되고 단체로 함께 연주하는 것이　　　　　　더 재미있어 보였다
more fun / and was more satisfying.
　　　　　그리고 더 만족스러웠다

➡ 동명사구(Being … a group)가 주어로, 음악가가 되고 연주하는 것이 '만족감을
주는'이라는 능동의 의미이므로 현재분사 satisfying이 알맞다.

지문 해석

일부 지역 사회에서, 구겐하임 박물관이 빌바오에서 그랬던 것만큼 완전히, 음악과 공연이
전체 지역을 성공적으로 바꿔 놓았다. 브라질의 Salvador에서, 음악가인 Carlinhos
Brown은 이전에 위험했던 지역에 몇 개의 음악과 문화 센터를 세웠다. Brown이
태어난 Candeal에서, 지역 아이들은 드럼 동호회에 가입하고, 노래하고, 공연을 무대에
올리도록 권장되었다. 이런 활동에 활력을 얻은 아이들은 마약 거래를 외면하기 시작했다.
어린 범죄자가 되는 것이 더 이상 이들의 유일한 삶의 선택은 아니었다. 음악가가 되고
단체로 함께 연주하는 것이 더 재미있어 보였고 더 만족스러웠다. 조금씩 그 지역에서
범죄율이 떨어졌고, 희망이 돌아왔다. Brown의 본보기에 영감을 받은 것 같은 또 다른
빈민가 지역에서, 문화센터는 지역 아이들이 음악공연을 무대에 올리도록 격려하기
시작했고, 그 중 몇몇은 그들이 아직 회복 중인 비극을 극화했다.

어휘

community 몡 지역 사회 performance 몡 공연 transform 동 변형시키다;
*완전히 바꿔 놓다 neighborhood 몡 인근; *지역 profoundly 悍 깊이; *완전히
formerly 悍 이전에, 예전에 stage 동 무대에 올리다 energize 동 열기[열정]를
돋우다 deal 동 마약을 거래하다 criminal 몡 범인, 범죄자 option 몡 선택
inspire 동 격려하다; *영감을 주다 dramatize 동 각색하다, 극화하다 tragedy 몡
비극 recover 동 회복하다

| 01 ③ | 02 ⑤ | 03 ⑤ | 04 ② | 05 ① | 06 ② | 07 ⑤ | 08 ① |
| 09 ④ | 10 ② | | | | | | |

01   정답 ③   정답률 65%

정답 풀이

③ 주격 관계대명사

I thought / {that I would be able to find another job / [what
나는 생각했다   접속사   …할 수 있다   선행사
     내가 다른 일자리를 찾을 수 있을 것이라고
(→ which/that) was a better match]}.
   주격 관계대명사
   더 잘 맞는

➡ 명사 another job을 선행사로 하면서, 뒤의 관계대명사절에서 주어 역할을 하는 주격 관계대명사가 필요하므로 what을 which나 that으로 고쳐야 한다. 관계대명사 what은 선행사를 포함하므로 앞에 선행사가 오지 않는다.

| 친절한 오답 풀이 |

① 수동태

Soon after I got out of school, / I was offered a job.
직후에   get out of: …에서 떠나다
내가 학교를 떠난 직후   나는 일자리를 제안받았다

➡ 주어(I)가 일자리를 '제안받은' 것이므로 수동태 was offered가 오는 것이 적절하다.

② 구동사와 목적어

[After carefully considering the opportunity], / I decided to **turn**
접속사(… 후에)   접속사가 남아있는 분사구문   turn down: …을 거절하다
그 기회를 곰곰이 생각한 후,   나는 그것을 거절하기로 결심했다
it down.

➡ 「동사 + 부사」로 이루어진 구동사의 목적어가 대명사일 경우, 목적어는 동사와 부사 사이에 위치해야 하므로, turn it down은 어법상 바르다.

Grammar Tips

구동사와 목적어(명사)의 어순

「동사 + 부사」로 이루어진 구동사의 목적어가 명사일 경우, 「동사 + 부사 + 명사」와 「동사 + 명사 + 부사」가 모두 가능하다.

예) Before you go shopping, please **turn off** the television.
= Before you go shopping, please **turn** the television **off**.
(쇼핑을 가기 전에 TV를 꺼주세요.)

④ 「spend + 시간 + v-ing」

..., the economy soon grew worse quickly / and I spent months /
     grow + 형용사: …해지다   spend + 시간 + v-ing: …하는 데 시간을 보내다
경기는 곧 빠르게 더 나빠졌다   그리고 나는 수개월을 보냈다
looking for another job.
다른 일자리를 찾는 데

➡ 「spend + 시간 + v-ing」 구문으로 동명사 looking은 어법상 바르다.

⑤ 동명사의 부정

I kicked myself / for not taking that position, / [which started to
kick oneself: 자책하다   전치사(…에 대해)   선행사   계속적 용법의 주격 관계대명사
나는 자책했다   그 자리를 잡지 않은 것에 대해   그것은 보이기 시작했다
look / more and more appealing].
비교급 + and + 비교급: 점점 더 …한
점점 더 매력적으로

➡ taking은 전치사 for의 목적어로 쓰인 동명사로, 동명사의 부정은 동명사 앞에 not을 쓰므로 not taking은 어법상 바르다.

구문 분석 Plus

1행
It's important [**to remember** that good decisions can still *lead to* bad outcomes].
➡ It은 가주어, to remember 이하가 진주어
➡ lead to: …로 이어지다

지문 해석

좋은 결정도 나쁜 결과로 이어질 수 있음을 기억하는 것은 중요하다. 여기 한 가지 사례가 있다. 학교를 떠난 직후, 나는 일자리를 제안받았다. 나는 그것이 나에게 아주 잘 맞는 것인지 확신이 없었다. 그 기회를 곰곰이 생각한 후, 나는 그것을 거절하기로 결심했다. 나는 더 잘 맞는 다른 일자리를 찾을 수 있을 것이라고 생각했다. 유감스럽게도, 경기는 곧 빠르게 나빠졌고, 나는 다른 일자리를 찾는 데 수개월을 보냈다. 나는 그 자리를 잡지 않은 것에 대해 자책했고, 그 자리는 점점 더 매력적으로 보이기 시작했다. 나는 그 당시에 내가 가진 모든 정보에 기초하여 좋은 결정을 내렸지만, 단기적으로 그것은 그다지 좋은 결과로 이어지지 않았다.

어휘

outcome 명 결과, 성과   **offer** 동 제안하다   **fit** 명 …하게 맞는 것   **match** 명 잘 어울리는 것   **appealing** 형 매력적인, 흥미를 끄는   **base upon** …에 기초를 두다   **in the short run** 단기적인 관점에서 보면

02   정답 ⑤   정답률 75%

정답 풀이

⑤ 주격 관계대명사

In the south / there was London, already the largest city in the
                동격
남부에는   이미 세계에서 가장 큰 도시인 런던이 있었다
world, / {showing all the crime, evil, and misery / [whose(→ that)
     동시동작을 나타내는 분사구문
     모든 범죄, 악, 그리고 비극을 드러내며
result from overpopulation and unplanned growth]}.
인구 과밀과 계획되지 않은 성장으로 인한

➡ all the crime, evil, and misery를 선행사로 하고 관계대명사절 안에서 동사 result의 주어 역할을 해야 하므로, whose가 아닌 주격 관계대명사 that이 와야 한다.

| 친절한 오답 풀이 |

① 명사를 수식하는 과거분사

England became the first industrial nation in the world / and,
       동사   보어1
영국은 세계 최초의 산업 국가가 되었다   그리고
by 1850, / the first nation / to have more people employed in
          보어2
1850년까지   첫 번째 국가가 되었다   산업에 종사하는 사람이 농업에 종사하는 사람보다
industry than in agriculture.
더 많은

➡ 앞의 명사 people을 수식하는 분사로, '고용된'이라는 수동의 의미가 적절하므로 과거분사 employed가 어법상 바르다.

② 부사

Expanding trade coincided with the growth of the Empire / and
동명사구(주어)   동사
무역의 확장은 제국의 성장과 맞물렸다   그리고
brought great wealth to Britain, / but this wealth was not evenly
  동사2   동사   부사
영국에 큰 부를 가져왔다   그러나 이 부는 고르게 분배되지 않았다
distributed.
   동사

➡ 동사구 was not distributed를 수식하므로, 부사 evenly는 어법상 바르다.

③ 동사의 수 일치

Many enterprising individuals (the 'self-made men') rose / from
　　　　　　　　　　　　　　　　　　　　　　　　　　　　　from A to B: A에서 B로
많은 진취적인 개인들('자수성가한 사람들')이 올라섰다
humble origins to positions of wealth and influence, / but large
　　　　　　　　　　　　　　　　　　　　　　　　　　　　　주어
변변치 않은 출신에서 부와 영향력을 가진 지위로　　　　　　하지만 대다수의
sections of the working class were forced into the overcrowded
　　　　　전치사구
노동계급은 대도시의 과밀한 빈민가로 내몰렸다
slums of large cities / [where they worked long hours for low
　　　　　　　　　　　　　　관계부사
　　　　　　　　　　열악한 환경에서 저임금으로 장시간 노동하는
wages in unhealthy conditions].

➡ 전치사구(of the working class)의 수식을 받고 있는 large sections가 주어이므로 복수 동사 were는 어법상 바르다.

④ 병렬구조

The manufacturing towns of the north of England provided some
　　주어　　　　　　　　　전치사구　　　　　　　동사1
영국 북부의 제조업 도시들은 가장 열악한 사례 중 일부를 제공했다
of the worst examples / and inspired such socially conscious
　　　　　　　　　　　　　　동사2
　　　　　　　　　그리고 사회 의식이 있는 소설에 영감을 주었다
novels / as Kingsley's *Alton Locke*, Gaskell's *Mary Barton*, and
Kingsley의 *Alton Locke*, Gaskell의 *Mary Barton*, 그리고
Dickens's *Hard Times*.
Dickens의 *Hard Times*와 같은

➡ 등위접속사 and가 동사를 병렬 연결하고 있는 구조로, provided와 대등하도록 inspired가 오는 것이 어법상 바르다.

지문 해석

빅토리아 시대의 영국은 산업 혁명의 완전한 발전으로 특징지어진다. 영국은 세계 최초의 산업 국가가 되었고, 1850년까지 산업에 종사하는 사람이 농업에 종사하는 사람보다 더 많은 첫 번째 국가가 되었다. 무역의 확장은 제국의 성장과 맞물려 영국에 큰 부를 가져왔지만, 이 부는 고르게 분배되지 않았다. 많은 진취적인 개인들('자수성가한 사람들')이 변변치 않은 출신에서 부와 영향력을 가진 지위로 올라섰지만, 대다수의 노동계급은 열악한 환경에서 저임금으로 장시간 노동하는 대도시의 과밀한 빈민가로 내몰렸다. 영국 북부의 제조업 도시들은 가장 열악한 사례 중 일부를 제공하며, Kingsley의 *Alton Locke*, Gaskell의 *Mary Barton*, 그리고 Dickens의 *Hard Times*와 같은 사회 의식이 있는 소설에 영감을 주었다. 남부에는 이미 세계에서 가장 큰 도시인 런던이 있었고, 인구 과밀과 계획되지 않은 성장으로 인한 모든 범죄, 악, 그리고 비극을 드러냈다.

characterise 동 특징짓다　development 명 발전　industrial 형 산업의
agriculture 명 농업　expand 동 확장하다　coincide 동 동시에 일어나다
empire 명 제국　wealth 명 부　distribute 동 분배하다　enterprising 형
진취적인　humble 형 변변치 않은　origin 명 기원, 출신　overcrowded 형 너무
붐비는　wage 명 임금　manufacturing 명 제조　inspire 동 영감을 주다
conscious 형 의식이 있는　evil 명 악　misery 명 비극

03　　　　　　　정답 ⑤　　　정답률 27%

정답 풀이

⑤ 대명사 vs. 관계대명사

The koala is the only known animal / [its(→ whose) brain only
　　　　　　　　　　　　　　　　　　　　　　소유격 관계대명사
코알라는 알려진 유일한 동물이다　　　　　뇌가 겨우 두개골의 절반을 채운다고
fills half of its skull].

➡ 절과 절을 연결하는 접속사 역할과 앞의 명사구 the only known animal을 대신하는

대명사 역할을 해야 하므로, its를 관계대명사 whose로 고쳐야 한다.

▌친절한 오답 풀이▌

① 접속사

For a long time many scientists suspected / {that koalas were so
　　　　　　　　　　　　　　　　　　　　　　명사절(목적어)을 이끄는 접속사
오랫동안 많은 과학자들은 의심했다　　　　코알라들이 그렇게도 무기력한 상태에 있는 것이라고
lethargic / [because the compounds in eucalyptus leaves / kept
　　　　　　　　접속사　　　주어　　　　　　　　　　　　　동사
　　　　　왜냐하면 유칼립투스 잎 속의 화학물이
the cute little animals in a drugged-out state]}.
　　　목적어
그 작고 귀여운 동물들을 몽롱한 상태로 만들었기 때문에

➡ 뒤에 완전한 절이 이어지고 있으므로 접속사 because는 어법상 바르다.

② 「so + 형용사 + that ...」

But more recent research has shown / {that the leaves are simply
　　　　　　　　　　　　　　　　　　　명사절(목적어)을 이끄는 접속사
그러나 더 최근의 연구는 보여 주었다　　　그 잎들이 단순히 영양분이
so low in nutrients / [that koalas have almost no energy]}.
so+형용사+that ...:　　　　접속사
너무 ~해서 …하다
너무 적기 때문에　　　　　코알라가 거의 에너지가 없는 것임을

➡ 주절에 '너무 ~해서'라는 의미의 「so + 형용사」가 쓰였으므로, '…하다'라는 결과를 나타내는 접속사 that이 오는 것이 알맞다.

③ 동사를 강조하는 조동사 do

Therefore they tend to move as little as possible / — and when
　　　　　　　tend to-v:　　as + 형용사/부사 + as possible: 가능한 …한/하게
　　　　　　　…하는 경향이 있다
그래서 코알라들은 가능한 한 적게 움직이는 경향이 있다　　　그리고 그것들이
they do move, / they often look as though they're in slow motion.
　　조동사　　　　　　　　　　마치 …인 것처럼
실제로 움직일 때　　흔히 그것들은 마치 슬로 모션으로 움직이는 것처럼 보인다

➡ 동사의 의미를 강조할 때 「do/does/did + 동사원형」 형태로 쓴다. 이 문장의 시제가 현재이므로 조동사 do가 원형 동사 move 앞에 오는 것이 알맞다.

④ 완료부정사

In fact, koalas spend little time thinking; / their brains actually
　　　　　　　　　spend + 시간 + v-ing: …하는 데 시간을 쓰다
사실 코알라는 생각을 하는 데 시간을 거의 사용하지 않는다　그것들의 뇌는 실제로
appear to have shrunk / over the last few centuries.
　　　　완료부정사
크기가 줄어든 것처럼 보인다　　지난 몇 세기 동안

➡ 주절의 동사 appear는 현재 시제이고 지난 몇 세기 동안 코알라의 뇌가 줄어든 것은 그 이전의 일이므로 완료부정사 to have shrunk는 어법상 바르다.

지문 해석

코알라가 잘하는 것이 한 가지 있다면, 그것은 자는 것이다. 오랫동안 많은 과학자들은 유칼립투스 잎 속의 화학물이 그 작고 귀여운 동물들을 몽롱한 상태로 만들어서 코알라들이 그렇게도 무기력한 상태에 있는 것이라고 의심했다. 그러나 더 최근의 연구는 그 잎들이 단순히 영양분이 너무나도 적기 때문에 코알라가 거의 에너지가 없는 것임을 보여 주었다. 그래서 코알라들은 가능한 한 적게 움직이는 경향이 있다. 그리고 그것들이 실제로 움직일 때에는, 흔히 그것들은 마치 슬로 모션으로 움직이는 것처럼 보인다. 그것들은 하루에 16시간에서 18시간 동안 휴식을 취하는데, 의식이 없는 상태로 그 시간의 대부분을 보낸다. 사실 코알라는 생각을 하는 데에 시간을 거의 사용하지 않는데, 그것들의 뇌는 실제로 지난 몇 세기 동안 크기가 줄어든 것처럼 보인다. 코알라는 뇌가 겨우 두개골의 절반을 채운다고 알려진 유일한 동물이다.

suspect 동 의심하다　compound 명 화합물, 혼합 성분　state 명 상태　nutrient
명 영양분　as though 마치 …인 것처럼　unconscious 형 의식이 없는　shrink 동
줄어들다, 작아지다　skull 명 두개골

정답 풀이

② 전치사 + 관계대명사

They will even try to match gestures / [which(→ with which)
전치사 + 관계대명사
그들은 심지어는 제스처에 맞추려고 노력할 것이다   자신에게 다소 어려운

they have some difficulty], / {experimenting with their own
동시동작을 나타내는 분사구문
자기 얼굴로 실험하면서

faces / [until they succeed]}.
접속사(…할 때까지)
성공할 때까지

➡ 뒤에 완전한 절이 이어지므로 관계대명사 앞에 전치사를 쓰거나 관계부사를 써야 한다. have some difficulty에 이어지는 전치사 with를 써서 which 앞에 with를 쓰는 것이 어법상 적절하다.

┃친절한 오답 풀이┃

① 분사구문

From birth, / infants will orient preferentially towards the human
태어날 때부터   아기는 사람의 얼굴과 목소리 쪽으로 우선적으로 향하는 경향이 있다

face and voice, / {seeming to know / [that such stimuli are
부대상황을 나타내는 분사구문   명사절(목적어)을 이끄는 접속사
알고 있는 것 같으면서   이러한 자극이

particularly meaningful for them]}.
부사   형용사
특히 자신에게 의미가 있다는 것을

➡ 주어인 infants의 상태를 부가적으로 설명하는 분사구문으로 능동의 의미이므로, 현재분사 seeming은 어법상 바르다.

③ 동사를 강조하는 조동사 do

When they do succeed, / they show pleasure by a brightening of
조동사
그들이 정말로 성공하면   그들은 반짝이는 눈으로 기쁨을 표시한다

their eyes; / when they fail, / they show distress.
그들이 실패하면   그들은 괴로움을 나타낸다

➡ 동사의 의미를 강조할 때 「do/does/did + 동사원형」 형태로 쓴다. 이 문장의 시제가 현재이므로 조동사 do가 동사원형 succeed 앞에 오는 것은 어법상 바르다.

④ 대명사

In other words, / they not only have an innate capacity / for
다시 말해   그들은 타고난 능력을 지니고 있을 뿐만이 아니다

matching their own kinaesthetically experienced bodily
match A with B: A와 B를 일치시키다
운동감각적으로 경험한 그들 자신의 신체적 움직임과

movements with those of others [that are visually perceived]; /
주격 관계대명사
시각적으로 인지되는 다른 사람의 그것(신체적 움직임)을 일치시키는

they have an innate drive to do so.
그들은 그렇게 하려는 타고난 욕구도 지니고 있다

➡ 앞에 나온 bodily movements를 지칭하는 대명사로, 지칭하는 대상이 복수이므로 복수형 대명사 those가 알맞다.

⑤ to부정사

That is, / they seem to have an innate drive / to imitate others / [whom
seem to-v: …인 것 같다   목적격 관계대명사
즉   그들은 타고난 욕구가 있는 것 같다   타인을 모방하려는

they judge to be 'like me'].
'나와 비슷하다'라고 판단되는

➡ judge의 목적격보어 역할을 하는 명사적 용법의 to부정사로 어법상 바르다.

6행

Moreover, they register this connection actively, {imitating a variety of facial gestures [that are presented to them — tongue protrusions, lip tightenings, mouth openings]}.

➡ imitating 이하는 동시동작을 나타내는 분사구문
➡ that은 a variety of facial gestures를 선행사로 하는 주격 관계대명사

지문 해석

많은 연구가 사회적 자극에 차별적으로 반응하는 인간의 타고난 성향에 대한 상당한 증거를 제공한다. 태어날 때부터, 아기는 사람의 얼굴과 목소리 쪽으로 우선적으로 향하는 경향이 있는데, 이러한 자극이 특히 자신에게 의미가 있다는 것을 알고 있는 것 같다. 또한, 아기는 혀 내밀기, 입술 다물기, 입 벌리기와 같이 자신에게 보이는 다양한 얼굴 제스처를 모방하면서 이러한 연결을 적극적으로 마음속에 새긴다. 그들은 심지어는 성공할 때까지 자기 얼굴로 실험하면서 자신에게 다소 어려운 제스처에 맞추려고 노력할 것이다. 그들은 정말로 성공하면 반짝이는 눈으로 기쁨을 표시하고, 실패하면 괴로움을 나타낸다. 다시 말해, 그들은 운동감각적으로 경험한 그들 자신의 신체적 움직임과 시각적으로 인지되는 다른 사람의 신체적 움직임을 일치시키는 타고난 능력을 지니고 있을 뿐만 아니라, 그렇게 하려는 타고난 욕구도 지니고 있다. 즉, 그들은 '나와 비슷하다'라고 판단되는 타인을 모방하려는 타고난 욕구가 있는 것 같다.

어휘

substantial 형 상당한   evidence 명 증거   differentially 부 차별적으로   stimulus 명 자극(pl. stimuli)   infant 명 아기, 유아   orient 통 향하다   preferentially 부 우선(적으로)   register 통 등록하다; *마음속에 새기다   imitate 통 모방하다, 본뜨다   present 통 보여주다   protrusion 명 내밀기   experiment 통 실험하다   brighten 통 생기가 나다, 환해지다   distress 명 괴로움   perceive 통 지각하다   drive 명 욕구, 추진력, 투지

정답 풀이

(A) 능동태 vs. 수동태

They come from plants or animals, / or they are [dug / digging] from
= natural materials
그것들은 식물이나 동물로부터 나왔다   혹은 그들은 땅에서 캐어졌다

the ground.

➡ 접속사 or 뒤의 주어 they가 지칭하는 명사는 앞에 언급된 natural materials이다. 천연 물질들이 땅에서 '캐어진'이라는 수동의 의미이므로 수동태 are dug가 오는 것이 적절하다.

(B) 접속사 vs. 관계대명사

Plastics are synthetic materials, / {which **means** / [that / what
선행사   계속적 용법의 주격 관계대명사   접속사
플라스틱은 합성물질이다   이는 의미한다

they are made from chemicals / in factories]}.
be made from: …로 만들어지다
그것들이 화학물질로 만들어진다는 것을   공장에서

➡ 네모 이하는 동사 means의 목적어 역할을 하는 명사절로, 네모 뒤에 완전한 절이 이어지고 있으므로 접속사 that이 오는 것이 알맞다. 관계대명사 what은 불완전한 절을 이끈다.

Grammar Tips

> 「, which」 뒤에 오는 동사의 수
>
> 계속적 용법으로 쓰인 which는 앞 절의 일부나 앞 절 전체를 선행사로 할 수 있다. 이때 which는 단수 취급하며 뒤에 단수 동사가 온다.
>
> 예) *He decided to climb over the wall*, **which wasn't** *a good idea.*
> (그는 담을 넘기로 결정했지만, 그것은 좋은 생각이 아니었다.)

(C) 동사의 수 일치

> An important quality of plastics / [is / ~~are~~] [that they are easy to
> 　　　주어　　　　　　　　　 동사　　　명사절(보어)를 이끄는 접속사
> 플라스틱의 중요한 성질은　　　　　　　 그것들이 모양을 만들기 쉽다는 것이다
> shape].

➡ 문장의 주어가 단수 명사 An important quality이므로 뒤에 단수 동사 is가 오는 것이 적절하다.

지문 해석

우리는 목화, 양모, 금속과 같은 많은 천연 물질들을 사용한다. 그것들은 식물이나 동물로부터 나오거나, 혹은 땅에서 캐어졌다. 플라스틱은 천연 물질들을 대신해서 사용될 수 있고, 그것들은 옷, 자동차 부품, 그리고 많은 다른 제품을 만드는 데 사용된다. 플라스틱은 합성물질인데, 이는 그것들이 공장에서 화학물질로 만들어진다는 것을 의미한다. 화학물질은 주로 석유에서 나오지만, 또한 천연가스와 석탄에서도 나오기도 한다. 플라스틱의 중요한 성질은 모양을 만들기 쉽다는 것이다. 그것들은 모든 종류의 물체를 만드는 데 사용될 수 있다.

cotton 명 목화　wool 명 양모　dig 통 파다, 발굴하다　in place of … 대신에
chemical 명 화학 물질　mainly 부 주로　coal 명 석탄　quality 명 품질; *특성
object 명 물체, 물건

06　　　　　정답 ②　　　정답률 50%

정답 풀이

② 「전치사 + 관계대명사」

> There can never be a situation / {which(→ where/in which) a firm
> 상황은 절대 있을 수 없다　　　　　　한 회사가 물품을 팔 수 없게 되는
> finds [that it can't sell its goods] / and so has to dismiss workers /
> 　　명사절(목적어)를 이끄는 접속사 that
> 　　　　　　　　　　　　　　　　　　그래서 직원들을 해고해야 하고
> and close its factories}.
> 공장의 문을 닫아야 하는

➡ 뒤에 완전한 절이 이어지므로 which를 관계부사 where나 「전치사 + 관계대명사」의 형태인 in which로 고쳐야 한다. 관계대명사 뒤에는 불완전한 절이 온다.

친절한 오답 풀이

① be used to-v

> 　　　　　　　　　　　　　　　be used to-v: …하는 데 사용되다
> The money from anything [that's produced] / is used to buy
> 　　주어　　　　　　　 주격 관계대명사　　　　　동사
> 생산된 물품으로부터 나오는 돈은　　　　　　다른 물품을 사는 데 사용된다
> something else.

➡ 「be used to-v」는 '…하는 데 사용되다'라는 의미이고, '다른 물품을 사는 데 사용된다'라는 의미가 적절하므로 to 뒤에 동사원형 buy가 오는 것은 어법상 바르다.

③ 접속사

> Say's Law applies / [because people use all their earnings / to buy
> 　　　　　　　　　　　접속사　주어　　동사　　목적어
> Say의 법칙은 적용된다　사람들이 모든 수입을 사용하기 때문에　　　물품을 사는 데
> things].

➡ 뒤에 완전한 절이 이어지고 있으므로 접속사 because는 어법상 바르다.

④ 대명사

> But what happens / if people don't spend all their money, / [saving
> 　　　　　　　　　　　　　　　　　　　　　동시동작을 나타내는 분사구문
> 하지만 무슨 일이 일어날까　만약 사람들이 그들의 돈을 전부 사용하지 않는다면
> some of it instead]?
> 　= all their money
> 대신 돈의 일부를 모으면서

➡ 앞에 언급된 단수 명사 all their money를 대신하고 있으므로 단수형 대명사 it이 오는 것이 어법상 알맞다.

⑤ 병렬구조

> 　　　　　　　　　동명사의 의미상 주어
> That would mean / firms producing less / and dismissing some
> 　　　　　　　　　　 동명사(목적어)　　　　 동명사(목적어)
> 그것은 의미할 것이다　회사들이 더 적게 생산하는 것을　그리고 일부 직원들을
> of their workers.
> 해고하는 것을

➡ 등위접속사 and가 동사 mean의 목적어로 쓰인 동명사를 병렬 연결하고 있는 구조로, 앞의 동명사 producing과 대등한 동명사 dismissing은 어법상 바르다.

 구문 분석 Plus

> An economic theory **of** Say's Law holds {*that* everything [*that's* made] will get sold}.
> 1행
> ➡ of: An economic theory와 동격을 이루는 명사구 Say's Law를 이끄는 전치사
> ➡ 첫 번째 that: 동사 holds의 목적어 역할을 하는 명사절을 이끄는 접속사
> ➡ 두 번째 that: everything을 선행사로 하는 주격 관계대명사

지문 해석

경제이론인 Say의 법칙은 만들어진 모든 물품이 팔리기 마련이라고 주장한다. 모든 생산된 물품으로부터 나오는 돈은 다른 물품을 사는 데 사용된다. 한 회사가 물품을 팔 수 없게 되어서 직원들을 해고하고 공장의 문을 닫아야 하는 상황은 절대 있을 수 없다. 따라서, 경기 후퇴와 실업은 불가능하다. 지출의 정도를 욕조 안의 물 높이로 상상해 보아라. Say의 법칙은 사람들이 그들의 모든 수입을 물품을 사는 데 사용하기 때문에 적용된다. 하지만 만약 사람들이 그들의 돈을 전부 사용하는 대신, 돈의 일부를 모은다면 무슨 일이 일어날까? 경제에서 저축은 지출의 '누수'이다. 당신은 아마 물의 높이가 지금 낮아지고 있는 것, 즉 경제에서 지출이 적어지는 것을 상상하고 있을 것이다. 그것은 회사들이 더 적게 생산하고 일부 직원들을 해고하는 것을 의미할 것이다.

dismiss 통 묵살하다; *해고하다　unemployment 명 실업　apply 통 신청하다;
*적용되다　earning 명 소득, 수입　leakage 명 누출, 누수

정답 풀이

⑤ 대명사 vs. 관계대명사

[As they get older], / children will then start to write in important
접속사(…함에 따라)
아이들은 나이가 더 들어감에 따라 그다음에는 중요한 일들을 적어 넣기 시작할 것인데
things / for themselves, / it(→ which) further helps them develop
for oneself: 스스로, 혼자 힘으로   주격 관계대명사
       스스로   그것은 나아가 그들이 자신의 통제감을 발달시키는 데
their sense of control.
도움을 준다

➡ 절과 절을 연결하는 접속사로서 앞 절 전체를 선행사로 하고 동사 helps의 주어 역할을 해야 하므로, 대명사 it을 주격 관계대명사 which로 고쳐야 한다.

친절한 오답 풀이

① 동사 강조

[When children are young], / much of the work is demonstrating
접속사   much of + 셀 수 없는 명사 + 단수 동사
아이들이 어릴 때   일의 많은 부분은 그들에게 보여 주는 것이다
to them / [that they do have control].
      접속사   동사를 강조하는 조동사
      그들이 정말로 통제권을 가지고 있음을

➡ 밑줄 친 do는 동사 have를 강조하는 조동사로, 주어가 복수 명사(they)이고 문장의 시제가 현재이므로 do가 오는 것이 알맞다.

② 동사의 수 일치

One wise friend of ours / [who was a parent educator for twenty
      주어   주격 관계대명사
우리의 현명한 친구 한 명은   20년간 부모 교육자였던
years] / advises / giving calendars to preschool-age children /
       동사   목적어1
       조언한다   취학 전 연령의 아이들에게 달력을 주고
and writing down all the important events in their life, ...
       목적어2
       그들의 생활에서 중요한 모든 일을 적어 보라고

➡ 주어가 주격 관계대명사절(who ... years)의 수식을 받는 단수 명사(One wise friend of ours)이므로, 단수 동사 advises가 오는 것이 적절하다.

③ 「have(사역동사) + 목적어 + 동사원형」

Have them cross off days of the week / [as you come to them].
have + 목적어 + 동사원형(목적격보어)   접속사(…하면서)
아이들이 그 주의 요일을 지워가도록 하라   요일에 다가가면서

➡ 사역동사 have는 목적어와 목적격보어의 관계가 능동일 경우 목적격보어로 동사원형을 취하므로 동사원형 cross가 오는 것이 알맞다.

④ 주격보어

Spend time going over the schedule for the day, / {giving them
spend + 시간 + v-ing: …하는 데 (시간)을 쓰다   동시동작을 나타내는 분사구문
그날의 일정을 검토하는 데 시간을 보내라   아이들에게 선택권을 주면서
choice / in that schedule / [wherever (it is) possible]}.
(= as you give ...)   복합관계부사(…하는 곳은 어디든지) 주격보어
     그 일정에 대해   가능한 경우마다

➡ 복합관계부사가 이끄는 부사절에서 「주어 + be동사」가 생략될 수 있으므로, 주격보어로 쓰인 형용사 possible은 어법상 바르다.

지문 해석

아이들이 어릴 때, 일의 많은 부분은 아이들이 정말로 통제권을 가지고 있음을 그들에게 보여 주는 것이다. 20년간 부모 교육자였던 우리의 현명한 친구 한 명은 취학 전 연령의 아이들에게 달력을 주고 그들의 생활에서 중요한 모든 일을 적어 보라고 조언하는데, 이는 부분적으로 아이들이 시간의 흐름을 더 잘 이해하고 자신들의 하루하루가 어떻게 펼쳐질지 이해하는 데 도움을 주기 때문이다. 아이들이 자신의 하루를 통제하고 있다고

느끼도록 돕는 데 있어 달력이라는 도구의 중요성은 아무리 과장해도 지나치지 않다. 요일에 다가가면서, 아이들이 그 주의 요일을 지워가도록 하라. 가능한 경우마다 그 일정에 대해 아이들에게 선택권을 주면서 그날의 일정을 검토하는 데 시간을 보내라. 이러한 의사소통은 존중을 보여 주어, 아이들은 자신이 그저 여러분의 하루와 여러분의 계획에 붙어서 따라다니는 사람이 아니라는 것을 알게 되고, 어떤 일이 언제, 왜 일어날지 이해하게 된다. 아이들은 나이가 더 들어감에 따라, 그다음에는 스스로 중요한 일들을 적어 넣기 시작할 것이며, 그것은 나아가 그들이 자신의 통제감을 발달시키는 데 도움을 준다.

어휘

demonstrate 동 (실례를 통해) 보여 주다, 설명하다 preschool-age 명 취학 전 연령 passage 명 통행; *흐름, 추이 unfold 동 펼쳐지다, 전개되다 overstate 동 과장하다, 허풍을 떨다 cross off …을 지우다 go over …을 검토하다 tagalong 명 붙어서 따라다니는 사람 sense of control 통제감

정답 풀이

① 관계대명사 vs. 접속사

[Wherever the ad is placed], / many members of the target
복합관계부사(어디에 …하더라도)
광고가 어디에 위치하더라도   표적시장의 많은 구성원들이 그것을 놓칠 수 있다
market may miss it, / so by increaseing the frequency of an ad, /
                   by v-ing: …함으로써
              그래서 광고의 빈도를 높임으로써   that은 동격의 접속사
advertisers increase the likelihood / [which(→ that) members of
                                동격
광고주는 가능성을 높인다   표적시장의 구성원들이 그것에 노출될 것이다
the target market will be exposed to it].

➡ 앞의 the likelihood와 동격인 명사절이 뒤에 이어지므로 관계대명사 which를 접속사 that으로 고쳐야 한다.

친절한 오답 풀이

② 부사

[If advertising is on television], / the more frequently a
                            the + 비교급 …, the + 비교급 ~: …하면 할수록, 더 ~하다
광고가 TV에 나온다면   광고가 자주 방송되면 될수록
commercial is run, / the more people it will reach.
                   그것은 더 많은 사람들에게 닿을 것이다

➡ 부사 frequently가 동사 is run을 수식하고 있으므로 어법상 바르다.

③ 간접의문문

[If advertising is on a bulletin board], / the location will affect /
광고가 게시판에 게시된다면   그 위치가 영향을 미칠 것이다
[how many people see the ad].
간접의문문(의문사 + 주어 + 동사)
얼마나 많은 사람들이 그 광고를 볼 것인지에

➡ how 이하는 동사 affect의 목적어 역할을 하는 간접의문문으로, 뒤에 주어와 동사가 이어지고 있으므로 어법상 바르다.

④ 수량형용사

..., and if it is placed in a low-traffic zone, / fewer people will see it.
그리고 만약 그것이 통행이 적은 구역에 위치한다면   더 적은 사람들이 그것을 볼 것이다

➡ 셀 수 있는 명사의 복수형인 people을 수식하므로 수량형용사 fewer가 오는 것이 어법상 바르다.

⑤ 동명사 주어

However, [increasing the frequency of advertising] costs more
　　　　　　　동명사 주어　　　　　　　　　　　　　동사
하지만 광고의 빈도를 높이는 것은 더 많은 비용이 든다
money, / and advertising is most expensive / [where it is most
　　　　　　　　　　　　　　　　　　　　　　　접속사(…한 곳에서)
그리고 광고는 가장 비싸다　　　　　　　　　　　가장 효과적인 곳에서
effective].

➡ increasing은 문장의 주어 역할을 하는 동명사로, 어법상 바르다.

지문 해석

광고가 어디에 위치하더라도, 표적시장의 많은 구성원들이 그것을 놓칠 수 있으므로,
광고의 빈도를 높임으로써 광고주들은 표적시장의 구성원들이 광고에 노출될 가능성을
높인다. 광고가 TV에 나온다면, 광고가 자주 방송되면 될수록, 그것은 더 많은 사람들에게
닿을 것이다. 광고가 게시판에 게시된다면, 그 위치가 얼마나 많은 사람들이 그것을 볼
것인지에 영향을 미칠 것이다. 그것이 통행이 많은 구역에 위치한다면, 더 많은 사람들이
그것을 볼 것이고, 그것이 통행이 적은 구역에 위치한다면, 더 적은 사람들이 그것을 볼
것이다. 하지만 광고의 빈도를 높이는 것은 더 많은 비용이 들고, 광고는 가장 효과적인
곳에서 가장 비싸다. 그러므로 광고에 자금을 분배할 때 신중한 계획이 필수적이다.

어휘

target market 표적시장　frequency 몡 빈도 (frequently 뮈 자주, 흔히)
likelihood 몡 가능성　expose 동 노출시키다　commercial 몡 (텔레비전·라디오의)
광고　run 동 달리다; *진행되다　bulletin board 게시판　location 몡 장소, 위치
allocate 동 할당하다

09　　정답 ④　　정답률 35%

정답 풀이

④ 관계대명사 what

Together, these impressions prompted / [that(→ what) he called
　　　　　　　　　　　　　　　　　　call + 목적어 + 목적격보어: …을 ~라고 부르다
다 함께, 이런 느낌들은 불러일으켰다　　　그가 불렸던 것을
a "sixth sense of danger]."
　　　　목적격보어
'위험에 대한 육감'이라고

➡ 동사 prompted 뒤에 목적어이자 선행사의 역할을 하는 명사가 없고, 동사 called의
목적어가 빠진 불완전한 절이 뒤에 이어지고 있으므로, 관계대명사 that을 선행사를
포함한 관계대명사 what으로 고쳐야 한다.

친절한 오답 풀이

① 관계부사

The psychologist Gary Klein tells the story / of a team of
　　　　　　　　　　　　동격
심리학자인 Gary Klein이 이야기를 해준다　　　한 팀의 소방관들에 대한
firefighters / {that entered a house} [where the kitchen was on fire]}.
　　　　　　　　주격 관계대명사　　　　　관계부사
집으로 진입한　　　　　　　　　　부엌에 화재가 난

➡ 선행사(a house)가 장소를 나타내는 명사이고, 뒤에 완전한 절이 이어지고 있으므로
관계부사 where는 어법상 바르다.

② 재귀대명사

[Soon after they started hosing down the kitchen], / the commander
접속사(… 직후에)
그들이 호스로 부엌에 물을 뿌리기 시작한 직후,　　　　지휘관은
heard himself shout, / "Let's get out of here!" / without realizing why.
hear + 목적어 + 동사원형: ~가 ~하는 것을 듣다
자신이 외치는 소리를 들었다　"여기서 나가자!"　　이유도 알지 못하고

➡ 지휘관이 '자신이' 외치는 소리를 들은 것으로, 동사 heard의 목적어가 주어(the
commander)와 같은 대상을 가리키므로 재귀대명사 himself가 오는 것이 적절하다.

③ 도치

Only after the fact / did the commander realize / [that the fire had
　　부사구　　　　　조동사　　주어　　　　동사　　접속사
그 사실 이후에야　　지휘관은 깨달았다　　　　　불이 이상하게 잠잠했고
been unusually quiet] / and [that his ears had been unusually hot].
had v-ed: 대과거　　　　　　접속사
　　　　　　　　　　자신의 귀가 이상하게 뜨거웠다는 것을

➡ only로 시작하는 부사구가 문장 앞에 오고 동사가 일반동사인 경우 「do[does/did] +
주어 + 동사원형」의 어순이 되는 도치가 일어난다. 의미상 시제가 과거이고 일반동사가
쓰였으므로, 주어 the commander 앞에 쓰인 did는 어법상 바르다.

⑤ 과거완료 시제

It turned out / [that the heart of the fire had not been in the kitchen /
가주어　과거　진주어　　　　　　　　　had v-ed: 대과거, not A but B: A가 아니라 B
밝혀졌다　　화재의 중심이 부엌에 있지 않았다
but in the basement below].
그러나 아래의 지하실에 있었다는 것이

➡ 사실이 밝혀진 시점(과거)보다 화재가 있었던 시점이 더 앞선 일이므로, 대과거를
나타내는 과거완료 시제를 쓰는 것이 알맞다.

지문 해석

심리학자인 Gary Klein이 부엌에 화재가 난 집으로 진입한 한 팀의 소방관들에 대한
이야기를 해준다. 그들이 호스로 부엌에 물을 뿌리기 시작한 직후, 지휘관은 이유도 알지
못하고 자신이 "여기서 나가자!"라고 외치는 소리를 들었다. 소방관들이 빠져나온 거의
직후에 마루가 무너졌다. 그 사실 이후에야 지휘관은 불이 이상하게 잠잠했고 자신의
귀가 이상하게 뜨거웠다는 것을 깨달았다. 다 함께, 이런 느낌들은 그가 '위험에 대한
육감'이라고 불렀던 것을 불러일으켰다. 그는 무엇이 잘못되었는지 몰랐지만, 무언가
잘못되었다는 것을 알았다. 화재의 중심이 부엌이 아니라 아래의 지하실에 있었다는 것이
밝혀졌다.

어휘

psychologist 몡 심리학자　hose down 호스로 씻어 내리다　commander 몡
지휘관　collapse 동 붕괴하다　escape 동 탈출하다; *벗어나다, 빠져나오다
prompt 동 촉발하다　turn out …임이 밝혀지다[드러나다]　heart 몡 심장; *핵심
basement 몡 지하실

10　　정답 ②　　정답률 34%

정답 풀이

② 「전치사 + 관계대명사」

This was a fundamental new development, / which(→ for which)
　　　　　　선행사　　　　　　　　　　　　　　계속적 용법의
　　　　　　　　　　　　　　　　　　　　　　　목적격 관계대명사
이것은 근본적인 새로운 발전이었다
there were no precedents in big history.
거대한 역사에서 (그 발전과 같은) 전례가 없었다

➡ 선행사가 a fundamental new development이고 뒤에 완전한 절이 이어지고
있으므로, 「전치사 + 관계대명사」가 되어야 한다. 관계대명사절에서 '그 발전에 대한
선례'라는 의미가 되어야 하므로 전치사 for가 관계대명사 which 앞에 있어야 한다.

친절한 오답 풀이

① 주격보어

Not only are humans unique / in the sense that they began to use
부정어구(not only)　　　　　…라는 점에서
강조에 의한 도치
인간은 유일무이할 뿐만 아니라　　그들이 점점 확장되는 도구 세트를 이용하기 시작했다는 점에서
an ever-widening tool set, / we are also the only species on this

지구상 유일한 종이기도 하다
planet / {that has constructed forms of complexity / [that use
　　　　주격 관계대명사　　　　　　　　　　　　주격 관계대명사
　　　　복잡한 형태를 만들어 낸
external energy sources]}.
외부 에너지원을 이용하는

→ unique는 be동사 are의 주격보어로 쓰인 형용사로 어법상 바르다. 부정어구 Not only가 문두로 나와 강조되어 주어와 동사가 도치된 문장이다.

③ 동사의 수 일치

> From at least 50,000 years ago, / **some of the energy** [stored in
> 적어도 5만 년 전부터   주어   과거분사
>   기류 및 수류에 저장된 에너지의 일부가 운항에 사용되었다
>
> air and water flows] **was** used for navigation / and, much later,
>   동사
>   그리고 훨씬 후에
>
> also for powering the first machines.
>   동명사(전치사의 목적어)
> 최초의 기계에 동력을 제공하는 데에도 (사용되었다)

→ 「some of + 명사」 주어는 of 뒤 명사에 동사의 수를 일치시킨다. the energy는 단수 명사이므로 단수 동사 was는 어법상 바르다.

 Grammar Tips

> 「부분을 나타내는 표현 + of + 명사」의 수 일치
>
> all, most, a majority, some, the rest 등의 부분을 나타내는 표현이 주어로 쓰이면, of 뒤에 나오는 명사에 수 일치시킨다.
>
> 예) **All of** *the club members* are going to participate in the event.
> (클럽 회원 모두가 행사에 참가할 것이다.)
> **The rest of** *the money* was donated to the charity.
> (나머지 돈은 자선단체에 기부되었다.)

④ 병렬구조

> Around 10,000 years ago, / humans learned to cultivate plants
>   learn to-v: …하는 것을 배우다
> 1만 년 전 즈음에   인간은 식물을 경작하고
>
> and tame animals and thus control these important matter and
> 동물을 길들여서 이런 중요한 물질 및 에너지 흐름을 통제하는 법을 배웠다
> energy flows.

→ 동사 learned의 목적어로 쓰인 to부정사 to cultivate와 접속사 and로 병렬 연결된 구조이며 이때 to는 반복을 피해 주로 생략되므로 동사 tame은 어법상 바르다.

⑤ 분사구문

> About 250 years ago, / fossil fuels began to be used on a large
>   to be v-ed: to부정사의 수동태
> 약 250년 전에는   화석 연료가 대규모로 사용되기 시작했다
>
> scale / for powering machines of many different kinds, /
>   동명사(전치사의 목적어)
> 많은 다양한 종류의 기계에 동력을 공급하는 데
>
> thereby {creating the virtually unlimited amounts of artificial
>   연속동작을 나타내는 분사구문
> 그렇게 함으로써 사실상 무한한 양의 인공적인 복잡성을 만들어내었다
>
> complexity / [that we are familiar with today]}.
>   목적격 관계대명사
>   오늘날 우리에게 익숙한

→ creating 이하는 연속동작을 나타내는 분사구문으로, 생략된 주어는 주절의 주어(fossil fuels)와 같다. 주어와 분사가 능동 관계에 있으므로 현재분사 creating이 오는 것이 어법상 바르다.

 구문 분석 Plus

> 6행
>
> This capacity **may** first **have emerged** between 1.5 and 0.5 million years ago, *when* humans began to control fire.
> → may have v-ed: …했을지도 모른다(과거 일에 대한 추측)
> → when: 1.5 and 0.5 million years를 선행사로 하는 계속적 용법의 관계부사(= and then)

인간은 점점 확장되는 도구 세트를 이용하기 시작했다는 점에서 유일무이할 뿐만 아니라 외부 에너지원을 이용하는 복잡한 형태를 만들어 낸 지구상 유일한 종이기도 하다. 이것은 근본적인 새로운 발전이었는데 거대한 역사에서 (그 발전과 같은) 전례가 없었다. 이러한 능력은 인간이 불을 통제하기 시작했던 150만 년 전에서 50만 년 전 사이에 처음으로 생겨났을지도 모른다. 기류 및 수류에 저장된 에너지의 일부가 적어도 5만 년 전부터 운항에, 그리고 훨씬 후에, 최초의 기계에 동력을 제공하는 데에도 사용되었다. 1만 년 전 즈음에, 인간은 식물을 경작하고 동물을 길들여서 이런 중요한 물질 및 에너지 흐름을 통제하는 법을 배웠다. 곧 인간은 동물의 근력을 이용하는 법도 배우게 되었다. 약 250년 전에는, 많은 다양한 종류의 기계에 동력을 공급하는 데 화석 연료가 대규모로 사용되기 시작하였고, 그렇게 함으로써 오늘날 우리에게 익숙한 사실상 무한한 양의 인공적인 복잡성을 만들어내었다.

🔊 **어휘**

ever-widening 형 계속 커지는   **complexity** 명 복잡성   **external** 형 외부의   **fundamental** 형 근본적인   **precedent** 명 선례   **capacity** 명 능력   **emerge** 동 나오다, 드러나다   **navigation** 명 항해   **cultivate** 동 경작하다, 재배하다   **tame** 동 길들이다   **fossil fuel** 명 화석 연료   **scale** 명 규모   **virtually** 부 가상으로   **unlimited** 형 무제한의, 무한정의

UNIT 2 관계사 2

코드 접속하기
pp.63~65

출제코드 1 관계부사의 쓰임

A **1** when **2** where
B **1** ➡ how 삭제, 혹은 in which **2** ○ **3** ➡ where[in which]

해석과 정답 풀이

STEP 1
1 뉴욕은 미국 동부에 위치해 있다. 그는 그 도시에 산다.
  그가 사는 뉴욕은 미국 동부에 위치해 있다.
2 1) 나는 그녀에게 내가 회의에 참석할 수 없었던 이유를 말했다.
  2) 네가 그 기계를 고쳤던 방법을 나에게 보여줄 수 있니?
3 1) 내가 여름휴가를 보내는 조부모님의 통나무집은 내가 가장 좋아하는 장소들 중 하나이다.
  2) 이것은 우리 엄마가 돌아가시기 전에 나에게 주셨던 목걸이다.

STEP 2
1 1) 도시에 공원이 있는데, 거기서 당신은 당신의 개와 산책할 수 있다.
  2) 그녀는 방 안의 모든 사람들이 여전히 잠들어 있는 새벽에 잠에서 깼다.
2 1) 나는 학기말 리포트를 제출해야 하는 날짜를 잊어버렸다.
  2) 악기를 파는 가게가 문을 닫은 것이 사실이니?

STEP 3
A 1 그녀가 그녀의 두 번째 커피숍을 열었던 2012년에 매출이 그 어느 때보다 더 높았다.
  ➡ 연도를 나타내는 2012를 선행사로 하고, 뒤에 완전한 절이 이어지므로 때를 나타내는 관계부사 when이 와야 한다.
  2 긴 내리막길은 당신이 기본적인 스케이트보드 기술을 연습하는 장소가 될 수 있다.
  ➡ 앞의 명사 an area를 선행사로 하고, 뒤에 완전한 절이 이어지므로 장소를 나타내는 관계부사 where가 와야 한다.
B 1 내가 너에게 우리가 최고의 팀이 되었던 방법을 말해줄 것이다.
  ➡ 관계부사 how는 선행사 the way와 함께 쓸 수 없으므로 how를 생략해야 한다. 혹은 how를 「전치사 + 관계대명사」인 in which로 고쳐야 한다.
  2 그녀는 샌프란시스코에 대해 생각하곤 했는데, 그곳에서 그녀는 3년 동안 일했다.
  ➡ 앞의 San Francisco를 선행사로 하고, 뒤에 완전한 절이 이어지므로 장소를 나타내는 관계부사 where가 오는 것이 알맞다.
  3 이곳은 사람들이 사진 촬영을 하거나 영화를 만들 수 있는 건물이다.
  ➡ 앞의 명사 a building을 선행사로 하고, 뒤에 완전한 절이 이어지므로 장소를 나타내는 관계부사 where로 고치거나, 혹은 「전치사 + 관계대명사」인 in which로 고쳐야 한다.

출제코드 2 복합관계대명사 vs. 복합관계부사

A **1** however **2** Whatever **3** Whichever
B **1** ○ **2** ➡ whatever **3** ➡ However

해석과 정답 풀이

STEP 1
1 1) 너는 네가 좋아하는 사람은 누구든 파티에 데려올 수 있다.
  2) 무슨 일이 있더라도, 낙심하지 마라.
  3) 어떤 버스를 타더라도, 너는 그 역에 도착할 것이다.
2 1) 내가 우울해 할 때마다 그녀는 나를 격려해주곤 했다.
  2) 아무리 열심히 노력해도, 그는 인터넷에 접속할 수 없었다.

STEP 2
1 1) 실험실에서 작업할 때마다 학생들은 몇 가지 지침을 따라야 한다.
  2) 작가들이 그들의 작품에 무엇을 표현하든 그것은 그들의 사고방식을 반영한다.
  3) 그녀가 어느 팀에 있고 싶어하는지는 나에게 중요하지 않다.
  4) 아무리 똑똑해도 그는 단지 10살 아이에 불과하다.

2 1) 다른 사람들이 무슨 말을 할지라도 너는 너 자신을 믿어야 한다.
  2) 그가 어디를 가더라도 모든 사람들이 그가 누구인지 안다.

STEP 3
A 1 내가 아무리 열심히 노력해도 그 문을 열 수 없었다.
  ➡ '아무리 …할지라도'라는 의미의 부사절을 이끌며, 뒤에 「형용사 + 주어 + 동사」가 이어지므로 복합관계부사 however가 와야 한다.
  2 당신이 워크숍에서 무엇을 배우더라도, 그것은 교육적이고, 즐겁고, 보람있을 것이다.
  ➡ '무엇을 …하더라도'라는 의미로 부사절을 이끌며, 뒤에 목적어가 빠진 불완전한 절이 이어지므로 복합관계대명사 whatever가 와야 한다.
  3 모퉁이에 좋은 이탈리아 식당이 있다. 어떤 음식을 선택하더라도 당신은 만족할 것이다.
  ➡ '어떤 …을 ~하더라도'라는 의미의 부사절을 이끌며, 뒤따르는 명사(dish)를 수식해줄 수 있는 복합관계형용사 Whichever가 와야 한다.
B 1 그녀는 사교적인 사람이고 그녀가 어느 곳에 가더라도 항상 새로운 친구들을 사귄다.
  ➡ '어디에 …하더라도'라는 의미의 부사절을 이끌고 있으며, 뒤에 완전한 절이 이어지므로 복합관계부사 wherever가 오는 것이 어법상 바르다.
  2 그들은 우리가 우리의 계획을 수행하기 위해 필요한 어떤 도움이든지 제공할 준비가 되어 있다.
  ➡ '어떤 …든지'라는 의미로 문장에서 목적어 역할을 하는 명사절을 이끌고 있으며, 뒤따르는 명사(help)를 수식하므로 복합관계형용사 whatever로 고쳐야 한다.
  3 당신이 아무리 그 콘서트에 가고 싶어 할지라도, 지금 당장 남아있는 티켓이 없다.
  ➡ '아무리 …할지라도'라는 의미의 부사절을 이끌고 있으며, 뒤에 부사(badly)가 이어지므로 복합관계부사 However로 고쳐야 한다.

기출예제 Q1 정답 ① 정답률 43%

정답 풀이

① 관계대명사 vs. 관계부사

Competitive activities / can be more than just performance
                                              ··· 이상의
경쟁을 벌이는 활동은   단지 수행 기량을 보여주는 공개 행사 그 이상일 수 있다
showcases / [which(→ where) the best is recognized and the rest
              관계부사   be v-ed: 수동태
            최고는 인정받고 나머지는 무시되는
are overlooked].
  수동태

➡ performance showcases가 선행사이고, 뒤에 수동태의 구조를 가진 완전한 절이 이어지므로, 관계대명사 which를 관계부사 where로 고쳐야 한다.

친절한 오답 풀이

② 동사의 수 일치

The provision of timely, constructive feedback / to participants /
          주어   전치사구
시기적절하고 건설적인 피드백을 제공하는 것은   참가자에게
on performance / is an asset / [that some competitions and
                    동사   목적격 관계대명사
수행 기량에 대한   자산이다   일부 대회와 경연이 제공하는
contests offer].

➡ 문장의 주어(The provision)가 전치사구(of timely, constructive feedback)의 수식을 받는 단수 명사이므로, 단수 동사 is가 오는 것이 알맞다.

③ 부분부정 「not necessarily ….」

The provision of that type of feedback / can be interpreted / as
          주어   동사(수동태)   전치사(…로서)
그런 유형의 피드백을 제공하는 것은   해석될 수 있다
shifting the emphasis / to demonstrating superior performance /
                           전치사(…로)   동명사
강조점을 이동하는 것으로   우월한 수행 기량을 보여주는 것으로
but not necessarily (demonstrating) excellence.
    부사(반드시 …인 것은 아니다)   생략
반드시 탁월함(을 보여주는 것)은 아닌

➡️ 「not necessarily ....」는 '반드시 …인 것은 아니다'라는 의미로 부분부정을 나타내며, necessarily와 excellence 사이에 반복되는 동명사 demonstrating이 생략된 것으로 볼 수 있으므로, 동명사 demonstrating을 수식하는 부사 necessarily는 어법상 바르다.

④ 「전치사 + 동명사」, 동명사의 동사적 성질

> The emphasis on superiority / is [what we typically see / as
> 우월성에 대한 강조   관계대명사 see A as B: A를 B로 간주하다 전치사
>   우리가 일반적으로 간주하는 것이다
> fostering a detrimental effect of competition].
> 유해한 경쟁 효과를 조장하는 것이라고

➡️ 전치사 as의 목적어 역할을 하면서 명사구 a detrimental effect of competition을 목적어로 취할 수 있는 동명사 fostering이 오는 것이 알맞다.

⑤ 대동사 do

> Information about performance / can be very helpful, / not only
> 수행 기량에 관한 정보는   not only A but also B: A뿐만 아니라 B도
>   매우 도움이 될 수 있다
> to the participant [who does not win or place] / but also
>   주격 관계대명사
> 이기지 못하거나 입상하지 못하는 참가자뿐만 아니라   이기거나 입상하는
> to those [who do].
> = the ↑   주격 = win or place
> participants 관계대명사
> 참가자들에게도

➡️ 의미상 win or place를 대신하는 대동사로, 선행사가 복수 명사 those이므로 복수 동사 do가 오는 것이 어법상 바르다.

지문 해석

경쟁을 벌이는 활동은 최고는 인정받고 나머지는 무시되는, 단지 수행 기량을 보여주는 공개 행사 그 이상일 수 있다. 참가자에게 수행 기량에 대한 시기적절하고 건설적인 피드백을 제공하는 것은 일부 대회와 경연이 제공하는 자산이다. 어떤 의미에서는, 모든 대회가 피드백을 제공한다. 많은 경우에, 이것은 참가자가 수상자인지에 관한 정보에 제한된다. 그런 유형의 피드백을 제공하는 것은 반드시 탁월함(을 보여주는 것)은 아닌, 우월한 수행 기량을 보여주는 것으로 강조점을 이동하는 것으로 해석될 수 있다. 최고의 대회는 단순히 승리하는 것이나 다른 사람을 '패배시키는 것'만이 아니라, 탁월함을 장려한다. 우월성에 대한 강조는 우리가 일반적으로 유해한 경쟁 효과를 조장하는 것이라고 간주하는 것이다. 수행 기량에 대한 피드백은 프로그램이 '이기거나, 입상하거나, 또는 보여주는' 수준의 피드백을 넘어설 것을 요구한다. 수행 기량에 관한 정보는 이기지 못하거나 입상하지 못하는 참가자뿐만 아니라 이기거나 입상하는 참가자들에게도 매우 도움이 될 수 있다.

showcase 명 (사람의 재능·사물의 장점 등을 알리는) 공개 행사 recognize 동 인정하다, 인식하다 overlook 동 간과하다; *무시하다 provision 명 제공, 공급 timely 형 시기적절한 constructive 형 건설적인 asset 명 자산, 재산 restrict 동 제한하다, 한정하다 interpret 동 해석하다, 이해하다 emphasis 명 강조(점), 주안점 demonstrate 동 보여 주다, 입증하다 promote 동 장려하다, 증진하다 beat 동 패배시키다, 이기다 place 동 입상하다

| 01 ⑤ | 02 ① | 03 ④ | 04 ⑤ | 05 ⑤ | 06 ② | 07 ② | 08 ② |
| 09 ⑤ | 10 ② | | | | | | |

01   정답 ⑤   정답률 48%

정답 풀이

⑤ 관계부사

> Organic structures are more horizontal in nature, / [which(→
>   관계부사
> 유기적 구조는 본래 더 수평적이다
> where) decision making is less centralized / and spread across the
> 여기서는 의사결정이 덜 중앙집중화된다   그리고 조직 계층에 걸쳐 펼쳐진다
> plane of the organization.

➡️ 선행사 Organic structures에 대해 부연 설명하고 있고 뒤에 완전한 절이 이어지고 있으므로, 계속적 용법의 관계부사 where이 되어야 적절하다.

친절한 오답 풀이

① 동사의 수 일치

> From an organizational viewpoint, / one of the most fascinating
>   one of the+최상급+복수 명사: 가장 …한 것들 중 하나
> 조직의 관점에서   가장 매력적인 예시 중 하나
> examples / of [how any organization may contain many different
>   간접의문문(의문사+주어+동사)
>   어떤 조직이 어떻게 많은 다른 문화 유형들을 포함할 수 있는지에 대한
> types of culture] / is to recognize the functional operations of
>   명사적 용법의 to부정사(보어)
>   조직 내 다른 부서들의 기능적 운영을 인식하는 것이다
> different departments within the organization.

➡️ 주어가 전치사구(of the most fascinating examples)의 수식을 받는 one이므로 단수 동사 is는 어법상 바르다.

② 대명사

> A department and its members will acquire "tunnel vision" / {which
> 한 부서와 그 구성원들은 '터널 시야 현상'을 습득하게 될 것이다   주격 관계대명사
> disallows them to see things / [as others see them]}.
> = the department   …대로(접속사)
>   and its members
> 그들이 볼 수 없게 하는   다른 이들이 그것들을 보는 대로

➡️ 앞에 언급한 things를 대신하므로 복수형 대명사 them은 어법상 바르다.

③ 명사절을 이끄는 접속사

> [The choice of whether the structure is "mechanistic" or "organic"] /
> 주어
> 구조가 '기계적'인지 또는 '유기적'인지의 선택은
> can have a profound influence on conflict management.
> 갈등 관리에 깊은 영향을 미칠 수 있다

➡️ 뒤에 완전한 절이 이어지고 있고 전치사 of의 목적어 역할을 하는 명사절을 이끌고 있으므로 접속사가 와야 한다. 문맥상 '…인지'의 의미이므로 접속사 whether는 어법상 바르다.

④ 명사를 수식하는 과거분사구

> A mechanistic structure has a vertical hierarchy / {with many
>   전치사구(형용사)
> 기계적 구조는 수직적 위계를 갖는다   많은
> rules, many procedures, and many levels of management [involved
> 규칙, 많은 절차 그리고 의사결정에 포함된 많은 수준의 관리를 가진   과거분사구
> in decision making]}.

➡ 수식을 받는 명사구 many levels of management가 involve의 대상이므로 수동의 의미를 나타내는 과거분사 involved는 어법상 바르다.

지문 해석

조직의 관점에서, 어떤 조직이 어떻게 많은 다른 문화 유형들을 포함할 수 있는지에 대한 가장 매력적인 예시 중 하나는 조직 내 다른 부서들의 기능적 운영을 인식하는 것이다. 조직 내 다양한 부서와 과는 필연적으로 어떤 주어진 상황이라도 그들 자신만의 편향적이고 편파적인 관점에서 볼 것이다. 한 부서와 그 구성원들은 그들을 다른 이들이 그것들을 보는 대로 볼 수 없게 하는 '터널 시야 현상'을 습득하게 될 것이다. 조직의 구조 자체가 갈등을 만들어 낼 수 있다. 구조가 '기계적'인지 또는 '유기적'인지의 선택은 갈등 관리에 깊은 영향을 미칠 수 있다. 기계적 구조는 많은 규칙, 많은 절차 그리고 의사결정에 포함된 많은 수준의 관리를 가진 수직적 위계를 갖는다. 유기적 구조는 본래 더 수평적이고, 여기서는 의사결정이 덜 중앙집중화되고, 조직 계층에 걸쳐 펼쳐진다.

organizational 형 조직의 viewpoint 명 관점 fascinating 형 매력적인
contain 통 포함하다 recognize 통 인식하다 functional 형 기능적인
operation 명 운영 department 명 부서 varying 형 다양한 division 명
분할; *분과, 부, 국 inevitably 부 필연적으로 acquire 통 습득하다 disallow
통 허가하지 않다 conflict 명 갈등 mechanistic 형 기계적인 organic 형
유기적인 profound 형 깊은, 심오한 management 명 관리 vertical 형
수직적인 involve 통 수반하다, 포함하다 horizontal 형 수평적인 centralized
형 중앙집중화된

---

02 정답 ① 정답률 56%

정답 풀이

(A) 「keep + 목적어 + 형용사」

They help to keep a bird [warm / ~~warmly~~] by trapping
keep + 목적어 + 형용사: ~가 ~하게 유지하다   by v-ing: ~함으로써
그것들은 새가 따뜻하게 유지하도록 돕는다   열을 가둠으로써
heat / {produced by the body / [(which/that is) close to the
      과거분사   「주격 관계대명사 + be동사」 생략
      몸에서 생긴   피부의 표면과 가까운
surface of the skin]}.

➡ 네모는 동사 keep의 목적격보어 자리로, 형용사 warm이 오는 것이 알맞다. 부사는 보어가 될 수 없다.

(B) be used to-v

Feathers may also **be used to** [attract / ~~attracting~~] mates.
          be used to-v: ~하는 데 쓰이다
깃털은 또한 짝을 유혹하는 데 쓰일 수도 있다

➡ 「be used to-v」는 '~하는 데 쓰이다'라는 의미이고, 「be used to v-ing」는 '~하는 데 익숙하다'라는 의미이다. 깃털이 '짝을 유혹하는 데 쓰인다'라는 의미가 적절하므로, to 뒤에 동사원형 attract가 오는 것이 알맞다.

 Grammar Tips

혼동되는 표현

표현	의미	예
be used to-v	~하는 데 쓰이다	The money will **be used to help** them. (돈은 그들을 돕는 데 사용될 것이다.)
be used to v-ing	~하는 데 익숙하다	I'm **used to getting** up early. (나는 일찍 일어나는 것이 익숙하다.)
used to (조동사)	(과거에) ~하곤 했다, ~였다	She **used to live** in New York. (그녀는 뉴욕에 살았다.)

(C) 계속적 용법의 주격 관계대명사

The rest of the body / seems to have been covered / in much shorter
            have been v-ed: 현재완료 수동태   비교급 강조 부사
몸의 나머지 부분은   덮여있었던 것으로 보인다   훨씬 짧은 깃털로
feathers, / [[which / ~~that~~] would have kept out the cold].
선행사   계속적 용법의 주격 관계대명사
            그것이 추위를 막아 주었을 것이다

➡ 네모는 shorter feathers를 선행사로 하고, 뒤에 오는 동사의 주어 역할을 하는 주격 관계대명사 자리로, 계속적 용법으로 쓰였으므로 which가 오는 것이 알맞다. 관계대명사 that은 계속적 용법으로 쓸 수 없다.

지문 해석

현생 조류에 있어서, 깃털은 비행 이외에도 다른 많은 기능들을 가진다. 그것들은 피부의 표면과 가까운 몸에서 생긴 열을 가둠으로써 새가 따뜻하게 유지하도록 돕는다. 깃털은 또한 짝을 유혹하는 데 쓰일 수도 있다. 깃털공룡의 꼬리는 긴 깃털로 된 큰 부채를 가지고 다녔는데, 이러한 구조는 아주 인상적인 표현이 되었을 것이다. 몸의 나머지 부분은 훨씬 더 짧은 깃털로 덮여있었던 것으로 보이며, 그것이 추위를 막아 주었을 것이다. 팔에도 몇몇 큰 깃털이 있었으며, 이것도 과시 행동에 관여되었을 것이다.

feather 명 깃털 function 명 기능 other than ~ 외에 trap 통 가두다
surface 명 표면 attract 통 유혹하다 mate 명 친구; *(동물의) 짝 structure 명
구조 impressive 형 인상적인 display 명 전시; *표현, 과시 present 형 현재의;
*있는, 존재하는 be involved in ~에 관련되다

---

03 정답 ④ 정답률 67%

정답 풀이

(A) 명사를 수식하는 현재분사

On January 10, 1992, a ship [[~~traveled~~ / traveling] through rough
                주어   현재분사
1992년 1월 10일, 거친 바다를 항해하던 배 한 척이
seas] / lost 12 cargo containers, / [one of which held / 28,800
          동사   선행사   목적격 관계대명사
화물 컨테이너 12개를 잃었는데   그 중 하나는 담고 있었다
floating bath toys].
28,800개의 물에 뜨는 욕실 장난감을

➡ 앞의 명사 a ship을 수식하는 분사로, 배가 거친 바다를 '항해하는'이라는 능동의 의미이므로 현재분사 traveling이 오는 것이 알맞다.

(B) 관계대명사 vs. 관계부사

After seven months, the first toys made landfall / on beaches near
7개월 후에, 첫 번째 장난감들이 상륙했다   알래스카의 Sitka 근처 해변에
Sitka, Alaska, / 3,540 kilometers from (the place) [[~~what~~ / where]
                                        선행사 생략   관계부사
            잃어버린 장소에서 3,540킬로미터 떨어진
they were lost].

➡ 뒤에 완전한 절이 이어지고 있으므로 관계부사 where가 오는 것이 알맞다.

(C) 비교급 강조 부사

Some toy animals stayed at sea [even / ~~very~~] longer.
                                    부사(훨씬)
어떤 동물 장난감들은 바다에 훨씬 더 오래 있었다

➡ '훨씬'이라는 뜻으로 뒤에 오는 비교급 longer를 강조하는 부사 even이 오는 것이 알맞다. 부사 very는 비교급을 수식할 수 없다.

지문 해석

1992년 1월 10일, 거친 바다를 항해하던 배 한 척이 12개의 화물 컨테이너를 잃었는데, 그 중 하나는 28,800개의 물에 뜨는 욕실 장난감을 담고 있었다. 밝은 색의 오리, 개구리, 그리고 거북이들은 태평양 한가운데에 표류하게 되었다. 7개월 후에, 잃어버린 장소에서 3,540킬로미터 떨어진 알래스카의 Sitka 근처 해변에 첫 번째 장난감들이 상륙했다. 다른

장난감들은 알래스카 해안을 따라 그리고 베링 해를 가로질러 북쪽과 서쪽으로 떠다녔다. 어떤 동물 장난감들은 바다에 훨씬 더 오래 있었다. 그것들은 완전히 북태평양 해류를 따라 떠다녔고, 결국에는 Sitka로 되돌아갔다.

어휘

rough 혤 거친 **cargo** 몡 (선박·비행기의) 화물 **float** 통 떠가다, 흘러가다
brightly 뷘 밝게 **adrift** 혤 표류하는 **make landfall** 상륙하다 **completely** 뷘
완전히 **current** 몡 해류, 조류

04
정답 ⑤ 정답률 34%

정답 풀이

⑤ 관계대명사 vs. 관계부사

> Yet research shows / {that exclusivity in problem solving, / even
> 명사절(목적어)을 이끄는 접속사
> 그러나 연구는 보여준다 문제 해결에 있어서 배타성은 심지어 천재와
> with a genius, / is not as effective as inclusivity, / [which(→ where)
> as + 형용사/부사 + as ...: ···만큼 ~한[하게] 계속적 용법의 관계부사
> 함께하는 것이더라도 포용성만큼 효과적이지 않다 포용성이 있는 경우에는
> everyone's ideas are heard / and a solution is developed / through
> 모든 사람의 생각을 듣는다 그리고 해결책은 발전된다 협력을 통해
> collaboration]}.

➡ 뒤에 문장의 요소를 모두 갖춘 완전한 절이 이어지므로, 관계대명사인 which를 관계부사인 where로 바꿔야 한다.

친절한 오답 풀이

① 동사의 수 일치

> [While reflecting on the needs / of organizations, leaders, and
> 접속사가 남아있는 분사구문
> 요구에 관해 곰곰이 생각할 때 오늘날 조직, 지도자, 그리고 가족의
> 명사절(목적어)을 이끄는 접속사
> families today], / we realize [that one of the unique characteristics
> one of + 복수 명사: ··· 중의 하나
> 우리는 독특한 특성 중 하나가 포용성이라는 것을 깨닫는다
> is inclusivity].

➡ 주어가 「one of + 복수 명사」이므로 단수 동사 is는 어법상 알맞다.

② 관계대명사 what

> Because inclusivity supports / [what everyone ultimately wants /
> 관계대명사절 목적어
> 포용성은 뒷받침하기 때문이다 모든 사람이 궁극적으로 원하는 것을
> from their relationships]: / collaboration.
> 자신의 관계에서 협력

➡ 동사 supports의 목적어로 쓰인 명사절을 이끌며, 뒤에 오는 불완전한 절의 목적어 역할을 하고 있으므로 관계대명사 what이 오는 것이 바르다.

③ 분사구문

> Yet the majority of leaders, organizations, and families / are still
> 선행사
> 그러나 대다수의 지도자, 조직, 그리고 가족은
> using the language of the old paradigm / [in which one person
> 목적격 관계대명사 주어
> 여전히 오래된 패러다임의 언어를 사용하고 있다 거기서는 한 사람이
> — typically the oldest, most educated, and/or wealthiest — /
> 보통 가장 연장자, 가장 교육을 많이 받은 사람, 그리고/또는 가장 부유한 사람인데
> makes all the decisions], / and their decisions rule / with little
> 동사 형용사(거의 ··· 없는)
> 모든 결정을 내린다 그리고 그들의 결정이 지배한다
> discussion or inclusion of others, / [resulting in exclusivity].
> 결과를 나타내는 분사구문(= and it results ...)
> 토론이나 다른 사람을 포함시키는 것이 거의 없이 결과적으로 배타성을 초래한다

➡ resulting 이하는 결과를 나타내는 분사구문으로, result는 자동사이므로 현재분사 resulting이 오는 것이 알맞다.

---

④ 형용사

> to부정사의 의미상 주어
> There is no need / for others to present their ideas / [because
> 형용사적 용법의 to부정사
> 필요가 없다 다른 사람들이 자신의 생각을 제시할 왜냐하면
> they are considered inadequate].
> ···라고 여겨지다 목적격보어
> 왜냐하면 그것은 부적절한 것으로 여겨지기 때문이다

➡ consider는 5형식(주어 + 동사 + 목적어 + 목적격보어)에 쓰이는 동사로 수동태로 변환할 경우 뒤에 목적격보어가 그대로 남는다. 목적격보어 자리이므로 형용사 inadequate이 오는 것이 어법상 알맞다.

지문 해석

오늘날 조직, 지도자, 그리고 가족의 요구에 관해 곰곰이 생각할 때 우리는 독특한 특성 중 하나가 포용성이라는 것을 깨닫는다. 왜 그런가? 포용성은 모든 사람이 자신의 관계에서 궁극적으로 원하는 것인 협력을 뒷받침하기 때문이다. 그러나 대다수의 지도자, 조직, 그리고 가족은 여전히 오래된 패러다임의 언어를 사용하고 있고, 거기서는 한 사람이, 보통 가장 연장자, 가장 교육을 많이 받은 사람, 그리고/또는 가장 부유한 사람인데, 모든 결정을 내리고 토론이나 다른 사람을 포함시키는 것이 거의 없이 그들의 결정이 지배하고 결과적으로 배타성을 초래한다. 오늘날 이 사람은 어떤 조직의 관리자, 최고 경영자, 또는 다른 상급 지도자일 수 있다. 다른 사람들이 자신의 생각을 제시할 필요가 없는데 왜냐하면 그것은 부적절한 것으로 여겨지기 때문이다. 그러나 연구에 따르면 문제 해결에 있어서 배타성은, 심지어 천재와 함께하는 것이더라도, 포용성만큼 효과적이지 않은데, 포용성이 있는 경우에는 모든 사람의 생각을 듣게 되고 해결책은 협력을 통해 발전된다.

어휘

reflect on ···에 관해 곰곰이 생각하다 **characteristics** 몡 특성, 특징
inclusivity 몡 포용성 **ultimately** 뷘 궁극적으로 **collaboration** 몡 협력
paradigm 몡 패러다임 **typically** 뷘 보통, 일반적으로 **educated** 혤 많이 배운,
교양 있는 **rule** 통 지배하다 **exclusivity** 몡 배타성 **senior** 혤 상급의
inadequate 혤 부적절한

05
정답 ⑤ 정답률 40%

정답 풀이

⑤ 관계대명사 vs. 관계부사

> ..., Taoist and Confucian scholars engaged in a practice / [known
> 과거분사
> 도교와 유교의 학자은 관행에 참여했다
> as 'pure talk'] / {which(→ where) they debated spiritual and
> 전치사(···로) 관계부사
> '청담(淸談)'이라고 알려진 그들이 정신적이고 철학적인 문제를 토론했던
> philosophical issues / before audiences in contests / [that might
> 주격 관계대명사
> 대회의 관중 앞에서
> last for a day and a night]}.
> 하루 동안 주야로 계속되기도 하는

➡ 'pure talk'가 장소를 나타내는 선행사 역할을 하고 있고, 뒤에 완전한 절이 이어지므로, 관계대명사 which를 관계부사 where로 고쳐야 한다.

친절한 오답 풀이

① 동사의 수 일치

> In ancient Rome, / debate in the Senate was critical / to the
> 주어 동사
> 고대 로마에서 원로원에서의 토론은 대단히 중요했다
> conduct of civil society and the justice system.
> 시민 사회의 경영과 사법제도에

➡ 주어(debate)가 단수 명사이므로 단수 동사 was가 오는 것이 알맞다.

② 부사

In Greece, / advocates for policy changes / **would** routinely make
　　　　　　　　주어　　　　　　　　　…하곤 했다 부사　　　↑ 동사
그리스에서　　정책 변화에 대한 옹호자들이　　　　자신들의 주장을 일상적으로
their cases / before citizen juries / [composed of hundreds of
make one's case: …의 주장을 진술하다 ↑　　　　　　 과거분사, …로 구성된
진술하곤 했다　시민 배심원단 앞에서　　　 수백 명의 아테네인들로 구성된
Athenians].

➡ 부사 routinely가 동사구 make their cases를 수식하고 있으므로 어법상 바르다.

 Grammar Tips

혼동되는 조동사

조동사	의미	예시
would / used to	…하곤 했다 (과거의 반복된 동작)	She **would** take a walk after lunch. (그녀는 점심식사 후 산책을 하곤 했다.) He **used to** travel alone during his vacations. (그는 방학 동안 혼자 여행하곤 했다.)
used to	…였다 (과거의 상태)	This bookstore **used to** be a café. (이 서점은 카페였다.)

③ be used to-v

In India, / debate was used to settle religious controversies / and
　　　　　　 be used to-v: …하는 데 쓰이다
인도에서　 토론은 종교적 논란을 해결하는 데 이용되었다　　　　　그리고
was a very popular form of entertainment.
매우 인기 있는 오락의 한 형태였다

➡ be used 뒤에 to부정사가 오면 '…하는 데 쓰이다'로 해석 되는데, 토론이 '종교적 논란을 해결하는 데 이용되었다'고 해석하는 것이 적절하므로 settle은 어법상 바르다.

④ 분사구문

Indian kings sponsored great debating contests, / [offering prizes
　　　　　　　　　　　　　　　　 동시동작을 나타내는 분사구문(= as Indian kings offered …)
인도의 왕들은 대규모 토론 대회를 후원했다　　　　 승리자들에게 상을 주면서
for the winners].

➡ offering 이하는 동시동작을 나타내는 분사구문으로, 생략된 주어는 주절의 주어 (Indian kings)와 같다. 왕들이 상을 '주면서'라는 능동의 의미가 적절하므로 현재분사 offering이 오는 것이 알맞다.

지문 해석

토론은 언어 그 자체만큼이나 오래되었고 인간의 역사 내내 많은 형태들을 취해왔다. 고대 로마에서, 원로원에서의 토론은 시민 사회의 경영과 사법제도에 대단히 중요했다. 그리스에서, 정책 변화에 대한 옹호자들이 수백 명의 아테네인들로 구성된 시민 배심원단 앞에서 일상적으로 자신들의 주장을 진술하곤 했다. 인도에서, 토론은 종교적 논란을 해결하는 데 사용되었고 매우 인기 있는 오락의 한 형태였다. 인도의 왕들은 승리자들에게 상을 주면서 대규모 토론 대회를 후원했다. 중국은 자국만의 오래되고 유명한 토론 전통을 가지고 있다. 2세기 들어, 도교와 유교의 학자들은 '청담(淸談)'이라고 알려진 하루 동안 주야로 계속되기도 하는 대회에서 그들이 정신적이고 철학적인 문제를 관중 앞에서 토론했던 관행에 참여했다.

어휘

debate 동 토론하다 명 토론　**senate** 명 상원; *(고대 로마의) 원로원　**critical** 형 비판적인; *대단히 중요한　**conduct** 명 행동; *경영　**civil society** 시민 사회　**justice** 명 정의; *사법　**advocate** 명 옹호자, 지지자　**policy** 명 정책, 방침　**jury** 명 배심원단　**settle** 동 (논쟁 등을) 해결하다　**religious** 형 종교의　**controversy** 명 논란　**entertainment** 명 오락　**sponsor** 동 후원하다　**distinguished** 형 유명한, 성공한　**Taoist** 형 도교의　**Confucian** 형 유교의　**scholar** 명 학자　**practice** 명 실행; *관행　**spiritual** 형 영적인　**philosophical** 형 철학적인　**audience** 명 청중, 관중

정답 풀이

② 관계대명사 vs. 관계부사

One domain / [which(→ where) this is of considerable
　 ↑　　　　　　　　　관계부사 주어 동사　　　　보어
한 영역은　　　　　　　　이것이 상당히 중요한
significance] / is music's potentially damaging effects / on
　　　　　　　　　　　　　　 현재분사　　　 └────┘
음악의 잠재적으로 해로운 영향이다
the ability to drive safely.
└──────┘ 형용사적 용법의 to부정사
안전하게 운전하는 능력에 대한

➡ One domain이 장소를 나타내는 선행사 역할을 하고 있고 뒤에 완전한 절이 이어지므로, 관계대명사 which를 관계부사 where로 고쳐야 한다.

친절한 오답 풀이

① 보어 역할을 하는 현재분사

Given that music appears to enhance / physical and mental
…을 고려하면
음악이 향상시키는 것으로 보인다는 점을 고려하면　　　신체적, 정신적 기술을
skills, / are there circumstances / [where music is damaging to
　　　　　　　　　　　　　　　　　 관계부사　　 주격보어
　　　　　　　　상황이 있는가　　　 음악이 작업 수행에 해로운
performance]?

➡ 현재분사 damaging이 형용사처럼 관계부사절 안에서 주격보어로 쓰였으므로 어법상 바르다.

③ 수동태

Evidence suggests an association / between loud, fast music and
　　　　　　　　　　　　　　　 between A and B: A와 B 사이
증거는 연관성을 제시한다　　　　　 시끄럽고, 빠른 음악과 난폭한 운전 사이의
reckless driving, / but how might music's ability to influence
　　　　　　　　　 조동사　 주어 ↑　　　 형용사적 용법의
　　　　　　 하지만 어떻게 운전하는 데 대한 음악의 영향력이　　 to부정사
driving / in this way / be explained?
　　　　　　　　　　　　　 동사
　　 이런 방식으로　　 설명될까

➡ 의문사 how가 이끄는 의문문의 주어는 music's ability로, 능력이 '설명되는'이라는 수동의 의미가 적절하므로 수동태 be explained는 어법상 바르다.

④ 접속사 that

One possibility / is [that drivers adjust to temporal regularities
　　　　　　　　　 명사절(보어)을 이끄는 접속사
한 가지 가능성은　 운전자가 음악의 시간적 규칙성에 적응한다는 것이다
in music], / and [that their speed is influenced accordingly].
　　　　　 접속사　 명사절(보어)을 이끄는 접속사
　　　　　 그리고 그들의 속도가 그에 따라 영향을 받는다는 것이다

➡ 등위접속사 and가 주격보어 역할을 하는 that절(that drivers … music)과 that절 (that their … accordingly)을 병렬 연결하고 있는 구조로, 접속사 that이 완전한 절을 이끌고 있으므로 어법상 바르다.

⑤ 접속사

In other words, / just as faster music causes people to eat faster, /
　　　　　　　　　 (just) as … so ~: …인 것과 마찬가지로 ~하다　 cause A to-v: A가 …하게 하다
다시 말해서　　　　더 빠른 음악이 사람들이 더 빨리 먹도록 하는 것과 마찬가지로
so it causes people to drive / at faster speeds, ….
그것은 사람들이 운전하게 한다　　 더 빠른 속도로

➡ 「(just) as … so ~」 구문으로, 접속사 so 뒤에 완전한 절이 이어지고 있으므로 어법상 바르다.

지문 해석

음악이 신체적, 정신적 기술을 향상시키는 것으로 보인다는 점을 고려하면, 음악이 작업

수행에 해로운 상황이 있는가? 이것이 상당히 중요한 한 영역은 안전하게 운전하는 능력에 대한 음악의 잠재적으로 해로운 영향이다. 증거는 시끄럽고, 빠른 음악과 난폭한 운전 사이의 연관성을 제시하지만, 이런 방식으로 운전하는 데 대한 음악의 영향력이 어떻게 설명될까? 한 가지 가능성은 운전자가 음악의 시간적 규칙성에 적응한다는 것이고, 그들의 속도가 그에 따라 영향을 받는다는 것이다. 다시 말해서, 더 빠른 음악이 사람들이 더 빨리 먹도록 하는 것과 마찬가지로, 사람들이 계속 반복되는 음악의 구조와 정신적, 신체적으로 맞물리면서, 그것은 사람들이 더 빠른 속도로 운전하게 한다는 것이다.

enhance 통 향상시키다   circumstance 명 상황   domain 명 분야, 영역
considerable 형 상당한   significance 명 중요성   potentially 부 잠재적으로
association 명 연관성   reckless 형 난폭한, 무모한   adjust 통 적응하다
temporal 형 시간의   regularity 명 규칙성   accordingly 부 그에 맞춰   engage
통 (주의·관심을) 사로잡다; *맞물리다   ongoing 형 계속 진행 중인

07 　　　정답 ②　　　정답률 74%

정답 풀이

(A) 동사의 수 일치

One of the exercises / [(which/that) we were given] / was / ~~were~~
주어, one of + 복수 명사: … 중의 하나   목적격 관계대명사 생략   동사
과제들 중 하나는   우리에게 주어진   목록을 작성하는
to make a list / of the ten most important events / of our lives.
명사적 용법의 to부정사(보어)
것이었다   가장 중요한 10가지 사건들의   우리의 삶에서

➡ 「one of + 복수 명사」가 주어이므로, 단수 동사 was가 오는 것이 알맞다.

(B) 복합관계부사 vs. 복합관계대명사

Number one was: "I was born," / and you could put [[~~however~~ /
일 번은 "나는 태어났다"였다   그리고 당신이 좋아하는 것은 무엇이든 넣을 수 있었다
whatever] you liked] / after that.
복합관계대명사(…하는 것은 무엇이든)
그다음에

➡ however는 복합관계부사로 뒤에 완전한 절이 오고, whatever는 복합관계대명사로 뒤에 불완전한 절이 온다. 뒤에 동사(liked)의 목적어가 빠진 불완전한 절이 이어지고 있으므로, whatever가 오는 것이 알맞다.

(C) 대명사를 수식하는 과거분사

Being born was something [[done / ~~doing~~] to me], / but my own
동명사 주어   동사   과거분사
태어나는 것은 나에게 일어난 일이었다   하지만 내 자신의 삶은
life began / [when I first made out the meaning of a sentence].
접속사   make out: …을 알아보다
시작되었다   내가 처음으로 문장의 의미를 이해했을 때

➡ 네모는 앞의 대명사 something을 수식하는 분사로, '행해진'이라는 수동의 의미가 적절하므로 과거분사 done이 오는 것이 알맞다. 현재분사 doing은 '…을 하는'이라는 능동의 의미로, 뒤에 목적어가 필요하다.

지문 해석

나의 어린 시절로부터 가져온 가장 유용한 것은 독서에서의 자신감이었다. 얼마 전에, 나는 어떻게 살아야 할지에 대한 단서를 얻으려는 희망에서 주말의 자아 탐구 연수에 갔다. 우리에게 주어진 과제들 중 하나는 우리의 삶에서 가장 중요한 10가지 사건들의 목록을 작성하는 것이었다. 1번은 "나는 태어났다"였고, 그다음에 당신이 좋아하는 것은 무엇이든 넣을 수 있었다. 그것에 대해 생각도 해보지 않고, 나의 손이 2번에 "나는 읽는 것을 배웠다"라고 적었다. "나는 태어나서 읽는 것을 배웠다"가 많은 사람들에게 떠오르는 순서는 아닐 것이라고 나는 생각한다. 그러나 나는 내가 말하고자 하는 것을 알고 있었다. 태어나는 것은 나에게 일어난 일이었지만, 내 자신의 삶은 내가 처음으로 문장의 의미를 이해했을 때 시작되었다.

confidence 명 자신감   self-exploratory 형 자아 탐구의   workshop 명 워크숍,
연수회   clue 명 단서   exercise 명 연습; *연습문제   sequence 명 순서   occur
to …에게 생각이 떠오르다

08 　　　정답 ②　　　정답률 33%

정답 풀이

(A) 대동사 do

[As a company's executive put it], / "Many users probably spend
접속사(…듯이)   말하다   spend + 시간 + on + 명사: …에 시간을 쓰다
어떤 회사의 간부가 말했듯이,   "많은 사용자들이 아마도 더 많은 시간을
more time on the Internet / than they [do / ~~are~~] in their cars."
= spend
인터넷에서 보낸다   그들이 차에서 그러는 것보다"

➡ 앞에 나온 일반동사 spend를 대신하므로, 대동사 do가 오는 것이 알맞다.

(B) 복합관계형용사 vs. 복합관계부사

We live and work within a browser, / and it doesn't matter /
전치사(… 안에)   가주어
우리는 브라우저 안에서 살고 작업하며,   중요하지 않다
[[whichever / ~~however~~] browser it may be].
진주어, 복합관계형용사
그것이 어떤 브라우저인지는

➡ 가주어 it에 대한 진주어 역할을 하는 명사절을 이끌면서, 뒤에 오는 명사 browser를 수식하는 형용사 역할을 해야 하므로, 복합관계형용사 whichever가 오는 것이 알맞다. however는 복합관계부사로 부사절을 이끈다.

(C) 명사를 수식하는 과거분사

But for the companies [~~concerning~~ / concerned], / things are different.
과거분사
하지만 관련된 회사에게는   상황이 다르다

➡ 앞에 오는 명사 the companies를 수식하는 분사로, 회사들이 '관련된'이라는 수동의 의미가 적절하므로 과거분사 concerned가 오는 것이 알맞다.

코드+α 구문 분석 Plus

1행
We **spend** an excessive amount of time **browsing** the Web every day.
➡ spend + 시간/돈 + v-ing: …하는 데 시간/돈을 쓰다

지문 해석

우리는 매일 지나치게 많은 시간을 웹을 검색하며 보낸다. 어떤 회사의 간부가 말했듯이, "많은 사용자들이 아마도 그들이 차에서 보내는 것보다 인터넷에서 더 많은 시간을 보낸다." 하지만 우리들 대다수는 우리가 어떤 브라우저를 사용하는지 거의 알지 못한다. 그것이 우리가 이메일을 확인하고 쇼핑을 좀 하게 해주는 한, 우리는 컴퓨터에 탑재된 것이 무엇이든 계속 쓰는 경향이 있다. 우리는 브라우저 안에서 살고 작업하며, 그것이 어떤 브라우저인지는 중요하지 않다. 일이 수행되게 하기만 하면 충분하다. 하지만 관련된 회사에게는 상황이 다르다. 그들은 보안과 안정성을 갖춘 최고의 브라우저를 고안하기 위해 모든 노력을 다하고 있다.

excessive 형 지나친, 과도한   browse 통 둘러보다; *인터넷을 돌아다니다
executive 명 경영 간부   barely 부 간신히; *거의 … 아니게   hold on to 고수하다,
계속 유지하다   matter 통 중요하다   concern 통 (사람에게 영향을) 미치다,
관련되다   come up with …을 생각해내다   security 명 보안   stability 명 안정

정답 풀이

(A) 병렬구조

He remembered seeing a pocket compass / [when he was five
remember v-ing: …한 것을 기억하다   접속사
그는 작은 나침반을 본 것을 기억했다   그가 다섯 살 때
years old] / and marveling / marveled / [that the needle always
접속사   동명사 목적어   명사절(목적어)을 이끄는 접속사
그리고 놀랐던 일을   바늘이 항상 북쪽을 가리키는 것에
pointed north].

➡ 등위접속사 and가 동사 remembered의 동명사 목적어를 병렬 연결하고 있는 구조로, 동명사 seeing과 대등한 동명사 marveling이 오는 것이 알맞다.

(B) 부사 vs. 관계부사

…, his family enrolled him in the Luitpold Gymnasium, /
선행사
그의 가족은 그를 Luitpold Gymnasium에 등록시켰고
[there / where he developed a suspicion of authority].
계속적 용법의 관계부사
그곳에서 그는 권위에 대해 의심이 생겼다

➡ 절(his family … Gymnasium)과 절(he … authority)을 연결하는 접속사 역할을 해야 하므로 관계부사 where가 오는 것이 알맞다. there는 부사로 절과 절을 연결할 수 없다.

(C) 가목적어 진목적어 구문

His habit of skepticism / made him / it easy / [to question /
주어   동사   가목적어 형용사   진목적어
그의 회의론적 습관은   쉽게 해주었다   의문을 제기하는 것을
many long-standing scientific assumptions].
오랫동안 지속된 많은 과학적 가설에 대해

➡ 「make it(가목적어) + 형용사 + to-v(진목적어)」 구문으로, 뒤에 오는 진목적어(to question … assumptions)를 대신할 가목적어 it이 오는 것이 알맞다.

지문 해석

알버트 아인슈타인은 과학자로서의 자신의 삶에 영향을 미친 것에 대해 이야기했다. 그는 다섯 살 때 작은 나침반을 보고 바늘이 항상 북쪽을 가리키는 것에 놀랐던 일을 기억했다. 그 순간에, 아인슈타인은 "사물의 뒤에 깊이 숨겨진 무언가를 느꼈다"고 회상했다. 여섯 살 무렵, 아인슈타인은 바이올린을 배우기 시작했다. 몇 년 후 음악의 수학적 구조를 인식했을 때, 바이올린은 그의 평생의 친구가 되었다. 아인슈타인이 열 살이었을 때, 그의 가족은 그를 Luitpold Gymnasium에 등록시켰고, 그곳에서 그는 권위에 대해 의심이 생겼다. 그 특성은 아인슈타인이 훗날 과학자로서의 삶에 큰 도움이 되었다. 그의 회의론적 습관은 오랫동안 지속된 많은 과학적 가정에 대해 의문을 제기하는 것을 쉽게 해 주었다.

 어휘

influence 동 영향을 미치다   compass 명 나침반   marvel 동 놀라워하다, 감탄하다   needle 명 바늘   recall 동 기억해내다, 상기하다   mathematical 형 수학적인   lifelong 형 평생 동안의   enroll 동 입학시키다, 등록시키다   suspicion 명 의심   authority 명 권위   trait 명 특성   skepticism 명 회의론   long-standing 형 오래된   assumption 명 추정, 가정

정답 풀이

(A) 명사를 수식하는 과거분사

…, the habit of reading newspapers / has been on the decline / and
be on the decline: 감소하다
신문을 읽는 습관이   감소해오고 있다
some of the dollars / [previously spent / were spent on newspaper
주어 ↑   과거분사
그리고 돈의 일부가   전에 신문 광고에 쓰였던
advertising] / have migrated to the Internet.
동사
인터넷으로 이동해오고 있다

➡ and로 연결된 절의 주어는 some of the dollars이고 동사는 have migrated로, 동사가 더 필요하지 않다. 따라서 네모에는 앞의 명사(some of the dollars)를 수식하는 과거분사인 spent가 오는 것이 알맞다.

(B) 복합관계부사 vs. 복합관계형용사

We can read the news of the day, / or the latest on business,
우리는 오늘의 뉴스를 읽을 수 있다   또는 사업, 연예에 대한 최신 내용을
entertainment / or however / whatever news / on the websites of
복합관계형용사 ↑
또는 어떤 뉴스든지   뉴욕타임즈, 가디언의 웹사이트에서
the *New York Times*, the *Guardian* / or almost any other major
또는 세계의 거의 다른 어떤 주요 신문의
newspaper in the world.

➡ 뒤에 오는 명사 news를 수식하므로 '어떤 …이라도'의 의미인 복합관계형용사 whatever가 오는 것이 알맞다. however는 복합관계부사로 명사를 수식할 수 없다.

(C) 능동태 vs. 수동태

Advertising dollars have simply been followed / following /
주어   have been v-ing: 현재완료 진행형
광고비는 단순히 따라가고 있다
the migration trail across to these new technologies.
목적어
이러한 새로운 기술로 이동하는 코스를

➡ 주어와 네모의 분사가 의미상 능동 관계이므로, 현재분사 following이 오는 것이 알맞다. 목적어 the migration trail이 뒤에 이어지고 있으므로 수동태 been followed 는 쓰일 수 없다.

콘드+α 구문 분석 Plus

5행	… newspaper reading has been **due to** the fact [*that* we are doing more of our newspaper reading online]. ➡ due to: '… 때문에'라는 의미의 전치사 ➡ that: 앞의 명사 the fact와 동격을 이루는 명사절을 이끄는 접속사
12행	Increasingly, we can access these stories wirelessly by mobile devices **as well as** our computers. ➡ B as well as A: A뿐만 아니라 B도(= not only A but also B)

지문 해석

많은 나라의 더 젊은 사람들 사이에서, 신문을 읽는 습관이 감소해오고 있으며, 전에 신문 광고에 쓰였던 돈의 일부가 인터넷으로 이동해오고 있다. 물론, 신문 읽기의 이런 감소는 일부 우리가 신문 읽기를 온라인으로 더 많이 하고 있다는 사실 때문이다. 우리는 뉴욕타임즈, 가디언, 또는 세계의 거의 다른 어떤 주요 신문의 웹사이트에서 오늘의 뉴스나 사업, 연예에 대한 최신 내용, 또는 어떤 뉴스든지 읽을 수 있다. 점점 더, 우리는 컴퓨터는 물론 모바일 기기로 이런 이야기들에 무선으로 접근할 수 있다. 광고비는 이러한 새로운 기술로 이동하는 코스를 단순히 따라가고 있다.

 어휘

decline 명 감소   previously 부 이전에   migrate 동 이동하다 (migration 명 이주, 이동)   latest 형 최신의, 최근의   entertainment 명 연예, 오락   increasingly 부 점점 더   access 동 접근하나   wirelessly 부 무선으로

UNIT 3 전치사와 접속사

코드 접속하기

출제코드 1　　　　　　　　　　전치사 vs. 접속사

A　**1** like　**2** because of　**3** Though
B　**1 ➡** near　**2** ○　**3 ➡** because

해석과 정답 풀이

STEP 1

1　1) 나는 여름방학 동안 전국 일주 여행을 할 계획이다.
　　2) 식당의 서비스는 형편없었지만, 요리는 아주 맛있었다.
3　1) 어젯밤 마지막 리허설은 실제 콘서트 같았다.
　　2) 그녀와 그녀의 여동생은 여러 면에서 비슷하다.
　　3) Kaka의 집은 나의 사무실에서 가깝다. 걸어서 2분 밖에 걸리지 않는다.

STEP 2

1　1) 커피는 사람들이 깨어있고 정신이 맑게 느끼도록 돕기 때문에 인기가 있다.
　　2) 우리 할아버지는 베트남 전쟁 동안 팔에 총을 맞았다.
　　3) Tom은 의사의 경고에도 불구하고 그의 약을 복용하는 것을 잊어버렸다.

STEP 3

A　**1** Teddy는 유치원의 많은 아이들과 마찬가지로 그의 장난감에 민감하다.
　　➡ 뒤에 목적어 역할을 하는 명사구(many children in kindergarten)가 이어지고
　　　 있으므로 전치사 like가 오는 것이 알맞다.
　　2 어떤 아이들은 그들의 부모님 때문에 독립하는 법을 배우지 못하는데, 그들은
　　　 아이들을 위해 모든 것을 해준다.
　　➡ 뒤에 목적어 역할을 하는 명사(their parents)가 이어지고 있으므로 전치사
　　　 because of가 오는 것이 알맞다.
　　3 정부가 흡연을 막으려고 노력해왔음에도 불구하고, 흡연자들의 수는 늘어나고 있다.
　　➡ 뒤에 문장성분이 완전한 절이 이어지고 있으므로 접속사 Though가 오는 것이
　　　 알맞다.
B　**1** 정원을 향한 창문 가까이에 있는 세면대는 쉬운 발판대를 제공해주었다.
　　➡ '창문 가까이에'라고 해석되고 뒤에 목적어 역할을 하는 명사(the window)가
　　　 이어지므로 부사 nearly를 전치사 near로 고쳐야 한다. nearly는 '거의'라는
　　　 의미의 부사이다.
　　2 이 약을 복용하는 동안에는 음주는 엄격하게 금지된다는 것을 당신은 명심해야 한다.
　　➡ 뒤에 문장성분이 완전한 절이 이어지고 있으므로 접속사 while을 쓰는 것이 알맞다.
　　3 나는 일에 집중할 수 없기 때문에 나의 일을 내일까지 끝내지 못할까 봐 두렵다.
　　➡ 뒤에 문장성분이 완전한 절이 이어지고 있으므로 접속사 because로 고쳐야 한다.
　　　 because of는 전치사이므로 뒤에 명사(구)가 이어져야 한다.

출제코드 2　　　　　　　　　　종속접속사

A　**1** So　**2** if　**3** whether
B　**1 ➡** Whether　**2** ○

해석과 정답 풀이

STEP 1

1　1) 좋은 소식은 내가 은행에서 돈을 인출할 수 있다는 것이다.
　　2) 그녀는 그가 회의 후에 커피를 마실 시간이 있는지 물었다.
2　1) 날씨가 화창하든 아니든, 나는 아이들과 외출할 것이다.
　　2) 나는 너무 아파서 오늘밤 파티에 갈 수 없다.

STEP 2

1　나는 누군가가 이 영화의 제목을 알고 있는지를 궁금해 했다.
2　1) 이 새로운 프로그램은 아주 효율적이어서 우리는 작업을 평소보다 일찍 끝냈다.
　　2) 그것은 너무 슬픈 이야기여서 나는 울지 않을 수 없었다.
3　네가 이기든 아니든, 나는 네가 마라톤에서 뛰는 것을 즐길 것이라고 확신한다.

STEP 3

A　**1** 그는 너무 멍청해서 무슨 일이 일어날 수 있을지 생각하지도 않고 서둘러 결정을
　　　 내렸다.
　　➡ '너무 …해서 ~하다'라는 의미의 so/such … that 구문이 쓰였는데, 뒤에 형용사
　　　 stupid가 이어지고 있으므로 So가 오는 것이 알맞다.
　　2 그는 안내 데스크로 가서 그가 호텔의 금고에 그의 지갑을 맡길 수 있는지 아닌지를
　　　 물어보았다.
　　➡ 동사 asked의 목적어 역할을 하는 명사절을 이끌고, '그의 지갑을 보관할 수
　　　 있는지 아닌지'라고 해석되므로 접속사 if가 오는 것이 알맞다.
　　3 그것은 우리가 소수 의견을 들어야 하는지 아니면 그것을 무시해야 하는지에 대한
　　　 의문을 제기한다.
　　➡ 전치사 of의 목적어 역할을 하는 명사절이 와야 하고, '…인지'라는 의미로
　　　 해석되므로 접속사 whether가 오는 것이 알맞다.
B　**1** 그의 결정이 옳은지 틀린지는 너의 관점에 달려있다.
　　➡ 주어 역할을 하는 명사절을 이끌고 있고, '…인지'라는 의미로 해석되므로 접속사
　　　 That을 Whether로 고쳐야 한다.
　　2 너무 추운 날이라서 아무도 강을 따라 걸으러 밖에 나가지 않았다.
　　➡ 뒤에 「a(n) + 형용사 + 명사」가 오고 있으므로 such는 어법상 바르게 쓰였다.

기출예제 Q1　　　　정답 ②　　　　정답률 51%

정답 풀이

② 명사절을 이끄는 접속사

Those [who donate to one or two charities] / seek evidence about /
주어 ↑――― 주격 관계대명사　　　　　　　　　　　　　동사
한두 자선단체에 기부하는 사람들은　　　　　　　　　…에 관한 증거를 찾는다
[what the charity is doing / and what(→ whether) it is really
간접의문문(의문사+주어+동사)　　　　　　　　전치사 about의 목적어
그 자선단체가 무슨 일을 하고 있는지와　　그것이 실제로
having a positive impact].
긍정적인 영향을 끼치고 있는지

➡ 뒤에 완전한 절이 이어지고 있고 전치사 about의 목적어 역할을 하는 명사절을
이끌고 있으므로 접속사가 와야 한다. 문맥상 '…인지'의 의미가 들어가야 하므로 접속사
whether로 고쳐야 한다.

친절한 오답 풀이

① 동사의 수 일치

Psychologists [who study giving behavior] have noticed / {that
주어 ↑―――― 주격 관계대명사　　　　　　　　동사　　　　접속사
기부하는 행위를 연구하는 심리학자들은 알게 되었다
some people give substantial amounts to one or two charities, /
some … others ~: 어떤 것[사람]들은 … 다른 것[사람]들은 ~
어떤 사람들은 한두 자선단체에 상당한 액수를 기부하는 반면에
[while others give small amounts to many charities]}.
접속사
다른 사람들은 많은 자선단체에 적은 액수를 기부한다는 것을

➡ 주어는 뒤에 관계대명사절의 수식을 받는 Psychologists로 복수 명사이므로 수
일치하여 복수 동사 have가 왔다.

③ 현재진행 시제에 쓰이는 현재분사

Those [who give small amounts to many charities] are not so
주어 ↑――― 주격 관계대명사　　　　　　　　　　　　　동사
많은 자선단체에 적은 액수를 내는 사람들은 …에 많은 관심을 두지 않는다
interested in / {whether [what they are doing] helps others]} — /
　　　　　　　　접속사　관계대명사　주어　　　　동사
　　　　　　　그들이 하는 일이 다른 사람들을 돕는지
psychologists call them warm glow givers.
심리학자들은 그들을 따뜻한 불빛 기부자라고 부른다

➡ 현재진행 시제는 「be v-ing」로 나타내므로 be동사 뒤의 현재분사 doing은 어법상
알맞다.

④ 대명사

Knowing that they are giving makes them feel good, / regardless
　주어(동명사구)　　　　　　동사　목적어 목적격보어　전치사(…에 상관없이)
자신이 기부하고 있다는 것을 아는 것이 그들을 기분 좋게 해준다
of the impact of their donation.
그들이 내는 기부가 끼치는 영향과 관계없이

➡ 앞에 they를 받는 대명사로 동사 makes의 목적어이므로 목적격 them이 알맞다. 주어 Knowing that they are giving과 목적어가 가리키는 대상이 다르므로 재귀대명사가 쓰이지 않았다.

⑤ stop to-v

In many cases the donation is so small — $10 or less — / that if
　　　　　　　　　　　　　　so ... that ~: 너무 …해서 ~하다
많은 경우 기부금은 10달러 이하의 매우 적은 금액이어서
they stopped to think, / they would realize / {that the cost of
　　　　　　　　　　　　　　　　　　　　　접속사　주어
곰곰이 생각해 본다면　　　　그들은 알게 될 것이다　기부금을 처리하는 비용이
processing the donation is likely to exceed any benefit / [(that) it
　　　　　　　　　　　be likely to-v: …하기 쉽다　　목적격 관계대명사 생략
모든 이점을 넘어서기 쉽다는 것을　　　　　　　　　　　　　그것이
brings to the charity]}.
자선단체에 가져다주는

➡ 동사 stop은 뒤에 to부정사(…하기 위해)와 동명사(…하는 것)가 모두 올 수 있는데, 문맥상 '생각하기 위해 멈추다, 곰곰이 생각하다'라는 의미가 자연스러우므로 to부정사 형태가 알맞다.

지문 해석

기부하는 행위를 연구하는 심리학자들은 어떤 사람들은 한두 자선단체에 상당한 액수를 기부하는 반면에, 어떤 사람들은 많은 자선단체에 적은 액수를 기부한다는 것을 알게 되었다. 한두 자선단체에 기부하는 사람들은 그 자선단체가 무슨 일을 하고 있는지와 그것이 실제로 긍정적인 영향을 끼치고 있는지에 관한 증거를 찾는다. 자선단체가 정말로 다른 사람들을 도와주고 있다는 증거가 보여 줄 경우 그들은 상당한 기부금을 낸다. 많은 자선단체에 적은 액수를 내는 사람들은 그들이 하는 일이 다른 사람들을 돕는지에는 그렇게 많은 관심을 두지 않는다. 심리학자들은 그들을 따뜻한 불빛 기부자라고 부른다. 그들이 내는 기부가 끼치는 영향과 관계없이 자신들이 기부하고 있다는 것을 아는 것이 그들을 기분 좋게 해준다. 많은 경우 기부금은 10달러 이하의 매우 적은 금액이어서, 곰곰이 생각해 본다면, 그들은 기부금을 처리하는 비용이 그것(기부금)이 자선단체에 가져다주는 모든 이점을 넘어서기 쉽다는 것을 알게 될 것이다.

 어휘

substantial 형 상당한　charity 명 자선단체　evidence 명 증거　impact 명 영향
process 동 처리하다　exceed 동 넘어서다　benefit 명 이점

코드 공략하기
pp.73~75

| 01 ③ | 02 ⑤ | 03 ② | 04 ④ | 05 ③ | 06 ④ | 07 ② | 08 ⑤ |

01
정답 ③　　정답률 60%

정답 풀이

③ 전치사 vs. 접속사

But other educators say / {that children do not use their imagination
　　　　　　　　　　　　명사절(목적어)을 이끄는 접속사
그러나 다른 교육자들은 말한다　아이들이 자신의 상상력을 충분히 사용하지 않는다고
enough / [because of(→ because) the computer screen shows
부사(충분히)　　　　접속사
　　　　　　　컴퓨터 화면이 그들에게 모든 것을 보여주기 때문에
them everything]}.

➡ because of는 전치사로 뒤에 명사(구)가 와야 하지만, 뒤에 완전한 절이 오고 있으므로 because of를 접속사 because로 고쳐야 한다.

---

① 명사적 용법의 to부정사

At what age / should a child learn / to use a computer?
몇 살에　　　　어린이는 배워야 하는가　　컴퓨터 사용법을

➡ to use는 동사 learn의 목적어 역할을 하는 명사적 용법의 to부정사로 어법상 바르다.

② 접속사 that

Some early childhood educators believe / [that in modern society
　　　　　　　　　　　　　　　　　　　　명사절(목적어)을 이끄는 접속사
일부 유아 교육자들은 생각한다　　　　　　　현대 사회에서
computer skills are a basic necessity / for every child].
컴퓨터 기술은 기본적인 필수 요소라고　　모든 아이들에게

➡ that은 접속사로, 동사 believe의 목적어 역할을 하는 명사절을 이끌고 있으므로 어법상 바르다.

④ 부사

Physically, children / [who type for a long time / or use a computer
　　　　　　　　　　　주격 관계대명사　오랫동안
신체적으로, 아이들은　　　오랫동안 컴퓨터 자판을 두드리는　혹은 마우스를 너무 많이 사용하는
mouse too much] / can develop problems to their bodies.
　　　　　　부사
　　　　　　　　그들의 몸에 문제를 일으킬 수 있다

➡ too much는 '너무 많이'라는 뜻으로 부사 too가 부사 much를 수식해주고 있으므로 어법상 바르다.

⑤ 대명사

Perhaps the best way / for young children to use computers /
　　　　　　　　　　to부정사의 의미상 주어　형용사적 용법의 to부정사
아마도 최상의 방법은　　　　어린이들이 컴퓨터를 쓰는
is to use them / only for a short time each day.
명사적 용법의 to부정사(보어)
그것들을 사용하는 것이다　매일 잠깐씩만

➡ 복수 대명사 them이 앞에 나온 복수 명사 computers를 지칭하고 있으므로 어법상 바르다.

 구문 별더 Plus

3행
Some early childhood educators believe .... But **other** educators say ....
➡ some ... other ~: 어떤 (사람은) … 다른 (사람은) ~

지문 해석

어린이는 몇 살에 컴퓨터 사용법을 배워야 하는가? 그 답은 당신이 누구에게 묻는가에 따라 달라질 것 같다. 일부 유아 교육자들은 현대 사회에서 컴퓨터 기술은 모든 아이들에게 기본적인 필수 요소라고 생각한다. 그러나 다른 교육자들은 컴퓨터 화면이 아이들에게 모든 것을 보여주기 때문에 그들이 자신의 상상력을 충분히 사용하지 않는다고 말한다. 신체적으로, 오랫동안 컴퓨터 자판을 두드리거나 마우스를 너무 많이 사용하는 아이들은 그들의 몸에 문제를 일으킬 수 있다. 아마도 어린이들이 컴퓨터를 쓰는 최상의 방법은 매일 잠깐씩만 그것들을 사용하는 것이다.

어휘

childhood 명 어린 시절, 아동기　educator 명 교육자　necessity 명 필요(성); *필수품　imagination 명 상상력　physically 부 신체적으로　develop 동 발달시키다; *(병이) 생기다

02 정답 ⑤ 정답률 51%

지문 해석

내가 어린 소녀였을 때, 내 방은 항상 엉망진창이었다. 어머니는 나에게 "가서 방 치워!"라고 말씀하시며 내가 방을 정돈하게 하려고 항상 노력하셨다. 나는 그때마다 어머니에게 저항했다. 나는 무엇을 해야 할지 듣는 것을 싫어했다. 나는 내가 원하는 방식으로 방을 두기로 결심했다. 내가 정말로 지저분한 방에서 사는 것을 좋아하느냐 아니냐는 완전히 다른 문제였다. 나는 깨끗한 방을 갖는 것의 이점들에 대해 전혀 멈추어서 생각하지 않았다. 나에게는, 내 방식대로 하는 것이 더 중요했다. 그리고 대부분의 다른 부모님들처럼, 어머니는 내가 그 이점들을 스스로 깨닫도록 하지 않았다. 대신에 그녀는 잔소리를 선택했다.

정답 풀이

(A) 능동태 vs. 수동태

I hated to [tell̶ / be told] / [what to do].
to be v-ed: to부정사의 수동태   what to-v: 무엇을 해야 할지
나는 듣는 것을 싫어했다   무엇을 해야 할지

➡ 주어(I)가 무엇을 해야 할지 '말하는' 것이 아니라 '말을 듣게 되는' 것이므로 수동태 be told가 오는 것이 적절하다.

(B) 접속사

[Because̶ / Whether] I actually liked living in a messy room or
   whether ... or not: …인지 아닌지
내가 정말로 지저분한 방에서 사는 것을 좋아하느냐 아니냐는
not] / was another subject altogether.
   동사   완전히
완전히 다른 문제였다

➡ 접속사 whether는 명사절과 부사절 모두를 이끌 수 있는 반면에 접속사 because는 부사절만 이끌 수 있다. 이 문장에서는 동사 was의 주어 역할을 하는 명사절을 이끌어야 하므로 접속사 Whether가 들어가는 것이 적절하다.

(C) 전치사

And my mother, / [alike̶ / like] most other parents, / did not get
   전치사(… 같이)   get A to-v: A가 …하도록 시키다
그리고 어머니는   대부분의 다른 부모님들처럼   내가 이 이점들을 깨닫도록
me to realize the benefits / for myself.
   for oneself: 스스로, 혼자 힘으로
하지 않았다   스스로

➡ alike는 서술어로만 쓰이는 형용사로 명사를 수식할 수 없고, like는 전치사로 뒤에 목적어 역할을 하는 명사(구)가 와야 한다. 네모 뒤에 명사 most other parents가 쓰였으므로, 전치사 like가 오는 것이 알맞다.

어휘

mess 명 엉망진창 (messy 형 지저분한)   straighten up …을 정돈하다, …을 정리하다   resist 동 저항하다   determined 형 단단히 결심한   subject 명 주제, 문제   benefit 명 이점   get one's own way 마음대로 하다   lecture 동 강의하다; *잔소리하다

Grammar Tips

사역의 의미를 갖는 동사 get의 목적격보어

동사 get은 사역동사처럼 '…하도록 시키다'라는 의미를 가지지만, 사역동사처럼 목적격보어로 동사원형을 쓰지 않고, to부정사, 현재분사, 과거분사를 목적격보어로 쓴다.

형태	뜻	예시
get + 목적어 + to-v	…가 ~하도록 시키다	I'll **get** him **to lock** the door. (나는 그가 문을 잠그게 할 것이다.)
get + 목적어 + v-ing (목적어와 목적격보어가 능동 관계)	…가 ~하게 하다	He couldn't **get** the car **running**. (그는 차가 달리게 할 수 없었다.)
get + 목적어 + v-ed (목적어와 목적격보어가 수동 관계)	…가 ~되게 하다	She **got** her bike **fixed** yesterday. (그녀는 어제 자전거를 수리받았다.)

구문 분석 Plus

2행
My mother was always trying to get me to **straighten it up**, [*telling* me, "Go clean your room!"]
➡ 동사와 부사로 이루어진 구동사의 목적어로 대명사 it이 오면서, 동사와 부사 사이에 위치함
➡ telling 이하는 '…하면서'의 의미로 동시동작을 나타내는 분사구문 (= as she told ...)

---

03 정답 ② 정답률 63%

정답 풀이

② 관계대명사 vs. 접속사

Many of the manufactured products [made today] contain /
   ↑ 과거분사
오늘날 만들어진 제조 식품 다수가 함유하고 있어서
so many chemicals and artificial ingredients / which (→ that) it
   가주어
너무 많은 화학물질과 인공 재료를
is sometimes difficult {to know exactly / [what is inside them]}.
   진주어   간접의문문(의문사(주어) + 동사)
때로는 정확히 알기가 어렵다   그 안에 무엇이 들어 있는지

➡ 완전하며 결과를 나타내는 절이 뒤에 이어지므로 관계대명사 which를 결과를 나타내는 접속사 that으로 고쳐야 한다.

친절한 오답 풀이

① be used to-v

That phrase **is** often **used to show** the relationship / between
   be used to-v: …하는 데 사용되다   between A and B: A와 B 사이
그 구절은 흔히 관계를 보여주는 데 사용된다
the foods [(which/that) you eat] and your physical health.
   ↑ 목적격 관계대명사 생략
여러분이 먹는 음식과 여러분의 신체 건강 사이의

➡ 「be used to-v」는 '…하는 데 사용되다'라는 의미이고, 먹는 음식과 신체 건강 사이의 '관계를 보여주는 데 사용된다'라는 의미가 적절하므로 to 뒤에 동사원형 show가 오는 것은 어법상 바르다.

③ 형용사적 용법의 to부정사

Food labels are a good way / to find the information / about
   형용사적 용법의 to부정사
식품 라벨은 좋은 방법이다   정보를 알아내는
the foods [(which/that) you eat].
   ↑ 목적격 관계대명사 생략
여러분이 먹는 식품에 관한

➡ 앞의 명사 a good way를 수식하는 형용사적 용법의 to부정사로, 어법상 적절하다.

④ 전치사

Labels on food are like the table of contents / [found in books].
   ↑ 전치사구   전치사   전치사의 목적어   과거분사
식품 라벨은 목차와 같다   책에서 발견되는

➡ 뒤에 전치사의 목적어 역할을 하는 명사구(the table of contents)가 있으므로 전치사 like는 어법상 바르다.

⑤ 동사의 수 일치

The main purpose of food labels / is to inform you / [what is inside
　　주어　　　　　전치사구　　　동사　　　간접의문문(의문사(주어) + 동사)
식품 라벨의 주된 목적은　　　　　여러분에게 알려주는 것이다　식품 안에 무엇이

the food] / [(which/that) you are purchasing].
　　　　　└─────목적격 관계대명사 생략
들어 있는지　　여러분이 구입하고 있는

➡ 문장의 주어는 전치사구(of food labels)의 수식을 받는 The main purpose로
주어가 단수 명사이므로 단수 동사 is가 오는 것이 알맞다.

지문 해석

'당신이 먹는 음식이 바로 당신이다.' 그 구절은 흔히 여러분이 먹는 음식과 여러분의 신체
건강 사이의 관계를 보여주는 데 사용된다. 하지만 여러분은 가공식품, 통조림 식품과
포장 된 식품을 살 때 자신이 무엇을 먹고 있는 것인지 정말 아는가? 오늘날 만들어진
제조 식품 다수가 너무 많은 화학물질과 인공 재료를 함유하고 있어서 때로는 정확히 그
안에 무엇이 들어 있는지 알기가 어렵다. 다행히도, 이제는 식품 라벨이 있다. 식품 라벨은
여러분이 먹는 식품에 관한 정보를 알아내는 좋은 방법이다. 식품 라벨은 책에서 발견되는
목차와 같다. 식품 라벨의 주된 목적은 여러분이 구입하고 있는 식품 안에 무엇이 들어
있는지 여러분에게 알려주는 것이다.

phrase 몡 구절　relationship 몡 관계　physical 혱 신체의　processed food
가공식품　canned food 통조림 식품　chemical 몡 화학물질　artificial 혱 인공
적인　ingredient 몡 재료　food label 식품 (영양 성분) 라벨　inform 통 알리다
purchase 통 구입하다

04　　정답 ④　　정답률 34%

정답 풀이

④ 명사절을 이끄는 접속사

..., I met my wife and son and asked / {that (→ whether/if) they
　　　　　　　　　　　　　　　　동사 asked의 목적어로 쓰인 명사절을 이끄는 접속사
나는 아내와 아들을 만나서 물었다　　　　그들이 아는지

knew / [who was shouting encouragement in the stand]}.
　　　　동사 knew의 목적어로 쓰인 간접의문문(의문사(주어) + 동사)
누가 관중석에서 응원을 외쳤는지

➡ 동사 asked의 목적어로 쓰인 명사절을 이끌고 있고, 그들이 '아는지'라고 해석되므로
접속사 that을 접속사 whether나 if로 바꿔야 한다.

친절한 오답 풀이

① 문장의 동사

[After moving to a new city], / I joined the company baseball team.
접속사가 남아있는 분사구문(= After I moved ...)
새로운 도시로 이사한 후　　　　　　나는 회사 야구팀에 가입했다

➡ 주절의 주어 I의 동사로, 어법상 바르다.

② 수량형용사

During one game, / I made a few mistakes.
전치사(… 동안)　　　　a few: 조금 있는
한 경기 중에　　　나는 약간의 실수를 했다

➡ a few는 '조금 있는'이라는 의미로, 셀 수 있는 명사의 복수형 앞에 쓰인다. 복수 명사
mistakes 앞에 a few가 쓰였으므로 어법상 바르다.

(a) few vs. (a) little

단어	뜻	예시
few + 복수 명사	거의 없는	There were **few** *people* in the library. (도서관에 사람이 거의 없었다.)
a few + 복수 명사	조금 있는	A **few** *cars* were parked on the street. (거리에 차 몇 대가 주차되어 있었다.)
little + 셀 수 없는 명사	거의 없는	There is **little** *money* left. (돈이 거의 남지 않았다.)
a little + 셀 수 없는 명사	조금 있는	I poured a **little** *water* into a bottle. (나는 물을 병에 조금 부었다.)

③ keep v-ing

Then / I kept hearing someone shouting, ...
　　　　keep v-ing: 계속해서 …하다　hear + 목적어 + v-ing: …가 ~하는 것을 듣다
그때　　　나는 어떤 사람이 소리치는 것을 계속 들었다

➡ 동사 kept의 목적어로 쓰인 동명사 hearing은 어법상 바르다.

⑤ 목적격보어로 쓰인 to부정사

I asked / [why he was calling me Mr. Green] / and he replied, /
동사 asked의 목적어로 쓰인 간접의문문(의문사 + 주어 + 동사), call A B: A를 B라고 부르다
나는 물었다　　왜 그가 나를 Green 씨라고 불렀는지　　　그리고 그는 대답했다

"I didn't want anyone to know / [that I'm your son]."
　　want A to-v: A가 …하는 것을 원하다　명사절(목적어)을 이끄는 접속사
저는 다른 사람이 알기를 원하지 않았어요　제가 아빠 아들이라는 것을

➡ want가 5형식 동사로 쓰일 때 to부정사를 목적격보어로 취하므로 to know는 어법상
바르다.

지문 해석

새로운 도시로 이사한 후, 나는 회사 야구팀에 가입했다. 나이가 제일 많은 선수여서, 나는
외야수로 뛰어야 했다. 한 경기 중에, 나는 약간의 실수를 했다. 그때 나는 어떤 사람이
"Green 씨, 잘해요."와 "Green 씨, 당신은 할 수 있어요."라고 소리치는 것을 계속
들었다. 나는 이 낯선 도시에서 누군가가 내 이름을 알고 있다는 것에 대해 놀랐다. 경기
후에, 나는 아내와 아들을 만나서 누가 관중석에서 응원을 외쳤는지를 아는지 물었다.
아들이 소리를 높여 "아버지, 그건 저였어요."라고 말했다. 나는 왜 그가 나를 Green
씨라고 불렀는지 물었고 그는 "저는 다른 사람이 제가 아빠 아들이라는 것을 알기를
원하지 않았어요."라고 대답했다.

play the outfield 외야수 역할을 하다　shout 통 외치다, 소리[고함]치다　way to
go 잘한다, 훌륭해　encouragement 몡 격려　reply 통 대답하다

05　　정답 ③　　정답률 67%

정답 풀이

(A) 명사를 수식하는 과거분사

Or they often teach moral lessons or values / [considered /
　　　　　　　　　　　　　　　　　　　　　　　　　　　　　과거분사
또는 그것들은 종종 도덕적 교훈이나 가치를 가르친다　　　　사회에서 중요하다고 여겨지는

considering important in a society] / and are also used to send
　　　　　　　　　　　　　　　　　be used to-v: …하는 데 사용되다
　　　　　　　　　　　　　　　　　그리고 또한 정치적 메시지를 전달하는 데

political messages / or draw attention to social issues.
　　　　　　　　　　　　　　…에 관심을 끌어들이다
사용된다　　　　또는 사회 문제에 관심을 끌어들이는 데

➡ 네모는 앞의 명사를 수식하는 분사로, 도덕적 교훈이나 가치가 중요하다고 '여겨지는' 것으로 수동의 의미를 나타내는 과거분사 considered가 오는 것이 적절하다. 동사 consider는 타동사로, 능동태로 쓰일 경우 뒤에 목적어가 필요하므로 현재분사는 적절하지 않다.

(B) 부사절을 이끄는 종속접속사

Yet the question is posed / [~~which~~ / whether the arts should
하지만 문제가 제기된다   접속사
         예술이 사회의 기준들을 반영해야 하는지
reflect society's standards / or question them].
         아니면 그것들에 대해 의문을 가져야 하는지

➡ 문장의 부사절을 이끌고 있고, '…인지'라고 해석되므로 접속사 whether가 오는 것이 적절하다. 뒤에 완전한 절이 이어지므로 관계대명사 which는 적절하지 않다.

(C) 접속사 vs. 전치사

It is ~~because~~ / because of their communicative properties that
It is ... that 강조구문, 전치사구(because of ... properties) 강조
바로 그것의 소통적 특성 때문이다
intense debates continue / over the true role of the arts in today's
격렬한 논쟁이 계속되는 것은   오늘날의 세계에서 예술의 진정한 역할에 대해
world.

➡ 뒤에 목적어 역할을 하는 명사구(their communicative properties)가 이어지므로 전치사 because of가 오는 것이 적절하다.

지문 해석

의심할 여지 없이, 예술은 어떤 사회에서나 중요한 역할을 한다. 그것들은 사건이나 개인을 기념하는 데 쓰일 수 있다. 또는 그것들은 종종 사회에서 중요하다고 여겨지는 도덕적 교훈이나 가치를 가르치고 정치적 메시지를 전달하거나 사회 문제에 관심을 끌어들이는 데 사용된다. 하지만 예술이 사회의 기준들을 반영해야 하는지 아니면 그것들에 대해 의문을 가져야 하는지 문제가 제기된다. 예술과 예술가는 또한 엘리트주의라는, 보통 사람들의 마음을 끄는 예술을 만들어 내지 않는 것에 대해 신랄하게 비난받는다. 오늘날의 세계에서 예술의 진정한 역할에 대해 격렬한 논쟁이 계속되는 것은 바로 예술의 소통적 특성 때문이다.

unquestionably ⒝ 의심할 여지 없이   play a role in …에서 역할을 하다
significant ⒣ 중대한   commemorate ⒯ 기념하다   moral ⒣ 도덕적인   lesson
⒨ 수업; *교훈   political ⒣ 정치적인   social issue 사회 문제   reflect ⒯
반사하다; *반영하다   standard ⒨ 기준   criticize ⒯ 비판[비난]하다   elitist ⒣
엘리트주의의   appeal ⒯ 호소하다; *관심을 끌다   ordinary ⒣ 보통의
communicative ⒣ 통신의; *소통의   property ⒨ 재산; *특성   intense ⒣ 극심한,
강렬한   debate ⒨ 토론; *논쟁

06   정답 ④   정답률 51%

정답 풀이

④ 접속사 vs. 전치사

The dummy's job is to simulate a human being / while(→ during)
      명사적 용법의 to부정사(보어)   접속사   전치사
마네킹의 임무는 인간을 모방하는 것이다   충돌하는 동안
                 주격 관계대명사
a crash, / {collecting data / [that would not be possible to collect /
         동시동작을 나타내는 분사구문(= As it collects ...)
         데이터를 수집하면서   수집하는 것이 가능하지 않을
from a human occupant]}.
인간 탑승자로부터

➡ 뒤에 목적어 역할을 하는 명사(a crash)가 있으므로 접속사 while을 전치사 during으로 고쳐야 한다. 접속사 while 뒤에는 완전한 절이 와야 한다.

① 현재완료 시제

Since the introduction of automotive crash-testing, / the number of
전치사(… 이래로)   the number of + 복수 명사: …의 수
자동차 충돌 시험이 도입된 이후로,   사람들의 수는
people / [killed and injured by motor vehicles] / has decreased in
      과거분사구   많은 나라에서 감소해왔다
      차량으로 죽거나 다친
many countries.

➡ 자동차 충돌 실험 도입 이후 죽거나 다친 사람들의 수가 계속 감소해왔다는 의미이므로, 현재완료 has decreased가 오는 것이 적절하다. 전치사 since는 '… 이래로'라는 의미로, 현재완료 시제와 자주 함께 쓰인다.

② 가주어 진주어 구문

Obviously, it would be ideal / [to have no car crashes].
         가주어   진주어
분명히, 이상적일 것이다   차량 충돌이 발생하지 않는 것이

➡ 앞에 오는 it은 가주어이고, to have 이하가 진주어인 to부정사구로 어법상 바르다.

③ 동사의 수 일치

One of the reasons / [(why) cars have been getting safer] / is [that
주어, one of + 복수 명사: … 중 하나 관계부사 생략   명사절(보어)을 이끄는 접속사
이유 중 하나는   자동차가 더 안전해지고 있는
we can conduct a well-established crash test / with test dummies].
우리가 안정된 충돌 시험을 실시할 수 있다는 것이   충돌 시험용 마네킹들로

➡ 문장의 주어가 「one of + 복수 명사」이므로 단수 동사 is가 오는 것이 알맞다.

⑤ 명사를 수식하는 과거분사

So far, they have provided invaluable data / on [how human
지금까지   전치사(…에 대해) 간접의문문(의문사 + 주어 + 동사)
지금까지, 그들은 귀중한 데이터를 제공해왔다   어떻게 인간의 신체가
bodies react in crashes] / and have contributed greatly
                                contribute to: …에 공헌하다
충돌에서 반응하는지에 대한   그리고 개선된 차량 설계에 크게 공헌해왔다
to improved vehicle design.
    과거분사

➡ 뒤에 오는 명사를 수식하는 분사로, 차량 설계가 '개선된'이라는 수동의 의미이므로 과거분사 improved가 오는 것이 적절하다.

지문 해석

당신이 구매하려는 새 차 혹은 중고 차가 안전하다고 생각하는가? 자동차 충돌 시험이 도입된 이후로, 많은 나라에서 차량으로 죽거나 다친 사람들의 수가 감소해왔다. 분명히, 차량 충돌이 발생하지 않는 것이 이상적일 것이다. 하지만 차량 충돌사고는 현실이며 당신은 생존의 가능성이 최대한 높기를 바란다. 자동차들은 어떻게 점점 더 안전해지고 있는가? 자동차가 더 안전해지고 있는 이유 중 하나는 우리가 충돌 시험용 마네킹들로 안정된 충돌 시험을 실시할 수 있다는 것이다. 마네킹의 임무는 충돌하는 동안 인간 탑승자로부터 수집하는 것이 가능하지 않을 데이터를 수집하면서 인간을 모방하는 것이다. 지금까지, 그들은 어떻게 인간의 신체가 충돌에서 반응하는지에 대한 귀중한 데이터를 제공해왔고 개선된 차량 설계에 크게 공헌해왔다.

vehicle ⒨ 차량, 탈 것   introduction ⒨ 소개; *도입   automotive ⒣ 자동차의
crash ⒨ 충돌 사고   injure ⒯ 부상을 입다[당하다]   ideal ⒣ 이상적인   chance
⒨ 기회; *가능성   survival ⒨ 생존   conduct ⒯ 수행하다   well-established
⒣ 안정된   test dummy 충돌 시험용 마네킹   simulate ⒯ 모방하다   occupant
⒨ 사용자; *(차량 등에) 타고 있는 사람   invaluable ⒣ 귀중한   contribute ⒯
기부하다; *공헌하다

정답 풀이

(A) 부정형용사

When he went on board, / he found / [(that) another / other
go on board: 승선하다　　接속사 생략　another + 단수 명사
그가 배에 탔을 때　　그는 알게 되었다　　또 다른 승객이

passenger was to share the cabin with him].
예정을 나타내는 be to-v(…할 예정이다)
그와 선실을 함께 사용하게 될 것이라는 것을

➡ another 뒤에는 단수 명사가, other 뒤에는 복수 명사가 와야 하는데, 뒤에 단수 명사 (passenger)가 왔으므로 another가 오는 것이 적절하다.

(B) 명사절을 이끄는 종속접속사

After going to see the accommodations, / he came up to the purser's
접속사가 남아있는 분사구문(= After he went …)
숙박시설을 살펴본 후에　　　　그는 선박 사무장의 책상으로 와서 물었다

desk and inquired / [if / that he could leave his valuables / in
接속사(…인지)
그가 자신의 귀중품들을 맡길 수 있는지

the ship's safe.]
배의 금고에

➡ 동사 inquired의 목적어 역할을 하는 명사절을 이끌고 있고, '…인지'의 의미를 나타내므로 접속사 if가 오는 것이 알맞다.

(C) 병렬구조

The purser accepted the responsibility for the valuables / and
주어　　　동사1　　　　　　　　　　　　　　　　接속사
선박의 사무장은 귀중품에 대한 책임을 받아들였다　　　　　그리고 말했다

remarking / remarked, ….
동사2

➡ 등위접속사 and에 의해 문장의 동사가 병렬 연결된 구조로, 앞의 동사 accepted와 대등하도록 and 뒤에 과거형 동사 remarked가 오는 것이 적절하다.

구문 분석 Plus

10행
[Judging from his appearance], he was afraid [that he might not be a very trustworthy person].
➡ Judging 이하는 때를 나타내는 분사구문(= As he judged from his appearance)
➡ that: 감정의 원인을 나타내는 접속사 that

지문 해석

Potter 씨는 가장 큰 대서양 횡단 여객선 중 하나를 타고 유럽으로 가고 있었다. 배에 탔을 때, 그는 또 다른 승객이 자신과 선실을 함께 사용하게 될 것이라는 것을 알게 되었다. 숙박시설을 살펴본 후에, 그는 선박 사무장의 책상으로 와서 자신의 귀중품들을 배의 금고에 맡길 수 있는지를 물었다. Potter 씨는 평소에는 그러한 특권을 전혀 이용하지 않지만, 자신의 선실에 갔었는데 다른 한 쪽 침대를 사용하는 남자를 만났다고 설명했다. 그의 외모로 판단하건대, 그는 그 사람이 그다지 신뢰할 만한 사람이 아닐지도 모른다는 것이 걱정되었다. 선박의 사무장은 귀중품에 대한 책임을 받아들이면서 "괜찮습니다. 손님을 위해서 기꺼이 그것들을 보관해 드리겠습니다. 다른 한 분도 여기에 와서 그와 똑같은 이유로 귀중품들을 맡겨 놓으셨습니다."라고 말했다.

transatlantic 형 대서양 횡단의　**liner** 명 여객선　**passenger** 명 승객　**share** 동 공유하다, 함께 쓰다　**cabin** 명 선실, 객실　**accommodation** 명 숙박시설　**inquire** 동 묻다　**valuables** 명 (pl.) 귀중품　**safe** 명 금고　**ordinarily** 부 평상시에는, 보통　**avail oneself of** …을 이용하다　**privilege** 명 특권　**occupy** 동 차지하다　**appearance** 명 모습, 외모　**trustworthy** 형 신뢰할 수 있는　**accept** 동 받아들이다　**responsibility** 명 책임　**remark** 동 언급[말]하다

정답 풀이

(A) 접속사 vs. 전치사

[Although / Despite various state-law bans and nationwide
전치사(…에도 불구하고)
다양한 주의 금지법과 전국적인 캠페인에도 불구하고

campaigns / to prevent texting from behind the wheel], /
형용사적 용법의 to부정사　　　　　운전 중에
운전 중에 문자 보내는 것을 막는

the number of people / {texting [while (they are) driving]} /
the number of + 복수 명사: …의 수　현재분사　接속사　「주어 + 동사」 생략
사람들의 수는　　　　　　운전하는 도중에 문자를 보내는

is actually on the rise, ….
be on the rise: 증가하다
실제로 증가하고 있다

➡ 뒤에 목적어 역할을 하는 명사구(various … campaigns)가 있으므로 전치사 Despite가 오는 것이 적절하다. Although는 접속사로 뒤에 완전한 절이 와야 한다.

(B) 동사의 수 일치

According to the Traffic Safety Administration (TSA), / the
전치사(…에 따르면)
교통안전국(TSA)에 의하면

percentage of drivers / {who send texts and use mobile devices /
주어　　　　　　　　　주격 관계대명사
운전자의 비율은　　　　　문자를 보내고 모바일 기기를 사용하는

[while (they are) on the road]} / have / has jumped from 0.6% in
接속사　주어 + 동사 생략　　　　　동사　from A to B: A에서 B까지
운전 중에　　　　　　　　　　　　　　　　2009년 0.6%에서 2010년 0.9%로 급증했다

2009 to 0.9% in 2010.

➡ 주어가 단수 명사 the percentage이므로 단수 동사 has가 오는 것이 적절하다.

(C) 목적격보어

In fact, the Safety Board is working / to make cellphone use from
make + 목적어 + 형용사: …을 ~하게 만들다
사실, 안전위원회는 작업 중이다　　　　　핸즈프리로 대화하는 것부터

talking hands-free to texting illegal / illegally / in all states.
from A to B: A에서 B까지　　　　　　동사 make의 목적격보어
문자 보내기에 이르기까지의 휴대전화 사용을 불법으로 만들기 위해　모든 주에서

➡ 동사 make의 목적격보어의 자리이므로, 형용사 illegal이 오는 것이 어법상 적절하다. 부사는 보어의 자리에 올 수 없다.

구문 분석 Plus

13행
The TSA said {that drivers [using mobile devices in any situation] are four times more likely to have an accident …}.
➡ that: said의 목적어 역할을 하는 명사절을 이끄는 접속사
➡ using 이하는 앞의 명사 drivers를 수식하는 현재분사구
➡ be likely to-v: …하기 쉽다, …할 가능성이 높다

지문 해석

운전 중에 문자 보내는 것을 막는 다양한 주의 금지법과 전국적인 캠페인에도 불구하고, 운전하는 도중에 문자를 보내는 사람들의 수는 실제로 증가하고 있다고, 새로운 연구는 주장한다. 교통안전국(TSA)에 의하면, 운전 중에 문자를 보내고 모바일 기기를 사용하는 운전자의 비율은 2009년 0.6%에서 2010년 0.9%로 급증했다. 자동차 제작자와 입법자들이 주의가 산만한 운전의 위험성에 대한 의식을 좀 더 높이려고 할 때 이 뉴스가 나온다. 사실 안전위원회는 모든 주에서 핸즈프리로 대화하는 것부터 문자 보내기에 이르기까지의 휴대전화 사용을 불법으로 만들기 위해 작업 중이다. 교통안전국에서는 어떤 상황에서든 휴대기기를 사용하는 운전자들이 사고를 내고 자신이나 타인을 다치게 할 가능성이 4배나 높다고 말했다.

어휘

state-law 명 주의 법   ban 명 금지(법)   nationwide 형 전국적인
administration 명 행정부   percentage 명 백분율, 퍼센트; *비율   device 명 장치,
기구   jump 동 뛰다; *급증하다   automaker 명 자동차 제작자   lawmaker 명
입법자   awareness 명 의식, 관심   distract 동 주의를 산만하게 하다   board 명
판자; *위원회   hands-free 형 손을 쓰지 않고 이용할 수 있는   illegal 형 불법적인

4 문장 구조

UNIT 1 문장의 구조

코드 접속하기   pp.77~80

출제코드 1   문장의 동사

A **1** allows **2** improve **3** is
B **1** ➡ erupted **2** ○ **3** ➡ tend

해석과 정답 풀이

STEP 1
1 1) 다행히, 그녀는 의사가 되었다.
    2) 경찰은 학생들의 가방을 훔친 도둑을 체포했다.
2 1) 나의 연필이 없어졌다.
    2) 그들은 아주 화가 나 보일지도 모른다.
    3) 그는 기타 치는 것을 즐긴다.
    4) 나는 Carl 씨에게 엽서 몇 장을 보냈다.
    5) 우리 부모님은 내가 더 빨리 오기를 원하셨다.

STEP 2
1 1) 최고의 요리는 볶음밥인 것으로 드러났다.
    2) 그녀는 사회적 이슈를 둘러싼 문제는 그들의 문화적 민감함이라고 말했다.
    3) 우리를 살아있고 활동적이게 하는 산소는 연소할 때 부산물을 내보낸다.

STEP 3
A **1** 챔피언이 되려는 그의 투지는 그가 우승을 하게 한다.
    ➡ 주어는 to부정사구(to be a champion)의 수식을 받는 명사 His determination
     으로, 뒤에 문장의 동사가 와야 하므로 allows가 오는 것이 알맞다.
  2 신문을 자주 읽는 사람들은 그들의 읽기 능력을 향상시킨다.
    ➡ 주어는 주격 관계대명사절(who ... newspaper)의 수식을 받는 People로, 뒤에
     동사가 와야 하므로 improve가 알맞다.
  3 사실, 당신이 게시한 모든 것들은 인터넷에서 모든 사람들이 볼 수 있다.
    ➡ 주어는 목적격 관계대명사절((that) you posted)의 수식을 받는 everything으로,
     뒤에 동사 is가 와야 한다.
B **1** 그 화산이 너무 강력하게 폭발해서 사람들이 놀랐다.
    ➡ 주어는 The volcano이고 so 이하는 부사절로, 문장의 동사가 없으므로
     erupting을 동사 erupted로 고쳐야 한다.
  2 갑자기, 내가 신문에서 한 번 읽었던 구절이 내 마음 속에 떠올랐다.
    ➡ 주어는 목적격 관계대명사절((which/that) I ... newspaper)의 수식을 받는
     a phrase이고 came은 동사로 어법상 바르다.
  3 엄마들은 그들의 아이가 울기 시작하면 어떤 상황에서도 즉각 반응하는 경향이 있다.
    ➡ 주어 Mothers에 대한 동사가 없으므로 tending을 동사 tend로 고쳐야 한다.

출제코드 2   병렬구조

A **1** try **2** making **3** healthy
B **1** ➡ eating **2** ➡ changed **3** ➡ playing

해석과 정답 풀이

STEP 1
1 1) 나는 음악을 듣는 것이 우리가 일에 집중하도록 돕는지 아니면 방해하는지
     궁금하다.
    2) Hailey는 책 읽기와 이야기 쓰기를 모두 좋아한다.
2 1) 수진이는 나에게 컵케이크를 주고 집으로 돌아갔다.
    2) 그는 교통사고가 났지만 꽤 침착했다.
3 1) *Harry Potter*는 소설로서 뿐만 아니라 영화로서도 큰 성공을 거뒀다.
    2) 문제는 언제 자느냐가 아니라 어디서 자느냐이다.

STEP 2
1 1) 그는 큰 바구니로 달려가 그것을 자신 위로 뒤집어 썼다.
   2) 이 살균제는 세균을 없앨 뿐만 아니라 좋은 향이 난다.
2 우리는 식당을 개조하고 새로운 메뉴를 개발하는 것에 대해 생각해야 한다.
3 나는 그가 밤새 일한 후 지치고 약해진 것을 알아챘다.

STEP 3
A 1 당신이 가지지 않은 것에 대해 생각하는 것을 멈추고 스스로 해결책을 찾으려고
     노력해라.
   ➡ 등위접속사 and가 명령문의 동사를 병렬 연결하고 있으므로, 동사 Stop과
     대등하도록 동사원형 try가 오는 것이 알맞다.
   2 인공지능이 악기를 연주하고 음악을 만드는 것이 가능해졌다.
   ➡ 등위접속사 and가 전치사 of의 목적어인 동명사를 병렬 연결하고 있으므로,
     playing과 대등하도록 동명사 making이 오는 것이 알맞다.
   3 그 캠프장은 울창한 숲으로 둘러싸여 있고, 신선한 공기는 우리가 활동적이고
     건강하게 해준다.
   ➡ 등위접속사 and가 동사 keeps의 목적격보어를 병렬 연결하고 있으므로, 형용사
     energetic과 대등하도록 형용사 healthy가 오는 것이 알맞다.
B 1 잘 자고 규칙적으로 식사를 하는 것은 당신의 기분이 나아지게 할 것이다.
   ➡ 등위접속사 and가 문장의 주어로 쓰인 동명사를 병렬 연결하고 있으므로,
     Sleeping과 대등하도록 동사 eat을 동명사 eating으로 고쳐야 한다.
   2 기후 변화는 몇몇 바다 물고기들을 멸종시켰을 뿐만 아니라 해양 생태계를
     변화시켰다.
   ➡ 상관접속사 not only A but also B에 의해 문장의 동사가 병렬 연결되어
     있으므로, 동사 wiped와 대등하도록 to change를 changed로 고쳐야 한다.
   3 밴드에 가입하고 공연에서 연주하기 전에, Dan은 그의 오래된 기타를 바꾸길
     원했다.
   ➡ 등위접속사 and가 전치사 Before의 목적어인 동명사를 병렬 연결하고 있으므로,
     joining과 대등하도록 played를 동명사 playing으로 고쳐야 한다.

기출예제 Q1　　정답 ④　　정답률 51%

정답 풀이
④ 문장의 동사

> {Thinking of himself as a boy [who is smart and knows how to
> 　주어(동명사구)　　　　　　　　　　↑　주격 관계대명사
> 스스로를 똑똑하고 일을 어떻게 하는지 아는 소년으로 생각하는 것은
> do things]} / being(→ is) likely to make him endure longer in
> 　　　　　　　　　　　make + 목적어 + 동사원형: …가 ~하게 하다
> 　　　　　　　　　그가 문제 해결 노력에 있어 더 오래 지속하도록 할 가능성이 높다
> problem-solving efforts / and (to) increase his confidence in
> 　　　　　　　　　　　　　　　to make와 병렬 연결됨
> 　　　　　　　　　　그리고 새롭고 어려운 일을 시도하는 것에 있어
> trying new and difficult tasks.
> 동명사(전치사 in의 목적어)
> 그의 자신감을 증가시킬 (가능성이 높다)

➡ 문장의 주어는 동명사구 Thinking of ... do things이다. 이 주어에 상응하는 동사가
와야 하며 동명사구는 단수 취급하므로 is로 고쳐야 한다.

친절한 오답 풀이
① 대명사

> Preschoolers believe / [what their parents tell them] in a very
> 　주어　　　　동사　　관계대명사
> 미취학 아동들은 생각한다　　그들의 부모가 그들에게 하는 말을 매우 뜻깊게
> profound way.

➡ them은 앞의 Preschoolers를 지칭하는 대명사이다. 지칭하는 명사가 3인칭
복수이므로 복수 대명사 them은 어법상 알맞다.

② 부사

> They do not yet have the cognitive sophistication / to reason
> 　　　　　　　　　　　　　　　　　　　　　↑
> 　　　　　　　　　　　　　　　　　　　　　형용사적 용법의
> 　　　　　　　　　　　　　　　　　　　　　to부정사
> 그들은 인지적 정교함을 아직 가지고 있지 않다　　　분석적으로 추론하고
> analytically and (to) reject false information.
> 　　　　　　to reason과 병렬 연결됨
> 잘못된 정보를 거부할 수 있는

➡ 부사 analytically는 동사의 성질을 지닌 준동사인 to부정사 to reason을 수식하고
있으므로 어법상 알맞다.

③ 접속사

> {If a preschool boy consistently hears from his mother / [that he
> 접속사　　　　　　　　　　　　　　　　　　　　　명사절을 이끄는 접속사
> 만약 미취학 소년이 그의 어머니로부터 계속 듣는다면　　　　　그가
> is smart and a good helper]}, / he is likely to incorporate that
> 　　　　　　　　　　　　　　　be likely to-v: …할 가능성이 높다
> 똑똑하고 좋은 조력자라는 것을　　그는 그 정보를 그의 자아상으로 통합시킬 가능성이 높다
> information into his self-image.

➡ 동사 hears의 목적어 역할을 하는 명사절을 이끌고 있으므로 접속사 that은 어법상
알맞다.

⑤ 명사적 용법의 to부정사

> Similarly, / {thinking of himself as the kind of boy [who is a
> 　　　　　　주어(동명사구)　　　　　　　　↑　주격 관계대명사
> 마찬가지로　　자신을 좋은 조력자인 그런 부류의 소년으로 생각하는 것은
> good helper]} / will make him more likely to volunteer / to help
> 　　　　　　　make + 목적어 + 형용사: …을 ~하게 만들다　　volunteer의 목적어
> 　　　　　　　그가 자발적으로 할 가능성을 더 크게 만들 것이다　역할을 하는 to부정사
> with tasks at home and at preschool.
> 집에서 그리고 유치원에서 일을 돕는 것을

➡ 동사 volunteer는 to부정사를 목적어로 취하므로 to help는 어법상 알맞다.

지문 해석

칭찬은 어린 아이들의 행동을 개선하는 데 사용할 수 있는 가장 강력한 도구 중
하나이지만, 그것은 아이의 자존감을 향상시키는 데에도 똑같이 강력하다. 미취학
아동들은 그들의 부모가 그들에게 하는 말을 매우 뜻깊게 여긴다. 그들은 분석적으로
추론하고 잘못된 정보를 거부할 수 있는 인지적 정교함을 아직 가지고 있지 않다. 만약
미취학 소년이 그의 어머니로부터 그가 똑똑하고 좋은 조력자라는 것을 계속 듣는다면,
그는 그 정보를 그의 자아상으로 통합시킬 가능성이 높다. 스스로를 똑똑하고 일을 어떻게
하는지 아는 소년으로 생각하는 것은 그가 문제 해결 노력에 있어 더 오래 지속하도록
하고 새롭고 어려운 일을 시도하는 것에 있어 그의 자신감을 증가시킬 가능성이 높다.
마찬가지로, 자신을 좋은 조력자인 그런 부류의 소년으로 생각하는 것은 그가 집에서와
유치원에서 일을 자발적으로 돕게 할 가능성을 더 크게 만들 것이다.

praise 명 칭찬　self-esteem 명 자부심, 자존감　preschooler 명 취학 전의 아동
cognitive 형 인식[인지]의　reason 동 추론하다　analytically 부 분석적으로
false 형 틀린, 사실이 아닌　consistently 부 일관하여, 지속적으로　incorporate
동 통합시키다　endure 동 견디다, 참다　volunteer 동 자진하여 하다

정답 풀이

⑤ 병렬구조

The existence of Stonehenge, / [(which was) built by people
　　　　주어　　　　　　　　　　　　　　　　과거분사(수동)
스톤헨지의 존재는　　　　　　　　　　　글이 없던 시절 사람들이 세운

without writing], / bears silent testimony / both to the regularity
　　　　　　　　　　동사　　　　　　　　both A and B: A와 B 둘 다
말없이 증언해 준다　　　　　　　　　자연의 규칙성뿐만 아니라

of nature / and to the ability of the human mind / to see behind
　　　　　　　　　　　　　　　　　　　　　　　　형용사적 용법의
　　　　　　　　　　　　　　　　　　　　　　　　to부정사
인간의 정신적 능력을　　　　　　　　　　　눈앞에 보이는 모습의

immediate appearances / and (to) discovers(→ discover) deeper
이면을 보고　　　　　　사건에서 더 깊은 의미를 발견하는

meanings in events.

→ 등위접속사 and가 형용사적 용법의 to부정사인 to see와 (to) discover를 병렬 연결하고 있는 구조이므로, discovers를 discover로 고쳐야 한다.

친절한 오답 풀이

① 대명사

Early astronomy provided information / about when to plant crops /
　　　　　　　　　동사1　　　　　　　　　　when to-v: 언제 …할지
초기 천문학은 정보를 제공했다　　　　　　언제 작물을 심어야 하는지에 대한

and gave humans / their first formal method / of recording the
　　동사2
그리고 인간에게 주었다　　그들 최초의 공식적인 방법을　　시간의 흐름을 기록하는

passage of time.

→ 복수 명사인 humans의 소유격 대명사이므로, their는 어법상 알맞다.

② 동사의 수 일치

Stonehenge, the 4,000-year-old ring of stones in southern Britain, /
　　주어　└──동격──┘
영국 남부에 있는 4,000년 된 고리 모양을 하고 있는 스톤헨지는

is perhaps the best-known monument / to the discovery of
동사
아마도 가장 잘 알려진 기념비일 것이다　　　규칙성과 예측 가능성을 발견한

regularity and predictability / in the world [(which/that) we
　　　　　　　　　　　　　　　　　　　　　목적격 관계대명사 생략
우리가 살고 있는 세계에서

inhabit].

→ Stonehenge, the 4,000-year-old ring of stones in southern Britain에서 the 4,000-year-old 이하는 주어 Stonehenge를 부연 설명하는 동격어구이므로, 단수 동사 is는 어법상 알맞다.

③ 관계부사

The great markers of Stonehenge / point to the spots on the
　　　　　　　　　　　　　　　　　　　　　선행사
스톤헨지의 커다란 표식은　　　　　　지평선의 장소를 가리킨다

horizon / [where the sun rises at the solstices and equinoxes] — /
　　　　　관계부사
　　　　　지점과 분점에서 태양이 뜨는

the dates [(which/that) we still use / to mark the beginnings of
　　　　　└──────┘목적격 관계대명사 생략　부사적 용법의 to부정사(목적)
우리가 여전히 사용하는 날짜인　　　　　계절의 시작을 표시하기 위해

the seasons].

→ the spots가 장소 역할을 하는 선행사이고, 뒤에 완전한 절이 왔으므로, 관계부사 where는 어법상 바르다.

④ 능동태 vs. 수동태

The stones may even have been used / to predict eclipses.
　　　　　may have v-ed: …이었을지도 모른다　부사적 용법의 to부정사(목적)
그 돌들은 심지어 사용되었을지도 모른다　　(해·달의) 식을 예측하는 데

→ The stones는 use의 행위를 당하는 대상이므로 수동태를 써야 한다. 따라서, 현재 완료 수동태 형태인 have been v-ed의 been used는 어법상 알맞다.

 구문 분석 Plus

> 1행
>
> Most historians of science point to the need for a reliable calendar **to regulate** agricultural activity as the motivation for learning about [*what* we now call astronomy, the study of stars and planets].
>
> → to regulate: 앞에 있는 명사구 a reliable calendar를 수식하는 형용사적 용법의 to부정사
> → what: 전치사 about의 목적어 역할을 하는 명사절을 이끌면서 선행사를 포함하는 관계대명사

지문 해석

대부분의 과학 역사가들은 별과 행성에 대한 연구, 즉 우리가 현재 천문학이라 부르는 것에 대해 배우고자 하는 동기로 농업 활동을 규제하기 위한 신뢰할 만한 달력의 필요성을 지적한다. 초기 천문학은 언제 작물을 심어야 하는지에 대한 정보를 제공했고 인간에게 시간의 흐름을 기록하는 그들 최초의 공식적인 방법을 제공했다. 영국 남부에 있는 4,000년 된 고리 모양을 하고 있는 돌들인 스톤헨지는 아마도 우리가 살고 있는 세계에서 규칙성과 예측 가능성을 발견한 가장 잘 알려진 기념비일 것이다. 스톤헨지의 커다란 표식은 우리가 계절의 시작을 표시하기 위해 여전히 사용하는 날짜인 지점(至點)과 분점(分點)에서 태양이 뜨는 지평선의 장소를 가리킨다. 그 돌들은 심지어 (해·달의) 식(蝕)을 예측하는 데 사용되었을지도 모른다. 글이 없던 시절 사람들이 세운 스톤헨지의 존재는 자연의 규칙성뿐만 아니라 눈앞에 보이는 모습의 이면을 보고 사건에서 더 깊은 의미를 발견할 수 있는 인간의 정신적 능력을 말없이 증언해 준다.

어휘

reliable 형 믿을 만한　regulate 동 규제하다　agricultural 형 농업의　motivation 명 동기　astronomy 명 천문학　plant 동 심다　formal 형 공식적인　passage 명 흐름　regularity 명 규칙성　predictability 명 예측 가능성　inhabit 동 살다　horizon 명 수평선, 지평선　solstice 명 지점(至點)(태양이 적도로부터 북쪽 또는 남쪽으로 가장 치우쳤을 때)　equinox 명 분점(分點)　bear testimony to …에 대하여 증언[증명]하다　immediate 형 눈앞에 있는

코드 공략하기 01　　　　　　　pp.81~83

01 ④　02 ④　03 ③　04 ③　05 ④　06 ③　07 ④　08 ⑤
09 ②　10 ③

정답 풀이

④ 문장의 동사

People in today's fast-paced society engaging(→ engage) in this /
　　주어　　　　　　전치사구　　　　　　　동사, engage in: …에 참여하다
오늘날의 빠르게 돌아가는 사회의 사람들은 이것에 참여하고 있다

either for necessity or for entertainment.
either A or B: A 또는 B 둘 중 하나
필요에 의해서든 즐거움을 위해서든

→ People이 주어이고 in … society는 주어를 수식하는 전치사구로, 뒤에 문장의 동사가 와야 하므로 준동사 engaging을 동사 engage로 고쳐야 한다.

친절한 오답 풀이

① 주격 관계대명사

This is a method [that has been used for a long time] / and is
　　　　└──┘ 주격 관계대명사
이것은 오랫동안 사용되어 온 방법이다

possibly the longest method / of food searching, ...
그리고 아마도 가장 오래된 방법이다　　식량을 찾는

➡ that은 앞의 명사 a method를 수식하는 관계대명사절에서 주어 역할을 하는 주격 관계대명사로 어법상 바르다.

② 수동태

> In the past, people commonly foraged for food / in forests,
> 과거에는, 사람들이 보통 식량을 찾아다녔다　　　　　　　　　숲,
> riversides, caves, and virtually any place / [where food could
> 　　　　　　　　　　　　　　　　　　　　　　　관계부사
> 강가, 동굴, 그리고 거의 모든 곳에서　　　　　아마도 식량이 발견될 수 있는
> possibly be found].

➡ 관계부사 where가 이끄는 절의 주어는 food로, 음식이 '발견되는'이라는 수동의 의미이므로 수동태 be found가 오는 것이 어법상 바르다.

③ 동사의 수 일치

> Most of the foods [foraged before] / were root crops, weeds,
> most of: …의 대부분 ↑　　　과거분사
> 예전에 찾은 식량의 대부분은　　　　　　뿌리작물, 잡초,
> shrubs, and many more.
> 관목, 그리고 더 많은 것들이었다

➡ 「부분을 나타내는 말(most, some 등) + of + 명사」가 주어일 경우, of 뒤에 나오는 명사에 동사의 수를 일치시킨다. 이 문장에서 Most of 뒤에 복수 명사 the foods가 왔으므로 복수 동사 were가 오는 것이 알맞다.

⑤ 「find + 목적어 + 형용사」

> More and more people / find it quite a fulfilling task and very
> 비교급 + and + 비교급: 점점 더 …한　동사　목적어　　목적격보어1　　접속사
> 점점 더 많은 사람들이　　　　　그것이 꽤 성취감을 주는 일이고 매우 유익하다고 생각한다
> beneficial.
> 목적격보어2

➡ 동사 find의 목적격보어로 쓰인 명사구(a fulfilling task)와 형용사(beneficial)가 접속사 and로 연결되어 있는 구조로, 보어 자리에는 명사와 형용사가 모두 올 수 있으므로 형용사 beneficial은 어법상 바르다.

지문 해석

식량을 찾아다니는 것은 야생의 식량 자원을 탐색하는 수단이다. 이것은 오랫동안 사용되어 온 방법이고, 수천 년 전으로 거슬러 올라가는 아마도 가장 오래된 식량을 찾는 방법이다. 과거에는 사람들이 보통 숲, 강가, 동굴, 그리고 아마도 식량이 발견될 수 있는 거의 모든 곳에서 식량을 찾아다녔다. 예전에 찾은 식량의 대부분은 뿌리작물, 잡초, 관목 그리고 더 많은 것들이었다. 이제는 식량을 찾아다니는 것이 떠오르는 추세가 되었다. 오늘날의 빠르게 돌아가는 사회의 사람들은 필요에 의해서든 즐거움을 위해서든 이것에 참여하고 있다. 그 목적이 무엇이든 간에, 사람들은 이제 식량을 찾아다니는 것에 느리지만 확실하게 친숙해지고 있다. 점점 더 많은 사람들이 그것이 꽤 성취감을 주는 일이고 매우 유익하다고 생각한다.

means 몡 수단, 방법　resource 몡 자원　possibly 뷔 아마　trace back to …로 거슬러 올라가다　cave 몡 동굴　virtually 뷔 사실상, 거의　weed 몡 잡초　shrub 몡 관목　fast-paced 혱 빠르게 진행되는　necessity 몡 필요　acquainted with …을 잘 알고 있는　fulfilling 혱 성취감을 주는　beneficial 혱 유익한

정답 풀이

④ 병렬구조

> Gradually, these simple reminder notes allowed Greg to have a
> 　　　　　　　　　　　　　　　　　allow A to-v: A가 …하는 것을 허용하다　목적격보어1
> 점차, 이런 단순한 상기시키는 쪽지는 Greg이 다른 관점을 가지게 했다
> different point of view / and realized(→ to realize) /
> 　　　　　　　　　　接속사　　　목적격보어2
> 　　　　　　　　　　그리고 깨닫게 했다
> [that he didn't have to be perfect / at everything].
> 명사절(목적어)을 이끄는 접속사
> 그가 완벽할 필요가 없다는 것을　　　　　모든 것에

➡ 등위접속사 and가 동사 allowed의 목적격보어를 병렬 연결하고 있으므로, to have와 대등하도록 realized를 to realize로 고쳐야 한다.

┃친절한 오답 풀이┃

① 목적격보어로 쓰인 현재분사

> A grade of 95 left him asking, / "How did I fail to achieve 100?"
> 　　　　　　　　동사 목적어 목적격보어
> 95점의 점수는 그가 묻게 했다　　　　"어떻게 내가 100점을 받지 못했을까?"

➡ asking은 동사 left의 목적격보어로 쓰인 분사로, 목적어인 him과 능동 관계이므로 현재분사 asking이 오는 것이 알맞다.

② 명사적 용법의 to부정사

> He decided to work on stress management.
> 　　　　　　work on …에 착수하다
> 그는 스트레스 관리를 시작하기로 마음먹었다

➡ to work는 동사 decided의 목적어로 쓰인 명사적 용법의 to부정사로 어법상 바르다.

③ 「전치사 + 동명사」

> He came up with the creative idea / of posting notes everywhere
> come up with: …을 생각해내다　　　동격
> 그는 독창적인 아이디어를 생각해냈다　사방에 간단한 메시지를 담은 쪽지를 붙여놓는
> with the simple message, / "92 is still an A."
> 　　　　　　　　　　　　　"92점도 여전히 A이다."

➡ 앞에 전치사 of가 쓰였으므로, 전치사의 목적어 역할을 하는 동명사 posting이 오는 것이 알맞다.

⑤ 비교급 강조 부사

> He still could earn an "A" in class, / but with **much** less pressure.
> 　　　　　　　　　　　　　　　　　　　　　　　↑ little의 비교급
> 그는 여전히 수업에서 'A'를 받을 수 있었다　그러나 훨씬 더 적은 압박을 받으면서

➡ much는 뒤에 오는 비교급 less를 수식하여 비교의 의미를 강조하는 부사로, 어법상 바르다.

 Grammar Tips

> **비교급을 강조하는 부사**
>
> much, even, far, still, a lot 등의 부사는 '훨씬 더 …한'의 의미로 뒤에 나오는 비교급을 수식하여 비교의 의미를 강조한다. 단, very는 비교급을 수식할 수 없다.

지문 해석

Greg은 모든 개별 과제에서 만점을 받지 못하면 실패자처럼 느꼈다. 95점의 점수는 그가 "어떻게 내가 100점을 받지 못했을까?"라고 묻게 했다. Greg은 완벽주의에 대한 자신의 욕구가 자신을 지속적인 스트레스 상태로 몰아넣고 있다는 것을 깨달았다. 그는 스트레스 관리를 시작하기로 마음먹었다. 그는 "92점도 여전히 A이다."라는 간단한 메시지를 담은 쪽지를 사방에 붙여놓는 독창적인 아이디어를 생각해냈다. 점차, 이런 단순한 상기시키는 쪽지는 Greg이 다른 관점을 가지게 했고 모든 것에 완벽할 필요가 없다는 것을 깨닫게

했다. 그는 여전히 수업에서 'A'를 받을 수 있었지만, 훨씬 더 적은 압박을 받았다.

feel like …처럼 느끼다   failure 명 실패; *실패자   assignment 명 과제   drive
명 운전; *욕구   perfectionism 명 완벽주의   state 명 상태   constant 형
지속적인   creative 형 창의적인   gradually 부 점차   reminder 명 생각나게 하는
것   point of view 관점   pressure 명 압박(감)

03   정답 ③   정답률 75%

정답 풀이

③ 병렬구조

> ┌──비교급 수식
> But a human is much more capable / of operating those instruments
> be capable of: …할 수 있다   전치사의 목적어1
> 하지만 인간은 훨씬 더 잘할 수 있다   그런 도구들을 바르게 작동하는 것을
> correctly / and to place(→ placing) them in appropriate and useful
> 등위접속사   전치사의 목적어2
> 그리고 그것들을 적절하고 유용한 위치에 설치하는 것을
> positions.

➡ 등위접속사 and가 전치사 of의 목적어인 동명사를 병렬 연결하고 있으므로, operating과 대등하도록 to place를 동명사 placing으로 고쳐야 한다.

▌친절한 오답 풀이▐

① 부정대명사

> [While manned space missions are more costly than unmanned
> 과거분사 └──────────────┘
> 유인 우주 비행이 무인 우주 비행보다 비용이 더 많이 들기는 하지만
> ones], / they are more successful.
> 그것들은 더 성공적이다

➡ 앞에 나온 복수 명사 space missions를 대신하므로, 복수형 부정대명사 ones가 오는 것이 알맞다.

② 대명사 much

> Robots and astronauts / use much of the same equipment in space.
> 주어   동사   목적어
> 로봇과 우주 비행사는   우주 공간에서 대부분 똑같은 장비를 사용한다

➡ much of 뒤에는 셀 수 없는 명사가 오고, many of 뒤에는 셀 수 있는 명사의 복수형이 와야 한다. 밑줄 친 much 뒤에 of와 셀 수 없는 명사 equipment가 쓰였으므로 much는 어법상 바르다.

④ 동사의 수 일치

> Rarely is a computer more sensitive and accurate than a human /
> 부정부사 동사   주어   주격보어
> 컴퓨터는 인간보다 더 민감하지도 정확하지도 않다
> in managing the same geographical or environmental factors.
> 동일한 지역적인 혹은 환경적인 요소들을 관리하는 데 있어서

➡ 부정의 의미를 나타내는 부사 Rarely가 문장의 앞으로 나와 주어와 동사의 도치가 일어난 구문으로, 주어(a computer)가 단수 명사이므로 단수 동사 is가 오는 것이 알맞다.

⑤ 접속사

> Robots are also not equipped with capabilities like humans / to
> be equipped with: …을 갖추고 있다 └──────────────
> 로봇은 또한 인간처럼 능력을 갖추고 있지 않다
> solve problems / [as they arise], / and they often collect data /
> 형용사적   접속사(…할 때) = problems   = robots   선행사
> 용법의 to부정사
> 문제를 해결할   그것이 발생할 때   그리고 그들은 종종 자료를 수집한다
> [that are unhelpful or irrelevant].
> 주격 관계대명사
> 도움이 안 되거나 상관없는

➡ 뒤에 완전한 절이 이어지고 있으므로 접속사 as는 어법상 바르다.

지문 해석

유인 우주 비행이 무인 우주 비행보다 비용이 더 많이 들기는 하지만, 그것들은 더 성공적이다. 로봇과 우주 비행사는 우주 공간에서 대부분 똑같은 장비를 사용한다. 하지만 인간은 그런 도구들을 바르게 작동하고 그것들을 적절하고 유용한 위치에 설치하는 것을 훨씬 더 잘할 수 있다. 컴퓨터는 동일한 지역적인 혹은 환경적인 요소들을 관리하는 데 있어서 인간보다 더 민감하지도 정확하지도 않다. 로봇은 또한 인간처럼 문제가 발생할 때 그것을 해결할 능력을 갖추고 있지 않으며, 종종 도움이 안 되거나 상관없는 자료를 수집한다.

manned 형 유인의, 사람이 탑승한 (unmanned 형 무인의)   costly 형 많은 비용이
드는   astronaut 명 우주 비행사   equipment 명 장비   operate 동 작동하다,
조작하다   appropriate 형 적절한   rarely 부 좀처럼 …하지 않는   sensitive
형 민감한   accurate 형 정확한   manage 동 관리하다   geographical 형
지리적인   environmental 형 환경적인   factor 명 요소   capability 명 능력
unhelpful 형 도움이 되지 않는   irrelevant 형 무관한, 상관없는

04   정답 ③   정답률 59%

정답 풀이

③ 병렬구조

> The material [(which/that) they choose to publish] / must not only
> 주어 └── 목적격 관계대명사 생략   not only A but (also) B: A뿐만 아니라 B도
> 그들이 출판하기로 선택하는 자료는
> have commercial value, but being(→ be) very competently
> 동사1   동사2
> 상업적 가치가 있어야 할 뿐만 아니라 매우 잘 작성되어야 한다
> written / and (be) free of editing and factual errors.
> …이 없는
> 그리고 편집상이나 사실과 다른 오류가 없어야 한다

➡ 상관접속사 「not only A but (also) B」에 의해 must 뒤에 오는 동사원형이 병렬 연결된 구조이므로, 준동사 being을 동사원형 be로 고쳐야 한다.

▌친절한 오답 풀이▐

① 동사의 수 일치

> The competition [to sell manuscripts to publishers] is fierce.
> 주어 └── 형용사적 용법의 to부정사   동사
> 출판사에 원고를 팔려는 경쟁은 치열하다

➡ 문장의 주어(The competition)가 단수이므로 단수 동사 is가 알맞다.

② 명사를 수식하는 과거분사

> I would estimate / {that less than one percent of the material [sent
> 명사절(목적어)을 이끄는 접속사 └───
> 나는 추정한다   출판사에 보내진 자료 중 1% 미만이
> to publishers] / is ever published}.
> be v-ed: 수동태
> 출판되는 것으로

➡ 앞의 명사 the material을 수식하는 분사로, 자료가 '보내진'이라는 수동의 의미가 적절하므로 과거분사 sent가 오는 것이 알맞다.

④ 수량형용사

> Any manuscript [that contains errors] / stands little chance /
> 주어 └── 주격 관계대명사
> stand a chance: 가능성이 있다
> 오류를 포함하는 어떤 원고도   가능성이 거의 없다
> at being accepted for publication.
> being v-ed: 동명사의 수동태
> 출판을 위해 받아들여질

➡ 수량형용사 little(거의 없는)은 셀 수 없는 명사만을 수식할 수 있는데, 뒤에 오는 chance는 셀 수 없는 명사이므로 어법상 바르다.

⑤ 소유격 관계대명사

Most publishers will not want to waste time / with writers [whose
　　　　　　　　　　　　　　　　　　　　　　　　　　　　　　　↑────소유격
대부분의 출판사들은 시간을 낭비하고 싶지 않을 것이다　　　　　　　　관계대명사

material contains too many mistakes].
자료에 너무 많은 오류를 포함하고 있는 집필자들과

➡ writers가 선행사이고 관계사절 안에서 뒤에 이어지는 명사 material과 소유 관계에
있으므로, 소유격 관계대명사 whose는 어법상 바르다.

 구문 분석 Plus

4행
Since so much material *is being written*, publishers can be
very selective.
➡ Since: '… 때문에'의 의미로 부사절을 이끄는 접속사
➡ is being v-ed: '…되고 있다'라는 의미의 현재 진행형 수동태

지문 해석

출판사에 원고를 팔려는 경쟁은 치열하다. 출판사에 보내진 자료 중 1% 미만이 출판되는
것으로 나는 추정한다. 아주 많은 자료가 작성되고 있기 때문에, 출판사는 매우 까다로울
수 있다. 그들이 출판하기로 선택하는 자료는 상업적 가치가 있어야 할 뿐만 아니라 매우
잘 작성되어야 하며 편집상이나 사실과 다른 오류가 없어야 한다. 오류를 포함하는 어떤
원고도 출판을 위해 받아들여질 가능성이 거의 없다. 대부분의 출판사들은 자료에 너무
많은 오류를 포함하고 있는 집필자들과 시간을 낭비하고 싶지 않을 것이다.

어휘

competition 몡 경쟁　**manuscript** 몡 원고, 필사본　**publisher** 몡 출판인, 출판사
(**publish** 동 출판하다 **publication** 몡 출판)　**fierce** 혱 치열한　**estimate** 동
추정하다　**selective** 혱 선택적인; *까다로운　**commercial** 혱 상업적인
competently 튀 적절하게, 유능하게　**factual** 혱 사실에 기반을 둔　**contain** 동
포함하다

05　　　　정답 ④　　　정답률 47%

정답 풀이

④ 문장의 동사

Galileo, / [who heard about the Dutch spyglass and began
주어, 선행사　　계속적 용법의 주격 관계대명사
Galileo는　　　　네덜란드의 소형 망원경에 대해 듣고 자신만의 것을 만들기 시작했던

making his own], / realizing(→ realized) right away / [how
　　　　　　　　　　　　　　동사　　　　　　realized의 목적어로 쓰인 의문사절
　　　　　　　　　　　　　즉시 깨달았다

useful the device could be / to armies and sailors].
그 장치가 얼마나 유용할지를　　　　　군대와 선원들에게

➡ Galileo가 주어이고 의문사절(how … sailors)이 목적어로, 문장에서 동사가 빠져
있으므로 현재분사 realizing을 동사 realized로 고쳐야 한다.

친절한 오답 풀이

① 병렬구조

[Though he probably was not the first to do it], / Dutch eyeglass
접속사(비록 …일지라도)　　　　　　　　　　　　　형용사적 용법의 to부정사
그가 그것을 한 첫 사람은 아니었을지라도　　　　　　　네덜란드의 안경 알

maker Hans Lippershey gets credit for putting two lenses /
　　　　────동격────　get credit for: 공로를 인정받다　전치사의 목적어1
제작인인 Hans Lippershey는 두 개의 렌즈를 붙인 것에 대해 공을 인정받고 있다

on either end of a tube / in 1608 / and creating a "spyglass."
　　　　　　　　　　　　　　　　　　접속사 전치사의 목적어2
관의 양쪽 끝에　　　　　　　1608년에　　그리고 '소형 망원경'을 만든 것에 대해

➡ 등위접속사 and가 전치사 for의 목적어로 쓰인 동명사 putting과 creating을 병렬
연결하고 있으므로, 어법상 바르다.

---

② 접속사 that

…, it was not Lippershey but his children / {who discovered /
It is … who[that] 강조구문　　　not A but B: A가 아니라 B
　　Lippershey가 아니라 그의 아이들이었다　　　　　발견한 사람은

[that the double lenses made a nearby weathervane look bigger]}.
명사절(목적어)을 이끄는 접속사　　make + 목적어 + 동사원형: …가 ~하게 하다
두 개의 렌즈가 가까운 풍향계를 더 크게 보이게 한다는 것을

➡ 동사 discovered의 목적어 역할을 하는 명사절을 이끌고 있고, 뒤에 완전한 절이
이어지므로 접속사 that은 어법상 바르다.

 Grammar Tips

「It is … that[who/which]」 강조구문

It is와 that 사이에 강조하려는 말을 두는데, 강조할 말이 사람인 경우 관계대명사
who를, 사물인 경우 관계대명사 which를 that 대신 쓸 수 있다.

예) **It was** *Amy* **who[that]** sent me an email.
(내게 이메일을 보낸 사람은 바로 Amy였다.)
예) **It was** *an email* **which[that]** Amy sent me.
(Amy가 내게 보낸 것은 바로 이메일이었다.)

③ 비교급 강조 부사

These early instruments were not much more than toys / [because
　　　　　　　　　　　비교급 강조 부사└───┘　　　　　　접속사
이런 초기 도구들은 장난감에 지나지 않았다

their lenses were not very strong].
왜냐하면 그 렌즈들은 별로 강하지 않았기 때문에

➡ much는 뒤에 나오는 비교급 more을 수식하는 부사로, 어법상 바르다. not much
more than은 '꼭, 바로'라는 의미의 표현이다.

⑤ 명사적 용법의 to부정사

{As he made better and better spyglasses, / [which were later
　　　　　　비교급 and 비교급: 점점 더 …한　　선행사　　계속적 용법의 주격 관계대명사
그가 점점 더 좋은 소형 망원경을 만들면서　　　　　그것은 나중에

named telescopes]}, / Galileo decided to point one at the Moon.
망원경이라고 이름 붙여졌는데　　Galileo는 하나를 달을 향하게 하기로 결심했다

➡ to point는 동사 decide의 목적어로 쓰인 명사적 용법의 to부정사로, 어법상 바르다.

지문 해석

그가 그것을 한 첫 사람은 아니었을지라도, 네덜란드의 안경 알 제작인인 Hans
Lippershey는 1608년에 관의 양쪽 끝에 두 개의 렌즈를 붙이고 '소형 망원경'을 만든
것에 대해 공을 인정받고 있다. 심지어 그때도, 두 개의 렌즈가 가까운 풍향계를 더
크게 보이게 한다는 것을 발견한 사람은 Lippershey가 아니라 그의 아이들이었다. 그
렌즈들은 별로 강하지 않았기 때문에 이런 초기 도구들은 장난감에 지나지 않았다. 소형
망원경을 하늘로 향하게 한 첫 번째 사람은 Galileo Galilei라는 이름을 가진 이탈리아
수학자이자 교수였다. 네덜란드의 소형 망원경에 대해 듣고 자신만의 것을 만들기
시작했던 Galileo는 그 장치가 군대와 선원들에게 얼마나 유용할지를 즉시 깨달았다.
그가 점점 더 좋은 소형 망원경들을 만들면서, 그것은 나중에 망원경이라 불리게
되었는데, Galileo는 하나를 달을 향하게 하기로 결심했다.

어휘

eyeglass 몡 안경 알　**tube** 몡 관　**spyglass** 몡 소형 망원경　**nearby** 혱 가까운
instrument 몡 기구, 도구　**mathematician** 몡 수학자　**army** 몡 군대　**sailor** 몡
선원　**name** 동 이름을 지어주다, 명명하다　**telescope** 몡 망원경

06   정답 ③   정답률 44%

정답 풀이

③ 문장의 동사

[When you read the comics section of the newspaper], /
접속사
신문 만화란을 읽을 때,

cutting(→ cut) out a cartoon / [that makes you laugh].
선행사   주격   make(사역동사) + 목적어 + 동사원형:
관계대명사   …가 ~하게 하다
만화를 잘라 내라   여러분을 웃게 하는

➡ 접속사 When이 이끄는 부사절 다음에 주절이 이어져야 하는데 주절에 동사가 없으므로 준동사 cutting을 동사 cut으로 고쳐 명령문으로 만들어야 한다.

친절한 오답 풀이

① 병렬구조

This is worthwhile / not just because they will make you laugh /
not just A but (also) B: A뿐만 아니라 B도
이것은 가치가 있다   그것이 여러분을 웃게 만들 것이기 때문일 뿐만 아니라

but because they contain wisdom / about the nature of life.
그것이 지혜도 담고 있기 때문에   삶의 본질에 관한

➡ 상관접속사 「not just A but (also) B」에 의해 접속사 because가 이끄는 두 개의 절이 병렬 연결된 구조이므로, 접속사 because가 오는 것이 알맞다.

② 「help + 목적어 + (to) 동사원형」

Charlie Brown and *Blondie* are part of my morning routine /
동사1
'Charlie Brown'과 'Blondie'는 나의 아침 일과의 일부이다

and help me to start the day / with a smile.
접속사 동사2, help + 목적어 + (to) 동사원형: …가 ~하도록 돕다
그리고 내가 하루를 시작할 수 있도록 돕는다   미소로

➡ 동사 help는 목적격보어로 동사원형이나 to부정사를 취하므로, to start는 어법상 바르다.

④ 지각동사의 목적격보어

Post it {wherever you need it most, / [such as on your refrigerator
복합관계부사(…하는 곳이 어디든지)   전치사(…와 같은)
여러분이 가장 필요로 하는 곳 어디에든지 그것을 붙여라   냉장고 위나

or at work]} ─ / so that every time you see it, you will smile and
결과를 나타내는 접속사(그 결과 …하다)
직장과 같이   그러면 그것을 볼 때마다, 여러분은 미소를 지을 것이고

feel your spirit lifted.
feel(지각동사) + 목적어 + 과거분사: …가 ~됨을 느끼다
기분이 고양되는 것을 느낄 것이다

➡ lifted는 지각동사 feel의 목적격보어로 쓰인 과거분사로, feel의 목적어(your spirit)와 목적격보어가 수동 관계이므로 과거분사인 lifted는 어법상 바르다.

⑤ 주격 관계대명사

Take your comics with you / when you go to visit / sick friends
명령문의 동사   접속사
여러분의 만화를 가지고 가라   문병하러 갈 때

[who can really use a good laugh].
주격 관계대명사
크게 웃는 것이 정말로 필요한 아픈 친구들을

➡ sick friends를 선행사로 하고 관계대명사절 안에서 동사(can use)의 주어 역할을 하는 주격 관계대명사 who는 어법상 바르다.

 구문 분석 Plus

11행   Share your favorites with your friends and family **so that** everyone **can** get a good laugh, too.
➡ so that + 주어 + can …: ~가 …할 수 있도록

지문 해석

만화를 읽을 시간을 내라. 그것이 여러분을 웃게 만들 것이기 때문일 뿐만 아니라 그것이 삶의 본질에 관한 지혜도 담고 있기 때문에 만화를 읽는 것은 가치가 있다. 'Charlie Brown'과 'Blondie'는 나의 아침 일과의 일부이고 내가 미소로 하루를 시작할 수 있도록 돕는다. 신문 만화란을 읽을 때, 여러분을 웃게 하는 만화를 잘라 내라. 그것을 냉장고 위나 직장과 같이 여러분이 가장 필요로 하는 곳 어디에든지 붙여라, 그러면 그것을 볼 때마다 여러분은 미소를 지을 것이고 기분이 고양되는 것을 느낄 것이다. 모두가 역시 크게 웃을 수 있도록 여러분이 가장 좋아하는 것들을 친구들 및 가족과 공유해라. 크게 웃는 것이 정말로 필요한 아픈 친구들을 문병하러 갈 때 여러분의 만화를 가지고 가라.

어휘

comics 몡 (*pl.*) (신문의) 만화   **worthwhile** 혱 가치가 있는   **contain** 통 담다, 포함하다   **nature** 몡 자연; *본질   **routine** 몡 일과   **cut out** …을 잘라 내다   **post** 통 붙이다, 게시하다   **spirit** 몡 기분, 기운   **lift** 통 고양시키다   **favorite** 몡 특히 좋아하는 것   **use** 통 사용하다; *필요하다

---

07   정답 ④   정답률 51%

정답 풀이

④ 문장의 동사

These things, {by vastly reducing the amount of work [needed
주어   by v-ing: …함으로써   과거분사
이러한 것들은 가사에 필요한 일의 양을 막대하게 줄여줌으로써

for household chores]}, / allowing(→ allowed) women to enter
동사1, allow A to-v: A가 …하는 것을 허용하다
여성들이 노동시장에 진입하는 것을 허용했다

the labor market / and virtually got rid of professions
접속사   동사2, get rid of: …을 제거하다, 없애다
그리고 사실상 가사 서비스와 같은 직업을 없애 버렸다

[like domestic service].
전치사(…와 같은)

➡ These things가 주어이고, the labor market 뒤에 접속사와 동사가 이어지므로 앞에 동사가 하나 더 필요하다. 글 전체가 과거의 일을 이야기하고 있으므로 준동사 allowing은 과거시제의 동사 allowed로 고쳐야 한다.

친절한 오답 풀이

① 부정대명사

[In perceiving changes], / we tend to regard the most recent ones /
in v-ing: …하는 데 있어서   regard A as B: A를 B라고 간주하다
변화를 인식함에 있어   우리는 가장 최근의 변화들을 여기는 경향이 있다

as the most revolutionary.
가장 혁명적인 것으로

➡ 앞에 나온 복수 명사 changes를 대신하므로, 복수 부정대명사 ones가 어법상 바르다.

② 관계대명사 what

Recent progress in telecommunications technologies / is not
주어   동사
통신 기술에 있어서 최근의 발전은   더 혁명적이지는 않다

more revolutionary / than what happened [in the late nineteenth
비교급 + than …: …보다 더 ~한   관계대명사
19세기 말에 일어났던 일보다

century] / in relative terms.
상대적으로

➡ 앞에 선행사가 없고, 주어가 빠진 불완전한 절을 이끌고 있으므로 선행사를 포함한 관계대명사 what은 어법상 바르다.

---

③ 원급 비교

> Moreover, / in terms of the consequent economic and social
> 　　　　　　in terms of: …의 면에서
> 게다가　　　그 결과로 일어나는 경제적, 사회적 변화의 측면에서,
> changes, / the Internet revolution has not been as important as
> 　　　　　　주어　　　　　　　　　　　　as + 형용사 + as …: …만큼 ~한
> 　　　　　인터넷 혁명은 세탁기만큼 중요하지는 않았다
> the washing machine / and other household appliances.
> 　　　　　　　　　　그리고 다른 가전제품들만큼

➡ as와 as 사이에 오는 말이 주격보어 역할을 하고 있으므로 형용사 important가 오는 것이 알맞다.

⑤ 목적격보어로 쓰인 to부정사

> This leads us to make all sorts of wrong decisions / about
> 　lead A to-v: A가 …하도록 이끌다
> 이것은 우리로 하여금 모든 종류의 잘못된 결정을 내리도록 이끈다
> national economic policy, corporate policies, and our own careers.
> 국가의 경제 정책, 기업의 정책, 그리고 우리 자신의 경력에 관한

➡ 동사 lead는 목적격보어로 to부정사를 취하므로 to make는 어법상 바르다.

지문 해석

변화를 인식함에 있어, 우리는 가장 최근의 변화들을 가장 혁명적인 것으로 여기는 경향이 있다. 이는 종종 사실과 일치하지 않는다. 통신 기술에 있어서 최근의 발전은 19세기 말에 일어났던 일보다 상대적으로 더 혁명적이지는 않다. 게다가, 그 결과로 일어나는 경제적, 사회적 변화의 측면에서, 인터넷 혁명은 세탁기와 다른 가전제품들만큼 중요하지는 않았다. 이러한 것들은 가사에 필요한 일의 양을 막대하게 줄여줌으로써 여성들이 노동시장에 진입하는 것을 허용하였고 사실상 가사 서비스와 같은 직업을 없애 버렸다. 우리는 과거를 들여다볼 때 '망원경을 거꾸로 놓고' 옛것을 과소평가하고 새것을 과대평가해서는 안 된다. 이것은 우리로 하여금 국가의 경제 정책, 기업의 정책, 그리고 우리 자신의 경력에 관한 모든 종류의 잘못된 결정을 내리도록 이끈다.

perceive 동 인지하다　revolutionary 형 혁명적인 (revolution 명 혁명)
inconsistent 형 일치하지 않는　relative 형 상대적인　consequent 형 …의 결과로 일어나는　household appliance 가전 제품　vastly 부 대단히, 엄청나게
virtually 부 사실상, 거의　profession 명 직업　telescope 명 망원경
underestimate 동 과소평가하다　overestimate 동 과대평가하다　corporate 형 기업의

08　　정답 ⑤　　정답률 50%

정답 풀이

⑤ 문장의 동사

> And anyone [who has spent time with a five-year-old] knowing
> 　　　주어　　 ↑　주격 관계대명사
> 그리고 다섯 살짜리 아이와 시간을 보내본 사람은 안다
> (→ knows) / {that children this age can test the limits of your
> 　　동사　　　　명사절(목적어)을 이끄는 접속사
> 　　　　　이 나이의 아이들이 당신의 인내심의 한계를 시험할 수 있다는 것을
> patience / by trying to get explanations / for why everything
> 　　　 by v-ing: …함으로써　　　　　간접의문문(의문사 + 주어 + 동사)
> 　　　　설명을 얻으려고 애씀으로써　　　 왜 모든 것이 작동하는지에 대한
> works / [as it does]}.
> 　　　접속사(…처럼)
> 　　　지금처럼

➡ 주어는 anyone이고 who 이하는 anyone을 수식하는 주격 관계대명사절로, 뒤에 동사가 와야 하므로 준동사 knowing을 동사 knows로 고쳐야 한다.

① 과거분사

> The ability to think / about {why things work and what may be
> 　주어　　　형용사적 용법의　간접의문문(의문사 + 주어 + 동사)
> 생각하는 능력은　to부정사　왜 일이 진행되고 무엇이 문제를 일으키고 있는지에 대해
> causing problems / [when events do not go as (they are) expected]} /
> 　　　　　　　접속사(…할 때)　　　　　　　접속사(…대로)
> 　　　　　　일이 예상된 대로 진행되지 않을 때
> seems like an obvious aspect / of the way [(in which) we think].
> 동사, seem like: …처럼 보이다
> 명확한 측면처럼 보인다　　　　　우리가 생각하는 방식의

➡ 접속사 as 뒤에 they are가 생략되었는데, 일이 '예상된' 대로라는 수동의 의미이므로 과거분사 expected가 오는 것이 적절하다.

② 대명사

> It is interesting / {that this ability to think about [why things
> 가주어　　　　진주어　　　　　　간접의문문(의문사 + 주어 + 동사)
> 흥미롭다　　　왜 일이 발생하는지에 대해 생각하는 이 능력이
> happen] / is one of the key abilities / [that separates human
> 　　　　　one of + 복수 명사: … 중 하나 ↑　주격 관계대명사
> 　　　　중요한 능력들 중 하나라는 것은　　인간의 능력을 그것들(능력들)과 구별해 주는
> abilities from those / of just about every other animal on the planet]}.
> separate A from B: A를 B와 구분 짓다　　　　　　　지구상에서
> 지구상의 거의 모든 다른 동물들의

➡ 앞에 나온 abilities를 지칭하는 대명사로, 지칭하는 대상이 복수이므로 복수형 대명사 those가 알맞다.

③ 「see(지각동사) + 목적어 + 동사원형」

> Issac Newton didn't just see an apple fall from a tree.
> 　　　　　　　 see(지각동사) + 목적어 + 동사원형: …가 ~하는 것을 보다
> 아이작 뉴턴은 단지 사과가 나무에서 떨어지는 것을 본 것이 아니다

➡ fall은 지각동사 see의 목적격보어로 쓰인 동사원형으로, 어법상 바르다.

④ 접속사 that

> Your car mechanic doesn't just observe / [that your car is not
> 　　　　　　　　　　　　　　명사절(목적어)을 이끄는 접속사
> 당신의 자동차 정비공은 단지 관찰하는 것이 아니다　당신의 차가 작동하지 않는 것을
> working].

➡ that은 접속사로 동사 observe의 목적어 역할을 명사절을 이끌고 있고, 뒤에 완전한 절이 이어지므로 어법상 바르다.

 구문 분석 Plus

> 12행
> He figures out [why it is not working] {using knowledge about [why it usually does work properly]}.
> ➡ why 이하는 각각 구동사 figures out과 전치사 about의 목적어 역할을 하는 간접의문문(의문사 + 주어 + 동사)
> ➡ using 이하는 동시동작을 나타내는 분사구문(= as he uses …)

지문 해석

왜 일이 진행되고 일이 예상된 대로 진행되지 않을 때 무엇이 문제를 일으키고 있는지에 대해 생각하는 능력은 우리가 생각하는 방식의 명확한 측면처럼 보인다. 왜 일이 발생하는지에 대해 생각하는 이 능력이 인간의 능력을 지구상의 거의 모든 다른 동물들의 능력과 구별해 주는 중요한 능력들 중 하나라는 것은 흥미롭다. '이유'를 묻는 것은 사람들이 설명을 만들어내도록 해준다. 아이작 뉴턴은 단지 사과가 나무에서 떨어지는 것을 본 것이 아니다. 그는 그런 관찰을 사과가 왜 떨어졌는지 그가 이해하도록 돕는 데 사용했다. 당신의 자동차 정비공은 단지 당신의 차가 작동하지 않는 것을 관찰하는 것이 아니다. 왜 그것이 평상시에 제대로 작동하는지에 대한 지식을 사용하여 왜 그것이 작동하지 않는지를 알아낸다. 그리고 다섯 살짜리 아이와 시간을 보내본 사람은 이 나이의 아이들이 왜 모든 것이 지금처럼 작동하는지에 대한 설명을 얻으려 애씀으로써 당신의 인내심의 한계를 시험할 수 있다는 것을 안다.

cause 통 야기시키다 obvious 형 명확한 aspect 명 측면 explanation 명 설명
observation 명 관찰 figure out …을 이해하다[알아내다] mechanic 명 정비공
properly 부 제대로, 적절하게 limit 명 한계 patience 명 인내심

09 　　정답 ②　　정답률 68%

정답 풀이

② 문장의 동사

With this form of agency comes the belief / [that individual
　　전치사구(부사)　　　　　　　　동사　　주어　　동격의 접속사　주어
이러한 형태의 주체성의 결과로 믿음이 생긴다　　　　개인의 성공이
successes / depending(→ depend) primarily on one's own
　　　　　　　　　depend on: …에 달려 있다
　　　　　　　주로 자신의 능력과 행동에 달려 있다는
abilities and actions], ...

➡ 전치사구(With this form of agency)가 문장의 첫머리에 오면서 주어와 동사의
순서가 바뀌는 도치가 일어난 문장이다. the belief와 동격인 명사절을 이끄는 접속사
that 뒤에 완전한 절이 이어져야 하므로 주어(individual successes) 뒤의 준동사
depending을 현재형 동사 depend로 고쳐야 한다.

▮친절한 오답 풀이▮

① 접속사

People from more individualistic cultural contexts / tend to be
　　　　　　　　　　　　　　　　　　　　　　tend to-v: …하는 경향이 있다
더 개인주의적인 문화 환경에서 온 사람들은　　　　　　　　유지하도록
motivated to maintain / self-focused agency or control / [as these
be motivated to-v: …하도록 동기 부여되다　　자신에게 초점을 맞춘 주체성이나 통제력을　접속사(… 때문에) 주어
동기 부여되는 경향이 있는데
serve as the basis of one's self-worth].
동사　전치사(…로서)
이는 이러한 것들이 자아 존중감의 토대로 역할을 하기 때문이다

➡ 뒤에 완전한 절이 이어지고 있으므로 접속사 as는 어법상 바르다.

③ 수동태

The independent self may be more driven / to cope by appealing /
　　주어　　　　　　　　　　　　　　　　　by v-ing: …함으로써
독립적 자기는 더 많이 유도될 수도 있다　　　호소함으로써 대처하도록
to a sense of agency or control.
주체 의식이나 통제 의식에

➡ 주어 The independent self는 동작의 주체가 아니라 대상으로, 독립적 자기가
'유도된다'라는 수동의 의미가 적절하므로 수동태의 과거분사 driven은 어법상 바르다.

④ 접속사 that

Research has shown / [that East Asians prefer to receive, but not
　　　　　　　　　명사절(목적어)을 이끄는 접속사
연구는 보여 주었다　　　동아시아인들은 추구하지는 않되, 받는 것을 선호한다는 것을
seek, / more social support / rather than seek personal control in
　　　　　　　　　　　　　　A rather than B: B보다는 A
　　더 많은 사회적인 지원을　　　어떤 경우에 개인적인 통제를 추구하기보다는
certain cases].

➡ that은 동사 has shown의 목적어 역할을 하는 명사절을 이끄는 접속사로, 뒤에
완전한 절이 이어지고 있으므로 어법상 바르다.

⑤ 주격 관계대명사

Therefore, people [who hold a more interdependent self-
　　　　　　　　　　└───주격 관계대명사
그러므로 더 상호 의존적인 자기 구성을 지닌 사람들은
construal] / may prefer to cope / in a way [that promotes harmony /
　　　　　　　　　　　　　　　　　　　　　　　└─주격 관계대명사
　　　　　대처하는 것을 선호할 수도 있다　화합을 증진하는 방식으로
in relationships].
관계 속에서

➡ people을 선행사로 하고, 동사 hold의 주어 역할을 하는 주격 관계대명사 who가
쓰였으므로 어법상 바르다.

지문 해석

더 개인주의적인 문화 환경에서 온 사람들은 자신에게 초점을 맞춘 주체성이나 통제력을
유지하도록 동기 부여되는 경향이 있는데, 이는 이러한 것들이 자아 존중감의 토대로
역할을 하기 때문이다. 이러한 형태의 주체성의 결과로 개인의 성공이 주로 자신의
능력과 행동에 달려 있다는 믿음이 생기며, 따라서 환경에 영향을 미침에 의해서든,
자신의 상황을 받아들이려고 노력함에 의해서든, 통제력의 사용은 궁극적으로 개인에게
집중된다. 독립적 자기는 주체 의식이나 통제 의식에 호소함으로써 대처하도록 더 많이
유도될 수도 있다. 그러나 더 상호 의존적인 문화 환경에서 온 사람들은 개인의 성공과
주체성의 문제에 덜 집중하며, 집단의 목표와 화합 쪽으로 더 많이 동기 부여되는 경향이
있다. 연구는 동아시아인들은 어떤 경우에 개인적인 통제를 추구하기보다는, 오히려
더 많은 사회적인 지원을, 추구하지는 않되, 받는 것을 선호한다는 것을 보여 주었다.
그러므로 더 상호 의존적인 자기 구성을 지닌 사람들은 관계 속에서 화합을 증진하는
방식으로 대처하는 것을 선호할 수도 있다.

어휘

individualistic 형 개인주의적인 context 명 문맥; *환경 agency 명 주체성,
주도성 serve as …의 역할을 하다 self-worth 명 자아 존중감 primarily
부 주로 ultimately 부 궁극적으로, 결국 center on …에 집중하다 cope
통 대처하다 appeal 통 호소하다 interdependent 형 상호 의존적인

10 　　정답 ③　　정답률 74%

정답 풀이

③ 문장의 동사

The most common activity / among people [observed by Whyte] /
　　　주어　　　　　　　　　　　　　　　　　　과거분사
가장 흔한 행동은　　　　　　　　Whyte에 의해 관찰된 사람들 사이의
turning(→ turned) out to be watching other people.
　　　　　동사, turn out: …으로 드러나다[밝혀지다]
다른 사람들을 지켜보는 것임이 밝혀졌다

➡ 주어는 The most common activity이고 among ... Whyte는 주어를 수식하는
전치사구로, 뒤에 문장의 동사가 필요하므로 준동사 turning을 동사 turned로 고쳐야
한다.

▮친절한 오답 풀이▮

① 간접의문문

William H. Whyte turned video cameras on a number of spaces
　　　　　　　　　　turn on: …을 켜다　　　　　a number of + 복수 명사: 많은 …
William H. Whyte는 뉴욕시의 많은 장소에 비디오카메라를 켜두고
in New York City, / {watching to see [how people used the spaces]}.
연속동작을 나타내는 분사구문(= and he watched ...) 간접의문문(의문사 + 주어 + 동사)
　　　　　　　　　　사람들이 그 공간들을 어떻게 사용하는지를 알기 위해 지켜보았다

➡ how 이하는 동사 see의 목적어 역할을 하는 간접의문문으로, 의문부사 how 뒤에
완전한 절이 이어지고 있으므로 어법상 바르다.

② 대명사

> He made a number of fascinating findings, / and he had the video
> 　　　　　　　　많은
> 그는 많은 흥미로운 사실들을 발견했고　　　　　　그는 비디오 증거를 갖게 되었다
> evidence / to back them up.
> 　　　　　back up: …을 뒷받침하다
> 　　　　　그것들을 뒷받침해주는

➡ 문맥상 밑줄 친 them은 앞에 나오는 복수 명사 a number of fascinating findings를 가리키므로, 복수형 대명사 them이 오는 것이 어법상 적절하다.

④ 능동태

> Whyte expected lovers to be found in private, isolated spaces, /
> 　　　　　expect A to-v: A가 …할 것을 예상하다
> Whyte는 연인들이 사적이고 외진 공간에서 발견될 것이라 예상했다
> but most often they sat or stood right in the center of things /
> 그러나 그들은 모든 것들의 바로 중앙에 가장 자주 앉거나 서 있었다
> for everyone to see.
> to부정사의 의미상 주어
> 모든 사람들이 볼 수 있는

➡ 동사 expected의 목적어(lovers)에 대해 설명하는 목적격보어로 쓰인 to부정사로, 연인들이 '발견되는'이라는 수동의 의미가 적절하므로 수동태 be found가 오는 것이 알맞다.

⑤ 「force + 목적어 + to-v」

> Further, people [having private conversations] / would stand in
> 　　　　　　　　└현재분사┘　　　　　　과거의 습관(…하곤 했다)
> 더 나아가, 사적인 대화를 나누는 사람들은　　　　　　인도 한가운데 서 있곤 했다
> the middle of the sidewalk, / [forcing people to step around them].
> 동시동작을 나타내는 분사구문(= as they force …), force A to-v: A가 …하게 하다
> 사람들이 그들의 주위를 걸어가도록 만들면서

➡ 동사 force는 목적격보어로 to부정사를 취하므로 to step은 어법상 바르다.

지문 해석

William H. Whyte는 뉴욕시의 많은 장소에 비디오카메라를 켜두고, 사람들이 그 공간들을 어떻게 사용하는지 알기 위해 지켜보았다. 그는 많은 흥미로운 사실들을 발견했고, 그것들을 뒷받침해주는 비디오 증거를 갖게 되었다. 매우 붐비는 도시에서조차, 그는 보통 많은 도시의 공간들이 버려진다는 것을 발견했다. 사람들은 혼자 있으려고 할 때조차도 몇몇 분주한 광장에 모여들었다. 왜 그럴까? Whyte에 의해 관찰된 사람들 사이의 가장 흔한 행동은 다른 사람들을 지켜보는 것임이 밝혀졌다. 그리고 또한 사람들은 주목받는 것을 좋아하는 것이 밝혀졌다! Whyte는 연인들이 사적이고 외진 공간에서 발견될 것이라 예상했으나, 그들은 모든 사람들이 볼 수 있는 모든 것들의 바로 중앙에 가장 자주 앉거나 서 있었다. 더 나아가, 사적인 대화를 나누는 사람들은 다른 사람들이 그들의 주위를 걸어가도록 만들면서 인도 한가운데 서 있곤 했다.

어휘

fascinating 형 대단히 흥미로운　finding 명 결과, 사실　crowded 형 붐비는, 복잡한　urban 형 도시의　desert 동 버리다　flock 동 모이다, 떼를 짓다　isolated 형 고립된　further 부 더 나아가　sidewalk 명 인도　step around …의 주위를 걸어가다

01　　　　　　　정답 ⑤　　　정답률 60%

정답 풀이

⑤ 병렬구조

> Moreover, / when the doctor specializes in the provision of
> 　　　　　　　　　　specialize in: …을 전문으로 하다
> 더군다나　　　　의사가 진료 제공을 전문으로 하면
> physician services / and hiring(→ hires) someone [who has a
> 　　　　　　　　　　　　　　　　└───┘주격 관계대명사
> 그리고 자료 기록에 비교 우위를 가지고 있는 사람을 고용하면
> comparative advantage in record keeping], / costs will be lower
> 　　　　　　　　　　　　　　　　　그 비용은 더 낮아질 것이고
> and joint output (will be) larger / than would otherwise be
> 공동의 결과물이 더 커질 것이다　유사 관계대명사　그렇지 않으면
> 　　　　　　　　　　　　　　그렇게 하지 않으면 얻을 수 있는 것보다
> achievable.

➡ when절의 동사 specializes와 접속사 and로 병렬 연결된 구조이므로 hiring을 hires로 고쳐야 한다.

친절한 오답 풀이

① 「전치사 + 관계대명사」

> Trying to produce everything yourself would mean / {(that) you
> 　　주어(동명사구)　　　　　　　명사절(목적어)을 이끄는 접속사 that 생략
> 모든 것을 당신 스스로 생산하려고 노력하는 것은 의미할 것이다　당신의
> are using your time and resources / to produce many things [for
> 　　　　　　　　　　　　　　　부사적 용법의 to부정사
> 시간과 자원을 사용하고 있다는 것을　　당신이 고비용 공급자가 되는 많은 것들을 생산하기 위해
> which you are a high-cost provider]}.
> 당신이 고비용 공급자가 되는 많은 것들을 생산하기 위해

➡ 관계대명사 which는 many things를 선행사로 하고 있고, 관계대명사 절에서 전치사 for의 목적어 역할을 하므로 어법상 바르다. 「전치사 + 관계대명사」 뒤에는 완전한 절이 온다.

② 가주어 진주어 구문

> For example, / [even though most doctors might be good at
> 　　　　　접속사(비록 …일지라도)　　　　　　…에 능숙하다
> 예를 들면　　비록 대부분의 의사가 자료 기록과 진료 예약을 잡는 데 능숙할지라도
> record keeping and arranging appointments], / it is generally in
> 　　　　　동명사(전치사 at의 목적어)　　　　가주어
> 　　　　　　　　　　　　　　　　　일반적으로 그들에게 이익이 된다
> their interest / to hire someone to perform these services.
> 　　　　　　진주어
> 이러한 서비스를 수행하기 위해 누군가를 고용하는 것은

➡ to hire 이하는 진주어 역할을 하는 to부정사구이므로, 앞에 가주어 it이 오는 것이 알맞다.

③ 명사를 수식하는 과거분사

> Because the time [spent with their patients] is worth a lot, / the
> 　　　　　　　└───┘과거분사
> 그들이 환자와 보내게 되는 시간은 많은 가치를 가지기 때문에
> opportunity cost of record keeping for doctors / will be high.
> 　　　주어　　　　　　　　　　　　동사
> 의사들에게 자료 기록을 하는 기회비용은　　　　　높을 것이다

➡ 앞에 나오는 명사(the time)를 수식하는 분사로, 시간이 '보내게 되는'이라는 수동의 의미이므로 과거분사 spent가 오는 것이 알맞다.

④ 「find + 목적어 + 형용사」

> Thus, doctors will almost always find it advantageous / [to hire
> 　　　　　　　　　　　　　　　　　　　가목적어　목적격보어　　　진목적어
> 따라서 의사는 이득이라는 것을 거의 항상 알게 될 것이다　　　진료 기록을
> someone else to keep and (to) manage their records].
> 　　　　　　　부사적 용법의 to부정사 접속사 and에 의해 to keep과 병렬 연결됨
> 하고 그것을 관리하기 위해 누군가 다른 사람을 고용하는 것이

➡ 동사 find의 목적격보어로 쓰였으므로 형용사 advantageous는 어법상 바르다.

지문 해석

모든 것을 당신 스스로 생산하려고 노력하는 것은 당신이 고비용 공급자가 되는 많은 것들을 생산하기 위해 당신의 시간과 자원을 사용하고 있다는 것을 의미할 것이다. 이것은 더 낮은 생산과 수입으로 해석될 수 있다. 예를 들면, 비록 대부분의 의사가 자료 기록과 진료 예약을 잡는 데 능숙할지라도, 이러한 서비스를 수행하기 위해 누군가를 고용하는 것은 일반적으로 그들에게 이익이 된다. 기록을 하기 위해 의사가 사용하는 시간은 그들이 환자를 진료하면서 보낼 수 있었던 시간이다. 그들이 환자와 보내게 되는 시간은 많은 가치를 가지기 때문에 의사들에게 자료 기록을 하는 기회비용은 높을 것이다. 따라서 의사는 자료 기록을 하고 그것을 관리하기 위해 누군가 다른 사람을 고용하는 것이 이득이라는 것을 거의 항상 알게 될 것이다. 더군다나 의사가 진료 제공을 전문으로 하고, 자료 기록에 비교 우위를 가지고 있는 사람을 고용하면, 그렇게 하지 않으면 얻을 수 있는 것보다 그 비용은 더 낮아질 것이고 공동의 결과물이 더 커질 것이다.

어휘

provider 명 제공자　translate 동 번역하다, 옮기다　arrange 동 처리하다; 정리하다　perform 동 수행하다　worth 형 …의 가치가 있는　opportunity cost 기회비용　advantageous 형 이익이 되는　specialize 동 전문적으로 다루다　provision 명 공급, 제공　comparative 형 비교의, 상대적인　joint 형 합동의　output 명 생산량　achievable 형 성취할 수 있는

02　정답 ④　정답률 58%

정답 풀이

④ 준동사의 형용사적 성질

> Unfortunately we do not have a century or two / make(→ to
> 불행하게도 우리는 한두 세기의 시간이 없다
> make) the change.
> 변화를 만들어 낼

➡ 앞에 본동사 do not have가 있으므로, make는 to make가 되어 앞의 a century or two를 수식하는 형용사 역할을 하는 준동사가 되는 것이 적절하다.

친절한 오답 풀이

① 명사를 수식하는 현재분사구

> One well-known shift took place / when the accepted view —
> 　　　　　　　　　　　　　　　　　　　　　　　　　동격
> 잘 알려진 한 가지 변화가 일어났다　　　지구가 우주의 중심이라는 용인된 관점이
> that the Earth was the center of the universe — changed / to one /
> 바뀌었을 때　　　　　　　　　　　　　　　　　　　관점으로
> {where we understood / [that we are only inhabitants on one
> 　└─관계부사　　　　　접속사
> 우리가 이해하는　　　우리가 하나의 행성에 사는 거주자일 뿐이라고
> planet / orbiting the Sun]}.
> 　　　태양 주위를 궤도를 그리며 도는

➡ 분사가 수식하는 one planet이 orbit의 궤도를 그리며 도는 주체이므로 능동의 의미를 나타내는 현재분사 orbiting은 어법상 바르다.

② 가주어 진주어 구문

> With each person [who grasped the solar system view], / it became
> 　　　　　　　　└─주격 관계대명사　　　　　　　　　　　가주어
> 태양계의 관점을 이해하는 각각의 사람이 있어서　　　　가주어
> easier for the next person to do so.
> 　　　　의미상 주어　　　진주어
> 그다음 사람이 그렇게 하는 것이 더 쉬워졌다

➡ 진주어인 to부정사구(to do so)의 가주어 it은 어법상 바르다.

③ 병렬구조

> When this perspective shifts into place, / it will be obvious /
> 접속사　　　　　　　　　　　　　　　　　가주어
> 이러한 관점이 바뀌어 자리를 잡으면　　　분명해질 것이다
> {that our economic wellbeing requires / [that we account for, and
> 진주어(that은 접속사)　　　　　　　　　접속사
> 우리의 경제적 안녕이 필요로 한다는 것이　　우리가 생태학적 건강의 요인에
> respond to, factors of ecological health]}.
> 책임지고, 대응하는 것을

➡ 동사구 account for와 respond to가 등위접속사 and로 공통의 목적어 factors of ecological health에 병렬 연결되어 있는 형태로, account와 문법적으로 대등한 형태인 복수 동사 respond는 어법상 바르다.

⑤ 전치사 + 관계대명사

> By clarifying the nature of the old and new perspectives, / and
> by -ing: …함으로써
> 오래된 관점과 새로운 관점의 본질을 명확히 함으로써　　　　　　그리고
> by identifying actions [on which we might cooperate to move
> by -ing: …함으로써(병렬구조)　└────전치사+관계대명사　부사적 용법의
> 그 과정을 진전시키기 위해 협력할지도 모를 행동을 밝힘으로써　to부정사(목적)
> the process along], / we can help accelerate the shift.
> 우리는 그 변화를 가속화하는 데 도움을 줄 수 있다

➡ which는 actions를 선행사로 하는 관계대명사로, 뒤에 완전한 절이 이어지므로 전치사+관계대명사의 형태는 어법상 바르다.

지문 해석

지구가 우주의 중심이라는 용인된 관점이 우리가 태양 주위를 궤도를 그리며 도는 하나의 행성에 사는 거주자일 뿐이라고 이해하는 관점으로 바뀌었을 때 잘 알려진 한 가지 변화가 일어났다. 태양계의 관점을 이해하는 각각의 사람이 있어서, 그다음 사람이 그렇게 하는 것이 더 쉬워졌다. 세계가 인간의 경제를 중심으로 돌아간다는 개념도 마찬가지이다. 이것은 경제가 모든 생명체를 연결하는 물질 흐름의 더 거대한 시스템의 일부라는 관점으로 서서히 대체되고 있다. 이러한 관점이 바뀌어 자리를 잡으면, 우리의 경제적 안녕이 우리가 생태학적 건강의 요인에 책임지고, 대응하는 것을 필요로 한다는 것이 분명해질 것이다. 불행하게도 우리는 변화를 만들어 낼 한두 세기의 시간이 없다. 오래된 관점과 새로운 관점의 본질을 명확히 하고, 그 과정을 진전시키기 위해 협력할지도 모를 행동을 밝힘으로써 우리는 그 변화를 가속화하는 데 도움을 줄 수 있다.

어휘

shift 명 변화 동 바뀌다　inhabitant 명 거주자　orbit 동 주위를 궤도를 그리며 돌다　grasp 동 이해하다　notion 명 개념　revolve 동 돌다　replace 동 대체하다　material 명 물질　flow 명 흐름　perspective 명 관점　obvious 형 분명한　account for …에 대해 책임지다　factor 명 요인　ecological 형 생태학적인　clarify 동 명확히 하다　nature 명 본질　identify 동 밝히다, 확인하다　cooperate 동 협력하다　accelerate 동 가속화하다

03　정답 ④　정답률 41%

정답 풀이

④ 병렬구조

> He can take [what's offered] / or refused (→ refuse) to take
> 조동사 동사1 관계대명사　　　접속사　　　동사2
> 그는 제안되는 것을 받을 수 있다　　혹은 받는 것을 거절할 수 있다
> anything.

→ 등위접속사 or가 문장의 동사를 병렬 연결하고 있는 구조로, 동사 앞에 조동사 can이 쓰였으므로 동사 take와 대등하도록 refused를 동사원형 refuse로 고쳐야 한다.

친절한 오답 풀이

① 「so + 형용사 + that ...」

Humans are **so** averse to feeling / [**that** they're being cheated] /
so+형용사+that ...: 너무 ~해서 …하다　　동격　　접속사　　be being v-ed: 진행형 수동태
인간은 느낌을 너무 싫어해서　　　　　　　　　　그들이 속고 있다는
that they often respond / in ways / [**that** seemingly make little
그들은 흔히 반응한다　　　　방법으로　　겉보기에 거의 말이 되지 않는
주격 관계대명사
sense].

→ 주절에 '너무 ~해서'라는 의미의 「so+형용사」가 쓰였으므로, '…하다'라는 결과를 나타내는 접속사 that이 오는 것이 알맞다.

② 관계대명사 what

Behavioral economists — the economists / {**who** actually study
행동 경제학자들은　　　　경제학자들인　　주격 관계대명사　　사람들이 하는 행동을 실제로
[**what** people do]} / as opposed to the kind / {**who** simply assume /
관계대명사　　　　　…와는 달리　　주격 관계대명사
연구하는　　　　　부류와는 달리　　단순히 가정하는
[(**that**) the human mind works / like a calculator]} ....
접속사 생략
인간의 정신이 작동한다고　　　계산기처럼

→ 동사 study의 목적어 역할을 하면서 뒤에 오는 불완전한 절의 목적어 역할을 하고 있으므로, 관계대명사 what이 오는 것이 알맞다.

③ 가주어 진주어 구문

... — have shown again and again / {**that** people reject unfair
명사절(목적어)을 이끄는 접속사
반복해서 보여주었다　　　　사람들이 불공정한 제안을 거부한다는 것을
offers / [even if it costs them money / **to do so**]}.
접속사(비록 …일지라도), 가주어　　　　진주어
비록 그들에게 돈이 들더라도　　　그렇게 하는 것이

→ to do 이하는 문장의 진주어 역할을 하는 to부정사구이므로, 앞에 가주어 it이 오는 것이 알맞다.

⑤ 분사구문

Many people offer an equal split / to the partner, / [**leaving** both
결과를 나타내는 분사구문
많은 사람이 동등한 몫을 제안하며　　상대방에게　　그것은 두 사람을 모두
individuals happy / and willing to trust each other / in the
행복하게 하고　　　서로를 흔쾌히 신뢰할 수 있게 한다　　미래에
future].

→ leaving 이하는 결과를 나타내는 분사구문으로, 생략된 주어는 주절의 주어(Many people)와 같다. 주어와 분사가 능동 관계에 있으므로 현재분사 leaving이 오는 것이 알맞다.

지문 해석

인간은 자신이 속고 있다는 느낌을 너무 싫어해서 겉보기에 거의 말이 되지 않는 방법으로 흔히 반응한다. 인간의 정신이 계산기처럼 작동한다고 단순히 가정하는 부류와는 달리 사람들이 하는 행동을 실제로 연구하는 경제학자들인 행동 경제학자들은 비록 불공정한 제안을 거부하는 것이 사람들에게 돈이 들더라도 그들은 그것을 거부한다는 것을 반복해서 보여주었다. 대표적인 실험은 최후통첩 게임이라 불리는 과업을 이용한다. 그것은 상당히 간단하다. 두 사람 중 한 사람이 가령 10달러의 약간의 돈을 받는다. 그리고 그 사람은 상대방에게 그 돈의 일부를 제안할 기회를 가진다. 상대방은 두 가지 선택만 할 수 있다. 그는 제안되는 것을 받거나, 받는 것을 거절할 수 있다. 협상의 여지가 없으며, 그래서 이것이 최후통첩 게임이라 불린다. 일반적으로 무슨 일이 일어나는가? 많은 사람이 상대방에게 동등한 몫을 제안하며, 그것은 두 사람을 모두 행복하게 하고 미래에 서로를 흔쾌히 신뢰할 수 있게 한다.

cheat 통 속이다　seemingly 분 겉보기에는　behavioral 형 행동의, 행동에 관한　economist 명 경제학자　assume 통 …이라 가정하다, 간주하다　experiment 명 실험　straightforward 형 간단한, 쉬운　opportunity 명 기회　negotiation 명 협상　split 명 분열; *분할, 몫　individual 명 개인

04　　　정답 ④　　정답률 48%

정답 풀이

④ 병렬구조

...; **one half** moved to the mountains, / **and the other** half
주어1　 동사1　　　　　　　　　접속사　　 주어2
한쪽 반은 산으로 갔고,　　　　　나머지 반쪽은 남았다
staying(→ stayed) / near the beach.
동사2
해변 근처에

→ 두 개의 절이 접속사 and로 병렬 연결되어 있는 문장으로, 두 번째 절의 주어 the other half 뒤에 동사가 필요하므로, 준동사 staying을 동사 stayed로 고쳐야 한다.

 Grammar Tips

one ... the other ~
두 개의 사물 혹은 두 사람 중 하나를 one, 나머지 하나를 the other라고 칭한다.
예) **One** man shouted, but **the other** man couldn't understand him.
(한 사람이 외쳤지만, 나머지 한 사람은 그를 이해하지 못했다.)

친절한 오답 풀이

① 간접의문문

A legend from the Hawaiian island of Kauai explains / [**how** the
간접의문문
하와이의 Kauai섬의 한 전설은 설명한다
naupaka flower got its unusual shape].
(의문사 + 주어 + 동사)
어떻게 naupaka 꽃이 그 특이한 모양을 가지게 되었는지

→ 동사 explains의 목적어로 쓰인 간접의문문을 이끄는 의문사로, 뒤에 완전한 절이 이어지고 있고 문맥상 '어떻게'라는 의미가 적절하므로 의문부사 how가 오는 것이 알맞다.

② 동사의 수 일치

The legend says / [**that** the marriage of two young lovers on the
접속사　　주어
그 전설은 전한다　　그 섬에 있는 젊은 두 연인의 결혼이 반대에 부딪혔다
island **was** opposed / by both sets of parents].
양쪽 부모에 의해서

→ 접속사 that이 이끄는 절의 주어는 the marriage로 단수 명사이므로 단수 동사 was가 오는 것이 알맞다.

③ 부사적 용법의 to부정사

The parents found the couple together on a beach one day, /
그 부모들은 그 연인들이 어느 날 해변에 함께 있는 것을 발견했다
and **to prevent** them from being together, / one of the families
prevent A from v-ing : A가 …하는 것을 막다　　one of + 복수 명사: … 중 하나
그리고 그들이 함께 있는 것을 막기 위하여　　가족들 중 하나가
moved to the mountains, ...
산으로 이사했다

→ to prevent는 '…하기 위하여'의 의미로 뒤에 이어지는 절(one of the families ... mountains)을 수식하는 부사적 용법의 to부정사로, 어법상 바르다.

⑤ 목적격 관계대명사

This story is a good example of a legend / [which native people
이 이야기는 전설의 좋은 예이다   목적격 관계대명사   원주민들이 만들어낸
invented / to make sense of the world around them].
부사적 용법의 to부정사(목적)
그들 주변의 세계를 이해하기 위해서

➡ which는 a good example of a legend를 선행사로 하고 관계대명사절에서 목적어 역할을 하는 목적격 관계대명사로, 어법상 바르다.

지문 해석

원주민들은 그들의 환경에서의 특이한 사건들을 설명하기 위해 전설을 만들어낸다. 하와이의 Kauai섬의 한 전설은 어떻게 naupaka 꽃이 그 특이한 모양을 가지게 되었는지 설명한다. 그 꽃은 반쪽 짜리 작은 데이지 꽃처럼 생겼다. 그 전설에 따르면, 그 섬에 있는 젊은 두 연인의 결혼이 양쪽 부모의 반대에 부딪혔다. 어느 날 그 부모들은 그 연인들이 해변에 함께 있는 것을 발견했고, 그들이 함께 있는 것을 막기 위하여 가족들 중 하나가 산으로 이사해서 그 젊은 연인들을 영원히 떨어뜨려 놓았다. 그 결과, naupaka 꽃은 두 개의 반쪽으로 분리되었는데, 한쪽 반은 산으로 갔고, 나머지 반쪽은 해변 근처에 남았다. 이 이야기는 원주민들이 그들 주변의 세계를 이해하기 위해서 만들어낸 전설의 좋은 예이다.

native people 원주민   legend 명 전설   unusual 형 특이한   daisy 명 데이지 꽃
oppose 동 …에 반대하다   separate 동 분리하다; *헤어지게 하다   invent 동
발명하다; *지어내다   make sense of …을 이해하다

---

05   정답 ④   정답률 54%

정답 풀이

④ 문장의 동사

Judith Rich Harris, / [who is a developmental psychologist], /
주어, 선행사   계속적 용법의 주격 관계대명사
Judith Rich Harris는   발달 심리학자인데,
arguing(→ argues) / [that three main forces shape our development: /
동사   argues의 목적어로 쓰인 that절
주장한다   우리의 발달을 형성하는 세 가지 주요한 힘은
personal temperament, our parents, and our peers].
개인적인 기질, 우리의 부모, 우리의 또래들이라고

➡ 주어는 Judith Rich Harris이고 명사절을 이끄는 that절(that ... peers)을 목적어로 취하는 동사가 빠져 있으므로 arguing을 동사 argues로 고쳐야 한다.

│친절한 오답 풀이│

① 비교급 강조 부사

But even stronger (influences on us), / especially [when we're
반복으로 인한 생략   접속사
하지만 훨씬 더 강한 영향을 주는 것은   특히 우리가 어렸을 때
young], / are our friends.
주격보어 강조로 인한 도치
우리의 친구들이다

➡ even은 '훨씬'의 의미로 비교급을 수식하여 비교의 의미를 강조하는 부사이므로, 비교급 stronger는 어법상 바르다.

② 「전치사 + 동명사」, 동명사의 동사적 성질

We often choose friends / as a way of [expanding our sense of
전치사(…로서) 전치사 동명사(전치사의 목적어)
우리는 보통 친구들을 선택한다   우리의 정체성을 확장하는 방법으로
identity] / beyond our families.
가족을 넘어서

➡ 전치사 of의 목적어 역할을 하면서 명사구 our sense of identity를 목적어로 취할 수 있는 동명사 expanding이 오는 것이 알맞다.

---

③ 동사의 수 일치

As a result, / the pressure to conform / to the standards and
주어   형용사적 용법의 전치사
      to부정사
그 결과   부합해야 한다는 압박감이   기준과 기대에
expectations / of friends and other social groups / is likely to be
동사
be likely to-v: …할 가능성이 있다
친구와 다른 사회 집단의   거세질 가능성이 있다
intense.

➡ 문장의 주어(the pressure)가 단수이므로 단수 동사 is는 어법상 바르다.

⑤ 목적격 관계대명사

"The world / [that children share with their peers]," / [she says], /
목적격 관계대명사   삽입절
세상은   아이들이 그들의 또래들과 공유하는   그녀는 말한다
"is [what shapes their behavior ...].
관계대명사
그들의 행동을 형성하는 것이라고

➡ that은 The world를 선행사로 하고 관계대명사절에서 동사 share의 목적어 역할을 하는 목적격 관계대명사로, 어법상 바르다.

지문 해석

긍정적이든 부정적이든, 우리의 부모와 가족은 우리에게 강력한 영향을 미치는 사람들이다. 하지만 특히 우리가 어렸을 때, 훨씬 더 강한 영향을 주는 것은 우리의 친구들이다. 가족을 넘어서 우리의 정체성을 확장하는 방법으로 우리는 보통 친구들을 선택한다. 그 결과, 친구와 다른 사회 집단의 기준과 기대에 부합해야 한다는 압박감이 거세질 가능성이 있다. Judith Rich Harris는 발달 심리학자인데, 우리의 발달을 형성하는 세 가지 주요한 힘은 개인적인 기질, 우리의 부모, 우리의 또래들이라고 주장한다. 또래들의 영향은 부모의 영향보다 훨씬 더 강하다고 그녀는 주장한다. 그녀는 "아이들이 그들의 또래들과 공유하는 세상은 그들의 행동을 형성하는 것이고, 그들이 가지고 태어난 특성을 수정하는 것이며, 따라서 그들이 자라서 어떤 사람이 될지를 결정하는 것이다."라고 말한다.

conform 동 부합하다   modify 동 수정하다   hence 부 따라서   sort 명 종류, 부류;
*(특정한 부류의) 사람

---

06   정답 ③   정답률 62%

정답 풀이

③ 문장의 동사

However, the complexity of human language, / its ability to convey
주어1   주어2
하지만, 인간 언어의 복잡성   미묘한 차이가 있는 감정과
nuanced emotions and ideas, / and its importance for our existence
접속사   주어3
생각을 전달하는 능력   그리고 사회적 동물로서 우리의 존재에 대한 그것의 중요성은
as social animals / setting(→ set) it apart from the communication
동사, set A apart from B: A를 B와 구분 짓다
그것을 의사소통 체계와 구분 짓는다
systems / [used by other animals].
과거분사
다른 동물들에 의해 사용되는

➡ 등위접속사 and가 주어들을 병렬 연결하고 있고, 뒤에 문장의 동사가 이어져야 하므로 현재분사 setting을 동사로 고쳐야 한다. 주어가 A, B, and C 형태로 복수이므로 복수 동사 set이 와야 한다.

┃친절한 오답 풀이┃

① 동사 강조

Many animals, including dolphins, whales, and birds, / do indeed
주어   전치사(…을 포함하여)   동사를 강조하는 조동사
돌고래, 고래, 그리고 새를 포함한 많은 동물들이
communicate with one another / through patterned systems /
동사   서로 서로   전치사(…을 통해)
실제로 서로 의사소통을 한다   패턴화된 체계를 통해
of sounds, scents, and other chemicals, / or movements.
소리, 냄새, 그리고 다른 화학물질의   또는 움직임을 통해

➡ 밑줄 친 do는 동사 communicate를 강조하는 조동사로, 주어가 복수 명사(many animals)이고 문장의 시제가 현재이므로 do가 오는 것이 알맞다.

② 현재완료 수동태

Furthermore, some nonhuman primates have been taught /
                               have been v-ed: 현재완료 수동태
게다가, 인간이 아닌 어떤 영장류는 배워왔다
to use sign language / to communicate with humans.
명사적 용법의 to부정사   부사적 용법의 to부정사(목적)
수화를 사용하는 것을   인간과 의사소통을 하기 위해

➡ 어떤 영장류가 '가르침을 받아 온' 것이므로, 현재완료 수동태인 have been taught가 오는 것이 어법상 적절하다.

④ 「전치사 + 관계대명사」

It provides the single most common variable / [by which different
              선행사
그것은 단 하나의 가장 보편적인 변인을 제공한다
cultural groups are identified].
다양한 문화 집단이 식별되는

➡ which는 앞의 명사구(the single … variable)를 선행사로 하는 관계대명사로, 관계대명사절에서 전치사 by의 목적어 역할을 하고 있으므로 어법상 적절하다.

⑤ 병렬구조

Language not only facilitates the cultural diffusion of innovations, /
        not only A (but) also B: A뿐만 아니라 B도
언어는 혁신의 문화적 보급을 촉진할 뿐 아니라
it also helps to shape / the way[how] [we think about, perceive,
                 선행사   주어 동사1   동사2
그것은 또한 형성하도록 돕는다   우리가 환경을 생각하고, 인지하고, 이름을 붙이는 방식을
and name our environment].
접속사 동사3

➡ 등위접속사 and가 관계부사절 안의 동사 think, perceive, name을 병렬 연결하고 있으므로 어법상 바르다.

 구문 분석 Plus

| 1행 | Language is **one of the primary features** [that distinguishes humans from other animals].
 ➡ one of + 복수 명사: … 중 하나
 ➡ that 이하는 one of the primary features를 수식하는 주격 관계대명사절
 ➡ distinguish A from B: A를 B와 구분하다 |

지문 해석

언어는 인간을 다른 동물과 구분하는 주요한 특징 중 하나이다. 돌고래, 고래, 그리고 새를 포함한 많은 동물들이 소리, 냄새, 그리고 다른 화학물질의 패턴화된 체계, 또는 움직임을 통해 실제로 서로 의사소통을 한다. 게다가, 인간이 아닌 어떤 영장류는 인간과 의사소통을 하기 위해 수화를 사용하도록 배웠다. 하지만 인간 언어의 복잡성, 미묘한 차이가 있는 감정과 생각을 전달하는 능력, 그리고 사회적 동물로서 우리의 존재에 대한 그것의 중요성은 그것을 다른 동물들에 의해 사용되는 의사소통 체계와 구분 짓는다. 여러 가지 면에서, 언어는 문화의 본질이다. 그것은 다양한 문화 집단이 식별되는 단 하나의 가장 보편적인 변인을 제공한다. 언어는 혁신의 문화적 보급을 촉진할 뿐 아니라, 우리가 환경을 생각하고, 인지하고, 이름을 붙이는 방식을 형성하도록 돕는다.

 어휘

primary 휑 주요한   **feature** 뗑 특징   **distinguish** 통 구분하다   **chemical** 뗑 화학 물질   **primate** 뗑 영장류   **sign language** 수화   **convey** 통 전달하다   **nuanced** 휑 미묘한 차이가 있는   **existence** 뗑 존재, 실재   **essence** 뗑 본질   **variable** 뗑 변수, 변인   **facilitate** 통 촉진하다   **diffusion** 뗑 발산; *(문화 등의) 전파, 보급   **perceive** 통 인지하다

---

07   정답 ①   정답률 57%

정답 풀이

(A) 병렬구조

Stop thinking about [what you don't have] / and find / ~~finding~~ a
stop v-ing: …하는 것을 멈추다 관계대명사   접속사
당신이 가지고 있지 않은 것에 대해 생각하는 것을 멈추고   스스로 해결책을 찾아라
solution yourself!
     재귀대명사(강조 용법)

➡ 등위접속사 and가 명령문의 동사를 병렬 연결하고 있으므로, Stop과 대등하도록 동사원형 find가 오는 것이 적절하다.

(B) 목적격 관계대명사절의 동사

"Gym" teacher is an old-fashioned term / [that some people still
                                        목적격 관계대명사
'gym' 교사는 구시대 용어이다   일부 사람들이 여전히 사용하는
use / ~~use it~~ / to describe a physical educator], / and some people still
          부사적 용법의 to부정사(목적)
          체육 교사를 지칭하기 위해   그리고 일부 사람들은 여전히
use the word "gym" / to describe physical education.
                  부사적 용법의 to부정사(목적)
'gym'이라는 단어를 사용한다   체육 교육을 지칭하기 위해

➡ 네모는 목적격 관계대명사 that이 이끄는 절의 동사 자리로 use가 오는 것이 알맞다. 관계대명사 that이 관계대명사절에서 목적어 역할을 하고 있으므로 동사 use 뒤에 목적어 it은 올 수 없다.

(C) 문장의 동사

If you were trained to be a physical education teacher, / not having
                                                   동명사구 주어
만약 당신이 체육 교사가 되기 위해 훈련을 받았다면
a gym is / ~~being~~ not a huge problem.
      동사
체육관을 가지고 있지 않은 것이 큰 문제가 아니다

➡ 동명사구(not having a gym)가 주어이므로 동사 is가 뒤따르는 것이 어법상 적절하다. 동명사구가 주어로 오면 단수로 취급한다.

지문 해석

"아니, 이런! 'gym' 교사가 체육관 없이 무엇을 할 수 있단 말입니까?" 당신이 가지고 있지 않은 것에 대해 생각하는 것을 멈추고 스스로 해결책을 찾아라! 당신은 'gym' 교사가 되도록 훈련을 받은 것이 아니라, 체육 교육을 실시하도록 훈련을 받았다. 'gym' 교사는 일부 사람들이 체육 교사를 지칭하기 위해서 여전히 사용하고 있는 구시대의 용어이며, 일부 사람들은 여전히 체육 교육을 지칭하기 위해서 'gym'이라는 단어를 사용한다. 당신이 체육 교사가 되기 위해 훈련을 받았다면, 체육관을 가지고 있지 않은 것이 큰 문제가 아니다. 예를 들어, 당신은 학교 주차장에서 학생들에게 테니스의 공을 치는 기술을, 오래된 교회에서 농구의 드리블 기술을 가르칠 수 있을 것이다.

 어휘

gym 뗑 체육관   **physical education** 체육 교육   **old-fashioned** 휑 구식의   **term** 뗑 기간; *용어   **physical educator** 체육 교사   **strike** 통 (공을) 치다   **dribble** 통 (스포츠에서) 드리블하다

정답 풀이

② 병렬구조

Those [who have found deeper meaning in their careers] /
주어 ↑ └ 주격 관계대명사
자신의 직업에서 더 깊은 의미를 찾은 사람은   비교급 강조
find their days much more energizing and satisfying, / and
동사1 └ find+목적어+목적격보어: …가 ~하다고 생각하다
자신의 하루하루가 훨씬 더 활기차고 만족감을 준다고 생각한다   그리고
to count(→ count) their employment as one of their greatest
동사2   전치사(…로)
자신의 직업을 기쁨과 자부심의 가장 큰 원천 중 하나로 꼽는다
sources of joy and pride.

➡ 동사 두 개가 등위접속사 and에 병렬 연결된 형태로, find와 문법적으로 대등한 형태의 count가 되어야 한다.

친절한 오답 풀이

① 주격 관계대명사

It would be hard to overstate / [how important meaningful work
가주어   진주어   간접의문문
과장해서 말한다는 것은 어려울 것이다   인간에게 의미 있는 일이 얼마나 중요한지를
is to human beings / — {work [that provides a sense of fulfillment
                              └ 주격 관계대명사
                              즉 성취감과 권한을 제공하는 일이
and empowerment]}.   └ meaningful work의 부연 설명

➡ work를 선행사로 하고 뒤에 주어가 빠진 절이 이어지므로 주격 관계대명사 that은 어법상 바르다.

③ 명사를 수식하는 현재분사구

Sonya Lyubomirsky, professor of psychology at the University
                        └ 동격
University of California의 심리학 교수인 Sonya Lyubomirsky는
of California, / has conducted numerous workplace studies /
                                        수많은 업무 현장 연구를 수행했다
현재분사   접속사
{showing that / [when people are more fulfilled on the job, / they
└ 명사절(목적어)을
이끄는 접속사
보여 주는   사람이 직업에 더 많은 성취감을 느낄 때
not only produce higher quality work and a greater output, / but
not only A but also B: A뿐만 아니라 B도
그들은 더 질 높은 업무와 더 큰 성과를 만들어 낼 뿐만 아니라
also generally earn higher incomes]}.
일반적으로 더 높은 수입을 거둔다는 것을

➡ workplace studies를 수식하는 분사 자리로, show의 주체이므로 능동의 의미를 나타내는 현재분사는 어법상 바르다.

④ 동사의 수 일치

Those [(who are) most satisfied with their work] / are also much
주어   주격 관계대명사+be동사 생략   동사   비교급 강조
자신의 일에 가장 만족하는 사람은
more likely to be happier with their lives overall.
be more likely to-v: ~할 가능성이 더 높다
또한 전반적으로 자신의 삶에 더 행복해할 가능성이 훨씬 더 높다

➡ 주어가 복수 명사 Those이므로 복수 동사 are는 어법상 바르다.

⑤ 분사구문

For her book *Happiness at Work*, / researcher Jessica Pryce-
전치사(…을 위해)   └ 동격
자신의 저서 〈*Happiness at Work*〉를 위해   연구자 Jessica Pryce-Jones는
Jones conducted a study of 3,000 workers in seventy-nine
                                        전치사구
79개 국가의 3,000명의 근로자에 대한 연구를 수행했다
                    명사절(목적어)을 이끄는 접속사
countries, / {finding that / [those <who took greater satisfaction
        결과를 나타내는 분사구문   └ 주격 관계대명사
                알아냈다   자신의 일로부터 더 큰 만족감을 갖는 사람이
from their work> / were 150 percent more likely to have a
전반적으로 더 행복한 삶을 살 가능성이 150퍼센트 더 높다는 것을
happier life overall]}.

➡ 주절의 주어 Jessica Pryce-Jones가 생략된 '(그 결과) 알아냈다'는 의미인 분사구문의 분사 자리로, 주어와 능동 관계이므로 현재분사 finding은 어법상 바르다.

지문 해석

인간에게 의미 있는 일, 즉 성취감과 권한을 제공하는 일이 얼마나 중요한지를 과장해서 말한다는 것은 어려울 것이다. 자신의 직업에서 더 깊은 의미를 찾은 사람은 자신의 하루하루가 훨씬 더 활기차고 만족감을 준다고 생각하고, 자신의 직업을 기쁨과 자부심의 가장 큰 원천 중 하나로 꼽는다. University of California의 심리학 교수인 Sonya Lyubomirsky는 사람이 직업에 더 많은 성취감을 느낄 때 그들은 더 질 높은 업무와 더 큰 성과를 만들어 낼 뿐만 아니라 일반적으로 더 높은 수입을 거둔다는 것을 보여 주는 수많은 업무 현장 연구를 수행했다. 자신의 일에 가장 만족하는 사람은 또한 전반적으로 자신의 삶에 더 행복해할 가능성이 훨씬 더 높다. 자신의 저서 〈*Happiness at Work*〉를 위해 연구자 Jessica Pryce-Jones는 79개 국가의 3,000명의 근로자에 대한 연구를 수행했고, 자신의 일로부터 더 큰 만족감을 갖는 사람이 전반적으로 더 행복한 삶을 살 가능성이 150퍼센트 더 높다는 것을 알아냈다.

어휘

overstate 통 과장해서 말하다 **fulfillment** 명 성취감 **empowerment** 명 권한
energizing 형 활기찬 **satisfying** 형 만족감을 주는 **employment** 명 직업, 고용
source 명 원천 **psychology** 명 심리학 **conduct** 통 수행하다 **workplace**
명 업무 현장, 직장 **output** 명 성과 **generally** 부 일반적으로 **income** 명 수입
overall 부 전반적으로

정답 풀이

⑤ 병렬구조

                                        부사절의 주어
Babies [with sight] smile more at you / [when you look at them /
주어   └ 전치사구(형용사) 동사   부사절 부사절의 동사1
시력이 있는 아기들은 당신에게 더 많이 미소 짓는다   당신이 그들을 바라볼 때
or, better still, / smiling(→ smile) back at them].
                    부사절의 동사2
또는 더 나아가   그들에게 미소를 지어줄 (때)

➡ 부사절의 동사 두 개가 등위접속사 or로 병렬 연결된 형태로, look과 문법적으로 대등한 형태의 smile이 되어야 한다.

친절한 오답 풀이

① 접속사 that

The built-in capacity for smiling is proven / by the remarkable
미소 짓기에 대한 선천적인 능력은 증명된다   놀라운 관찰에 의해
                        that절의 주어 ↓
observation / {that babies [who are congenitally both deaf and
        └ 동격 ┘   ↑ 주격 관계대명사1
                        선천적으로 청각장애와 시각장애가 있는 아기들이
blind], / [who have never seen a human face], / also start to smile /
        주격 관계대명사2   that절의 동사
        사람 얼굴을 한 번도 본 적이 없는 (아기들이)   또한 미소를 짓기 시작한다는
at around 2 months}.
약 2개월 즈음에

➡ 앞의 명사구 the remarkable observation과 동격을 이루는 명사절을 이끄는 접속사 that은 어법상 바르다.

② 동사의 수 일치

> However, / [smiling in blind babies] eventually disappears / [if
> 　　　　　동명사구(주어)　　　　　　　　　동사　　접속사(…라면)
> 그러나　　시각장애를 가진 아기의 미소 짓기는 결국 사라진다
> nothing is done / to reinforce it].
> 　　　　　　　　부사적 용법의 to부정사(목적)
> 아무것도 행해지지 않으면　그것을 강화하기 위해

➡ 주어로 쓰인 동명사는 단수 취급하므로, 단수 동사 disappears는 어법상 바르다.

③ 대명사

> But here's a fascinating fact: / blind babies will continue to smile /
> 　　　　　　　　　　　　　　　　　continue to-v[v-ing]: 계속 …하다
> 하지만 여기에 흥미로운 사실이 있다　시각장애를 가진 아기들은 계속 미소를 지을 것이다
> [if they are cuddled, bounced, nudged, and tickled by an adult] /
> 접속사(…라면)　　　　　　　　　　　　　　　　　　　　　　　명사절(목적어)을
> 만약 그들이 어른에 의해서 안기고, 흔들리고, 슬쩍 찔리고, 간지럽혀지면　이끄는 접속사2
> — anything {to let them know / [that they are not alone] / and [that
> 　　　　　형용사적 용법의 to부정사　명사절(목적어)을 이끄는 접속사1
> 그들이 알게 하는 것　　　　그들이 혼자가 아니라는 것　　　　그리고
> someone cares about them]}.
> 누군가 그들에게 관심을 갖고 있다는 것을

➡ 복수 명사 blind babies를 대신하므로 복수형 대명사 them은 어법상 바르다.

④ 부사적 용법의 to부정사

> In this way, / early experience operates with our biology / to
> 　　　　　　　　　주어　　　　　동사
> 이런 방식으로　초기 경험은 우리의 생리 작용과 함께 작용한다
> establish social behaviors.
> (그 결과) 사회적 행동을 확립한다

➡ 문장의 동사 operates가 있으므로 준동사 형태가 되어야 한다. 따라서 부사적 용법의 to부정사는 어법상 바르다.

지문 해석

미소 짓기에 대한 선천적인 능력은 선천적으로 청각장애와 시각장애가 있고, 사람 얼굴을 한 번도 본 적이 없는 아기들도, 약 2개월 즈음에 미소를 짓기 시작한다는 놀라운 관찰에 의해 증명된다. 그러나, 시각장애를 가진 아기의 미소 짓기는 그것을 강화하기 위해 아무것도 행해지지 않으면 결국 사라진다. 적절한 피드백이 없으면, 미소 짓기는 사라진다. 하지만 여기에 흥미로운 사실이 있다. 만약 그들이 어른에 의해서 안기고, 흔들리고, 슬쩍 찔리고, 간지럽혀지면—그들이 혼자가 아니며 누군가 그들에게 관심을 갖고 있다는 것을 알게 하는 것—시각장애를 가진 아기들은 계속 미소를 지을 것이다. 이러한 사회적 피드백은 그 아기가 계속 미소를 지을 수 있도록 조장한다. 이런 방식으로, 초기 경험은 우리의 생리 작용과 함께 작용하여 사회적 행동을 확립한다. 사실, 당신은 이를 설명하기 위해 시각장애를 가진 아기의 사례들을 필요로 하지 않는다. 시력이 있는 아기들은 당신이 그들을 바라볼 때나, 더 나아가, 당신이 그들에게 미소를 지어줄 때, 당신에게 더 많이 미소 짓는다.

 어휘

capacity 명 능력　remarkable 형 놀라운　observation 명 관찰　eventually 부 결국　reinforce 통 강화하다　die out 사라지다　tickle 통 간지럽히다　establish 통 확립하다

정답 풀이

③ 문장의 동사

> No matter how it is conceptualized — / whether as
> = however(어떤 식으로 …하든)　　　　　　　whether A or B: A이든 B이든
> 그것이 어떤 식으로 개념화되든
> trustworthiness, cooperation, justice, or caring — /
> 신뢰성, 협력, 정의 혹은 보살핌이든지
> morality to be(→ is) always about the treatment of people /
> 　주어　　　　동사
> 도덕성은 항상 사람을 대하는 것에 관한 것이다
> in social relationships.
> 사회적 관계에서

➡ 문장의 주어는 morality이고 동사가 빠져 있으며 글 전체가 현재 시제로 쓰였으므로 to부정사 to be를 현재형 be동사 is로 고쳐야 한다.

친절한 오답 풀이

① 「전치사 + 관계대명사」

> In the interdependent groups / [in which humans and other
> 　　선행사　　　　　　　　　　　　　　　　　　other + 복수 명사
> 　　　　　　　　　　　　　　　　목적격 관계대명사
> 상호 의존적인 집단에서　　　　　인간과 그 외의 영장류들이 사는
> primates live], / individuals must have even greater common
> 　　　　　　　　　　　　　　　　　　　부사(훨씬)
> 　　　　　　　개인들은 훨씬 더 큰 공통의 기반을 가져야 한다
> ground / to establish and (to) maintain social relationships.
> 부사적 용법의 to부정사(목적)　접속사 and에 의해 to establish와 병렬 연결됨
> 사회적 관계를 확립하고 유지하기 위해

➡ 관계대명사 which는 the interdependent groups를 선행사로 하고, 관계대명사절에서 전치사 in의 목적어 역할을 하고 있으므로 어법상 바르다.

② 「전치사 + 동명사」, 동명사의 동사적 특징

> This is (the reason) why …: 이것이 …한 이유이다
> This is (the reason) / [why morality often is defined / as a shared
> 　　　　　　　　　　앞에 생략된 선행사 the reason을 수식하는 관계부사　수동태
> 이것이 이유이다　도덕성이 자주 정의되는　　　　　　　　　　공유된
> set of standards / for judging right and wrong / in the conduct of
> 　　　　　　　전치사 동명사(전치사의 목적어)
> 일련의 기준으로　옳고 그름을 판단하기 위한　　　　사회적 관계의 행위에서
> social relationships].

➡ 전치사 for의 목적어 역할을 하면서 명사구 right and wrong을 목적어로 취할 수 있는 동명사 judging이 오는 것이 알맞다.

④ 접속사 that

> This is likely why there is surprising agreement / across a wide
> 　　아마, 십중팔구　　　　　　　　　　　　전치사(… 전체에 걸쳐) 광범위한
> 이것이 아마 놀라운 일치가 있는 이유이다　광범위한 관점에 걸쳐
> range of perspectives / [that a shared sense of morality is
> 　　　　　　　　　　　동격　　that은 동격의 접속사
> 　　　　　　　　공유된 도덕 관념이 사회적 관계에 필수적이라는
> necessary to social relations].

➡ 앞의 명사 perspectives와 동격을 이루는 명사절을 이끄는 접속사로, 뒤에 완전한 절이 이어지고 있으므로 어법상 바르다.

⑤ 동사의 수 일치

> Evolutionary biologists, sociologists, and philosophers all / seem
> ⌐…처럼 보이다
> 진화 생물학자와 사회학자, 철학자 모두는
> to agree with (opinions of) social psychologists / {that the
> └…에 동의하다┘ └─────동격─────┘ └that은 동격의 접속사
> 사회 심리학자의 의견에 동의하는 것처럼 보인다
> interdependent relationships / within groups / [that humans
> └동격의 명사절의 주어┘ └전치사(… 안에)┘ └목적격 관계대명사
> 상호 의존적 관계가 집단 내에서의 인간이 의존하는
> depend on] / are not possible / without a shared morality}.
> └…에 의존하다┘ └동사┘ └전치사(… 없이)
> 가능하지 않다는 공유된 도덕성 없이는

➡ 접속사 that이 이끄는 동격의 명사절 내에서 주어(the interdependent relationships)가 복수 명사이므로 복수 동사 are가 오는 것이 알맞다.

지문 해석

모든 사회적 상호 작용은 관련된 당사자들이 그들의 행동을 조정할 수 있는 어떤 공통의 기반을 요구한다. 인간과 그 외의 영장류들이 사는 상호 의존적인 집단에서, 개인들은 사회적 관계를 확립하고 유지하기 위해 훨씬 더 큰 공통의 기반을 가져야 한다. 이러한 공통의 기반은 도덕성이다. 이는 도덕성이 사회적 관계의 행위에서 옳고 그름을 판단하기 위한 공유된 일련의 기준으로 자주 정의되는 이유이다. 그것이 어떤 식으로 개념화되든(신뢰성, 협력, 정의 혹은 보살핌이든지) 도덕성은 항상 사회적 관계에서 사람을 대하는 것에 관한 것이다. 이것이 아마 공유된 도덕 관념이 사회적 관계에 필수적이라는 광범위한 관점에 걸쳐 놀라운 일치가 있는 이유이다. 진화 생물학자와 사회학자, 철학자 모두는 인간이 의존하는 집단 내에서의 상호 의존적 관계가 공유된 도덕성 없이는 가능하지 않다는 사회 심리학자의 의견에 동의하는 듯하다.

common 형 공통의   ground 명 기반   party 명 당사자   coordinate 동 조정하다
interdependent 형 상호 의존적인   primate 명 영장류   establish 동 수립하다
morality 명 도덕성   conduct 명 행위   conceptualize 동 개념화하다
trustworthiness 명 신뢰성   caring 명 보살핌   treatment 명 (사람에 대한) 대우
agreement 명 일치   perspective 명 관점   sense 명 …감[의식/느낌], 관념
biologist 명 생물학자   sociologist 명 사회학자   philosopher 명 철학자

UNIT 2 문장의 형식

코드 접속하기
pp.87~90

출제코드 1 · 5형식 문장 구조와 목적격보어

A 1 recovered 2 difficult 3 to become
B 1 ➡ punished 2 ○

해석과 정답 풀이

STEP 1
1 우리는 그를 학급 회장으로 선출했다.
2 1) 그의 밝은 미소는 사람들을 행복하게 만든다.
  2) 그녀의 아버지는 그녀가 저녁 식사 전에 집에 올 것이라 기대했다.
  3) 사장은 그의 비서에게 오늘 점심 식사를 예약하게 했다.
  4) 그녀는 누군가가 그녀를 향해 조용히 걸어오고 있는 것을 알아챘다.
  5) Amy는 그녀의 이름이 스피커를 통해 크게 불리는 것을 들었다.

STEP 2
1 그 비극적인 교통 사고는 그가 그의 시력을 잃게 했다.
2 시진은 살아남아 자신이 운이 좋다고 여겼다.
3 1) 나는 내 여동생이 그녀의 고양이에게 먹이를 주는 것을 보았다.
  2) Josh는 2주 전에 그의 사랑니를 뺐다.

STEP 3
A 1 그는 컴퓨터 전문가에 의해 잃어버린 파일이 복구되게 해야 한다.
  ➡ 사역동사 have의 목적어(the lost files)와 목적격보어가 의미상 수동의 관계이므로 과거분사 recovered가 오는 것이 알맞다.
  2 얼마 후, 그는 작은 그림에서 세세한 것들을 보는 것이 어려워진 것을 알았다.
  ➡ 동사 found의 목적격보어 자리이므로 형용사 difficult가 오는 것이 알맞다.
  3 그가 자신의 실패에 좌절되는 것을 허용했다면, 그는 결코 그의 목표를 성취하지 못했을 것이다.
  ➡ 동사 allowed는 목적격보어로 to부정사를 취하므로 to become이 오는 것이 알맞다.
B 1 나는 항상 지각을 하는 Tom이 잘못된 행동으로 벌을 받는 것을 들었다.
  ➡ 지각동사 heard의 목적어(Tom)와 목적격보어가 의미상 수동의 관계에 있으므로 punish를 과거분사 punished로 고쳐야 한다.
  2 당신의 생일에 부모님이 당신을 울게 만드는 마음이 따뜻해지는, 감동적인 편지를 주었다고 상상해보라.
  ➡ 사역동사 make의 목적어(you)와 목적격보어가 의미상 능동의 관계이므로 동사원형 cry가 오는 것이 알맞다.

출제코드 2 · 2형식 문장 구조와 주격보어

A 1 sensitive 2 anxious 3 obvious
B 1 ○ 2 ➡ late 3 ➡ secure

해석과 정답 풀이

STEP 1
1 1) 그녀는 유명한 작곡가다.
  2) 난 학급 회의 동안에 침묵을 지켰다.
2 1) 그는 화가 나서 내 전화를 받지 않았다.
  2) 만약 포도잼이 너무 달다면, 버터나 마가린을 대신 먹어봐라.
  3) 내가 도서관 앞에서 Jenny를 만났을 때 그녀는 지쳐 보였다.

STEP 2
1 1) 테이블 위에 있는 사과 파이는 아주 맛있어 보인다.
  2) 향수는 서로 다른 사람들의 피부에서 다른 향기가 난다.
  3) 뚱뚱한 토끼는 느린 것처럼 보이지만, 사실은 매우 빠르게 움직일 수 있다.

STEP 3
A 1 심리학자들은 왜 사람들이 자기 자신의 결점들을 듣는 것에 대해 그렇게

민감해지는지에 관해 연구했다.
➡ 동사 studied의 목적어로 쓰인 간접의문문(why ... flaws)에서, 네모는 동사 become의 주격보어 자리이므로 형용사 sensitive가 오는 것이 알맞다.
2 그는 교수가 되기를 매우 열망해서 그의 어머니는 그를 다시 학교로 보냈다.
➡ be동사 was가 쓰인 2형식 문장의 주격보어 자리이므로 형용사 anxious가 오는 것이 알맞다.
3 이는 분명한 것처럼 들리지만, 오직 그 증상을 치료하는 것은 문제를 무시하는 것이다.
➡ 감각동사 sounds가 쓰인 2형식 문장의 주격보어 자리이므로 형용사 obvious가 오는 것이 알맞다.
B 1 그는 작은 비디오 카메라를 통해 상어들의 삶을 보는 것이 흥미로울 것이라고 생각했다.
➡ 동사 thought의 목적어로 쓰인 명사절(it ... camera)에서, 형용사 interesting이 주격보어로 쓰였으므로 어법상 바르다.
2 깨워서 미안하지만, 내가 오늘 밤에 조금 늦게 집에 갈 것 같아 전화할 수 밖에 없었다.
➡ be동사의 주격보어 자리이므로 형용사 late로 고쳐야 한다. 부사 lately는 '최근에'라는 의미를 가지며, 보어로 쓰일 수 없다.
3 많은 여성들이 오늘날의 이 무서운 세상에 대해 걱정하며 혼자 외출할 때 그들이 어떻게 안전하게 느낄 수 있는지를 궁금해한다.
➡ 동사 wonder의 목적어로 쓰인 간접의문문(how ... alone)에서, 밑줄 친 부분은 감각동사 feel의 주격보어 자리이므로 부사 securely를 형용사 secure로 고쳐야 한다.

기출예제 Q1   정답 ④   정답률 50%

정답 풀이

④ 목적격보어

In addition, / people engage with infants / by exaggerating their
         ···와 관계를 맺다   by v-ing: ···함으로써
또한   사람들은 유아들과 관계를 맺는다   얼굴 표정을 과장하고
facial expressions and inflecting their voices / in ways [that
                                                        ↑   목적격
목소리를 조정하면서   관계대명사
infants find fascinated(→ fascinating)].
                          목적격보어
유아들이 매력적이라고 느끼는 방식으로

➡ 동사 find의 목적격보어 자리이고, 목적어는 선행사인 ways이므로 목적어와 목적격보어가 의미상 능동 관계에 있다. 따라서 과거분사 fascinated를 현재분사 fascinating으로 고쳐야 한다.

친절한 오답 풀이

① 접속사 that

By noticing the relation / between their own actions and resultant
by v-ing: ···함으로써   between A and B: A와 B 사이에
관계를 알아차림으로써   자신의 행동과 그에 따른 외부 변화 사이에서의
external changes, / infants develop self-efficacy, / a sense [that
                                                          동격   동격의
                유아들은 자아 효능감을 발전시킨다   접속사
they are agents of the perceived changes].
즉 그들이 인지된 변화의 주체라는 인식

➡ 앞의 명사구 a sense와 동격을 이루는 명사절을 이끄는 접속사로, 뒤에 완전한 절이 이어지고 있으므로 어법상 바르다.

② 부사

[Although infants can notice the effect of their behavior / on the
접속사(비록 ···이긴 하지만)
유아들은 자신의 행동의 영향을 알아차릴 수 있지만
physical environment], / it is in early social interactions / that
                          It is ... that 강조구문
물리적 환경에 미치는   바로 초기 사회적 상호 작용을 통해서
infants most readily perceive the consequence of their actions.
  주어   부사 └─→ 동사
유아들은 매우 쉽게 자신의 행동의 결과를 인식한다

➡ 동사 perceive를 수식하고 있으므로 부사 readily가 오는 것이 알맞다.

③ 동사의 수 일치

People have perceptual characteristics /{that virtually assure [that
                                              주격 관계대명사   접속사
사람들은 지각과 관련된 특성을 가지고 있다   유아들이 그들에게 향하는 것을
infants will orient toward them]}.
                = people
실제로 확실하게 하는

➡ assure은 perceptual characteristics를 선행사로 하는 주격 관계대명사절의 동사로, 선행사가 복수 명사이므로 복수 동사가 오는 것이 알맞다.

⑤ 관계부사

Consequentially, / early social interactions provide a context / [where
                                                        ↑   관계
결과적으로   초기 사회적 상호작용은 맥락을 제공한다   부사
infants can easily notice the effect of their behavior].
유아들이 자신의 행동의 영향을 쉽게 알아차릴 수 있는

➡ where는 a context를 선행사로 하는 관계부사로, 뒤에 완전한 절이 이어지고 있으므로 어법상 바르다.

지문 해석

유아들은 자신의 행동과 그에 따른 외부 변화 사이에서의 관계를 알아차림으로써, 그들이 인지된 변화의 주체라는 인식, 즉 자아 효능감을 발전시킨다. 유아들은 자신의 행동이 물리적 환경에 미치는 영향을 알아차릴 수 있는데, 바로 초기 사회적 상호 작용을 통해서 유아들은 매우 쉽게 자신의 행동의 결과를 인식한다. 사람들은 유아들이 그들에게 향하는 것을 실제로 확실하게 하는 지각과 관련된 특성을 가지고 있다. 사람들은 시각적으로 구별되고 달라지는 얼굴 표정을 지닌다. 사람들은 소리를 만들고, 촉각을 제공하고, 흥미로운 냄새를 가지고 있다. 또한, 사람들은 유아들이 매력적이라고 느끼는 방식으로 얼굴 표정을 과장하고 목소리를 조절하면서 유아들과 관계를 맺는다. 그러나 다른 무엇보다 중요한 것은 이러한 익살스러운 행동은 유아들의 발성, 얼굴 표정, 몸짓에 대해 반응을 잘 한다는 것이다. 사람들은 유아들의 행동에 반응하여 자신들의 행동의 속도와 수준을 다양하게 한다. 결과적으로 초기 사회적 상호 작용은 유아들이 자신의 행동의 영향을 쉽게 알아차릴 수 있는 맥락을 제공한다.

어휘

resultant 형 그 결과로 생긴   external 형 외부의   self-efficacy 명 자아 효능감   agent 명 대리인; *행위자   readily 부 쉽게   perceive 동 인지하다   perceptual 형 지각의   characteristic 명 특징   assure 동 확실하게 하다   orient 동 (어떤 방향으로) 향하다   responsive 형 즉각 반응하는   context 명 맥락, 문맥

기출예제 Q2   정답 ②   정답률 60%

정답 풀이

② 목적격보어

The problem is [that globalization pushes in the opposite
      명사절(보어)을 이끄는 접속사   반대 방향으로
문제는 세계화가 반대 방향으로 밀어낸다는 것이다
direction]; by placing a premium on high skills / [that make
              place a premium on: ···을 높이 평가하다   주격 관계대명사   동사
              고도의 기술을 높이 평가함으로써
workers more competitively(→ competitive)], ...
           목적어   목적격보어
근로자들을 더 경쟁적으로 만드는

➡ 동사 make의 목적격보어 자리이므로 부사 competitively를 형용사 competitive로 고쳐야 한다. 부사는 보어 자리에 쓰일 수 없다.

① be to-v 용법

Democracies require more equality / if they **are to** grow stronger.

민주주의는 더 많은 평등을 필요로 한다 / be to-v 용법(의도) / 만약 그들이 더 강력해지려 한다면

➡ '…하려고 하다'라는 의미로 의도를 나타내는 be to-v가 쓰였으므로 어법상 바르다.

③ 가주어 진주어 구문

In this situation, / it is not sufficient / [to reduce economic

이러한 상황에서 / 가주어 / 충분하지 않다 / 진주어 / 경제적인 불안정을 감소시키는 것은

insecurity / by expanding the social safety net].

by v-ing: …함으로써 / 사회 안전망을 확대함으로써

➡ 앞의 it이 가주어, to reduce 이하가 진주어로 쓰인 to부정사구로 어법상 바르다.

④ 병렬구조

..., with an emphasis on creating a more highly skilled labor

전치사 / 동명사1 / 더욱 고도로 숙련된 노동력을 창출하는 것을 강조하면서

force / and improving access to the labor market for women ....

접속사 / 동명사2 / 그리고 여성의 노동시장에의 접근성을 높이는 것을

➡ 등위접속사 and가 전치사 on의 목적어 역할을 하는 동명사를 병렬 연결하고 있는 구조로, 동명사 creating과 대등한 동명사 improving이 왔으므로 어법상 바르다.

⑤ 수동태

Only then can social policies be considered / key factors of

부사구 / 조동사 / 주어 / 동사 / 생산의 주요 요소로
그때서야 사회 정책들은 간주될 수 있다

production ....

➡ 부사구 Only then이 강조를 위해 문장 앞으로 나가면서 「조동사 + 주어 + 동사」 형태로 도치가 일어난 문장이다. 사회 정책들이 '간주되는'이라는 수동의 의미이므로 수동태 be considered가 오는 것이 알맞다.

지문 해석

민주주의가 더 강력해지려 한다면 더 많은 평등을 필요로 한다. 문제는 세계화가 반대 방향으로 밀어낸다는 것이다. 근로자들을 더 경쟁적으로 만드는 고도의 기술을 높이 평가함으로써, 세계화는 고도로 숙련된 소수와 나머지 사이의 소득 불평등을 증가시킨다. 이러한 상황에서 사회 안전망을 확대함으로써 경제적인 불안정을 감소시키는 것은 충분하지 않다. 대신에, 국가는 복지국가에서 노동 후생국가로 이행하기 시작해야 하는데, 더욱 고도로 숙련된 노동력을 창출하고, 여성과 저소득 청년의 노동시장에의 접근성을 높이는 것을 강조해야 한다. 일자리 창출을 확대하려면, 새로운 사회 정책은 또한 창업 의욕과 혁신에 대한 더 나은 인센티브를 제공해야 한다. 그때서야 사회 정책은 사회 보호의 도구로서의 역할을 넘어서 생산의 주요 요소로 간주될 수 있다.

democracy 몡 민주주의 require 통 요구하다 equality 몡 평등 (inequality 몡 불평등) globalization 몡 세계화 opposite 혱 정반대의 direction 몡 방향 competitively 픠 경쟁적으로 minority 몡 소수 sufficient 혱 충분한 insecurity 몡 불안정성 expand 통 확장하다 transition 몡 (다른 상태로의) 이행 welfare state 복지국가 workfare state 노동 후생국가 emphasis 몡 강조 labor force 노동력 access 몡 접근 incentive 몡 유인책, 인센티브 innovation 몡 혁신 production 몡 생산 instrument 몡 도구 protection 몡 보호

---

01 ①	**02** ③	**03** ⑤	**04** ⑤	**05** ②	**06** ④	**07** ②	**08** ⑤
09 ②	**10** ①						

01 정답 ① 정답률 50%

정답 풀이

(A) 주격보어

Many parents worry about the state of the world today / and

많은 부모들은 오늘날 세상의 상태를 걱정한다 / 그리고

wonder / {how they can feel safe / safely / [when raising kids

간접의문문(의문사 + 주어 + 동사), feel + 형용사: …하게 느끼다 / 접속사가 남아있는 분사구문 (= when they raise …)
궁금해한다   그들이 어떻게 안전하게 느낄 수 있을지 / 이 무서운 세상에서

in this scary world]}.

아이들을 기를 때

➡ 감각동사 feel의 보어 자리이므로 형용사 safe가 오는 것이 알맞다.

(B) 분사구문

The other boy put his arm in front of his friend, / [~~motioned~~

다른 남자아이가 팔로 친구의 앞을 막았다

/ motioning for me to go ahead].

동시동작을 나타내는 분사구문(= as he motioned …)
내가 먼저 가라고 손짓을 하면서

➡ 네모는 동시동작을 나타내는 분사구문의 분사로, 생략된 주어는 주절의 주어(The other boy)와 같다. 주어와 분사가 능동 관계에 있으므로 현재분사 motioning이 오는 것이 알맞다.

(C) 접속사 that

I promised myself at that moment / [when / that I would raise

부사구 / 명사절(목적어)을 이끄는 접속사
나는 그때 스스로에게 다짐했다 / 내 아이를 그와 같이 기르겠다고

my children to be like him].

전치사(…와 같은)

➡ 동사 promised의 목적어 역할을 하는 명사절을 이끌며, 뒤에 완전한 절이 이어지고 있으므로 접속사 that이 오는 것이 알맞다.

지문 해석

많은 부모들이 오늘날 세상의 상태를 걱정하고 이 무서운 세상에서 아이들을 기를 때 어떻게 안전하게 느낄 수 있을지 궁금해한다. 그러나 나는 여전히 희망은 있다는 것을 발견했다. 내가 막 엄마가 되었을 때, 두 명의 십 대 남자아이들과 함께 엘리베이터를 탔다. 엘리베이터 문이 열리자, 한 소년이 먼저 내리려 했다. 다른 남자아이가 내게 먼저 가라고 손짓을 하면서 팔로 친구의 앞을 막았다. 나는 그의 작지만 사려 깊은 행동과 훌륭한 매너에 감동을 받았다. 나는 소년에게 고맙다고 말했고, 또한 그의 어머니에게 이렇게 예의 바른 청년을 기르는 멋진 일을 하신 것에 대해 나의 감사를 전해달라고 부탁했다. 나는 그때 내 아이들을 그와 같이 기르겠다고 스스로에게 다짐했다.

state 몡 상태 raise 통 들어올리다; *(아이를) 키우다 scary 혱 무서운 brand-new 혱 아주 새로운 teenage 혱 십 대의 be about to-v 막 …하려고 하다 motion 통 손짓을 하다 thoughtfulness 몡 사려 깊음, 친절 polite 혱 예의 바른 promise 통 약속하다

02

정답 ③ 정답률 65%

정답 풀이

③ 목적격보어

> Cognitive psychologist David Perrett studies / [what makes faces
> ┗━━━━━━ 동격 ━━━━━━┛ 간접의문문(의문사(주어) + 동사) 동사 목적어
> 인지심리학자인 David Perrett은 연구한다 무엇이 얼굴을 매력적으로 만드는지를
> attractively(→ attractive).
> 목적격보어

➡ 동사 make의 목적격보어의 자리이므로 부사 attractively를 형용사 attractive로 고쳐야 한다. 부사는 보어로 쓰일 수 없다.

친절한 오답 풀이

① 관계대명사 what

> The latest studies indicate / {that [what people really want] is
> 접속사 관계대명사
> 최근 연구는 나타낸다 사람들이 정말로 원하는 것은 배우자라는 것을
> a mate / [that has qualities like their parents]}.
> ┗━━ 주격 관계대명사 전치사(…와 같은)
> 그들의 부모와 같은 특징을 지닌

➡ what은 선행사를 포함하는 관계대명사로, that절의 주어인 명사절을 이끌고 있으므로 어법상 바르다.

② 전치사

> Women are after a man [who is like their father] / and men want
> be after: …을 찾다 주격 관계대명사 전치사(…와 같은)
> 여성들은 그들의 아버지와 닮은 남성을 찾고 남성들은 자신의 어머니를
> to be able to see their own mother / in the woman of their dreams.
> 볼 수 있기를 원한다 이상적인 여성에게서

➡ after는 '…을 찾는'이라는 의미의 전치사로, 뒤에 명사(a man)를 목적어로 취하고 있으므로 어법상 바르다.

④ 문장의 동사

> Perrett suggests / [that we find our own faces charming] ....
> 접속사 find + 목적어 + 형용사(목적격보어): …을 ~라고 여기다[생각하다]
> Perrett은 말한다 우리가 우리 자신의 얼굴이 매력적이라고 생각한다고

➡ find는 동사 suggests의 목적어로 쓰인 명사절의 동사로 어법상 바르다.

⑤ remind A of B

> ... because they remind us of the faces / [(which/that) we looked
> remind A of B: A에게 B를 상기시키다 ┗━ 목적격 관계대명사 생략
> 그것들이 우리에게 얼굴들을 상기시키기 때문에 우리가 어린 시절에 계속해서 본
> at constantly in our early childhood years] — / Mom and Dad.
> 즉 엄마와 아빠를

➡ 「remind A of B」 구문에서 of는 전치사로, 뒤에 명사(the faces)를 목적어로 취하고 있으므로 어법상 바르다.

지문 해석

최근 연구는 사람들이 정말로 원하는 것은 그들의 부모와 같은 특징을 지닌 배우자라는 것을 나타낸다. 여성들은 그들의 아버지와 닮은 남성을 찾고 남성들은 이상적인 여성에서 자신의 어머니를 볼 수 있기를 원한다. 인지심리학자인 David Perrett은 무엇이 얼굴을 매력적으로 만드는지를 연구한다. 그는 자신의 욕구에 맞도록 얼굴을 계속해서 조정할 수 있는 컴퓨터 영상정보처리 시스템을 개발했다. Perrett은 우리의 얼굴이 우리가 어린 시절에 계속해서 본 얼굴들, 즉 엄마와 아빠를 상기시키기 때문에 우리가 우리 자신의 얼굴이 매력적이라고 생각한다고 말한다.

어휘

indicate 통 나타내다 cognitive 형 인지적인 psychologist 명 심리학자 attractively 부 매력적으로 computerized 형 컴퓨터화된 morphing 명 모핑 (컴퓨터 그래픽스로 화면을 차례로 변형시키는 특수 촬영 기술) endlessly 부 끝없이 adjust 통 조정하다 charming 형 매력적인 constantly 부 끊임없이 childhood 명 유년시절

03

정답 ⑤ 정답률 39%

정답 풀이

⑤ 사역동사의 목적격보어

> So many presents and so much money all at once / made her eyes
> 갑자기 사역동사 목적어
> 갑자기 그렇게 많은 선물과 돈은 그녀의 눈을 반짝이게 했다
> shone(→ shine).
> 목적격보어

➡ 동사 make는 사역동사이고 목적어(her eyes)와 목적격보어가 능동 관계이므로 과거분사 shone을 동사원형 shine으로 고쳐야 한다.

친절한 오답 풀이

① 과거완료

> ..., and a pair of very old silver earrings from Chris, /
> 한 쌍의 선행사
> 그리고 Chris는 아주 오래된 은귀걸이 한 쌍을 가지고 왔는데,
> [who said (that) she had had them / since she was a little girl].
> 계속적 용법의 주격 관계대명사 접속사(…한 이래로)
> 그녀는 그 귀고리를 가지고 있었다고 말했다 그녀가 어린 아이였을 때부터

➡ Chris가 말했던 시점(과거)보다 더 이전의 일이고, 그녀가 어렸을 때부터 계속 가지고 있었던 것이므로 계속을 나타내는 과거완료 had had가 오는 것이 어법상 바르다.

② 간접의문문

> Uncle Jack gave a lengthy speech / about [how Mary was like a
> 간접의문문(의문사 + 주어 + 동사) 전치사(…와 같은)
> Jack 삼촌은 장황한 연설을 했다 Mary가 얼마나 딸 같은지에 관해
> daughter / to him and to Aunt Barbara].
> 그와 Barbara 숙모에게

➡ 밑줄 친 how는 전치사 about의 목적어로 쓰인 간접의문문을 이끄는 의문부사로, 뒤에 빠진 문장성분이 없고 문맥상 '얼마나'라는 의미가 적절하므로 how가 오는 것이 알맞다.

③ 「전치사 + 관계대명사」

> And then, he handed her an envelope / [in which was tucked
> 선행사 ┗━ 동사
> 그러고 나서, 그는 그녀에게 봉투를 건네주었다 50달러짜리 지폐가 담긴
> a fifty-dollar bill].
> 주어, 장소 부사 역할을 하는 「전치사 + 관계대명사」가 앞에 나오면서 주어와 동사가 도치됨

➡ an envelope을 선행사로 하고, 관계대명사절에서 전치사 in의 목적어 역할을 하는 목적격 관계대명사 which는 어법상 바르다.

④ 재귀대명사

> Mary was to buy herself some new clothes / with Aunt Barbara's
> be to-v 용법(가능) 간접목적어 직접목적어
> Mary는 새 옷을 몇 벌 살 수 있게 되었다 Barbara 숙모의 도움과 조언으로
> help and advice.

➡ 주어와 목적어가 동일인을 지칭할 때는 목적어 자리에 재귀대명사를 쓴다. 간접목적어가 주어인 Mary와 동일 인물을 지칭하므로 herself는 어법상 바르다.

지문 해석

Mary의 열세 번째 생일이었다. 또한 삼촌 집에서 맞는 첫 번째 생일이기도 했다. 모두가 Mary를 위해 선물들을 가져왔는데, Elena는 스타킹, Steve는 지갑, Chris는 아주

오래된 은귀고리 한 쌍을 가지고 왔는데, 그녀는 어린 아이였을 때부터 그 귀고리를 가지고 있었다고 했다. Jack 삼촌은 그와 Barbara 숙모에게 Mary가 얼마나 딸 같은지에 대해 장황한 연설을 했다. 그러고 나서, 그는 50달러짜리 지폐가 담긴 봉투를 그녀에게 건네주었다. Barbara 숙모의 도움과 조언으로, Mary는 새 옷을 몇 벌 살 수 있게 되었다. 기적이었다! 갑자기 그렇게 많은 선물과 돈은 그녀의 눈을 반짝이게 했다. 그녀는 모두에게 입을 맞추고 싶었다.

purse 명 지갑 lengthy 형 장황한 speech 명 연설 envelope 명 봉투 tuck 동 밀어넣다 bill 명 지폐 shine 동 빛나다, 반짝이다

04 　　　　　　　정답 ⑤　　　정답률 51%

정답 풀이

(A) 목적격보어

That causes many boats and ships [erash / to crash] onto the rock.
앞 문장 내용 cause A to-v: A가 ~하도록 하다　　목적격보어
그것은 많은 소형 배와 큰 선박들이 그 바위에 충돌하게 한다

→ 동사 cause는 목적격보어로 to부정사를 취하므로, to crash가 오는 것이 알맞다.

(B) 동사의 수 일치

The rock is so close to the top of the water / {that all the vessels [that
so + 형용사/부사 + that ...: 너무 ~해서 …하다　　　주어　주격 관계대명사
그 암초는 물의 상층부에 너무 가까워서　　　　그 위로 항해하려는 모든 배들은
try to sail over it] / hit / hits it}.
= the rock　= the rock
　　그것에 부딪친다

→ 네모는 주격 관계대명사절(that try … it)의 수식을 받는 all the vessels를 주어로 하는 동사로, 주어가 복수 명사이므로 복수 동사인 hit이 와야 한다.

(C) 목적격 관계대명사

So he fastened a floating mark to the rocks / with a strong chain, /
fasten to: ~에 고정시키다　선행사
그래서 그는 부표를 암초에 고정시켰다　　　　단단한 체인으로
on top of [it / which] a bell was attached.
　　　　목적격 관계대명사
그 부표의 꼭대기에 종 하나가 달려있었다

→ 절과 절을 연결하는 접속사 역할과 선행사(a floating mark)를 대신하는 대명사의 역할을 하는 관계대명사 which가 오는 것이 적절하다. 대명사 it은 접속사의 역할을 할 수 없다.

 구문 분석 Plus

7행	He thought {that it was tragic for so many sailors [to die on that hidden rock]}. → that: 동사 thought의 목적어 역할을 하는 명사절을 이끄는 접속사 → it은 가주어, to die 이하가 진주어 → for so many sailors: to부정사의 의미상 주어
10행	When ships came near, the waves **made** the mark **float** back and forth and the bell **ring** clearly. → make(사역동사) + 목적어 + 동사원형(목적격보어): …가 ~하게 하다 → 등위접속사 and에 의해 사역동사 made의 목적어와 목적격보어가 병렬 연결되어 있음

지문 해석

The Inchcape Rock은 북해에 있는 큰 암초이다. 대부분의 시간 동안 그것은 물로 덮여있다. 그것은 많은 소형 배와 큰 선박들이 그 바위에 충돌하게 한다. 그 암초는 물의 상층부에 너무 가까워서 그 위로 항해하려는 모든 배들은 그것에 부딪친다. 100여 년 전에, 한 인정 많은 사람이 근처에 살았다. 그는 그렇게 많은 선원들이 그 숨겨진 암초 때문에 죽는 것이 비극적이라고 생각했다. 그래서 그는 단단한 체인으로 부표를 암초에 고정시켰는데, 그 부표의 꼭대기에 종 하나가 달려있었다. 배들이 가까이 왔을 때, 파도가

그 부표를 앞뒤로 떠다니게 만들어 그 종이 또렷하게 울리게 했다. 이제 선원들은 더 이상 그곳의 바다를 건너는 것을 두려워하지 않았다.

crash 동 충돌하다 vessel 명 (대형) 선박 kind-hearted 형 마음씨 고운, 인정 많은 tragic 형 비극적인 fasten 동 묶다 floating mark 부표 attach 동 붙이다 back and forth 앞뒤로

05 　　　　　　　정답 ②　　　정답률 60%

정답 풀이

② 주격보어

The families were made miserably(→ miserable) / by the noise, ...
　　　　　　동사　　　　　　　　　　　보어　　　　　　소음으로
그 가족들은 괴롭게 되었다

→ 5형식 문장(The noise made the families miserable)이 수동태로 전환된 문장으로, 5형식 문장의 목적격보어가 주격보어로 전환되었다. 보어 자리에는 부사가 올 수 없으므로, 부사 miserably를 형용사 miserable로 고쳐야 한다.

▌친절한 오답 풀이 ▌

① 주격 관계대명사

An environment-agency official tells a surprising incident /
어느 환경청 공무원은 놀라운 사건을 이야기해준다
about some people / {who lived in an apartment building / [(which
　　　　　　　　　주격 관계대명사　　　　「주격 관계대명사 + be동사」 생략
어떤 사람들에 관한　　　아파트에 살았던
was) close to a busy state highway]}.
번잡한 주(州) 고속도로 근처의

→ some people을 선행사로 하고 관계사절 내에서 동사(lived)의 주어 역할을 하는 주격 관계대명사 who는 어법상 바르다.

③ 동사 ask의 종속절의 동사

City officials went to the state capital again and again / to **ask**
　　　　　　　　　　　　　　　　　　　　몇 번이고 반복해서 부사적 용법(목적)
시 공무원들은 여러 차례 주 의회에 갔다　　　　　　　　　요구하기 위해서
[that something (shoud) be done / about quieting the highway noise].
명사절(목적어)을 이끄는 접속사　　　　　　고속도로의 소음을 줄이는 일에 대해
어떤 조치가 취해져야 한다는 것을

→ 동사 ask가 '요청하다'의 의미일 경우 뒤에 오는 that절의 동사는 「should + 동사원형」 형태로 쓰며, should는 생략할 수 있다. 동사 ask의 종속절인 that절에 should가 생략되고 동사원형 be가 쓰였으므로 어법상 바르다.

 Grammar Tips

제안(suggest), 요구(demand, ask), 주장(insist), 명령(order) 등을 나타내는 동사 뒤에 오는 that절의 동사는 「should + 동사원형」 형태로 쓰며, 종종 should는 생략된다.

예) They **insisted** that she (should) **be** expelled from school.
　　(그들은 그녀가 퇴학당해야 한다고 주장했다.)

④ 동사를 강조하는 조동사 do

The trees made hardly any difference / in the amount of noise, /
　　　　　　거의 … 없는　　　　　　　소음의 양에
그 나무들은 거의 차이를 만들지 않았다
but they did block the view of the highway.
그러나 그것들은 고속도로의 모습이 보이지 않게 했다

→ 동사의 의미를 강조할 때 「do/does/did + 동사원형」 형태로 쓴다. 이 문장의 시제가 과거이므로 조동사 did가 원형 동사 block 앞에 오는 것이 알맞다.

⑤ 수량형용사

> After that, there were very few **complaints** from the people / in the
> 거의 없는
> 그 이후로, 사람들에게서 불평이 거의 없었다   그 건물의
> building.

➡ few는 셀 수 있는 명사의 복수형 앞에 쓰이는 수량형용사로, 뒤에 복수 명사 complaints가 있으므로 어법상 적절하다. '거의 없는'이라는 의미로 셀 수 없는 명사를 수식할 때는 형용사 little을 사용한다.

지문 해석

눈으로 소리를 듣는 것은 아니지만, 가끔은 마치 우리가 거의 그러는 것처럼 보인다. 어느 환경청 공무원이 번잡한 주(州)고속도로 근처의 아파트에 살았던 어떤 사람들에 관한 놀라운 사건을 이야기해준다. 그 가족들은 소음으로 괴로워져서 시청에 항의를 했다. 시 공무원들은 고속도로의 소음을 줄이는 일에 관해 어떤 조치가 취해져야 한다는 것을 요구하기 위하여 여러 차례 주 의회에 갔다. 그들은 여러 차례 발뺌을 당했다. 마침내 시 공무원들은 좋은 수를 생각해냈다. 그들은 아파트 앞에 한 줄로 나무를 심었다. 그 나무들이 소음의 양에는 거의 차이를 만들지 않았지만, 그것들은 고속도로의 모습이 보이지 않게 했다. 그 이후로, 그 건물의 사람들에게서 불평이 거의 없었다.

environment-agency official 환경청 공무원 incident 몡 사건 busy 혱 바쁜; *붐비는 state capital 주 의회 quiet 통 조용히 시키다 put off (핑계를 대어 사람·요구 등을) 피하다, 발뺌하다 row 몡 열, 줄

---

06 정답 ④ 정답률 64%

정답 풀이

④ 목적격보어

> However, this process removes the important plant cover /
> 선행사
> 그러나 이런 과정은 중요한 땅 표면의 식물들을 없앤다
> [that holds soil particles in place], / [making soil defenselessly
> 주격 관계대명사   그 자리에   목적어
>   결과를 나타내는 분사구문(= and it makes …)
> 토양의 미세 입자들을 그 자리에 붙잡아 두는   땅을 무방비 상태로 만들면서
> (→ defenseless) / to wind and water erosion].
>   목적격보어
>   바람이나 물에 의한 침식에

➡ 앞에 오는 분사 making의 목적격보어의 자리이므로 부사 defenselessly를 형용사 defenseless로 고쳐야 한다.

친절한 오답 풀이

① 부사적 용법의 to부정사

> Farmers plow more and more fields / to produce more food /
> 비교급 + and + 비교급: 점점 더 …한   부사적 용법의 to부정사(목적)
> 농부들은 점점 더 많은 땅을 일군다   더 많은 식량을 생산하기 위하여
> for the increasing population.
> 늘어나는 인구를 위해

➡ to produce는 앞의 동사 plow를 수식하는 부사적 용법의 to부정사로 어법상 바르다.

② 대명사

> Farmers plow soil / to improve it for crops.
>   부사적 용법의 to부정사(목적)
> 농부들은 땅을 일군다   농작물을 위해 그것을 향상시키기 위해

➡ 앞에 언급된 단수 명사 soil을 단수형 대명사 it이 대신하고 있으므로 어법상 바르다.

③ 분사구문

> They turn and loosen the soil, / [leaving it in the best condition
> = farmers   결과를 나타내는 분사구문(= and they leave …)
> 그들은 토양을 뒤엎고 느슨하게 한다   그것을 농사를 짓기에 최상의 상태로 둔다
> for farming].

➡ leaving 이하는 결과를 나타내는 분사구문으로, 생략된 주어는 주절의 주어(They)와 같다. 그들이 토양을 최상의 상태에 '두는'이라는 능동의 의미이므로 현재분사 leaving이 오는 것이 알맞다.

⑤ 비교급 강조 부사

> Soil erosion in many places occurs at a much **faster** rate /
>   부사(훨씬)
> 토양의 침식이 많은 곳에서 훨씬 더 빠른 속도로 일어난다
> than the natural processes of weathering can replace it.
> 접속사   주어   동사   목적어
> 자연적인 풍화작용이 그것을 대체할 수 있는 속도보다

➡ much는 '훨씬'의 의미로 뒤에 오는 비교급 faster를 수식하여 비교의 의미를 강조하는 부사로, 어법상 바르다.

지문 해석

농부들은 늘어나는 인구를 위해 더 많은 식량을 생산하기 위하여 점점 더 많은 땅을 일군다. 이것은 우리의 토양 자원에 압박을 증가시킨다. 농부들은 농작물을 위해 땅을 향상시키기 위해 땅을 일군다. 그들은 토양을 뒤엎고 느슨하게 해서, 농사를 짓기에 최상의 상태에 둔다. 그렇지만 이러한 과정은 토양의 미세 입자들을 그 자리에 붙잡아 두는 중요한 땅 표면의 식물들을 없애서, 땅을 바람이나 물에 의한 침식에 무방비 상태로 만든다. 때때로 바람이 갈아 엎어 놓은 경작지에서 흙을 날려버리기도 한다. 많은 곳에서 자연적인 풍화작용이 대체할 수 있는 속도보다 훨씬 더 빠른 속도로 토양의 침식이 일어난다.

plow 통 (땅을) 갈다, 경작하다 soil resources 토양 자원 loosen 통 느슨하게 하다 condition 몡 상태 particle 몡 (아주 작은) 입자 defenseless 혱 무방비의 erosion 몡 침식 rate 몡 비율; *속도 weathering 몡 풍화(작용)

---

07 정답 ② 정답률 69%

정답 풀이

(A) 접속사 that

> Many social scientists have believed for some time / [**that** / ~~what~~
>   한동안 명사절(목적어)을 이끄는 접속사
> 많은 사회과학자들은 한동안 믿어 왔다
> birth order directly affects / both personality and achievement in
>   both A and B: A와 B 둘 다
> 출생 순서가 직접적으로 영향을 준다는 것을 성격과 성인기의 삶의 성취에
> adult life].

➡ 동사 believed의 목적어 역할을 하는 명사절을 이끌며, 뒤에 완전한 절이 이어지고 있으므로 접속사 that이 오는 것이 어법상 바르다. 관계대명사 what은 주어나 목적어가 빠진 불완전한 절을 이끈다.

(B) 주격보어

> …, because I'm the youngest child / and thus less ~~aggressively~~ /
>   보어1   접속사
> 나는 막내이기 때문에   그러므로 덜 적극적이다
> **aggressive** / than my older brothers and sisters.
> 보어2
>   나의 형이나 누나들보다

➡ 2형식 문장의 주격보어 자리이므로 형용사 aggressive가 오는 것이 어법상 바르다. 부사는 보어 자리에 올 수 없다.

(C) 분사구문

> …, but as you mature into adulthood, / [~~accepted~~ / **accepting** other
> 접속사(…함에 따라서)   동시동작을 나타내는 분사구문(= as you accept …)
>   그러나 당신이 성인으로 성장함에 따라   다른 사회적 역할들을 받아들이면서
> social roles], / birth order becomes insignificant.
>   출생 순서는 사소해진다

➡ 네모는 동시동작을 나타내는 분사구문의 분사로, 생략된 주어는 앞 절의 주어(you)와

같다. 당신이 다른 사회적 역할을 '받아들이는'이라는 능동의 의미이므로 현재분사 accepting이 알맞다.

 지문 해석

많은 사회과학자들은 한동안 출생 순서가 성격과 성인기의 삶의 성취에 직접적으로 영향을 준다고 믿어 왔다. 사실, 사람들은 공격적인 행동이나 수동적인 기질과 같은 성격 요인을 설명하기 위해 출생 순서를 사용해 왔다. 한 사람은 "아, 나는 세 자매 중에 맏이라서, 내가 거만해지는 것을 피할 수 없어." 또는 "나는 막내이고 형이나 누나들보다 덜 적극적이기 때문에 사업에 그다지 성공적이지 못해."라고 말할 수도 있다. 그러나 최근의 연구들은 이러한 믿음이 잘못된 것이라는 것을 입증했다. 다시 말해, 출생 순서가 가족 안에서 당신의 역할을 규정지을 수는 있지만, 당신이 성인으로 성장함에 따라, 다른 사회적 역할들을 받아들이면서, 출생 순서는 사소해진다.

어휘

social scientist 사회과학자 **birth order** 출생 순서 **directly** 閉 직접적으로 **personality** 명 성격 **achievement** 명 성취 **account for** …을 설명하다 **aggressive** 형 공격적인, 대단히 적극적인 **passive** 형 수동적인 **temperament** 명 기질 **overbearing** 형 고압적인; *거만한 **prove** 통 입증하다, 증명하다 **belief** 명 믿음 **define** 통 정의하다, 규정하다 **mature** 통 (어른이) 되다, 성숙해지다 **adulthood** 명 성인 **insignificant** 형 사소한, 하찮은

08 　정답 ⑤ 　정답률 37%

정답 풀이

(A) 목적격보어

> The question asks the listeners [choosing / to choose] / among
> ask A to-v: A가 …하도록 요청하다　　　목적격보어
> 그 질문은 듣는 사람이 선택하게 한다　　　　여러 대안들 중에
> several alternatives.

➡ 동사 ask는 목적격보어로 to부정사를 취하므로, to choose가 어법상 적절하다.

(B) 전치사

> Dilemma tales are [like / alike] folk tales / in that they are usually
> 전치사(…와 같은)　　　…라는 점에서, that은 접속사
> 딜레마 이야기는 민간 설화와 비슷하다　　그들이 주로 짧고, 단순하며, 전적으로
> short, simple, and driven entirely by plot.
> 줄거리에 의해 전개된다는 점에서

➡ 명사 folk tales를 목적어로 가질 수 있는 전치사 like가 오는 것이 어법상 적절하다. 서술적 용법으로만 쓰이는 형용사 alike는 문장에서 보어가 되어 주어나 목적어를 설명하는 역할만을 하며, 명사를 수식할 수 없다.

 Grammar Tips

서술적 용법으로 쓰이는 형용사의 종류
주로 접두사 a-가 붙은 형용사들이 이에 속한다.
afraid, alike, alive, alone, aware, asleep, ashamed 등

(C) 수동태

> Their stories and tales / are meant to [tell / be told] aloud.
> be meant to-v: …하기로 되어 있다
> 그들의 이야기와 설화는　　크게 소리 내어 말해지도록 되어 있다

➡ 문맥상 그들의 이야기와 설화가 크게 '말해지는' 것이므로 수동태 be told가 오는 것이 어법상 적절하다.

 구문 분석 Plus

8행 **As** you read a dilemma tale, you need to keep in mind [*that* most African cultures were traditionally oral ones]:
➡ As: '…할 때'라는 의미의 접속사(= when)
➡ that: keep in mind의 목적어의 역할을 하는 명사절을 이끄는 접속사
➡ ones: 복수 명사 cultures를 받는 대명사

지문 해석

딜레마 이야기는 질문으로 끝맺음을 하는 아프리카의 이야기 형식이다. 그 질문은 듣는 사람이 여러 대안들 중에서 선택하게 한다. 딜레마 이야기는 활발한 토론을 조장함으로써 청중으로 하여금 사회 안에서의 옳고 그른 행동에 대해 생각하게 이끈다. 딜레마 이야기는 주로 짧고, 단순하며, 전적으로 줄거리에 의해 전개된다는 점에서 민간 설화와 비슷하다. 당신이 딜레마 이야기를 읽을 때, 대부분의 아프리카 문화들은 전통적으로 구술문화였다는 점을 명심할 필요가 있다. 즉, 그들의 이야기와 설화는 크게 소리 내어 말해지도록 되어 있다.

어휘

alternative 명 대안 **encourage** 통 조장하다 **folk tale** 민간 설화 **entirely** 閉 전적으로 **keep in mind** …을 명심하다 **traditionally** 閉 전통적으로 **oral** 형 구두의

09 　정답 ② 　정답률 70%

정답 풀이

(A) 문장의 동사

> Mirror neurons were first discovered by Italian scientists / {who,
> 　　　　　　　　　　　　　　　　　　　　주격 관계대명사
> 거울 뉴런은 이탈리아 과학자들에 의해 처음 발견되었다
> [while looking at the activity of individual nerve cells /
> 접속사가 남아있는 분사구문(= while they looked …)
> 그들이 개별 신경 세포의 활동을 보는 동안에
> inside the brains of monkeys], / [noticed / noticing] [that neurons
> 　　　　　　　　　　　　　　　　동사　　　　　접속사
> 원숭이 뇌 속의　　　　　　　　뇌의 똑같은 영역의 뉴런이 활성화된다는 것을 알아차린
> in the same area of the brain were activated …]}.

➡ 네모는 Italian scientists를 선행사로 하는 주격 관계대명사 who의 동사 자리이므로 noticed가 오는 것이 적절하다.

(B) 지각동사의 목적격보어

> A similar phenomenon takes place / [when we watch someone
> take place: 발생하다 watch + 목적어 + v-ing: …가 ~하는 것을 보다
> 비슷한 현상이 발생한다　　　　　　　우리가 어떤 사람이 감정을 겪는 것을 보고
> [experiencing / experienced] an emotion / and feel the same
> 목적격보어
> 　　　　　　　　　　　　　　　그에 반응해서 똑같은 감정을 느낄 때
> emotion in response.

➡ 네모는 동사 watch의 목적격보어 자리로, 누군가가 감정을 '겪는' 것을 본다라는 의미로 목적어(someone)와 목적격보어가 능동 관계이므로 현재분사 experiencing이 오는 것이 알맞다.

(C) 주격 관계대명사

> The same neural systems get activated in a part of the insula, /
> 　　　　　　　　　　　　　　　　　　　　　선행사
> 똑같은 신경 체계가 뇌도의 한 영역에서 활성화되는데
> [[it / which] is part of the mirror neuron system], ….
> 계속적 용법의 주격 관계대명사
> 그것은 거울 뉴런 조직의 일부이다

➡ 절과 절을 연결하는 접속사 역할과 선행사(a part of the insula)를 대신하는 대명사의 역할을 해야 하므로, 주격 관계대명사 which가 오는 것이 알맞다. 대명사 it은 접속사의

역할을 할 수 없다.

 구문 분석 Plus

8행	... **whether** the animals were performing a particular movement **or** simply *observing another monkey perform* the same action. ➡ whether A or B: A이든 B이든 ➡ observe(지각동사) + 목적어 + 동사원형: …가 ~하는 것을 관찰하다
10행	It appeared **as though** the cells in the observer's brain "mirrored" the activity in the performer's brain. ➡ as though: 마치 …인 것처럼(= as if)

지문 해석

공감은 거울 뉴런이라 불리는 특별한 신경세포 그룹에 의해 가능해진다. 이러한 특별한 세포들은 우리가 감정을 '반영할' 수 있도록 해준다. 거울 뉴런은 이탈리아 과학자들에 의해 처음 발견되었는데, 그들은 원숭이 뇌 속의 개별 신경 세포의 활동을 보는 동안에, 그 동물들이 특정한 행동을 하든지 또는 단지 다른 원숭이가 똑같은 행동을 하는 것을 관찰하든지 간에 뇌의 똑같은 영역의 뉴런이 활성화된다는 것을 알아차렸다. 그것은 마치 관찰자의 뇌 세포들이 행위자의 뇌의 활동을 '반영하는' 것처럼 보였다. 우리가 어떤 사람이 감정을 겪는 것을 보고 그에 반응해서 똑같은 감정을 느낄 때 비슷한 현상이 발생한다. 똑같은 신경 체계가 거울 뉴런 조직의 일부인 뇌도의 한 영역과 관찰된 감정과 관련이 있는 감정 뇌 영역에서 활성화된다.

 어휘

empathy 명 공감　nerve cell 신경세포　mirror neuron 거울 뉴런, 반사경 뉴런 mirror 통 반영하다　activity 명 활동 (activate 통 활성화시키다)　observe 통 관찰하다　phenomenon 명 현상　in response …에 반응하여　neural system 신경망 체제　insula 명 (고대 로마의) 집단 주택; *(뇌·췌장의) 섬

10 　　정답 ①　　정답률 48%

정답 풀이

(A) 주격보어

Sometimes the variation is as subtle / ~~subtly~~ as a pause.
as + 형용사/부사 + as: …만큼 ~한/하게
때때로 그 변화는 멈추는 것만큼 미묘하다

➡ 동사 is의 보어로 형용사 subtle이 오는 것이 어법상 적절하다. 부사는 보어로 쓰일 수 없다.

(B) 주격 관계대명사

I recently saw a news interview with an acquaintance / [who /
나는 최근에 아는 사람의 뉴스 인터뷰를 봤다　　　　　　　　　주격 관계대명사
~~whom~~ **I was certain** / was going to lie about a few particularly
　　　　　삽입절　　　　　동사
내가 확신했던　　몇 가지 특별히 민감한 문제에 대해 거짓말을 할 것이라고
sensitive issues], / and lie she did.
그리고 그녀는 정말 거짓말을 했다

➡ an acquaintance를 선행사로 하고, 관계대명사절에서 동사 was going to lie의 주어 역할을 하는 주격 관계대명사 who가 오는 것이 알맞다.

 Grammar Tips

삽입절

I am sure / it seems (to me) / I believe[think, hear, suggest, etc.] 등은 문장 중간에 자주 삽입되는 절이다. 삽입절은 문장 맨 앞에 두고 해석하면 자연스럽다.

예) She has a book which **I think** would be very useful to you.
(내 생각에 그녀는 너한테 매우 유용할 것 같은 책을 가지고 있다.)

(C) 문장의 동사

It is true [that the questions dealt / ~~dealing~~ with very personal
가주어　　　진주어　　　주어　　　동사, deal with: …을 다루다
그 질문들이 아주 사적인 문제를 다룬 것은 사실이다
issues], / but I have found / {[that in general, no matter how
　　　　　　　접속사　　일반적으로　= however(아무리 …하더라도)
　　　　　하지만 나는 알았다　　일반적으로 질문이 아무리 민감하더라도
touchy the question], / if a person is telling the truth] / his or her
　　　　　　　　누군가가 진실을 말하고 있다면　　　그 혹은 그녀의
manner will not change / significantly or abruptly}.
태도가 변하지는 않을 것이다　　상당히 또는 갑작스럽게

➡ 진주어인 that절의 주어는 the questions이고 뒤에 동사가 이어져야 하므로 deal의 과거형인 dealt가 오는 것이 어법상 적절하다.

지문 해석

누군가가 거짓말을 할 때 그 사람의 평소 패턴으로부터 벗어난 점을 알아채기 위해서는 그것에 세심한 주의를 기울여야 한다. 때때로 그 변화는 멈추는 것만큼 미묘하다. 어떤 때는 그것은 명백하고 갑작스럽다. 나는 최근에 몇 가지 특별히 민감한 문제에 대해 거짓말을 할 것이라고 내가 확신했던 아는 사람의 뉴스 인터뷰를 봤는데, 그녀는 정말 거짓말을 했다. 인터뷰하는 동안 대부분 그녀는 차분하고 솔직했지만, 거짓말을 하기 시작했을 때, 그녀의 태도는 극적으로 변했다. 그녀는 머리를 뒤로 젖히고, '불신'의 웃음을 짓고, 머리를 앞으로 흔들었다. 그 질문들이 아주 사적인 문제를 다룬 것은 사실이지만, 일반적으로 질문이 아무리 민감하더라도 누군가가 진실을 말하고 있다면, 그 혹은 그녀의 태도가 상당히 또는 갑작스럽게 변하지는 않을 것이라는 점을 나는 알았다.

 어휘

deviation 명 일탈, 탈선　variation 명 변화　subtle 형 미묘한, 감지하기 힘든 pause 명 (말·행동 등의) 멈춤　obvious 형 명백한　abrupt 형 갑작스러운 (abruptly 부 갑작스럽게)　acquaintance 명 아는 사람, 지인　sensitive 형 민감한 direct 형 솔직한, 단도직입적인　dramatically 부 극적으로　disbelief 명 불신 touchy 형 과민한, 다루기 힘든　significantly 부 상당히

UNIT 3 기타 주요 구문

코드 접속하기

pp.95~97

출제코드 1
간접의문문, 도치구문, 강조구문

A **1** did **2** that **3** when
B **1** ○ **2** ➡ that[who]

해석과 정답 풀이

STEP 1
1 1) 그는 마침내 왜 그의 부모님이 그들의 집을 지었는지 깨달았다.
　　2) 그녀는 누가 그녀 방의 창문을 깼는지 궁금했다.
2 1) 나는 John이 오늘밤에 올 것이라고 전혀 기대하지 않았다.
　　2) 나는 여기를 떠나기 싫고, 그도 그렇다.
3 1) 내가 극장에서 만났던 사람은 바로 Nick이었다.
　　2) 내가 찾고 있었던 것은 바로 그 책이다.

STEP 2
1 1) 모든 사람들이 어떻게 그녀가 젓가락을 잡으려 하는지 지켜봤다.
　　2) 우리는 달이 무엇으로 구성되어있는지 궁금해했다.
2 1) 그들은 대립되는 견해를 가지고 있어서 정치에 대해 거의 이야기하지 않는다.
　　2) 그녀는 비행기가 착륙하자 안심했고, 그녀의 남편도 그랬다.
3 처음으로 카푸치노를 만들기 시작했던 것은 바로 이탈리아인들이었다.

STEP 3
A **1** 그는 공부를 별로 잘하지 못했고, 나아질 것 같지도 않았다.
　➡ nor이 문장 앞에 나와서 주어와 동사의 도치가 일어난 구문으로, 주절의 시제가 과거이므로 과거형 조동사 did가 오는 것이 알맞다.
　2 어떤 사진의 "모양"을 결정하는 것은 바로 카메라 렌즈의 사용이다.
　➡ '~한 것은 바로 …이다'의 의미로 the use of camera lenses를 강조하는 「It is ... that」 강조구문으로, that이 오는 것이 알맞다.
　3 사자가 얼룩말을 추격할 때, 그들은 그것이 언제 왼쪽 혹은 오른쪽으로 뛰어갈지 알 수 없다.
　➡ 동사 tell의 목적어 역할을 하는 간접의문문을 이끄는 의문사로, 뒤에 완전한 절이 이어지므로 의문부사 when이 오는 것이 알맞다.
B **1** 꿈을 이루기 위해, 그녀는 항상 어떻게 유명인사들이 성공했는지에 대해 생각한다.
　➡ 전치사 about의 목적어 역할을 하는 간접의문문을 이끄는 의문사로, 뒤에 완전한 절이 이어지므로 방법을 나타내는 의문부사 how가 오는 것이 알맞다.
　2 내가 영화를 보고 난 직후에 그 극장에서 봤던 사람은 바로 할리우드 스타였다.
　➡ '~한 것은 바로 …였다'의 의미로 a Hollywood star를 강조하는 「It is ... that[who]」 강조구문이므로, when을 that이나 who로 고쳐야 한다.

출제코드 2
가주어 진주어, 가목적어 진목적어 구문

A **1** to persuade **2** to recognize **3** that
B **1** ○ **2** ➡ it

해석과 정답 풀이

STEP 1
1 1) 한자를 읽고 쓰는 법을 배우는 것은 어렵다.
　　2) 그가 혼자 이집트를 여기저기 여행했다는 것은 믿기 어렵다.
2 그들은 그 언어를 영어로 번역하는 것이 어렵다는 것을 알았다.

STEP 2
1 1) 영화 속에서 영웅들이 부활하는 것을 보는 것은 흔한 일이다.
　　2) 사람들이 웹에서 그들이 필요한 정보를 얻는다는 것은 잘 알려져 있다.
2 1) 내가 목표를 세웠을 때 연습하는 것이 더 재미있다는 것을 알았다.
　　2) 그의 호기심은 그가 많은 과학적 가설에 의문을 제기하는 것을 쉽게 해주었다.

STEP 3
A **1** 그들이 그 캠페인에 참여하도록 설득하는 것은 거의 불가능하다.

　➡ It은 가주어로, 뒤에 진주어 역할을 하는 to부정사 to persuade가 오는 것이 알맞다.
　2 얼룩말 줄무늬는 사실 얼룩말들이 서로 알아보는 것을 더 쉽게 해준다.
　➡ 동사 make 뒤에 오는 it은 가목적어로, 뒤에 진목적어 역할을 하는 to부정사 to recognize가 오는 것이 알맞다.
　3 기차의 탈선으로 인한 사상자가 없었다는 것은 정말로 다행이었다.
　➡ 앞에 가주어 It이 있고, 뒤에 완전한 절이 이어지므로 진주어절을 이끄는 접속사인 that이 오는 것이 알맞다.
B **1** 당신이 고속도로에서 운전하는 동안 뻥 뚫린 도로를 달리는 것은 이상적일 것이다.
　➡ It은 가주어로, 뒤에 진주어 역할을 하는 to부정사 to have가 오는 것이 알맞다.
　2 몇몇 연구 후에, 과학자들은 결론을 내리는 것이 어렵다는 것을 알았다.
　➡ to make a conclusion이 동사 found의 진목적어이므로, 가목적어 자리에 쓰인 them을 it으로 고쳐야 한다.

기출예제 Q1
정답 ⑤　　**정답률 61%**

정답 풀이

⑤ 「so + 동사 + 주어」 도치구문

> These experts are still with us, / and as a result so does(→ is) the
> 이런 전문가들은 여전히 우리와 함께 있다　　그리고 그 결과 그 말 또한 그렇다 （부사）
> phrase.

➡ 「so + 동사 + 주어」 도치구문으로, 앞 절에 be동사 are가 쓰였으므로 도치구문의 동사도 be동사를 써야 한다. 주어(the phrase)가 단수이므로 does를 단수형 be동사 is로 고쳐야 한다.

친절한 오답 풀이

① 명사를 수식하는 과거분사

> The phrase, 'jack-of-all-trades' is a shortened version /
> 　　　　　　　　　　　　　　　　　　　（과거분사）
> 'jack-of-all-trades(만물박사)'라는 말은 축약된 형태이다
> of 'jack of all trades and master of none.'
> 'jack of all trades and master of none(모든 일을 다 하지만 정말 잘하는 것은 없는 사람)'의

➡ 밑줄 친 부분은 뒤의 명사 version을 수식하는 분사로, '줄여진'이라는 수동의 의미이므로 과거분사 shortened가 오는 것이 알맞다.

② 동사의 수 일치

> It refers to those / [who claim to be proficient at countless tasks, /
> 　　　　　　　　　　（주격 관계대명사）
> 그것은 사람들을 말한다　　수많은 일에 능숙하다고 주장하는
> but cannot perform a single one of them well].
> 그러나 그것들 중 단 한 가지도 잘 수행하지 못하는

➡ claim은 those를 선행사로 하는 주격 관계대명사절의 동사로, 선행사가 복수 대명사이므로 복수 동사가 오는 것이 알맞다.

③ 분사구문

> A large number of efficiency experts set up shop in London, /
> a number of + 복수 명사: 많은 …
> 많은 효율성 전문가들이 런던에 사무소를 차렸다
> [advertising themselves as knowledgeable / about every type of
> 연속동작을 나타내는 분사구문(= and they advertised ...)
> 그리고 자신들이 많이 안다고 광고했다　　　　모든 유형의
> new manufacturing process, trade, and business].
> 새로운 제조 과정, 거래, 사업에 대해

➡ advertising 이하는 연속동작을 나타내는 분사구문으로, 생략된 주어는 주절의 주어(A large ... experts)와 같다. 주어와 분사가 의미상 능동 관계이므로 현재분사 advertising이 오는 것이 알맞다.

④ 주격보어

> But it soon became evident / [that their knowledge was limited
> 　　　　　　　　　　가주어　　　　　보어　　　　　진주어
> 하지만 곧 분명해졌다　　　　　　　　그들의 지식은 제한되어 있으며 유용한 가치가 없다는 것이
> and of no practical value].

➡ became은 2형식 동사로 뒤에 보어를 취하므로 형용사 evident가 오는 것이 알맞다.

지문 해석

'jack-of-all-trades(만물박사)'라는 말은 'jack of all trades and master of none (모든 일을 다 하지만 정말 잘하는 것은 없는 사람)'이 축약된 형태이다. 그것은 수많은 일에 능숙하다고 주장하지만, 그것들 중 단 한 가지도 잘 수행하지 못하는 사람들을 말한다. 그 말은 산업혁명이 시작될 때에 영국에서 처음 사용되었다. 많은 효율성 전문가들이 런던에 사무소를 차렸고, 자신들을 모든 유형의 새로운 제조 과정, 거래, 사업에 대해 많이 안다고 광고했다. 상당한 수수료를 받고, 그들은 자신들의 지식을 고객들에게 전했다. 하지만 곧 그들의 지식은 제한되어 있으며 유용한 가치가 없다는 것이 분명해졌다. 의심을 품게 된 생산업자들은 이러한 자칭 전문가라고 주장하는 사람들을 'jacks of all trades and masters of none'이라고 부르기 시작했다. 이러한 전문가들은 아직도 우리와 함께 있으며, 그 결과 그 말 또한 그렇다.

jack-of-all-trades 만물박사, 팔방미인 (실제로는 잘 하는 것은 없는 사람들)
shorten 图 짧게 하다　refer to …을 나타내다　proficient 图 능숙한, 숙달된
countless 图 무수한　phrase 图 구; *관용구　Industrial Revolution 산업혁명
efficiency 图 효율성　expert 图 전문가　set up …을 건립하다[세우다]
advertise 图 광고하다　knowledgeable 图 아는 것이 많은　manufacture
图 제조[생산]하다　trade 图 거래, 무역　business 图 사업　substantial
图 상당한　fee 图 수수료　impart 图 전하다　client 图 고객　evident 图
분명한　practical 图 현실적인; *유용한　value 图 가치　doubtful 图 의심을
품은　industrialist 图 기업가　self-appointed 图 자기 혼자 정한, 자칭의

코드 공략하기

pp.98~99

| 01 ③ | 02 ④ | 03 ③ | 04 ⑤ | 05 ④ | 06 ③ |

01　　　정답 ③　　　정답률 64%

정답 풀이

(A) 분사구문

> Instead, it moves quickly back and forth, / [[forcing / forced] the
> 　　　　　　　　　　　　　　연속동작을 나타내는 분사구문(= and it forces ...)
> 대신, 그것은 이리저리 빠르게 움직인다　　　그래서 코요테 역시 방향을 바꾸고
> coyote to change direction and (to) make sharp turns, too].
> force A to-v: A가 …하게 하다
> 급선회를 하게 한다

➡ 네모는 연속동작을 나타내는 분사구문의 분사로, 생략된 주어는 주절의 주어(it = a rabbit)와 같다. 주어와 분사가 능동 관계이므로 현재분사 forcing이 오는 것이 알맞다.

(B) 간접의문문

> The coyote also cannot tell / [[what / when] the rabbit will run this
> 　　　　　　　　　　　　　간접의문문(의문사 + 주어 + 동사)
> 코요테는 또한 알 수 없다　　　언제 토끼가 이쪽 혹은 저쪽으로 뛸지
> way or that], / so it cannot plan its next move.
> 　　　　　그래서 자신의 다음 움직임을 계획할 수 없다

➡ 동사 tell의 목적어로 쓰인 간접의문문을 이끄는 의문사로, 뒤에 완전한 절이 이어지고 문맥상 '언제'라는 의미가 오는 것이 적절하므로 의문사 when이 알맞다.

(C) 목적격보어

> In this way, the rabbit makes the chase more [difficult / difficultly]
> 　　　　　　　　　　make + 목적어 + 형용사: …을 ~하게 만들다　목적격보어1
> 이런 식으로, 토끼는 추격을 더 어렵고 피곤하게 만든다
> and tiring / for the coyote.
> 접속사　목적격보어2
> 　　　코요테에게

➡ 네모는 동사 make의 목적격보어 자리이다. 보어 자리에는 명사와 형용사만이 올 수 있으므로, 형용사 difficult를 쓰는 것이 알맞다. 부사는 보어로 쓰일 수 없다.

 코드 +α 구문 분석 Plus

11행
> **Though** a coyote may still succeed in catching its prey, there
> is a chance [*that* it may tire out, give up, and go look for an
> easier meal].
> ➡ though: '비록 …이긴 하지만'이라는 의미의 접속사
> ➡ that: 앞의 명사 a chance와 동격인 명사절을 이끄는 접속사

지문 해석

추격자를 더 힘들게 하는 한 가지 방법은 지그재그로 움직이는 것이다. 예를 들어, 코요테로부터 도망가는 토끼는 일직선으로 끊임없이 달리지 않는다. 대신, 그것은 이리저리 빠르게 움직여서 코요테 역시 방향을 바꾸고 급선회를 하도록 한다. 지그재그로 움직이는 것은 몸집이 더 큰 코요테보다 몸집이 작은 토끼에게 더 쉽다. 코요테는 또한 언제 토끼가 이쪽 혹은 저쪽으로 뛸지 알 수 없어서, 자신의 다음 움직임을 계획할 수 없다. 이런 식으로, 토끼는 코요테에게 추격을 더 어렵고 피곤하게 만든다. 코요테가 그 먹이를 잡는 데 여전히 성공할지는 모르지만, 그것이 기진맥진해지고, 포기하고, 그리고 더 쉬운 먹이를 찾으러 갈 가능성이 있다.

pursuer 图 추격자　zigzag 图 지그재그로 나아가다　endlessly 图 끝없이
back and forth 앞 뒤로; *왔다갔다　tell 图 말하다; *알다, 판단하다　chase 图 추격
tiring 图 피곤한　succeed in …에 성공하다　prey 图 먹이, 사냥감　chance 图
기회; *가능성　tire out 녹초가 되게 만들다

02　　　정답 ④　　　정답률 52%

정답 풀이

(A) 부사적 용법의 to부정사

> The university catalog can be used to [help / helping] the freshman /
> 　　　　　　　　　　　　　be used to-v: …하는 데 사용되다　　선행사
> 대학 편람은 신입생들을 돕는 데 사용될 수 있다
> [who is confused by university life].
> 주격 관계대명사
> 대학 생활에 혼란스러워하는

➡ '…하는 데 사용되다'라는 의미이므로, be used 뒤에 목적을 나타내는 부사적 용법의 to부정사가 와야 한다. 「be used to v-ing」 구문은 '…하는 데 익숙하다'의 의미로 문맥상 적절하지 않다.

(B) 부사

> These courses are arranged [alphabetical / alphabetically] /
> 　　　　　　　　　　　　　　　　　　　　　　　　부사
> 이 교육과정들은 알파벳순으로 정리되어 있다
> by each department / in order that the student may choose /
> 각 과별로　　　　　　…하기 위해서
> 　　　　　　　　　　학생이 선택할 수 있도록
> [which courses he wants to take].
> 간접의문문(의문사 + 주어 + 동사)
> 자신이 어떤 과목을 듣고 싶은지

➡ 동사 are arranged를 수식하고 있으므로 부사 alphabetically가 오는 것이 알맞다.

(C) 「It is ... that」 강조구문

It is also from this list of courses of each department / while / **that**
It is ... that 강조구문
또한 바로 각 학과의 이런 교육과정 목록으로부터이다

a degree plan for the student can be devised, / which will be
<u>선행사</u>   계속적 용법의 주격 관계대명사
그 학생을 위한 학위 계획이 만들어질 수 있는 것은   이 계획은

within the limits of the regulations of the university.
대학 규정의 범위에 들어 있을 것이다

➡ 부사구(from ... department)를 강조하는 「It is ... that」 강조구문이므로 that이
와야 한다.

 지문 해석

대학 편람은 대학 생활에 혼란스러워하는 신입생들을 돕는 데 사용될 수 있다. 그것은
최신(판)이 되도록 매년 개정된다. 무엇보다, 이 편람에는 대학에 의해 제공되는 모든
교육과정 목록이 들어 있다. 이 교육과정은 자신이 어떤 과목이 듣고 싶은지 학생이
선택할 수 있도록 각 과목별로 알파벳순으로 정리되어 있다. 또한 그 학생을 위한 학위
계획이 만들어질 수 있는 것은 바로 각 학과의 이런 교육과정 목록으로부터이며, 이
계획은 대학 규정의 범위에 들어 있을 것이다.

어휘

catalog 명 목록; *대학 요람[편람]   freshman 명 신입생   revise 통 변경하다;
*개정하다   up-to-date 형 현대식의; *최근의, 최신의   arrange 통 마련하다;
*정리하다, 배열하다   alphabetically 부 알파벳순으로   department 명 부서, 학과
degree 명 (온도 단위인) 도; *학위   devise 통 창안[고안]하다   limit 명 한계; *제한,
허용치   regulation 명 규정

03 　　　　　　　정답 ③　　　정답률 83%

정답 풀이

③ 가주어 진주어 구문

[As technology and the Internet are a familiar resource for young
접속사(~ 때문에)
과학기술과 인터넷이 젊은이들에게 친숙한 자원이기 때문에

people], / it is logical [what(→ that) they would seek assistance
　　　　　　　가주어　　　　　진주어
　　　　　　그들이 이 정보원에서 도움을 구할 것이라는 것은 논리적이다

from this source].

➡ 밑줄 친 부분은 가주어 it에 대한 진주어절을 이끄는 접속사 자리로, 진주어절 내에 빠진
문장성분이 없으므로 what을 접속사 that으로 고쳐야 한다.

친절한 오답 풀이

① 「with + (대)명사 + 분사」

Adolescents have been quick to immerse themselves in
　　　　　　　　　　　　　　immerse oneself in: ~에 몰두하다
청소년들은 빠르게 과학기술에 몰두해 왔다
technology / with most using the Internet / to communicate.
　　　　　with + (대)명사 + v-ing: ~가 ~한 채로　　　부사적 용법의 to부정사(목적)
　　　　　대부분이 인터넷을 사용하면서　　　　　　　소통하기 위해

➡ '~가 ~한[된] 채로'라는 의미의 「with + (대)명사 + 분사」 구문으로, (대)명사와 분사의
관계가 능동이면 현재분사를, 수동이면 과거분사를 쓴다. 문맥상 대부분의 청소년들이
인터넷을 '사용하면서'라는 능동의 의미이므로 현재분사 using이 오는 것이 알맞다.

② 부사

Young people also increasingly access social networking websites.
　　　　　　　　　　　　　부사└──────┘
젊은이들은 또한 소셜 네트워킹 사이트에 점점 더 많이 접속한다

➡ 부사 increasingly가 뒤에 오는 동사 access를 수식하고 있으므로 어법상 바르다.

---

④ 동사의 수 일치

A number of 'youth friendly' mental health websites have been
a number of + 복수 명사: 많은 ...　　　　　　　　　have been v-ed: 현재완료 수동태
많은 '젊은이 친화적인' 정신 건강 웹사이트들이 개발되었다
developed.

➡ 주어가 복수 명사(youth ... websites)이므로 뒤에 복수 동사 have가 오는 것이
알맞다. A number of 뒤에는 복수 명사가 와야 한다.

 코드
+α　Grammar Tips

a number of (많은 ...) vs. the number of (...의 수)
• a number of + 복수 명사 + 복수 동사
• the number of + 복수 명사 + 단수 동사
예) **A number of students were** participating in the campaign.
(많은 학생들이 그 캠페인에 참여하고 있다.)
The number of participants has doubled over the past few
years. (참가자들의 수가 지난 몇 년에 걸쳐 두 배로 증가했다.)

⑤ 명사를 수식하는 과거분사

The information presented often takes the form / of Frequently
　　　　　주어↑└──────┘과거분사　　동사
제시되는 정보는 종종 형태를 띤다　　　　　　　　　　　　자주 묻는 질문,
Asked Questions, fact sheets and suggested links.
　　　　　　　　　　　　　　과거분사└──────┘
자료표, 추천 링크의

➡ 앞에 나오는 명사(The information)를 수식하는 분사로, 정보가 '제시되는'이라는
수동의 의미이므로 과거분사 presented가 오는 것이 알맞다.

지문 해석

인터넷과 통신 기술은 선진사회의 젊은이들의 사회생활에서 점점 더 큰 역할을 수행한다.
대부분이 소통하기 위해 인터넷을 사용하면서 청소년들은 빠르게 과학기술에 몰두해
왔다. 젊은이들은 휴대전화를 생활의 필수품으로 다루고 친구들과 소통하기 위해 문자
메시지를 사용하기를 종종 선호한다. 젊은이들은 또한 소셜 네트워킹 사이트에도 점점
더 많이 접속한다. 과학기술과 인터넷이 젊은이들에게 친숙한 자원이기에, 그들이 이
정보원에서 도움을 구할 것이라는 것은 논리적이다. 이것은 젊은이들을 위한 치료법
정보를 제공하는 웹 사이트의 증가로 증명되었다. 많은 '젊은이 친화적인' 정신 건강 웹
사이트들이 개발되었다. 제시되는 정보는 종종 자주 묻는 질문, 자료표, 추천 링크의
형태를 띤다. 그러므로 젊은이들에게 온라인상담을 제공하는 것은 논리적으로 보일
것이다.

어휘

ever-increasing 형 계속 증가하는   adolescent 명 청소년   treat 통 다루다,
취급하다   essential 형 필수적인   necessity 명 필수품   increasingly 부 점점 더
access 통 접속하다   resource 명 자원   assistance 명 도움   therapeutic 형
치료(법)의   fact sheet 자료표   suggest 통 제안하다; *추천하다   counselling 명
상담, 카운슬링

04 　　　　　　　정답 ⑤　　　정답률 41%

정답 풀이

(A) 간접의문문

They wondered / [**if** / what the moon was made of].
　　　　　　　　간접의문문(의문사 + 주어 + 동사), be made of: ...로 구성되다
그들은 궁금했다　　달이 무엇으로 만들어졌는지

➡ 동사 wondered의 목적어로 쓰인 간접의문문을 이끌며, 간접의문문 안에서 전치사
of의 목적어 역할을 하는 의문사 what이 오는 것이 적절하다.

(B) 수량형용사

Scientists developed [many / ~~much~~] different theories, or guesses, /
과학자들은 많은 다양한 이론이나 추측을 발전시켰다
but they could not prove / [that their ideas were correct].
　　　　　　　　　　　　　명사절(목적어)을 이끄는 접속사
하지만 그들은 증명할 수 없었다　　　자신들의 생각이 옳다는 것을

➡ 뒤에 복수 명사(different theories, or guesses)가 왔으므로 many가 오는 것이
알맞다. much는 셀 수 없는 명사와 함께 쓰인다.

(C) 병렬구조

Then, between 1969 and 1972, the United States sent astronauts
그러다, 1969년과 1972년 사이에, 미국은 우주비행사들을 달에 보냈다
to the moon / for their studying the moon and [returned /
전치사　　　전치사의 목적어1
　　　　　　그들이 달을 연구하고 지구로 돌아오도록
[returning] to Earth / with rock samples.
전치사의 목적어2
　　　　　　　　암석 표본을 가지고

➡ 등위접속사 and가 전치사 for의 목적어로 쓰인 동명사를 병렬 연결하고 있으므로, 앞의
동명사 studying과 대등하도록 동명사 returning이 오는 것이 알맞다.

지문 해석

수천 년 동안 사람들은 밤하늘을 올려다보고 달을 보아 왔다. 그들은 달이 무엇으로
만들어졌는지 궁금했다. 그들은 달이 얼마나 크지 그리고 얼마나 멀리 떨어져 있는지 알고
싶었다. 가장 흥미로운 질문 중 하나는 "달이 어디서 생겨났는가?"였다. 누구도 확실히
알지 못했다. 과학자들은 많은 다양한 이론이나 추측을 발전시켰지만, 자신들의 생각이
옳다는 것을 증명할 수 없었다. 그러다, 1969년과 1972년 사이에 미국은 달을 연구하고
암석 표본을 지구로 가지고 돌아오도록 우주비행사들을 달에 보냈다.

theory 몡 이론　　guess 몡 추측, 짐작　　prove 통 입증하다, 증명하다　　astronaut
몡 우주비행사

05　정답 ④　정답률 63%

정답 풀이

④ 가목적어 진목적어 구문

However, this lack of time for relaxation makes it more difficult /
　　　　　　　　　주어　　　　　　　동사 가목적어 목적격보어
하지만, 이런 휴식 시간의 부족은 더 어렵게 만든다
[get(→ to get) the most out of your studies].
　　　　진목적어, get the most out of: …을 최대한 활용하다
공부를 최대한 활용하는 것을

➡ 동사 makes 뒤에 오는 it은 가목적어로, 뒤에 진목적어 역할을 하는 to부정사가 와야
하므로 get을 to부정사인 to get으로 고쳐야 한다.

친절한 오답 풀이

① 「전치사 + 동명사」, 동명사의 동사적 성질

Activities, friends, and pastimes may cause some difficulties / in
　　　　　　　　　　　　　　　　　　　　　　　　　　전치사
활동, 친구들, 그리고 오락은 약간의 어려움을 야기할 수 있다
your performing the real job / at hand.
동명사의 의미상 주어
당신이 실질적인 일을 수행하는 데　　코앞에 닥친

➡ 전치사 in의 목적어 역할을 하면서 명사 the real job을 목적어로 취할 수 있는 동명사
performing이 오는 것이 알맞다.

② 감정을 나타내는 분사

When you are feeling overwhelmed / by presentations, paper
　　　　　　　　feel + 형용사: …하게 느끼다
당신이 압도당하는 느낌이 들 때　　　　　　발표, 보고서 마감시간, 혹은 시험에 의해
deadlines, or tests, ...

➡ 감각동사 feel의 보어 역할을 하는 분사로, 주어(you)가 '압도당하는'이라는 의미이므로
과거분사 overwhelmed가 오는 것이 알맞다.

③ 부사적 용법의 to부정사

..., you will probably spend all your time studying / to deal with
　　　　　　　　spend + 시간 + v-ing: …하는 데 (시간)을 쓰다　부사적 용법의
당신은 아마도 공부하는 데 당신의 모든 시간을 쓸 것이다　　　to부정사(목적)
these pressures.
이런 긴급한 일을 처리하기 위해

➡ 앞의 동사 spend를 수식하는 부사적 용법의 to부정사로 어법상 바르다.

⑤ 재귀대명사

(You) Promise yourself / {that [no matter how much work you
　　　　　　　　　　　　접속사　아무리 …하더라도(= however)
자신에게 약속해라　　　　　　아무리 당신이 일이 많더라도
have], / you will always relax / during one full evening}.
　　　　　　항상 쉬겠다고　　　하루 저녁은 온전히

➡ 명령문에서 생략된 주어(You)와 동사 Promise의 목적어가 동일인을 지칭하므로,
목적어 자리에 재귀대명사 yourself가 오는 것이 알맞다.

지문 해석

대학 생활은 바쁘다. 당신의 계획에 요구사항들이 너무 많다. 활동, 친구들, 그리고 오락은
당신이 코앞에 닥친 실질적인 일을 수행하는 데 약간의 어려움을 야기할 수 있다. 발표,
보고서 마감시간, 혹은 시험에 의해 압도당하는 느낌이 들 때, 당신은 아마도 이런 긴급한
일들을 처리하기 위해 공부하는 데 모든 시간을 쓸 것이다. 하지만, 이런 휴식 시간의
부족은 공부를 최대한 활용하는 것을 더 어렵게 만든다. 아무리 당신이 일이 많더라도
항상 하루 저녁은 온전히 쉬겠다고 자신에게 약속해라. 휴식을 위해서 시간을 낸다면
당신은 일을 더 잘하게 될 것이다.

demand 몡 요구사항, 필요사항　　pastime 몡 오락, 기분전환　　perform 통 수행하다
overwhelm 통 압도하다　　presentation 몡 발표　　deadline 몡 기한, 마감시간
pressure 몡 압박(감), 긴급　　lack 몡 부족, 결핍　　relaxation 몡 휴식

06　정답 ③　정답률 38%

정답 풀이

③ 도치구문

[Just as saying sorry matters], / so does remember(→ remembering)
꼭 …처럼　　　　주어　　　　동사　　　동사　　　　　주어
미안하다고 말하는 것이 중요한 것처럼　사람들에게 감사하는 것을 기억하는 것도 그렇다
to thank those / [who help you move forward].
　　　　　　　　주격 관계대명사　help + 목적어 + 동사원형: …가 ~하도록 돕다
당신이 앞으로 나아가도록 돕는

➡ 부사 so가 앞으로 나가면서 주어와 동사의 도치가 일어난 구문으로, 동사 뒤에 주어가
나와야 하므로 remember를 동명사 remembering으로 고쳐야 한다. 「just as ...,
so ~」는 '…한 것처럼 ~도 역시 그렇다'라는 의미의 구문이다.

① forget to-v

> In business settings, / it's really easy [to **forget to take** the time / to
> 가주어   진주어   명사적 용법의   형용사적 용법의
>   to부정사   to부정사
> 사업 현장에서   시간을 내는 것을 잊기가 정말 쉽다
> say Thank-You], / and yet, it's an essential part of interaction
> 고마움을 표할   하지만, 그것은 다른 사람과의 교류에서 필수적인 부분이다
> with others.

➡ 문맥상 '시간을 내는 것을 잊다'의 의미이므로 forget의 목적어로 to부정사가 오는 것이 알맞다.

 Grammar Tips

> **과거의 동명사, 미래의 to부정사**
> 동사 forget과 remember는 to부정사와 동명사를 모두 목적어로 취할 수 있는데, 과거의 일을 나타낼 때는 동명사를, 미래의 일을 나타낼 때는 to부정사를 쓴다.
> • forget[remember] to-v: (미래에) …할 것을 잊다[기억하다]
> • forget[remember] v-ing: (과거에) …한 것을 잊다[기억하다]

② 주격보어

> It's important to people / [that they feel valid, important, and
> 가주어   진주어   감각동사 보어1   보어2   접속사
> 사람들에게 중요하다   그들이 정당하고, 중요하며, 존중받고 있다고 느끼는 것이
> respected].
> 보어3

➡ 감각동사 feel의 보어가 등위접속사 and에 의해 병렬 연결된 구조로, 주어(they)가 '존중받는 것'이라는 수동의 의미이므로 과거분사 respected가 오는 것이 알맞다.

④ 비교급 강조 부사

> A personal note [written by your own hand] / matters far more /
>   과거분사   부사
> 당신의 손으로 직접 쓴 개인적인 편지는   훨씬 더 많이 중요하다
> than a few lines of typing into a window / [that's so easily
>   주격 관계대명사
> (컴퓨터) 화면에 입력해서 넣은 몇 줄보다   당신의 손끝으로 아주 쉽게 이용할 수 있는
> available at your fingertips].

➡ far는 '훨씬'의 의미로 뒤에 나오는 비교급 more을 수식하여 비교의 의미를 강조하는 부사로, 어법상 바르다.

⑤ 병렬구조

> One more thing: [if you're going to go this route], put in the extra
>   명령문의 동사1
> 한 가지 더, 당신이 이렇게 할 것이라면, 추가 몇 분을 더 들여라
> few minutes / to purchase a nice card / and use a pen [that gives
>   부사적 용법의 to부정사(목적)   명령문의 동사2   주격 관계대명사
>   좋은 카드를 구입하기 위해   그리고 당신이 잘 쓰게 하는 펜을 써라
> you a decent flow].

➡ 등위접속사 and가 명령문의 동사를 병렬 연결하고 있으므로, 동사 put과 대등하도록 동사원형 use가 오는 것이 알맞다.

 구문 분석 Plus

> 7행
> And I think [(that) **it's** *much* nicer **to send** along a physical
> card than an email].
> ➡ it은 가주어, to send 이하가 진주어
> ➡ much: '훨씬'의 의미로 비교급을 강조하는 부사

사업 현장에서, 고마움을 표할 시간을 내는 것을 잊기가 정말 쉽지만, 그것은 다른 사람과의 교류에서 필수적인 부분이다. 사람들에게 그들이 정당하고, 중요하며, 존중받고 있다고 느끼는 것이 중요하다. 미안하다고 말하는 것이 중요한 것처럼, 당신이 앞으로 나아가도록 돕는 사람들에게 감사하는 것을 기억하는 것도 중요하다. 그리고 나는 이메일보다 실제 카드를 보내는 것이 훨씬 더 좋다고 생각한다. 당신의 손으로 직접 쓴 개인적인 편지는 당신의 손끝으로 아주 쉽게 이용할 수 있는 (컴퓨터) 화면에 입력해서 넣은 몇 줄보다 훨씬 더 중요하다. 한 가지 더, 당신이 이렇게 할 것이라면, 좋은 카드를 구입하기 위해 추가 몇 분을 더 들이고 당신이 잘 쓰게 하는 펜을 써라.

 어휘

setting 몡 환경   essential 혱 필수적인   interaction 몡 상호 작용   valid 혱 타당한, 정당한   respected 혱 훌륭한, 존경받는   matter 통 중요하다   physical 혱 육체의; *물질[물리]적인   available 혱 구할[이용할]수 있는   route 몡 길; *방법 decent 혱 괜찮은, 제대로 된

5 대명사, 형용사, 부사

UNIT 1 대명사

코드 접속하기

pp.101~104

출제코드 1 | 대명사의 수와 격

A **1** it **2** that **3** mine
B **1** → yours **2** → it **3** ○

해석과 정답 풀이

STEP 1

1 1) Hailey는 팔찌를 받았으나, 그것을 좋아하지 않았다.
 2) 나는 가게에서 많은 모자를 써 보았으나, 그것들 중 어떤 것도 맞지 않았다.
 3) 나는 규칙적으로 운동하는데, 그것은 나를 건강하게 유지시켜 준다.
2 1) 그녀의 소설은 아주 인기가 있어서, 그것은 그녀를 베스트셀러 작가로 만들었다.
 2) 내가 오늘 아침에 산 스마트폰은 그의 것과 다르다.

STEP 2

1 1) 그녀가 그 영화에 아주 감동을 받아서 그것을 10번 보았다.
 2) 그들의 다양한 정책들로 인해 유럽 국가들의 출생률이 증가하기 시작했다.
2 Andrew는 그의 작품이 상을 받았어야 했다고 생각했지만, 심판들은 그녀의 작품을 더 선호했다.

STEP 3

A **1** 무엇이 정의인가? 각기 다른 철학자들은 그것을 아주 다르게 정의한다.
 ➡ 단수 명사 justice를 지칭하고 있으므로 단수 대명사 it이 알맞다.
 2 정원으로 들어갔을 때, 나는 잔디가 담장 다른 편에 있는 것보다 더 푸르다는 것을 알아차렸다.
 ➡ 단수 명사 the grass를 지칭하고 있으므로 단수 대명사 that이 알맞다.
 3 나의 친구는 종이 더미를 보고 "내가 네 일을 먼저 도와줄게. 나는 나중에 내 일을 끝낼 수 있어."라고 말했다.
 ➡ 문맥상 '나의 일'이라는 의미가 적절하므로 소유대명사 mine이 알맞다.
B **1** 너는 이름이 너의 이름과 같은 친구가 있니?
 ➡ 문맥상 '너의 이름'이라는 의미가 적절하므로 you를 소유대명사 yours로 고쳐야 한다.
 2 나는 빨리 나의 걱정들에 대해 메모를 썼고 그것을 탁자 위에 두었다.
 ➡ 대명사가 단수 명사 a note를 지칭하고 있으므로 복수 대명사 them을 단수 대명사 it으로 고쳐야 한다.
 3 극장의 3층 좌석들은 1층 좌석들보다 더 싸다.
 ➡ 대명사가 복수 명사 The seats를 지칭하고 있으므로 복수 대명사 those가 오는 것이 알맞다.

출제코드 2 | 부정대명사

A **1** other **2** both **3** Both
B **1** → either[each] **2** → another **3** → both

해석과 정답 풀이

STEP 1

1 1) 그녀는 빨간 사과보다 초록 사과를 더 좋아한다.
 2) 몇몇 사람들은 개고기를 좋아하는 반면, 다른 사람들은 그것을 정말로 싫어한다.
 3) 그들은 둘 다 같은 학교에 다니지만, 각자 전공이 다르다.
 4) 나는 이 셔츠의 색깔이 마음에 들지 않아요. 다른 색상으로 나오는 것이 있나요?
2 1) 내가 화났던 또 다른 이유는 어떤 통지도 없이 회의가 취소되었다는 것이다.
 2) 당신이 추천한 호텔들 어떤 것도 좋아 보인다.
 3) 각각의 박스는 무작위로 선택된 몇 개의 품목들을 담고 있다.

STEP 2

1 1) 파업이 끝난 후에 그들 둘 다 해고되었다.
 2) Charley는 그의 감사함을 보여주는 다른 방법들을 알기를 원한다.
2 1) 길의 양쪽에 오렌지 나무들이 있다.
 2) 나의 가족은 다음 달에 다른 도시로 이사를 갈 것이다.

STEP 3

A **1** 몇몇은 그들의 노트에 열심히 필기를 하는 반면, 다른 학생들은 경악하여 필기하는 것을 포기한다.
 ➡ 뒤에 복수 명사 students가 이어지고 있으므로 부정형용사 other가 오는 것이 알맞다. 부정형용사 another 뒤에는 단수 명사가 온다.
 2 렌즈와 각막은 손상되기 쉬운 부위이다. 태양에 너무 많이 노출된다면 그들은 둘 다 손상을 받는다.
 ➡ 뒤에 복수 동사 are가 이어지고 있으므로 부정대명사 both가 오는 것이 알맞다. 부정대명사 each 뒤에는 단수 동사가 온다.
 3 두 소년 모두 그들의 팀을 대표해서 시상식에 참석하도록 요청 받았다.
 ➡ 뒤에 복수 명사 boys와 복수 동사 were가 이어지고 있으므로 부정대명사 Both가 오는 것이 알맞다. Each 뒤에는 단수 명사와 단수 동사가 온다.
B **1** 케이크와 아이스크림은 좋은 디저트들이므로, 어느 것이든 나는 괜찮다.
 ➡ 뒤에 단수 대명사 one과 단수 동사 is가 이어지고 있으므로 both를 부정형용사 either이나 each로 고쳐야 한다.
 2 당신이 그 식당에 만족하지 못하신다면, 제가 당신에게 또 다른 식당을 추천해드리겠습니다.
 ➡ 뒤에 단수 대명사 one(= restaurant)이 이어지고 있으므로 부정형용사 another가 오는 것이 알맞다. 부정형용사 other 뒤에는 복수 명사가 온다.
 3 두 도둑이 마침내 잡혔고, 경찰은 두 남자를 심문했다.
 ➡ 뒤에 복수 명사 men이 있으므로 each를 부정형용사 both로 고쳐야 한다. 부정형용사 each 뒤에는 단수 명사가 온다.

출제코드 3 | 재귀대명사

A **1** him **2** themselves **3** yourself
B **1** → them **2** ○ **3** → herself

해석과 정답 풀이

STEP 1

1 1) Julia는 그녀 자신에게 꽃 한 다발을 사주었다.
 2) 나는 실수로 칼에 베였을 때, 고통으로 울었다.
 3) Jamie는 그 스스로 작업을 완수하려 노력했다.

STEP 2

2 1) Angela는 항상 작은 일들에 대해 걱정하고, 그녀 자신을 다른 사람들과 자주 비교한다.
 2) 그가 문을 열었을 때, 그의 어린 딸이 그에게 달려왔다.
 3) 대회에서 우승한 후에, 그는 그 자신을 최고의 사진작가라고 불렀다.

STEP 3

A **1** 그가 당황하지 않도록, 그 연회에 있는 마을 사람들은 아무 일도 일어나지 않은 것처럼 행동했다.
 ➡ 동사 save의 목적어와 주절의 주어(the villagers)가 일치하지 않으므로 인칭대명사 him이 오는 것이 알맞다.
 2 디자이너들은 그들 자신을 작품 속에 표현할 수 있어야 한다.
 ➡ 동사 express의 목적어와 주어(Designers)가 일치하므로 재귀대명사 themselves가 오는 것이 알맞다.
 3 당신이 실패할 때, 당신이 과거에 했던 일들에 대해 자신을 책망하지 마라.
 ➡ 명령문의 생략된 주어(you)와 동사 blame의 목적어가 지칭하는 대상이 같으므로 재귀대명사 yourself가 오는 것이 알맞다.
B **1** 몇몇의 한국 부모들은 그들의 아이들이 "alpha kids"가 되도록 준비시키기 위해 그들을 열심히 공부하게 한다.
 ➡ 문장의 주어(Some Korean parents)와 동사 prepare의 목적어가 지칭하는 대상이 다르므로 재귀대명사 themselves를 인칭대명사 them으로 고쳐야 한다.
 2 David는 거울 속에서 자신을 보고 그가 그의 어머니를 전혀 닮지 않았다는 것을 깨달았다.
 ➡ 문장의 주어(David)와 동사 looked at의 목적어가 지칭하는 대상이 같으므로

재귀대명사 himself가 오는 것이 알맞다.

3 Laura는 항상 바이올린을 연주하기를 원했고, 그래서 어느 날 그녀는 독학하기로 결심했다.

➡ so가 이끄는 절의 주어(she)와 동사 teach의 목적어가 지칭하는 대상이 같으므로 her를 재귀대명사 herself로 고쳐야 한다.

기출예제 Q1 정답 ② 정답률 28%

정답 풀이

② 재귀대명사

Clothes are part of [how people present them(→ themselves) to
옷은 사람들이 자신을 세상에 보여주는 방식의 일부이고   관계부사
the world], / and fashion locates them in the present, / relative to
패션은 그들을 현재에 위치시킨다
[what is happening in society] and to fashion's own history.
관계사
사회에서 일어나고 있는 일 그리고 패션 자체의 역사와 관련하여

➡ 관계부사절 내의 주어 people과 목적어가 가리키는 대상이 같으므로, 목적어로는 재귀대명사 themselves가 와야 한다. people이 복수 명사이므로 대명사도 복수형이 와야 한다.

친절한 오답 풀이

① 접속사

The most common explanation / {offered by my informants / as to
                        주어   과거분사   ~에 관해
가장 흔한 설명은   나의 정보 제공자들이 제공한
[why fashion is so appealing]} / is [that it constitutes a kind of
간접의문문(의문사 + 주어 + 동사)   동사 접속사
왜 패션이 그렇게 매력적인지에 대해   그것이 일종의 연극적인 의상을 구성한다는 것이다
theatrical costumery].

➡ 동사 is의 보어 역할을 하는 명사절을 이끌며, 뒤에 완전한 절이 이어지므로, 접속사 that은 어법상 알맞다.

③ 명사를 수식하는 과거분사

As a form of expression, / fashion contains a host of ambiguities, /
전치사(…로서)   다수의
표현 형태로서   패션은 다수의 모호함을 담고 있어
{enabling individuals to recreate the meanings [associated with
결과를 나타내는 분사구문   과거분사
개인이 특정한 옷과 연관된 의미를 재창조할 수 있게 한다
specific pieces of clothing]}.

➡ 과거분사 associated는 앞의 명사구 the meanings를 수식하고 있다. 의미는 '연관되어진' 것이므로 수식을 받는 명사와 분사의 의미상 관계가 수동이므로 과거분사 associated는 어법상 알맞다.

④ 부사

Fashion is among the simplest and cheapest methods of
패션은 자기표현의 가장 단순하고 값싼 방법 중 하나이다
self-expression: / clothes can be inexpensively purchased / [while
                        동사   접속사를 생략하지
                옷은 저렴하게 구매할 수 있으며   않은 분사구문
making it easy to convey notions of wealth, intellectual stature,
       가목적어   진목적어
부, 지적 능력, 휴식 또는 환경 의식에 대한 개념을 쉽게 전달할 수 있다
relaxation or environmental consciousness], / [even if none of
                                                접속사
                                          비록 이것 중 어느 것도
these is true].
사실이 아니라 해도

➡ 부사 inexpensively는 동사 can be purchased를 수식하고 있으므로 어법상 알맞다.

---

⑤ 분사구문

Fashion can also strengthen agency in various ways, / [opening
                                          결과를 나타내는 분사구문
패션은 또한 다양한 방법으로 행동성을 강화하여
up space for action].
행동을 위한 공간을 열어 줄 수 있다

➡ opening 이하는 결과를 나타내는 분사구문으로, 분사의 의미상 주어는 주절의 주어 Fashion과 동일하다. 의미상 주어와 분사의 관계가 능동이므로 현재분사 opening은 적절하다.

지문 해석

유행은 사람들이 자신을 재조정할 새로운 기회를 끊임없이 제시하고 변화의 때를 나타낸다. 유행이 궁극적으로 어떻게 개인에게 힘과 자유를 줄 수 있는지를 이해하기 위해서는 먼저 변화를 위한 기반으로서의 패션의 중요성에 대해 논의해야 한다. 왜 패션이 그렇게 매력적인지에 대해 나의 정보 제공자들이 한 가장 흔한 설명은 그것이 일종의 연극적인 의상을 구성한다는 것이다. 옷은 사람들이 자신을 세상에 보여주는 방식의 일부이고 패션은 사회에서 일어나고 있는 일 그리고 패션 자체의 역사와 관련하여 그들을 현재에 위치시킨다. 표현 형태로서 패션은 다수의 모호함을 담고 있어 개인이 특정한 옷과 연관된 의미를 재창조할 수 있게 한다. 패션은 자기표현의 가장 단순하고 값싼 방법 중 하나로 옷은 저렴하게 구매할 수 있으며 부, 지적 능력, 휴식 또는 환경 의식에 대한 개념을 비록 이것 중 어느 것도 사실이 아니라 해도 쉽게 전달할 수 있다. 패션은 또한 다양한 방법으로 행동성을 강화하여 행동을 위한 공간을 열어 줄 수 있다.

어휘

occasion 명 때, 경우   ultimately 부 궁극적으로   informant 명 정보 제공자
appealing 형 매력적인   constitute 동 구성하다   costumery 명 의상, 복장
ambiguity 명 모호함   convey 동 전달하다   consciousness 명 의식
strengthen 동 강화하다

코드 공략하기 pp.105~107

01 ③ **02** ② **03** ② **04** ⑤ **05** ② **06** ⑤ **07** ⑤ **08** ⑤

---

01 정답 ③ 정답률 35%

정답 풀이

③ 대명사

These microplastics are very difficult to measure / {once they
                                                        접속사
이러한 미세 플라스틱은 측정하기가 매우 어렵다   일단 그것들이
are small enough / to pass through the nets / [typically used /
형용사/부사 + enough to-v: …할 만큼 충분히 ~한/하게   과거분사
충분히 작으면   그물망을 통과할 만큼   일반적으로 사용되는
to collect themselves (→ them)]}.
                    = microplastics
그것들을 수거하는 데

➡ 의미상 주체가 되는 the nets와 collect의 목적어가 서로 다르므로, 목적격 대명사인 them으로 고쳐야 한다.

친절한 오답 풀이

① 주격 관계대명사

Plastic is extremely slow to degrade / and tends to float, /
                                          tend to-v: …하는 경향이 있다
플라스틱은 매우 느리게 분해되고   물에 떠다니는 경향이 있는데
[which allows it to travel in ocean currents / for thousands of
계속적 용법의 주격 관계대명사
   이는 플라스틱이 해류를 따라 이동하게 한다   수천 마일을
miles].

➡ 앞 절 전체를 선행사로 하고, 뒤에 이어지는 관계사절에서 동사 allows의 주어 역할을 할 수 있는 관계대명사 which가 오는 것이 알맞다.

② 분사구문

> Most plastics break down into smaller and smaller pieces /
> 대부분의 플라스틱은 점점 더 작은 조각으로 분해되어
> [when (they are) exposed to ultraviolet (UV) light], / [forming
> 접속사 「주어 + 동사」 생략　　　　　　　　　　결과를 나타내는 분사구문
> 자외선에 노출될 때　　　　　　　　　　　　　　미세 플라스틱을
> microplastics].
> (= and they form ...)
> 형성한다

➡ forming 이하는 결과를 나타내는 분사구문으로, 생략된 주어는 주절의 주어(Most plastics)와 같다. 주어와 분사가 의미상 능동 관계에 있으므로 현재분사 forming이 오는 것이 알맞다.

④ 동사의 수 일치

> [Because most of the plastic particles / in the ocean / are so
> 접속사　　　　　　주어　　　　　　　　　　　　　　동사
> 대부분의 플라스틱 조각들은　　　　　바닷속에 있는　　매우 작기 때문에
> small], / there is no practical way / to clean up the ocean.
> 　　　　　　　　　　　　　　　　　　　형용사적 용법의 to부정사
> 실질적인 방법은 없다　　　　　바다를 청소할

➡ 「부분을 나타내는 말(most, some 등) + of + 명사」가 주어일 경우, of 뒤에 나오는 명사에 동사의 수를 일치시킨다. 이 문장에서 most of 뒤에 복수 명사 the plastic particles가 왔으므로 복수 동사 are가 오는 것이 알맞다.

⑤ 부사

> One would have to filter enormous amounts of water / to collect
> 　　　　　　　　　　　　　　　　　　　　　부사적 용법의 to부정사(목적)
> 엄청난 양의 물을 여과해야 할 수도 있다　　　　　　　　비교적 적은 양의
> a relatively small amount of plastic.
> 　　부사
> 플라스틱을 수거하기 위해

➡ 부사 relatively가 형용사 small을 수식하고 있으므로 어법상 바르다.

지문 해석

플라스틱은 매우 느리게 분해되고 물에 떠다니는 경향이 있는데, 이는 플라스틱이 해류를 따라 수천 마일을 이동하게 한다. 대부분의 플라스틱은 자외선에 노출될 때 점점 더 작은 조각으로 분해되어 미세 플라스틱을 형성한다. 이러한 미세 플라스틱은 일단 그것들을 수거하는 데 일반적으로 사용되는 그물망을 통과할 만큼 충분히 작으면 측정하기가 매우 어렵다. 미세 플라스틱이 해양 환경과 먹이 그물에 미치는 영향은 아직도 제대로 이해되지 않고 있다. 이 작은 조각들은 다양한 동물에게 먹혀 먹이 사슬 속으로 들어간다고 알려져 있다. 바닷속에 있는 대부분의 플라스틱 조각들은 매우 작기 때문에 바다를 청소할 실질적인 방법은 없다. 비교적 적은 양의 플라스틱을 수거하기 위해 엄청난 양의 물을 여과해야 할 수도 있다.

어휘

extremely 閉 극도로, 극히　ocean current 閔 해류　break down into ~로 분해되다　expose 통 드러내다, 노출시키다　ultraviolet light 閔 자외선　microplastic 閔 미세 플라스틱　measure 통 측정하다　impact 閔 영향, 충격　marine 휄 바다의, 해양의　food web 閔 먹이 그물　particle 閔 (아주 작은) 입자[조각]　various 휄 다양한　filter 통 여과하다, 거르다　enormous 휄 거대한, 막대한, 엄청난　relatively 閉 비교적

02　　　　　정답 ②　　　정답률 63%

정답 풀이

(A) 동사의 수 일치

> [Taking photos on sunny, hot days] / is / ~~are~~ just as dangerous
> 동명사구 주어　　　　　　　　as + 형용사 + as: ···만큼 ~한
> 화창하고 더운 날 사진을 찍는 것은　　　　당신에게 위험하다
> for you / as it is for your camera.
> 당신의 카메라에 만큼이나

➡ 주어가 동명사구(Taking ... days)로, 동명사구는 단수 취급하므로 단수 동사 is를 써야 한다.

(B) 동명사

> { Keep / Keeping the lens covered / [when you aren't using it]} /
> 동명사 주어, keep + 목적어 + v-ed: ···을 ~한 채로 유지하다　접속사
> 카메라 렌즈를 덮어 두는 것이　　　　　　　　당신이 그것을 사용하고 있지 않을 때
> is recommended.
> 동사
> 권장된다

➡ 네모는 동사 is recommended의 주어 역할을 하는 명사구를 이끄는 자리이므로 동명사 Keeping이 오는 것이 알맞다.

(C) 부정대명사

> The lens is related to the human eye; / both / ~~each~~ are damaged /
> be related to: ···와 관계가 있다　　　　　　　　　　　둘 다 손상을 입는다
> 렌즈는 인간의 눈과 관계가 있다
> by directly peering at the light.
> 빛을 직접 봄으로써

➡ 앞에 언급된 The lens와 the human eye를 지칭하며, 뒤에 복수 동사 are가 이어지고 있으므로 '둘 다'라는 뜻의 부정대명사 both가 적절하다. each는 '개개의 것'이라는 의미로 단수 취급한다.

지문 해석

화창하고 더운 날 사진을 찍는 것은 당신의 카메라에 만큼이나 당신에게 위험하다. 당신은 햇빛으로 인한 단순 화상을 처리할 수 있지만, 카메라는 너무 많이 햇볕에 노출되면 영구적인 손상에 직면할 수 있다. 당신이 카메라를 사용하고 있지 않을 때 렌즈를 덮어 두는 것이 권장된다. 일출과 일몰 사진은 언제나 찍는 것도 재미있고 나중에 보는 것도 재미있지만, 당신의 카메라 렌즈를 직접적으로 햇볕을 향하게 하는 것은 카메라에 손상을 입힐 수 있다. 렌즈는 인간의 눈과 관계가 있다. 둘 다 빛을 직접적으로 봄으로써 손상을 입게 된다.

어휘

sunburn 閔 햇볕으로 입은 화상　permanent 휄 영구적인　damage 閔 손상 통 손상을 주다　exposure 閔 노출　sunrise 閔 일출　sunset 閔 일몰　directly 閉 곧장, 똑바로　peer 통 응시하다

03　　　　　정답 ②　　　정답률 80%

정답 풀이

(A) 명사를 수식하는 과거분사

> "Working memory," or "short-term memory" is a term / {used /
> '작동 기억' 또는 '단기 기억'은 용어이다　　　　　　　　과거분사
> ~~using~~ to describe the fact / [that one can hold only a given
> 부사적 용법(목적)　　　　　　동격　　that은 접속사
> 사실을 설명하기 위해 사용되는　　　사람이 오직 주어진 양의 자료만을 기억할 수 있다는
> amount of material in mind / at one time].
> 한 번에

➡ 앞의 명사 a term을 수식하는 분사로, 용어가 '사용되는'이라는 수동의 의미이므로 과거분사 used가 오는 것이 알맞다.

(B) 부정대명사

> ...; some write furiously in their notebooks, / while ~~other~~ / others
> some ... others ~: (여럿 중에서) 어떤 것[사람]들은 ~ 다른 것[사람]들은 ~
> 어떤 이들은 공책에 맹렬히 필기한다　　　　　　　반면에 다른 이들은
> give up writing in complete discouragement.
> 완전히 낙담해서 필기를 포기한다

➡ 앞 절에 '(여럿 중에서) 어떤 사람들'이라는 의미의 복수형 대명사 some이 쓰였고, 네모 뒤에 복수 동사 give가 이어지고 있으므로 복수 대명사 others가 오는 것이 알맞다.

(C) 구동사와 대명사 목적어

> Note taking thus is <u>dependent on</u> one's ability / {to maintain
> 동명사 주어 　　　 be dependent on: …에 의존하다 　　 형용사적 용법, 부정사1
> 따라서 필기는 개인의 능력에 의존하고, 　　　　　　　　　　 집중을 유지하고,
> attention, (to) <u>understand</u> [what is being said], and (to) <u>hold</u> it in
> 　　　　 부정사2 　　　　 관계대명사 　　　 접속사 　 부정사3
> 강의되고 있는 것을 이해하고, 그것을 작동 기억 속에 지니는
> working memory / long enough to | <del>write down it</del> / write it down |}.
> 　　　　　　　　 형용사/부사 + enough to-v: ~할 만큼 충분히 …한/하게
> 　　　　　　　　 그것을 필기할 만큼 충분히 오래

➡ 「동사 + 부사」로 이루어진 구동사의 목적어가 명사일 경우 목적어의 위치는 부사 앞이나 뒤 모두 가능하다. 그러나 목적어가 대명사일 경우 반드시 동사와 부사의 사이에 쓰인다. 이 문장에서, 구동사 write down의 목적어가 대명사 it이므로, write it down으로 쓰는 것이 어법상 바르다.

지문 해석

필기는 학생들이 집중한 상태를 유지하기 위해 시도하는 활동 중 하나이지만, 그것은 또한 기억하는 것을 도와준다. '작동 기억' 또는 '단기 기억'은 사람이 한 번에 오직 주어진 양의 자료만을 기억할 수 있다는 사실을 설명하기 위해 사용되는 용어이다. 강사가 연속적으로 새로운 개념을 제시하면, 학생들의 얼굴은 고통과 좌절의 기색이 보이기 시작한다. 어떤 학생들은 공책에 맹렬히 필기하는 반면, 다른 학생들은 완전히 낙담해서 필기를 포기한다. 따라서 필기는 집중을 유지하고, 강의되고 있는 것을 이해하고, 그것을 필기할 만큼 충분히 오래 작동 기억 속에 지닐 수 있는 개인의 능력에 의존한다.

어휘

attempt 통 시도하다 　**attentive** 형 집중하는 (**attention** 명 집중) 　**aid** 명 원조, 지원 　**material** 명 자료 　**present** 통 제시하다 　**succession** 명 연속 **concept** 명 개념 　**anguish** 명 고통 　**frustration** 명 좌절 　**furiously** 부 맹렬히 **discouragement** 명 낙담 　**maintain** 통 유지하다

04　　　　　　　정답 ⑤　　　정답률 26%

정답 풀이

⑤ 재귀대명사

> There is absolutely no reason / [why any e-commerce enterprise
> 　　　　　　　　　　　　　　　　　　　　 관계부사
> 이유가 전혀 없다 　　　　　　　 어떤 전자 상거래 기업도 스스로를 국한시켜야 할
> should limit themselves(→ itself) / to marketing and selling one
> 　　　　　　　　　　　　　　　 한 생산자의 상품을 마케팅하고 판매하도록
> maker's products].

➡ 관계부사절에서 동사 limit의 목적어가 가리키는 대상이 주어인 any e-commerce enterprise와 같고, 주어가 단수 명사이므로 themselves를 단수형 재귀대명사 itself로 고쳐야 한다.

친절한 오답 풀이

① 관계대명사 what

> E-commerce is to the information revolution / what the railroad
> A is to B what C is to D: A와 B의 관계는 C와 D의 관계와 같다 　관계대명사
> 전자 상거래와 정보혁명과의 관계는 　　　　　　　　　 철도와 산업혁명과의 관계와 같다
> was to the industrial revolution.

➡ 「A is to B what C is to D」 구문으로, 관계대명사 what은 어법상 바르다.

② 목적격보어

> The Internet provides enterprises with the ability / [to link one
> 　　　　　　 provide A with B: A에게 B를 제공하다 　　　　 형용사적 용법의
> 　　　　　　　　　　　　　　　　　　　　　　　　　　 to부정사
> 인터넷은 기업에 능력을 제공한다 　　　　　　　　　 하나의 활동을
> activity to another and to <u>make</u> real-time data widely available].
> 　　　　　　 make + 목적어 + 형용사: …을 ~하게 만들다 　　　 목적격보어
> 다른 것과 연결하고 실시간 자료를 폭넓게 이용할 수 있게 하는

➡ 동사 make의 목적격보어 자리에 형용사 available이 쓰였으므로 어법상 바르다.

③ 형용사적 용법의 to부정사

> It strengthens the move to break up the big corporation of today.
> 　　　　　　　　　　　　　　 형용사적 용법의 to부정사
> 그것은 오늘날의 거대 기업을 세분화하는 움직임을 강화한다

➡ 앞의 명사 the move를 수식하는 형용사적 용법의 to부정사로 어법상 적절하다.

④ 복합관계대명사

> But, the greatest strength of e-commerce / is {that it provides the
> 　　　　　 주어 　　　　　　　　　　 동사 　 명사절(보어)을 이끄는 접속사
> 그러나, 전자 상거래의 최대 강점은 　　　　　　 그것이 소비자에게
> consumer with a whole range of products, / [whoever makes them]}.
> 　　　　　　　　　　　　　　　　　　　 복합관계대명사(= no matter who)
> 광범위한 종류의 제품을 제공한다는 것이다 　　　　 누가 그것을 만들더라도

➡ 양보의 부사절을 이끌며 뒤에 불완전한 문장이 이어지고, 문맥상 '누가 …하더라도'의 의미를 나타내므로 복합관계대명사 whoever가 오는 것이 알맞다.

지문 해석

전자 상거래와 정보혁명과의 관계는 철도와 산업혁명과의 관계와 같다. 철도가 거리를 정복한 반면, 전자상거래는 거리를 없앴다. 인터넷은 기업에 하나의 활동을 다른 것과 연결하고 실시간 자료를 폭넓게 이용할 수 있게 하는 능력을 제공한다. 그것은 오늘날의 거대 기업을 세분화하는 움직임을 강화한다. 그러나, 전자 상거래의 최대 강점은 누가 만들더라도 소비자들에게 광범위한 종류의 제품을 제공한다는 것이다. 전자상거래는 처음으로 판매와 생산을 분리시킨다. 판매는 더 이상 생산이 아닌 분배와 연관되어 있다. 어떤 전자 상거래 기업도 한 생산자의 상품을 마케팅하고 판매하도록 스스로를 국한시켜야 할 이유가 전혀 없다.

어휘

e-commerce 명 전자 상거래 　**revolution** 명 혁명 　**railroad** 명 철도 　**industrial** 형 산업[공업]의 　**master** 통 정복하다 　**eliminate** 통 제거하다 　**enterprise** 명 기업, 회사 　**real-time** 형 실시간의 　**strengthen** 통 강화하다 (**strength** 명 강점) **corporation** 명 기업, 회사 　**separate** 통 분리하다 　**distribution** 명 분배 　**limit** 통 제한하다

05　　　　　　　정답 ②　　　정답률 56%

정답 풀이

(A) 재귀대명사

> Aging is a result of the gradual failure / of the body's cells and
> 노화는 점진적인 실패의 결과이다 　　　　　　　　 신체의 세포와 기관들의
> organs / to replace and repair | <del>them</del> / themselves |.
> 　　　　 형용사적 용법의 to부정사구, the gradual failure 수식
> 　　　　 스스로를 교체하고 회복하는

➡ 문맥상 to부정사 to replace and repair의 주체와 목적어가 모두 같은 대상(the body's cells and organs)이므로, 재귀대명사 themselves가 오는 것이 알맞다.

(B) 부사

> Sometimes the new cells [that are produced] have defects / or do
> 　　　　　　　　　　　　　 주격 관계대명사 　 동사1 　　 접속사
> 때때로 생성되는 새로운 세포는 결함을 가지고 있거나
> not carry out their usual task | <del>effective</del> / effectively |.
> 　 동사2 　　　　　　　　　　　　　　　　 부사
> 늘 하던 일을 효율적으로 수행하지 못한다

➡ 네모가 동사구 do not carry out을 수식하므로, 부사 effectively가 오는 것이 알맞다.

(C) 문장의 동사

Organs can then begin to fail, tissues change in structure, /
그러면 기관들이 작동이 안 되기 시작할 수 있고, 조직들은 구조에 변화를 일으키며
and the chemical reactions [that power the body] become /
접속사　　　　주어　　　　　주격 관계대명사　　　　동사
그리고 신체에 활력을 공급하는 화학 반응이 덜 효율적이게 된다
~~becoming~~ less efficient.

→ and 이하 절에서, 주어는 the chemical reactions이고 that ... body는 주어를 수식하는 관계대명사절로, 뒤에 동사가 이어져야 하므로 become이 오는 것이 알맞다.

 구문 분석 Plus

12행
The brain cells become **short of** oxygen and nutrients, *leading* to forgetfulness.
→ short of: ⋯이 부족한
→ leading: 연속동작을 나타내는 분사구문(= and they lead ...)

 지문 해석

노화는 신체의 세포와 기관들이 스스로를 교체하고 회복하는 것에 대한 점진적인 실패의 결과이다. 이것은 각 세포가 분열할 수 있는 횟수에 한계가 있기 때문이다. 신체의 세포가 이 한계에 거의 근접하기 시작하면서, 그것들이 분열하는 속도가 느려진다. 때때로 생성되는 새로운 세포는 결함을 가지고 있거나 늘 하던 일을 효율적으로 수행하지 못한다. 그러면 기관들이 작동이 안 되기 시작할 수 있고, 조직들은 구조에 변화를 일으키며, 신체에 활력을 공급하는 화학 반응이 덜 효율적이게 된다. 때로는 뇌로 혈액 공급이 원활하게 되지 않는다. 뇌세포는 산소와 영양분이 부족해져서, 망각 증세로 이어진다.

어휘

gradual 휑 점진적인　cell 명 감방; *세포　organ 명 (인체 내의) 장기[기관]　replace 동 대체하다　rate 명 속도　defect 명 결함　carry out ⋯을 수행[이행]하다　tissue 명 조직　chemical reaction 화학 반응　supply 명 공급　oxygen 명 산소　nutrient 명 영양소　forgetfulness 명 망각

06 　　　정답 ⑤　　정답률 59%

정답 풀이

(A) 명사를 수식하는 현재분사

Yet throughout history, unpaid amateurs, / [~~worked~~ / working
　　　　　　　　　　　　　주어　　　　　　　현재분사
하지만 역사적으로, 무보수로 일했던 아마추어들은
for themselves, their families or their communities], /
자신, 가족, 혹은 지역사회를 위해 일하는
have made remarkable achievements / in a wide variety of fields, /
동사　　　　　　　　　　　　　　　매우 다양한
놀랄만한 업적을 쌓아왔다　　　　　　　　매우 다양한 분야에서
including science and technology.
전치사(⋯을 포함하여)
과학과 기술을 포함한

→ 앞의 명사(unpaid amateurs)를 수식하는 분사로, 아마추어들이 '일하는'이라는 능동의 의미를 나타내므로 현재분사 working이 오는 것이 알맞다.

(B) 대명사

Many gained a living / as paid professionals in one field / but
대명사　동사1　　　　　전치사(⋯로서)　　　　　　　　접속사
많은 이들이 생계를 유지했다　　한 분야에서 급여를 받는 전문가로서
made [his / their] greatest contributions to history as amateurs.
동사2, make a contribution to: ⋯에 공헌하다
하지만 아마추어로서 역사에 큰 공헌을 했다

→ 앞의 '다수의 사람'이라는 뜻의 복수 대명사 주어 Many를 지칭하는 소유격 대명사로 their가 오는 것이 알맞다.

(C) 소유격 관계대명사

Pierre de Fermat, / [~~who~~ / whose] 'last theorem' puzzled
　　　주어　　　　　소유격 관계대명사
피에르 드 페르마는　　　'마지막 정리'로 수 세기동안 수학자들을 혼란스럽게 만든
mathematicians for centuries], / was a lawyer.
　　　　　　　　　　　　　　　　변호사였다

→ 네모는 Pierre de Fermat을 선행사로 하는 관계대명사로, 'Pierre de Fermat의 마지막 정리'라는 의미로 뒤에 이어지는 'last theorem'과 소유 관계이므로 소유격 관계대명사 whose가 적절하다.

 지문 해석

오늘날의 매우 전문화된 세상에서, '아마추어'라는 용어는 회사의 간부들이나 경제학자들에게는 거부감을 일으킨다. 하지만 역사적으로, 자신과 가족, 혹은 지역사회를 위해 무보수로 일했던 아마추어들은 과학과 기술을 포함한 매우 다양한 분야에서 놀랄만한 업적을 쌓아왔다. 과학은 아직 돈을 벌 수 있는 직종이 아니었기 때문에, 초기의 과학자들은 거의 모두 아마추어들이었다. 많은 이들이 한 분야에서 급여를 받는 전문가로서 생계를 유지했지만, 아마추어로서 역사에 큰 공헌을 했다. 정치가로서 벤자민 프랭클린은 바다 가장자리의 해류를 연구해서 번개가 전기의 한 형태라는 것을 증명했다. '마지막 정리'로 수 세기 동안 수학자들을 혼란스럽게 만든 피에르 드 페르마는 변호사였다.

어휘

highly 부 몹시, 매우　professionalized 형 전문화된 (profession 명 직업[직종]　professional 명 전문가)　invite 동 초대하다; *불러들이다　rejection 명 거절　executive 명 경영[운영] 간부　economist 명 경제학자　unpaid 형 아직 돈을 내지 않은; *무보수의　remarkable 형 놀랄 만한　achievement 명 업적　paying 형 돈이 벌리는　gain a living 생계를 꾸리다　contribution 명 기여　demonstrate 동 증명하다　lightning 명 번개　theorem 명 (특히 수학에서의) 정리(定理)　puzzle 동 혼란스럽게 하다　mathematician 명 수학자

07 　　　정답 ⑤　　정답률 46%

정답 풀이

(A) 「전치사 + 관계대명사」

There is a huge body of scientific research / to explain the
　　　　　　　많은 양의　　　　　　　　　　　형용사적 용법의 to부정사
많은 양의 과학적 연구가 있다　　　　　　　그 메커니즘을 설명하는
mechanism / [~~which~~ / by which] routine enables difficult things
선행사　　　　　　　　　　　　　enable A to-v: A가 ⋯하는 것을 가능하게 하다
　　　　　　　　　　　　　　정해진 절차가 어려운 일들이 쉬워지는 것을 가능하게 하는
to become easy].

→ the mechanism을 선행사로 하는 관계대명사절에서 선행사가 '⋯에 의해'라는 의미의 전치사 by의 목적어 역할을 해야 하므로 「전치사 + 관계대명사」 형태인 by which가 어법상 적절하다.

(B) 문장의 동사

One simplified explanation / is {that [as we repeatedly do a
　　　　　　　　　　　　　접속사　접속사(⋯할 때)
한 가지 간단한 설명은　　　　　　　우리가 반복적으로 어떤 과제를 수행할 때
certain task] / the neurons, or nerve cells, [make / ~~making~~] new
　　　　　　　　　주어　　　　　　　　동사　　　　　목적어
　　　　　　　뉴런, 혹은 신경세포들이 새로운 연결을 만든다
connections / through communication gateways called 'synapses'}.
　　　　　　　　　　　　　　　　　　　　　　　과거분사구
'시냅스'라고 불리는 전달 관문을 통해

→ that절의 주어는 the neurons, or nerve cells로 뒤에 동사가 이어져야 하므로 make가 오는 것이 어법상 적절하다.

(C) 대명사

To recall the word later you will need to activate the same
부사적 용법의 to부정사(목적)   need to-v: …할 필요가 있다
나중에 그 단어를 기억하기 위해 당신은 똑같은 시냅스를 활성화시킬 필요가 있을 것이다
synapses / [until eventually you know the word / without
       접속사(…때까지)
       결국 그 단어를 알게 될 때까지
consciously thinking about [it / ~~them~~]].
그것에 대해 의식적으로 생각하지 않고도

➡ 앞에 언급된 the word를 지칭하는 대명사로, 지칭하는 명사가 단수이므로 단수 대명사 it이 오는 것이 알맞다.

지문 해석

정해진 절차를 만들어 둔다면, 우리는 매일 모든 일에 우선순위를 정하는 데 소중한 에너지를 쏟을 필요가 없다. 우리는 정해진 절차를 만들기 위해 단지 적은 양의 초기 에너지만 쓰면 되고, 그리고 나서 해야 할 남은 일은 그것을 따르는 것이다. 정해진 절차가 어려운 일들이 쉬워지는 것을 가능하게 하는 메커니즘을 설명하는 많은 양의 과학적 연구가 있다. 한 가지 간단한 설명은 우리가 반복적으로 어떤 과제를 수행할 때 뉴런 혹은 신경세포가 '시냅스'라고 불리는 전달 관문을 통해 새로운 연결을 만든다는 것이다. 반복을 통해, 그 연결이 강력해지고 뇌가 그 연결을 활성화시키는 것이 더 쉬워진다. 예를 들어, 당신이 새로운 단어 하나를 배울 때 그 단어가 숙달되기 위해서는 다양한 간격으로 여러 번 반복이 필요하다. 나중에 그 단어를 기억하기 위해서 당신은 그것에 대해 의식적으로 생각하지 않고도 결국 그 단어를 알게 될 때까지 똑같은 시냅스를 활성화시킬 필요가 있을 것이다.

routine 명 정해진 절차 expend 동 (에너지를) 쏟다 prioritize 동 우선순위를 정하다 initial 형 초기의 mechanism 명 기계 장치; *방법, 메커니즘 simplified 형 단순화한, 간소화한 neuron 명 뉴런, 신경세포 gateway 명 관문 repetition 명 반복 strengthen 동 강화하다 activate 동 작동시키다; *활성화시키다 interval 명 간격 recall 동 기억해내다 consciously 부 의식적으로

08   정답 ⑤   정답률 41%

정답 풀이

(A) 접속사

The name implies / [[what / that] the event includes three jumps], /
       명사절(목적어)을 이끄는 접속사
그 이름은 암시한다   경기가 세 번의 점프를 포함하고 있다는 것을
but it is made up of a hop, a skip, and a jump.
       be made up of: …로 구성되다
하지만 그것은 hop, skip, jump로 구성되어 있다

➡ 동사 implies의 목적어인 명사절을 이끄는 접속사로, 뒤에 빠진 문장성분이 없는 완전한 절이 이어지므로 접속사 that이 오는 것이 알맞다.

(B) 부정형용사

[Another / ~~The other~~] event is the hammer throw.
      └─ 단수 명사
또 다른 경기는 해머던지기이다

➡ 문맥상 올림픽의 여러 경기들 중 '또 다른' 경기를 나타내고, 단수 명사 event가 뒤따르고 있으므로 Another가 오는 것이 알맞다. another는 '(여러 개 중) 또 다른 하나의'를 뜻하고, the other는 '(두 개 중) 나머지 하나의'를 뜻하는 부정형용사이다.

 Grammar Tips

> 부정대명사/부정형용사 another, other, the other, the others
> • 둘 중, 하나는 one / 나머지 하나는 the other
> • 셋 중, 하나는 one / 또 다른 하나는 another / 나머지 하나는 the other
> • 정해진 복수 명사 중, 일부는 some / 나머지는 the others
> • 정해지지 않은 복수 명사 중, 일부는 some / 나머지는 others

(C) 병렬구조

The athlete holds the handle with both of his or her hands, /
      동사1
선수는 양손으로 손잡이를 잡고
spins around to build power, / and then [releasing / releases] the
   동사2   부사적 용법의 to부정사(목적) 접속사   동사3
힘을 가하기 위해 회전하고   그리고 나서 공중으로 해머를 던진다
hammer into the air.

➡ 등위접속사 and가 동사를 병렬 연결하고 있는 구조로, holds, spins와 대등하도록 releases가 오는 것이 알맞다.

 구문 분석 Plus

> The athletes [who compete in this event] look as if they are dancing as they bounce down the runway.
> 5행
> ➡ who: The athletes를 선행사로 하는 주격 관계대명사
> ➡ look as if: 마치 …처럼 보이다
> ➡ as: '…할 때'라는 의미의 접속사

지문 해석

하계 올림픽 경기에는 오해를 불러일으키는 이름을 가진 많은 종목들이 있다. 예를 들어, 3단 뛰기는 육상경기 종목이다. 그 이름은 경기가 세 번의 점프를 포함하고 있다는 것을 암시하지만, 그것은 hop, skip, jump로 구성되어 있다. 이 종목에서 경기하는 선수들이 주로를 깡충깡충 뛰어갈 때 마치 춤을 추는 것처럼 보인다. 또 다른 경기는 해머 던지기이다. 이 종목의 이름은 해머가 전혀 목수의 도구처럼 보이지 않기 때문에 오해를 일으킨다. 올림픽 경기에서의 해머는 철사로 된 손잡이에 매달린 금속 공이다. 선수는 양손으로 손잡이를 잡고, 힘을 가하기 위해 회전하고 나서, 공중으로 해머를 던진다.

contain 동 포함하다 event 명 사건; *(스포츠) 경기 misleading 형 오해하게 만드는 track and field event 육상경기 imply 동 넌지시 나타내다; *암시[시사]하다 athlete 명 선수 compete 동 경쟁하다 bounce 동 깡충깡충 뛰다 runway 명 주로, 활주로 carpenter 명 목수 release 동 석방하다; *날려보내다

UNIT 2 형용사, 부사

코드 접속하기

pp.108~111

출제코드 1 | 형용사 vs. 부사

A **1** happy **2** alphabetically **3** naturally
B **1** ○ **2** ➡ increasingly **3** ➡ highly

해석과 정답 풀이

STEP 1
1 1) 나는 매일 아침으로 신선한 과일 샐러드를 먹는다.
  2) 십 대 소녀들은 그들의 체중에 민감하다.
  3) 그의 태도 때문에, 우리는 그가 그 임무에 적합하다고 생각했다.
  4) 그들은 돌고래를 살아있게 하기 위해 모든 노력을 했다.
2 1) 그는 특정 상황에서 공격적으로 반응한다.
  2) 그녀는 그 문제를 완전히 다른 방식으로 해결하고 싶어 했다.
  3) Tom은 항상 놀랍도록 빠르게 복잡한 수학 문제를 푼다.
  4) 이 정책의 초점은 주로 테러 방지에 있다.
  5) 다행히도, 경찰이 실종된 아이를 동굴에서 찾아냈다.

STEP 2
1 1) 정기적인 회의에서, 동호회 구성원들은 자신의 의견들을 공유한다.
  2) 지방을 효율적으로 저장하는 능력은 소중한 생리학적인 기능이다.

STEP 3
A 1 작년에 산타클로스 복장을 한 남자의 방문은 아이들을 행복하게 했다.
  ➡ 동사 made의 목적격보어 자리이므로, 형용사 happy가 오는 것이 알맞다. 부사는 보어로 쓰일 수 없다.
  2 학생들의 이름은 각 학과마다 알파벳 순으로 정렬되어 있다.
  ➡ 앞의 동사 are arranged를 수식하고 있으므로 부사 alphabetically가 오는 것이 알맞다.
  3 이산화탄소가 주요 오염원으로 비난 받고 있지만, 그것은 자연스럽게 발생하는 식물의 생명선이다.
  ➡ 뒤의 현재분사 occurring을 수식하고 있으므로 부사 naturally가 오는 것이 알맞다.
B 1 기회가 있을 때마다 낚시를 하러 가는 것은 그에게 꽤 많은 돈이 들었다.
  ➡ 형용사 costly는 문장에서 주격보어로 쓰이므로 어법상 적절하다. costly는 -ly 형태이지만, 형용사임에 유의한다.
  2 요즘, 사람들이 점점 더 많이 소셜 네트워킹 사이트에 접속하고 있다.
  ➡ 뒤에 오는 현재진행형의 현재분사 accessing을 수식하고 있으므로 형용사 increasing을 부사 increasingly로 고쳐야 한다.
  3 이 잡지는 세계의 최신 패션 경향을 다루고 있기 때문에 매우 권장된다.
  ➡ 뒤에 오는 수동태의 과거분사 recommended를 수식하고 있으므로 형용사 high를 부사 highly로 고쳐야 한다.

출제코드 2 | 비교구문과 비교급을 강조하는 부사

A **1** still **2** explicitly
B **1** ➡ deeper **2** ➡ easily **3** ○

해석과 정답 풀이

STEP 1
1 1) 이 책은 지난 번 책보다 더 흥미롭다.
  2) 매일 충분한 물을 마시는 것은 매일 운동하는 것만큼 중요하다.
  3) 당신이 고른 그 신발은 우리 가게에서 제일 비싼 것이다.
2 1) 이 지역에서 토양 침식은 정상보다 훨씬 더 빠른 속도로 일어난다.
  2) 이것은 내가 사용해본 것 중 단연 최고의 사전이다.
3 1) 가능한 한 빨리 저에게 다시 전화해주세요.
  2) 북극에 있는 얼음이 점점 더 빠르게 녹고 있다.
  3) 당신이 더 많이 연습하면 할수록, 더 잘 연주할 수 있다.

STEP 2
1 1) 정부는 그 법안을 훨씬 더 널리 도입하기로 결정했다.
  2) 그들은 이전의 장난감들보다 물속에서 훨씬 더 오래 있을 수 있는 장난감을 개발했다.
2 1) 이 생물의 독은 전갈의 독만큼이나 독성이 있다.
  2) 차가운 경주용 자동차 타이어는 그것들이 따뜻할 때만큼 효과적으로 기능할 수 없다.

STEP 3
A 1 어떤 사람들은 심지어 나이가 들어가면서 훨씬 더 뚜렷해질 수 있는 기억력을 가지고 있다.
  ➡ 뒤에 오는 비교급 sharper를 수식하는 부사 자리이므로 비교급 강조 부사인 still이 오는 것이 알맞다.
  2 애매모호함을 피하는 유일한 방법은 가능한 명쾌하게 말하는 것이다.
  ➡ as와 as 사이에 오는 말이 구동사 spell out을 수식하고 있으므로 부사 explicitly가 오는 것이 알맞다.
B 1 모순적이게도, 당신이 더 많이 허우적댈수록, 더 깊이 유사에 빠질 것이다.
  ➡ 「the + 비교급 …, the + 비교급 ~」 구문으로, 형용사 원급 deep을 비교급 deeper로 고쳐야 한다.
  2 이 소프트웨어로, 나는 전문가만큼 쉽게 사진을 편집할 수 있다.
  ➡ as와 as 사이의 말이 동사 can edit를 수식하고 있으므로 형용사 easy를 부사 easily로 고쳐야 한다.
  3 민지는 다른 도시로 이사를 갈 수 있다면 그녀의 삶이 훨씬 더 나아졌을 것이라 생각했다.
  ➡ 비교급 강조 부사 much가 뒤에 오는 비교급 better를 수식하고 있으므로 어법상 적절하다.

출제코드 3 | 수량형용사

A **1** much **2** few
B **1** ○ **2** ➡ few **3** ➡ much

해석과 정답 풀이

STEP 1
1 1) 과학자들은 많은 이론들을 발전시켰지만, 그것들 모두를 소개할 수 없었다.
  2) 영화 촬영을 위한 많은 장비가 오래되고 결함이 있었다.
2 1) 방에 카펫을 깐 후로, 그들은 소음에 대한 불평을 거의 받지 않았다.
  2) 사과 주스가 캔에 조금 있었고, 그것이 몇 마리의 벌들을 끌어들였다.
  3) 그녀는 그 문을 여는 것을 약간 두려워하는 것처럼 보였다.

STEP 2
1 1) 교수님은 우리에게 기말고사를 위해 읽을 많은 책들을 주셨다.
  2) 내가 무대를 걸었을 때 어떻게 느꼈는지를 묘사할 말이 거의 없다.
2 1) 그 항공사는 승객들의 짐을 분실한 후 많은 비난을 받았다.
  2) 심지어 소량의 카페인도 내가 밤에 잠드는 것을 어렵게 만든다.

STEP 3
A 1 그는 올림픽에 출전할 자격을 얻기 위해 많은 노력을 하지 않았다.
  ➡ 뒤의 명사 effort는 셀 수 없는 명사이므로 형용사 much가 오는 것이 알맞다.
  2 초창기 이후에는, 그들의 적을 계속 공격했던 개미들은 거의 없었다.
  ➡ 뒤에 복수 명사 ants가 왔으므로 형용사 few가 오는 것이 알맞다.
B 1 운이 좋게도, 많은 환자들은 신약으로 치료되었다.
  ➡ 뒤에 복수 명사 patients가 있으므로, 형용사 many는 어법상 바르다.
  2 지구 온난화 때문에, 북극곰이 서식할 수 있는 지역이 거의 없다.
  ➡ 뒤에 복수 명사 areas가 있고, '거의 없는'이라는 의미이므로 little을 형용사 few로 고쳐야 한다.
  3 그 상사는 재정적인 문제를 다룬 경험이 많지 않은 사람들을 원하지 않는다.
  ➡ experience는 셀 수 없는 명사이므로, many를 같은 뜻을 가진 형용사 much로 고쳐야 한다. many는 셀 수 있는 명사의 복수형 앞에 쓰인다.

정답 풀이

⑤ 형용사 vs. 부사

so + 형용사/부사 + that ...: 너무 ~해서 …하다

So uniformly(→ uniform) is this expectation, indeed, / [that the
　　　　　　　　　　　동사　　　주어　　　　　　　　접속사
실제로 이러한 예상은 너무나도 획일적이어서

odd exception is noteworthy, / and generally established for a
특이한 예외는 주목할 만하며　　　　일반적으로 특정한 목적을 위해 설정된다

specific purpose].

➡ 「so + 형용사/부사 + that ...」 구문에서 강조를 위해 so 이하가 문장 앞으로 나가 주어와 동사의 도치가 일어난 문장이다. be동사 is가 있으므로 부사 uniformly를 형용사 uniform으로 바꿔야 한다.

친절한 오답 풀이

① 대명사

The world's first complex writing form, Sumerian cuneiform, /
　　　　　　　주어　　　　　　　　　　동격
세계 최초의 복잡한 쓰기 형태인 수메르 쐐기 문자는

followed an evolutionary path, / [moving around 3500 BCE / from
동사　　　　　　　　　　　　　동시동작을 나타내는 분사구문(= as it moved ...)
진화적 경로를 따라갔다　　　　　　기원전 3500년경에 나아가며

pictographic to ideographic representations, / from the depiction
그림 문자에서 표의 문자적 표현으로　　　　　　　　사물의 묘사에서 추상적

of objects to that of abstract notions].
　　　　　　　　= the depiction
개념의 그것(묘사)으로

➡ that은 앞에 언급된 the depiction을 지칭하는 대명사로, 지칭하는 명사가 단수이므로 단수 대명사 that이 오는 것은 어법상 알맞다.

② 분사구문

Sumerian cuneiform was a linear writing system, / [its symbols
　　　주어　　　　　동사　　　　　　　　　　　　　그것의 기호가
수메르 쐐기 문자는 선형적 쓰기 체계였다

usually set in columns, / read from top to bottom and from left
주어가 남아 있는 분사구문(= as its symbols were usually set ...)
보통 세로 단에 놓인 채로　　　위에서 아래로 그리고 왼쪽에서 오른쪽으로 읽혔다

to right].

➡ its symbols 이하는 주어가 남아있는 분사구문으로, 주어와 분사가 수동 관계에 있으므로 과거분사 set이 오는 것이 어법상 바르다. 이어지는 read 이하도 its symbols를 주어로 하는 분사구문이다.

③ 재귀대명사

This regimentation was a form of abstraction: / the world is not a
이 조직화는 일종의 추상 개념이었다　　　　　　　세상은 선형적 공간이 아니라

linear place, / and objects do not organize themselves /
　　　　　　　그리고 사물은 스스로를 구조화하지 않는다

horizontally or vertically in real life.
실제 삶에서 수평적으로나 수직적으로

➡ 동사의 목적어가 주어와 동일한 대상을 지칭하므로, 목적어로 쓰인 재귀대명사 themselves는 어법상 바르다.

④ 부사적 용법의 to부정사

Early rock paintings, / [thought to have been created for ritual
　　　주어　　　　　　　　　　　　　삽입구
초기의 암각화들은　　　　　　　　의례적 목적으로 만들어졌다고 여겨지는

purposes], / were possibly shaped and organized / to follow the
　　　　　　　　동사
　　　　　　　아마도 형상화되고 구조화됐을 것이다

walls of the cave, or the desires of the painters, / [who may have
　　　　　　　　　　　　　　　　선행사　　　　　계속적 용법의 주격 관계대명사
동굴의 벽이나 화가의 바람을 따르도록　　　　　　　　　그들은

organized them symbolically, or artistically, or even randomly].
　　　　　= rock paintings
상징적으로, 예술적으로, 심지어는 무작위로 그것들을 구조화했을지도 모른다

➡ to follow는 were possibly shaped and organized를 수식하는 부사적 용법의 to부정사로 어법상 바르다.

지문 해석

세계 최초의 복잡한 쓰기 형태인 수메르 쐐기 문자는 기원전 3500년경에 그림 문자에서 표의 문자적 표현으로, 즉 사물의 묘사에서 추상적 개념의 그것(묘사)으로 나아가며 진화적 경로를 따라갔다. 수메르 쐐기 문자는 선형적 쓰기 체계였는데, 보통은 그것의 기호가 세로 단에 놓인 채로 위에서 아래로 그리고 왼쪽에서 오른쪽으로 읽혔다. 이 조직화는 일종의 추상 개념으로, 세상이 선형적 공간이 아니고 사물은 실제 삶에서 수평적으로나 수직적으로 스스로를 구조화하지 않는다는 것이었다. 의례적 목적으로 만들어졌다고 여겨지는 초기의 암각화들은 아마도 동굴의 벽이나 화가의 바람을 따르도록 형상화되고 구조화됐을 것이었고, 그들(화가)은 상징적으로, 예술적으로, 심지어는 무작위로 그것(암각화)들을 구조화했을지도 모른다. 하지만 쐐기 문자 이후에는 등장한 사실상 모든 형태의 문자는 분명한 시작과 종료 지점이 있는 줄로 나열되어 왔다. 실제로 이러한 예상은 너무나도 획일적이어서 특이한 예외는 주목할 만하며 일반적으로 특정한 목적을 위해 설정된다.

어휘

evolutionary 혱 진화의, 점진적인 　pictographic 혱 그림 문자의 　ideographic 혱 표의 문자의 　representation 몡 묘사, 표현 　depiction 몡 묘사 　abstract 혱 추상적인 　notion 몡 개념 　linear 혱 직선의, 선형적 　horizontally 븻 수평으로 　vertically 븻 수직으로 　ritual 혱 의식상의, 의식을 위한 　symbolically 븻 상징적으로 　artistically 븻 예술적으로 　randomly 븻 무작위로, 임의로 　virtually 븻 사실상, 거의 　uniformly 븻 획일적으로, 균일하게 　exception 몡 예외 　noteworthy 혱 주목할 만한

코드 공략하기

pp.112~113

01 ③   **02** ④   **03** ③   **04** ③   **05** ①   **06** ④

정답 풀이

(A) 형용사 vs. 부사

Just like people, / no two places can be exact / exactly alike.
전치사(…처럼)　　　　　　　　　　　　　　　　　　　　부사
사람들과 마찬가지로,　　　어떠한 두 장소도 정확히 똑같을 수 없다

➡ 뒤에 나오는 형용사 alike를 수식하므로 부사 exactly가 오는 것이 알맞다.

(B) 명사를 수식하는 과거분사

Many large cities have very tall buildings / called / calling
　　　　　　　　　　　　　　　　　　　　　　　　　　　　과거분사
많은 대도시들은 아주 높은 건물들을 가지고 있다　　마천루라 불리는

skyscrapers.

➡ 앞에 오는 명사구 very tall buildings를 수식하는 분사로, 건물들이 마천루라고 '불리는' 것이므로 과거분사 called가 오는 것이 알맞다.

(C) 동사 수 일치

[Learning about these patterns] / help / helps us to understand
　동명사구 주어　　　　　　　 help + 목적어 + to-v: …가 ~하는 것을 돕다
이런 패턴들에 대해서 아는 것은　　 우리가 세상을 좀 더 잘 이해하도록 돕는다
the world a little better.

➡ 동명사구 Learning ... patterns가 주어이므로 뒤에 단수 동사 helps가 오는 것이
알맞다.

 구문 분석 Plus

9행 | Other patterns can be found in the foods [(which/that) **we eat**], the way [*we dress*], or the way [*we grow crops*].
➡ we eat은 선행사 the foods를 수식하는 관계대명사절로 앞에 목적격 관계대명사 which 혹은 that이 생략되어 있음
➡ we dress와 we grow crops는 각각 앞의 the way를 수식하는 관계부사절로, the way는 관계부사 how로 바꿔쓸 수 있음

지문 해석

지구상의 모든 장소는 다르다. 사람들과 마찬가지로, 어떠한 두 장소도 정확히 똑같을 수 없다. 그러나 몇몇 장소는 어떤 면에서는 유사하다. 사람들이 살아가는 방식이나 그 땅을 이용하는 방법에 패턴들이 있다. 건물의 설계가 한 가지 패턴을 보여준다. 많은 대도시들은 마천루라 불리는 아주 높은 건물들을 가지고 있다. 땅이 충분하지 않아서, 사람들은 하늘 높이 지어 올려 더 많은 공간을 만든다. 다른 패턴들은 우리가 먹는 음식, 우리가 입는 방식, 또는 우리가 작물을 재배하는 방식에서 발견될 수 있다. 이런 패턴들에 대해서 아는 것은 우리가 이 세상을 좀 더 잘 이해하도록 돕는다.

어휘

exactly 閉 정확하게　alike 閉 같은　similar 閉 비슷한　certain 閉 확실한; *어떤
skyscraper 閉 높은 건물, 마천루　room 閉 공간　crop 閉 작물

02　　　　정답 ④　　　정답률 59%

정답 풀이

④ 원급 비교구문

Flocks of birds enjoyed them as many as(→ as much as) I did /
　　　　　　　　　　　　　　　　　　 …만큼
새 무리들이 내가 그러는 것만큼 그것들을 좋아했다
and would gather together in the tree, / eating the fruit quickly
…하곤 했다(과거의 습관) 모이다　　 연속동작을 나타내는 분사구문(= and they eat ...)
나무에 모여들곤 했다　　　　　　　 열매를 빨리, 열심히 먹었다
and eagerly / [whenever I wasn't there].
　　　　　 복합관계부사(…할 때마다)
　　　　　 내가 그곳에 없을 때마다

➡ 원급 비교구문의 as와 as 사이에는 수식 대상에 따라 형용사와 부사가 모두 들어갈 수 있다. 이 문장에서는 동사 enjoyed를 수식하고 있으므로, 형용사 many를 동사를 수식할 수 있는 부사 much로 고쳐야 한다.

│친절한 오답 풀이│

① 관계부사

Every summer [when the cherries began to ripen], ...
　　　　　　　　　　　　　　　 관계부사
버찌가 익기 시작했던 매 여름마다

➡ 시간을 나타내는 명사 Every summer를 선행사로 하고, 뒤에 완전한 절이 이어지므로 관계부사 when은 어법상 바르다.

② spend + 시간 + v-ing

..., I would spend hours high in the tree / picking and eating the
…하곤 했다(과거의 습관)　spend + 시간 + v-ing:　　　 접속사
　　　　　　　　　　　 …하는 데 시간을 보내다
나는 나무 높은 곳에서 여러 시간을 보내곤 했다　 달콤하고 햇볕을 받아 따뜻한
sweet, sunwarmed cherries.
버찌를 따고 먹으며

➡ 「spend + 시간 + v-ing」 구문으로, 동명사 picking이 오는 것이 알맞다.

③ 대동사 do

My mother always worried about my falling out of the tree, /
　　　　　　　　　　　　　　 동명사의 의미상 주어
엄마는 늘 내가 나무에서 떨어질까 걱정했다
but I never did.
　　　 = fell out of the tree
그러나 나는 결코 그러지 않았다

➡ 의미상 fell out of the tree를 대신하는 대동사로, 문장의 시제가 과거이므로 과거형 did가 오는 것이 알맞다.

⑤ 부정대명사

I used to wonder / [why the grown-ups never ate **any** of the
…하곤 했다(과거의 습관)　 간접의문문(의문사 + 주어 + 동사)
나는 궁금해하곤 했다　　 왜 어른들이 버찌를 절대 먹지 않는지
cherries].

➡ 부사 never가 쓰인 부정문이므로, '어떤 것도'라는 의미의 부정대명사 any가 오는 것이 알맞다.

 Grammar Tips

some vs. any

some과 any는 막연한 수나 양을 나타내는 말로, 대명사와 형용사로 쓰일 수 있다. some은 주로 긍정문에 쓰이고, any는 주로 부정문, 의문문, 조건절에 쓰인다.

예) **Some** students were absent from school because of flu.
(몇몇 학생들은 독감 때문에 학교에 결석했다.)
Do you have **any** questions about this? (이에 대해 질문이 있습니까?)

지문 해석

내가 자랄 때, 가장 좋아했던 장소 중의 하나는 뒷마당의 버찌나무였다. 버찌가 익기 시작했던 매 여름마다, 나는 나무 높은 곳에서 여러 시간을 달콤하고 햇볕을 받아 따뜻한 버찌를 따고 먹으며 보내곤 했다. 엄마는 늘 내가 나무에서 떨어질까 걱정했지만, 나는 결코 그러지 않았다. 그렇지만 나에게는 버찌를 노리는 경쟁자가 있었다. 새 무리들이 내가 그러는 것만큼 그것들을 좋아했고 내가 그곳에 없을 때마다 나무에 모여들어 열매를 빨리, 열심히 먹었다. 나는 왜 어른들이 버찌를 절대 먹지 않는지 궁금해하곤 했다.

어휘

cherry tree 버찌나무　yard 閉 마당　ripen 動 익다, 숙성하다　pick 動 고르다;
*(과일 등을) 따다　sun-warmed 閉 햇볕을 받아 따뜻한　competition 閉 경쟁;
*경쟁자　flock 閉 (양·염소·새의) 떼　eagerly 閉 열망하여, 열심히　wonder 動
궁금해하다　grown-up 閉 어른

정답 풀이

(A) 계속적 용법의 목적격 관계대명사

But [when a robot scans a room], / it sees nothing but a vast
접속사(…할 때)   오직(= only)
그러나 로봇이 방을 살펴볼 때   그것은 오직 직선과 곡선의 방대한 집합체만 본다

collection of straight and curved lines, / which / what it
선행사   계속적 용법의 목적격 관계대명사
                           그것을 화소로 전환한다

converts to pixels.

➡ 관계대명사절에서 동사 converts의 목적어 역할을 하면서, a vast … lines를 선행사로 하는 계속적 용법의 목적격 관계대명사인 which가 오는 것이 알맞다.

(B) 분사구문

Spending / Spent an enormous amount of computing time, /
때를 나타내는 분사구문(= After a robot spends …)
상당한 양의 계산 시간을 보내고 난 후

a robot might finally recognize the object / as a table.
                             전치사(…로)
로봇은 마침내 그 물체를 인식할지도 모른다   탁자로

➡ 네모는 때를 나타내는 분사구문의 분사로, 생략된 주어는 주절의 주어(a robot)와 같다. 로봇이 시간을 '보내는'이라는 능동의 의미이므로 현재분사 Spending이 오는 것이 어법상 바르다.

(C) 비교급 강조 부사

In other words, robots can see, / and in fact they can see
즉, 다시 말해서
다시 말해서, 로봇은 볼 수 있다   그리고 사실 그들은 인간보다 훨씬 더 잘 볼 수 있다

much / very better than humans, / but they don't understand /
                                  하지만 그들은 이해하지는 않는다

[what they are seeing].
관계대명사
그들이 보고 있는 것을

➡ 뒤에 오는 비교급 better를 수식하고 있으므로 비교급 강조 부사 much가 와야 한다. 부사 very는 비교급을 수식하는 부사로 쓸 수 없다.

 구문 분석 Plus

5행 | **It takes** an enormous amount of computing time **to make sense** out of this jumble of lines.
➡ It takes + 시간/노력/돈 + to-v: …하는 데 ~가 걸리다

지문 해석

우리가 방에 들어갈 때, 즉시 바닥, 의자, 가구, 탁자 등을 인식한다. 그러나 로봇이 방을 살펴볼 때, 오직 직선과 곡선의 방대한 집합체만 보며, 그것을 화소로 전환한다. 이런 뒤죽박죽 섞인 선들을 이해하는 데 상당한 양의 계산 시간이 든다. 컴퓨터는 오직 원, 타원, 나선, 직선, 곡선, 모퉁이 등의 한 집합체만 본다. 상당한 양의 계산 시간을 보내고 난 후, 로봇은 마침내 그 물체를 탁자로 인식할지도 모른다. 그러나 당신이 그 이미지를 회전시키면, 컴퓨터는 모든 것을 다시 시작해야 한다. 다시 말해서, 로봇은 볼 수 있고, 사실 인간보다 훨씬 더 잘 볼 수 있지만, 그들은 보고 있는 것을 이해하지는 않는다.

 어휘

immediately ⊞ 즉시 **recognize** 동 인식하다 **and so forth** … 등등 **scan** 동 살피다 **vast** 형 방대한 **collection** 명 수집품; *더미 **straight** 형 곧은, 똑바른 **curved** 형 곡선의, 약간 굽은 **convert** 동 전환하다 **pixel** 명 화소 **enormous** 형 거대한 **compute** 동 계산하다 **make sense** 의미가 통하다; *이해가 되다 **oval** 명 타원 **spiral** 명 나선, 나선형 **corner** 명 모퉁이 **rotate** 동 회전시키다

정답 풀이

(A) 관계대명사 what

If you need to buy food, there is probably a shop or a department
                                         선행사
당신이 음식을 사야 한다면, 아마 상점이나 백화점이 있을 것이다

store / close to your home / {that sells just [which / what you want]}.
           형용사구   주격 관계대명사
     당신의 집 근처에   당신이 원하는 바로 그것을 파는

➡ 앞에 선행사가 없고, 동사 sells의 목적어 역할을 하는 명사절을 이끌며, 뒤에 불완전한 절이 이어지고 있으므로, 선행사를 포함하는 관계대명사 what이 오는 것이 알맞다.

(B) 수량형용사

The first shops sold just a few / a little products / such as meat
                                        전치사(…와 같은)
최초의 상점은 단지 소수의 상품들만 팔았다   고기와 빵과 같은

and bread.

➡ 수량형용사 a few 뒤에는 셀 수 있는 명사의 복수형이 a little 뒤에는 셀 수 없는 명사가 오는데, 복수 명사 products가 뒤따르고 있으므로 a few가 오는 것이 알맞다.

(C) 동명사의 능동태 vs. 수동태

They replaced the old methods of serving customers individually /
그것들은 고객들에게 개별적으로 서비스하던 옛날 방식을 대체했다

by selling / being sold prepackaged goods straight from the
by v-ing: …함으로써   부사
미리 포장되어 있는 상품들을 선반에서 곧바로 판매함으로써

shelves.

➡ 전치사 by의 목적어로 쓰인 동명사로, 뒤에 목적어(prepackaged goods)를 취하며 상품이 팔리는 것이 아니라 '파는' 것이므로 능동형 동명사 selling이 오는 것이 알맞다. 동명사의 수동태는 being v-ed의 형태로 쓴다.

 구문 분석 Plus

9행 | In 1850, **the first department store**, **a shop** [which sells many different items under one roof], opened in Paris.
➡ the first department store와 a shop은 동격
➡ which: a shop을 선행사로 하는 주격 관계대명사

지문 해석

당신이 음식을 사야 한다면, 아마 당신의 집 근처에 당신이 원하는 바로 그것을 파는 상점이나 백화점이 있을 것이다. 그러나 쇼핑이 항상 그렇게 쉬웠던 것은 아니었다. 상점들은 단지 화폐가 도입되면서 시작되었다. 초기 시절에는, 사람들은 작물이나 그들이 만든 물건들을 그들이 필요했던 상품들과 교환했다. 최초의 상점은 고기와 빵과 같은 단지 소수의 상품들만 팔았다. 1850년에, 한 지붕 아래서 많은 다양한 품목들을 파는 상점인 최초의 백화점이 파리에서 문을 열었다. 셀프서비스 가게들은 1930년대에 미국에서 발달했다. 그것들은 미리 포장되어 있는 상품들을 선반에서 곧바로 판매함으로써 고객들에게 개별적으로 서비스하던 옛날 방식을 대체했다.

 어휘

department store 백화점 **introduction** 명 도입 **trade** 동 교환하다 **object** 명 물건, 물체 **in exchange for** … 대신에, …와 교환하여 **item** 명 물품, 항목 **replace** 동 대체하다 **method** 명 방법 **individually** ⊞ 개별적으로 **prepackaged** 형 미리 포장되어 있는 **shelf** 명 선반

정답 풀이

(A) 문장의 동사

[Wherever (it is) possible], / { choose / ~~choosing~~ books or articles /
복합관계부사(…하는 곳은 어디든지)　명령문의 동사　　　　선행사
가능한 곳은 어디든지　　　　책이나 기사를 선택하라

[which encourage you to read on]}.
주격 관계대명사
당신이 계속해서 읽도록 해주는

➡ 명령문인 절 내에 다른 동사가 없으므로 동사 choose가 오는 것이 알맞다.

(B) 부사

Rather than working with word lists, / it is usually / ~~usual~~ best /
전치사(…하기 보다는)　　　　　　　　　가주어　부사
단어 목록을 가지고 공부하기보다는　　　　　　　　보통 가장 좋다

[to see new words in context].
진주어
문맥 속에서 새로운 단어를 보는 것이

➡ 뒤에 나오는 최상급의 형용사 best를 수식하는 부사 자리이므로 usually가 와야 한다.

(C) 소유격 대명사

[As you read a new word in context], / there is a very good
접속사(…할 때)　　　　　　　　　　　　　　　　　아주 좋은 기회가 있다
당신이 문맥 속에서 새로운 단어를 읽을 때

chance / [that you will be able to guess its / ~~their~~ meaning].
　　└ 동격 ┘　　　　　　　　　　　　　　　　　= a new word's
당신이 그것의 의미를 추측해 볼 수 있는

➡ 앞에 나온 단수 명사 a new word를 지칭하므로 단수형 소유격 대명사 its가 오는 것이 알맞다.

 구문 분석 Plus

| 1행 | **The more** you read, **the more** you will build up your vocabulary and develop your reading skills.
➡ the + 비교급 …, the + 비교급 ~: …하면 할수록 더 ~하다 |
| 4행 | Make sure [(**that**) they are at your level, or only a little above your level, *neither* too difficult *nor* too easy].
➡ Make sure의 목적어절을 이끄는 접속사 that이 생략되어 있음
➡ neither A nor B: A도 아니고 B도 아니다 |

지문 해석

많이 읽으면 읽을수록, 당신은 더 많이 어휘를 쌓고 읽기 능력을 향상시킬 것이다. 가능한 곳은 어디든지, 당신이 계속해서 읽도록 해주는 책이나 기사를 선택하라. 그것들이 당신의 수준이거나 당신의 수준보다 약간 높은 것이어야 하며, 너무 어려워도 너무 쉬워도 안 된다. 단어 목록을 가지고 공부하기보다는 문맥에서 새로운 단어를 보는 것이 보통 가장 좋다. 그러면 당신은 그것들이 어떻게 사용되는지를 이해할 것이다. 당신이 문맥 속에서 새로운 단어를 읽을 때, 그것의 의미를 추측해 볼 수 있는 아주 좋은 기회가 있다.

 어휘

build up 쌓아올리다, 높이다　**vocabulary** 몡 어휘　**reading skill** 읽기 능력
article 몡 기사　**encourage** 통 격려[고무]하다　**context** 몡 맥락　**meaning** 몡 뜻, 의미

정답 풀이

(A) 접속사

[~~Then~~ / When I left the field at the end of a period], / he would
접속사(…할 때)　　　　　　　　　　　　　　　　…하곤 했다(과거의 습관)
한 쿼터가 끝나고 내가 경기장을 떠날 때　　　　　　　그는 나를 부르곤 했다

call me over / with his hands.
　　　　　　손짓으로

➡ 두 개의 절이 연결되어야 하므로, 주어 I 앞에 '때'를 나타내는 접속사 When이 오는 것이 알맞다. Then은 부사로, 절과 절을 연결하는 접속사의 역할을 할 수 없다.

(B) 부사

Bend your knees / a few / a little more.
　　　　　　　　　　　　　　부사　　부사
무릎을 구부려라　　　조금 더

➡ 네모는 동사 Bend를 수식하는 부사 more를 수식하는 부사 자리이므로 a little이 오는 것이 알맞다. a few는 형용사로, 부사를 수식할 수 없다.

(C) 병렬구조

I would respond to his comments / by bending my knees more
…하곤 했다(과거의 습관)　　　　　　　by v-ing: …함으로써 전치사의 목적어1
나는 그의 말에 응하곤 했다　　　　　　　　　무릎을 더 굽히고 더 빨리 달림으로써

and ~~to run~~ / running faster / [when I got back in the game].
접속사　　전치사의 목적어2　　　접속사(…할 때)
　　　　　　　　　　　　　다시 경기로 돌아갔을 때

➡ 등위접속사 and가 전치사 by의 목적어인 동명사를 병렬 연결하고 있으므로, bending과 대등하도록 동명사 running이 오는 것이 알맞다.

 구문 분석 Plus

| 6행 | {(**Being**) Not quite sure of [*what* he was talking about]}, he always said the same thing.
➡ Not 이하는 동시동작을 나타내는 분사구문으로, 앞에 Being이 생략되어 있음 (= As he was not quite sure of …)
➡ what 이하는 전치사 of의 목적어 역할을 하는 간접의문문 |

지문 해석

아버지는 내가 경기를 할 때마다 미식축구 경기에 오셨다. 아버지는 사이드라인에 서서 경기를 주의 깊게 지켜 보셨다. 나는 경기장에 오는 방법을 아버지께 결코 말씀드리지 않았지만, 아버지는 어쨌든 나타나셨다. 한 쿼터가 끝나고 내가 경기장을 떠날 때, 아버지는 손짓으로 나를 부르곤 하셨다. 자신이 무슨 말을 하고 있는지 확신하지 못하면서, 아버지는 항상 같은 말을 하셨다. "Ron, 잘 하고 있어. 무릎을 조금 더 굽혀." 다시 경기로 돌아갔을 때 나는 무릎을 더 굽히고 더 빨리 달리는 것으로 아버지의 말에 응하곤 했다.

 어휘

sideline 몡 사이드라인, 옆선　**attentively** 뮈 주의 깊게　**show up** 나타나다
bend 통 구부리다　**knee** 몡 무릎　**respond** 통 대답[응답]하다　**comment** 몡 논평, 말

UNIT 1 어휘 의미

코드 접속하기

pp.115~118

출제코드 1 　　　　　　　　　 반의어

A **1** damaged **2** contract **3** vulnerable **4** confident
　　5 honor **6** superior

해석과 정답 풀이

STEP 2

A **1** 항공사들은 문제에 신속히 대응해야 한다. 만약 그들이 그러지 않으면, 그들의 평판은 손상될 수 있다.
➡ 항공사의 평판이 '손상되다'가 문맥상 자연스러우므로 damaged가 알맞다. recover는 '회복하다'라는 의미의 반의어이다.

2 겨울에, 당신의 혈관은 수축하기 쉽고, 이것은 당신의 혈압이 높아지게 한다.
➡ 겨울에 혈관이 '수축하기' 쉽다는 의미가 문맥상 자연스러우므로 contract가 알맞다. expand는 '확장시키다'라는 의미의 반의어이다.

3 십 대들은 특히 약물 사용에 취약하다. 그들의 뇌는 여전히 성장하고 있으므로 약물은 심각한, 장기적인 영향을 미칠 수 있다.
➡ 십 대들이 약물 사용에 '취약하다'가 문맥상 자연스러우므로 vulnerable이 알맞다. immune은 '면역성이 있는'이라는 의미의 반의어이다.

4 "소비자들이 제품의 성분들에 대한 세부적인 정보를 얻게 될 때, 그들은 자신의 결정에 대해 더 확신하게 된다."라고 Harry M. Kaiser가 말했다.
➡ 세부적인 정보를 얻게 되어 선택에 '확신하게 된다'라는 의미가 문맥상 자연스러우므로 confident가 오는 것이 알맞다. insecure는 '자신이 없는'이라는 의미의 반의어이다.

5 에베레스트산 정상에 도달하는 것은 과거에 놀라운 업적으로 여겨졌다. 정상에 도달하는 데 성공한 등반가가 있다는 것은 국가적인 영예였다.
➡ 에베레스트산 등반에 성공한 등반가가 있는 것은 국가적인 '영예'라는 의미가 문맥상 자연스러우므로 honor가 오는 것이 알맞다. dishonor는 '불명예'라는 의미의 반의어이다.

6 자신 위에 있는 다른 사람들을 늘 신경 쓰는 사람은 자존감이 낮다. 그들이 우월하다고 믿기 때문에, 그는 결코 그들의 능력 수준까지 도달할 수 없다고 생각한다.
➡ 자신 위에 있는 사람들을 '우월하다'고 믿는다는 의미가 문맥상 자연스러우므로 superior가 알맞다. inferior는 '열등한'이라는 의미의 반의어이다.

출제코드 2 　　　　　　　　　 문맥상 적절한 단어

A **1** protects **2** delay **3** ignored **4** experience
　　5 awareness **6** chosen **7** specialized

해석과 정답 풀이

STEP 1

어떤 가족들은 일련의 가정 규칙들이 있으면 더 잘 협력한다. 이러한 규칙들은 가족이 한 집단으로 함께 살아갈 수 있도록 기대 사항과 지침을 규정한다. 명확한 가정 규칙들은 청소년기에 아주 중요해질 수 있다.

STEP 2

A **1** 당신은 피부의 기능에 대해서 생각해본 적이 있는가? 우리 대부분은 피부가 우리를 열, 추위, 그리고 먼지로부터 보호해준다고 알고 있다.
➡ 피부의 기능은 우리를 '보호하는' 것이라는 의미가 문맥상 자연스러우므로 protect가 알맞다. select는 '선택하다'라는 의미이다.

2 아무도 다른 사람들을 화나게 하는 것을 좋아하지 않는다. 많은 사람들은 "안돼"라고 말하기를 주저하지만, 우리는 나쁜 소식을 전하는 것을 연기해서는 안 된다.
➡ 나쁜 소식을 전하는 것을 '연기하면' 안 된다는 의미가 문맥상 자연스러우므로

---

delay가 알맞다. continue는 '계속하다'라는 의미이다.

3 대부분의 여성들이 집에서 오랜 시간을 일한다. 그러나 가정에서 여성의 공헌은 가족의 번영을 고려할 때 종종 무시된다.
➡ 오랜 시간의 노동에도 여성의 가정에 대한 공헌이 '무시된다'가 문맥상 자연스러우므로 ignored가 알맞다. include는 '…을 포함하다'라는 의미이다.

4 대부분의 사람들이 장기 여행을 떠난다면, 많은 장비를 가져가야 한다고 생각한다. 그러나 전문 배낭 여행가의 경험은 우리에게 정반대의 것을 가르쳐준다.
➡ 전문 배낭 여행가의 '경험'이 가르쳐준다는 의미가 문맥상 자연스러우므로 experience가 알맞다. absence는 '결석, 부재'라는 의미이다.

5 그 기사는 스마트폰 중독에 대한 대중의 인식을 높이고, 정신적인 그리고 신체적인 건강 문제를 예방하는 것을 돕기 위해 쓰여졌다.
➡ 스마트폰 중독에 대한 사람들의 '인식'을 높이기 위해 기사가 쓰였다는 의미가 문맥상 자연스러우므로 awareness가 알맞다. admiration은 '존경'이라는 의미이다.

6 연구는 살충제 사용이 세 배 증가한 반면, 해충 피해로 인한 곡식 손실은 두 배 늘어났음을 보여준다. 이는 살충제 사용보다 자연 통제가 선택되어야 한다는 것을 보여준다.
➡ 비효율적인 살충제 사용보다 자연 통제가 '선택되어야' 한다는 내용이 문맥상 자연스러우므로 chosen이 알맞다. avoid는 '피하다'라는 의미이다.

7 한 사람이 모든 일을 혼자서 할 수는 없다. 대신에, 우리는 빵을 굽거나 건물을 설계하는 것과 같이 각자 매우 특화된 한 가지 일을 하면서 하나의 사회로 기능을 한다.
➡ 개인이 각자 '특화된' 일을 한다는 의미가 문맥상 자연스러우므로 specialized가 알맞다. urgent는 '긴급한'이라는 의미이다.

기출예제 Q1 　　　　　 정답 ⑤ 　　　　 정답률 55%

정답 풀이

⑤ 반의어(laboriously → easily)
➡ 앞에서 순록이 물에 떠 있는 동안에는 공격받기 쉬운 상태가 되고 '쉽게' 따라 잡힌다고 했으므로 ⑤의 laboriously(힘들게)를 easily(쉽게)와 같은 낱말로 고쳐야 한다.

친절한 오답 풀이

① uncertain 혱 불확실한
② weakness 몡 약점
③ vulnerable 혱 약점이 있는; *공격받기 쉬운
④ advantage 몡 이점

코드+α 구문 분석 Plus

2행	Even **under** ideal **circumstances**, [hunting these fast animals with spear or bow and arrow] *is* an uncertain task. ➡ under circumstances: …의 상황 하에서 ➡ 주어인 동명사구 hunting these fast ... arrow에 수 일치하여 단수 동사 is
4행	The reindeer, however, had a weakness [**that** mankind would mercilessly exploit]: *it* swam poorly. ➡ that: a weakness를 선행사로 하는 목적격 관계대명사 ➡ 대명사 it은 앞의 The reindeer를 지칭함

지문 해석

유럽 최초의 '호모 사피엔스'는 주로 큰 사냥감, 특히 순록을 먹고 살았다. 심지어 이상적인 상황에서도, 이런 빠른 동물을 창이나 활과 화살로 사냥하는 것은 불확실한 일이다. 그러나 순록에게는 인류가 인정사정없이 이용할 약점이 있었는데, 그것은 순록이 수영을 잘 못한다는 것이었다. 순록은 물에 떠 있는 동안, 코를 물 위로 내놓으려고 애쓰면서 가지진 뿔을 높이 쳐들고 천천히 움직이기 때문에, 유례없이 공격받기 쉬운 상태가 된다. 어느 시점에선가, 석기 시대의 한 천재가 수면 위를 미끄러지듯이 움직일 수 있음으로써 자신이 얻을 엄청난 사냥의 이점을 깨닫고 최초의 배를 만들었다. 힘들게(→ 쉽게) 따라잡아서 도살한 먹잇감을 일단 배 위로 끌어 올리면, 사체를 부족이 머무는 곳으로 가지고 가는 것은 육지에서보다는 배로 훨씬 더 쉬웠을 것이다. 인류가 이런 장점을 다른 물품에 적용하는 데는 긴 시간이 걸리지 않았을 것이다.

game 뗑 사냥감　reindeer 뗑 순록　spear 뗑 창　mercilessly 톙 인정사정없이,
무자비하게　antler 뗑 (사슴의) 가지진 뿔　overtake 톙 따라잡다

기출예제 Q2　　정답 ③　　정답률 70%

정답 풀이

(A) 문맥상 적절한 단어(warn / exhaust)
➡ 아기의 뇌는 전체 에너지의 65퍼센트를 사용하기 때문에 성장하는 뇌가 그들을
'기진맥진하게 만들다'라는 의미가 문맥상 자연스럽다. 따라서 exhaust가 들어가야 한다.
warn은 '경고하다'라는 의미이다.

(B) 반의어(more / less)
➡ 뒤에 우리의 기관 중에 뇌가 가장 에너지 소모가 많다고 했으므로, 뇌는 다른 기관보다
훨씬 '더 많은' 에너지를 사용한다는 의미가 문맥상 자연스럽다. 따라서 more가 들어가야
한다. less는 '더 적은'이라는 의미이다.

(C) 문맥상 적절한 단어(creative / efficient)
➡ 뇌는 하루 동안 블루베리 머핀에서 얻을 수 있는 약 400칼로리의 에너지만을 필요로
한다고 했으므로, 뇌가 '효율적인'이라는 의미가 문맥상 자연스럽다. 따라서 efficient가
들어가야 한다. creative는 '창의적인'이라는 의미이다.

코드 +α 구문 분석 Plus

3행	That's partly [**why** babies *sleep* all the time — their growing brains exhaust them — and *have* a lot of body fat, to use as an energy reserve when (it is) needed]. ➡ why 이하는 문장의 보어 역할을 하는 간접의문문 ➡ sleep과 have가 병렬구조를 이룸 ➡ when (it is) needed: when 뒤에 「주어 + be동사」인 it is가 생략된 형태로, 시간과 조건의 부사절에서 주절과 같은 주어와 뒤따르는 be동사는 종종 생략됨
12행	**Try** running your laptop for twenty-four hours on a muffin and **see** [*how* far you get]. ➡ Try와 see가 병렬구조를 이룸 ➡ how 이하는 동사 see의 목적어 역할을 하는 「how + (형용사/부사) + 주어 + 동사」 어순의 간접의문문으로, how는 형용사 far를 수식하는 의문부사로 쓰임

지문 해석

뇌는 우리 몸무게의 2퍼센트만을 차지하지만 우리 에너지의 20퍼센트를 사용한다. 갓
태어난 아기의 경우, 그 비율은 65퍼센트나 된다. 그것은 부분적으로 아기들이 항상 잠을
자고 (성장하는 뇌는 그들을 기진맥진하게 만들고), 많은 체지방을 보유하는 이유인데,
필요할 때 예비 에너지로 사용하기 위한 것이다. 우리의 근육은 전체의 약 4분의 1 정도로
훨씬 더 많은 에너지를 사용하기도 하지만, 우리는 많은 근육을 가지고 있기도 하다.
실제로, 물질 단위당, 뇌는 다른 기관보다 훨씬 더 많은 에너지를 사용한다. 그것은 우리의
기관 중 뇌가 가장 에너지 소모가 많다는 것을 의미한다. 하지만 그것은 또한 놀랍도록
효율적이다. 우리 뇌는 하루에 약 400칼로리의 에너지만을 필요로 하는데, 이는 우리가
블루베리 머핀에서 얻는 것과 같다. 한 개의 머핀으로 24시간 동안 노트북을 작동시켜서
얼마나 가는지 보라.

newborn 뗑 신생아　no less than 다름 아닌 …이다　reserve 뗑 예비, 비축
quarter 뗑 4분의 1　per …당[마다]　organ 뗑 (인체 내의) 장기[기관]
marvelously 톙 놀랍게도

01　　정답 ⑤　　정답률 51%

정답 풀이

(A) 반의어(common / unique)
➡ 숲을 지키고 싶어 하는 사람들은 그것이 '독특한(unique)' 것이고 보호돼야 한다고
생각한다는 의미가 문맥상 자연스럽다. common은 '일반적인'이라는 의미의 반의어이다.

(B) 반의어(sustainable / unsustainable)
➡ 뒤에 자원을 현명하게 사용하면 미래에도 여전히 자원을 가지게 될 것이라고 했으므로
앞 문장에 자원을 '지속 가능한(sustainable)' 것으로 만든다는 내용이 들어가야
자연스럽다. unsustainable은 '지속 불가능한'이라는 의미의 반의어이다.

(C) 반의어(changing / preserving)
➡ 앞 문장에 우리에게 환경을 돌볼 책임이 있다고 했으므로, 원주민으로부터 환경을
'보존하는(preserving)' 것의 중요성을 배울 수 있다는 내용이 이어지는 것이 자연스럽다.
changing은 '바꾸는 것'이라는 의미의 반의어이다.

코드 +α 구문 분석 Plus

7행	Most people are **in favor of** *using* our resources wisely. ➡ in favor of: …에 찬성[지지]하여 ➡ using: 전치사 of의 목적어로 쓰인 동명사
15행	[**What** you inherited and live with] will become the inheritance of future generations. ➡ What 이하는 문장의 주어 역할을 하는 관계대명사절

지문 해석

Ontario 주, Temagami 지역 근처에 원시림이 있다. 어떤 사람들은 목재용으로 그
나무들을 베고 싶어 한다. 다른 사람들은 그것을 그대로 지키고 싶어 한다. 그들은 그것이
독특하고 다음 세대를 위해 보호되어야 한다고 믿는다. 많은 사람들은 일부는 사용하고
일부는 보호하기를 원하면서, 중간의 어딘가에 있다. 대부분의 사람들은 우리의 자원을
현명하게 사용하는 것을 찬성한다. 그들은 우리의 자원을 지속 가능하게 만드는 관행을
선호한다. 즉, 우리는 현재 우리의 자원을 현명하게 사용해야 하고 그러면 우리는 미래를
위해 여전히 더 많은 자원을 가지게 될 것이다. 우리 모두는 환경을 돌볼 책임이 있다.
우리는 미래 세대를 위해 환경을 보존하는 것의 중요성을 오랫동안 알아왔던 캐나다
원주민으로부터 배울 수 있다. 당신이 물려받았고 더불어 살아가고 있는 것이 미래 세대의
유산이 될 것이다.

old-growth forest 원시림　lumber 뗑 목재　common 톙 흔한　unique 톙
유일무이한, 독특한　generation 뗑 세대　practice 뗑 실행; *관행　sustainable
톙 지속 가능한 (unsustainable 톙 지속 불가능한)　be responsible for …에
책임이 있다　look after …을 맡다[돌보다]　preserve 톙 보존하다　inherit 톙
물려받다 (inheritance 뗑 유산)

02　　정답 ⑤　　정답률 60%

정답 풀이

(A) 문맥상 반의어(ignore / magnify)
➡ 자존감이 낮은 사람들은 자신에 대한 판단이 부정적이라고 했으므로, 자신의 실패의
중요성을 '확대한다(magnify)'는 의미가 들어가는 것이 문맥상 자연스럽다. ignore은
'무시하다'라는 의미이다.

(B) 반의어(accurately / inaccurately)
➡ 자존감이 낮은 사람들은 자신의 실패의 중요성을 확대하므로, 부정적인 피드백을 받을
때 그것들이 그들의 자기가치감을 '정확하게(accurately)' 반영한다고 믿는다는 내용이

문맥상 자연스럽다. inaccurately는 '부정확하게'라는 의미의 반의어이다.

(C) 문맥상 반의어(hurts / improves)
➡ 자존감이 낮은 사람이 우울해질 위험이 평균보다 높다는 사실은 그것이 개인의 정신적, 정서적 안녕과 신체적 건강 그리고 사회적 관계의 질을 '해친다(hurts)'는 내용이 문맥상 자연스럽다. improve는 '개선하다'의 의미이다.

 구문 분석 Plus

6행	And [**when** they get negative feedback, such as a bad evaluation at work or a disrespectful remark from someone (whom/that) they know], they are likely to believe that it accurately reflects their self-worth. ➡ when: 부사절을 이끄는 접속사 ➡ someone 뒤에 someone을 선행사로 하는 목적격 관계대명사가 생략됨 ➡ that: 동사 believe의 목적어 역할을 하는 명사절을 이끄는 접속사
11행	This hurts **not only** an individual's mental and emotional wellbeing **but also** his or her physical health and the quality of his or her social relationships. ➡ not only A but also B: A뿐만 아니라 B도

지문 해석

때때로 자신에 대한 우리의 판단은 터무니없이 부정적이다. 이것은 자존감이 낮은 사람들에게 특히 그러하다. 몇몇 연구는 그런 사람들이 자신의 실패의 중요성을 확대하는 경향이 있다는 것을 보여주었다. 그들은 자주 자신의 능력을 과소평가한다. 그리고 직장에서의 나쁜 평가나 그들이 아는 누군가로부터의 무례한 말과 같은 부정적인 피드백을 받을 때, 그들은 그것이 자신의 자기가치감을 정확하게 반영한다고 믿을 가능성이 있다. 자존감이 낮은 사람들은 또한 우울해질 위험이 평균보다 높다. 이것은 한 개인의 정신적 그리고 정서적 안녕뿐만 아니라 그 사람의 신체적 건강과 사회적 관계의 질 또한 해친다.

 어휘

judgment 명 판단 **unreasonably** 부 비이성적으로 **self-esteem** 명 자부심, 자존감 **underestimate** 동 과소평가하다 **evaluation** 명 평가 **disrespectful** 형 무례한, 실례되는 **remark** 명 발언 **reflect** 동 비추다; *반영하다 **self-worth** 명 자아 존중감, 자부심 **risk** 명 위험 **depressed** 형 우울한 **mental** 형 정신의, 마음의 **wellbeing** 명 안녕, 행복

---

03 정답 ④ 정답률 80%

정답 풀이

④ 반의어(weaken → strengthen)
➡ 사람들이 자주 회의와 같은 모임을 갖게 되면 관계가 강화된다는 의미가 되어야 하므로 weaken(약화시키다)을 strengthen(강화시키다)으로 고치는 것이 적절하다.

┃친절한 오답 풀이┃
① coordination 명 합동, 조화
② frequently 부 자주, 흔히
③ shared 형 공유된
⑤ help 동 돕다

 구문 분석 Plus

10행	He explains, "The rhythm [**that** frequency generates] *allows* relationships *to strengthen*, personal habits *to be understood*, and stressors *to be identified*. ➡ that: 선행사 The rhythm을 수식하는 목적격 관계대명사 ➡ allow A to-v: A가 …하는 것을 허용하다 ➡ 동사 allows의 목적어와 목적격보어가 A, B, and C의 구조로 병렬 연결되어 있으며, relationships, personal habits, stressors가 각각 목적어, to strengthen, to be understood, to be identified가 각각 목적격보어임
13행	All of this **helps** the members of the team **understand** *not only* their roles *but also* [how they can get the best out of one another]. ➡ help + 목적어 + 동사원형: …가 ~하는 것을 돕다 ➡ not only A but also B: A뿐만 아니라 B도 ➡ how 이하는 동사 understand의 목적어 역할을 하는 간접의문문

지문 해석

사람들이 똑같은 매일, 매주, 매달 그리고 계절 리듬을 공유할 때, 그들 사이의 관계는 더욱 빠르게 형성되고 더욱 강한 상태를 유지한다. 사람들은 서로를 더욱 깊이 신뢰하고, 협력도 더 쉬워진다. 결국, 그들은 빈번하게 똑같은 일들을 하고 똑같은 문제들을 함께 해결한다. 사실, 몇몇 조직들은 강한 결속력을 유지하고 공유된 사고방식을 강화하기 위해 정기 스탠딩 회의를 이용한다. 한 식품 회사의 최고 경영자는 그의 팀과 함께 매일 하는 짧은 회의에 대해 말한다. 그는 "빈번함이 만들어내는 리듬은 관계가 약화되도록(→ 강화되도록) 하고, 개인의 습관이 이해되게 하고, 스트레스 요인도 확인되게 한다. 이 모든 것은 팀의 구성원들이 자신의 역할 뿐만 아니라 그들이 어떻게 서로에게서 최상의 것을 얻어낼 수 있는지를 이해하도록 도와준다."라고 설명한다.

 어휘

organization 명 조직 **maintain** 동 유지하다 **bond** 명 유대 **reinforce** 동 강화하다 **mindset** 명 사고방식 **frequency** 명 빈도, 잦음 **generate** 동 만들어내다 **stressor** 명 스트레스 요인 **identify** 동 확인하다 **one another** 서로서로

---

04 정답 ⑤ 정답률 43%

정답 풀이

⑤ 반의어(relieved → nervous)
➡ 서커스 공연을 예로 들어 긴장감이 주는 즐거움에 대해 서술하는 내용이므로, '편안한' 상태가 아니라 '긴장된' 상태로 기다리는 것을 좋아한다는 내용이 되어야 한다. 따라서 relieved(편안한)를 nervous(긴장된)로 바꾸는 것이 적절하다.

┃친절한 오답 풀이┃
① beforehand 부 사전에, 미리
② fail 동 실패하다
③ increase 동 증가시키다
④ hesitate 동 망설이다, 주저하다

 구문 분석 Plus

7행	Even the deliberate manner [**in which** he arranges the opening scene] increases our expectation. ➡ which는 the deliberate manner를 선행사로 하며, 관계대명사절에서 전치사 in의 목적어 역할을 하는 목적격 관계대명사
13행	We **not only** like to wait, [*feeling nervous*], **but** we appreciate [what we wait for]. ➡ not only A but (also) B: A뿐만 아니라 B도 ➡ feeling nervous: 동시동작을 나타내는 분사구문(= as we feel nervous) ➡ what: '…하는 것'의 의미로 선행사를 포함한 관계대명사

긴장감은 삶에서 우리의 흥미의 많은 부분을 차지한다. 당신이 줄거리를 미리 안다면 연극이나 소설은 종종 대부분의 흥미가 사라진다. 우리는 결과에 대해 계속 추측하기를 좋아한다. 서커스 곡예사는 의도적으로 여러 번 실행하는 것을 실패한 후 재주를 성공할 때 이 원칙을 사용한다. 심지어 그가 시작 장면을 준비하는 고의적인 태도조차 우리의 기대를 증가시킨다. 극의 마지막 연기에서, 작은 서커스 개는 코 위에서 공의 균형을 잡는다. 어느 날 밤 그 개는 재주를 실행하기 전 오랫동안 주저하고 시도를 했을 때, 그 개는 한 번에 기술을 행했을 때보다 훨씬 더 많은 박수를 받았다. 우리는 편안한(→ 긴장된) 기분으로 기다리기를 좋아할 뿐만 아니라, 우리가 기다린 것의 진가를 인정한다.

suspense 圏 긴장   take up 차지하다   be robbed of …을 강탈당하다   as to …에 관해서는   outcome 圏 결과   acrobat 圏 곡예사   employ 圏 고용하다; *사용하다   feat 圏 위업; *솜씨, 재주   purposely 圉 고의로, 일부러   deliberate 圏 고의적인   expectation 圏 기대   applause 圏 박수   appreciate 圏 진가를 인정하다

---

05 정답 ④ 정답률 55%

정답 풀이

④ 반의어(unaware → aware)
➡ 계통 오차는 반복적으로 측정해도 오차가 드러나거나 제거되지 않는 반면 임의 오차는 최종적으로 큰 값의 오차로 나타남으로써 사람들이 결과의 부정확함을 '알게' 된다는 내용이 되어야 하므로 unaware(모르는)를 aware(알고 있는)로 바꾸는 것이 적절하다.

┃친절한 오답 풀이┃

① repeat 圏 반복하다
② reveal 圏 드러내다
③ dangerous 圏 위험한
⑤ reliable 圏 믿을[신뢰할] 수 있는

 구문 분석 Plus

5행
Neither of these points **is** true for a systematic error.
➡ Neither of + 복수 명사 + 단수 동사: …의 어느 쪽도 아니다

6행
Repeated measurements with the same apparatus **neither** reveal **nor** do they eliminate a systematic error.
➡ neither A nor B: A도 아니고 B도 아니다
➡ 부정어(nor) 뒤에 주어와 동사가 도치된 형태로, 동사(eliminate)가 일반동사이므로 주어(they) 앞에 do가 쓰임

 Grammar Tips

neither의 수 일치

• neither A nor B → B에 수 일치
예)**Neither** *the teacher* **nor** *the students* are happy with the announcement. (교사도 학생들도 발표에 기쁘지 않다.)

• neither of + 복수 명사 → 단수 취급
예)Unfortunately, **neither of** *us* has a solution right now.
(안타깝게도 지금은 우리 둘 다 해결책이 없다.)

지문 해석

임의 오차는 측정을 반복하면 발견될 수 있다. 그뿐만 아니라, 더욱더 많은 측정값을 구함으로써 우리는 참값에 더욱더 가까운 값을 산술 평균으로부터 얻는다. 이 두 가지 사실 중 어떤 것도 계통 오차에는 적용되지 않는다. 동일한 도구를 가지고 하는 반복적인 측정은 계통 오차를 드러내거나 제거하지도 않는다. 이런 이유로 계통 오차는 임의 오차보다 잠재적으로 더 위험하다. 만약 어떤 실험에서 큰 임의 오차가 존재하면, 그것은

최종적으로 매겨진 오차의 큰 값으로 나타날 것이다. 그리하여 모든 사람이 결과의 부정확함을 모르게(→ 알게) 되는데, 실험자의 결과에 아무도 주목하지 않을 때는 어쩌면 실험자의 자존심에 (가해질 수 있는 해) 말고는 어떠한 해도 가해지지 않는다. 그러나 계통 오차의 숨겨진 존재는, 추정된 오차가 작다면, 언뜻 신뢰할 수 있는 것처럼 보이는 결과로 이어질 수 있는데, 그것은 사실 심각하게 잘못된 것이다.

random error 임의 오차, 무작위 오차   detect 圏 발견하다   measurement 圏 측정   reading 圏 측정값   obtain 圏 얻다   systematic error 계통 오차   eliminate 圏 제거하다   manifest 圏 나타나다   quoted 圏 (가격 따위가) 견적된   imprecision 圏 부정확함   ego 圏 자존심, 자아   take notice of …에 주목하다   conceal 圏 숨기다   apparently 圉 보기에

---

06 정답 ② 정답률 29%

정답 풀이

② 문맥상 반의어(object → cling)
➡ 문장의 주어인 Many는 과학의 힘을 신봉하는 사람들이므로 이들은 과학의 힘에 열정을 가지고 계속 '반대하는' 것이 아니라 '집착한다'는 의미가 문맥상 자연스럽다. 따라서, object(반대하다)를 cling(집착하다) 등으로 바꿔주는 것이 적절하다.

┃친절한 오답 풀이┃

① ignore 圏 무시하다
③ counter 圏 반격하다, 반박하다
④ concern 圏 관련된 것이다
⑤ deny 圏 부정하다

 구문 분석 Plus

1행
Those [**who** limit themselves to Western scientific research] have virtually ignored anything that *cannot be perceived* by the five senses and repeatedly *measured* or *quantified*.
➡ who: Those를 선행사로 하는 주격 관계대명사
➡ 조동사 cannot 뒤에 쓰인 수동태가 and와 or로 병렬 연결된 구조로 measured와 quantified 앞에 be가 생략되었다.

지문 해석

서양의 과학 연구에 국한된 사람들은 오감으로 감지할 수 없고 반복적으로 측정하거나 정량화할 수 없는 것은 무엇이든 거의 무시해 왔다. 연구는, 원인과 결과에 의해 과학적으로 설명될 수 없으면, 미신적이고 무효한 것으로 일축된다. 많은 사람이 과학의 힘, 더 구체적으로 과학이 그들에게 주는 힘에 대한 이 문화적 패러다임에 거의 종교적 열정을 가지고 계속 반대한다(→ 집착한다). 비서양의 과학적 패러다임을 기껏해야 열등하고 최악의 경우 부정확하다고 일축함으로써, 종래의 서양 의학 연구 단체의 가장 완고한 구성원들은 대체 의학 요법과 연구가 자신들의 연구, 자신들의 행복, 그리고 자신들의 세계관에 가하는 위협에 반격하려 한다. 그럼에도 불구하고, 생물 의학 연구는 돌봄 치료 과정과 관련하여 대체 의학 시술자들과 관련된 현상 중 많은 것에 대해 설명할 수 없다. 침술이나 동종 요법 같은 치료법이 생물 의학적 모델에 의해 설명될 수 없는 생리적 또는 임상적 반응을 초래하는 것이 관찰될 때, 많은 사람이 과학적인 모델을 수정하기보다는 그 결과를 부정하려 애써 왔다.

virtually 圉 사실상, 거의   perceive 圏 감지하다   measure 圏 측정하다, 재다   quantify 圏 정량화하다   dismiss 圏 일축하다, 묵살하다   superstitious 圏 미신적인   invalid 圏 무효한, 효력 없는   religious 圏 종교적인   paradigm 圏 패러다임   inferior 圏 열등한   at best 기껏   inaccurate 圏 부정확한   at worst 최악의 경우에   rigid 圏 완고한, 엄격한   conventional 圏 전통적인, 종래의   counter 圏 반격하다, 반박하다   alternative 圏 대체 의학의, 대체의   pose 圏 가하다, 제기하다   biomedical 圏 생물 의학의   phenomenon 圏 현상 ((pl. phenomena))   practitioner 圏 시술자, (전문직 종사자, 특히) 의사   physiological 圏 생리적인   modify 圏 수정하다

07   정답 ⑤   정답률 45%

⑤ 반의어(less → more)

→ 기술이 발달할수록 인간은 점점 더 그것에 의존하게 되지만 예상치 못한 일이 발생할 때는 인간만이 그 문제에 유연하게 대처할 수 있다고 했으므로, 대형 여객기의 조종에서 인간 조작자가 관리를 포기하면 사고를 겪을 가능성은 더 많을 것이다. 따라서 less(더 적게)를 more(더욱)로 바꾸는 것이 적절하다.

┃친절한 오답 풀이┃

① paradox 명 역설
② distracted 형 산만해진
③ passive 형 수동적인
④ flexibility 명 유연성, 융통성

 구문 분석 Plus

2행
They are **so** unstable **that** they require an automated system [*that* can sense and act more quickly than a human operator to maintain control].
→ so + 형용사 + that ...: 너무 ~해서 …하다
→ that: an automated system을 선행사로 하는 주격 관계대명사
→ to maintain: 목적을 나타내는 부사적 용법의 to부정사

지문 해석

가장 진보된 군사용 제트기는 전자식 비행 조종 장치이다. 그것들은 매우 불안정해서 계속 제어하기 위해서는 인간 조작자보다 더 빠르게 감지하고 행동할 수 있는 자동화된 시스템이 필요하다. 스마트 기술에 대한 우리의 의존은 역설로 이어졌다. 기술이 향상될수록 그 기술은 신뢰성과 효율성이 더 높아지고, 인간 조작자들은 훨씬 더 그것에 의존한다. 결국, 그들은 집중력을 잃고, 산만해지며, 시스템이 스스로 작동하도록 내버려 둔 채로 떠난다. 가장 극단적인 경우, 대형 여객기를 조종하는 것은 TV를 보는 것과 같은 수동적인 직업이 될 수 있다. 이것은 예상치 못한 일이 일어나기 전까지는 괜찮다. 예상치 못한 일은 인간의 가치를 드러낸다. 우리가 제시하는 것은 새로운 상황에 대처할 수 있는 유연성이다. 기계는 공동의 목표를 추구하기 위해 협력하는 것이 아니라 단지 도구의 역할을 할 뿐이다. 따라서 인간 조작자가 관리를 포기하면 그 시스템이 심각한 사고를 겪을 가능성이 더 적을(→ 많을) 것이다.

어휘

unstable 형 불안정한   extreme 형 극도의, 극심한   massive 형 거대한, 엄청나게 큰   airliner 명 여객기   collaborate 동 협력하다, 부역하다   in pursuit of …을 추구하여   oversight 명 관리, 감독

08   정답 ⑤   정답률 59%

(A) 문맥상 반의어(promoted / eliminated)

→ 앞서 슬픔은 부정적인 감정으로 여겨진다고 했으므로, 슬픔이 '제거될' 필요가 있는 문제 감정의 범주에 들어간다는 의미가 문맥상 자연스럽다. 따라서 eliminated가 들어가야 한다. promote는 '촉진하다'라는 의미이다.

(B) 문맥상 반의어(accpeted / discouraged)

→ 슬픔과 우울이라는 감정을 부정적으로 보는 현재와 달리, 과거에는 이러한 감정들이 '수용되었다'라는 의미가 문맥상 적절하므로, accepted가 들어가야 한다. discourage는 '막다, 좌절시키다'라는 의미이다.

(C) 문맥상 반의어(destructive / instructive)

→ 고전 철학자나 문학 작품들은 슬픔을 포함한 여러 감정들을 탐험하는 것을 '유익한' 것으로 여겼다는 의미가 문맥상 자연스러우므로 instructive가 들어가야 한다. destructive는 '파괴적인'이라는 의미이다.

 구문 분석 Plus

16행
It is only recently **that** a thriving industry promoting positivity has *managed to remove* this earlier and more balanced view of human affectivity.
→ 부사구 only recently 를 강조하는 「It is ... that」 강조구문
→ manage to-v: 간신히 …하다

지문 해석

우리 문화에서 슬픔은 종종 불필요하고 바람직하지 않은 감정으로 여겨진다. 수많은 자기 계발서들은 긍정적 사고와 긍정적 행동의 장점을 장려하고, 대개 부정적인 감정, 특히 슬픔을 제거될 필요가 있는 '문제 감정'의 범주에 지정한다. 심리학 종사자의 대부분은 슬픔을 관리하고 완화하는 일에 종사한다. 그러나 어느 정도의 슬픔과 우울은 오늘날의 경우보다 이전 역사 시대에는 훨씬 더 많이 수용되어 왔다. 고전 철학자부터 셰익스피어를 거쳐 체호프, 입센, 그리고 19세기의 위대한 소설에 이르기까지, 슬픔, 갈망, 그리고 우울이라는 감정을 탐험하는 것은 유익한 것으로 오랫동안 여겨져 왔다. 긍정성을 장려하는 번창하는 산업이 인간 정서에 대한 더 이전의 그리고 더 균형적인 이러한 관점을 어떻게든 없앤 것은 불과 최근이다.

어휘

unnecessary 형 불필요한   undesirable 형 바람직하지 않은   self-help book 자기 계발서   assign 동 지정하다   affect 명 감정, 정서   psychology 명 심리학   profession 명 직업; *종사자들   employ 동 고용하다   depression 명 우울증; *우울함   historical 형 역사적, 역사상의   classic 형 고전의, 고전적인   philosopher 명 철학자   longing 명 갈망, 열망   thriving 형 번창하는   affectivity 명 정서

09   정답 ①   정답률 50%

(A) 문맥상 적절한 단어(resistance / connection)

→ 문맥상 특정 분야에 대한 학습 '거부' 때문에 사각지대(blind spots)가 생기는 것이므로 resistance가 들어가는 것이 알맞다. connection은 '관련성'이라는 의미이다.

(B) 문맥상 반의어(flooded / limited)

→ 사각지대의 예시로, 재정 분야에서는 지식이 뛰어나지만 사람 관리에 대한 이해는 '제한될' 수 있다는 내용이 문맥상 자연스러우므로 limited가 들어가는 것이 알맞다. flooded '넘치는'이라는 의미이다.

(C) 문맥상 적절한 단어(prospect / retrospect)

→ 앞에서 그 경영자는 남들의 의견을 받아들이려 하지 않는다고 했으므로 자신의 경영 방식을 바꾸는 것에 대한 '전망'조차 거부한다는 내용이 이어지는 것이 자연스럽다. 따라서 prospect가 들어가는 것이 알맞다. retrospect는 '회상'이라는 의미이다.

 구문 분석 Plus

4행
At the root of many of our blind spots are a number of emotions or attitudes — [*fear being* the most obvious], but also pride, self-satisfaction, and anxiety.
→ 부사구(At the root of many of our blind spots)가 문장 맨 앞에 오면서 주어(a number of emotions or attitudes)와 동사(are)가 도치됨
→ fear being 이하는 주절의 주어와 분사구문의 주어가 달라 주어 fear를 생략하지 않은 독립분사구문

지문 해석

사각지대는 지식의 단순한 부족과 같지 않다. 사각지대는 특정 분야의 학습에 대한 거부에서 나온다. 우리의 사각지대의 뿌리에는 많은 감정들 또는 태도들이 있는데, 가장 분명한 것은 두려움이지만, 자만, 자기만족, 그리고 불안도 있다. 예를 들어 한 경영자는 재정 분야에서 탁월한 지식을 가지고 있지만, 사람 관리에 대한 이해는 한계가 있을지도 모른다. 사람들은 그녀가 차갑고 냉담하다는 것을 알고 있고 그녀가 보다 자문적이고 팀원들과 함께 어울리게 되기를 원한다. 그러나 그녀는 자신의 경영 스타일에 대한

피드백을 받아들이려고 하지 않고 심지어 자신의 경영 스타일의 변화에 대한 전망을 고려하는 것조차 거부한다.

blind spot 사각지대 (잘 모르는 분야) lack 명 부족, 결핍 emerge 동 나오다, 생겨나다 resistance 명 저항 connection 명 관련, 연관 particular 형 특정한 attitude 명 태도 obvious 형 분명한 pride 명 자만 self-satisfaction 명 자기만족 anxiety 명 걱정, 근심 unsurpassed 형 타의 추종을 불허하는 financial 형 재정적인 understanding 명 이해 management 명 경영; *(사람의) 관리 flooded 형 물에 잠긴; *넘쳐나는 consultative 형 고문(자문)의, 상담의 involved 형 관여하는, 관련된 accept 동 수용하다, 받아들이다 refuse 동 거절하다 consider 동 고려하다 prospect 명 전망 retrospect 명 회상, 회고

10   정답 ④   정답률 40%

정답 풀이

(A) 문맥상 적절한 단어(based / lost)
➡ 자신만의 시각을 가지고 혼자서 일하는 교사들에게 더 잘 가르치는 교사가 있을 수 있다는 사실이 '이해되지 않는다'라는 의미가 문맥상 자연스러우므로 lost가 들어가는 것이 알맞다. based는 '기반을 둔'이라는 의미이다.

(B) 반의어(allows / forbids)
➡ 뒤에 교사들에게 자신만의 관점 하나만 남겨진다고 했으므로, 더 잘하는 사람을 벤치마킹할 수 있게 '허용하는(allow)' 과정이 없었다라는 내용이 문맥상 자연스럽다. forbid는 '금지하다'라는 의미의 반의어이다.

(C) 반의어(mostly / never)
➡ 앞서 같은 과목을 가르치는 다른 교사들이 수업하는 방식에 대해 거의 알지 못했다고 했으므로, 다른 교사들과 정보 공유하고자 하는 생각이 '결코 없었다'라는 내용이 자연스러우므로 never가 들어가는 것이 알맞다. mostly는 '주로'라는 의미의 반의어이다.

코드 +α   구문 분석 Plus

> 2행
>
> The fact {**that** there might be someone somewhere in the same building or district [*who* may be more successful at teaching this or that subject or lesson]} is lost on teachers [*who* close the door and work their way through the school calendar virtually alone].
> ➡ that은 The fact와 동격인 명사절을 이끄는 접속사
> ➡ 첫 번째 who는 someone somewhere in the same building or district를, 두 번째 who는 teachers를 수식하는 주격 관계대명사

지문 해석

교사들이 홀로 일할 때, 그들은 한 쌍의 눈, 즉 자기 자신의 눈을 통해 세상을 보는 경향이 있다. 이러저러한 과목이나 수업을 가르치는 데 더 성공적일지도 모르는 누군가가 같은 건물이나 구역 어딘가에 있을지도 모른다는 사실은 문을 닫고 사실상 혼자서 학사 일정에 따라 자신의 방식으로 일하는 교사들에게는 이해되지 않는다. 일을 더 잘 하거나 적어도 다르게 하는 사람들을 벤치마킹할 수 있게 해주는 과정이 없는 경우, 교사들에게는 자기 자신만의 관점 하나만 남겨진다. 나는 사회과라는 상위교과 하에 있는 다양한 과목들을 가르쳤고 같은 과목을 가르치는 동료 교사들이 어떻게 일하는지에 대해 거의 알지 못했다. 의견을 교환하고, 공동 평가를 계획하고, 우리가 잘한 것을 공유하기 위해 정기적으로 모이자는 생각은 우리에게 결코 일어나지 않았다. 오히려, 우리는 사회과 교무실에서 시간 부족에 대해 불평하고 남을 비난하면서 많은 시간을 보냈다.

in isolation 별개로, 홀로 district 명 지역, 구역 be lost on …에게 이해를 못 얻다 school calendar 학교의 연간 행사 예정표 virtually 부 사실상 in the absence of …이 없을 때에 benchmark 동 벤치마킹하다 perspective 명 관점, 시각 social studies (교과목) 사회 compare notes 의견을 교환하다 assessment 명 평가 blame game 비난 게임

코드 공략하기 02   pp.123~126

01 ⑤   02 ③   03 ④   04 ③   05 ②   06 ②   07 ③   08 ③   09 ③   10 ①

01   정답 ⑤   정답률 80%

정답 풀이

⑤ 반의어(disrespect → respect)
➡ 다른 문화권 사람의 언어로 의사소통하려고 노력하는 것은 그들에 대한 '존중'을 보여주는 것이므로 disrespect(무례함)을 respect(존중)로 고치는 것이 적절하다.

┃친절한 오답 풀이┃
① foreign 형 외국의
② gap 명 차이, 격차
③ preparation 명 준비
④ basic 형 기본적인

코드 +α   구문 분석 Plus

> 5행
>
> A language gap is a great opportunity **for good manners** to shine.
> ➡ for good manners: to부정사의 의미상 주어
> ➡ to shine: a great opportunity를 수식하는 형용사적 용법의 to부정사

지문 해석

세상은 좁고, 사업은 모든 문화권의 사람들을 한데 모은다. 당신은 외국 방문객과 함께 회의에 참석하거나, 당신이 이해하지 못하는 언어를 사용하는 국가로 파견될 수도 있다. 언어의 차이는 훌륭한 예절이 빛을 발할 아주 좋은 기회이다. 가장 좋은 행동 방침은 약간의 준비이다. 당신은 상용 회화집을 구하여 "안녕하세요," "부탁합니다," "고맙습니다," "만나서 반갑습니다," "안녕히 가세요."와 같은 몇 가지 기본 표현을 배울 수 있다. 다른 사람의 언어로 의사소통하려고 노력하는 것은 그 사람에 대한 무례함(→ 존중)을 보여준다.

attend 동 참석하다 send off 파견하다, 보내다 opportunity 명 기회 obtain 동 구하다 make an effort 노력하다, 애쓰다

02   정답 ③   정답률 64%

정답 풀이

③ 문맥상 반의어(disproved → reinforced)
➡ 빵 굽는 냄새가 눈에 보이지 않는 작은 빵 입자의 존재(원자)에 대한 아이디어를 주었고, 날씨의 순환이 이러한 생각을 '강화했다'라는 의미가 문맥상 자연스럽다. 따라서, disproved(틀렸음을 입증했다)를 reinforced(강화했다) 등으로 바꿔주는 것이 적절하다.

┃친절한 오답 풀이┃
① detect 동 감지하다
② exist 동 존재하다
④ conserve 동 보존하다
⑤ late 형 늦은

구문 분석 Plus

12행	They reasoned that there must be particles of water [**that** *turn into* steam, *form* clouds, and *fall to* earth], so that the water is conserved even though the little particles are **too** small **to see**. ➡ that 이하는 선행사 particles of water를 수식하는 주격 관계대명사절로 복수 명사인 선행사에 수 일치하여 turn into, form, fall to가 병렬 연결됨 ➡ , so that + 주어 + 동사: 그래서 …하다 ➡ too + 형용사/부사 + to-v: 너무 …해서 ~할 수 없다

지문 해석

나는 어느 여름날 저녁 스페인의 한 식당 밖에 앉아 저녁 식사를 기다리고 있었다. 주방의 향기가 나의 미뢰를 자극했다. 내가 먹을 식사는, 너무 작아 눈으로 볼 수는 없지만 코로는 감지되는, 공중을 떠다니는 분자의 형태로 내게 오고 있었다. 고대 그리스인들은 이런 식으로 원자의 개념을 최초로 떠올렸는데, 빵 굽는 냄새는 그들에게 작은 빵 입자들이 눈에 보이지 않게 존재한다는 생각이 들게 했다. 날씨의 순환이 이 생각이 틀렸음을 입증했다(→ 이 생각을 강화했다). 땅 위의 물웅덩이는 점차 말라 사라지고, 그런 다음 나중에 비가 되어 떨어진다. 수증기로 변하여 구름을 형성하고 땅으로 떨어지는 물 입자가 존재하는 게 틀림없고, 그래서 그 작은 입자들이 너무 작아 눈에 보이지 않더라도 그 물은 보존된다고 그들은 추론했다. 스페인에서의 나의 파에야가 원자 이론에 대한 공로를 인정받기에는 4천 년이나 너무 늦게 내게 영감을 주었다.

excite 동 자극하다   drift 동 떠다니다, 떠돌다   come upon 우연히 떠오르다   suggest 동 암시하다; *생각나게 하다   particle 명 알갱이, 입자   vision 명 시야   puddle 명 물웅덩이   gradually 부 점차   reason 동 추론하다   steam 명 수증기   inspire 동 영감을 주다   take the credit for …에 대한 공로를 인정받다   atomic 형 원자의   theory 명 이론

03   정답 ④   정답률 41%

정답 풀이

④ 문맥상 반의어(accommodating → managing)
➡ 도시 교통 전문가들이 도시의 자동차 수요에 부응하기보다는 관리해야 한다는 견해를 따르고 있다고 했으며, 이를 위한 구체적인 전략이 소개되고 있다. 이 전략 중 하나인 자동차 여행을 더 비싸게 만들거나 행정 규정으로 제한하는 것은 자동차 수요에 '부응하는 것'이 아니라 '관리하는 것'이므로 accommodating(부응하기)을 managing(관리하기)과 같은 단어로 바꿔주는 것이 적절하다.

친절한 오답 풀이

① limit 동 제한하다
② persuade 동 설득하다
③ alternative 형 대안적인, 대체의
⑤ reinforce 동 강화하다

 구문 분석 Plus

11행	As a result, **as** cities develop and their residents become more prosperous, [*persuading* people *to choose* not to use cars] becomes an increasingly key focus of city managers and planners. ➡ as: '…함에 따라' 의미의 접속사 ➡ persuade + 목적어 + to-v: ~가 ~하도록 설득하다 ➡ becomes: 주절의 동사로 주어는 동명사구 persuading people … cars이다.

지문 해석

최근 몇 년 동안 전 세계적으로 도시 교통 전문가들은 도시의 자동차 수요에 부응하기보다는 관리해야 한다는 견해를 대체로 따랐다. 소득 증가는 필연적으로 자동차 보급의 증가로 이어진다. 기후 변화로 인한 불가피성이 없다 하더라도, 인구 밀도가

높은 도시의 물리적 제약과 그에 상응하는 접근성, 이동성, 안전, 대기 오염, 그리고 도시 거주 적합성에 대한 요구 모두가 단지 이러한 증가하는 수요에 부응하기 위해 도로망을 확장하는 선택권을 제한한다. 결과적으로, 도시가 발전하고 도시의 거주자들이 더 부유해짐에 따라, 사람들이 자동차를 사용하지 '않기로' 결정하도록 설득하는 것이 도시 관리자와 계획 설계자들의 핵심 중점 사항이 된다. 걷기, 자전거 타기, 대중교통과 같은 대안적인 선택 사항의 질을 향상하는 것이 이 전략의 핵심 요소이다. 하지만 자동차 수요에 부응하는(→ (를) 관리하는) 가장 직접적인 접근 방법은 자동차 여행을 더 비싸게 만들거나 행정 규정으로 그것을 제한하는 것이다. 자동차 여행이 기후 변화의 원인을 제공하는 것이 이런 불가피성을 강화한다.

urban 형 도시의   transport 명 교통, 수송   professional 명 전문가   accommodate 동 (요구 등에) 부응하다, 맞추다   inevitably 부 불가피하게   motorization 명 자동차 보급, 전동화   densely inhabited 인구 밀도가 높은   corresponding 형 상응하는   accessibility 명 접근성, 접근   mobility 명 이동성   livability 명 거주 적합성, 살기 좋음   expand 동 확장하다   resident 명 거주자   prosperous 형 번영하는   alternative 형 대안적인, 대체의   direct 형 직접적인   restrict 동 제한하다   administrative 형 행정의   contribution 명 원인 제공, 기여

04   정답 ③   정답률 70%

정답 풀이

③ 반의어(easy → difficult)
➡ 작은 변화가 결과로 빨리 이어지지 않아 이전의 일상으로 다시 돌아가게 한다고 했으므로, 변화의 느린 속도는 나쁜 습관을 깨기 '어렵게' 만든다는 의미가 문맥상 자연스럽다. 따라서, easy(쉬운)를 difficult(어려운) 등으로 바꿔주는 것이 적절하다.

친절한 오답 풀이

① matter 동 중요하다
② quickly 부 빨리
④ repeat 동 반복하다
⑤ problem 명 문제

 구문 분석 Plus

7행	The slow pace of transformation also **makes** *it* **difficult** [to *break* a bad habit]. ➡ make + 목적어 + 형용사: …을 ~하게 만들다 ➡ it은 가목적어, to break 이하가 진목적어

지문 해석

우리는 작은 변화들이 당장 크게 중요한 것 같지 않아서 보통 그것들을 무시한다. 지금 돈을 약간 모아도, 당신은 여전히 백만장자가 아니다. 오늘 밤에 스페인어를 한 시간 동안 공부해도, 여러분은 여전히 그 언어를 익힌 것은 아니다. 우리는 약간의 변화를 만들어 보지만, 그 결과는 결코 빨리 오지 않는 것 같고 그래서 우리는 이전의 일상으로 다시 빠져든다. 변화의 느린 속도는 또한 나쁜 습관을 깨기 쉽게(→ 어렵게) 만든다. 오늘 몸에 좋지 않은 음식을 먹어도 저울 눈금은 크게 움직이지 않는다. 하나의 결정은 무시하기 쉽다. 하지만 우리가 잘못된 결정을 반복적으로 따름으로써 작은 오류를 날마다 반복한다면, 우리의 작은 선택들이 모여 좋지 않은 결과를 만들어낸다. 많은 실수는 결국 문제로 이어진다.

ignore 동 무시하다   in the moment 당장은   millionaire 명 백만장자   slide into …로 빠져들다   previous 형 이전의, 앞의   routine 명 일상, 판에 박힌 일   pace 명 속도   transformation 명 변화, 변형   unhealthy 형 몸에 좋지 않은   scale 명 저울 눈금   day after day 날마다   add up to (결과가) …가 되다   misstep 명 실수   eventually 부 결국

05   정답 ②   정답률 41%

정답 풀이

② 문맥상 반의어(believe → challenge)

➡ 뒤에 소문이 오래된 것이면 전통으로 불리기 시작하고 사람들이 그것을 더 믿는다고 했으므로, 기적에 대한 소문이 책에 쓰여지고 그 책이 옛날의 것이라면 그 소문은 '믿기' 힘든 것이 아니라 '이의를 제기하기' 힘들다는 의미가 문맥상 자연스럽다. 따라서 believe(믿다)를 challenge(이의를 제기하다)로 바꿔주는 것이 적절하다.

┃친절한 오답 풀이┃

① thrill 몡 스릴, 전율
③ old 혱 오래된
④ distorted 혱 왜곡된, 곡해된
⑤ recently 및 최근에

 구문 분석 Plus

9행

This is rather odd because you might think (**that**) they would realize that older rumors have had more time to get distorted than younger rumors [*that* are close in time to the alleged events themselves].
➡ think의 목적어로 쓰인 명사절을 이끄는 접속사 that은 종종 생략됨
➡ that 이하는 선행사 younger rumors를 수식하는 주격 관계대명사절
➡ themselves는 the alleged events를 강조하는 재귀대명사

지문 해석

스릴 넘치는 유령 이야기는 정말 무섭다면 들려주기에 재밌고, 만약 당신이 그 이야기가 사실이라고 주장하면 훨씬 더 그렇다. 사람들은 그런 이야기를 전달하는 것으로부터 스릴을 느낀다. 이것은 기적 이야기에도 동일하게 적용된다. 만약 기적에 대한 소문이 어떤 책에 쓰인다면, 특히 그 책이 먼 옛날의 것이라면, 그 소문은 믿기(→ 이의를 제기하기) 힘들어진다. 만약 소문이 충분히 오래된 것이라면, 그것은 대신 '전통'으로 불리기 시작하고, 그러고 나서 사람들은 그것을 더욱더 믿는다. 이것은 다소 이상한데, 그 이유는 그들이 (근거 없이) 주장된 사건 그 자체에 시간상 가까운 최근의 소문보다 오래된 소문이 왜곡될 시간이 더 있다는 것을 깨달을 것이라고 당신이 생각할 수 있기 때문이다. Elvis Presley와 Michael Jackson은 전통이 생겨나기에는 너무 최근에 살아서 '화성에서 목격된 Elvis'와 같은 이야기를 믿는 사람은 많지 않다.

 어휘

spine-tingling 혱 스릴 넘치는   apply to …에 적용되다   rumor 몡 소문   all the more 더욱더, 오히려   odd 혱 이상한   alleged 혱 (근거 없이) 주장된   grow up (사태·관습이) 생기다

06   정답 ②   정답률 55%

정답 풀이

(A) 문맥상 적절한 단어(conformity / individuality)

➡ 20세기에 이를 때까지 고전음악은 기본적인 규칙을 따랐고, '개성'을 발휘할 여지는 있었으나 항상 기본적인 비율과 논리가 있었다는 것이 문맥상 자연스럽다. 따라서 individuality가 알맞다. conformity는 '순응'이라는 의미이다.

(B) 문맥상 반의어(maintained / overturned)

➡ 급진적인 개념으로 규칙이 '뒤집어진' 이후에도 작곡가들은 여전히 종합적이고 통일적인 구조를 생산해내는 방식을 택했다는 내용이 문맥상 자연스러우므로 overturned가 알맞다. maintain은 '유지하다'라는 의미이다.

(C) 반의어(approachable / inaccessible)

➡ 앞 문장에서 여전히 작곡가들이 통일적인 구조를 생산해내는 방식으로 생각을 구성했다고 했으므로, 모더니즘 작품들이 복잡함에도 불구하고 '이해하기 쉽다'라는 의미가 문맥상 자연스럽다. 따라서 approachable이 알맞다. inaccessible은 '이해할 수 없는'이라는 의미의 반의어이다.

 구문 분석 Plus

10행

..., **composers**, more often than not, still **organized** their thoughts in ways [*that* produced an overall, unifying structure].
➡ composers, organized: 주절의 주어, 동사
➡ that: ways를 선행사로 하는 주격 관계대명사

13행

That's one reason (**why**) the atonal, *incredibly complex works by Arnold Schönberg or Karlheinz Stockhausen*, to name two twentieth-century Modernists, *are* nonetheless approachable.
➡ 선행사 one reason 뒤에 관계부사 why가 생략됨
➡ the atonal ... Stockhausen, are: 관계부사절의 주어와 동사

지문 해석

작곡가들이 형식과 디자인을 자유롭게 실험하기 시작했던 20세기에 이를 때까지, 고전 음악은 화음은 말할 것도 없이, 구조와 관련 있는 기본적인 규칙들을 계속 따랐다. 여전히 개성을 발휘할 여지는 있었지만 (위대한 작곡가들은 규칙을 따르지 않고, 규칙이 그들을 따르도록 만들었다) 디자인 이면에는 항상 기본적인 비율과 논리가 있었다. 많은 규칙이 최근 들어 급진적인 개념에 의해 뒤집어진 이후에도, 여전히 작곡가들은 대개 종합적이고 통일적인 구조를 생산해내는 방식으로 자신들의 생각을 구성했다. 그것이 20세기 모더니즘 작곡가 두 명을 예로 들면, Arnold Schönberg나 Karlheinz Stockhausen에 의해 작곡된 무조(無調)의 매우 복잡한 작품들이 그럼에도 불구하고 이해하기 쉬운 한 가지 이유이다. 그 소리는 매우 이상할지 모르지만, 그 결과는 여전히 구성의 측면에서 분명히 고전적이다.

 어휘

composer 몡 작곡가   experiment 됨 실험하다   not to mention …은 말할 것도 없고   fundamental 혱 근본적인   proportion 몡 비율   radical 혱 급진적인   more often than not 자주, 대개   overall 혱 종합적인   unifying 혱 통일적인   complex 혱 복잡한   name 됨 이름을 대다, 말하다   nonetheless 및 그렇기는 하지만   decidedly 및 확실히, 분명히   organization 몡 구성

07   정답 ③   정답률 88%

정답 풀이

(A) 반의어(enhanced / hindered)

➡ 디지털 혁명이 의사소통을 '향상시킨' 것이라는 의미가 자연스러우므로 enhanced가 들어가는 것이 적절하다. hinder는 '저해하다, 방해하다'라는 의미의 반의어이다.

(B) 문맥상 적절한 단어(object / reconnect)

➡ 전화, 텔레비전, 인터넷 등을 이민자들이 그들의 옛 문화에 '다시 연결되게' 할 것이라는 의미가 문맥상 자연스럽다. 따라서 reconnect가 들어가는 것이 적절하다. object는 '반대하다'라는 의미이다.

(C) 반의어(abandon / maintain)

➡ 문맥상 출신 국가와의 빈번한 접촉이 고국의 문화 양식을 '유지하도록' 할 것이므로 maintain이 들어가는 것이 적절하다. abandon은 '버리다, 유기하다'라는 의미의 반의어이다.

 구문 분석 Plus

15행

..., and **result in** *more immigrant families* being influenced to maintain cultural patterns from the homeland, ...
➡ result in: … 결과를 가져오다
➡ more immigrant families: 뒤에 오는 동명사구의 의미상 주어
➡ being influenced: 전치사 in의 목적어로 쓰인 동명사구

지문 해석

20세기 중반까지, 단지 소수의 이민자만이 죽기 전에 한두 번 고국을 방문했을 뿐,

대부분은 자기가 태어난 땅으로 다시는 돌아가지 못했다. 이러한 경향은 의사소통을 향상시킨 디지털 혁명과 더불어 세계화의 도래로 완전히 바뀌었다. 결과적으로, 이민은 과거의 것과는 매우 다른 경험이다. 이민자 가족들이 전화와 텔레비전과 인터넷을 통하여 그들의 옛 문화에 다시 연결될 수 있다는 것은 주류 미국 사회 속으로의 통합에 대한 그들의 접근방식을 바꾸었다. 이것은 또한 어린이들에 대한 이민자들의 사회화 관행에도 크게 영향을 미쳤다. 출신 국가와의 접촉은 이제 더 빈번하며, 더 많은 이민자 가족들이 고국에서 가져온 문화 양식을 유지하고 그들의 자녀들도 그것을 유지하도록 영향을 주려고 시도하도록 영향 받게 되는 결과를 초래한다.

immigrant 뗑 (다른 나라로 온) 이민자 (immigration 뗑 이민)   pay a visit 방문을 하다   homeland 뗑 고국   completely 뷔 완전히   advent 뗑 도래, 출현   globalization 뗑 세계화   coupled with …과 결부된   digital revolution 디지털 혁명   enhance 통 향상시키다   hinder 통 저해하다, 방해하다   object 통 반대하다   reconnect 통 다시 연결하다   via 전 …을 통하여   integration 뗑 통합   mainstream 뗑 주류, 대세   socialization 뗑 사회화   contact 뗑 접촉   abandon 통 버리다   maintain 통 유지하다

08   정답 ③   정답률 36%

정답 풀이

③ 문맥상 반의어(solidify → counter)
➡ 기존 고객들의 요구를 더 완벽히 충족시키는 것에 집중하는 전략에 대한 이야기이므로, 여러 다른 회사에서 각각의 금융 서비스를 이용하는 기존 소비자들의 편의를 위해 이러한 구매 패턴에 '대항하여' 많은 회사들이 현재 모든 서비스를 한 곳에서 제공하고 있다고 하는 것이 문맥상 자연스럽다. 따라서 solidify(확고히 하다)를 counter(대항하다) 등으로 바꿔주는 것이 적절하다.

▌친절한 오답 풀이 ▌

① acquire 통 습득하다; *획득하다
② different 혱 다른
④ current 혱 현재의, 지금의
⑤ little 혱 거의 없는

  구문 분석 Plus

3행

This strategy **involves** abandon**ing** the old notions *of* [acquiring new customers and increasing transactions] to focus instead on more fully <u>serving</u> the needs of existing customers.
➡ 동사 involve는 목적어로 동명사를 취함
➡ of는 동격의 전치사로 the old notions와 acquiring new … transactions는 동격 관계임
➡ serving은 전치사 on의 목적어로 쓰인 동명사

지문 해석

고객 관계를 구축하기 위한 가장 생산적인 전략들 중 하나는 회사의 시장 점유율보다 그것의 고객 점유율을 높이는 것이다. 이러한 전략은 대신에 기존 고객들의 요구를 더 완벽히 충족시키는 것에 집중하기 위해 신규 고객들을 확보해서 거래를 늘린다는 오래된 개념을 버리는 것을 포함한다. 금융 서비스들이 이것의 좋은 예시이다. 대부분의 소비자들은 다른 회사들로부터 금융 서비스를 구매한다. 그들은 한 기관과 은행 거래를 하고, 또 다른 기관으로부터 보험을 구매하며 그리고 다른 곳에서 자신들의 투자금을 처리한다. 이러한 구매 패턴을 확고히하기(→ 대항하기)위해 많은 회사들이 현재 이 모든 서비스를 한 곳에서 제공한다. 예를 들어, Regions Financial Corporation은 1,500개가 넘는 지사의 네트워크에서 고객들에게 소매 및 상업 은행업, 신탁, 담보 대출, 그리고 보험 상품을 제공한다. 그 회사는 그것의 현재 고객들의 금융적 요구를 더 완벽히 충족시키려고 노력하며, 그것에 의해 각 고객의 금융 거래에서 더 큰 점유율을 획득한다. 이러한 유형의 관계를 형성함으로써 고객들은 자신들의 금융 서비스 요구를 충족시키기 위해 경쟁 회사를 찾을 동기를 거의 가지지 않는다.

productive 혱 생산적인   abandon 통 버리다, 유기하다   transaction 뗑 거래, 매매   serve 통 …의 요구를 충족시키다   needs 뗑 ((pl.)) 요구   insurance 뗑 보험   trust 뗑 신뢰; *신탁   mortgage 뗑 담보 대출   incentive 뗑 동기   seek out …을 찾아내다   fulfill 통 충족시키다

09   정답 ③   정답률 55%

정답 풀이

(A) 문맥상 적절한 단어(controlling / raising)
➡ 기대감이 높아질수록 만족하기는 더욱 어려워진다는 앞의 내용으로 보아, 기대감을 '통제함'으로써 삶에서 느끼는 만족감을 향상할 수 있다는 것이 문맥상 자연스러우므로 controlling이 들어가는 것이 적절하다. raise는 '높이다'라는 의미이다.

(B) 반의어(frequent / rare)
➡ 뒤에서 특별한 경우를 위해 훌륭한 와인을 아껴두라고 이야기하고 있으므로 적절한 기대감을 가지기 위한 한 방법은 멋진 경험들을 '드문' 상태로 유지하는 것이라는 내용이 와야 한다. 따라서, rare가 들어가는 것이 적절하다. frequent는 '잦은, 빈번한'이라는 의미를 가진 반의어이다.

(C) 문맥상 적절한 단어(familiarity / pleasure)
➡ 앞에서 품위 있는 실크 블라우스를 특별한 즐거움이 되게 하라고 이야기하고 있으므로 그것은 당신이 '즐거움'을 계속해서 경험할 수 있도록 보장해 주는 방법이라는 내용이 이어져야 한다. 따라서, pleasure가 들어가는 것이 적절하다. familiarity는 '익숙함, 낯익음'이라는 의미이다.

  구문 분석 Plus

9행

[**No matter what** you can afford], save great wine for special occasions.
➡ no matter what: '무엇을 …하더라도'의 의미로, 복합관계대명사 whatever로 바꿔 쓸 수 있음

지문 해석

사람들은 삶이 나아질수록 더 높은 기대감을 지닌다. 하지만 기대감이 더 높아질수록 만족하기는 더욱 어려워진다. 우리는 기대감을 통제함으로써 삶에서 느끼는 만족감을 향상할 수 있다. 적절한 기대감은 많은 경험들을 즐거운 놀라움이 되도록 하는 여지를 남긴다. 문제는 적절한 기대감을 가지는 방법을 찾는 것이다. 이것을 위한 한 방법은 멋진 경험들을 드문 상태로 유지하는 것이다. 당신이 무엇이든 살 여유가 있더라도, 특별한 경우를 위해 훌륭한 와인을 아껴두어라. 품위 있는 실크 블라우스를 특별한 즐거움이 되게 하라. 이것은 당신의 욕구를 부정하는 행동처럼 보일 수도 있지만, 내 생각은 그렇지 않다. 반대로, 그것은 당신이 즐거움을 계속해서 경험할 수 있도록 보장해 주는 방법이다. 훌륭한 와인과 멋진 블라우스가 당신을 기분 좋게 만들지 못한다면 무슨 의미가 있겠는가?

expectation 뗑 예상, 기대   satisfaction 뗑 만족(감)   adequate 혱 적절한, 적당한   proper 혱 적절한   afford 통 …할 여유가 있다   occasion 뗑 (특정한) 때, 경우   treat 뗑 만족[즐거움]을 주는 것   desire 뗑 욕구

10   정답 ①   정답률 37%

정답 풀이

(A) 문맥상 적절한 단어(perceived / hidden)
➡ 뒤에서 완벽해 보이는 사람들이 실수를 저지르는 것은 다른 사람들에게 그들의 인간미가 사랑스럽도록 만들 것이라 말하고 있으므로, 한 개인의 인지된 매력도는 그 사람의 '인지된' 능력에 따라 증가하거나 감소한다는 것을 추론할 수 있다. 따라서, perceived가 들어가는 것이 적절하다. hidden은 '숨겨진, 숨은'이라는 의미이다.

(B) 문맥상 적절한 단어(creates / narrows)
➡ 완벽성, 혹은 그 자질을 개인들에게 귀속하는 것은 일반 대중들이 공감할 수 없는

인지된 거리감을 '만든다'는 의미가 문맥상 자연스러우므로 creates가 들어가는 것이 적절하다. narrow는 '좁히다'라는 의미이다.

(C) 반의어(more / less)
➡ 앞서 언급한 것과 정반대의 효과를 가진다고 기술하고 있으므로 인지된 평균 혹은 그 이하의 능력을 가진 사람이 실수를 저지른다면 그는 다른 사람들에게 '덜' 매력적이고 호감을 '덜' 주게 될 것이라는 내용이 와야 한다. 따라서, less가 들어가는 것이 적절하다. more는 '더'라는 의미를 가진 반의어이다.

구문 분석 Plus

12행	Perfection, or the attribution of that quality to individuals, creates a perceived distance [**that** the general public cannot relate to]—*making* those [who never make mistakes] *perceived* as being less attractive or likable. ➡ that 이하의 선행사 a perceived distance를 수식하는 목적격 관계대명사절 ➡ make(사역동사) + 목적어 + v-ed: …가 ~되게 하다 ➡ who 이하의 선행사 those를 수식하는 주격 관계대명사절

지문 해석

사회 심리학의 한 현상인 Pratfall Effect는 한 개인의 인지된 매력도가 그 사람이 실수를 한 후에 그 사람의 인지된 능력에 따라 증가하거나 감소한다고 말한다. 유명인사들은 일반적으로 능력 있는 사람들로 여겨지고 어떤 측면에서는 흔히 흠이 없고 완벽하다고도 보이기 때문에, 실수를 저지르는 것은 그 사람의 인간미를 다른 사람들에게 사랑스럽도록 만들 것이다. 기본적으로, 실수를 전혀 저지르지 않는 사람들은 이따금 실수를 저지르는 사람들에 비해 덜 매력적이고 덜 '호감을 주는' 것으로 인지된다. 완벽성, 혹은 그 자질을 개인들에게 귀속하는 것은 일반 대중들이 공감할 수 없는 인지된 거리감을 만들며 실수를 전혀 저지르지 않는 사람들을 덜 매력적이거나 호감이 덜 가도록 만든다. 하지만 이것은 정반대의 효과도 가지는데, 인지된 평균 혹은 그 이하의 능력을 가진 사람이 실수를 저지른다면, 그 사람은 다른 사람들에게 덜 매력적이고 호감을 덜 주게 될 것이다.

어휘

phenomenon 명 현상 **social psychology** 명 사회 심리학 **state** 동 말하다, 진술하다 **attractiveness** 명 매력 **depending on** …에 따라 **competence** 명 능력, 역량 (**competent** 형 유능한, 능력이 있는) **celebrity** 명 유명인사 **flawless** 형 흠이 없는 **aspect** 명 측면 **commit** 동 (죄·과오 등을) 범하다, 저지르다 **humanness** 명 사람됨, 인간성[미] **endearing** 형 사랑스러운 **basically** 부 근본적으로; *기본적으로 **likable** 형 호감이 가는, 마음에 드는 **occasional** 형 가끔의 **attribution** 명 귀속 **relate to** ~을 이해[공감]하다

코드 공략하기 03
pp.127~130

01 ① **02** ③ **03** ⑤ **04** ③ **05** ③ **06** ③ **07** ② **08** ②
09 ② **10** ④

01
정답 ①　　정답률 49%

정답 풀이

(A) 반의어(allow / forbid)
➡ 글의 흐름상 마찰을 피하기 위해 동료가 자신의 에너지를 빼앗도록 '허용할' 지도 모른다는 내용이 와야 하므로 allow가 들어가는 것이 알맞다. forbid는 '금지하다'라는 의미의 반의어이다.

(B) 반의어(frustrated / satisfied)
➡ 가족 구성원들에게 거절당한다는 느낌을 주지 않기 위해 항상 그렇다고 답하는 것이 결국 자신에게는 '좌절감'을 준다는 내용이 문맥상 자연스러우므로 frustrated이 들어가는 것이 알맞다. satisfied는 '만족한'이라는 의미의 반의어이다.

(C) 반의어(ignoring / fulfilling)
➡ 뒤에 우리가 의미 있는 삶을 살게 하는 것을 포기한다는 내용이 이어지는 것으로 보아 앞에 자신의 욕구를 '무시한다'는 내용이 들어가는 것이 알맞다. 따라서 ignoring이 들어가야 한다. fulfill은 '성취하다'라는 의미의 반의어이다.

구문 분석 Plus

6행	At home you may say yes to family members [**who** give you a hard time to avoid their emotional rejection], *only to feel* frustrated by the lack of quality time that you have for yourself. ➡ who: family members를 선행사로 하는 주격 관계대명사 ➡ only to-v: '(…했으나 결국) ~하고 말았다'는 의미로, 결과를 나타내는 부사적 용법의 to 부정사

지문 해석

우리 대부분은 죄책감을 느끼거나 다른 사람들을 실망하게 할 수 있는 가능성에 직면했을 때 우리의 욕구를 제쳐둠으로써 위험을 무릅쓰지 않는다. 직장에서 당신은 마찰을 피하기 위해 불평하는 직장 동료가 계속 당신의 에너지를 빼앗아가는 것을 허용하여, 결국 당신의 직업을 싫어하게 될지도 모른다. 집에서 당신은 정서적인 거절을 피하기 위하여 당신을 힘들게 하는 가족 구성원들에게 '그래'라고 말해, 결국 당신 자신을 위해 가지는 양질의 시간의 부족으로 좌절하게 될지도 모른다. 우리는 자신의 욕구를 무시한 채로 다른 사람들의 (우리에 대한) 인식을 관리하기 위해 열심히 노력하고, 결국 우리가 의미 있는 삶을 살도록 해줄 바로 그것을 포기한다.

어휘

play it safe 안전책을 강구하다 **put aside** …을 제쳐두다 **guilty** 형 죄책감을 느끼는 **allow** 동 허용하다 **forbid** 동 금지하다 **conflict** 명 마찰, 갈등 **end up** 결국 …하게 되다 **rejection** 명 거부, 거절 **frustrated** 형 좌절한 **satisfied** 형 만족한 **quality** 형 질 좋은 **manage** 동 관리하다 **perception** 명 인식 **ignore** 동 무시하다 **fulfill** 동 채우다, 성취하다 **in the end** 결국

02
정답 ③　　정답률 69%

정답 풀이

③ 반의어(improbable → possible)
➡ 음악가들이 음악을 기억할 때 한 음 한 음 개별적으로 기억하는 것이 아니라 음악이 연주되는 과정을 기억한다고 했으므로, 음악가들이 음악적인 과정을 기억함으로써 기억의 성취가 '일어날 것 같지 않게 되는' 것이 아니라 '가능해지는' 것이다. 따라서 improbable(일어날 것 같지 않은)을 possible(가능한) 등으로 바꾸는 것이 적절하다.

친절한 오답 풀이

① struggle 동 분투하다
② memory 명 기억
④ mentally 부 정신적으로, 마음[머릿]속으로
⑤ start 명 시작, 처음

구문 분석 Plus

1행	If we **had** to encode it in our brains note by note, we**'d struggle** to make sense of anything *more complex than* the simplest children's songs. ➡ If + 주어 + 동사의 과거형 …, 주어 + 조동사의 과거형 + 동사원형 …: 현재 사실과 반대되는 일을 가정하는 가정법 과거 ➡ 비교급 + than: …보다 더 ~한
15행	It's rather like describing [**how** you drive to work]: …. ➡ how 이하는 동명사 describing의 목적어 역할을 하는 관계부사절

지문 해석

덩어리로 나누는 것은 음악을 인식하기 위해 필수적이다. 만일 우리가 그것을 한 음 한 음 우리의 뇌에서 부호화해야 한다면 우리는 가장 간단한 동요보다 더 복잡한 어느

것이든 이해하기 위해 분투하게 될 것이다. 물론, 대부분의 기량이 뛰어난 음악가들은 한 음도 틀리지 않고 수천 개의 음을 포함하는 작품을 완전히 기억해서 연주할 수 있다. 그렇지만 겉보기에는 굉장한 것 같은 이러한 기억의 성취는 보통 말하는 그런 개별적인 음을 기억하는 것이 아니라 음악적인 '과정'을 기억함으로써 일어날 것 같지 않게 되는(→ 가능해지는) 것이다. 만일 피아니스트에게 모차르트 소나타를 41번 마디부터 시작해 달라고 요청하면, 그녀는 아마도 그 음악을 처음부터 머릿속으로 재생해서 그 마디까지 와야 할 것이다. 그 악보는 그저 그녀의 머릿속에 펼쳐져 있어서 어떤 임의의 지점부터 읽힐 수 있는 것이 아니다. 그것은 흡사 여러분이 운전해서 직장에 가는 방법을 설명하는 것과 같다. 여러분은 추상적인 목록으로 길의 이름을 단순히 열거하는 것이 아니고 머릿속에서 그것을 되짚어감으로써 여러분의 경로를 구성해야 한다. 음악가들이 리허설 중에 실수한다면, 그들은 다시 시작하기 전에 한 악구의 처음으로 되돌아간다('2절부터 다시 합시다').

vital 휑 필수적인 encode 동 부호화하다 note 명 메모; *음 accomplished 휑 기량이 뛰어난 composition 명 작품 seemingly 튐 겉보기에는 recall 명 기억(하는 능력) as such 보통 말하는 그런 score 명 득점; *악보 lay ... out …을 펼치다 random 휑 임의의, 무작위의 recite 동 열거하다 abstract 휑 추상적인 retrace 동 되짚어가다 wind back 원래 방향으로 되돌아가다 phrase 명 악구 verse 명 (노래의) 절

03 정답 ⑤ 정답률 34%

정답 풀이

⑤ 반의어(encouraged → limited)
➡ 과학기술의 발전이 불러오는 변화는 때론 불편하며 사람들은 본능적으로 이러한 불편함을 싫어한다고 했다. 따라서 새로운 과학기술이 우리의 삶을 향상할 수 있다는 생각은 편안함을 추구하는 욕구로 '장려되는(encouraged)' 것이 아니라 '제한될(limited)' 수 있다.

친절한 오답 풀이

① threat 명 위협
② hate 명 증오; 아주 싫은 것[사람]
③ least 휑 가장 적은
④ unrealized 휑 실현되지 않은

코드+α 구문 분석 Plus

2행
This is **one of the main reasons** why technology is often resisted and why some perceive it as a threat.
➡ one of + 복수 명사: … 중 하나
➡ why: reasons를 선행사로 하는 관계부사
➡ perceive A as B: A를 B로 인식하다

4행
It is important [**to understand** our natural hate of *being* uncomfortable] when we consider the impact of technology on our lives.
➡ It은 가주어, to understand ... uncomfortable이 진주어
➡ being은 전치사 of의 목적어로 쓰인 동명사

지문 해석

과학기술의 발전은 흔히 변화를 강요하는데, 변화는 불편하다. 이것은 과학기술이 흔히 저항을 받고 일부 사람들이 그것을 위협으로 인식하는 주된 이유 중 하나이다. 과학기술이 우리 삶에 끼치는 영향력을 고려할 때 우리는 불편함에 대한 우리의 본능적인 싫어함을 이해하는 것이 중요하다. 사실, 우리의 대부분은 최소한의 저항의 길을 선호한다. 이 경향은 많은 사람들에게 새로운 무엇인가를 시작하는 것이 너무 힘든 일일 뿐이기 때문에 새로운 과학기술의 진정한 잠재력이 실현되지 않은 채로 남아 있을 수 있다는 것을 의미한다. 심지어 새로운 과학기술이 어떻게 우리의 삶을 향상할 수 있는가에 관한 우리의 생각은 편안함을 추구하는 욕구로 장려될(→ 제한될) 수 있다.

force 동 강요하다 uncomfortable 휑 불편한 resist 동 저항하다 (resistance 명 저항[반대]) perceive 동 인식하다 impact 명 영향, 충격 tendency 명 경향 potential 명 잠재력 struggle 명 투쟁; *힘든 것 enhance 동 강화하다 desire 명 욕망 comfort 명 안락, 편안

04 정답 ③ 정답률 30%

정답 풀이

③ 반의어(cultivate → intrude on)
➡ 청소년의 감정 조절을 위해서는 부모가 자율적 감정 조절을 간접적으로 지원해야 한다는 글이므로, 직접적인 위로와 지시가 청소년의 자율성 추구에 방해가 된다는 내용이 되어야 한다. 따라서 cultivate(장려하다)를 intrude on(방해하다) 등으로 바꾸는 것이 적절하다.

친절한 오답 풀이

① primary 휑 주된
② similar 휑 유사한
④ adjust 동 조정하다
⑤ indirect 휑 간접적인

코드+α 구문 분석 Plus

7행
For example, their own responses **to** emotional situations serve as a role model for emotion regulation, {*increasing* the likelihood [**that** their children will show similar reactions in comparable situations]}.
➡ to는 '…로(에)'의 의미인 전치사
➡ increasing 이하는 결과를 나타내는 분사구문
➡ that은 the likelihood와 동격 관계의 절을 이끄는 접속사

지문 해석

다른 사람들로부터 감정과 감정을 다루는 방법을 배우는 감정 사회화는 어릴 때부터 시작되며 감정 조절 발달에 기초적인 역할을 한다. 청소년기에는 또래나 미디어와 같은 가족 이외의 영향이 중요해지지만, 부모는 여전히 주된 사회화 주체이다. 예를 들어, 감정적 상황에 대한 부모 자신의 반응이 감정 조절의 롤모델이 되어 자녀가 비슷한 상황에서 유사한 반응을 보일 가능성을 높인다. 자녀가 정서적 어려움에 직면했을 때 부모의 (습관적) 행동 또한 감정 조절 발달에 영향을 미친다. 직접적인 위로와 어떻게 해야 하는지에 대한 지시적 안내가 어린 자녀에게는 도움이 되지만, 청소년의 자율성 추구를 장려할(→ 방해할) 수 있다. 결과적으로 부모의 행동이 조정되지 않는다면, 청소년은 정서적 위기 상황에서 부모에게 의지하기보다 오히려 부모로부터 멀어질 수 있다. 청소년기에 더 적합한 것은 청소년의 정서적 경험에 대한 인식과 무비판적 수용뿐만 아니라 (그에 대한) 관심, 그리고 청소년이 대화하고 싶을 때 곁에 있어 주는 것과 같은 방법으로 자율적 감정 조절을 간접적으로 지원하는 것이다.

socialization 명 사회화 foundational 휑 기초적인 regulation 명 조절 extrafamilial 휑 가족 이외의 adolescence 명 청소년기 agent 명 주체, 행위자 likelihood 명 가능성 comparable 휑 비슷한 practice 명 (습관적) 행동 whereas 접 반면에 soothing 명 위로 directive 휑 지시적인 beneficial 휑 도움이 되는 autonomy 명 자율성 striving 명 추구 turn toward …에 의지하다 suitable 휑 적합한 awareness 명 인식 nonjudgmental 휑 무비판적인

05 정답 ③ 정답률 50%

정답 풀이

③ 문맥상 반의어(hard-earned → sudden)
➡ 갑작스럽게 성공했을 때 우리가 성공은 노력을 해야 얻을 수 있다는 기본적인 지혜를 보지 못한다고 했으므로, '갑작스러운' 이익에 있어 운이 하는 역할을 고려하지 않는다는 의미가 문맥상 자연스럽다. 따라서 hard-earned(애써서 얻은)를 sudden(갑작스러운)

등으로 바꾸는 것이 적절하다.

 친절한 오답 풀이

① repeat 통 반복하다
② lose 통 잃다
④ resistant 형 저항하는
⑤ fall 명 추락; *하락

 구문 분석 Plus

15행	Because this cannot be sustained, we experience an inevitable fall, {**which** is all the more painful, [*leading* to the depression part of the cycle]}. ➡ which 이하는 선행사 an inevitable fall을 부연 설명하는 계속적 용법의 주격 관계대명사절 ➡ leading 이하는 결과를 나타내는 분사구문(= therefore it leads to ...)

지문 해석

갑작스러운 성공이나 상금은 아주 위험할 수 있다. 신경학적으로 흥분과 에너지의 강력한 분출을 유발하는 화학물질들이 뇌에서 분비되고, 이 경험을 반복하고자 하는 욕구로 이어진다. 그것이 어떤 종류의 중독 또는 광적 행동의 출발점일 수 있다. 또한, 이익이 빨리 얻어질 때, 우리는 진정한 성공이 정말 지속되기 위해서는 노력을 해야 한다는 기본적인 지혜를 보지 못하는 경향이 있다. 우리는 그처럼 어렵게 얻은(→ 갑작스러운) 이익에 있어 운이 하는 역할을 고려하지 않는다. 우리는 그렇게 많은 돈이나 관심을 얻는 것에서 오는 그 황홀감을 되찾기 위해 계속해서 시도한다. 우리는 우월감을 얻게 된다. 우리는 특히 우리에게 경고하려고 하는 사람에게 저항하게 된다. 그들은 이해하지 못한다고 우리 자신에게 이야기한다. 이것은 지속될 수 없기 때문에 우리는 필연적인 하락을 경험하는데, 그것은 더 고통스러우며, 그 사이클의 우울한 시기로 이어진다. 도박꾼들이 가장 이러기 쉽지만, 이것은 거품 경제일 때의 사업가들과 대중으로부터 갑작스러운 관심을 얻은 사람들에게도 똑같이 적용된다.

 어휘

winning 명 승리; 《*pl.*》 *상금 (**win** 통 이기다; *얻다)   **neurologically** 부 신경학적으로   **release** 통 발산하다   **burst** 명 분출   **addiction** 명 중독   **manic** 형 (열의·흥분·걱정 등으로) 미친 듯한   **gain** 명 《*pl.*》 이익   **lose sight of** …을 못 보다   **take into account** 고려하다   **recapture** 통 (과거의 느낌·경험을) 되찾다   **high** 명 황홀감   **superiority** 명 우월성   **sustain** 통 지속시키다   **inevitable** 형 불가피한   **gambler** 명 도박꾼   **be prone to-v** …하기 쉽다   **businesspeople** 명 사업가들   **bubbles** 명 〈경제〉 거품   **public** 명 대중, 일반 사람들

06　　　　정답 ③　　　정답률 43%

정답 풀이

③ 반의어(benefits → drawbacks)
➡ 소수의 작물에만 의존하는 것은 인류를 기아나 농업의 손실에 취약한 상태에 둘 수 있으며, 생물의 다양성을 고려해야 한다는 내용이므로 단일 경작이 가져올 잠재적 '이점'이 아니라 '결점'을 인식해야 한다는 것이 문맥상 자연스럽다. 따라서 benefits(이점)를 drawbacks(결점)로 고치는 것이 적절하다.

친절한 오답 풀이

① vulnerable 형 취약한
② primarily 부 주로
④ ensure 통 보장하다
⑤ balance 명 균형

 구문 분석 Plus

1행	Human innovation in agriculture has unlocked modifications in apples, tulips, and potatoes that never would **have been realized** .... ➡ have been realized: '…되어 왔다'라는 뜻의 현재완료 수동태
4행	This cultivation process has created some of the recognizable vegetables and fruits [[**which/that**] consumers look for in their grocery stores]. ➡ consumers ... stores: 선행사 some of the recognizable vegetables and fruits를 수식하는 목적격 관계대명사절로, 앞에 which나 that이 생략돼 있음

지문 해석

농업에서 인류의 혁신은 식물의 자연적 번식 주기를 통해서는 결코 실현할 수 없었을 사과, 튤립, 감자에 있어 개량을 가능케 했다. 이러한 경작 과정은 소비자들이 식료품 가게에서 찾는, 몇몇의 알아볼 수 있는 채소나 과일을 만들어냈다. 그러나 만약 추수가 망쳐지면 소수의 재배된 작물에만 의존하는 것은 인류를 기아나 농업의 손실에 취약한 상태에 둘 수도 있다. 예를 들어, 아일랜드 사람들이 영양학적으로 균형 있는 식사를 마련하기 위해 주로 감자와 우유에 의존했기 때문에, 아일랜드 감자 기근 (사태) 동안 백만 명의 사람들이 3년의 추이에 걸쳐 사망했다. 재배 식물과 공생 관계를 유지하려면, 인류는 생물의 다양성을 고려해야만 하고 식물의 단일 경작이 가져올 수 있는 잠재적 이점(→ 결점)에 대해서도 인식해야만 한다. 설령 그것들이 당장은 유용하고 이득이 된다고 보이지는 않아도 모든 종류의 씨앗을 심는 것은 다가올 세대들을 위해 그러한 식물들이 오래 지속되는 것을 보장해 줄 수 있다. 야생에 대한 자연의 능력과 통제에 대한 인간의 욕망 사이에서 균형은 유지되어야 한다.

 어휘

modification 명 수정, 변경   **reproductive** 형 생식의, 번식의   **cultivation** 명 경작, 재배   **vulnerable** 형 취약한   **starvation** 명 기아, 굶주림   **harvest** 명 수확, 추수   **famine** 명 기근   **primarily** 부 주로   **nutritionally** 부 영양학적으로   **biodiversity** 명 생물 다양성   **potential** 형 잠재적인   **monoculture** 명 단일 경작   **profitable** 형 수익성이 있는, 이득이 되는   **ensure** 통 보장하다   **longevity** 명 오래 지속됨   **generation** 명 세대   **capacity** 명 능력   **desire** 명 욕구, 욕망

07　　　　정답 ②　　　정답률 58%

정답 풀이

(A) 반의어(complexity / simplicity)
➡ 바로 뒤에서 군집의 종이 풍부할수록 더 안정적이라 말하고 있으므로, 군집 안정성은 군집 '복잡성'의 결과임을 알 수 있다. 따라서, complexity가 들어가는 것이 적절하다. simplicity는 '단순성'이라는 의미의 반의어이다.

(B) 반의어(likely / unlikely)
➡ 군집 안에 종이 다양하면 하나의 종의 중요도는 낮아진다는 앞의 내용으로 보아, 어떤 단 하나의 교란이 군집 체계의 기능에 영향을 미칠 가능성이 '적으므로' unlikely가 들어가는 것이 적절하다. likely는 '…할 것 같은'이라는 의미의 반의어이다.

(C) 반의어(common / uncommon)
➡ 글의 흐름상, 군집 복잡성이 높은 자연 군집에서보다 군집 복잡성이 낮은 경작지에 해충의 피해가 더 '흔하게' 나타날 것임을 추론할 수 있다. 따라서, common이 들어가는 것이 적절하다. uncommon은 '흔하지 않은'이라는 의미의 반의어이다.

구문 분석 Plus

8행	According to this view, **the greater** the species richness, **the less** critically important any single species should be. ➡ the + 비교급 ..., the + 비교급 ~: …하면 할수록 더 ~하다
14행	Evidence for this hypothesis includes the fact {**that** destructive outbreaks of pests are more common in cultivated fields, [*which* are low-diversity communities], than in natural communities with greater species richness}. ➡ that: the fact와 동격인 명사절을 이끄는 접속사 ➡ which: cultivated fields를 선행사로 하는 계속적 용법의 주격 관계대명사

지문 해석

전통적으로, 대부분의 생태학자는 한 군집이 환경 교란을 견디는 능력인 군집 안정성이 군집 복잡성의 결과라고 추정했다. 즉, 종 풍부도가 높은 군집이 종 풍부도가 덜한 군집보다 더 잘 기능하고 더 안정적일 수 있다. 이 관점에 의하면, 종의 풍부도가 높으면 높을수록 어떤 하나의 종은 결정적으로 덜 중요할 것이다. 군집 안에서 가능한 많은 상호작용으로, 어떤 단 하나의 교란이 그 체계의 기능에서 중대한 차이를 가져올 만큼 체계의 구성 요소에 영향을 미칠 수 있을 것 같지는 않다. 이 가설의 증거는 파괴적인 해충의 발생이 종 풍부도가 높은 자연 군집에서보다 다양성이 낮은 군집인 경작지에서 더 흔하다는 사실을 포함한다.

 어휘

ecologist 뗑 생태학자 **assume** 뚱 추정하다 **stability** 뗑 안정, 안정성 (**stable** 뗑 안정적인) **withstand** 뚱 견디다 **disturbance** 뗑 교란 **consequence** 뗑 결과 **complexity** 뗑 복잡성 **simplicity** 뗑 단순성 **considerable** 뗑 상당한, 많은 **species richness** (해양과학) 종 풍부도 **critically** 뿌 결정적으로 **component** 뗑 요소 **hypothesis** 뗑 가설 **destructive** 뗑 파괴적인 **outbreak** 뗑 발생 **cultivated field** 경작지 **diversity** 뗑 다양성

08 정답 ② 정답률 60%

정답 풀이

(A) 문맥상 적절한 단어(creating / forgiving)
➡ 관계를 형성하기 위해 다른 사람과 경쟁하기도 한다고 했으므로, 소문을 통해 잠재적인 적을 '만들어낸다'라는 의미의 creating이 들어가는 것이 알맞다. forgiving은 '용서하다'라는 의미이다.

(B) 문맥상 반의어(harmony / tension)
➡ 라이벌 관계에 있는 파티나 더 많은 친구와 팔로워를 얻기 위해 경쟁을 하는 소셜 미디어에서 이러한 '긴장감'을 볼 수 있다는 내용이 자연스러우므로 tension이 들어가는 것이 알맞다. harmony는 '화합'이라는 의미이다.

(C) 문맥상 반의어(generate / prevent)
➡ 고등학교 친목 동아리와 컨트리 클럽에서의 경쟁적 배제가 충성과 지속적인 유대를 형성하게 한다고 했으므로 경쟁적 배제가 협력을 '만들어낸다'는 의미의 generate가 들어가는 것이 알맞다. prevent는 '막다'라는 의미이다.

 구문 분석 Plus

1행	Social connections are **so** essential for our survival and well-being **that** we *not only* cooperate with others to build relationships, we *also* compete with others for friends. ➡ so + 형용사 + that ...: 너무 ~해서 …하다 ➡ not only A (but) also B: A뿐만 아니라 B도
15행	...: **It is** through selective inclusion and exclusion **that** they produce loyalty and lasting social bonds. ➡ 부사구 through selective inclusion and exclusion을 강조하는 「It is ... that」 강조구문

지문 해석

사회적 관계는 우리의 생존과 행복을 위해 매우 필수적이어서 우리는 관계를 형성하기 위해 다른 사람들과 협력할 뿐만 아니라, 친구를 얻기 위해 다른 사람들과 경쟁하기도 한다. 그리고 우리는 자주 동시에 둘 다를 한다. 소문을 생각 해보자. 소문을 통해 우리는 친구들과 흥미로운 세부 사항을 공유하면서 유대를 형성한다. 그러나 동시에 우리는 소문의 대상들 중에서 잠재적인 적을 만들어낸다. 또는 누가 '그들의' 파티에 참석할 것인지를 알아보기 위해 경쟁하는 라이벌 관계의 휴일 파티를 생각해 보라. 우리는 심지어 소셜 미디어에서도 사람들이 가장 많은 친구와 팔로워를 얻기 위해 경쟁할 때 이러한 긴장감을 볼 수 있다. 동시에 경쟁적 배제는 협력도 만들어낼 수 있다. 고등학교 친목 동아리와 컨트리 클럽은 이러한 공식을 사용하여 큰 효과를 발휘한다. 그들이 충성과 지속적인 사회적 유대를 형성하는 것은 바로 선택적인 포함과 '배제'를 통해서이다.

 어휘

well-being 뗑 (건강과) 행복, 웰빙 **cooperate** 뚱 협력하다 (**cooperation** 뗑 협력) **gossip** 뗑 소문, 험담 **bond** 뚱 유대를 형성하다; 뗑 유대 **potential** 뗑 잠재적인 **rival** 뗑 경쟁하는 **attend** 뚱 참석하다 **exclusion** 뗑 배제 **formula** 뗑 공식, …식 **selective** 뗑 선택적인 **inclusion** 뗑 포함 **loyalty** 뗑 충성 **lasting** 뗑 지속적인

09 정답 ② 정답률 36%

정답 풀이

② 반의어(forbid → encourage)
➡ 불신을 받는다는 인식은 자기 성찰의 동기를 제공한다고 했으므로 자신에 대한 타인의 불신을 깨달은 직원은 그들의 신뢰를 받을 수 있는 방식으로 자신의 의무를 수행하도록 고무될 것이다. 따라서 불신은 그 직원이 자기 성찰을 통해 자신의 의무를 수행하도록 '금지하는(forbid)' 것이 아니라 '고무한다(encourage)'라는 내용으로 고치는 것이 알맞다.

▌친절한 오답 풀이▐

① realize 뚱 깨닫다
③ sincere 뗑 진실된, 진정한
④ suspicious 뗑 의심스러운
⑤ break 뚱 (법·약속 등을) 어기다

 구문 분석 Plus

3행	An employee [**who** realizes she *isn't being trusted* by her co-workers with shared responsibilities at work] might, upon reflection, identify areas [**where** she has consistently let others down or failed to follow through on previous commitments]. ➡ who: An employee를 선행사로 하는 주격 관계대명사 ➡ is being v-ed: '… 되고 있다'라는 의미의 현재 진행형 수동태 ➡ where: areas를 선행사로 하는 관계부사
10행	But distrust of one [**who** is sincere in her efforts *to be* a trustworthy and dependable person] can be disorienting and might cause her *to doubt* her own perceptions and *to distrust* herself. ➡ who: one을 선행사로 하는 주격 관계대명사 ➡ to be: 앞의 명사 efforts를 수식하는 형용사적 용법의 to부정사 ➡ cause A to-v: A가 …하게 하다, cause의 목적격보어로 쓰인 to부정사 to doubt와 to distrust가 접속사 and로 병렬 연결됨

지문 해석

때때로 불신을 받는다는 인식은 자기 성찰에 필요한 동기를 제공할 수 있다. 자신이 직장에서의 공유하는 책임을 가진 동료들로부터 신뢰를 받지 못하고 있다는 것을 깨달은 직원은, 성찰하자마자 자신이 다른 사람들을 지속적으로 실망시키거나 이전의 책무를 끝내지 못했던 영역을 확인할 수 있을 것이다. 그러면 그에 대한 다른 사람들의 불신은 자신이 그들의 신뢰를 받을 만한 가치가 더 있도록 만드는 방식으로 자신의 몫의 의무를 수행하도록 금지할(→ 고무할) 수도 있을 것이다. 그러나 믿음직하고 신뢰할 수 있는 사람이 되기 위한 노력을 진실되게 하는 사람에 대한 불신은 방향감각에 혼란을 가져올 수 있고 그 자신의 인식을 의심하게 하고 자신을 불신하도록 야기할 수도 있다. 예를 들어,

밤에 외출할 때 부모가 의심하고 불신하는 10대 청소년을 생각해 보라. 비록 그가 자신의 계획에 대해 솔직하고 합의된 어떤 규칙도 어기고 있지 않더라도, 존경할 만한 도덕적인 주체로서의 그녀의 정체성은 기만과 배신을 예상하는 널리 스며있는 부모의 태도에 의해 훼손된다.

awareness 몡 인식 distrust 통 불신하다 incentive 몡 동기 self-reflection 몡 자기 성찰 identify 통 확인하다(identity 몡 정체) consistently 븐 지속적으로 follow through …을 끝내다 commitment 몡 책무 worthy 헹 …을 받을 만한 dependable 헹 신뢰할 수 있는 disorient 통 …의 방향 감각을 혼란시키다 perception 몡 인식 distrustful 헹 불신하는 respectable 헹 존경할 만한 moral 헹 도덕적인 undermine 통 훼손하다 deceit 몡 기만

10   정답 ④   정답률 55%

정답 풀이

④ 반의어(inappropriate → appropriate)
➡ 뒤에서 의도적인 운영 체계가 피로나 스트레스, 정서적인 요인에 의한 인지 부하의 증가로 작동이 멈추면 부적절한 생각이 들 수 있다고 했으므로, 의도적인 운영 체계가 정상적으로 작동할 때는 의도된 생각과 일치하지 않는 생각이 '적절한' 생각으로 대체된다는 의미가 문맥상 자연스럽다. 따라서, inappropriate(부적절한)를 appropriate(적절한) 등으로 바꿔주는 것이 적절하다.

친절한 오답 풀이

① more 븐 더
② ironic 헹 역설[모순]적인, 아이러니한
③ unrelated 헹 관련 없는
⑤ accessible 헹 접근하기 쉬운

코드+α 구문 분석 Plus

11행
This dual-process system involves, first, an intentional operating process, {**which** consciously attempts to locate thoughts [*unrelated* to the suppressed ones]}.
➡ which 이하는 선행사 an intentional operating process을 부연 설명하는 계속적 용법의 주격 관계대명사절
➡ unrelated 이하는 thoughts를 수식하는 과거분사구

지문 해석

내가 여러분에 '흰곰을 생각하지 말라.'라고 말하면, 여러분은 흰곰을 생각하지 않는 것이 어렵다는 것을 알게 될 것이다. 이런 식으로, '사고의 억제가 실제로는 억누르고 싶은 생각을 가라앉히는 대신, 생각을 증가시킬 수 있다'. 이것의 한 가지 흔한 예는 다이어트를 하고 있어서 음식에 대해 생각하지 않으려고 노력하는 사람들이 흔히 음식에 대해 훨씬 더 많이 생각하기 시작한다는 것이다. 따라서 이 과정은 '반동 효과'라고도 알려져 있다. 그 아이러니한 결과는 관련된 두 가지 인지 과정의 상호 작용에 의해 야기되는 것 같다. 우선, 이 이중 처리 체계는 의도적인 운영 과정을 포함하는데, 그것은 억제된 생각과 무관한 생각을 의식적으로 찾아내려고 한다. 다음으로, 그리고 동시에, 무의식적인 감시 과정은 운영 체계가 효과적으로 작동하고 있는지 검사한다. 감시 체계가 의도된 생각과 일치하지 않는 생각을 마주치는 경우, 그것은 의도적인 운영 과정을 자극하여 반드시 이러한 생각이 부적절한(→ 적절한) 생각으로 대체되도록 한다. 그러나 주장되는 바로는, 의도적인 운영 체계는 피로, 스트레스와 정서적 요인에 의해 생긴 증가된 인지 부하로 인해 작동을 멈출 수 있고, 그래서 감시 과정이 부적절한 생각을 의식으로 스며들게 해, 그것을 매우 접근하기 쉽게 만든다는 것이다.

suppression 몡 억제, 억압 (suppress 통 억압하다; *억누르다) rebound effect (심리학) 반동 효과 (흰곰을 떠올리지 말라고 요구하면 흰곰만 생각하게 되는 것처럼, 의도한 것과 반대 효과가 나타나는 것) interplay 몡 상호 작용 cognitive 헹 인지의 dual 헹 이중의 intentional 헹 의도적인 consciously 븐 의식적으로 locate 통 찾아내다 simultaneously 븐 동시에 unconscious 헹 무의식적인 monitor 통 감시하다 encounter 통 마주치다 inconsistent with …와 일치하지 않는 prompt 통 자극하다 ensure 통 반드시 …하게 하다 replace 통 대체하다 load 몡 부담; *부하 fatigue 몡 피로 filter 통 거르다; *스며들게 하다

UNIT 2 어휘 형태

코드 접속하기   pp.131~133

출제코드 1   유사한 형태

A 1 corrected 2 delicate 3 provide 4 attention
   5 transfer   6 lacking   7 crucial

해석과 정답 풀이

STEP 2

A 1 마침내, 그녀는 그녀의 실수를 알아챘고 그것을 고쳤다.
➡ 실수를 '고쳤다'가 문맥상 자연스러우므로 corrected가 오는 것이 알맞다. collect는 '모으다, 수집하다'라는 의미이다.
  2 바나나 나무의 몸통은 많은 양의 물을 함유하고 있고 매우 연약하다.
➡ 나무의 몸통이 '연약하다'가 문맥상 자연스러우므로 delicate이 오는 것이 알맞다. deliberate는 '고의의'라는 의미이다.
  3 다람쥐들은 추운 겨울에 그들 자신에게 음식을 공급하기 위해 여름과 가을 동안 견과류를 묻어둔다.
➡ 음식을 '공급하다'가 문맥상 자연스러우므로 provide가 오는 것이 알맞다. prohibit은 '금하다, 금지하다'라는 의미이다.
  4 어떤 회사들은 프로 스포츠 팀을 후원하는데, 이는 대중의 관심을 끌어모은다.
➡ 대중의 '관심'을 끄는 것이라는 의미가 문맥상 자연스러우므로, attention이 오는 것이 알맞다. intention은 '의도'라는 의미이다.
  5 올림픽 규정에 따르면, 사람들은 표를 다른 누군가에게 양도할 수는 있지만, 재정적 이익을 위한 것이어서는 안 된다.
➡ 표를 다른 사람에게 '양도하다'가 문맥상 자연스러우므로 transfer가 오는 것이 알맞다. transform은 '변형시키다'라는 의미이다.
  6 그녀는 그 영화가 흥미로운 줄거리와 현실적인 등장인물이 부족했기 때문에 지루하다고 느꼈다.
➡ 흥미로운 줄거리와 현실적인 등장인물이 '부족하다'가 문맥상 자연스러우므로 lacking이 오는 것이 알맞다. leak는 '새게 하다'라는 의미이다.
  7 우리가 도미노 집 쌓기를 거의 다 마쳤을 때, Josh가 너무 결정적인 실수를 해서 그것이 무너졌다.
➡ '결정적인' 실수로 도미노 집이 무너졌다는 것이 문맥상 자연스러우므로 crucial이 오는 것이 알맞다. cruel은 '잔인한'이라는 의미이다.

출제코드 2   파생어

A 1 prescribed   2 attend   3 interrupted 4 contain
   5 contributing 6 observe 7 popularity   8 perform

해석과 정답 풀이

STEP 2

A 1 몇몇 약은 피부의 노화과정을 늦추기 위해 처방된다.
➡ 약이 '처방된다'가 문맥상 자연스러우므로 prescribed가 오는 것이 알맞다. subscribe는 '(신문 등을) 구독하다'라는 의미이다.
  2 많은 학생들이 직업 교육을 위한 지역 전문대학에 다닌다.
➡ 학생들이 대학에 '다닌다'가 문맥상 자연스러우므로 attend가 오는 것이 알맞다. intend는 '의도하다'라는 의미이다.
  3 어젯밤 음악회는 음향 장치 고장으로 중단되었다.
➡ 음악회가 '중단되었다'가 문맥상 자연스러우므로 interrupted가 오는 것이 알맞다. erupt는 '분출하다'라는 의미이다.
  4 에너지 음료는 당신의 건강에 해로운 높은 수치의 카페인과 설탕을 함유한다.
➡ 음료가 카페인과 설탕을 '함유하다'가 문맥상 자연스러우므로 contain이 오는 것이 알맞다. sustain은 '지속하다'라는 의미이다.
  5 그 영화배우는 자선 단체에 많은 돈을 기부하는 것으로 유명하다.
➡ 자선 단체에 돈을 '기부하는 것'이 문맥상 자연스러우므로 contributing이 오는 것이 알맞다. attribute는 '…의 탓으로 돌리다'라는 의미이다.
  6 연구자들은 재난으로 이어지는 환경 조건을 관찰하기 위해 위성 자료를 사용한다.
➡ 환경 조건을 '관찰하다'가 문맥상 자연스러우므로 observe가 오는 것이 알맞다. preserve는 '보존하다'라는 의미이다.

7 새로운 자전거 공유 프로그램 덕분에 그 도시에서 도심 자전거 타기가 대단한 인기를 얻었다.

➡ 자전거 타기가 '인기'를 얻었다는 의미가 문맥상 자연스러우므로 popularity가 오는 것이 알맞다. population은 '인구'라는 의미이다.

8 만약 당신이 유연성을 유지한다면 긴장된 근육을 혹사하지 않고 일상활동을 할 수 있을 것이다.

➡ 활동을 '행하다'가 문맥상 자연스러우므로 perform이 오는 것이 알맞다. inform은 '알리다, 통지하다'라는 의미이다.

기출예제 Q1   정답 ②   정답률 53%

정답 풀이

(A) 유사한 형태(hesitancy / consistency)
➡ 앞에 프랑스인들은 새 기술을 쓰는 것이 느렸다고 언급했고, 이런 '주저함'에 몇 가지 이유가 있었다는 내용이 이어지는 것이 문맥상 자연스러우므로 hesitancy가 오는 것이 알맞다. consistency는 '일관성'이라는 의미이다.

(B) 유사한 형태(distribution / description)
➡ 앞에 텔레비전 프로그램 개발 비용이 많이 들어 산출량이 적었다고 언급했고, 빈약한 '배급'으로 제품 구입을 유인하지 못했다는 내용이 이어지는 것이 문맥상 자연스러우므로 distribution이 오는 것이 알맞다. description은 '묘사'라는 의미이다.

(C) 반의어(optimistic / skeptical)
➡ 프랑스 엘리트들이 텔레비전을 미국화와 대중문화의 전령으로 여겼다는 내용이 뒤에 이어지는 것으로 보아, 앞에 이들이 텔레비전에 대해 '회의적'이었을 것이라는 내용이 오는 것이 문맥상 자연스러우므로 skeptical이 오는 것이 적절하다. optimistic은 '낙관적인'이라는 의미의 반의어이다.

지문 해석

텔레비전 방송의 첫 번째 실험은 1930년대에 프랑스에서 시작되었지만, 프랑스인들은 그 새로운 기술을 사용하는 것이 느렸다. 이런 주저함에는 몇 가지 이유가 있었다. 라디오가 정부 자원의 대부분을 써버렸고, 프랑스 정부는 텔레비전 방송을 위한 전국적인 방송망을 개발하는 재정적인 부담을 떠맡는 것을 꺼려했다. 텔레비전의 프로그램을 짜는 비용은 너무 높았고, 그에 상응하는 프로그램의 산출량은 낮았다. 아주 적은 제공 편수와 결합된 빈약한 배급은 그 새로운 상품을 구매할 유인을 거의 제공하지 않았다. 뿐만 아니라, 텔레비전 수상기는 특히 1930년대와 1940년대에 변변찮은 생활 수준이 사치스런 상품의 취득을 허용하지 않았던 일반 대중의 수입을 넘어서서 가격이 매겨져 있었다. 이데올로기적인 영향력도 또한 요인에 들어 있었다. 엘리트들이 특히 텔레비전에 대해 회의적이었고, 그것을 대중문화와 미국화의 전령으로 인식했다.

어휘

experiment 몡 실험   **broadcasting** 몡 방송   **employ** 통 고용하다; *쓰다, 이용하다   **absorb** 통 흡수하다; *(돈·시간을) 잡아먹다   **majority** 몡 대부분   **reluctant** 혱 꺼리는, 주저하는   **shoulder** 통 떠맡다   **financial** 혱 재정적인   **burden** 몡 부담   **output** 몡 산출(량)   **correspondingly** 뮈 상응하여, 일치하여   **minimal** 혱 최소한의   **incentive** 몡 유인, 동기   **means** 몡 수단; *(pl.) 재력, 수입   **modest** 혱 수수한, 하찮은   **living standard** 생활 수준   **acquisition** 몡 취득, 습득   **luxury** 혱 사치스런   **perceive** 통 감지[인지]하다   **messenger** 몡 전령, 사자   **mass culture** 대중문화

코드 공략하기   pp.134~136

01 ①   **02** ①   **03** ②   **04** ③   **05** ②   **06** ①   **07** ⑤   **08** ③

---

01   정답 ①   정답률 73%

정답 풀이

(A) 유사한 형태(poverty / property)
➡ 교육의 기회를 증진시키는 것이 '빈곤'을 줄이는 열쇠라는 의미가 문맥상 자연스러우므로,

---

poverty가 들어가는 것이 알맞다. property는 '재산'이라는 의미이다.

(B) 유사한 형태(receive / deceive)
➡ 뒤에 여자 아이들은 돈을 벌거나 가족을 돌보기 위해 학교를 다니지 않는다고 했으므로 교육을 '받기' 어렵다는 내용이 와야 한다. 따라서, receive가 들어가는 것이 적절하다. deceive는 '속이다, 기만하다'라는 의미이다.

(C) 반의어(strengthens / weakens)
➡ 교육으로 여자 아이들이 좋은 직업을 가진 여성으로 성장하면 장기적인 면에서 경제가 '강화되는' 것이므로 strengthens가 들어가는 것이 적절하다. weaken은 '약화시키다'라는 의미의 반의어이다.

 구문 분석 Plus

> **9행**
> A great deal of research shows an important connection **between** *increasing* educational opportunities ***and*** *improving* the economic conditions of poor countries.
> ➡ between A and B: A와 B 사이에
> ➡ increasing과 improving이 이끄는 동명사구가 접속사 and에 의해 병렬 연결되어 있음

지문 해석

유니세프(국제아동기금)에 따르면, 개발도상국가에서 빈곤을 감소시키는 열쇠 중 하나는 아이들, 특히 여자 아이들에게 교육의 기회를 증진시키는 것이다. 가난한 국가에서 여자 아이들이 교육을 받는 것은 종종 어렵다. 여자 아이들은 일을 하거나 가족을 돌봐야 하기 때문에 종종 학교에 다니지 않거나 중도에 그만두어야 한다. 상당량의 조사는 교육의 기회를 증가시키는 것과 가난한 국가들의 경제적 상황을 개선하는 것 사이의 중요한 관계를 보여준다. 교육은 여자 아이들이 좋은 직업을 가진 여성으로 자라도록 도와줄 수 있다. 이것이 장기적인 면에서 경제를 강화시킨다.

 어휘

poverty 몡 빈곤   **property** 몡 재산   **opportunity** 몡 기회   **deceive** 통 속이다, 기만하다   **attend** 통 참석하다   **drop out** 중퇴하다   **strengthen** 통 강화하다   **weaken** 통 약화시키다   **in the long term** 장기적으로

---

02   정답 ①   정답률 54%

정답 풀이

(A) 유사한 형태(accumulate / stimulate)
➡ 일부만 사용되고 나머지는 배출되는 비타민과 달리 비타민 A와 D는 몸에 '축적되어' 건강에 해를 줄 수 있다는 의미가 되어야 하므로 accumulate가 들어가는 것이 적절하다. stimulate는 '자극하다, 활성화시키다'라는 의미이다.

(B) 유사한 형태(version / vision)
➡ 비타민 A의 과다 복용으로 인한 부작용에 대해 이야기하고 있으므로 '시력'이 약해진다는 내용이 와야 한다. 따라서 vision이 들어가는 것이 알맞다. version은 '-판'이라는 의미이다.

(C) 유사한 형태(prescribed / subscribed)
➡ 뒤에 이어지는 예로 보아 어떤 비타민은 의학적인 목적을 위해 '처방되기도' 한다는 내용이 와야 한다. 따라서, prescribed가 들어가는 것이 알맞다. subscribe는 '구독하다'라는 의미이다.

 구문 분석 Plus

> **4행**
> Other vitamins, especially Vitamins A and D, accumulate in the body and can cause damage **if** (**they are**) **taken** in extremely high amounts over a period of time.
> ➡ if taken: if 뒤에 「주어 + be동사」인 they are가 생략됨. 시간과 조건의 부사절에서 주절과 같은 주어와 뒤따르는 be동사는 종종 생략됨

비타민제는 당신의 건강에 위험할 수 있을까? 만약 당신이 너무 많이 복용하면, 그렇다. 어떤 비타민의 경우, 몸은 필요한 만큼만 사용하고 나머지는 배출해버린다. 다른 비타민들, 특히 비타민 A와 D는 일정 기간 동안 과하게 많은 양이 섭취되면 몸에 축적되어 해를 줄 수 있다. 예를 들어, 과하게 많은 양의 비타민 A는 결국 간 손상과 시력 저하로 이어질 수 있다. 반면에 종합비타민제를 정기적으로 복용하는 것은 안전하며, 어떤 비타민들은 심지어 의학적인 목적으로 처방되기도 한다. 예를 들면, 니아신은 엄격한 의학적 통제하에 콜레스테롤 수치를 낮추기 위해 아주 다량 사용된다.

 어휘

pill 명 알약, 정제 rest 명 나머지 accumulate 동 축적하다; *모이다 stimulate 동 자극하다 extremely 부 극도로 liver 명 간 blurred 형 흐릿한 version 명 –판, 형태 vision 명 시력 prescribe 동 처방하다 subscribe 동 (신문 등을) 구독하다 dosage 명 (약의) 정량, 복용량 strict 형 엄격한 supervisioin 명 감독, 통제 lower 동 낮추다

03 　　　　　정답 ②　　　정답률 67%

정답 풀이

(A) 문맥상 반의어(remove / reproduce)
➡ 문맥상 손을 씻는 것이 불가능할 때 물티슈, 크림, 그리고 스프레이는 세균을 '제거하는' 데 도움이 될 것이므로 remove가 들어가는 것이 적절하다. reproduce는 '번식시키다'라는 의미로 문맥상 반의어이다.

(B) 반의어(valuable / valueless)
➡ 물티슈, 크림, 그리고 스프레이는 손 씻기를 대체할 수 없지만 '소중한' 두 번째 방어선이 될 수는 있다는 의미가 되어야 하므로, valuable이 들어가는 것이 알맞다. valueless는 '무가치한'이라는 의미의 반의어이다.

(C) 유사한 형태(organism / organization)
➡ 앞에 나온 Environmental Working Group은 비영리 '단체'일 것이므로 organization이 들어가는 것이 알맞다. organism은 '유기체'라는 의미이다.

 구문 분석 Plus

1행	It's well known {that washing your hands with good old-fashioned soap and water is a great way [to help prevent disease]}. ➡ It은 가주어, that 이하가 진주어 ➡ to help: a great way를 수식하는 형용사적 용법의 to부정사
4행	There are plenty of wipes, creams, and sprays on store shelves [that promise to remove germs without the addition of running water]. ➡ that: plenty ... shelves를 선행사로 하는 주격 관계대명사

지문 해석

옛날식의 좋은 비누와 물로 손을 씻는 것이 질병을 예방하는 데 도움을 주는 훌륭한 방법이라는 것은 잘 알려져 있다. 그 방법을 선택할 수 없을 때 당신은 어떻게 하는가? 상점의 선반에 수돗물을 추가로 사용하지 않고도 세균을 제거한다고 보장하는 많은 물티슈, 크림, 그리고 스프레이들이 있다. 그것들이 통상적인 손 씻기를 대체할 수는 없지만, 소중한 두 번째 방어선이 될 수는 있다. 이런 제품들의 대부분은 알코올이 기본 성분이다. 개인 관리 제품들에 관해 폭넓은 연구를 해온 비영리 단체인 Environmental Working Group의 선임 분석가인 Sonya Lunder에 따르면 알코올은 일반적으로 안전하고 효과적이다.

 어휘

old-fashioned 형 옛날식의, 구식의 prevent 동 예방하다 wipe 명 물티슈 remove 동 제거하다 reproduce 동 번식시키다 germ 명 세균, 미생물 addition 명 덧셈; *추가 running water 수돗물 substitute 명 대체물 valuable 형 소중한, 귀중한 valueless 형 무가치한 defense 명 방어 analyst 명 분석가 non-profit 형 비영리적인 organism 명 유기체 organization 명 단체 extensive 형 아주 넓은; *광범위한, 폭넓은

04 　　　　　정답 ③　　　정답률 54%

정답 풀이

(A) 유사한 형태(collected / corrected)
➡ 문맥상 작가 생텍쥐페리가 하인을 돕기 위해 천 프랑을 '모았다'가 되어야 하므로, collected가 들어가는 것이 알맞다. correct는 '바로잡다, 정정하다'라는 의미이다.

(B) 유사한 형태(general / generous)
➡ 문맥상 하인이 가장 좋은 식당으로 가서 '후한' 팁을 주었다가 되어야 하므로, generous가 들어가는 것이 알맞다. general은 '일반적인'이라는 의미이다.

(C) 유사한 형태(instrument / investment)
➡ 고향에 가서 돈을 많이 쓴 하인은 고향 사람들의 관심을 얻고, 직장도 얻을 수 있을 것이므로, 그의 행동은 사람에 대한 '투자'임을 추론할 수 있다. 따라서, investment가 들어가는 것이 알맞다. instrument는 '도구'라는 의미이다.

 구문 분석 Plus

13행	[Spending in that way], he managed to win all over again the respect of his countrymen, and they will offer him a job. ➡ Spending: 이유를 나타내는 분사구문(= Because he spent ...) ➡ manage to-v: 간신히 ···하다

지문 해석

작가 생텍쥐페리가 아프리카의 비행 기지에 머물고 있었을 때, 모로코 출신 하인이 고향으로 돌아가는 것을 도우려고 동료들로부터 천 프랑을 모금했다. 그 하인을 그의 고향까지 태워다 준 조종사 중 한 명이 "그는 도착하자마자, 가장 좋은 식당으로 가서, 후한 팁을 주고, 모든 사람의 음식과 술값을 내고, 마을 아이들에게 인형을 사주더군. 이 사람은 경제관념이라고는 조금도 없었어."라고 말했다. "그 반대일세. 그는 세상에서 가장 좋은 투자는 사람에게 있다는 것을 알았다는 걸세. 그렇게 돈을 썼기 때문에, 그는 고향 사람들의 관심을 다시 얻을 수 있게 되고, 그들이 그에게 일자리를 제공할 거네."라고 생텍쥐페리는 답했다.

 어휘

air base 공군 기지 collect 동 모으다 correct 동 바로잡다, 정정하다 servant 명 하인 hand out 나누어 주다 general 형 일반적인 generous 형 후한, 넉넉한 all round 모든 사람에게 slight 형 약간의 notion 명 개념 opposite 형 정반대의 instrument 명 도구 investment 명 투자 all over again 다시 countryman 명 (어떤 고장의) 출신자, 주민

05 　　　　　정답 ②　　　정답률 48%

정답 풀이

(A) 유사한 형태(daybreak / outbreak)
➡ 앞에서 세계적으로 많은 사람들이 말라리아에 걸린다고 했으므로, 역사상 가장 큰 규모의 말라리아 '발병' 사례가 이어지는 것이 적절하다. 그러므로 outbreak가 들어가야 한다. daybreak는 '새벽'이라는 의미이다.

(B) 유사한 형태(thrive / thrill)
➡ 바로 뒤에 모기가 남극에 넘쳐난다는 내용이 오는 것으로 보아, 모기는 추운 온도에서 '창궐한다'는 것을 추론할 수 있다. 따라서 thrive가 들어가는 것이 알맞다. thrill은 '열광시키다'라는 의미이다.

(C) 유사한 형태(transmit / transcribe)
➡ 전체 380여 종의 모기 중 60종만이 기생충을 '옮긴다'는 내용이 문맥상 적절하므로, transmit이 들어가는 것이 알맞다. transcribe는 '기록하다'라는 의미이다.

 구문 분석 Plus

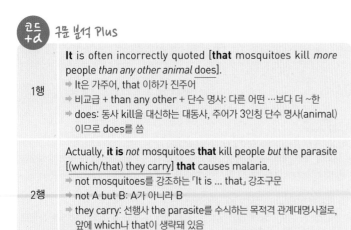

1행	It is often incorrectly quoted [**that** mosquitoes kill *more* people *than any other animal* does]. ➡ It은 가주어, that 이하가 진주어 ➡ 비교급 + than any other + 단수 명사: 다른 어떤 …보다 더 ~한 ➡ does: 동사 kill을 대신하는 대동사, 주어가 3인칭 단수 명사(animal)이므로 does를 씀
2행	Actually, **it is** *not* mosquitoes **that** kill people *but* the parasite [(which/that) they carry] **that** causes malaria. ➡ not mosquitoes를 강조하는 「It is ... that」 강조구문 ➡ not A but B: A가 아니라 B ➡ they carry: 선행사 the parasite를 수식하는 목적격 관계대명사절로, 앞에 which나 that이 생략돼 있음 ➡ that: the parasite를 선행사로 하는 주격 관계대명사

지문 해석

다른 어떤 동물들이 그러는 것보다 모기가 더 많은 사람을 죽인다고 종종 부정확하게 인용되고 있다. 사실, 사람을 죽이는 것은 모기가 아니라 모기가 옮기고 다니는 말라리아를 유발하는 기생충이다. 세계적으로 대략 3억 명의 사람들이 말라리아에 걸리고 매년 150만 명의 사람들이 말라리아로 죽는다. 알려진 가장 엄청난 말라리아의 발병은 1920년대 러시아에서 일어났는데 1,300만 명이 말라리아에 걸렸고 60만 명이 죽었다. 또한 모기는 추운 온도에서 창궐하는 것으로 증명됐다. 모기는 남극에서 넘쳐난다. 전 세계에 약 380종의 모기가 있으나, 60종만이 기생충을 옮긴다.

어휘

quote 圄 인용하다, 전달하다 mosquito 圀 모기 approximately 凰 대략 affect 圄 영향을 끼치다; *병에 걸리다 daybreak 圀 새벽 outbreak 圀 발병 thrive 圄 창궐하다 thrill 圄 열광시키다 temperature 圀 온도, 기온 abundant 圀 넘치는 Antarctica 圀 남극 대륙 transmit 圄 전송하다; *전염시키다 transcribe 圄 기록하다

06   정답 ①   정답률 35%

정답 풀이

(A) 파생어(popularity / population)
➡ 전국적인 '인기'를 얻고 있는 팀이 수백만 달러의 가치가 있을 것이라는 의미가 문맥상 자연스러우므로 popularity가 들어가야 한다. population은 '인구'라는 의미이다.

(B) 유사한 형태(attention / intention)
➡ 대학은 선수에 대한 투자로 돈을 벌고 '주목'을 받을 것이므로 attention이 들어가는 것이 알맞다. intention은 '의도'라는 의미이다.

(C) 반의어(valued / neglected)
➡ 뒤에 학생 선수들이 운동 말고는 배우는 것이 없다고 이야기하는 것으로 보아 앞에 대학선수들이 대학생보다는 운동선수로 더 '존중되는' 것처럼 보인다는 내용이 오는 것이 알맞다. 따라서 valued가 들어가야 한다. neglected는 '방치된'이라는 의미의 반의어이다.

 구문 분석 Plus

5행	The athletes often get a free education and gain experience [**that** might lead to a chance *to play* professionally]. ➡ that: experience를 선행사로 하는 주격 관계대명사 ➡ to play: a chance를 수식하는 형용사적 용법의 to부정사
10행	They say {**that** some players [*who* finish college] never really learn anything except their sport}. ➡ that: 동사 say의 목적어 역할을 하는 명사절을 이끄는 접속사 ➡ who: some players를 선행사로 하는 주격 관계대명사

지문 해석

대학 스포츠는 하나의 큰 산업이다. 전국적인 인기를 얻고 있는 팀은 수백만 달러의 가치가 있을 수 있다. 그래서 대학들은 그들의 선수에게 투자를 하고, 그 대신 학교는 돈을 벌고 주목을 받는다. 선수들은 흔히 무료 교육을 받으며, 프로선수로 활동할 기회로 이어질 수도 있는 경험을 얻는다. 하지만 이를 비난하는 사람들은 대학선수들이 대학생으로보다는 운동선수로 더 존중되는 것처럼 보일 수도 있는 상황의 도덕성에 의문을 제기한다. 그들은 대학을 마친 몇몇 운동선수들이 운동을 제외하고는 정말로 아무것도 배우는 것이 없다고 말한다.

어휘

industry 圀 산업 nationwide 圀 전국적인 popularity 圀 인기 population 圀 인구 invest 圄 투자하다 in return 대신에 attention 圀 관심, 주목 intention 圀 의도 athlete 圀 (운동)선수 morality 圀 도덕(성) valued 圀 존중되는 neglected 圀 방치된

07   정답 ⑤   정답률 42%

정답 풀이

(A) 반의어(familiar / unfamiliar)
➡ 아이들의 두려움이 정상적인 이유는 아이들이 경험하는 것 중 많은 것들이 '친숙하지 않기' 때문일 것이다. 따라서, unfamiliar가 들어가는 것이 알맞다. familiar는 '친숙한'이라는 의미의 반의어이다.

(B) 파생어(sensitive / sensible)
➡ 대부분의 아이들과 달리 일부 아이들이 두려움을 극복하는 데 힘든 시간을 보내는 이유는 두려움에 '민감하기' 때문일 것이다. 따라서 sensitive가 와야 한다. sensible은 '분별[지각]있는, 현명한'이라는 의미이다.

(C) 유사한 형태(expended / expected)
➡ 문맥상 두려움을 극복할 것으로 '예상되는' 나이를 넘어서 지속될 때, 그 사람은 지나친 두려움과 불안을 겪고 있다는 신호일 것이다. 따라서, expected가 들어가는 것이 알맞다. expended는 '소비되는'이라는 의미이다.

 구문 분석 Plus

12행	When fears last beyond the expected age, it might be a sign [**that** someone is overly fearful, worried, or anxious]. ➡ that 이하는 앞의 명사 a sign과 동격을 이루는 명사절

지문 해석

어린 시절에 어떤 두려움은 정상적인 것이다. 그것은 두려움이 불확실한 감정에 대한 자연스러운 반응일 수 있고, 아이들이 경험하는 많은 것들이 익숙하지 않기 때문이다. 어린 아이들은 종종 어둠, 혼자 있는 것, 낯선 사람, 괴물 또는 다른 무서운 상상의 생물체에 대한 두려움을 가지고 있다. 학령기의 아이들은 폭풍이 몰아치거나 처음으로 집 밖에서 잘 때 무서워할지 모른다. 대부분의 아이들은 어른의 도움을 받으며 성장하고 학습함에 따라, 천천히 이러한 두려움을 정복하고 그것들에서 벗어날 수 있다. 어떤 아이들은 두려움에 더 예민해져서 그것을 극복하는 데 힘든 시간을 보낼지도 모른다. 두려움이 예상되는 나이를 넘어서 지속될 때, 그것은 그 사람이 과도하게 두려워하거나, 걱정하거나, 또는 근심한다는 신호일 수 있다. 두려움이 너무 강하거나 너무 오랫동안 지속되는 사람들은 그것을 극복하기 위해 도움이나 후원을 필요로 할지 모른다.

unsure 형 불확실한 stranger 명 낯선[모르는] 사람 scary 형 무서운, 겁나는 imaginary 형 상상의, 가상의 sleep-over 명 외박 conquer 통 정복하다, 물리치다 outgrow 통 …에서 벗어나다 sensitive 형 민감한, 예민한 sensible 형 분별[지각]있는, 현명한 tough 형 힘든, 어려운 overcome 통 극복하다 expend 통 소비하다 expect 통 기대하다 intense 형 극심한, 강렬한 support 명 지원, 후원

---

08   정답 ③   정답률 65%

정답 풀이

(A) 유사한 형태(assists / resists)

➡ 뒤에 이어지는 내용으로 보아, 실질적으로 도움이 되는 선물이 이상적이지만, 우리 마음 속 다른 부분은 그 생각에 '저항한다'고 기술하고 있으므로 resists가 들어가는 것이 알맞다. assist는 '돕다'라는 의미이다.

(B) 유사한 형태(originality / utility)

➡ 100달러를 현금으로 선물 받아, 자신에게 필요한 타이어를 산다면 '효용성'이 극대화될 것이다. 따라서 utility가 들어가는 것이 알맞다. originality는 '독창성'이라는 의미이다.

(C) 반의어(luxurious / ordinary)

➡ 앞에서 사랑하는 사람이 생일 선물로 자동차 타이어를 준다면 기쁘지 않을 것이라고 했으므로, 대부분 선물을 주는 사람이 덜 '평범한' 것을 주기를 바란다는 내용이 적절하다. 따라서 ordinary가 들어가는 것이 알맞다. luxurious는 '호화로운'이라는 의미의 반의어이다.

> **콘드+α 구문 분석 Plus**
>
> 3행
>
> He offers a good counterexample to the practical notion {that the ideal gift is an item [(which/that) we would have bought for ourselves]}: ....
>
> ➡ that: the practical notion과 동격을 이루는 명사절을 이끄는 접속사
>
> ➡ we ... ourselves: 선행사 an item을 수식하는 목적격 관계대명사절로, 앞에 목적격 관계대명사 which나 that이 생략돼 있음

지문 해석

"내 마음 속의 경제학자는 가장 좋은 선물이 현금이라고 말한다."라고 경제학자이자 블로거인 Alex Tabarrok은 쓰고 있다. "내 안의 나머지는 저항한다." 그는 이상적인 선물은 우리가 우리 자신을 위해서 구입했을 물건이라는 실리적인 생각에 대한 좋은 반례를 제공하고 있다. 누가 당신에게 100달러를 주어서, 당신이 자동차 타이어 한 세트를 산다고 가정하자. 이것은 효용을 극대화하는 것이다. 그러나 사랑하는 사람이 당신의 생일 선물로 자동차 타이어를 준다면 당신은 별로 기뻐하지 않을지도 모른다. Tabarrok이 지적하는 바에 따르면, 대부분의 경우, 우리는 선물을 주는 사람이 우리에게 덜 평범한 것을 사주기를 바란다. 적어도 우리는 가까운 사람들로부터, "야성적인 자아, 열정적인 자아, 낭만적인 자아"에게 호소하는 선물을 더 받고 싶어 한다.

economist 명 경제학자 assist 통 돕다 resist 통 저항하다 counterexample 명 반례 practical 형 실질적인, 실리적인 notion 명 개념, 생각 maximize 통 극대화하다 originality 명 독창성 utility 명 (경제) 효용, 유용성 luxurious 형 호화로운 ordinary 형 평범한 intimate 명 절친한 친구 speak to …에 호소하다 self 명 자신; *자아 passionate 형 열정적인

모의고사 1회   pp.138~140

01 ② 02 ① 03 ③ 04 ⑤ 05 ⑤ 06 ③ 07 ⑤ 08 ③
09 ② 10 ③

---

01   정답 ②   정답률 39%

정답 풀이

② 지각동사의 목적격보어

> I enjoyed the ride home / and **watched** my fellow passengers
> 나는 집에 버스 타고 가기를 즐겼다   그리고 동행 승객들이 내리는 것을 지켜보았다
> wacth + 목적어 + 동사원형/v-ing: …가 ~하는[하고 있는] 것을 보다
> got off(→ get[getting] off) / at their stops.
> 정류장에서

➡ 지각동사 watched의 목적격보어로, 목적어와 목적격보어가 능동 관계에 있으므로 got off를 동사원형 get off나 현재분사 getting off로 고쳐야 한다.

> **콘드+α   Grammar Tips**
>
> **지각동사의 목적격보어**
>
> see, look at, watch, observe, hear, listen to, feel, notice, perceive 등의 지각동사는 동사원형, 현재분사, 과거분사를 목적격보어로 취할 수 있다.
>
> | 형태 | 의미 | 예시 |
> |---|---|---|
> | 지각동사 + 목적어 + **동사원형** (목적어와 목적격보어가 능동 관계) | …가 ~하는 것을 (동사)하다 | I **heard** her **sing** in the bathroom. (나는 그녀가 화장실에서 노래하는 것을 들었다.) |
> | 지각동사 + 목적어 + **현재분사** (목적어와 목적격보어가 능동 관계이고, 동작이 진행 중일 때) | …가 ~하고 있는 것을 (동사)하다 | I **heard** her **singing** in the bathroom. (나는 그녀가 화장실에서 노래하고 있는 것을 들었다.) |
> | 지각동사 + 목적어 + **과거분사** (목적어와 목적격보어가 수동 관계) | …가 ~되는 것을 (동사)하다 | I **heard** my name **repeated** several times. (나는 내 이름이 여러 번 반복되는 것을 들었다) |

친절한 오답 풀이

① 접속사

> It was late in the evening / when I finished, / so I ran down the
>   접속사
> 늦은 저녁이었다   내가 일을 마쳤을 때   그래서 나는 거리를 뛰어내려갔다
> street / to the bus stop.
> 버스 정류장까지

➡ when은 접속사로, 절과 절을 이어주고 있고, when 뒤에 완전한 절이 이어지고 있으므로 어법상 바르다.

③ 명사를 수식하는 과거분사

> After a while, I was the only one / [left on the bus].
>   과거분사
> 잠시 뒤, 내가 유일한 사람이었다   버스에 남겨진

➡ 앞의 대명사 the only one을 수식하는 분사로, 버스에 '남겨진'이라는 수동의

의미이므로 과거분사 left의 쓰임은 적절하다.

④ 접속사

> I explained to him / [that I lived just up the next street].
> 나는 그에게 설명했다　　명사절(목적어)을 이끄는 접속사　바로 다음 거리에 산다고

➡ 동사 explained의 목적어의 역할을 하는 명사절을 이끌고 있고, 뒤에 완전한 절이 이어지고 있으므로 접속사 that은 어법상 바르다.

⑤ 분사구문

> I thanked the bus driver and walked to my door, / {knowing [that
> 나는 버스 기사에게 고맙다고 했고 문으로 걸어갔다　동시동작을 나타내는 분사구문(= as I knew ...) 접속사　그의 친절함을 절대 잊지
> I would never forget his kindness]}.
> 않을 것이라 생각하면서

➡ knowing 이하는 동시동작을 나타내는 분사구문으로, 생략된 주어는 주절의 주어(I)와 같다. 주어와 분사가 능동 관계이므로 현재분사 knowing이 오는 것이 알맞다.

지문 해석

나는 양로원에서 일하고 있었다. 내가 일을 마쳤을 때 늦은 저녁이었고, 그래서 나는 버스 정류장까지 거리를 뛰어내려갔다. 나는 집에 버스 타고 가기를 좋아했고, 동행 승객들이 정류장에서 내리는 것을 지켜보았다. 잠시 뒤에, 내가 버스에 남겨진 유일한 사람이었다. 버스가 내가 내릴 정거장에 다가왔을 때, 버스 기사가 나에게 "어디 사세요?"라고 소리쳤다. 나는 그에게 바로 다음 거리에 산다고 설명했다. 그러자 그는 나를 집 앞에 내려주겠다고 제안했다. 나는 그의 제안이 매우 고마웠다. 나는 버스 기사에게 고맙다고 했고, 그의 친절함을 절대 잊지 않을 것이라 생각하면서 문으로 걸어갔다.

nursing home 양로원　fellow 몡 동료　passenger 몡 승객　get off 내리다
approach 통 다가가다　offer 통 제안하다 몡 제안　drop 통 내려주다　grateful
톙 고마워하는, 감사하는　kindness 몡 친절함

02　　　정답 ①　　정답률 51%

정답 풀이

(A) 반의어(available / unavailable)

➡ 더 안전한 대안이 비슷한 비용으로 '이용될 수 있는데(available)' 업계에서는 이 사실을 거부한다는 내용이 문맥상 자연스럽다. unavailable은 '이용할 수 없는'이라는 의미를 가진 반의어이다.

(B) 유사한 형태(predicting / preventing)

➡ 화학 업계에서는 냉장하지 않으면 경제적인 재앙과 수많은 사망자가 발생할 거라고 '예측했다(predicting)'는 의미가 문맥상 자연스럽다. prevent는 '막다'라는 의미이다.

(C) 반의어(necessary / unnecessary)

➡ 살충제 업계에서 합성 살충제가 식량을 재배하는 데 '필요하다(necessary)'고 주장했으나 유기농 농부들은 그들이 틀렸음을 입증하고 있다는 내용이 문맥상 자연스럽다. unnecessary는 '불필요한'이라는 의미를 가진 반의어이다.

코드 +α 구문 분석 Plus

> 9행
> The chemical industry denied {that there were practical alternatives to ozone-depleting chemicals, [*predicting* not only economic disaster but numerous deaths because food and vaccines would spoil without refrigeration]}.
> ➡ that: denied의 목적어 역할을 하는 명사절을 이끄는 접속사
> ➡ predicting 이하는 동시동작을 나타내는 분사구문
> ➡ not only A but (also) B: A뿐만 아니라 B도

지문 해석

오늘날 사용 중인 모든 독성 물질, 공정, 혹은 제품에는 — 이미 존재하거나 인간의 지력,

독창성, 그리고 노력의 적용을 통해 발견되기를 기다리고 있는 — 더 안전한 대안이 있다. 거의 모든 경우에, 더 안전한 대안이 비슷한 비용으로 이용될 수 있다. 업계는 이러한 사실을 거부하고 높은 실행 비용에 대해 불평할지도 모르지만, 역사가 그런 내용을 바로잡는다. 화학 업계에서는 냉장하지 않으면 식품과 백신이 상할 것이라는 이유로 경제적인 재앙뿐만 아니라 수많은 사망자를 예측하면서 오존을 고갈시키는 화학 물질에 대한 실용적인 대안이 있다는 것을 부인했다. 그들은 틀렸다. 자동차 업계는 처음에 자동차가 대기 오염을 유발한다는 것을 부인하였고, 그다음에는 자동차로부터의 오염을 줄이는 어떤 기술도 존재하지 않는다고 주장했으며, 나중에 대기 오염을 줄이는 장치를 설치하면 자동차가 엄청나게 비싸질 것이라고 주장했다. 그들은 매번 틀렸다. 살충제 업계에서는 합성 살충제가 식량을 재배하기 위해 절대적으로 필요하다고 주장한다. 수많은 유기농 농부들은 그들이 틀렸음을 입증하고 있다.

toxic 톙 독성의　substance 몡 물질　process 몡 과정; *공정　alternative
몡 대안　in existence 현존하는　application 몡 적용　intellect 몡 지력,
지성　ingenuity 몡 독창성　comparable 톙 비슷한　reject 통 거부하다
set the record straight (일반적으로 잘못 알려진 내용을) 바로잡다　practical
톙 실용적인　disaster 몡 재해, 재앙　numerous 톙 많은　spoil 통 상하다
refrigeration 몡 냉장　initially 뮈 처음에　claim 통 요구하다; *주장하다
install 통 설치하다　device 몡 장치　absolutely 뮈 절대적으로

03　　　정답 ③　　정답률 62%

정답 풀이

③ 가주어 진주어 구문

> It is better / [what(→ that) you make your mistakes early on /
> 가주어　　진주어, that은 접속사　　초기에
> 더 낫다　　일찍이 실수를 저지르는 것이
> rather than later in life].
> 인생에서 나중보다

➡ 가주어 It에 대한 진주어 역할을 하는 명사절을 이끌고 있고 뒤에 완전한 절이 이어지므로 관계대명사 what을 접속사 that으로 고쳐야 한다.

친절한 오답 풀이

① 대동사 do

> You may make some foolish spending choices, / but if you do, /
> 당신은 몇 가지 어리석은 소비 선택을 할 수도 있다　　　그러나 당신이 그런다면
> the decision to do so is your own ....
> 그렇게 하려는 결정은 당신 자신의 것이다　　　형용사적 용법의 to부정사

➡ 밑줄 친 do는 앞에 나온 동사구(make ... choices)를 대신하는 대동사로 어법상 바르다.

② 동사의 수 일치

> Much of learning occurs / through trial and error.
> much of + 셀 수 없는 명사 + 단수 동사　　　시행착오
> 배움의 많은 부분이 일어난다　　　시행착오를 거쳐서

➡ much of 뒤에는 셀 수 없는 명사와 단수 동사가 이어져야 하므로, 단수 동사 occurs는 어법상 바르다.

④ 명사적 용법의 to부정사

> Explain / {that you will have a family someday / and you need to
> 명사절(목적어)을 이끄는 접속사　　　need to-v: …할 필요가 있다
> 설명해라　당신이 언젠가는 가정을 갖게 될 것이라는 것과　당신이 알 필요가 있다는 것을
> know / [how to manage your money]}.
> how to-v: …하는 법
> 자신의 돈을 관리하는 법을

➡ 의문사 how 뒤에 쓰인 to manage는 명사적 용법의 to부정사로 어법상 바르다.

⑤ 수동태

> Not everything is taught at school!
> 모든 것이 …인 것은 아니다(부분부정)
> 모든 것이 다 학교에서 가르쳐지는 것은 아니다!

➡ 주어 everything은 동작의 주체가 아니라 대상으로, '가르쳐지는'이라는 수동의 의미가 적절하므로 수동태 is taught가 오는 것이 알맞다.

 지문 해석

당신의 부모님은 당신이 용돈을 현명하게 쓰지 않을 것을 걱정할 수도 있다. 당신은 몇 가지 어리석은 소비 선택을 할 수도 있지만, 당신이 그런다면, 그렇게 하려는 결정은 당신 자신의 것이고, 바라건대 당신은 자신의 실수로부터 배울 것이다. 배움의 많은 부분이 시행착오를 거쳐서 일어난다. 돈은 당신이 남은 인생 동안 처리해야 할 어떤 것임을 당신의 부모님께 설명해라. 인생에서 나중보다 일찍이 실수를 저지르는 것이 더 낫다. 당신이 언젠가 가정을 갖게 될 것이라는 것과 자신의 돈을 관리하는 법을 알 필요가 있다는 것을 설명해라. 모든 것이 다 학교에서 가르쳐지는 것은 아니다!

allowance 명 용돈 **wisely** 부 현명하게 **choice** 명 선택 **decision** 명 결정 **hopefully** 부 바라건대 **occur** 통 일어나다, 발생하다 **manage** 통 관리하다

04 　　　　　정답 ⑤ 　　정답률 82%

정답 풀이

(A) 반의어(disgrace / honor)
➡ 에베레스트 산 정상에 오르는 것이 놀라운 업적이었던 때에, 등반에 성공한 등반가를 국가적 '영예(honor)'라는 의미가 문맥상 자연스럽다. disgrace는 '불명예'라는 의미의 반의어이다.

(B) 문맥상 반의어(difficult / possible)
➡ 앞에 과거와 달리 오늘날 에베레스트 산 등반에 성공한 사람 수가 크게 늘어났다고 했으므로, 많은 사람들의 성공이 '가능해진(possible)' 요인에 대한 내용이 이어지는 것이 문맥상 자연스럽다. difficult는 '어려운'이라는 의미이다.

(C) 문맥상 적절한 단어(lack / presence)
➡ 뒤에 오늘날에는 정확한 날씨 정보를 가지고 등반 시점을 정한다는 내용이 이어지고 있으므로, 이와 반대로 앞에는 과거의 정보 '부족(lack)'과 관련 내용이 들어가는 것이 문맥상 자연스럽다. presence는 '존재'라는 의미이다.

구문 분석 Plus

2행	It was even a national honor {**to have** a climber [*waving* a national flag there]}. ➡ It은 가주어, to have 이하가 진주어 ➡ waving 이하는 앞의 명사 a climber를 수식하는 현재분사구
4행	But [**now that** almost 4,000 people have reached its summit], the achievement means less than it *did* a half century ago. ➡ now that: …이기 때문에 ➡ did: 앞의 일반동사 means를 대신하는 대동사로 과거를 나타내는 부사구 a half century ago와 함께 쓰여 과거형으로 쓰임
9행	Then what makes **it** possible *for so many people* [**to reach** the summit]? ➡ it은 가목적어, to reach 이하가 진목적어 ➡ for so many people: to부정사의 의미상 주어

지문 해석

에베레스트 산 정상에 도달하는 것은 한때 놀라운 업적으로 여겨졌다. 그곳에서 국기를 흔드는 등반가를 갖는 것은 심지어 국가적 영예였다. 그러나 거의 4,000명이 그곳의 정상에 도달했기 때문에, 그 업적은 반세기 전에 그랬던 것보다 의미하는 바가 더 적다. 1963년에, 6명이 정상에 도달했지만, 2012년 봄에, 정상은 500명 이상의 사람들로 붐볐다. 그렇다면 그렇게 많은 사람들이 정상에 도달하는 것을 가능하게 만든 것은 무엇인가? 한 가지 중요한 요인은 향상된 일기예보이다. 과거에, 정보의 부족은 팀

구성원들이 준비가 될 때마다 원정대가 정상 등반을 시도하게 했다. 오늘날, 초정밀 위성 예보로, 모든 팀들은 언제 날씨가 등반을 위해 완벽해질지를 정확하게 알며, 그들은 자주 같은 날에 정상을 향해 간다.

achievement 명 업적 **summit** 명 정상 **disgrace** 명 불명예 **national flag** 국기 **factor** 명 요인 **weather forecasting** 일기예보 **lack** 명 부족 **presence** 명 존재 **expedition** 명 탐험, 원정; *탐험[원정]대 **attempt** 통 시도하다 **hyper-accurate** 형 초정밀의 **satellite** 명 위성

05 　　　　　정답 ⑤ 　　정답률 72%

정답 풀이

⑤ 문맥상 반의어(lacked → had)
➡ 앞에서 실험자들이 잠재 의식적으로 자신들이 발견할 것이라 예상한 것과 일치하는 결과만을 받아들여 '편향'이라는 오류가 나타난다고 했는데, 이러한 패턴은 실험자들이 자신들이 예상한 결과가 아닌 실제 측정된 결과를 보고할 용기가 '있었을' 때가 되어서야 바뀌었다는 의미가 문맥상 적절하다. 따라서 lacked(부족했다)를 had(가지고 있었다) 등으로 바꿔주는 것이 적절하다.

친절한 오답 풀이

① quantity 명 양, 수량
② opposite 형 반대의
③ match 통 일치하다, 아주 비슷하다
④ influence 통 영향을 주다[미치다]

구문 분석 Plus

10행	This kind of error, [**where** results are always on one side of the real value], is called "bias." ➡ where 이하는 선행사 This kind of error를 부연 설명하는 계속적 용법의 관계부사절
18행	The pattern only changed when someone had the courage **to report** what was actually measured instead of [*what was expected*]. ➡ to report: 명사구 the courage를 수식하는 형용사적 용법의 to부정사 ➡ what 이하는 전치사 of의 목적어로 쓰인 관계대명사절

지문 해석

편승 효과가 어떻게 발생하는지는 빛의 속도 측정의 역사로 입증된다. 이 빛의 속도는 상대성 이론의 기초이기 때문에, 과학에서 가장 빈번하고 면밀하게 측정된 수량 중 하나이다. 우리가 아는 한, 빛의 속도는 시간이 흘러도 아무 변화가 없었다. 그러나 1870년부터 1900년까지 모든 실험에서 너무 높은 속도를 발견했다. 그러고 나서, 1900년부터 1950년까지 그 반대 현상이 일어나, 모든 실험에서 너무 낮은 속도를 발견했다! 결과치가 항상 실제 값의 어느 한쪽에 있는 이런 형태의 오류를 '편향'이라고 한다. 그것은 아마 시간이 지나면서 실험자들이 자신들이 발견할 것이라 예상한 것과 일치하도록 잠재 의식적으로 결과를 조정했기 때문에 생겨났을 것이다. 결과가 그들이 예상한 것과 부합하면, 그들은 그것을 유지했다. 결과가 부합하지 않으면, 그들은 그것을 버렸다. 그들은 의도적으로 부정직한 것은 아니었고, 단지 일반 통념에 의해 영향을 받았을 뿐이었다. 그 패턴은 누군가가 예상된 것 대신에 실제로 측정된 것을 보고할 용기가 부족했을(→ 있었을) 때가 되어서야 바뀌었다.

demonstrate 통 입증하다; 보여주다 **measurement** 명 측정, 측량 **basis** 명 근거; *기반, 기초 **relativity** 명 상대성 **as far as** …하는 한 **experiment** 명 실험 (**experimenter** 명 실험자) **bias** 명 편견, 편향 **probably** 부 아마 **subconsciously** 부 잠재 의식적으로 **fit** 통 맞다 **throw out** (제안·아이디어 등을) 물리치다[버리다] **intentionally** 부 의도적으로, 고의로 **conventional wisdom** 일반 통념 **report** 통 알리다, 보고하다

06 정답 ③ 정답률 41%

정답 풀이

(A)「전치사 + 관계대명사」

Select clothing / {appropriate for the temperature and
의류를 선택하라 ／ 형용사구 기온과 환경 조건에 적합한
environmental conditions / [which / in which you will be doing
선행사 ／ 당신이 운동하고 있을
exercise]}.

➡ 네모 이하는 선행사 environmental conditions를 수식하는 관계대명사절로 네모 뒤에 완전한 절이 이어지므로「전치사 + 관계대명사」의 형태인 in which가 와야 한다. 관계대명사 뒤에는 불완전한 절이 온다.

(B) 동사의 수 일치

In warm environments, / clothes [that have a wicking capacity] /
주어 ↑ 주격 관계대명사
따뜻한 환경에서는 수분을 흡수하거나 배출할 수 있는 기능을 가진 옷이
is / are helpful in dissipating heat from the body.
동사 동명사(전치사의 목적어)
몸에서 열을 발산하는 데 도움이 된다

➡ 네모는 문장의 동사 자리로, 문장의 주어에 수를 일치시켜야 한다. 문장의 주어(clothes)가 복수 명사이므로 복수 동사 are가 알맞다.

(C) 형용사

In contrast, / it is best [to face cold environments with layers] /
가주어 진주어
반면 겹겹이 입어서 추운 환경에 대처하는 것이 최선이다
so (that) you can adjust your body temperature / to avoid
so (that) + 주어 + can ...: ~가 ...할 수 있도록 부사적 용법의 to부정사(목적)
체온을 조절하려면 땀을 흘리는 것을 피하고
sweating and (to) remain comfortable / comfortably .
보어
쾌적한 상태를 유지하기 위해

➡ 동사 remain의 보어 자리이므로 형용사 comfortable이 오는 것이 어법상 바르다. 부사는 보어 자리에 올 수 없다.

지문 해석

운동하는 동안 편안함을 제공하기 위해 의류가 비쌀 필요는 없다. 기온과 운동하고 있을 환경 조건에 적절한 의류를 선택하라. 운동과 계절에 적절한 의류는 운동 경험을 향상시킬 수 있다. 따뜻한 환경에서는 수분을 흡수하거나 배출할 수 있는 기능을 가진 옷이 몸에서 열을 발산하는 데 도움이 된다. 반면, 땀을 흘리는 것을 피하고 쾌적한 상태를 유지하기 위해 체온을 조절하려면 겹겹이 입어서 추운 환경에 대처하는 것이 최선이다.

어휘

comfort 명 편안함 **appropriate** 형 적절한 **temperature** 명 기온
environmental condition 환경 조건 **improve** 동 향상시키다 **capacity** 명
능력 **in contrast** 반면 **layer** 명 겹 **adjust** 동 조절하다 **remain** ···한
상태를 유지하다 **comfortable** 형 쾌적한

---

07 정답 ⑤ 정답률 47%

정답 풀이

⑤ 능동태 vs. 수동태

[Although the living supplies for the settlers would send(→ be sent) /
접속사(비록 ···이긴 하지만) 주어 동사
비록 정착민들을 위한 생필품들이 보내지긴 하겠지만
from Earth], / taking the risk of exchanging life for dreams is tough.
동명사구 주어, take the risk of: ···의 위험을 무릅쓰다, exchange A for B: A와 B를 교환하다
지구로부터 꿈과 목숨을 맞바꾸는 위험을 무릅쓰는 것은 힘든 일이다

➡ 생필품이 '보내지는'이라는 수동의 의미가 적절하므로 능동태 send를 수동태 be sent로 고쳐야 한다.

친절한 오답 풀이

① 병렬구조

The U. S. space agency NASA is currently on the Hundred
미 항공 우주국 NASA는 현재 Hundred Years Starship이라는 프로젝트를 추진하고 있다
Years Starship, a project / of exploring new habitable planets /
동격 전치사 전치사의 목적어1
거주 가능한 새로운 행성을 탐사하는
and helping people settle down there.
접속사 전치사의 목적어2 help + 목적어 + 동사원형: ···가 ~하도록 돕다
그리고 사람들이 그곳에 정착하도록 도와주는

➡ 등위접속사 and가 전치사 of의 목적어로 쓰인 동명사를 병렬 연결하고 있는 구조로, 앞의 동명사 exploring과 대등한 동명사 helping은 어법상 바르다.

② 부정형용사

If settlers succeed / in making another planet their home, / it will
···에 성공하다
정착민들이 성공한다면 또 다른 행성을 자신들의 집으로 만드는 데 그것은
become one of the most revolutionary events / in history.
one of the + 최상급 + 복수 명사: 가장 ···한 것들 중 하나
가장 혁명적인 사건 중 하나가 될 것이다 역사상

➡ '또 다른 하나의'라는 의미의 부정형용사 another는 단수 명사와 함께 쓰이는데, 뒤에 단수 명사 planet이 쓰였으므로 어법상 바르다.

③ 수동형 분사구문

(Being) Assumed to have a substantial amount of water, / Mars is
이유를 나타내는 분사구문(= As Mars is assumed ...)
상당한 양의 물이 있다고 추정되므로 화성은
probably most habitable / out of all the planets / in our solar system.
··· 중에
아마도 가장 살 만한 곳이다 모든 행성 중에서 우리 태양계에 있는

➡ 밑줄 친 부분은 이유를 나타내는 분사구문으로, 생략된 주어는 주절의 주어(Mars)와 같다. 화성이 상당한 양의 물을 가지고 있다고 '추정되는' 것으로 주어와 분사가 수동 관계이므로 과거분사 Assumed가 오는 것이 알맞다.

④ 목적격보어

However, this project would take time / since the cost will make a
접속사(··· 때문에)
그러나, 이 프로젝트는 시간이 걸릴 것이다 비용이 지구로의 귀환 비행을
return flight to Earth almost impossible.
make + 목적어 + 형용사: ···을 ~하게 하다
거의 불가능하게 할 것이기 때문에

➡ 동사 make의 목적격보어 자리이므로, 형용사 impossible은 어법상 바르다.

지문 해석

미 항공 우주국 NASA는 거주 가능한 새로운 행성을 탐사하고 사람들이 그곳에 정착하도록 도와주는 Hundred Years Starship이라는 프로젝트를 현재 추진하고 있다. 정착민들이 또 다른 행성을 자신들의 집으로 만드는 데 성공한다면, 그것은 역사상 가장 혁명적인 사건 중 하나가 될 것이다. 상당한 양의 물이 있다고 추정되므로, 화성은 아마도 우리 태양계에 있는 모든 행성들 중에서 가장 살 만한 곳이다. 그러나 비용이 지구로의 귀환 비행을 거의 불가능하게 할 것이기 때문에 이 프로젝트는 시간이 걸릴 것이다. 비록 정착민들을 위한 생필품들이 지구로부터 보내지긴 하겠지만, 꿈과 목숨을 맞바꾸는 위험을 무릅쓰는 것은 힘든 일이다.

어휘

space agency 항공 우주국 **currently** 부 현재, 지금 **habitable** 형 거주할 수
있는 **settle down** 정착하다 **settler** 명 정착민 **succeed in** ···에 성공하다
revolutionary 형 혁명적인 **assume** 동 추정하다 **substantial** 형 상당한
solar system 태양계 **living supply** 생필품 **tough** 형 힘든, 어려운

08   정답 ③   정답률 55%

정답 풀이

③ 문맥상 반의어(benefits → constraints)

➡ 대규모 유기농 경작 방식은 작물의 산출량을 감소시키고 생산비를 증가시키며, 화학 비료가 사용되지 않으면 잡초 방제가 어렵고 일손이 많이 필요하다는 내용의 글이므로, 거름이나 콩과 식물의 광범위한 사용에는 '이점'이 있는 것이 아니라 '제약'이 있다는 것이 문맥상 자연스럽다. 따라서 benefits(이점)를 constraints(제약) 등으로 바꿔주는 것이 적절하다.

친절한 오답 풀이

① reduce 통 감소시키다
② essential 형 필수적인
④ fewer 형 더 적은
⑤ contribution 명 기여, 이바지

구문 분석 Plus

1행

It has been suggested {that "organic" methods, *defined* as those [in which only natural products can be used as inputs], would be less damaging to the biosphere}.

➡ It은 가주어이고, that 이하가 진주어
➡ defined 이하는 앞에 있는 명사 "organic" methods를 수식하는 과거분사구
➡ in which: which는 those를 선행사로 하는 관계대명사로, 관계사절에서 전치사 in의 목적어 역할을 하고 있음. 선행사인 those는 앞에 나온 methods를 가리킴

지문 해석

천연 제품들만 투입물로 사용되는 방식으로 정의되는 '유기농' 방식은 생물권에 해를 덜 끼친다고 시사되어 왔다. 그러나 '유기농' 경작 방식의 대규모 채택은 많은 주요 작물의 산출량을 감소시키고 생산비를 증가시키게 된다. 무기질 질소 공급은 많은 비(非)콩과 작물 종의 생산성을 중상 수준으로 유지하는 데 필수적인데, 그것은 질소성 물질의 유기적 공급이 무기 질소 비료보다 자주 제한적이거나 더 비싸기 때문이다. 게다가, '친환경적인 거름' 작물로 거름이나 콩과 식물의 광범위한 사용에는 이점(→ 제약)이 있다. 많은 경우, 화학 물질이 사용될 수 없으면 잡초 방제가 매우 어렵거나 많은 손일이 필요할 수 있는데, 사회가 부유해짐에 따라 이 작업을 기꺼이 하려는 사람이 더 적을 것이다. 그러나 돌려짓기의 합리적인 사용과 경작과 가축 경영의 특정한 조합과 같은 '유기농' 경작에서 사용되는 몇몇 방식들은 농촌 생태계의 지속 가능성에 중요한 이바지를 할 수 있다.

어휘

organic 형 유기농의, 유기의, 화학 비료를 쓰지 않는   input 명 투입(물)   damaging 형 해로운   biosphere 명 생물권   adoption 명 채택   yield 명 산출량, 수확물   crop 명 작물 통 경작하다   inorganic 형 무기질의   moderate 형 중간의   non-leguminous 비(非)콩과의   nitrogenous material 질소성 물질   extensive 형 광범위한   chemical 명 화학 물질   sensible 형 합리적인   crop rotation 돌려짓기, 윤작   combination 명 조합   livestock 명 가축   enterprise 명 기업; *사업, 경영   contribution 명 기여, 이바지   sustainability 명 지속 가능성

---

09   정답 ②   정답률 53%

정답 풀이

(A) 병렬구조

In 1856, / he waterproofed a simple box camera, / attached it to a
                     동사1   동사2
1856년에   그는 간단한 상자형 카메라를 방수 처리하고   막대에 부착하여
pole, / and ⎣lowered / ~~lowering~~⎦ it / beneath the waves / off the
      접속사   동사3
             내려보냈다   바닷속으로
coast of southern England.
영국 남부 연안의

➡ 등위접속사 and가 문장의 동사를 병렬 연결하는 구조로, 앞의 waterproofed, attached와 대등하도록 과거형 동사 lowered가 오는 것이 알맞다.

(B) 관계부사 vs. 관계대명사

Near the surface, / [⎣where / ~~which~~⎦ the water is clear / and there
      선행사   관계부사
수면 근처에서는   물이 맑고   충분한 빛이 있는
is enough light], / it is quite possible / for an amateur photographer /
                가주어   to부정사의 의미상 주어
                가능성이 상당히 높다   아마추어 사진작가가
[to take great shots / with an inexpensive underwater camera].
    진주어
   멋진 사진을 찍을   저렴한 수중 카메라로

➡ 장소(the surface)를 선행사로 하며 뒤에 완전한 절이 이어지고 있으므로, 관계부사 where가 오는 것이 알맞다.

(C) 능동태 vs. 수동태

At greater depths — it is dark and cold there — photography is
더 깊은 곳에서는   그곳은 어둡고 차갑다
the principal way of exploring a mysterious deep-sea world, /
                        동격   선행사
사진술이 신비로운 심해 세계를 탐험하는 주요한 방법인데
[95 percent of which has never ⎣seen / been seen⎦ before].
계속적 용법의 목적격 관계대명사, have been v-ed: 현재완료 수동태
그곳의 95%는 예전에는 전혀 볼 수 없었다

➡ 관계대명사 which의 선행사는 a mysterious deep-sea world로, 신비로운 심해 세계의 95%는 예전에는 전혀 '보여질' 수 없었던 것이므로 수동태 been seen이 오는 것이 알맞다.

지문 해석

최초의 수중 사진은 William Thompson이라는 영국인에 의해 촬영되었다. 1856년에 그는 간단한 상자형 카메라를 방수 처리하고 막대에 부착하여 영국 남부 연안의 바닷속으로 내려보냈다. 10분간의 노출 동안 카메라에 서서히 바닷물이 차올랐지만 사진은 온전했다. 수중 사진술이 탄생한 것이다. 물이 맑고 충분한 빛이 있는 수면 근처에서는 아마추어 사진작가가 저렴한 수중 카메라로 멋진 사진을 찍을 가능성이 상당히 높다. 더 깊은 곳에서는 — 그곳은 어둡고 차갑다 — 사진술이 신비로운 심해 세계를 탐험하는 주요한 방법인데, 그곳의 95%는 예전에는 전혀 볼 수 없었다.

어휘

underwater 형 물속의, 수중의   waterproof 통 방수 처리를 하다   attach 통 부착하다   lower 통 ~을 낮추다, 내리다   beneath 전 아래[밑]에   flood 통 물에 잠기다   inexpensive 형 비싸지 않은, 값이 싼   depth 명 깊이   principal 형 주요한, 주된   explore 통 탐험[답사]하다

---

10   정답 ③   정답률 56%

정답 풀이

(A) 반의어(clear / unclear)

➡ 뒤에서 한 살 미만 영아는 시력이 미숙하여 화면에 초점을 맞출 수 없다고 했으므로, 컴퓨터를 얼마나 빨리 시작해야 하는지에 대한 대답은 '분명하다(clear)'라는 의미가 들어가는 것이 문맥상 자연스럽다. unclear는 '불확실한'이라는 의미의 반의어이다.

(B) 반의어(agree / disagree)

➡ 컴퓨터 대신 다른 방식으로 아이들을 자극해야 한다는 내용이 뒤에 이어지고 있으므로, 어떤 사람들은 세 살짜리 아이들의 컴퓨터 노출에 '동의하지 않는다(disagree)'라는 의미가 들어가는 것이 문맥상 자연스럽다. agree는 '동의하다'라는 의미의 반의어이다.

(C) 문맥상 적절한 단어(familiarity / reluctance)

➡ 앞에 컴퓨터에 일찍 노출되게 하는 것이 도움이 된다는 주장이 언급됐으므로, 일찍 시작할수록 디지털 기기에 '친숙함(familiarity)'을 가지게 될 것이라는 의미가 들어가는 것이 문맥상 자연스럽다. reluctance는 '마지못해 함'이라는 의미이다.

구문 분석 Plus

13행
They believe **the earlier** kids start to use computers, **the more** familiarity they will have [*when using* other digital devices].
➡ the + 비교급 ..., the + 비교급 ~: ···하면 할수록 더 ~하다
➡ when using 이하는 접속사가 남아있는 분사구문(= when they use ...)

지문 해석

얼마나 일찍 아이들이 컴퓨터를 시작해야 너무 일찍 시작하는 것이 될까? 당신의 아기가 한 살 미만이라면, 대답은 분명하다. 왜냐하면 아기의 시력은 화면에 집중할 수 있을 정도로 충분히 발달되지 않았고, 심지어 혼자 앉아 있을 수조차 없기 때문이다. 그러나 첫 돌이 지나면, 사람들은 그 질문에 대해 다양한 대답을 가지고 있다. 몇몇 사람들은 세 살짜리 아이들을 컴퓨터에 노출시키는 것에 동의하지 않는다. 그들은 부모가 컴퓨터 대신 독서, 운동, 놀이를 통한 전통적인 방식으로 아이들에게 자극을 줘야 한다고 주장한다. 다른 사람들은 컴퓨터에 일찍 노출되는 것이 디지털 세계에 적응하는 데 도움이 된다고 주장한다. 그들은 아이들이 컴퓨터를 일찍 사용하면 할수록, 다른 디지털 기기를 사용할 때 더 많은 친숙함을 가질 것이라고 믿는다.

vision 몡 시력, 눈 **expose** 통 드러내다; *노출시키다 (**exposure** 몡 노출) **insist** 통 주장하다 **stimulate** 통 자극하다 **instead of** ··· 대신에 **adapt** 통 맞추다, 조정하다; *적응하다 **familiarity** 몡 친숙함 **reluctance** 몡 마지못해 함 **device** 몡 장치, 기구

모의고사 2회
pp.141~143

01 ③ 02 ⑤ 03 ④ 04 ③ 05 ⑤ 06 ② 07 ⑤ 08 ②
09 ② 10 ⑤

01
정답 ③ 정답률 64%

정답 풀이

(A) 능동태 vs. 수동태

Let's say / a product, / [even if it has been out there for a while], /
가정해보자   한 상품이   even if(접속사, 비록 ···일지라도), 삽입절   그것이 한동안 그곳에 나와있었을지라도
is not ⎡advertising / advertised⎤.
광고되지 않았다

➡ 주어는 a product로, 상품이 '광고되지' 않았다는 수동의 의미가 적절하므로 수동태의 과거분사 advertised가 오는 것이 알맞다.

(B) 대명사

Not knowing / [that the product exists], / customers would probably
이유를 나타내는 분사구문(= As customers don't know ...)   that은 접속사
알지 못했기 때문에   그 상품이 존재하는 것을   소비자들은 아마도 그것을 사지 않을
not buy it / [even if the product may have worked for ⎡it / them⎤].
것이다   그 상품이 그들에게 유용했을지라도   may have v-ed: ···했[였]을지도 모른다

➡ 앞의 복수 명사 customers를 대신하므로 복수 대명사 them이 오는 것이 알맞다.

(C) 관계대명사 what

..., they are able to compare them and make purchases / {so that
접속사(그래서)
그들은 그것들을 비교하고 구입할 수 있다   그래서 그들은
they get ⎡t̶h̶a̶t̶ / what⎤ they desire / with their hard-earned money]}.
관계대명사
바라는 것을 얻는다   그들이 힘들게 번 돈으로

➡ 동사 get의 목적어 역할을 하는 명사절을 이끌고 있고, 뒤에 동사의 목적어가 빠진 불완전한 절이 이어지므로 선행사를 포함한 관계대명사 what이 오는 것이 알맞다. 접속사 that은 뒤에 완전한 절이 와야 한다.

지문 해석

많은 소비자들은 상품이 시장에서 구입 가능하다는 것을 알게 된 후에야 상품을 구매한다. 한 상품이 시장에 한동안 나와있었을지라도 광고되지 않았다고 가정해보자. 그렇다면 어떤 일이 일어날까? 그 상품이 존재하는 것을 알지 못했기 때문에, 그 상품이 소비자들에게 유용했을지라도 그들은 아마 그것을 사지 않을 것이다. 광고는 또한 사람들이 그들 자신에게 최적의 상품을 찾을 수 있도록 돕는다. 그들이 모든 다양한 상품들을 알게 되었을 때, 그것들을 비교하고 구입할 수 있어서 그들이 힘들게 번 돈으로 그들이 바라는 것을 얻는다. 그래서 광고는 모든 사람의 일상생활에서 필수적인 것이 되었다.

aware 몡 알고 있는 **available** 몡 이용할 수 있는 **exist** 통 존재하다 **a range of** 다양한 **purchase** 몡 구입, 구매 **desire** 통 바라다, 원하다 **necessity** 몡 필요(성); *필수품

02
정답 ⑤ 정답률 45%

정답 풀이

⑤ 문맥상 반의어(maintain → delay)

➡ 혁신적인 기술이 출현할 때 우리가 새로운 그 기술 세계로 가는 것이 아니라 그 기술이 우리의 삶으로 흡수되어 인간에게 적응해야 한다는 내용의 글이다. 따라서 컴퓨터가 우리를 신세계로 데려다 줄 것이라고 오래 믿을수록 우리는 컴퓨터와 우리 삶의 자연스러운 융합을 더 오래 '지연시키게' 될 것이다. 따라서 maintain(유지하다)을 delay(지연시키다) 등으로 바꿔주는 것이 적절하다.

친절한 오답 풀이

① remote 혱 외진, 외딴
② absorption 몡 흡수
③ affect 통 영향을 미치다
④ adapt 통 적응하다

지문 해석

우리가 고개를 돌리는 곳 어디서든 우리는 전능하신 '사이버공간'에 대해 듣는다! 과대 광고는 우리가 지루한 삶을 떠나 고글과 바디 수트를 착용하고, 어떤 금속성의, 3차원의, 멀티미디어로 만들어진 다른 세계로 들어갈 것이라고 약속한다. 위대한 혁신인 모터와 함께 산업 혁명이 도래했을 때 우리는 어떤 외딴 모터 공간으로 가기 위해 우리의 세상을 떠나지 않았다! 반대로, 우리는 모터를 자동차, 냉장고, 드릴 프레스, 연필깎이와 같은 것들로 우리 삶에 가져왔다. 이 흡수는 매우 완전해서 우리는 그것들의 '모터성'이 아니라 그것들의 사용을 분명하게 밝히는 이름으로 이 모든 도구를 지칭한다. 이러한 혁신품들은 정확히 우리의 일상생활에 들어와 깊은 영향을 미쳤기 때문에 주요한 사회경제적 운동으로 이어졌다. 사람들은 수천 년 동안 근본적으로 변하지 않았다. 기술은 끊임없이 변화한다. 우리에게 적응해야 하는 것은 바로 그것이다. 그것이 바로 인간 중심의 컴퓨터 사용 하에 정보 기술과 그 장치들에 일어날 일이다. 컴퓨터가 우리를 마법 같은 신세계로 데려다 줄 것이라고 계속해서 더 오래 믿게 될수록 컴퓨터와 우리 삶의 자연스러운 융합이 더 오래 유지될(→ 지연될) 것인데, 이는 사회경제적 혁명이라고 불리기를 열망하는 모든 주요 운동의 특징이다.

almighty 혱 전능한 **metallic** 혱 금속성의 **complete** 혱 완벽한; *완전한 **declare** 통 분명하게 밝히다 **usage** 몡 사용 **socioeconomic** 혱 사회 경제적인 **profoundly** 凰 깊이 **fundamentally** 凰 근본적으로 **fusion** 몡 융합 **aspire** 통 열망하다

정답 풀이

④ 병렬구조

A designer <u>must</u> first <u>document</u> / the existing conditions of a
　　　　　　조동사　　　　동사1
디자이너는 우선 기록해야 한다　　　　　　문제의 기존 상황을

problem / <u>and collecting</u>(→ collect) relevant data to be analyzed.
　　　접속사　　　동사2　　　　　　　　　　↑ 형용사적 용법의
　　　　　그리고 분석되어야 할 관련 있는 자료를 수집해야 한다　　to부정사

➡ 등위접속사 and가 문장의 동사를 병렬 연결하고 있는 구조로, 동사 앞에 조동사 must가 쓰였으므로 동사 document와 대등하도록 collecting을 동사원형 collect로 고쳐야 한다.

‖친절한 오답 풀이‖

① 부사

These conditions may be <u>purely functional</u> / in nature, ...
　　　　　　　　　　　　　부사└───┘형용사
이런 상황들은 순전히 기능적일 수 있다　　　　　　　　근본적으로

➡ 부사 purely가 형용사 functional을 수식하고 있으므로 어법상 바르다.

② 비교급 강조 부사

In any case, / it is assumed / [that the existing set of conditions is
　　　　　　　가주어　　　　　진주어1, that은 접속사
어떤 경우든　　여겨진다　　　　기존 상황들이 훨씬 덜 만족스러운 것이라고

<u>much less</u> satisfactory] / and [that a new set of conditions would
부사└─┘
　　　　　　　　　　　　　　　진주어2, that은 접속사
　　　　　　　　　　　　그리고 새로운 상황이 바람직할 것이라고

be desirable].

➡ much가 '훨씬'의 의미로 비교급 less의 의미를 강조하고 있으므로 어법상 바르다.

③ 형용사적 용법의 to부정사

The initial phase of any design process / is the recognition of a
어느 디자인 과정의 첫 단계는　　　　　　　　문제가 있는 상황의 인식이다
problematic condition / and <u>the decision to find</u> a solution to it.
　　　　　　　　　　　↑────────┘ 형용사적 용법의 to부정사
그리고 그것의 해결책을 찾는 결정이다

➡ to find는 앞의 명사 the decision을 수식하는 형용사적 용법의 to부정사로, 어법상 바르다.

⑤ 수동태

This is the critical phase of the design process / {since the nature
　　　　　　　　　　　　　　　　　접속사(… 때문에)
이것은 디자인 과정의 중요한 단계이다　　　　　　해결책의 본질이
of a solution is related / to [how a problem is defined]}.
　　be related to: …와 관계가 있다　간접의문문(의문사 + 주어 + 동사)
관계가 있기 때문이다　　　　　　　문제가 어떻게 정의되는가와

➡ 전치사 to의 목적어 역할을 하는 간접의문문에서 주어는 a problem으로, 문제가 '정의되다'라는 수동의 의미가 적절하므로 수동태 is defined는 어법상 바르다.

지문 해석

건축은 일반적으로 기존 상황에 대한 반응으로 구상되고, 설계되고, 실현된다. 이러한 상황들은 근본적으로 순전히 기능적일 수 있거나, 사회적, 정치적, 경제적 분위기를 다양하게 반영할 수도 있다. 어떤 경우든, 기존 상황들이 훨씬 덜 만족스럽고, 새로운 상황들이 바람직할 것이라고 여겨진다. 어느 디자인 과정의 첫 단계는 문제가 있는 상황의 인식과 그것의 해결책을 찾는 결정이다. 디자인은 무엇보다도 의도적인 노력이다. 디자이너는 우선 문제의 기존 상황을 기록하고 분석되어야 할 관련 자료를 수집해야 한다. 이것은 디자인 과정의 중요한 단계인데, 해결책의 본질이 문제가 어떻게 정의되는가와 관계가 있기 때문이다.

어휘

architecture 몡 건축학[술], 건축　conceive 됭 구상하다　realize 됭 깨닫다; *실현하다　existing 혱 기존의, 현재 사용되는　condition 몡 상태; *(pl.) 환경, 상황　purely 閂 순전히, 전적으로　functional 혱 기능적인　reflect 됭 반사하다; *반영하다　climate 몡 기후; *분위기　satisfactory 혱 만족스러운　desirable 혱 바람직한　initial 혱 처음의, 초기의　phase 몡 단계　recognition 몡 인식　problematic 혱 문제가 있는　above all 무엇보다도　purposeful 혱 목적의식이 있는　endeavor 몡 노력, 시도　document 됭 기록하다　relevant 혱 관련 있는　analyze 됭 분석하다　critical 혱 중요한

정답 풀이

③ 문맥상 반의어(prevent → accommodate)

➡ 자연 발생적인 강의 불규칙하고 복잡한 형태는 강의 기능에 필수적이라는 내용의 글로 강의 자연적인 형태가 수위와 속도 변화를 '막는' 것이 아니라 '조절한다'는 것이 문맥상 자연스럽다. 따라서 prevent(막다)를 accommodate(조절하다) 등으로 바꿔주는 것이 적절하다.

‖친절한 오답 풀이‖

① straighten 됭 똑바르게 하다, 직선화하다
② irregular 혱 불규칙적인
④ destroy 됭 파괴시키다
⑤ controlled 혱 통제된

콘드 +α 구문 보석 Plus

2행	The attempt **to straighten** rivers and **give** them regular cross-sections is perhaps the most disastrous example of this form-and-function relationship. ➡ to straighten: 명사구 The attempt를 수식하는 형용사적 용법의 to부정사이며 and로 (to) give와 병렬 연결됨
6행	The natural river has a very irregular form: it curves a lot, spills across floodplains, and leaks into wetlands, [**giving** it an ever-changing and incredibly complex shoreline]. ➡ giving 이하는 결과를 나타내는 분사구문

지문 해석

지난 20년 혹은 30년 동안의 상세한 연구는 자연계의 복잡한 형태가 그것의 기능에 필수적이라는 것을 보여주고 있다. 강을 직선화하고 규칙적인 횡단면으로 만들고자 하는 시도는 아마도 이러한 형태, 기능 관계의 가장 막심한 피해 사례가 될 수 있다. 자연 발생적인 강은 매우 불규칙한 형태를 가지고 있다. 그것은 많이 굽이치고, 범람원을 가로질러 넘쳐 흐르고, 습지로 스며 들어가서 끊임없이 변화하여, 엄청나게 복잡한 강가를 만든다. 이것은 강의 수위와 속도 변화를 막을(→ 조절할) 수 있게 한다. 강을 질서정연한 기하학적 형태에 맞춰 넣는 것은 기능적 수용 능력을 파괴하고 1927년과 1993년의 Mississippi강의 홍수와, 더 최근에는, 허리케인 Katrina와 같은 비정상적인 재난을 초래한다. Louisiana에서 "강을 자유롭게 흐르도록 두라.(let the river loose.)"라는 500억 달러 계획은 통제된 Mississippi강이 매년 그 주의 24제곱마일을 유실시키고 있다는 것을 인정한 것이다.

어휘

detailed 혱 상세한　complex 혱 복잡한　attempt 몡 시도　straighten 됭 똑바르게 하다, 직선화하다　cross-section 몡 횡단면　disastrous 혱 처참한　curve 됭 곡선을 이루다　spill 됭 넘치다　floodplain 몡 (홍수의) 범람원　leak 됭 새다　wetland 몡 습지　ever-changing 혱 늘 변화하는, 변화무쌍한　shoreline 몡 강가, 해안선　square mile 제곱마일

05

정답 풀이

⑤ 문장의 동사

> ..., and the resulting explosion of personal liberty creating
> 　　　　　　　　　　주어
> 그리고 결과적으로 나타난 개인적 자유의 폭발은
> (→ created) an array of options, alternatives, and decisions / [that
> 　동사
> 일련의 선택, 대안, 그리고 결정을 만들어냈다　　　　　　　　목적격 관계대명사
> our ancestors never faced].
> 우리의 조상이 결코 마주하지 못했던

➡ 절 안에 주어(the resulting ... liberty)에 대한 동사가 없으므로 creating을 동사 created로 바꿔주는 것이 어법상 적절하다.

친절한 오답 풀이

① 동사의 수 일치

> Making these decisions is such a natural part of adulthood /
> 　동명사구 주어　　　　　such a(n) + 형용사 + 명사 + that ...: 너무 ~해서 …하다
> 이런 결정을 내리는 것은 성인의 삶에 있어 너무나 자연스러운 부분이어서
> that it is easy {to forget / [that we are among the first human
> 　가주어　　　　진주어　　접속사
> 잊어버리기 쉽다　　　　　우리가 최초의 인간에 속한다는 것을
> beings / to make them]}.
> 형용사적 용법의 to부정사 = these decisions
> 　　그런 결정을 하는

➡ 동명사구(Making these decisions)가 문장의 주어이므로 뒤에 단수 동사 is가 오는 것이 알맞다.

② 접속사

> For most of recorded history, / people lived [where they were
> 　　　　　　　　　　　　　　　접속사(…한 곳)
> 기록된 역사 대부분에서,　　　　　사람들은 그들이 태어난 곳에 살았다
> born], / did [what their parents had done], ...
> 　　　　관계대명사
> 　　　그들의 부모가 했던 일을 했다

➡ where는 동사 lived 뒤에서 부사절을 이끄는 접속사로, 뒤에 완전한 절이 이어지고 있으므로 어법상 바르다.

③ 주격 관계대명사

> Social and physical structures were the great dictators / {that
> 　　　　　　　　　　　　　　　　　　　　　　　　주격 관계대명사
> 사회적, 물리적인 구조는 위대한 지배자였다
> determined / [how and where people would spend their lives]}.
> 　　　　　간접의문문(의문사 + 주어 + 동사)
> 결정하는　　어떻게 그리고 어디서 사람들이 그들의 삶을 보낼지를

➡ the great dictators를 선행사로 하고 관계대명사절 안에서 동사 determined의 주어의 역할을 할 수 있는 주격 관계대명사 that이 쓰였으므로 어법상 바르다.

④ for oneself

> This left most folks with little to decide / for themselves.
> 　　　　　　　　　　　　　　　　for oneself: 혼자 힘으로, 스스로
> 이것은 대부분의 사람들에게 결정할 것을 거의 남기지 않았다　그들 스스로

➡ 문맥상 대부분의 사람들(most folks)이 '그들 스스로' 결정할 일이므로 재귀대명사 themselves가 오는 것이 어법상 바르다.

지문 해석

우리들 대부분은 우리의 삶에서 적어도 세 가지 중요한 결정을 한다. 어디에 살지, 무엇을 할지, 그리고 누구와 그것을 할지. 우리는 우리의 마을, 직업, 그리고 배우자와 친구를 선택한다. 이런 결정을 내리는 것은 성인의 삶에 있어 너무나 자연스러운 부분이어서 우리가 그런 결정을 하는 최초의 인간에 속한다는 것을 잊어버리기 쉽다. 기록된 역사 대부분에서, 사람들은 태어난 곳에서 살았고, 그들의 부모가 했던 일을 했고, 그리고 같은

일을 하는 사람들과 사귀었다. 사회적, 물리적인 구조는 어떻게 그리고 어디서 사람들이 그들의 삶을 보낼지를 결정하는 위대한 지배자였다. 이것은 대부분의 사람들에게 그들 스스로 결정할 것을 거의 남기지 않았다. 하지만 산업 기술 혁명은 그 모든 것들을 바꾸었고, 결과적으로 나타난 개인의 자유의 폭발은 우리의 조상이 결코 마주하지 못했던 일련의 선택, 대안, 그리고 결정을 만들어냈다.

어휘

spouse 몡 배우자　associate 통 연관짓다; *어울리다　physical 혱 신체의; *물리적인　dictator 몡 독재자; *지배자　determine 통 결정하다　folk 몡 (일반적인) 사람들　industrial 혱 산업의　technological 혱 기술적인　resulting 혱 결과로 초래된　explosion 몡 폭발　liberty 몡 자유　an array of 다수의　option 몡 선택 사항　alternative 몡 대안　ancestor 몡 조상

06

정답 풀이

(A) 반의어(fair / unjust)

➡ Dworkin은 한 사람의 운명이 그 사람의 통제 내에 있는 것들에 의해 결정되어야 한다고 했으므로, 행복에서의 차이가 개인의 통제 밖에 있는 환경에 의해 결정되는 것은 '불공평'하다고 하는 것이 문맥상 자연스럽다. 따라서 'unjust'가 적절하다. fair는 '공평한'이라는 의미의 반의어이다.

(B) 반의어(acceptable / intolerable)

➡ 행복의 차이가 개인의 통제 밖에 있는 환경에 의해 결정되는 것은 불공평하지만, 개인의 선택이나 취향 차이에 의한 불평등은 '허용할 수 있다'는 의미가 문맥상 자연스럽다. 따라서 acceptable이 적절하다. intolerable은 '참을 수 없는'이라는 의미의 반의어이다.

(C) 문맥상 적절한 단어(ensuring / neglecting)

➡ 행복의 불평등을 제거하는 것은 기회의 평등이나 자원의 접근에의 평등을 '보장함'으로써 이룰 수 있는 것이므로 ensuring이 알맞다. neglect는 '방치하다, 도외시하다'라는 의미이다.

코드+α 구문 분석 Plus

2행	From Dworkin's view, justice **requires** {that a person's fate **be** determined by things [that are within that person's control], not by luck}. ➡ 요구를 나타내는 동사 require 뒤에 오는 that절의 동사는 「should + 동사원형」 형태로 쓰며, should는 종종 생략됨 ➡ that: 동사 requires의 목적어 역할을 하는 명사절을 이끄는 접속사 ➡ that: things를 선행사로 하는 주격 관계대명사
5행	{If differences in wellbeing are determined by circumstances [lying outside of an individual's control]}, they are unjust. ➡ If: 부사절을 이끄는 접속사 ➡ lying ... control은 앞의 명사 circumstances를 수식하는 현재분사구
10행	But we should seek to eliminate inequality of wellbeing {that is driven by factors [that are not an individual's responsibility] and [which prevent an individual from achieving what he or she values]}. ➡ that: inequality of wellbeing을 선행사로 하는 주격 관계대명사 ➡ that, which: factors를 선행사로 하는 주격 관계대명사 ➡ what: 선행사를 포함한 관계대명사

지문 해석

Dworkin은 특정한 종류의 기회의 평등에 관한 고전적 주장을 제시한다. Dworkin의 관점에서 정의는 한 사람의 운명이 운이 아닌 그 사람의 통제 내에 있는 것들에 의해 결정되는 것을 필요로 한다. 행복에서의 차이가 개인의 통제 밖에 있는 환경에 의해 결정된다면, 그 차이는 불공평하다. 이 주장에 따르면, 개인의 선택이나 취향의 차이에 의한 행복의 불평등은 허용할 수 있다. 그러나 우리는 개인의 책임이 아니면서 개인이

자신이 중요하게 여기는 것을 성취하지 못하게 막는 요소에 의해 만들어지는 행복의 불평등을 제거하기 위해 노력해야 한다. 우리는 기회의 평등 또는 기본적인 자원에의 접근의 평등을 보장함으로써 그렇게 한다.

argument 명 주장   equality 명 평등 (inequality 명 불평등)   fate 명 운명
determine 통 알아내다; *결정하다   circumstance 명 《pl.》 환경, 상황   taste
명 맛; *기호, 취향   eliminate 통 제거하다   factor 명 요소   responsibility 명
책임   value 통 소중하게 생각하다   access 명 접근   fundamental 형 기본적인

07 　　　　　　　　　정답 ⑤　　　정답률 42%

지문 해석

⑤ 접속사 that

[What(→ That) some organisms must starve / in nature] / is
　접속사　　　　　주어　　　　　　　　동사
일부 유기체들이 굶주려야 한다는 것은　　　자연에서
deeply regrettable and sad.
매우 유감스럽고 슬프다

➡ 문장의 주어 역할을 하며 뒤에 완전한 절이 이어지므로 What을 명사절을 이끄는
접속사 That으로 고쳐야 한다.

친절한 오답 풀이

① 「전치사 + 관계대명사」

It also is part of the process / of selection / [by which biological
　　　　　　　　　　　　　　　　　　　　　　which는 목적격 관계대명사
그것은 또한 과정의 일부이기도 하다　　선택의　　　생물학적 진화가 기능하게 되는
evolution functions].

➡ which는 the process of selection을 선행사로 하고, 관계대명사절에서 전치사
by의 목적어로 쓰였으므로 「전치사 + 관계대명사」 형태인 by which는 어법상 바르다.
「전치사 + 관계대명사」 뒤에는 완전한 절이 온다.

② 재귀대명사

Starvation helps filter out / those less fit to survive, / those less
　　　　　　　　　　　　　　　　　　　한 것들
기아는 걸러 내는 데 도움을 준다　　살아남기에 덜 적합한 것들을　　즉 수완이 부족한
resourceful / in finding food / for themselves and their young.
것들을　　　　　먹이를 찾는 데　　자신과 자신의 새끼들을 위한

➡ 앞서 언급된 those less resourceful과 가리키는 대상이 같으므로 재귀대명사
themselves가 오는 것이 어법상 바르다.

③ 형용사적 용법의 to부정사

In some circumstances, / it may pave the way / for genetic
　　　　　　　　　　　　　　　　to부정사의 의미상 주어
몇몇 상황에서　　　　　기아는 길을 열어줄지도 모른다
variants to take hold in the population of a species / and
　　형용사적 용법의 to부정사
유전적 변종들이 종의 개체군을 장악할 수 있는　　　　　그리고
eventually allow the emergence of a new species / in place of
　　　　　　　　　　　　　　　　　　　　　　　… 대신에
결국에는 새로운 종이 출현할 수 있게 할지도 모른다　　이전의 종을 대신하여
the old one.
　= species

➡ to take는 앞의 명사 the way를 수식하는 형용사적 용법의 to부정사로 어법상 바르다.
for genetic variants는 to부정사의 의미상 주어이다.

---

④ 목적격보어

Thus starvation is a disvalue / [that can help make possible /
　　　　　　　　　　　　　　　　주격 관계대명사 make + 목적어 + 형용사:
따라서 기아는 부정적 가치이다　　　　　가능하게 하는 데 도움이 될 수 있는
the good of greater diversity].
…을 ~하게 만들다
더 큰 다양성이 주는 이익을

➡ 동사 make의 목적격보어로 형용사 possible은 어법상 바르다. 목적어 the good of
greater diversity가 길어서 목적격보어와 도치된 형태이다.

지문 해석

모든 유기체가 생존하기에 충분한 먹이를 구할 수는 없으므로, 기아는 자연에서 흔히
발견되는 일종의 부정적 가치이다. 그것은 또한 생물학적 진화가 기능하게 되는 선택
과정의 일부이기도 하다. 기아는 살아남기에 덜 적합한 것들, 즉 자신과 자신의 새끼들을
위한 먹이를 찾는 데 수완이 부족한 것들을 걸러 내는 데 도움을 준다. 몇몇 상황에서
기아는 유전적 변종들이 종의 개체군을 장악할 수 있는 길을 열어주고 결국에는 이전의
종을 대신하여 새로운 종이 출현할 수 있게 할지도 모른다. 따라서 기아는 더 큰 다양성이
주는 이익을 가능하게 하는 데 도움이 될 수 있는 부정적 가치이다. 기아가 고유한
부정적 가치가 되는 바로 그 순간, 실용적인, 즉 도움이 되는 가치를 지닐 수 있다. 일부
유기체들이 자연에서 굶주려야 한다는 것은 매우 유감스럽고 슬프다. 기아가 때로 좋은
목적에 공헌할 수도 있기는 하지만, 그 말은 여전히 확고하게 진실이다.

organism 명 유기체   sufficient 형 충분한   starvation 명 기아, 굶주림
(starve 통 굶주리다)   disvalue 명 무시; *부정적 가치   selection 명 선발, 선택
biological 형 생물학적인   evolution 명 진화   function 통 기능하다   filter out
…을 걸러 내다   resourceful 형 지략 있는, 수완이 비상한   circumstance 명
상황   pave the way (…을 위한) 길을 닦다   variant 명 변종   take hold 장악하다,
사로잡다   emergence 명 출현, 발생   diversity 명 다양성   instrumental 형
도움이 되는   even as …하는 바로 그 순간   intrinsic 형 고유한   regrettable 형
유감스러운

08 　　　　　　　　　정답 ②　　　정답률 44%

정답 풀이

② 반의어(found → lost)

➡ 지식 탐구 목적의 고고학자는 아주 오랜 시간이 필요하지만, 상업적인 고고학자는
유물을 팔기 전까지 오랜 시간을 기다릴 수 없다고 설명하고 있다. 그러므로 보물
탐사 기업에 고용된 상업적인 고고학자에게 연구를 위한 6개월이 주어지기만 하면
어떠한 역사적 지식도 '사라지지' 않을 것이라는 의미가 문맥상 자연스럽다. 따라서,
found(발견된)를 lost(사라진)로 바꿔주는 것이 적절하다.

친절한 오답 풀이

① time 명 시간
③ catalog 통 목록을 작성하다
④ learn 통 배우다, 학습하다
⑤ wait 통 기다리다

코드+α 구문 분석 Plus

15행
… before they could even catalog all the finds from an
eleventh-century AD wreck (which/that) they had excavated.
➡ they had excavated: 선행사 all the finds (from an … wreck)를
수식하는 목적격 관계대명사절로, 앞에 which나 that이 생략돼 있음

지문 해석

일부 저명한 언론인들은 보물 사냥꾼이 과거에 대해 많은 것을 드러낼 수 있는 가치 있는
역사적 유물을 축적해 왔기 때문에 고고학자는 보물 사냥꾼과 협업해야 한다고 말한다.
그러나 도굴꾼 또한 가치 있는 역사적 유물을 가지고 있긴 하지만, 고고학자는 도굴꾼과
협력하도록 요구받지는 않는다. 이윤 추구와 지식 탐구는 시간이라는 요인 때문에
고고학에서 공존할 수 없다. 상당히 믿기 어렵지만, 보물 탐사 기업에 의해 고용된 한
고고학자는 난파선의 유물이 판매되기 전에 그것들을 연구할 수 있도록 고고학자들에게

6개월의 시간이 주어지기만 하면, 어떠한 역사적 지식도 발견되지(→ 사라지지) 않는다고 말했다! 그와는 반대로, 해양고고학 연구소(INA)의 고고학자들과 보조원들은 그들이 발굴한 서기 11세기 난파선의 모든 발굴물의 목록을 만들 수 있기까지 10년 이상의 기간 내내 보존이 필요했다. 그리고 나서, 그러한 발굴물을 해석하기 위해서 그들은 러시아어, 불가리아어, 그리고 루마니아어를 배워야만 했는데, 그렇게 하지 않았다면 그들은 유적지의 실체를 결코 알지 못했을 것이다. '상업적인 고고학자'가 발굴물을 팔기 전에 10여 년 이상의 기간을 기다릴 수 있었겠는가?

archaeologist 몡 고고학자 **accumulate** 동 모으다, 축적하다 **valuable** 혱 귀중한, 가치가 큰 **artifact** 몡 (고고학) 인공 유물 **cooperate with** …와 협력하다 **tomb robber** 도굴꾼 **quest** 몡 탐구, 탐색 **coexist** 동 동시에 있다, 공존하다 **shipwrecked** 혱 난파한 **conservation** 몡 보호, 보존 **find** 몡 (흥미롭거나 가치 있는) 발견물 **interpret** 동 (의미를) 설명하다; *(특정한 뜻으로) 이해[해석]하다

09 　　　　　정답 ②　　　정답률 67%

정답 풀이

② 문장의 동사

The combustion of oxygen / [that keeps us alive and active] /
　　　　주어　　　　　　　주격 관계대명사
산소의 연소는　　　　　우리를 살아있고 활동적이게 유지해주는
sending(→ sends) out by-products / [called oxygen free radicals].
　　　동사　　　　　　　　　　　과거분사
부산물을 내보낸다　　　　　　　활성 산소라고 불리는

→ 문장의 주어는 The combustion of oxygen이고 that ... active는 주어를 수식하는 관계대명사절로, 뒤에 문장의 동사가 이어져야 한다. 따라서 준동사 sending을 동사 sends로 고쳐야 한다.

┃친절한 오답 풀이┃

① 주격 관계대명사

The ultimate life force / lies in tiny cellular factories of energy, / called
궁극적인 생명력은　　　아주 작은 에너지 세포 공장에 있다　　　선행사　　과거분사
　　　　　　　　　　　　　　　　　　　　　　　　　　　　　　　불리는
mitochondria, / {that burn nearly all the oxygen / [(which/that)
　　　주격 관계대명사
미토콘드리아라고　　거의 모든 산소를 태우는　　　　목적격 관계대명사 생략
we breathe in]}.
우리가 들이쉬는

→ 밑줄 친 that은 tiny cellular factories of energy를 선행사로 하는 주격 관계대명사로 어법상 바르다.

③ 부사적 용법의 to부정사

..., [when the body mobilizes / to fight off infectious agents], /
접속사　　　　　　　　　　부사적 용법의 to부정사(목적)
신체가 동원될 때　　　　　　감염원과 싸워 물리치기 위해
it generates a burst of free radicals / to destroy the invaders
= the body　　　　　　　　　　　　　부사적 용법의 to부정사(목적)
그것은 한바탕 활성 산소를 생산한다　　침입자들을 매우 효율적으로 파괴하기 위해
very efficiently.

→ 밑줄 친 to fight는 앞의 동사 mobilizes를 수식하는 부사적 용법의 to부정사로 어법상 바르다.

④ 부사

On the other hand, / free radicals move uncontrollably / through
　　　　　　　　　　　　　　　　　　　　　　　부사
다른 한편으로　　　활성 산소는 통제할 수 없게 돌아다닌다　　　신체를
the body, / [attacking cells, rusting their proteins, piercing their
　　　　　　　동시동작을 나타내는 분사구문(= as they attack ..., rust ..., pierce ..., and corrupt ...)
　　　　　　　세포를 공격하고, 세포의 단백질을 부식시키고, 세포막을 뚫고
membranes and corrupting their genetic code ...].
세포의 유전 암호를 변질시키면서

→ uncontrollably는 동사 move를 수식하는 부사로 어법상 바르다.

⑤ 명사를 수식하는 과거분사

These fierce radicals, / [built into life as both protectors and
　　　　　　　　　　　　　　　　과거분사　　　both A and B: A와 B 둘 다
이런 사나운 활성 산소는　　　　　보호자인 동시에 보복자로서 생명체로 만들어진
avengers], / are potent agents of aging.
　　　　　　　노화의 강력한 동인이다

→ 앞의 명사 These fierce radicals를 수식하는 분사로, 활성산소가 생명체로 '만들어지는'이라는 수동의 의미이므로 과거분사 built가 오는 것이 알맞다.

지문 해석

가장 중요한 것은 바로 산소이다. 얄궂게도, 우리에게 생명을 주는 것이 결국 그것을 죽인다. 궁극적인 생명력은 우리가 들이쉬는 거의 모든 산소를 태우는, 미토콘드리아라고 불리는 아주 작은 에너지 세포 공장에 있다. 그러나 호흡에는 대가가 있다. 우리를 살아있고 활동적이게 유지해주는 산소의 연소는 활성 산소라고 불리는 부산물을 내보낸다. 그것들은 지킬박사와 하이드 씨의 특징을 가지고 있다. 한편으로, 그것들은 우리의 생존을 보장하도록 돕는다. 예를 들어, 감염원과 싸워 물리치기 위해 신체가 동원될 때, 그것은 침입자들을 매우 효율적으로 파괴하기 위해 한바탕 활성 산소를 생산한다. 다른 한편으로, 활성 산소는 세포가 제대로 기능을 하지 못하게 되고 때로는 포기하여 죽어버릴 때까지 세포를 공격하고, 세포의 단백질을 부식시키고, 세포막을 뚫고 세포의 유전 암호를 변질시키면서 통제할 수 없게 신체를 돌아다닌다. 보호자인 동시에 보복자로서 생명체로 만들어진 이런 사나운 활성 산소는 노화의 강력한 동인이다.

cellular 혱 세포의 **combustion** 몡 연소 **by-product** 몡 부산물 **mobilize** 동 동원되다 **infectious** 혱 전염되는, 전염성의 **agent** 몡 요인, 동인(動因) **invader** 몡 침입자 **uncontrollably** 뷔 통제할 수 없게 **rust** 동 부식하다 **protein** 몡 단백질 **pierce** 동 뚫다 **corrupt** 동 변질시키다 **genetic code** 유전 암호 **dysfunctional** 혱 제대로 기능을 하지 않는 **fierce** 혱 사나운 **avenger** 몡 보복자 **potent** 혱 강력한

10 　　　　　정답 ⑤　　　정답률 50%

정답 풀이

⑤ 반의어(expanded → limited)

→ 글에 제시된 예들을 통해, 현대 화가들뿐 아니라 고대 화가들 역시 제한된 색을 사용했다는 것을 알 수 있다. 따라서 이러한 제한된 색의 사용이 명확성과 이해 가능성에 도움을 주었다고 하는 것이 문맥상 자연스러우므로 expanded(확대된)를 limited(제한된)로 바꿔주는 것이 적절하다.

┃친절한 오답 풀이┃

① explosion 몡 폭발; 폭발적인 증가
② restrictive 혱 제한하는
③ enough 혱 충분한
④ new 혱 새로운

코드+α 구문 분석 Plus

11행
There was **nothing new** in this: the Greeks and Romans *tended to* use just red, yellow, black and white.
→ -thing으로 끝나는 대명사는 형용사가 뒤에서 수식함
→ tend to-v: …하는 경향이 있다

지문 해석

이론상으로 화가들은 무한한 범위의 색을 마음대로 사용할 수 있는데, 합성 화학을 통한 유채색의 폭발적 증가를 이룬 현대에 특히 그렇다. 그러나 화가들이 모든 색을 동시에 사용하는 것은 아닌데, 사실 많은 화가들은 눈에 띄게 제한적으로 색을 선택하여 사용해 왔다. Mondrian은 자신의 검정색 선이 그려진 격자무늬를 채우기 위해 대개 빨강, 노랑, 그리고 파랑의 3원색으로 스스로를 제한했고, Kasimir Malevich는 비슷하게 스스로 부과한 제한에 따라 작업했다. Yves Klein에게는 한 가지 색이면 충분했고, Franz Kline의 예술(작품)은 보통 흰색 바탕 위에 검정색이었다. 이것에는 새로울 것이 없었는데, 그리스와 로마 사람들은 단지 빨간색, 노란색, 검정색 그리고 흰색만을

사용하는 경향이 있었다. 왜 그랬을까? 일반화할 수는 없지만, 고대와 현대에 모두 (범위가) 확대된(→ 제한된) 팔레트가[색이] 명확성과 이해 가능성에 도움을 주고 중요한 구성요소인 모양과 형태에 주의를 집중할 수 있도록 도움을 주었을 것 같다.

---

in principle 이론상으로   infinite 형 무한한   at one's disposal …의 마음대로 사용할 수 있게   synthetic 형 합성의   chemistry 명 화학   primary 명 원색 self-imposed 형 자진해서 하는   antiquity 명 고대   modernity 명 현대(성) palette 명 팔레트, 색   aid 동 돕다   clarity 명 명료성   comprehensibility 명 이해할 수 있음   component 명 구성요소

MEMO

MEMO

MEMO

독해

READING EXPERT

중고등 대상 7단계 원서 독해 교재

Level 1 | Level 2 | Level 3 | Level 4 | Level 5 |
Advanced 1 | Advanced 2

기강 잡고

기본을 강하게 잡아주는 고등영어

독해 잡는 필수 문법 | 기초 잡는 유형 독해

빠른독해 바른독해

빠른 독해를 위한 바른 선택

기초세우기 | 구문독해 | 유형독해 | 수능실전

The 상승

독해 기본기에서 수능 실전 대비까지

직독직해편 | 문법독해편 | 구문편 |
수능유형편 | 어법·어휘+유형편

수능

맞수

맞춤형 수능영어 단기특강 시리즈

구문독해 | 기본편 | 실전편
수능유형 | 기본편 | 실전편
수능문법어법 | 기본편 | 실전편
수능듣기 | 기본편 | 실전편
빈칸추론

핵심만 콕 찍어주는 수능유형 필독서

독해 기본 | 독해 실력 | 듣기

특급

수능 1등급 만드는 특급 시리즈

독해 유형별 모의고사 | 듣기 실전 모의고사 24회 |
어법 | 빈칸추론 | 수능·EBS 기출 VOCA

얇빠 얇고 빠른 미니 모의고사 10+2회

수능 핵심유형들만 모아 얇게! 회당 10문항으로 빠르게!

입문 | 기본 | 실전

수능만만

만만한 수능영어 모의고사

기본 영어듣기 20회 | 기본 영어듣기 35회+5회 |
기본 영어독해 10+1회 | 기본 문법·어법·어휘 150제 |
영어듣기 20회 | 영어듣기 35회 |
영어독해 20회 | 어법·어휘 228제

NE능률 영어교육연구소

NE능률 영어교육연구소는 전문성과 탁월성을 기반으로
영어 교육 트렌드를 선도합니다.

2025 학평대비 다빈출 코드 어법·어휘

펴 낸 날	2024년 12월 20일 (개정판 제1쇄)
펴 낸 이	주민홍
펴 낸 곳	(주)NE능률
지 은 이	NE능률 영어교육연구소
개 발 책 임	김지현
개 발	신유승
영 문 교 열	Curtis Thompson
디 자 인 책 임	오영숙
디 자 인	안훈정
제 작 책 임	한성일

등 록 번 호	제1-68호
I S B N	979-11-253-4913-6

대 표 전 화	02 2014 7114
홈 페 이 지	www.neungyule.com
주 소	서울시 마포구 월드컵북로 396(상암동) 누리꿈스퀘어 비즈니스타워 10층